MODERN COPYRIGHT FUNDAMENTALS

Key Writings on Technological and Other Issues

Edited by

Ben H. Weil

Ben H. Weil, Inc.
Warren, NJ

and

Barbara Friedman Polansky

American Chemical Society
Washington, DC

Published by Learned Information, Inc.
for the American Society for Information Science

Manufactured in the United States of America

Learned Information, Inc.
143 Old Marlton Pike
Medford, NJ 08055

Library of Congress Cataloging-in-Publication Data

Modern copyright fundamentals.

    Bibliography: p.
    Includes index.
    1. Copyright—United States. I. Weil, Ben H.
II. Polansky, Barbara Friedman.
KF2994.M58 1989   346.7304'82   89-2586
ISBN 0-938734-33-4   347.306482

Contents

Publishers

Other Owners

III: USERS

Educators

Bibliographic Services

V: BASIC ISSUES

Fair Use

Abstracts

Contents By Author

Foreword

Would that fine editors of the stature of Ben Weil and Barbara Friedman Polansky had done for earlier copyright statutes what has now been done for the current law. The myth of the arcane and the esoteric that we copyright lawyers have long perpetuated can be dispelled only by an excellent volume such as this. To understand the significance and the ramifications of a statute, one needs more than merely the words of Congress. For proper understanding, one needs a compilation of varying views from differing perspectives. This is such a compilation.

A "compilation" is defined in the Copyright Act as a work "formed by the collection and assembly of preexisting materials or of data that are selected, coordinated, or arranged in such a way that the resulting work as a whole constitutes an original work of authorship." If the work is such an "original work of authorship," the Act provides that "copyright protection subsists" in it. The definition is apt here, because it is obvious that the compilation of articles and papers comprising *Modern Copyright Fundamentals* is an original, dynamic work of authorship. And what could be more suitable than for the field of copyright itself to have a compilation tailored to its intricasies and needs?

Since the passage of the comprehensive general revision of the copyright law in 1976, considerable and meaningful literature has appeared on all aspects of copyright. This literature is widely scattered among law school and other reviews, journals and magazines in the professions and industries concerned, and the general and business press. Although much of it is indexed or abstracted, the number of references on a topic may intimidate the unititiated, and the diversity of viewpoints may confuse as often as it enlightens.

The editors of *Modern Copyright Fundamentals* are therefore to be commended for sifting through this vast literature, selecting works from among it that are representative and instructive, and organizing their selections in a manner well suited to the needs of prospective readers.

The title and subtitle of this book are also particularly appropriate to the present copyright scene and to the editors' treatment of it. "Modern," "technological," and "issues" are keywords of real significance, and the editors have also paid close attention to the "copyright fundamentals" involved.

The array of authors whose papers are included is impressive, and their papers have much to say. So do the editors' Commentaries, an unusual feature in a compendium, and one that lends valuable context. Equally valuable are the bibliographies at the end of each of the nine sections of the book.

I know the editors, and I know they are well qualified to prepare this useful book. I recommend it wholeheartedly to those who want information and insight on copyright today.

MORTON DAVID GOLDBERG
Schwab Goldberg Price & Dannay
New York, New York

Preface

"Copyright" means many things to many people. Almost everyone knows that the Copyright Statute, enacted by Congress, is based on a Constitutional grant "to Promote the Progress of Science and the Useful Arts." However, agreement as to exactly what that means often ends right there. To the creators and other proprietors of copyrighted works, copyright is normally a foundation or bulwark for protecting the fruits of their efforts. To some scholars and librarians, and to certain manufacturers and many home users of technological products, it seems to be a confusing and unfair barrier to desirable activities, and therefore to progress itself.

Not surprisingly, quite a number of books and articles have been written on copyright and its aspects. These include books for lawyers, authors, publishers, and users. Some of these publications are scholarly treatises on the nature and faults of copyright itself. Others, especially articles and papers, range from lengthy analyses of major or minor aspects of the law to news accounts about specific problems or challenges and judicial or legislative actions.

So, why another book on copyright? In recent years, particularly, copyright issues have been much in the public eye. However, these issues have had numerous confusing aspects, many of them at the cutting edge of technology. The "Williams and Wilkins" litigation of the early 1970s, on library photocopying, has given way in the mid-1980s to issues involving technology and the home, such as the "Betamax" case on home videotape recording off the air, and to technology on a broader basis, such as debate and action on computer programs, computer chips, and optical/video discs.

Moreover, in this age of home and office computers, legal questions have been raised about several issues involving users, including unauthorized "downloading" from online computer data-bases. Therefore, it seemed to us that many people need to know more about how copyright relates to the modern scene—to understand both the fundamentals of copyright and their very real impacts.

Also, enough time has now passed since the enactment of the U.S. Copyright Statute of 1976, which became effective January 1, 1978, for practitioners and students of copyright, as well as other members of the concerned public, to write some really illuminating explanations and interpretations of the law in legal, other scholarly, and news publications. These articles have explored both copyright basics and key issues. However, this burgeoning literature has appeared in widely scattered sources. Some of the best are *The Journal of the Copyright Society of the U.S.A., Publishers Weekly, Information Hotline, Rights,* and *American Libraries,* but even these cover only a fraction of the copyright information.

As copyright users and administrators, and as authors ourselves in this field,* we therefore became receptive to suggestions that we prepare this compendium of key writings on technological and other issues related to modern copyright fundamentals. In attempting this compilation, we found ourselves able to include informative articles on such important subjects as how copyright and related issues affect authors, publishers, and other proprietors; the specific copyright concerns and problems of users and intermediaries; a wide variety of legal and commercial issues; the interplay of the copyright law and the new technologies; vital legislative and judicial aspects; and, finally, some thoughts about the future of copyright.

In making our selections from the several hundred good papers available, we have been acutely aware not only of existing issues and controversies, but also that the copyright-related scene is constantly changing. Therefore, we have not hesitated to include or cite some substantive papers that do not represent our own points of view and with which we disagree. Moreover, we are well aware that future judicial decisions based on the "new" copyright law will continue to alter previous truisms. Also, applications of the new technologies will outstrip our previous imaginings and will raise new copyright challenges. Congress will occasionally consider and pass amendments to the copyright statute. We have kept all these points in mind by selecting articles that we hope will explain and illuminate such happenings for some time to come.

We know of other books on copyright that go into greater detail on some "how to do it" matters, but we have not neglected these. What we have tried to stress in our selections are the "this is what it's all about" aspects—the key issues, the players, and why both are important.

The intricacies of copyright are many indeed, as are its effects on communication. Books and periodicals will probably remain with us for a long time, but they will be increasingly joined by electronic communications of all types. Television, videorecordings, online access from personal computers, videodiscs—what will be next? Creators, marketers, and users all have their stakes here. Therefore, it is important for all of us to understand copyright and to be aware of its possible implications and consequences. We hope that this book will help.

ACKNOWLEDGEMENTS

We sincerely thank Toni Carbo Bearman and Rita Lerner, who encouraged us to prepare this book.

We deeply appreciate the suggestions and permissions of many distinguished authors and publishers. Jon A. Baumgarten, Morton David Gold-

*We must make a disclaimer that we are not attorneys, nor do we pretend to practice law in this book. We leave that properly to lawyers, many of whom have authored papers that appear here. Also, the views expressed in this book are not necessarily those of the American Chemical Society.

berg, and Charles H. Lieb suggested many valuable papers. Other who made helpful suggestions include Joseph S. Alen, Robert Frase, Dennis D. McDonald, Patricia H. Penick, Kurt D. Steele, and Paul G. Zurkowski.

The late Kate McKay of The Copyright Society of the U.S.A. was gracious and helpful in making her library and that of the New York University Law Center accessible to us. We also thank D. H. Michael Bowen and Helen D. Coleman of the American Chemical Society for their interest and moral support.

We are particularly grateful to Margaret H. Graham and Frank A. Merola, formerly of Exxon Corporation Research and Engineering Company, and to Vincent F. Bick, Jr., and Mary Kay Moynihan of the Exxon Corporation Law Department for obtaining for us—legally—the copies of photocopies of many of the papers that we have considered for inclusion in this book. Robert J. Allan of Exxon Research was also helpful with bibliographic references. Many others deserve our thanks.

Last but not least, we extend special thanks to our spouses, Carolyn L. Weil and the late Michael S. Polansky, for their understanding and support during the many months that we worked on this book.

Addendum to the Revised Second Printing

We are honored and pleased that the revised second printing of our book makes it part of the ASIS Monograph Series.

It is not yet time for a second edition. Copyright and the fields with which it interacts continue to move on, and at an accelerating pace, but few changes have been made in the Copyright Statute, and those that are pending or recently passed have not yet had time to yield many definitive analyses. The new literature is indeed vast, but it is also vastly repetitive. We are convinced that this first edition will continue to serve a wide variety of readers for some years.

However, we have seized the opportunity of this second printing to bring this book largely up to date for those willing to look beyond its basic papers. We have added a brief COPYRIGHT UPDATE section, including a substantial number of recent references. We know these will be of value.

BEN H. WEIL

BARBARA FRIEDMAN POLANSKY

INTRODUCTION

"Copyright" is technically a right defined by law (principally a national law) to make and sell copies of creative works or to perform or display them. In the United States "creative works" include literary works, musical compositions, dramatic works, pantomimes, choreographic works, works of art (pictorial, graphic, sculptural), motion pictures and other audiovisual works, sound recordings, and computer programs. It is thus a *proprietary* right, with overtones of *exclusive*. But because the framers of our Constitution saw it in a broad social context, it is a right that is part of a bargain and one that is Congress' to establish and define.

Article I, Section 8 of the U.S. Constitution states that:

The Congress shall have the Power . . . to Promote the Progress of Science and the Useful Arts, by securing for limited Times to Authors and Inventors the exclusive Rights to their respective Writings and Discoveries.

Laws are by nature complex, which is why we frequently need lawyers and courts. Indeed, a law passed by a legislature is commonly called a statute, which requires fleshing out by judicial decisions (and then perhaps amendments) before it is fully established. Thus, it is not surprising that Public Law 94-553, a completely amended Title 17 of the United States Code that was passed in 1976 with an effective date of January 1, 1978, should already be the center of judicial argument, and actual and proposed amendments—even though it was an omnibus copyright revision that reflected some 20 years of drafting, debate, and compromise.

It is not our intent to go on substantively here. A real introduction to U.S. copyright is the function of Paper 1. All that we will say further here is the obvious—that the U.S. Copyright Statute is complex and ever in need of interpretation and updating; that copyright reaches into many corners of commerce, the arts, and the home in this age of information—this age of electronics; and that even the large collection of targeted key writings on copyright that we have collected here can serve only to introduce one to modern copyright fundamentals—hence the title of our book.

There are many ways that phases of copyright can be addressed. We have chosen to gather and arrange the key writings under copyright basics and formalities, creators and owners, users, intermediaries, basic issues, technological issues, legislative and judicial issues, international aspects, and future developments. In this way, we progress from the more familiar fundamentals to those involved with the new technologies, and sometimes new points of commerce and law. If our division of the subject does not always work perfectly, it at least serves to highlight the most important aspects and their interrelations.

We begin each Part of the book with editors' commentaries that highlight both that phase of copyright and the purpose and contents of the papers themselves. Most commentaries also end with a Bibliography—the best of the hundreds of pertinent papers that we could not find room to include.

In our Preface we have already thanked the authors of the papers in this compendium. We can but hope that readers will agree with the value and context of our selections.

I: OVERVIEW AND BASICS

Papers 1 Through 4: Commentary

"Copyright" is defined in *Webster's Seventh New Collegiate Dictionary* as "the exclusive legal right to reproduce, publish, and sell the matter and form of a literary, musical, or artistic work." Both published and unpublished works are protected by copyright at the moment original works of authorship are fixed in a tangible medium of expression. In other words, copyright begins from the moment that pen touches paper.

Except for *fair use*, which is covered later in this book, a copyright owner has the exclusive rights to do and to authorize the following, according to Section 106 of the Copyright Statute:

(1) to reproduce the copyright works in copies or phono-records

(2) to prepare derivative works based upon the copy-righted work;

(3) to distribute copies or phonorecords of the copyrighted work to the public by sale or other transfer of ownership, or by rental, lease, or lending;

(4) in the case of literary, musical, dramatic, and choreographic works, pantomimes, and motion pictures and other audio-visual works, to perform the copyrighted work publicly; and

(5) in the case of literary musical, dramatic, and choreo-graphic works, pantomimes, and pictorial, graphic, or sculp-tural works, including the individual images of a motion picture or other audiovisual work, to display the copyrighted work publicly.

As simple as all this may sound, copyright is a complex law, open to con-troversial interpretations, heated discussions, and a myriad of misunder-standings.

In Paper 1 we (Weil and Polansky) have tried to present an unbiased review of the basics of copyright, as well as some predictions of their con-sequences. Although we did not deal exhaustively with all of the chapters of the U.S. Copyright Law in our paper, we have included articles in this com-pendium that do address the other copyright issues.

The second paper in this section is the U.S. Copyright Office's Circular R1, *Copyright Basics.* This publication is a fine informational item that cov-ers topics such as what copyright is, who can claim copyright, what works are protected, what is not protected by copyright, notice of copyright, how long copyright endures, transfer of copyright, termination of transfers, copyright registration, mandatory deposit for works published in the United States with notice of copyright, fees, and more. This circular is must reading for anyone who is interested in learning the basics of copyright.

In her 1974 Bowker Memorial Lecture, "The Demonology of Copyright" (Paper 3), Barbara Ringer, former U.S. Register of Copyrights, presented the origins of copyright, analyzed the changes in and effectiveness of the law, and offered some words of wisdom. Her powerful paper, although presented several years ago, still holds basic truths. For instance, she wrote:

> New services, such as cable systems, photocopy machines, and computers, have emerged without clearcut copyright guidelines, and people have come to rely on them in their businesses and their very lives. These services cannot be cut off, but somehow the copyright law must find a way to insure that the interests of authors and copyright owners are protected at the same time . . . .

The last paper that we have included in the Overview and Basics section is Jon Baumgarten's article, "Decoding the Copyright Act, A Course in the Formalities" (Paper 4). In it, he details the principal formalities of the Copyright Law, including registration, which is now permissive and is not a condition of copyright protection. Baumgarten goes into great depth on this subject, showing the advantages of registering works with the U.S. Copyright Office; he also presents the disadvantages to registration.

Another formality covered in Baumgarten's paper is the copyright notice. He addresses the fact that omission of a notice does not invalidate copyright provided that certain conditions are met. He concludes by writing, "Adoption of the principle of 'automatic copyright' marks a welcome movement in the United States law toward recognition of proprietary rights as a natural attribute of creative effort."

U.S. adherence to the Berne Convention in 1989, discussed in the Copyright Update, will remove the necessity for many of thee formalities, but not recessarily the value of adhering to them.

BIBLIOGRAPHY

Of course, there are many other good sources that present an overview and/or the basics of copyright. From among them we have selected the following citations for your information:

Cost-Benefit Study of U.S. Copyright Formalities, 1982, *Inf. Hotline* **14**(2):3.

Levine, A. J., 1978, Subject Matter of Copyright, *Copr. Soc. U.S.A. Bull.* **25**(3):201-203.

Lieb, C. H., 1976, An Overview of the New Copyright Law, *New Copyright Law: Overview,* Association of American Publishers, Inc., New York and Washington, D.C.

Roth, E., 1982, Is Notice Necessary? An Analysis of the Notice Provisions of the Copyright Law Revision, *ASCAP Copr. Law Symp.* **27**:245-284.

Books

Our compendium is composed almost exclusively of articles and papers, these being the types of documents that are concerned with very specific aspects of a subject and that can be targeted to a variety of concerned audiences in a variety of media. However, it is inherently the role of books to organize and present more information on a broad subject than can be done in individual, shorter papers—indeed, that is the purpose of this book—so we felt it desirable to refer readers to a few of the many books on copyright that are currently in print. Those wanting a more complete list should refer to *Books in Print,* which can be found in most libraries.

Bush, G.P., and Dreyfus, R. H., eds., 1979, *Technology and Copyright: Sources and Materials,* 2nd rev. ed., Lomond Books, Mt. Airy, Maryland.

Copyright Office, 1977, *General Guide to the Copyright Act of 1976,* Library of Congress, Washington, D.C.

Henn, H. C., 1988, *Copyright Law: A Practioner's Guide,* 2nd Ed., Practicing Law Institute, New York.

Johnson, D. F., 1978, *Copyright Handbook,* Bowker, New York and London.

Nimmer, M. B., 1984 (revised annually), *Nimmer on Copyright,* 4 vols., Matthew Bender, New York.

Patry, W. F., 1986, *Latman's The Copyright Law,* 6th ed., Bureau of National Affairs, Washington, D.C.

Pearle, E. G. and Williams, J. T., 1988 *The Publishing Law Handbook,* Prentice Hall Law & Business, Clifton, NJ.

Ploman, E. W., and Hamilton, L. C., 1980, *Copyright: Intellectual Property in the Information Age,* Routledge & Kegan, London, Boston, and Henley.

1: COPYRIGHT BASICS AND CONSEQUENCES

Ben H. Weil

Ben H. Weil, Inc.
Warren, N.J. 07060

Barbara Friedman Polansky

American Chemical Society
Washington, D.C. 20036

The U.S. Copyright Statute has complexities that affect the well being of the scientific and engineering communities, among others, and that are often not fully understood by them. To provide a better background for future consideration of specific copyright issues, this feature article reviews the basics of the current copyright statute and then interprets these in terms of such business, professional, emotional, and ethical aspects as print publications, library photocopying, videodiscs, downloading from bibliographic databases, and videotape recording off the air.

In recent years, literally thousands of articles have appeared that attempt to explain, interpret, or comment on the Copyright Statute of 1976, which became effective on January 1, 1978, and which culminated well over 20 years of legislative study and debate on how best to modify and update the Copyright Law of 1909. Because the new law—as for all copyright laws—is complex and far from unambiguous, it provides a veritable feast of opportunity for lawyers and for the pleaders of special causes, legitimate or sometimes less so.

Although only 7 years have passed since the statute was enacted, many questions have already been posed as to its adequacy to protect the more technological forms of expression. Depending on who is speaking, copyright can be rated on a scale ranging from a boon for "authors" to a barrier to communication.

Many articles and books on copyright rush quickly from references to its origins to details on its functions or malfunctions, presuming—probably incorrectly—that everyone knows what the Copyright Law is all about and what it actually says that gives rise to such a myriad of interpretations. Actually, it is important to be *certain* that readers know the basics of copyright if they are to really understand the more complicated issues in which copyright protection or the use of copyrighted material are involved. Accordingly, in this feature article we will review the fundamentals of copyright and will then discuss their impacts on uses and users—"copyright consequences".

GENERAL BACKGROUND

Two important U.S. laws—the copyright law and the patent law—are based on the same brief portion of the Constitution of the United States (Article I, Section 8):

"The Congress shall have the Power...to Promote the Progress of Science and the Useful Arts, by securing for limited Times to Authors and Inventors the exclusive Rights to their respective Writings and Discoveries..."

This passage has been subject to many shadings of interpretation. To those to whom monopolies of any type or degree are anathema, emphasis is always placed on the public-welfare implications and on diminishing rights for authors and inventors. However, for those to whom creative entrepreneurship within the free-enterprise system is a way of life, it is clear that the exclusive rights granted are proper business awards.

Moreover, while the Constitution speaks of "Authors", in modern terminology this term has been broadened to include composers, artists, and even computer programmers, as well as employers. In our capitalistic society, relatively few of these creators of "intellectual property" can actually produce, reproduce, adapt, or perform their works to optimal economic advantage, so they usually assign (or are required to assign) such rights to publishers, recording firms, and similar enterprises, thereby providing these organizations with the requisite economic incentive.

The original U.S. copyright statute was patterned after the 1710 British law known as the Statute of Anne, which was an "Act for the Encouragement of Learning by Vesting the Copies of Printed Books in Authors of Such Copies During the Times Therein Mentioned". Protection for the author had by then succeeded the original British purpose for statutory copyright, which was the stifling of religious heresy. To achieve the latter, a royal decree in 1556 had given the Stationers' Company (an organization of the leading London publishers) a monopoly over all printing.

In 1790, 3 years after the U.S. Constitution was approved, Congress enacted its first copyright statute. This protected books, maps, and charts, but subsequent 19th Century versions broadened the areas of protection to include prints, musical compositions, photographs, works of fine art, translation rights, public performance (first for drama, then for musical compositions), and the right to dramatize nondramatic literary works. Thus, Congress did not restrict "writings" to the printed word (Gutenberg technology) and laid the groundwork for such later, esoteric compositions as computer software.

To receive copyright protection, a "writing" must be a fixed product of original or creative thought and work; unlike for a patentable invention, it need not be novel. "To be eligible for protection, however, the work must take some tangible form; ideas, plans, methods, and systems, as such, are not copyrightable, although the writing that expresses or describes them is subject to copyright. At present, words, names, titles, and slogans are also not eligible for copyright, but Congress probably has the Constitutional authority to extend protection to these 'writings' if it should so elect. Facts, news, and other commonly held information are not protectable, since they do not meet the requirement of 'originality'."[1]

Further history and background on copyright is available in numerous books and articles, including the above-referenced work[1] in whose preparation B.H.W. played a major role on behalf of the American Chemical Society and several other scientific and engineering societies.

THE LAW ITSELF

To understand copyright, nothing is as important as the 1976 Copyright Statute itself. While available space obviously does not permit us to reproduce this here, we strongly urge serious scholars to obtain a copy of this statute, in addition to copies of the forms, regulations, and circulars that are part of the Copyright Office Information Kit available from the Copyright Office, Library of Congress, Washington, DC 20559.

The copyright statute, which is Title 17 of the U.S. Code, is divided into eight chapters, each of which has numbered sections and further subdivisions. Chapters include:
1. Subject matter and scope of copyright.
2. Copyright ownership and transfer.
3. Duration of copyright.
4. Copyright notice, deposit, and registration.
5. Copyright infringement and remedies.
6. Manufacturing requirements and importation.
7. Copyright Office.
8. Copyright Royalty Tribunal.

We will concentrate on the first four of these chapters, but will touch briefly on the others, as appropriate. Our emphasis in this article will be on matters of direct importance to scientists and engineers as authors and users of copyrighted works, but not so much on copyright formalities.

Subject Matter and Scope. Almost half of the copyright statute is concerned with Chapter 1, which is subdivided into 18 sections that address the subject matter and scope of copyright:
101. Definitions.
102. Subject matter of copyright: In general.
103. Subject matter of copyright: Compilations and derivative works.
104. Subject matter of copyright: National origin.
105. Subject matter of copyright: United States Government works.
106. Exclusive rights in copyrighted works.
107. Limitations on exclusive rights: Fair use.
108. Limitations on exclusive rights: Reproduction by libraries and archives.
109. Limitations on exclusive rights: Effect of transfer of particular copy or phonorecord.
110. Limitations on exclusive rights: Exemption of certain performances and displays.
111. Limitations on exclusive rights: Secondary transmissions.
112. Limitations on exclusive rights: Ephemeral recordings.
113. Scope of exclusive rights in pictorial, graphic, and sculptural works.
114. Scope of exclusive rights in sound recordings.
115. Scope of exclusive rights in nondramatic musical works: Compulsory license for making and distributing phonorecords.
116. Scope of exclusive rights in nondramatic musical works: Public performances by means of coin-operated phonorecord players.
117. Scope of exclusive rights: Use in conjunction with computers and similar information systems.
118. Scope of exclusive rights: Use of certain works in conjunction with noncommercial broadcasting.

Definitions. Section 101 contains many definitions that are vital to a clear understanding of the statute, but it is too lengthy to include here. A few examples must suffice to depict its importance:

A "collective work" is a work, such as a periodical issue, anthology, or encyclopedia, in which a number of contributions, constituting separate and independent works in themselves, are assembled into a collective whole.

A "compilation" is a work formed by the collection and assembling of preexisting materials or of data that are selected, coordinated, or arranged in such a way that the resulting work as a whole constitutes a work of authorship. The term "compilation" includes collective works.

"Copies" are material objects, other than phonorecords, in which a work is fixed by any method now known or later developed, and from which the work can be perceived, reproduced, or otherwise communicated, either directly or with the aid of a machine or device. The term "copies" includes the material object, other than a phonorecord, in which the work was first fixed.

A "derivative work" is a work based on one or more preexisting works, such as a translation, musical arrangement, dramatization, fictionalization, motion picture version, sound recording, art reproduction, abridgement, condensation, or any other form in which a work may be recast, transformed, or adapted. A work consisting of editorial revisions, annotations, elaborations, or other modifications which, as a whole, represent an original work of authorship, is a "derivative work".

A work is "fixed" in a tangible medium of expression when its embodiment in a copy or phonorecord, by or under the authority of the author, is sufficiently permanent or stable to be perceived, reproduced, or otherwise communicated for a period of more than transitory duration. A work consisting of sounds, images, or both that are being transmitted, is "fixed" ... if a fixation of the work is being made simultaneously with its transmission.

"Literary works" are works, other than audiovisual works, expressed in words, numbers, or other verbal or numerical symbols or indicia, regardless of the nature of the material objects, such as books, periodicals, manuscripts, phonorecords, film, tapes, disks, or cards, in which they are embodied.

"Publication" is the distribution of copies or phonorecords of a work to the public by sale or other transfer of ownership, or by rental, lease, or lending. The offering to distribute copies or phonorecords to a group of persons for purposes of further distribution, public performance, or public display, constitutes publication. A public performance or display of a work does not of itself constitute publication.

Other pertinent terms defined include "display", "joint work", "perform", "transfer of copyright ownership", "transmit", "work of the United States Government", and "work made for hire".

Subject Matter in General. Section 102 states that "copyright protection subsists ... in original works of authorship fixed in any tangible medium of expression, now known or later developed, from which they can be perceived, later reproduced, or otherwise communicated, either directly or with the aid of a machine or device". Works of authorship include (1) literary works; (2) musical works, including any accompanying words; (3) dramatic works, including any accompanying music; (4) pantomimes and choreographic works; (5) pictorial, graphic, and sculptural works; (6) motion pictures and other audiovisual works; (7) sound recordings.

However, copyright protection does not extend to "any idea, procedure, process, system, method of operation, concept, principle, or discovery, regardless of the form in which it is described, explained, illustrated, or embodied in such works".

Other Subject Matter. Section 103 extends the specification of subject matter eligible for copyright to compilations and derivative works, including preexisting copyrighted material as long as it has been used lawfully. Section 104 extends copyright protection to unpublished works without regard to nationality or domicile; however, protection of published works is limited to U.S. citizens and those of countries that are members of the Universal Copyright Convention (UCC) or other copyright treaties to which the U.S. is a party. Also, the work must be published in the U.S., in a country that is party to the UCC, by the United Nations or any of its agencies, or by the Organization of American States.

Section 105 denies copyright protection to "any work of the United States Government", which "is a work prepared by an officer or employee of the United States Government as part of that person's official duties". However, this does not preclude a U.S. Government employee from holding copyright if the work was not prepared as part of his or her official duties. Also, the U.S. Government may receive and hold copyrights that might be transferred to it by assignment, bequest, or otherwise.

Exclusive Rights. Subject to limitations expressed in the remaining sections of Chapter 1, Section 106 states that the copyright owner "has the exclusive rights to do and to authorize any of the following:

(1) to reproduce the copyrighted work in copies or phonorecords;

(2) to prepare derivative works based upon the copyrighted work;

(3) to distribute copies or phonorecords of the copyrighted work by sale or other transfer of ownership, or by rental, lease, or lending;

(4) in the case of literary, musical, dramatic, and choreographic works, pantomimes, and motion pictures and other audiovisual works, to perform the copyrighted work publicly; and

(5) in the case of literary, musical, dramatic, and choreographic works, pantomimes, and pictorial, graphic, or sculptural works, including the individual images of a motion picture or other audiovisual work, to display the copyrighted work publicly."

Fair Use Exceptions. Section 107, which concerns "fair use" exceptions to the aforementioned exclusive rights, codifies what had previously been judicial doctrine. It was not intended to change, narrow, or enlarge it in any way. According to Section 107, "the fair use of a copyrighted work, including such use by reproduction in copies or purposes such as criticism, comment, new reporting, teaching (including multiple copies for classroom use), scholarship, or research, is not an infringement of copyright. In determining whether the use made of a work in any particular case is a fair use the factors to be considered shall include: (1) the purpose and character of the use, including whether such is of a commercial nature or is for nonprofit educational purposes; (2) the nature of the copyrighted work; (3) the amount and substantiality of the portion used in relation to the copyrighted work as a whole; and (4) the effect of the use upon the potential market for or value of the copyrighted work."

These criteria are not necessarily the sole ones to consider in determining fair use. Some examples of fair use that appear on page 65 of House of Representatives Report 94-1476, dated September 3, 1976, include "quotation of excerpts in a review or criticism for purposes of illustration or comment; quotation of short passages in a scholarly or technical work, for illustration or clarification of the author's observation; summary of an...article, with brief quotations, in a news report; and reproduction by a teacher or student of a small part of a work to illustrate a lesson".

The courts have found it quite difficult to state a concise definition of fair use. To quote again from the above-mentioned House Report, "since the doctrine is an equitable rule of reason, no generally applicable definition is possible, and each case raising the question must be decided on its own facts". Taking this statement into consideration, some groups that were particularly concerned with copying for teacher and classroom use and with photocopying of music, tried to work out some compromises. As a result of their successful efforts, guidelines for such uses were accepted by both the House and the Senate. Although these guidelines are not included in the copyright statute, they were published in the aforementioned House Report.

Reproduction by Libraries and Archives. In the years preceding the passage of the 1976 law, Congress also paid considerable attention to balancing the rights of authors and publishers with the needs of libraries for the benefit of users. Previously, most libraries had depended for their photocopying on an interpretation of "fair use" that permitted them to provide a "single copy" of a portion of a copyrighted work (including an entire article) to any user, locally or through "interlibrary loan". Congress agreed that "reproduction by libraries and archives" warranted some amplification and definition over "simple" fair use, including definition of limitations.

Accordingly, Section 108 permits a library or archives to produce or distribute a single copy of a work in its collection if this is done "without any purpose of direct or indirect commercial advantage", if its collections are "open to the public" or available "to persons doing research in a specialized field" as well as to affiliated researchers, and if the copy "includes a notice of copyright". A damaged, lost, or stolen copy may be duplicated in facsimile form "if the library or archives has, after a reasonable effort, determined that an unused replacement cannot be obtained at a fair price".

Under Section 108, a library or archives may make for a user, or may request in his or her behalf from another library or archives, "no more than one article or other contribution to a copyrighted collection or periodical issue...or a small part of any other copyrighted work". However, the copy must become the property of the user, and the library or archives may prepare or obtain it only when it "has had no notice that the copy or phonorecord would be used for any other purpose than private study, scholarship, or research" and when "a warning of copyright", as prescribed by the Register of Copyrights, is displayed "where orders are accepted" and is included on the library's order form. Moreover, with the same provisos, a copy of an entire work or a substantial portion of it may be requested "if the library or archives has first determined, on the basis of a reasonable investigation, that a copy or photorecord of the copyrighted work cannot be obtained at a fair price".

A library or archives is not liable for what is done at unsupervised reproducing equipment located on its premises, provided that a notice is posted "to the effect that the making of a copy may be subject to the copyright law". An individual using such equipment or requesting a photocopy from the library or archives can be held liable "for copyright infringement if his act...or later use...exceeds fair use as provided in Section 107".

Library copying under Section 108 is further restricted to "isolated and unrelated reproduction of a single copy or phonorecord of the same material on separate occasions". The right to do such copying "does not extend to cases where the library...or its employee—(1) is aware or has substantial reason to believe that it is engaging in related or concerted reproduction or distribution of multiple copies or phonorecords of the same material, whether made on one occasion or over a period of time, and whether intended for aggregate use by one or more individuals or for separate use by the individual members of a group; or (2) engages in the systematic reproduction or distribution of single or multiple copies or phonorecords...: *Provided*, That nothing in this clause prevents a library or archive from participating in interlibrary arrangements that do not have, as their purpose or effect, that the library or archives receiving such copies or phonorecords for distribution does so in such aggregate quantities as to substitute for a subscription to or purchase of such work."

Under guidelines on "Photocopying—Interlibrary Arrangements" developed in 1976 by the National Commission on New Technological Uses for Copyrighted Works (CONTU), just in time to be included by the House and Senate in their (copyright statute) "Conference Report" (H.R. 94-1733, dated September 29, 1976), libraries or archives are permitted to request from other libraries or archives up to five copies of articles published in the last 5 years in a given periodical, as long as they maintain proper records of such requests.

The Conference Report, in interpreting "indirect commercial advantage"—mentioned earlier as one barrier to library eligibility for Section 108 privileges—went on to say that if other criteria in Section 108(a) were met, "the conferees consider that the isolated, spontaneous making of single photocopies by a library or archives in a for-profit organization without any commercial motivation, or participation by such a library or archives in interlibrary arrangements, would come within the scope of Section 108". However, the Association of American Publishers believes that such private-library copying is very strictly limited, because of examples of violations included in the earlier Senate Report (94-473, dated November 20, 1975), basing the priority for this report on the fact that neither the House nor the Conference Committee made any changes in the related wording of the statute.

Section 108 also states that its provisions do not apply to musical works, graphic works, motion pictures, etc. It concludes with a provision that, every 5 years after 1978, the Register of Copyrights shall prepare and submit to Congress a report on the extent to which Section 108 "has achieved the intended statutory balancing of the rights of the creators and the needs of users" and that this report should also include recommendations for any legislative changes needed to solve any problems that may exist. The Register's report submitted in 1983 noted an apparent lack of library clarity on the stringencies in Section 108 and a need for further studies. The Register recommended a few statutory changes, including addition of an "umbrella statute" to limit statutory damages, for users complying with certain requirements, for the copying of technical or business periodicals beyond fair use or Section 108; this limitation would apply only for publishers who have not registered their periodicals with the Copyright Clearance Center or otherwise specified payments for such copying.

Other Exceptions and Statements of Scope. Section 109 makes it lawful for the owner of a copy of a copyrighted work to sell or otherwise dispose of that copy without the authority of the copyright owner, or similarly to display it publicly (including projection of one image at a time) or to authorize someone else to do the same. Such rights do not extend, without the permission of the copyright owner, to those who rent, lease, or borrow the copy without actually owning it.

Sections 110–116 and 118 do not often relate directly to scientists and engineers as authors or users, although Section 110 does permit certain performances and displays for classroom purposes.

Section 117, which was amended in 1980, relates importantly to the limitations on exclusive rights concerning computer programs and use. The original Section 117 mentioned that the copyright owner was not afforded any "greater or lesser rights with respect to the use of the [copyrighted] work in conjunction with automatic systems capable of storing, processing, retrieving, or transferring information, or in conjunction with any similar device, machine, or process, than those afforded to works under the law...in effect on December 31, 1977, ..." The amended Section 117 allows "the owner of a copy of a computer program to make or authorize the making of another copy or adaptation...", provided that such action is essential to use of the computer program and that the new copy is not used in any other manner or that the making of the new copy or adaptation is for archival purposes only; when the owner of the computer program no longer has the right to possess it, all archival copies must be destroyed.

Copyright Ownership and Transfer. Chapter 2 of the 1976 copyright statute deals with copyright ownership and transfer; it contains five sections:

201. Ownership of copyright.
202. Ownership of copyright as distinct from ownership of material object.
203. Termination of transfers and licenses granted by the author.
204. Execution of transfers of copyright ownership.
205. Recordation of transfers and other documents.

Section 201 makes it clear that the author of a work eligible for copyright is the initial owner of it, with the authors of a joint work coowners of it. However, in the case of a "work made for hire, the employer or other person for whom the work was prepared is considered the author...[and] owns all of the rights...unless the parties have explicitly agreed otherwise" in writing.

Authors of scientific and engineering books have long been accustomed to assigning the ownership of copyright in their books to publishers as part of their book contracts, although not always for subsidiary rights in the case of works of fiction, where authors more generally hold their own copyrights. However, prior to the 1976 copyright statute, there was usually little in writing between publishers and the authors of journal articles beyond (in some cases) statements in society bylaws and on reprint order forms that papers published in a given journal were the property of the given society or other publisher. It was normally assumed that copyright transfer took place upon publication in the case of papers in journals and other collective works. It was also assumed that the copyright of the collective work also held for the individual papers.

Now, however, the copyright in each paper "is distinct from copyright in the collective work as a whole, and [not only] vests initially in the author of the [separate] contribution", but also continues to be his or hers "in the absence of express transfer [in writing] of the copyright or of any of the rights under it". Without such written transfer, the copyright owner of the collective work—usually a publisher—is "presumed to have acquired only the privilege of reproducing and distributing the contribution as part of that particular collective work, any revision of that collective work, and any later collective work in the same series".

Accordingly, most publishers of scientific and engineering books, journals, and proceedings (the American Chemical Society was a leader here) now require written copyright transfers before publication, "to protect their reputations, and ours as authors, against misuse of our writings, and centrally to represent authors in a variety of ways"; without such transfers, these publishers "are unable to grant even royalty-free permissions, much less licenses, for anyone to make photocopies of their papers, and they cannot make their papers available in digital form for [on-line, full-text] searching".[2] Actually, "it goes without saying that you must be the copyright owner of requested material in order to grant... permissions".[3] On the other side of the coin, requestors find it easier to obtain permissions from a publisher rather than from a multiplicity of individual authors.

Chapter 2 of the statute also contains sections on the recordation of transfers and other documents in the U.S. Copyright Office and the termination of transfers and licenses granted by authors. As provided for in Section 203, "in the case of any work other than a work made for hire...", termination of the transfer may be made at any time in years 36–41 from the data of the original transfer.

Duration of Copyright. Chapter 3 of the copyright statute contains five sections, as follow:

301. Preemption with respect to other laws.
302. Duration of copyright: Works created on or after January 1, 1978.
303. Duration of copyright: Works created but not published or copyrighted before January 1, 1978.
304. Duration of copyright: Subsisting copyrights.
305. Duration of copyright: Terminal data.

To align U.S. practice with that in most countries, the term of copyright for works created on or after January 1, 1978, is generally the life of the author plus 50 years. In the case of joint works prepared by two or more authors, the copyright term is 50 years after the death of the last surviving author. For anonymous works, pseudonymous works, and works made for hire, copyright endures for a term of 75 years from first publication or 100 years from the work's creation, whichever expires first.

Works only in their (old law) first term of copyright on January 1, 1978, continue in copyright for the balance of this original term of 28 years; they are then eligible, upon application, for a renewal term of 47 years. The duration of copyright for works already in their renewal term on January 1, 1978, was automatically extended to 75 years from their original date of copyright.

Copyright Notice, Deposit, and Registration. Chapter 4 of the copyright statute has 12 sections, as follow:

401. Notice of copyright: Visually perceptible copies.
402. Notice of copyright: Phonorecords of sound recordings.
403. Notice of copyright: Publications incorporating United States Government works.
404. Notice of copyright: Contributions to collective works.
405. Notice of copyright: Omission of notice.
406. Notice of copyright: Error in name or date.
407. Deposit of copies or phonorecords for Library of Congress.
408. Copyright registration in general.
409. Application for copyright registration.
410. Registration of claim and issuance of certificate.
411. Registration as prerequisite to infringement suit.
412. Registration as prerequisite to certain remedies for infringement.

Whenever a work that is eligible for copyright protection is published, a copyright notice as provided by Section 401 "shall be placed on all publicly distributed copies from which the work can be visually perceived...". The notice consists of three elements: "(1) the symbol © (the letter C in a circle), or the word 'Copyright', or the abbreviation 'Copr.'; (2) the year of first publication of the work;...and (3) the name of the

the owner of copyright in the work...", e.g.

Copyright © 1984 American Chemical Society

Phonorecords must show a similar notice, except that the letter P is used instead of C.

A separate contribution to a collective work may bear its own notice of copyright, if permitted by the publisher. However, "a single notice applicable to the collective work as a whole is sufficient to satisfy the requirements...with respect to the separate contributions it contains..., regardless of the ownership of copyright in the contributions and whether or not they have been previously published" (Section 404).

Section 407 requires the copyright owner to deposit within 3 months, for use by the Library of Congress, two complete copies of the best edition of the published work or phonorecord. Certain exceptions are or may be made, such as for motion pictures and very limited editions ("less than five copies"). Fines may be levied if the deposit copies are not delivered after they are requested in writing by the Register of Copyrights.

Copyright registration, *which is not required for copyright ownership*, may be obtained from the Copyright Office when delivering the deposit copies "if they are accompanied by the prescribed application and fee, and by any additional identifying material that the Register may, by regulation, require". Registration may also be obtained after the 3-month deadline for deposit of copies. However, according to Section 407, "the certificate of registration made before or within five years after first publication of the work shall constitute prima facie evidence of the validity of the copyright and of the facts stated in the certificate. The evidentiary weight to be accorded the certificate of registration made thereafter shall be within the discretion of the court."

Registration is a prerequisite to infringement suits. According to Section 411, "no action for infringement of copyright in any work shall be instituted until registration of the copyright claim has been made". Section 412 states that "no award of statutory damages or of attorney's fees, as provided in Sections 504 and 505, shall be made for any infringement of copyright...commenced before the effective data of its registration", unless in the case of a published work, "such registration is made within three months after the first publication of the work".

Other Chapters. While important, the remaining chapters of the copyright statute are not usually the concern of individual scientists and engineers—unless, indeed, they have innocently or willfully violated the law.

One pertinent exception to the imposition of statutory damages (which can be as high as $50 000) occurs in Section 504(c) (2), where "the court shall remit statutory damages in any case where an infringer believed and has reasonable grounds for believing that his or her use of the copyrighted work was a fair use under Section 107, if the infringer was...an employee or agent of a nonprofit educational institution, library, or archives acting within the scope of his or her employment who, or such institution, library, or archives itself, which infringed by reproducing the work in copies or phonorecords; ...". As an attorney for a publisher's association has put it, however, this exception allows "only one free bite".

Chapter 6, as amended in 1982, protects domestic printers and publishers by prohibiting, prior to July 1, 1986, importation into the U.S. of nondramatic literary works in the English language unless manufactured in the U.S. or Canada. This chapter also prohibits (as an infringement of copyright) the unauthorized importation of copies or phonorecords. However, importation of such copies is not actionable where "an organization operated for scholarly, educational, or religious purposes and not for private gain [imports] no more than one copy of an audiovisual work solely for its archival purposes, and no more than five copies or phonorecords of any work for

10

its library lending or archival purposes, unless the importation of such copies or phonorecords is part of an activity consisting of systematic reproduction or distribution, engaged in by such organization in violation of Section 108(g) (2)". Systematic importation of photocopies from the British Library Lending Division without payment of copy fees may presently fall into the latter category.

Chapter 8 describes the establishment, purpose, and procedures of the Copyright Royalty Tribunal, which was created to determine reasonable royalty rates concerned with the compulsory licensing of the use of phonorecords and remote TV signals. If the statute is changed, this Tribunal may eventually be concerned with copyright areas that more directly affect scientists and engineers, as such.

COPYRIGHT CONSEQUENCES

By now, if you are new to copyright, you probably feel that we have told you everything you ever wanted to know about copyright, and much more. You have probably been amazed at the detailed, complex, and convoluted phraseology and have gained a glimmer of what we meant earlier by "feast for lawyers". But if you are not new to copyright, the personal and professional emotions that this subject always evokes have probably long since started your adrenalin flowing in disagreement with some of our comments to date, and in anticipation of what you fear we have yet to say. The significance—consequences—of this statute is/are such that few people ever agree completely on many points or, if they do, at least one will want a statutory change.

Business, Professional, Emotional, and Ethical Aspects. Neither of us is an economist, sociologist, psychologist, or attorney, but both of us have long been aware that copyright has many of the aspects that are studied by such professionals. We are also aware that copyright is unique, because the creative "writings" it protects are not used up by either fair or unfair use, although awareness of possible losses from the latter may discourage or prevent publication-"distribution". Even not-for-profit organizations such as scientific and engineering societies need break-even revenues from marketing their publications to support their efforts to disseminate information, and such revenues may not be sufficiently forthcoming if they are circumvented by too many for-free channels.

What is really important is that users of information, who are also often its creators, make certain that decision makers in their management chains, including information managers and corporate counsel, understand clearly the consequences to communications if every loophole in the copyright law is fully exploited. A dollar saved may not be a dollar earned if creative authors are no longer able to publish new, useful information because publishers no longer receive sufficient revenues from organizational subscriptions, page charges, or copyright copying fees to continue operations. Enlightened managements know this, but rapidly advancing technology often obscures what is going on.

In addition, many of us have professional drives that hide such facts even from ourselves. As scientists and engineers, we are strongly motivated to share our findings with colleagues, in order to be properly evaluated by them and to spur both our and their work. We want to communicate, and we really do not worry about the communication channels unless they become clogged. So strong is this drive that we sometimes even have trouble in observing proprietary niceties.

Moreover, many of our information managers, including librarians, are so well indoctrinated in the service ethic that they rebel instinctively against anything (especially legal artificialities) that could impede their ability to serve their individual clients optimally. Beginning—decades ago—with photocopying, they have become increasingly alert to tech-

nological developments, such as on-line computer networks and (soon) electronic copy delivery, that will expedite their services. Moreover, acute budgetary stringencies have reduced their ability to subscribe to publications (now more numerous and more expensive than ever) and have made them instinctively unsympathetic to new charges such as copyright royalty fees for copying.

B.H.W. has written before on the need for empathy and ethics in areas of information such as this,[4] and we will not belabor the subject further here. In regard to the copyright area, we can but laud such corporate policies as those that call for *strict* compliance with the law—all laws—as being most in keeping with the public welfare. And we hope that the philosophical points we have raised here will serve as minimum background to the discussions that follow.

Print Publications and Related Technological Developments. The copyright law is still the principal foundation upon which rests the protection of print publications. It establishes basic author rights. When copyright ownership is transferred to publishers, it gives them a legal basis from which to proceed against print piracy and other nonfair uses. Until photocopying became inexpensive—"single copy publishing" as some publishers call it—the copyright law provided a good set of rules for most of the print–publishing businesses. Lately, however, other technological challenges have arisen, as we have indicated, and revisions to the law or agreement on what the revisions mean seem not to have kept pace.

Except (for now) for long, entire works, users are turning increasingly to "document-delivery services"—libraries and information businesses—for copies of even current short documents—articles and the like. More and more, they are identifying the pertinent documents by on-line computer searching of bibliographic databases or computerized full-text versions of the documents themselves and less and less by subscribing to current issues of the printed publications. Not all of these new channels contribute presently or potentially to publishing revenues.

As we have seen, Sections 107 and 108 govern most of the print–publication copying and permit a considerable amount of it "for free" for classroom use and by/in libraries, especially where profit is not involved. Availability, convenience, and speed of delivery are the chief driving forces for users; real costs for the copies are considerable, although royalty fees—when paid—are seldom a major portion, at least so far.

To make it possible for users to legally make or obtain copies when these would otherwise fall outside of Section 107 and 108 privileges, the Association Publishers (AAP), jointly with certain users, helped to establish the Copyright Clearance Center, Inc. (CCC), in 1977. Under the CCC's "transactional" system, users may copy articles or chapters from publications that are registered with the CCC, provided that they report their copying to the CCC and, when billed by it, pay the per-copy fees that have been preset by each publisher. Under the CCC's Annualized Authorization Service, an industrial organization may sign a license agreement and pay a lump sum, based on a 90-day survey of its copying, for the right to copy from all CCC-registered publications. Because of the convenience of this latter program, and perhaps spurred by AAP litigation against some large companies, use of the CCC is increasing rapidly, and significant revenue for journal publishers is projected for 1985.

For-profit suppliers of copyrighted-document copies can either pay copying royalty fees through the CCC or, like others, they can attempt to negotiate copying licences with publishers. For copying billed as CCC-fee paid, the CCC has a monitoring program based on user-assisted sampling.

The library-copying program is considerably more confusing. The aforementioned 1983 5-year report of the Register of

Copyrights indicated that a considerable amount of library copying exceeded statutory fair use and exempted library use, especially the nearly 30% that were multiple copies. Less than 1% of total library copying was copy-fee paid. The Register's 1982 attempt to have representatives of the library and publishing communities resolve some of their disagreements and arrive at some definitions was unsuccessful.

Indeed, organized consultation between these communities is at a low ebb concerning copyright, especially in the area of photocopying. In 1979, librarians and publishers did meet to discuss the prospect of a National Periodicals Center that would have provided fee payments to publishers for its copying; however, somewhat premature legislation to establish it thereupon foundered, at least partially because of poor communications and a lack of mutual trust.

Both communities and some information businesses are now interested in document storage and supply on videodiscs, which can hold digitalized images of as many as 20 000 pages each. Several European groups have separately been studying this media, including a combine of five private publishers that considered the British Library Lending Division as the operator. This latter group, which also had at one stage proposed to transmit images to the U.S. by satellite for printout and mailing of copies from regional stations, has suspended its efforts because of technical and economic difficulties.

In the U.S., interest has centered on an "experimental" videodisc project of the Library of Congress, which has asked a number of publishers for permission to put a few years of their most recent issues on videodiscs; the experiment would be limited to local (Washington, DC) Library of Congress users. Copying charges were not initially proposed, nor were royalty fees; the stated purpose of the project centers around document preservation. However, the data to be collected will be pertinent for the copying of recent publications. Separate advisory groups of librarians and publishers (including information businesses) have been appointed.

Would-be producers of videodiscs, including customized ones, were very much in evidence at the November 1983 conference of the Information Industry Association. What was emphasized was direct, local use of videodiscs instead of microfiche, microfilm, or paper copies; on-line transmission was not mentioned. Copyright aspects were hardly touched on, but were implied.

Meanwhile, an on-line interlibrary loan network is being centralized by OCLC, the Online Computer Library Service, Inc. Also, on-line ordering (from designated document suppliers) of desired documents identified in on-line searching is currently available from some vendors of bibliographic databases.

In the meantime, the increasing electronic composition of print media is yielding digitalized versions that are in some cases being put on-line for searching and printout. In other cases, "electronic publishing" yields the latter type of product exclusively.

The copyright law is very much involved in all this. Technology is advancing so quickly here, however, that some people question whether copyright can protect the proprietary works involved. We will touch on this again later.

Bibliographic Databases; "Downloading". As we have mentioned, bibliographic databases—sometimes known as "secondary publications" or access services—are increasingly being used to identify pertinent documents, copies of which are then obtained by/for the individuals desiring information. Prior to the advent of on-line, remote computer searching of these databases in the 1970s—until lately almost entirely through "database vendors" ("on-line services")—such searching was exclusively done through printed publications (hence the phrase, "secondary publications"). However, by the mid 1960s, the advent of computer typesetting for these had permitted computer searching of new-issue tapes to identify references pertinent to the interests of individuals or groups ("SDI", or "selective dissemination of information").

Under the 1909 copyright law, relatively little attention was given to the copyright status of bibliographic databases and their constituent references and abstracts. In 1973, however, this subject was reviewed as part of the background for a study on impacts of the proposed new law.[1] By then, dissension had arisen in one scientific community (physics) as to whether an unaffiliated service could extensively use the "author abstracts" from another organization's primary-journal articles without a license. The unaffiliated service had then shifted to its own writing of "original abstracts" for these papers.

No legal challenge occurred. Moreover, the aforementioned study of proposed copyright-law changes[1] held essentially that, beyond some limited fair use, the copyright of "author abstracts" was probably the property of the primary journals in which they first appeared (although their free use by secondary journals was almost universally encouraged and permitted). The study also held that original abstracts could probably be written without the permission of the primary journals (and could be copyrighted themselves) as long as they did not become "derivative works"; in other words, if they were not so long and so comprehensive that their use could be substituted for the original works.

These conclusions still hold for the copyright status of abstracts under the 1976 statute, according to a recent study made by representatives of the Information Industry Association (IIA) and the National Federation of Abstracting and Information Services (NFAIS).[5] However, a strong dissent to these conclusions, especially in regard to the copyrightability of abstracts, has been expressed by the head of a major scientific-abstracting service.

In regard to original abstracts, the IIA/NFAIS study[5] differentiated between the typical 100–250-word abstracts of 5000–8000-word articles, which can seldom be derivative works, and the short "news" abstracts of newspaper and similar stories, which can sometimes contain all of the information in these items and, hence, might be derivative works. However, for these short-item abstracts, attention was called to the fair-use privileges afforded to "news stories" in Section 107 of the copyright statute.

There seems to be general agreement that the elements of bibliographic references, including document titles, are not copyrightable but that copyright protection extends to "compilations" of data (such as directories and, by inference, bibliographic databases) that contain such data in meaningful arrangements.[6] If so, this compilation protection would seem to be particularly strong for databases that contain copyrighted abstracts.

Under these circumstances, there would seem to be little question as to the copyright status of and protection afforded to bibliographic databases when they are made accessible via on-line computers. In addition to copyright protection, database information is usually further protected by limitations that are spelled out in contracts between database suppliers and on-line customers. Nevertheless, technology has put a strain on both copyright and contract protection. It is now possible for on-line users to easily "download" extensive portions of databases digitally, for later internal, payment-free use, without detection by the database suppliers. While some users have been asking for permission to download, others have even frankly admitted to what may amount to database misappropriation.

Nevertheless, recent studies indicate that unauthorized downloading is not as widespread as had been feared. Moreover, some of the major bibliographic-database

services—such as Chemical Abstracts Service and BIOSIS—
have announced licensing programs that permit such reuse in
a controlled manner. Continued attention to downloading
seems warranted, however, because it adds to the economic
impact of the on-line databases on subscriptions to the printed
versions.

It is too early to tell if and/or in what areas the use of on-line
searching of full-text databases will seriously impact on (replace rather than augment) the use of the bibliographic databases. Unfair copyright use of full-text databases appears
less attractive, because whole articles would have to be
downloaded. Public vendors of full-text databases would
certainly have to operate under licenses from the primary
publishers if, indeed, the primary publishers do not have their
own full-text on-line services.

Other Aspects. The recent decision of the Supreme Court
on the "Betamax" case will probably have wide repercussions.
As most of us know, this was a case in which a motion picture
studio sued a Japanese manufacturer of TV videotape recorders, claiming that their sale (and home use of) for off-
the-air taping of its copyrighted movies constituted contributory copyright infringement. The Supreme Court disagreed.
However, it was widely believed that, regardless of the outcome
of the case, Congress might counteract the decision, such as
by exempting videotape recorder sale and use if the motion
picture producer had won or by levying a sales charge on the
recorders to compensate the copyright owners for compulsory
use if—as happened—the manufacturer of videotape recorders
was held noninfringing.

The Supreme Court's decision, with or without modification
by Congress, is almost certain to have significant copyright
consequences in other areas of application. Copyright protection in general may well have been weakened by such
broadening of public rights at the expense of the copyright
owners. It was always inconceivable that the public use of such
appliances would be blocked, nor were the copyright owners
really seeking that, but even legislated compulsory licensing
does not strengthen copyright in general.

So rapidly is technology developing—so broad are its
applications—that we could go on almost indefinitely in discussing the resulting copyright consequences. We must content
ourselves and readers by mentioning only one more
consequence—the recent amendment to Section 117 under
which it became clear that computer programs could be
protected by copyright. This was an uneasy choice; indeed,
a minority opinion in CONTU held that neither copyright nor
patenting was applicable and that a new type of protection was
needed. As mentioned, copyright normally protects the expression, not the contents, of writings.

Those who are really uneasy about this are further concerned about pending legislation that would make it possible
to copyright the screens used to produce computer "chips",
contending that this would further distort the copyright concept. It will be interesting to see how this comes out; apparently, U.S. manufacturers of computer chips need some
protection against unfair foreign competition. Hopefully, the
form of this protection will not be to the detriment of the
copyright system.

CONCLUSIONS

So there you have it—our review on copyright basics and
consequences. Frankly, this field is so complex that we see
no other mechanism that presently could work better. We can
only urge patience, good ethical practices, and cooperation
instead of confrontation. If these can prevail, perhaps we can
all withstand—to coin a phrase—the temptations of technology.

REFERENCES AND NOTES

(1) Cambridge Research Institute "Omnibus Copyright Revision: Comparative Analysis of the Issues"; ASIS: Washington, DC, 1973.
(2) Weil, Ben H. "Why Should Chemists Care about Copyright?" *J.
Chem. Inf. Comput. Sci.* **1982**, *22*, 61–63.
(3) Friedman, Barbara A. "Copyright from a Permissions Person's Point
of View". *J. Chem. Inf. Comput. Sci.* **1982**, *22*, 70–72.
(4) Weil, Ben H. "Information Transfer in a Time of Transition: The Need
for Community, Organizational, and Individual Empathy and Ethics".
In "Abstracting and Indexing Services in Perspective: Miles Conrad
Memorial Lectures 1969–1983"; Neufeld, M. Lynne; Cornog, Martha;
Sperr, Inez L., Eds.; Information Resources Press: Arlington, VA,
1983.
(5) Weil, Ben H.; Steele, Kurt D.; Goldberg, Morton David; Neufeld, M.
Lynne; Granick, Lois W. "Proprietary Aspects of Abstracts". *ASIS
Bull.* **1983**, *9* (Apr), 18–21; *9* (June), 25–27.

2: COPYRIGHT BASICS

U.S. Copyright Office

On January 1, 1978, the Copyright Act of 1976 (title 17 of the United States Code) came into effect. This general revision of the copyright law of the United States, the first such revision since 1909, makes important changes in our copyright system and supersedes the previous Federal copyright statute. For highlights of the overall changes in the copyright law, request Circular R99 from the Copyright Office.

WHAT COPYRIGHT IS

Copyright is a form of protection provided by the laws of the United States (title 17, U.S. Code) to the authors of "original works of authorship" including literary, dramatic, musical, artistic, and certain other intellectual works. This protection is available to both published and unpublished works. Section 106 of the Copyright Act generally gives the owner of copyright the exclusive right to do and to authorize others to do the following:

- *To reproduce* the copyrighted work in copies or phonorecords;
- *To prepare derivative works* based upon the copyrighted work;
- *To distribute copies or phonorecords* of the copyrighted work to the public by sale or other transfer of ownership, or by rental, lease, or lending;
- *To perform the copyrighted work publicly,* in the case of literary, musical, dramatic, and choreographic works, pantomines, and motion pictures and other audiovisual works, and
- *To display the copyrighted work publicly,* in the case of literary, musical, dramatic, and choreographic works, pantomimes, and pictorial, graphic, or sculptural works, including the individual images of a motion picture or other audiovisual work.

It is illegal for anyone to violate any of the rights provided to the owner of copyright by the Act. These rights, however, are not unlimited in scope. Sections 107 through 118 of the Copyright Act establish limitations on these rights. In some cases, these limitations are specified exemptions from copyright liability. One major limitation is the doctrine of "fair use," which is now given a statutory basis by section 107 of the Act. In other instances, the limitation takes the form of a "compulsory license" under which certain limited uses of copyrighted works are permitted upon payment of specified royalties and compliance with statutory conditions. For further information about the limitations of any of these rights, consult the Copyright Act or write to the Copyright Office.

WHO CAN CLAIM COPYRIGHT

Copyright protection subsists from the time the work is created in fixed form; that is, it is an incident of the process of authorship. The copyright in the work of authorship *immediately* becomes the property of the author who created it. Only the author or those deriving their rights through the author can rightfully claim copyright.

In the case of works made for hire, the employer and not the employee is presumptively considered the author. Section 101 of the copyright statute defines a "work made for hire" as:

(1) a work prepared by an employee within the scope of his or her employment; or

(2) a work specially ordered or commissioned for use as a contribution to a collective work, as a part of a motion picture or other audiovisual work, as a translation, as a supplementary work, as a compilation, as an instructional text, as a test, as answer material for a test, or as an atlas, if the parties expressly agree in a written instrument signed by them that the work shall be considered a work made for hire. . . .

The authors of a joint work are co-owners of the copyright in the work, unless there is an agreement to the contrary.

Copyright in each separate contribution to a periodical or other collective work is distinct from copyright in the collective work as a whole and vests initially with the author of the contribution.

Two General Principles

- Mere ownership of a book, manuscript, painting, or any other copy or phonorecord does not give the possessor the copyright. The law provides that transfer of ownership of any material object that embodies a protected work does not of itself convey any rights in the copyright.

Reprinted from *Circular R1*, Library of Congress, Washington, D.C., 1983, pp. 3-12.

• Minors may claim copyright, but state laws may regulate the business dealings involving copyrights owned by minors. For information on relevant state laws, it would be well to consult an attorney.

COPYRIGHT AND NATIONAL ORIGIN OF THE WORK

Copyright protection is available for all unpublished works, regardless of the nationality or domicile of the author.

Published works are eligible for copyright protection in the United States if any one of the following conditions is met:

• On the date of first publication, one or more of the authors is a national or domiciliary of the United States or is a national, domiciliary, or sovereign authority of a foreign nation that is a party to a copyright treaty to which the United States is also a party, or is a stateless person wherever that person may be domiciled; or

• The work is first published in the United States or in a foreign nation that, on the date of first publication, is a party to the Universal Copyright Convention; or the work comes within the scope of a Presidential proclamation.

THE MANUFACTURING CLAUSE

The manufacturing clause in the copyright law, section 601 of the 1976 Copyright Act (title 17, U.S. Code), was extended by Congress in July 1982 until July 1, 1986; without this congressional action, the manufacturing provisions in the copyright law would have expired on July 1, 1982.

The manufacturing clause applies only to published works, primarily textual, written by United States authors or domiciliaries. The provisions require that copies of a work "consisting preponderantly of nondramatic literary material that is in the English language" be manufactured in the United States or Canada in order to be lawfully imported and publicly distributed in the United States. There are several exceptions to the provisions; they relate to three general categories: the nature of the work, the processes used to manufacture the copies, or certain facts existing at the time of importation or distribution of copies in the United States. One of the exceptions of the third type provides for the issuance of an Import Statement which will permit the importation of up to 2,000 copies of a foreign edition when certain conditions are met.

For further information on the issuance of import statements (Form IS), please write to:

Information and Publications Section, LM-455
Copyright Office
Library of Congress
Washington, D.C. 20559

WHAT WORKS ARE PROTECTED

Copyright protection exists for "original works of authorship" when they become fixed in a tangible form of expression. The fixation does not need to be directly perceptible, so long as it may be communicated with the aid of a machine or device. Copyrightable works include the following categories:

(1) literary works;
(2) musical works, including any accompanying words;
(3) dramatic works, including any accompanying music;
(4) pantomimes and choreographic works;
(5) pictorial, graphic, and sculptural works;
(6) motion pictures and other audiovisual works; and
(7) sound recordings.

This list is illustrative and is not meant to exhaust the categories of copyrightable works. These categories should be viewed quite broadly so that, for example, computer programs and most "compilations" are registrable as "literary works"; maps and architectural blueprints are registrable as "pictorial, graphic, and sculptural works."

WHAT IS NOT PROTECTED BY COPYRIGHT

Several categories of material are generally not eligible for statutory copyright protection. These include among others:

• Works that have *not* been fixed in a tangible form of expression. For example: choreographic works which have not been notated or recorded, or improvisational speeches or performances that have not been written or recorded.

• Titles, names, short phrases, and slogans; familiar symbols or designs; mere variations of typographic ornamentation, lettering, or coloring; mere listings of ingredients or contents.

• Ideas, procedures, methods, systems, processes, concepts, principles, discoveries, or devices, as distinguished from a description, explanation, or illustration.

15

- Works consisting *entirely* of information that is common property and containing no original authorship. For example: standard calendars, height and weight charts, tape measures and rules, and lists or tables taken from public documents or other common sources.

HOW TO SECURE A COPYRIGHT

Copyright Secured Automatically Upon Creation

The way in which copyright protection is secured under the present law is frequently misunderstood. No publication or registration or other action in the Copyright Office is required to secure copyright under the present law, unlike the previous law, which required either publication with the copyright notice or registration in the Copyright Office (see NOTE below). There are, however, certain definite advantages to registration. (See page 9.)

Under the present law, copyright is secured *automatically* when the work is created, and a work is "created" when it is fixed in a copy or phonorecord for the first time. In general, "copies" are material objects from which a work can be read or visually perceived either directly or with the aid of a machine or device, such as books, manuscripts, sheet music, film, videotape, or microfilm. "Phonorecords" are material objects embodying fixations of sounds (excluding, by statutory definition, motion picture soundtracks), such as audio tapes and phonograph disks. Thus, for example, a song (the

> **NOTE:** Before 1978, statutory copyright was generally secured by the act of publication with notice of copyright, assuming compliance with all other relevant statutory conditions. Works in the public domain on January 1, 1978 (for example, works published without satisfying all conditions for securing statutory copyright under the Copyright Act of 1909) remain in the public domain under the current Act.
>
> Statutory copyright could also be secured before 1978 by the act of registration in the case of certain unpublished works and works eligible for ad interim copyright. The current Act automatically extends to full term copyright (section 304 sets the term) for all works in which ad interim copyright was subsisting or was capable of being secured on December 31, 1977.

"work") can be fixed in sheet music ("copies") or in phonograph disks ("phonorecords"), or both.

If a work is prepared over a period of time, the part of the work existing in fixed form on a particular date constitutes the created work as of that date.

PUBLICATION

Publication is no longer the key to obtaining statutory copyright as it was under the Copyright Act of 1909. However, publication remains important to copyright owners.

The Copyright Act defines publication as follows:

"Publication" is the distribution of copies or phonorecords of a work to the public by sale or other transfer of ownership, or by rental, lease, or lending. The offering to distribute copies or phonorecords to a group of persons for purposes of further distribution, public performance, or public display, constitutes publication. A public performance or display of a work does not of itself constitute publication.

A further discussion of the definition of "publication" can be found in the legislative history of the Act. The legislative reports define "to the public" as distribution to persons under no explicit or implicit restrictions with respect to disclosure of the contents. The reports state that the definition makes it clear that the sale of phonorecords constitutes publication of the underlying work, for example, the musical, dramatic, or literary work embodied in a phonorecord. The reports also state that it is clear that any form of dissemination in which the material object does not change hands, for example, performances or displays on television, is *not* a publication no matter how many people are exposed to the work. However, when copies or phonorecords are offered for sale or lease to a group of wholesalers, broadcasters, or motion picture theaters, publication does take place if the purpose is further distribution, public performance, or public display.

Publication is an important concept in the copyright law because upon publication, several significant consequences follow. Among these are:

- When a work is published, all published copies should bear a notice of copyright. (See discussion below of "notice of copyright.")
- Works that are published with notice of copyright in the United States are subject to mandatory deposit with the

Library of Congress. (See discussion on page 10 on "mandatory deposit.")

● Publication of a work can affect the limitations on the exclusive rights of the copyright owner that are set forth in sections 107 through 118 of the law.

● The year of publication is used in determining the duration of copyright protection for anonymous and pseudonymous works (when the author's identity is not revealed in the records of the Copyright Office) and for works made for hire.

● Deposit requirements for registration of published works differ from those for registration of unpublished works. (See discussion on page 9 of "copyright registration" procedures.)

NOTICE OF COPYRIGHT

When a work is published under the authority of the copyright owner, a notice of copyright should be placed on all publicly distributed copies and on all publicly distributed phonorecords of sound recordings. This notice is required even on works published outside of the United States. Failure to comply with the notice requirement can result in the loss of certain additional rights otherwise available to the copyright owner.

The use of the copyright notice is the responsibility of the copyright owner and does not require advance permission from, or registration with, the Copyright Office.

Form of Notice for Visually Perceptible Copies

The notice for visually perceptible copies should contain all of the following three elements:

1. *The symbol ©* (the letter C in a circle), or the word "Copyright," or the abbreviation "Copr."
2. *The year of first publication* of the work. In the case of compilations or derivative works incorporating previously published material, the year date of first publication of the compilation or derivative work is sufficient. The year date may be omitted where a pictorial, graphic, or sculptural work, with accompanying textual matter, if any, is reproduced in or on greeting cards, postcards, stationery, jewelry, dolls, toys, or any useful articles.
3. *The name of the owner of copyright* in the work, or an abbreviation by which the name can be recognized, or a generally known alternative designation of the owner.
Example: © 1982 John Doe

The "C in a circle" notice is required only on "visually perceptible copies." Certain kinds of works, for example, musical, dramatic, and literary works, may be fixed not in "copies" but by means of sound in an audio recording. Since audio recordings such as audio tapes and phonograph disks are "phonorecords" and not "copies," there is no requirement that the phonorecord bear a "C in a circle" notice to protect the underlying musical, dramatic, or literary work that is recorded.

Form of Notice for Phonorecords of Sound Recordings

The copyright notice for phonorecords of sound recordings* has somewhat different requirements. The notice appearing on phonorecords should contain the following three elements:

● *The symbol ℗* (the letter P in a circle); and
● *The year of first publication* of the sound recording; and
● *The name of the owner of copyright* in the sound recording, or an abbreviation by which the name can be recognized, or a generally known alternative designation of the owner. If the producer of the sound recording is named on the phonorecord labels or containers, and if no other name appears in conjunction with the notice, the producer's name shall be considered a part of the notice.
Example: ℗ 1982 A.B.C., Inc.

> **NOTE:** Because of problems that might result in some cases from the use of variant forms of the notice, any form of the notice other than these given here should not be used without first seeking legal advice.

Position of Notice

The notice should be affixed to copies or phonorecords of the work in such a manner and location as to "give reasonable notice of the claim of copyright." The notice on phonorecords may appear on the surface of the phonorecord or on

---

*Sound recordings are defined as "works that result from the fixation of a series of musical, spoken, or other sounds, but not including the sounds accompanying a motion picture or other audiovisual work, regardless of the nature of the material objects, such as disks, tapes, or other phonorecords, in which they are embodied."

the phonorecord label or container, provided the manner of placement and location gives reasonable notice of the claim. The three elements of the notice should ordinarily appear together on the copies or phonorecords. The Copyright Office has issued regulations concerning the form and position of the copyright notice in the *Code of Federal Regulations* (37 C.F.R. Part 201); copies of these regulations are available from the Copyright Office as Circular R96 201.20.

Publications Incorporating United States Government Works

Whenever a work is published in copies or phonorecords consisting preponderantly of one or more works of the United States Government, the notice of copyright shall also include a statement identifying, either affirmatively or negatively, those portions of the copies or phonorecords embodying any work or works protected by title 17 of the United States Code.

Unpublished Works

The copyright notice is not required on unpublished works. To avoid an inadvertent publication without notice, however, it may be advisable for the author or other owner of the copyright to affix notices, or a statement such as *Unpublished Work* © 1982 John Doe, to any copies or phonorecords which leave his or her control.

Effect of Omission of the Notice or of Error in the Name or Date

Unlike the law in effect before 1978, the new Copyright Act, in sections 405 and 406, provides procedures for correcting errors and omissions of the copyright notice on works published on or after January 1, 1978.

In general, the omission or error does not automatically invalidate the copyright in a work if registration for the work has been made before or is made within 5 years after the publication without notice, and a reasonable effort is made to add the notice to all copies or phonorecords that are distributed to the public in the United States after the omission has been discovered.

HOW LONG COPYRIGHT PROTECTION ENDURES

Works Originally Copyrighted on or After January 1, 1978

A work that is created (fixed in tangible form for the first time) on or after January 1, 1978, is automatically protected from the moment of its creation, and is ordinarily given a term enduring for the author's life, plus an additional 50 years after the author's death. In the case of "a joint work prepared by two or more authors who did not work for hire," the term lasts for 50 years after the last surviving author's death. For works made for hire, and for anonymous and pseudonymous works (unless the author's identity is revealed in Copyright Office records), the duration of copyright will be 75 years from publication or 100 years from creation, whichever is shorter.

Works that were created before the present law came into effect, but had neither been published nor registered for copyright before January 1, 1978, have been automatically brought under the statute and are now given Federal copyright protection. The duration of copyright in these works will generally be computed in the same way as for works created on or after January 1, 1978: the life-plus-50 or 75/100-year terms will apply to them as well. However, all works in this category are guaranteed at least 25 years of statutory protection.

Works Copyrighted Before January 1, 1978

Under the law in effect before 1978, copyright was secured either on the date a work was published, or on the date of registration if the work was registered in unpublished form. In either case, the copyright endured for a first term of 28 years from the date it was secured. During the last (28th) year of the first term, the copyright was eligible for renewal. The new copyright law has extended the renewal term from 28 to 47 years for copyrights that were subsisting on January 1, 1978, making these works eligible for a total term of protection of 75 years. However, the copyright *must* be timely renewed to receive the 47-year period of added protection. For more detailed information on the copyright term, write to the Copyright Office and request Circulars R15a and R15t. For information on how to search the Copyright Office records concerning the copyright status of a work, ask for Circular R22.

TRANSFER OF COPYRIGHT

Any or all of the exclusive rights, or any subdivision of those rights, of the copyright owner may be transferred, but the transfer of *exclusive* rights is not valid unless that transfer is in writing and signed by the owner of the rights conveyed (or such owner's duly authorized agent). Transfer of a right on a nonexclusive basis does not require a written agreement.

A copyright may also be conveyed by operation of law and may be bequeathed by will or pass as personal property by the applicable laws of intestate succession.

Copyright is a personal property right, and it is subject to the various state laws and regulations that govern the ownership, inheritance, or transfer of personal property as well as terms of contracts or conduct of business. For information about relevant state laws, consult an attorney.

Transfers of copyright are normally made by contract. The Copyright Office does not have or supply any forms for such transfers. However, the law does provide for the recordation in the Copyright Office of transfers of copyright ownership. Although recordation is not required to make a valid transfer as between the parties, it does provide certain legal advantages and may be required to validate the transfer as against third parties. For information on recordation of transfers and other documents related to copyright, write to the Copyright Office for Circular R12.

TERMINATION OF TRANSFERS

Under the previous law, the copyright in a work generally reverted to the author, if living, or if the author was not living, to other specified beneficiaries, provided a renewal claim was registered in the 28th year of the original term. The present law drops the renewal feature except for works already in their first term of statutory protection when the present law took effect. Instead, the present law generally permits termination of a grant of rights after 35 years under certain conditions by serving written notice on the transferee within specified time limits.

For works already under statutory copyright protection, the present law provides a similar right of termination covering the newly added years that extended the former maximum term of the copyright from 56 to 75 years. For further information, write to the Copyright Office for Circulars R15a and R15t.

INTERNATIONAL COPYRIGHT PROTECTION

There is no such thing as an "international copyright" that will automatically protect an author's writings throughout the entire world. Protection against unauthorized use in a particular country depends, basically, on the national laws

of that country. However, most countries do offer protection to foreign works under certain conditions, and these conditions have been greatly simplified by international copyright treaties and conventions. For a list of countries which maintain copyright relations with the United States, write to the Copyright Office and ask for Circular R38a.

The United States is a member of the Universal Copyright Convention (the UCC), which came into force on September 16, 1955. Generally, a work by a national or domiciliary of a country that is a member of the UCC or a work first published in a UCC country may claim protection under the UCC. If the work bears the notice of copyright in the form and position specified by the UCC, this notice will satisfy and substitute for any other formalities a UCC member country would otherwise impose as a condition of copyright. A UCC notice should consist of the symbol © accompanied by the name of the copyright proprietor and the year of first publication of the work.

An author who wishes protection for his or her work in a particular country should first find out the extent of protection of foreign works in that country. If possible, this should be done before the work is published anywhere, since protection may often depend on the facts existing at the time of **first** publication.

If the country in which protection is sought is a party to one of the international copyright conventions, the work may generally be protected by complying with the conditions of the convention. Even if the work cannot be brought under an international convention, protection under the specific provisions of the country's national laws may still be possible. Some countries, however, offer little or no copyright protection for foreign works.

COPYRIGHT REGISTRATION

In general, copyright registration is a legal formality intended to make a public record of the basic facts of a particular copyright. However, except in two specific situations,* registration is not a condition of copyright protection.

---

*Works published with notice of copyright prior to January 1, 1978, must be registered and renewed during the first 28-year term of copyright to maintain protection.

Under sections 405 and 406 of the Copyright Act, copyright registration may be required to preserve a copyright that would otherwise be invalidated because the copyright notice was omitted from the published copies or phonorecords, or the name or year date was omitted, or certain errors were made in the year date.

Even though registration is not generally a requirement for protection, the copyright law provides several inducements or advantages to encourage copyright owners to make registration. Among these advantages are the following:

● Registration establishes a public record of the copyright claim;

● Registration is ordinarily necessary before any infringement suits may be filed in court;

● If made before or within 5 years of publication, registration will establish prima facie evidence in court of the validity of the copyright and of the facts stated in the certificate; and

● If registration is made within 3 months after publication of the work or prior to an infringement of the work, statutory damages and attorney's fees will be available to the copyright owner in court actions. Otherwise, only an award of actual damages and profits is available to the copyright owner.

Registration may be made at any time within the life of the copyright. Unlike the law before 1978, when a work has been registered in unpublished form, it is not necessary to make another registration when the work becomes published (although the copyright owner may register the published edition, if desired).

NOTE: Before 1978, the copyright law required, as a condition for copyright protection, that all copies published with the authorization of the copyright owner bear a proper notice. If a work was published under the copyright owner's authority before January 1, 1978, without a proper copyright notice, all copyright protection for that work was permanently lost in the United States. The new copyright law does not provide retroactive protection for those works.

REGISTRATION PROCEDURES

In General

To register a work, send the following three elements to the Copyright Office *in the same envelope or package* to the Register of Copyrights, Copyright Office, Library of Congress, Washington, D.C. 20559: (see page 12 for what happens if the elements are sent separately).

1. A properly completed application form;
2. A nonreturnable filing fee of $10 for each application;
3. A deposit of the work being registered. The deposit requirements will vary in particular situations. The general requirements are as follows:

● If the work is unpublished, one complete copy or phonorecord.

● If the work was first published in the United States on or after January 1, 1978, two complete copies or phonorecords of the best edition.

● If the work was first published in the United States before January 1, 1978, two complete copies or phonorecords of the work as first published.

● If the work was first published outside the United States, whenever published, one complete copy or phonorecord of the work as first published.

● If the work is a contribution to a collective work, and published after January 1, 1978, one complete copy or phonorecord of the best edition of the collective work.

NOTE: COMPLETE THE APPLICATION FORM USING BLACK INK PEN OR TYPEWRITER. After registration is completed, the application form becomes a part of the official permanent records of the Copyright Office so the application forms must meet archival standards. Therefore, applications should be submitted on the forms printed and issued by the Copyright Office. Because the certificate itself will be reproduced from the application by xerographic process, it should be completed legibly in black ink or typewritten.

20

Unpublished Collections

A work may be registered in unpublished form as a "collection," with one application and one fee, under the following conditions:

- The elements of the collection are assembled in an orderly form;
- The combined elements bear a single title identifying the collection as a whole;
- The copyright claimant in all the elements and in the collection as a whole is the same; and
- All of the elements are by the same author, or, if they are by different authors, at least one of the authors has contributed copyrightable authorship to each element.

Unpublished collections are indexed in the *Catalog of Copyright Entries* only under the collection titles.

Special Deposit Requirements

The Copyright Act gives the Register of Copyrights authority to issue regulations making adjustments in the statutory deposit requirements. These regulations as now issued require or permit, for particular classes, the deposit of identifying material instead of copies or phonorecords, the deposit of only one copy or phonorecord where two would normally be required, and in some cases material other than complete copies of the best edition. For example, the regulations ordinarily require deposit of identifying material, such as photographs or drawings, when the work being registered has been reproduced in three-dimensional copies.

If you are unsure of the proper deposit required for your work, write to the Copyright Office for that information and describe the work you wish to register.

NOTE: LIBRARY OF CONGRESS CATALOG CARD NUMBERS.
A Library of Congress Catalog Card Number is different from a copyright registration number. The Cataloging in Publication (CIP) Division of the Library of Congress is responsible for assigning LC Catalog Card Numbers and is operationally separate from the Copyright Office. A book may be registered in or deposited with the Copyright Office but not necessarily cataloged and added to the Library's collections. For information about obtaining an LC Catalog Card Number, contact the CIP Division, Library of Congress, Washington, D.C. 20540.

CORRECTIONS AND AMPLIFICATIONS OF EXISTING REGISTRATIONS

To deal with cases in which information in the basic registration later turns out to be incorrect or incomplete, the law provides for "the filing of an application for supplementary registration, to correct an error in a copyright registration or to amplify the information given in a registration." The information in a supplementary registration augments but does not supersede that contained in the earlier registration. Note also that a supplementary registration is not a substitute for an original registration or for a renewal registration. Form CA is available from the Copyright Office for making a supplementary registration. For further information about supplementary registrations, write for Circular R8.

MANDATORY DEPOSIT FOR WORKS PUBLISHED IN THE UNITED STATES WITH NOTICE OF COPYRIGHT

Although a copyright registration is not required, the Copyright Act establishes a mandatory deposit requirement for works published with notice of copyright in the United States (see definition of "publication" on page 5). In general, the owner of copyright, or the owner of the right of first publication in the work, has a legal obligation to deposit in the Copyright Office, within 3 months of publication in the United States, 2 copies (or, in the case of sound recordings, 2 phonorecords) for the use of the Library of Congress. Failure to make the deposit can result in fines and other penalties, but does not affect copyright protection.

The Copyright Office has issued regulations *exempting* certain categories of works *entirely* from the mandatory deposit requirements, and reducing the obligation for certain other categories. For further information about mandatory deposit, please write to the Copyright Office for Circular R7d.

USE OF MANDATORY DEPOSIT TO SATISFY REGISTRATION REQUIREMENTS

With respect to works published in the United States the Copyright Act contains a special provision under which a single deposit can be made to satisfy both the deposit requirements for the Library and the registration requirements. The provision requires that, in order to have this dual effect, the copies or phonorecords must be "accompanied by the prescribed application and fee" for registration.

WHO MAY FILE AN APPLICATION FORM

The following persons are legally entitled to submit an application form:

- The author. This is either the person who actually created the work, or, if the work was made for hire, the employer or other person for whom the work was prepared.

- The copyright claimant. The copyright claimant is defined in Copyright Office regulations as either the author of the work or a person or organization that has obtained ownership of all the rights under the copyright initially belonging to the author. This category includes a person or organization who has obtained by contract the right to claim legal title to the copyright in an application for copyright registration.

- The owner of exclusive right(s). Under the new law, any of the exclusive rights that go to make up a copyright and any subdivision of them can be transferred and owned separately, even though the transfer may be limited in time or place of effect. The term "copyright owner" with respect to any one of the exclusive rights contained in a copyright refers to the owner of that particular right. Any owner of an exclusive right may apply for registration of a claim in the work.

- The duly authorized agent of such author, other copyright claimant, or owner of exclusive right(s). Any person authorized to act on behalf of the author, other copyright claimant, or owner of exclusive right(s) may apply for registration.

There is no requirement that applications be prepared or filed by an attorney.

APPLICATION FORMS

For Original Registration

Form TX: for published and unpublished non-dramatic literary works

Form SE: for serials, works issued or intended to be issued in successive parts bearing numerical or chronological designations and intended to be continued indefinitely (periodicals, newspapers, magazines, newsletters, annuals, journals, etc.)

Form PA: for published and unpublished works of the performing arts (musical and dramatic works, pantomimes and choreographic works, motion pictures and other audiovisual works)

Form VA: for published and unpublished works of the visual arts (pictorial, graphic, and sculptural works)

Form SR: for published and unpublished sound recordings

For Renewal Registration

Form RE: for claims to renewal copyright in works copyrighted under the law in effect through December 31, 1977 (1909 Copyright Act)

For Corrections and Amplifications

Form CA: for supplementary registration to correct or amplify information given in the Copyright Office record of an earlier registration

Other Forms for Special Purposes

Form GR/CP: an adjunct application to be used for registration of a group of contributions to periodicals in addition to an application Form TX, PA, or VA

Form IS: request for issuance of an import statement under the manufacturing provisions of the Copyright Act

Application forms are supplied by the Copyright Office free of charge.

FORMS HOTLINE

NOTE: Requestors may order application forms at any time by telephoning (202) 287-9100. Orders will be recorded automatically and filled as quickly as possible.

MAILING INSTRUCTIONS

All applications and materials related to copyright registration sent to the Copyright Office should be addressed to the Register of Copyrights, Copyright Office, Library of Congress, Washington, D.C. 20559.

The application, deposit (copies or phonorecords), and nonreturnable filing fee should be mailed in the same package.

WHAT HAPPENS IF THE THREE ELEMENTS ARE NOT RECEIVED TOGETHER

Applications and fees received without copies or phonorecords will not be processed and will ordinarily be returned. Unpublished deposits alone will ordinarily be returned, also. Published deposits received without applications and fees will be immediately transferred to the collections of the Library of Congress. This practice is in accordance with section 408 of the law which provides that the published deposit required for the collections of the Library of Congress may be used for registration only if the deposit is "accompanied by the prescribed application and fee . . ."

After the deposit is received and transferred to another department of the Library for its collections or other disposition, it is no longer available to the Copyright Office; the custody of that deposit has also been transferred to the other department. Then, if you wish to make copyright registration, you must deposit additional copies or phonorecords with your application and fee.

FEES

Do not send cash. Fees sent to the Copyright Office should be in the form of a money order, check, or bank draft payable to the Register of Copyrights; it should be securely attached to the application.

EFFECTIVE DATE OF REGISTRATION

Please note that **a copyright registration is effective on the date of receipt in the Copyright Office of all the required elements in acceptable form,** regardless of the length of time it takes thereafter to process the application and mail the certificate of registration. The length of time required by the Copyright Office to process an application varies from time to time, depending on the amount of material received and the personnel available to handle it. It must also be kept in mind that it may take a number of days for mailed material to reach the Copyright Office and for the certificate of registration to reach the recipient after being mailed by the Copyright Office.

If you are filing an application for copyright registration in the Copyright Office, you *will not* receive an acknowledgement that your application has been received (the Office receives more than 500,000 applications annually), but you can expect:

- A letter or telephone call from a copyright examiner if further information is needed;
- A certificate of registration to indicate the work has been registered, or if the application cannot be accepted, a letter explaining why it has been rejected.

You may not receive either of these until 90 days have passed.

If you want to know when the Copyright Office receives your material, you should send it via registered or certified mail and request a return receipt.

AVAILABLE INFORMATION

This circular attempts to answer some of the questions that are frequently asked about copyright. For a list of other material published by the Copyright Office, write for "Publications on Copyright." Any requests for Copyright Office publications or special questions relating to copyright problems not mentioned in this circular should be addressed to the Information and Publications Section, LM-455, Copyright Office, Library of Congress, Washington, D.C. 20559.

The Copyright Office is not permitted to give legal advice. If you need information or guidance on matters such as disputes over the ownership of a copyright, suits against possible infringers, the procedure for getting a work published, or the method of obtaining royalty payments, it may be necessary to consult an attorney.

3: THE DEMONOLOGY OF COPYRIGHT

Barbara Ringer

In her Bowker Memorial Lecture for 1974,
Barbara Ringer, recently appointed U.S. Register of Copyrights,
stresses that the rights of the author must remain
paramount in any changes in copyright law

Photographs by Helen Marcus

This is a very slightly abridged version of the lecture Ms. Ringer gave at Lincoln Center, New York, on October 24 as part of the continuing series of Bowker Memorial Lectures on Book Publishing. The series, sponsored jointly by the R.R. Bowker Company and the School of Library Service at Columbia University, was instituted in 1935 as a tribute to Richard Rogers Bowker, for many years editor and publisher of PW. *The lectures were discontinued in 1967 and resumed last year, and this was the second of the new series.*

In choosing to give this lecture the rather enigmatic title of "The Demonology of Copyright," I do not mean to suggest either that copyright itself is a form of devil worship or, conversely, that copyright offers a form of salvation from the powers of darkness. Like any other law, copyright is a pragmatic response to certain felt needs of society and, like any other law, must change in scope and direction as these needs change. But changing any law is never an easy matter, and the case of copyright is made much more difficult by the religious fervor and theological arguments thrown at each other by the contending parties. The personal anger, the emotion, the presentation of viewpoints in stark black-and-white terms, are quite different in degree and character from what one might find in

disputes over admiralty or insurance law.

It is easy to make fun of the kind of confrontation I am talking about, where the mere mention of a word like "monopoly" or "property" will cause chairs to be pushed back from tables, faces to redden, breathing to shorten and bitter words to be exchanged. This naturally prolongs discussions and makes compromise more difficult to achieve, assuming it is compromise you want. But I for one have seen this sort of exchange too often not to take it seriously; and to ask whether there is something special about copyright that provokes these strong and diametrically opposed expressions of feeling.

Justice Story once called copyright "the metaphysics of the law," and I think most people sense the truth of this aphorism without really knowing what it means. If metaphysics is the study of human generation, regeneration—of the relation of man to his natural and supernatural environment and to the past and future of his species—then copyright as a legal system can indeed be linked closely to this study. In a religious sense, it is man's creative acts that bring him closest to the godhead, and it is precisely these acts that copyright is concerned with.

Perhaps one of the problems with copyright is that some people have elevated it to a sanctified or divine plane, and that authors have been looked on as saints or angels, if not demigods. Before you laugh, think about how you or people you know regard the contributions of Shakespeare and Tolstoy, Beethoven and Toscanini to your own life and psyche.

But if people feel really strongly about gods and angels there will be a tendency

to assume the existence of demons and witches, and to worship evil and combat heresy with equal vigor. Perhaps it is an extreme example, but you will find precisely what I am talking about in the writings of Ezra Pound, where the creative act of authorship is exalted and any attempt to limit or exploit it is deplored as usury, Pound's ultimate devil. At the other extreme, there are plenty of legal philosophers and politicians who attack incremental changes in copyright protection and in some cases attack as evil the very existence of a copyright law.

My purpose here is to analyze this dialectic in terms of the changes the copyright laws of the world are now undergoing, and to determine whether the charge and counter-charges of the pro- and anti-copyright forces can help us in adapting to these changes. Before doing so I should do what Professor Ben Kaplan did in his 1966 Carpentier lectures, collected under the title "An Unhurried View of Copyright": to admit the personal bias I bring to the subject. Professor Kaplan acknowledged candidly that he had "introduced throughout a calculated low-protectionist bias which I associate with a concern for easy public access to, and use and improvement of products of the mind." My bias is just the opposite: I believe it is society's duty to go as far as it can possibly go in nurturing the atmosphere in which authors and other creative artists can flourish. I agree that the copyright law should encourage widespread dissemination of works of the mind. But it seems to me that, in the long pull, it is more important for a particular generation to produce a handful of great

Reprinted from *Publ. W'kly* **206**(21):26-30 (1974).

creative works than to shower its school-children with unauthorized photocopies or to hold the cost of a jukebox play down to a dime, if that is what it is these days.

The Origins of Copyright

It is interesting, though of debatable significance, that copyright as we know it originated in England during the 16th and 17th centuries. This was a period of great religious ferment and political unrest during which witchcraft and devil worship were at their height, and repressive measures against all forms of heresy were widespread. The pro-copyright theologians argue that copyright as a natural property right of the author emerged from the mists of the common law and took definite form as the result of the invention of the printing press and the increase in potential and actual piracy after 1450. They dismiss the historical ties between copyright and the Crown's grants of printing monopolies, its efforts to suppress heretical or seditious writing and to exercise censorship control over all publications. This line of argument tends to infuriate the anti-copyright scholars who point out that the first copyright statute in history, the Statute of Anne of 1710, was a direct outgrowth of an elaborate series of monopoly grants, Star Chamber decrees, licensing acts, and a system involving mandatory registration of titles with the Stationer's Company. This system operated both as a means of exercising control over freedom of the press, generating revenues for the Crown, and giving certain printers monopoly protection as against unlicensed printers. The author was the forgotten figure in this drama, which was played out during the 16th and 17th centuries in England, France, and other Western European countries where the invention of movable type and its increasing use collided with the desire of the governments to suppress dissident writing. The beneficiaries of these primitive copyrights were the publishers who agreed to buy monopolies in exchange for freedom of the press. Authors were paid off in lump sums, usually quite low.

Now it is true in general that under this system copyright was equated with heresy. But is this any basis for damning copyright as a tool of autocratic power, political or economic, and for linking copyright with efforts to suppress freedom of the press and freedom of speech? This question is a much more lively one than you might think.

Many of you will remember Admiral Rickover's efforts in the early 1960s to prevent the unauthorized publication by

Barbara Ringer

Public Affairs Press of several of his speeches on education and atomic energy. At the heart of the dispute was the question of whether the author's efforts to control publication and assert economic rights in his writings amounted to interference with the public's right of free access. Justice Stanley Reed, who by that time had retired from the Supreme Court but was sitting on the Circuit Court of Appeals by designation, wrote the opinion of the court upholding the Admiral's right to secure copyright, and later described the case as the most fascinating in his entire career on the bench. The Supreme Court ducked the issue, but the defendant felt strongly enough to write a book on the question, publishing it under the title "Constraint by Copyright." It certainly belongs in anyone's library of copyright demonology.

The theme of copyright and its possible repressive effect on matters of urgent public concern or curiosity runs through a whole series of front-page events over the last decade or so: Martin Luther King's "I Have a Dream" speech, Senator Dodd's files, Oswald's diaries, interviews given by Howard Hughes and the Beatles, Hemingway's personal conversations, the dispute over Manchester's book on Kennedy's assassination, and other affairs, some frivolous and others deadly serious. The question rose to the surface in the Pentagon Papers affair, dramatizing the close relationship between systems of security classification and copyright, and the various recent assertions of executive privilege and ownership over Presidential tapes and documents all have direct copyright implications.

The most recent *cause célèbre* in copyright is the infringement suit brought by CBS against Vanderbilt University concerning its archive of video tapes of nightly network news broadcasts. The case, which has its complications as well as its fascinations, has not yet been argued; judging from the briefs I have seen there appears to be a deliberate effort to provoke a confrontation over the extent to which copyright should be allowed to control the fixation and later dissemination of matters of current interest and historical value. Vanderbilt seems much less interested in defending the case on the basis of fair use than on the ground that copyright registration over material such as national news broadcasts should be sharply limited or eliminated altogether. A major argument in the University's briefs rests on the analogy between the efforts of CBS to license the videotaping of its newscasts and to control the conditions under which the tapes are disseminated, and the efforts of the Tudor and Stuart monarchies, and their successors, to control the press through monopolies and licensing.

Somebody who had read the Vanderbilt brief called and asked me whether it was true that copyright really started as a censorship device aimed at suppressing dissident writing and limiting the public to information favorable to the regime. I said that the facts were right but that they should be looked at in a broader historical context. Although a few extreme demonologists might argue otherwise, it is plain to see that English copyright in 1974 is as fundamentally different from English copyright in 1600 as the powers of Elizabeth II are from those of Elizabeth I.

In the first place, to look only at English constitutional history for a moment, it is important to recognize that the Statute of Anne of 1710, the first copyright statute anywhere and the mother of us all, was enacted precisely because the whole autocratic censorship/monopoly/licensing apparatus had broken down completely. As a result of the bloodless revolution taking place in the English constitutional system, basic individual freedoms, notably freedom of speech and freedom of the press, were becoming established under common law principles. The Statute of Anne marked the end of autocracy in English copyright and established a set of democratic principles: recognition of the individual author as the ultimate beneficiary and fountainhead of protection and a guarantee of legal protection against unauthorized use for limited times, without any elements of prior restraint of censorship by government or its agents. The great English copyright cases of the 18th century, in construing the law as it had been changed by the Statute of Anne, established three fundamental principles; looked at with late 20th century eyes, these principles can be considered a revolutionary "declaration of human rights" for authors:

First, under English common law, the individual author has absolute and perpetual rights in his works. As long as he chooses to leave his work unpublished, the law has an unqualified obligation to protect him against unauthorized publication or other use.

Second, this common law right is not destroyed by publication. The very purpose of authorship is to reach the minds of others through publication, and it is the law's duty to continue to protect an author's work even after he has voluntarily released its contents to the public and thus lost any power to control it physically.

Third, if the law offers protection to the work by means of a copyright statute, common law protection ends and is superseded by protection under the specific terms and conditions written down in the statute. In other words, if the government chooses to offer protection to published works under specified terms and conditions, the author is guaranteed protection, but only on the terms and conditions laid down in the statute.

If, as I believe, the Statute of Anne was a product of the bloodless revolution that established democracy in England, the copyright laws of the United States were an even more immediate result of the American Revolution. The new country was seized with nationalistic fervor, and copyright, as a means of promoting native authorship, was identified as a leading article in the creed of influential nationalists such as Noah Webster. Under the Articles of Confederation 12 of the 13 original states adopted copyright statutes based on the Statute of Anne. But it soon became apparent that separate systems of legal protection, even if adopted and enforced in all of the states, could not be effective to protect intangible property as capable of flowing across state borders as easily as books and other publications. Thus, the power of Congress at the federal level to "promote the progress of science and useful arts by securing to authors and inventors the exclusive rights to their respective writings and discoveries" was guaranteed directly and explicitly in the first Article of the Constitution.

Listen to Madison's words on this guarantee in the Federalist Papers: do they suggest any direct or indirect purpose to use copyright protection for purposes of repression or censorship?

The utility of this power will scarcely be questioned. The copyright of authors has been solemnly adjudged, in Great Britain, to be a right of common law. The right to useful inventions seems with equal reason to belong to the inventors. The public good fully coincides in both cases with the claims of individuals.

It is striking that the second and third copyright statutes in the world—those of the United States of America and of France—were adopted immediately following the revolutions in those countries that overthrew autocratic government and were based on ideals of personal liberty and individual freedom. The Rights of Man in both cases certainly included the Rights of the Author, and the French word for copyright, "le droit d'auteur," reflects this philosophical approach literally. The American statute of 1790 followed the Statute of Anne and broke little new ground, but the French statute of 1793 was based on the philosophical recognition of copyright as a natural right of the author and of the author as a creative individual rather than merely as a property owner. Among other revolutionary changes, the French statute established a term of copyright based on the life of the author. A hypothesis well worth exploring is that the copyright statutes adopted one after the other in Europe during the 19th century were the direct product of the Age of Revolution and the political upheavals in each of those countries.

To summarize this point, I don't agree with the charge that copyright originated as a marriage between tyranny and greed, arranged by the devil. Regardless of its origins, however, the concept of copyright changed radically as a result of the revolutionary political movements of the late 18th and 19th centuries, and the first copyright statutes were based on a rejection of autocratic repression and monopoly control and upon a new recognition of individual liberty and the human rights of authors. But nothing ever stays the same, and the main thing all this teaches me is that copyright does have the capacity to do good or evil, promote or suppress individual freedom of expression, depending upon how it is implemented.

Monopoly versus Property

Over the years, I have listened with increasing impatience to hundreds of debates as to whether copyright is monopoly or property. Certainly no single issue divides the pro-copyright and anti-copyright forces more sharply, and the arguments are invariably put forward in stark either/or terms, as if something that is a monopoly could not possibly also be property, or vice versa. This is an extreme example of what has been called "the tyranny of labels," and its results have been both time-consuming and pernicious.

I have seen too many cases where a judge or lawmaker, coming upon copyright for the first time and looking for guidance on a particular issue, assumes either that he is dealing with a monopoly in which protection should be granted grudgingly and to the bare extent necessary or, conversely, that property rights are involved and that any limitations must be fully justified. Monopoly, property, and personal rights are merely terms describing certain legal concepts; copyright has some of the characteristics of all three of these concepts, but not others. Copyright is, as a legal concept, unique and can be defined only in terms of its own special characteristics.

Be that as it may, the demonologists who have attacked copyright as a "monopoly" (sometimes also referred to as a "tax") have had a considerable influence upon the development of the law throughout the world, and cannot be dismissed as doctrinaire theorists. The greatest of them, the British historian Thomas Babington Macaulay, made a speech on the subject in Parliament in 1841, which probably has more influence today than when it was delivered:

Copyright is monopoly, and produces all the effects which the general voice of mankind attributes to monopoly. The effect of monopoly generally is to make articles scarce, to make them dear, and to make them bad. It is good that authors should be remunerated; and the least exceptionable way of remunerating them is by a monopoly. Yet monopoly is an evil. For the sake of the good we must submit to the evil; but the evil ought not to last a day longer than is necessary for the purpose of securing the good.

Lord Macaulay refused to consider copyright as a form of property. He pointed out that, if the arguments for extending the copyright term were carried to their logical conclusion, the result would be a perpetual copyright, with the benefits going to monopolists rather than the author or his immediate family. His pithy if hopelessly simplistic conclusion: "The principle of copyright is this. It is a tax on readers for the purpose of giving a bounty to writers."

Macaulay's words and sentiments live on 130 years later, notably in one of the most provocative articles on copyright published in recent years: "The Uneasy Case for Copyright" by Professor Stephen Breyer, published in the *Harvard Law Review* in 1970. Despite the title he chose, Breyer's argument cannot really be considered a "case for copyright," uneasy or otherwise. Like Macaulay from whom he quotes liberally, Breyer strongly opposes any augmentation in the term or scope of the present, 65-year-old U.S. copyright law.

Breyer stops short, just barely, of advocating outright abolition of the copyright law, but puts forward an argument that the results of abolition would not be disastrous and might be beneficial, especially when it comes to textbooks. He acknowledges the cost advantage that a pirate would have over the originating publisher, but argues that, even so, the latter could stay in business through his advantage of "lead time" (being on the market first) and possible "retaliation" (bringing out "punitive editions" priced below the pirate's cost and thus driving him out of business). He suggests the possibility that buyers of textbooks might, despite anit-trust problems, be able to or-

ganize in ways that, either directly or with government support, would enable them to contract with a publisher in advance of publication to insure both a reasonable price and a reasonable profit.

For me the most significant possibility explored in Professor Breyer's article is that, at least in respect to textbooks, government subsidy be substituted entirely for copyright to insure adequate revenue to both publishers and authors. He recognizes two obvious dangers: that the government will subsidize only what it wants to see published, and that it will censor what it subsidizes. Yet, on balance, he seems to prefer this approach to the evils of what he regards as the copyright monopoly. While mostly disagreeing with his conclusions, I admire Professor Breyer's courage and skill in saying what he thinks, but I must say that at this point he scared me.

Professor Ben Kaplan's famous and controversial book preceded and in some ways anticipated Breyer's article. It consists of three lectures published under the title "An Unhurried View of Copyright" and, despite its level tone and expansive

outlook, many proponents of copyright found it an anathema and many anti-copyright demonologists welcomed it as scripture.

One of Kaplan's main points is contained in his second lecture, dealing with plagiarism, and it seems a pity that it has been obscured in the controversy over the book as a whole. His argument is that, before copyright was systematized in statutory form, authors were free to recast works into different forms and to draw freely on elements of plot, characterization, setting and theme from other writers. He felt that this freedom resulted in a flourishing of literature such as that found during the Elizabethan Age in England. By broadening the scope of copyright protection to inhibit or prohibit the kind of untrammeled adaptations, dramatizations, translations, and abridgments that were formerly normal procedure in all artistic pursuits, Kaplan considered that the courts and legislatures have dampened creativity and narrowed the scope of original works available to the public. Some of this makes good sense to me, and I think it is just as

The Lincoln Center library auditorium audience listens to Ms. Ringer

indefensible to ignore reasonable warnings about the inhibiting effects of expanding the scope or term of copyright too far as it is to claim that every expansion is automatically against the public interest.

At the other extreme from the anti-monopoly arguments of the professors is the anti-copyright philosophy sometimes expressed on behalf of authors: that an author's work is property generically like any other but qualitatively much more valuable, and that in simple justice society should protect it without any limitations whatever in term or scope. Under this theory, copyright statutes containing limitations on protection are positive detriments to the author's interests, and if all the copyright statutes were repealed society would find a way to provide authors with more effective protection.

Admittedly, there has been a recent resurgence of copyright protection under state common law principles, thanks to the phenomenon of record piracy and the failure of the federal law to deal with it effectively until the problem was out of hand. Nevertheless, experience has proved more than once that local laws are ineffective to deal with problems on a national or international scale. In any case, I doubt whether most copyright owners would agree to run the risk of relying on the vagaries of 50 state copyright laws, even if they existed. They would prefer to do everything they can to seek stronger protection under the existing federal system, but this is proving increasingly difficult.

The Impact of Technology

In 1945, 29 years ago, Zechariah Chafee, Jr., wrote what is probably the best single work on copyright law ever published in English. The opening paragraph of his article entitled "Reflections on the Law of Copyright," published in two parts in the *Columbia Law Review*, was both perceptive and foresighted:

Copyright is the Cinderella of the law. Her rich older sisters, Franchises and Patents, long crowded her into the chimney-corner. Suddenly the Fairy Godmother, Invention, endowed her with mechanical and electrical devices as magical as the pumpkin coach and the mice footmen. Now she whirls through the mad mazes of a glamorous ball.

Although Chafee mentioned specifically, as examples of these magical devices, only motion pictures and radio, he was perfectly aware that new pumpkin coaches and mice footmen were waiting to be summoned. He lived to see some, but not all, of the mad mazes technology had in store for copyright: television and its stepchild cable TV, audio tape recording, video tape recording, photocomposition and electronic typesetting, automatic storage and retrieval devices, satellites, and our present Prince Charming, photocopying. Reprography seems to me the most serious immediate problem in copyright law, but I have come to feel that satellites represent the most important development in human history since the printing press.

What has happened in the 29 years since Chafee wrote his article is so staggering that words are literally inadequate to describe it. The copyright law that was Cinderella in 1945 has aged considerably, but seems still to be dancing in a mad ball. The changes in communications have produced whole new generations of pressure groups, making statutory reform much more difficult, but the courts have become reluctant to extend the old 1909 Act to cover things Teddy Roosevelt never dreamed of. New services, such as cable systems, photocopy machines, and computers, have emerged without clear-cut copyright guidelines, and people have come to rely on them in their businesses and their very lives. These services cannot be cut off, but somehow the copyright law must find a way to insure that the interests of authors and copyright owners are protected at the same time. Increasingly, the answer being suggested to this problem nationally and internationally involves systems of compulsory licensing: free access with payment of reasonable compensation on some sort of blanket or bulk basis.

In recent years the entire structure of international copyright has been shaken by two new and unexpected factors: the challenge of the developing countries, which have demanded and gotten concessions in their international copyright obligations consistent with their economic and educational problems, and the adherence of the Soviet Union to the Universal Copyright Convention, which has introduced a whole new system and concept of copyright law into the international scheme. Demonology flourishes where there is uncertainty and a need for simple explanations for complex situations, and the new developments in international copyright have brought the demonologists out in force all over the world. The onslaught of the new technology, combined with the introduction into the international copyright system of countries with different needs and with conflicting economic and political concepts, leaves the future of copyright very much in question.

Copyright's Ultimate Goals

In his 1945 article, Chafee suggested six ideals to which a copyright statute should aspire: (1) complete coverage; (2) unified protection, enabling the author to control all the channels through which the work reaches the public; (3) international protection, with no discrimination against foreign authors; (4) protection that does not go substantially beyond the purposes it seeks to serve; (5) protection that is not so broad as to stifle independent creation by others; and (6) legal rules that are convenient to handle.

These goals are still worthy and unattained today; the failure of the 1909 Act to meet them is much more serious in 1974 than in 1945. The current revision bill, while a considerable improvement over the present law in many respects, would be far from a complete fulfillment of Chafee's six objectives.

There is a seventh goal, which Chafee could not have been as aware of in 1945 as he would be today, and which in fact may be the most important copyright goal of all. It can be stated very simply: a substantial increase in the rights of the author, considered not as a copyright owner but as a separate creative individual. It involves a recognition that committees don't create works and corporations don't create works and machines don't create works. If, for the sake of convenience, of companies or societies or governments, the copyright law forces individual authors back into a collective straitjacket or makes them into human writing machines, it will indeed have become a tool of the devil.

I think I know a little of why copyright engenders such sensitivity and emotion, such aggressiveness and defensiveness, such extremes of position. It is because at its root there is one beneficiary of protection and one only, and that is the independent author who, as we have seen in the cataclysmic events in our own country of the past 18 months, can change the course of history.

If the copyright law is to continue to function on the side of light against darkness, good against evil, truth against newspeak, it must broaden its base and its goals. Freedom of speech and freedom of the press are meaningless unless authors are able to create independently from control by anyone, and to find a way to put their works before the public. Economic advantage and the shibboleth of "convenience" distort the copyright law into a weapon against authors. Anyone who cares about freedom and authorship must insure that, in the process of improving the efficiency of our law, we do not throw it all the way back to its repressive origins in the Middle Ages.

4: DECODING THE COPYRIGHT ACT:
A Course in the Formalities

Jon A. Baumgarten

[*Editors' Note:* The boldfaced superscript letters in the text did not appear in the original. They have been added in this reprinting to accommodate addenda by the author that are given at the end of the article.]

INTRODUCTION

On January 1, 1978, after a legislative revision effort that lasted more than twenty years, a new copyright law came into effect in the United States. This act, now codified in Title 17 of the United States Code, made numerous substantial changes in the copyright law of this country. One of the most fundamental and much heralded changes was the adoption of a principle of "automatic copyright." Under this principle, works created on and after January 1, 1978, are copyrighted under the federal statute "automatically" upon their creation (§302(a)). In effect, this means that if a work created after that date is "copyrightable," it *is* copyrighted *ab initio*. For these purposes, a work is "created" as soon as it is fixed in some tangible form of more than transitory stability (§101)—e.g., written or drawn on paper or canvas; sculpted or manufactured; captured on film, disc, videotape or holoform; or recorded on audio tape or microfilm.

Neither registration with the U.S. Copyright Office nor use of a copyright notice is a condition of securing copyright for works created on and after January 1, 1978. However, the "formalities" of registration and notice, and certain other conditions, remain of considerable importance under the new law. In some cases, a failure to observe these formalities may affect the scope or degree of available protection; in others, it actually may forfeit the initial, automatic, copyright.

For at least three related reasons, a general understanding of these formalities is important to any lawyer whose clients may wish to prevent or control the reproduction, distribution, performance,

Jon A. Baumgarten is a partner in Paskus, Gordon & Hyman of Washington, D.C. and New York City. He is a former general counsel of the U.S. Copyright Office.

or display of documents, products, information, or other materials. These are:

1. *The extraordinary breadth of subject matter covered by U.S. copyright.* Of course, works of the literary, musical, fine, cinematographic, and allied "arts" are included, such as poems, novels, stories, articles, texts and reference books; musical and dramatic compositions; paintings, drawings, sculpture, and photographs; motion pictures, stage presentations, and television programs; and cartographic, choreographic, and pantomimic works. So are many works of "applied art" and artistic craftsmanship, such as jewelry, toys, fabric designs, and even the embellishments of furniture, architecture, appliances, and a host of other industrial or functional products. But the importance of copyright cannot be limited to the practices of "publishing," "entertainment," "art" or "design" lawyers. At bottom, virtually every concrete, fixed expression of intellect, whether of a "personal" nature such as private letters and diaries, or "business" significance—such as directories, manuals, instructions, and specifications; memoranda, reports, studies, and documented, filmed, or taped presentations; schematics, layouts, and models; lists and tabulated or compiled facts, figures, or data; promotional materials and correspondence; and computer programs and automated data bases—is subject to copyright protection against certain forms of unauthorized use.

2. *The fact that all such subject matter, whether created before or after January 1, 1978, now falls within the province of the Federal Copyright Act, without regard to whether or not it has been published or disseminated (§301).* (Prior to the new Act, unpublished materials were protectable by "common law copyright" under the laws of the individual states, without formalities.)

3. *The Copyright Act's preemption of all common law and state rights that are "equivalent" to copyright protection (§301(a)).* The precise scope of the preemptive effect of the law is yet to be fully determined; but the potential impact of this rule on various forms of action heretofore

available under trade secret, unfair competition/misappropriation, tort, and conversion law must be considered carefully.

The purpose of this article is to survey the principal formalities attendant upon copyright protection under the new Copyright Act. Before doing so, however, it must be noted that works created *before* January 1, 1978, generally had to secure and maintain statutory copyright by publication with a specified notice of copyright (in a limited number of cases, statutory copyright could also be secured by registration of unpublished versions with the Copyright Office; but those works required use of a notice upon their subsequent publication.) As a general rule, if a work was published before January 1, 1978, without an adequate copyright notice (or if a first term of copyright secured before January 1, 1978, expired without filing of a renewal in the Copyright Office), it entered the public domain in this country. Nothing in the new Act protects or resurrects protection for works that entered the public domain before January 1, 1978.

A. REGISTRATION OF CLAIMS TO COPYRIGHT

Under the new Act, registration of claims to copyright with the U.S. Copyright Office may be made for all works, before or after publication (§408(a)). Registration is now clearly "permissive" only, and is not a condition of copyright (*id.*) However, the new statute provides a number of advantages or "inducements" to registration in general, and to prompt registration in particular. There can be no general answer to the oft-asked question of clients: should I regularly register our [publications] for copyright? The circumstances of each client, and each class of work produced by that client, must be considered separately with reference to these inducements. Factors such as the client's financial position, the likelihood and importance of prospective infringements, the likely timing of such infringements (e.g., are the works held in close security so as to be unavailable for copying, at least before general dissemination?), and the importance of various types of remedies for infringement (e.g., will injunctions generally be a sufficient remedy?; are unauthorized foreign reproductions a particular problem so as to emphasize protection at ports of entry?) must be reviewed carefully in each case. Of course, counsel cannot be expected to have a definitive view of all possible future occurrences; however, reasoned judgments can and must be made. In some cases, consideration of registration is not a matter of regular client procedures, but rather of serving a particular need (such as curing deficiencies arising under other provisions of the statute, or facilitating or barring certain imports) under the circumstances.

The statutory "inducements" to registration are the following:

1. In most cases, registration must be made before instituting an action for copyright infringement (§411). Registration may be made at the "eleventh hour" and suit brought, after registration, for infringements committed earlier; however, in that case (i.e., infringement commenced before registration) no award of statutory damages or attorneys' fees generally may be made (§412). "Statutory damages" are a monetary award courts may make, at plaintiff's election, in lieu of actual damages and profits (§504). Because non-speculative damages are frequently difficult to prove in copyright infringement actions, statutory damages are commonly an important element in copyright litigation. Equally important, the *possibility* of statutory damages being awarded is often a significant consideration in settlement negotiations. Remedies other than statutory damages and attorneys' fees — i.e., actual damages, profits, injunctions, impounding, and discretionary costs — are not negated by the comparative dates of registration and infringement.

It is sometimes said that registration is a "condition" to statutory damages and attorneys' fees; this is inaccurate. The deprivation of these remedies does *not* apply: (a) to infringements commenced after publication and before registration if registration is made within a "grace period" of three months after first publica-

tion;[1] and (b) to infringements commenced after registration, regardless of when registration is made (see §412).

If registration for a work has not been made and it is important to institute an infringement action promptly, recourse may be had to Copyright Office procedures for "special handling" of applications. At the present time, no additional fees beyond the usual registration fee of ten dollars are imposed for special handling of such cases. However, this procedure disrupts the normal work flow of the Copyright Office, creates significant administrative burdens, and ultimately works to the disadvantage of all other applicants for registration whose works are being processed in the normal manner. It is possible that, in the near future, the Copyright Office will seek to impose a substantial fee on special handling cases.[a]

2. A certificate of registration made before or within five years after first publication of a work is *prima facie* evidence of the validity of the copyright, and of the facts (e.g., authorship and ownership) stated in the certificate (§410(c)). A certificate of registration made after five years from first publication is entitled to only such evidentiary weight as a court may accord in its discretion (*id.*). The *prima facie* evidentiary effect of registration is frequently important to plaintiffs in copyright litigation, both (a) in substantially easing the road to preliminary injunctive relief, and (b) in favorably ordering the burden of proof on the merits.

3. Registration of a claim to copyright in a work may be required for a recorded document transferring or affecting ownership of rights therein to be given constructive notice and priority over conflicting transfers (§205).

4. Registration is required in order to obtain a Copyright Office "Import Statement" that will permit the importation into the United States of a limited number of copies of English-language literary works (i.e., those consisting preponderantly of textual material) by American authors that are (a) manufactured by certain processes outside the United States or Canada, and (b) not otherwise exempt from the requirement of the new law that such works be produced in the United States or Canada

as a condition to domestic importation or distribution in some cases (§601). (Importation and distribution in violation of these requirements do not invalidate copyright, but may provide a complete defense to actions for unauthorized reproduction (§601(d)).)

5. Under the new Act, the United States Customs Service may bar the importation of "piratical" copies of copyrighted works or articles—i.e., copies unlawfully produced abroad, and seeking entry into the United States without the authority of the domestic copyright owner (§602(b)). The ability to bar infringing materials at the point of entry is frequently helpful to copyright owners, for example, in avoiding the possible necessity of instituting multiple infringement actions further down the chain of distribution. Although the Customs Service has not yet issued regulations for the exclusion of piratical copies under the new Act,[b] copyright registration may be helpful in connection with such proceedings, and appears to be required for these purposes for domestic works under existing customs regulations issued under the prior law. (In a recent proceeding, the United States International Trade Commission also indicated that it would require copyright registration as a condition to the entry of exclusion orders against infringing merchandise.)

6. To be entitled to receive royalties under a compulsory "mechanical" license for making records and audio tapes established in the Act, the copyright owner of a nondramatic musical work "must be identified in the registration or other public records" of the Copyright Office (§115).

7. The information contained in a registration certificate also may effect a change in the duration of copyright normally applicable to anonymous and pseudonymous works. Under the new law, copyright in works created on and after January 1, 1981, generally endures for the life of the author and fifty years after his or her death (§302(a)). (In the case of jointly authored works, the postmortem period is measured from the death of the last surviving author (§302(b).) Post-January 1, 1978 works that identify their authors by a pseudonym, or that bear no author iden-

tification, are subject to a special rule: copyright therein endures for a term of seventy-five years from publication, or one hundred years from creation, whichever first expires; however, if the identity of one or more authors is revealed in a registration or in certain other Copyright Office records, the term of protection of such works is then converted to the general rule of "life plus fifty" based on the life of the revealed authors (§302(c)). (Post-January 1, 1978 works created by employees, and *certain* works created on commission, are also protected for seventy-five years from publication or one hundred years from creation, rather than "life plus fifty." However, unlike anonymous and pseudonymous works, the copyright term in such works "made for hire" is not subject to conversion.)

8. Registration also may serve certain rehabilitative purposes. Thus, it may be used to cure the omission of a copyright notice from published copies in certain cases (§405(a)(3), discussed below). The presence of a copyright registration in the proper owner's name also may avoid defenses otherwise available to infringers who mistakenly rely upon dealings with a person misnamed as the owner of copyright in a copyright notice (§406(a)(1)). In addition, registration is one step by which a copyright owner may reinstate remedies otherwise unavailable against unauthorized reproduction of American-authored textual works that have been imported or distributed in violation of the manufacturing provisions of the new Act noted above (see §601(d)(3)).

In addition to the foregoing statutory advantages to registration, it wants to be noted that in a variety of circumstances — notably where works are being widely offered or disclosed for consideration by publishers, producers, customers, etc., and especially outside of established channels — registration may have the practical advantage of emphasizing one's claim of ownership and serving as a warning against unauthorized use. Also, ownership of a registration certificate may offer prac-

tical advantages in facilitating negotiations and commercial dealings; indeed, in some cases the certificate may approach a virtual condition to closing or obtaining financing for creative projects.

Although we have referred to registration under the Copyright Act as "permissive," as does the statute itself (§408(a)), this should not obscure a very important point *with respect to works copyrighted before January 1, 1978*, by publication with notice (or, in some cases, registration in unpublished form). It must be kept in mind that *renewal registration* in the Copyright Office is an absolute condition to extending the copyright in such works beyond a first term of twenty-eight years from the year in which the work was first published (or, in the case of the limited category of works that secured copyright by registration in unpublished form under the old law, from the year of registration (§§304(a), 305)). Application for renewal of works so copyrighted before January 1, 1978, must be made before the end of the twenty-eighth year from first publication (or, in the case of the aforesaid limited class of works, from registration). If renewal is not made on time, those works will enter the public domain in the United States at the expiration of those twenty-eight years (§304(a)). If timely renewal is made, it will secure a second term of forty-seven additional years (*id.*). In the case of works published before January 1, 1978, these rules operate regardless of whether any registration has been made earlier. (Under current practice, the Copyright Office will require an original (i.e., first-term) registration before a renewal registration will be made for works published before January 1, 1978. However, the original registration may be made simultaneously with the application for renewal.)*c*

Are there any *disadvantages* to registration? Beyond the potential economic burden on clients seeking assurance of full protection for substantial numbers of works, an additional possible drawback to registration should be considered in the

case of materials that are unpublished, or even if technically "published" within the definition of the Copyright Act, are normally subject to a significantly restricted dissemination and not made generally available to the public. Applications for registration in the Copyright Office must be accompanied by a "deposit," which usually will consist of a copy of the work (§408(b) and (c)). After registration, this deposit will be open to public inspection, both under the organic Copyright Act (§705(b)) and the Freedom of Information Act provisions of the Administrative Procedure Act as specifically applied to the Copyright Office (see §701(d)). (However, the deposit copies are generally not subject to actual copying (see §706(b) and §701(d)).) Thus, if the work for which registration is considered includes secret, confidential, private, or secure matter—such as might be the case with certain computer programs marketed under lease-license relationships, company training or instruction manuals, documents containing customer lists, descriptions of secret processes, confidential analyses, or the like, private diaries or correspondence, and other materials—it must be taken into account that registration may result in opening this matter to perusal by the general public, competitors, or potential unauthorized users. Apart from these practical consequences of the availability of the deposit copy for public inspection, there is also an unanswered question of the impact of such availability on protection for confidential information disclosed in the deposit under the law of trade secrets.*d*

Although considerations such as the foregoing might be resolved simply by deferring copyright registration until it becomes necessary to register in order to institute an infringement action, this may not always be an adequate answer. First of all, there are the benefits of copyright registration — particularly with respect to statutory damages, attorneys' fees, and evidentiary effect — that may be lost by such a decision. Perhaps more important, it may become necessary to institute a copyright infringement action against *threatened* infringement, or against an infringer whose activities (e.g., unauthorized reproduction or distribution) have not yet resulted in wide dissemination of the infringing copies. In some cases, the very object of such infringement actions may be to restrain threatened or continued dissemination of infringing copies in order to preserve the confidential nature of the material disclosed therein. Indeed, this may be a more important objective than the possible financial recoveries in such an action. This problem is compounded further by the fact that actions for infringement of so-called "common law copyright" are no longer available, the sole possibility of copyright actions arising after January 1, 1978, being under the federal statute and subject to its registration requirements; and by the fact that common law actions brought under the guise of unfair competition or trade secret law may be subject to defenses of preemption by the Copyright Act (see §301(a)), particularly where the complaint is not based on elements of intrusion, stealth, misrepresentation, breach of trust or confidence, or the like, as distinguished from the mere act of unauthorized reproduction and/or distribution of copyrighted material. It will be seen that unless the problem posed by the public availability of the deposit is resolved, the price of instituting such an action may be the sacrifice of the very value of confidentiality, security, or privacy that the action is designed to preserve.[e]

This dilemma for some time has been felt particularly among some software houses that engage in the restricted marketing of computer programs under lease/licensing arrangements designed to preserve the confidentiality of material embodied in the programs. Because of both the movement of computer program marketing to mass market or public distribution in an era of "mini" and "home" computers and certain other alternatives available to applicants for registration of copyright in computer programs,[2] concern for this issue may have diminished somewhat in that sector; however, this concern is being increasingly felt in various other areas. At this writing, the

issue does not appear to have been adequately resolved, except with respect to one category of copyrightable works. This category is "secure tests," a Copyright Office regulatory classification covering testing materials (such as Bar examinations, and other tests used in measuring scholastic, professional, and related aptitudes and abilities) that are administered and maintained under strict conditions of supervision and security by the test sponsor (see 37 C.F.R. §202.20(b)(4)). Copyright Office regulations permit confidential examination of secure tests as part of the registration procedure and the return of the actual tests to the applicant for registration after such examination, subject to Copyright Office retention of only identifying portions, descriptions or the like sufficient to form an archival record of the registered work (37 C.F.R. §202.20(c)(2)(vi)). The purpose of the secure test regulation is to assure the availability of copyright registration for such works, while avoiding compromise of the value and continued utility of test items for future use and evaluation that would result from their public exposure.[3] The Copyright Office at one time held out the possibility of similar treatment being accorded to other confidential works under petitions for "special relief" from the usual deposit requirements; apparently, however, few if any such petitions are being granted under the office's current practices.[f]

The mechanics of copyright registration are not difficult. Registration is made by submitting an application on the appropriate official form—currently, Form TX for nondramatic textual works; Form PA for works of the performing arts such as musical and dramatic works and motion pictures; Form VA for pictorial, graphic and sculptural works; and Form SR for sound recordings—together with the required deposit as specified in office regulations[4] and fee (at this time $10, per work; fee increases are quite possible in the near future) to the Copyright Office. The office will examine the application and deposit principally to ensure that the work comprises copyrightable subject matter and that the requisite information has been given (§410(d)); it will generally not compare the work with others or examine for novelty, invention, or aesthetic merit since

such elements are not conditions of copyright protection.[5] Although the procedure is not complex, care should be taken in completing the application. Material omissions or misstatements may provide the basis for defenses of unclean hands or fraud on the Copyright Office, or may detract from the *prima facie* evidentiary effect otherwise accorded the facts stated in promptly made registrations. In addition, the forms call for a specification of the "nature" of the work or authorship for which registration is sought. Although completion of this entry does not require the detailed specificity of patent claims, it should be carefully drawn in order to obtain the full benefits of registration and to avoid potential disputes in litigation; this may be particularly true where the precise work represented by the deposit is subject to conflicting interpretations.[6]

If an error is discovered in the information given on the initial application after registration has been completed, application for "supplementary registration" may be made on Form C/A to correct it. Supplementary registration also may be made to amplify or clarify information originally given. It is important to note, however, that this device should not be used to reflect changes in ownership or allocation of rights among licensees that occur after original registration is made. In these cases, *recordation* of the actual transfer documents or licenses in the Copyright Office—rather than registration of the mere fact of such transfer or license—is the appropriate course. (Recordation of documents, like registration, is generally permissive only (§205(a).) However, the Act also induces recordation by according it certain advantages, such as constructive notice and priority over conflicting transfers and licenses in some cases (§205(c), (e)). Recordation of an assignment or exclusive license also may become necessary before the assignee or licensee can institute an action for infringement (§205(d)).[7] Supplementary registration also is not appropriate to file renewal of copyrights secured before January 1, 1978; instead, specific renewal applications should be made on time, as noted above, for such works on Copyright Office Form RE.

In most cases, separate applications (and fees) must be made for each individual work for which registration is sought. However, in a limited number of cases, a single application and fee may cover multiple works. Thus:

1. A single "group registration" may be made, using Copyright Office Form GR/CP, for a number of individual contributions to periodicals by the same author first published during any twelve-month period. (But note the possible loss of statutory damages and attorneys' fees under §412 for infringement of such of the "grouped" articles as are registered more than three months after publication.)

2. A single registration may be made under certain conditions for various unpublished works created by at least one common author (see 37 C.F.R. §202.3(b) (3)(i)(B)). At the present time, there is no numerical or thematic limitation on this device, although this may change with future Copyright Office regulations.

3. A single registration may be made for all works that are published in a single unit (e.g., an audiovisual "kit" including filmstrip, audio cassette, script, and manual) and in which the copyright owner is the same (37 C.F.R. §203.3(b)(3)(i)(A)).

The Copyright Act also gives the Copyright Office general authority to establish regulations governing a single registration for "a group of related works" (§408(c)(1)). Although the office has invited comments on possible criteria or candidates for this form of registration, no proposed or final regulation has yet been issued.

If the Copyright Office refuses registration, appeal may be taken through the appropriate section and division (no formal regulations governing the appeal procedure have been established). Under the new Act, the office's refusal to register a work will not bar an action for infringement, if notice is served on the Register of Copyrights so as to give the office the opportunity to participate in the action on the issue of registrability (§411(a)). This is a salutary change from the prior law. Before the effective date of the new Act, applicants whose claims were refused registration could not bring an infringe-ment action until after they had overturned the rejection by separate judicial action in the nature of mandamus against the office. But what if registration is refused, and the applicant desires registration for reasons, such as those discussed earlier, other than immediate prosecution of an infringement claim? It generally has been thought that an action in the nature of mandamus would continue to lie for such purposes. However, a recent unreported order of a California District Court may cast doubt on this conclusion and suggest that the sole remedy for any refusal to register is the right to bring an infringement action on notice to the Register under §411(a).[8] It is submitted that in view of the various statutory and practical benefits of registration mentioned above (as well as the potentially injurious effects of a record refusal of registration in the marketplace), such a result would be short-sighted and in error.

B. COPYRIGHT NOTICE

The new Act requires that whenever a copyrighted work is *published* "in the United States or elsewhere," a notice of copyright be placed on all publicly distributed copies (and phonorecords of sound recordings) (§§401, 402). In the case of copies and phonorecords distributed on and after January 1, 1978, the notice shall be affixed "in such manner and location as to give reasonable notice" of the claim to copyright (§§401(c), 402(c)).[9]

The Act requires the Copyright Office to prescribe specific methods of affixation and positions of notice that will satisfy this requirement; however, these are to be considered examples only and will not bar a showing that a notice otherwise affixed or placed is reasonable under the circumstances (§401(c)). The office has issued detailed proposed regulations for these purposes (see 42 Fed. Reg. 64374). At this writing, they have not been issued in final form, although that appears imminent. In any event, a conservative approach to copyright notice affixation and placement and close adherence to the regulations are generally advisable.[9]

"Publication" is now defined in Section 101 of the Act as (a) "the distribution of copies or phonorecords . . . to the public by sale or other transfer of ownership, or by rental, lease, or lending" (including, e.g., subscription, mailing list or retail distribution and some lease/license arrangements); and (b) "the offering to distribute copies or phonorecords to a group of persons for purposes of further distribution, public performance, or public display" (including, e.g., some syndications and offerings to wholesalers, theatres, performing groups, and broadcasters). The public performance or display of a work (e.g., a television or radio broadcast; an art exhibition where copies are not offered for sale) is not *itself* a "publication" (*id.*), but may amount to a "publication" if accompanied by other factors falling within the two preceding clauses.[10] Whether or not a publication is involved is not always clear; and the statutory definition does not resolve all questions that may arise. Insofar as the question of copyright notice is concerned, it is frequently advisable to assume publication in such cases and use a notice. However, other considerations, under the Copyright Act and otherwise (e.g., the possible impact of notice as an alleged concession of "publication" on trade secret protection), may be pertinent in particular cases.**h**

The elements of copyright notice are set out in §§401(b) and 402(b) of the Act. They consist of the symbol ©, the word "Copyright" or the abbreviation "Copr." (in the case of phonorecords of sound recordings, the symbol ℗ is to be used); the year of first publication of the work; and the name (or recognizable abbreviation or known alternative designation) of the copyright owner. Two commonly overlooked aspects of copyright notice under the new law are:

1. In the case of works "consisting

preponderantly of one or more works of the U.S. Government" (e.g., an official government report published with a privately authored preface or annotations), the notice also must include a statement identifying the copyrighted portions (§403); and

2. The year of publication may be omitted from the notices for graphic or sculptural works reproduced on certain items specified in §401(b)(2) of the Act. (These include greeting cards, stationery, toys, and functional devices.) However, year-dated notices are now required in all other cases, including certain pictorial and similar works that did not require such notices under the prior law.

It also should be observed that, except in the case of advertisements, a "blanket" copyright notice in the publisher's name or the like on a collective work such as a journal, magazine, or anthology is sufficient to cover each of the separate contributions therein (§404(a)). However, where the person named in the blanket notice is not the owner of copyright in the contribution, "innocent infringers" who deal with the person named in the notice may have a defense in certain cases (see §§404(b), 406(a)).

A point that often causes some confusion pertains to the appropriate copyright notice for "phonorecords"—i.e., phonograph record discs, audio tapes, and the like. This confusion is principally attributable to the fact that phonorecords commonly embody two entirely distinct copyrighted works (frequently owned by separate copyright proprietors). The first of these works is usually a musical composition (or, in the case of "spoken word" records, a dramatic work, poem, story or lecture) that has been recorded—this work represents the creative efforts of the composer or other author of the music, lyrics, or text, and happens to be embodied, in this instance, on a phonorecord rather than in book, sheet music, or manuscript form. A "©" copyright notice is not required to be placed on the phonorecord to protect the recorded musical, literary, or dramatic work (see §401 and pertinent definitions in §101).[11] The second work embodied in the phonorecord is the "sound recording"—that is, the aggregation of particular sounds representing the creative effort and interpretative rendition

of the performing artists, narrator, and/or production technicians. A "℗" is required to be placed on the phonorecord, or on its label or container, to protect the sound recording.

Substantially deficient or omitted notices on copies and phonorecords published before January 1, 1978, may have thrown the work into the public domain. As noted earlier, in that event the new law does not reinstate protection. However, notice omissions after January 1, 1978, will not invalidate the copyright in a work if any one of three conditions is met. For these purposes, "omissions" include the complete absence of notice from published copies, notices post-dated by more than one year, certain dispersed notices (see §406(b) and (c)), and notices failing to meet the special requirements for works "consisting preponderantly of one or more works of the U.S. Government" (see §§403, 405(a)).[12] These conditions are:

1. That notice was omitted "from no more than a relatively small number" of publicly distributed copies (§405(a)(1)). There is little guidance as to the meaning of a "small number" or "relatively" under this section.

2. That notice was omitted by a licensee or the like in breach of an "express requirement in writing" that the distributed copies or phonorecords bear notice (§405(a)(3)). This provision can assume considerable importance, and copyright owners would be well advised to insert appropriately worded clauses into their licensing and similar agreements; indeed, in some cases (such as non-exclusive licenses, which otherwise do not have to be in writing), it would not be overly cautious to use written documentation for just this purpose.

3. That the omission is *cured*: by making (a) registration for the work before or within five years after publication without notice; *and* (b) "a reasonable effort . . . to add notice to all copies or phonorecords distributed to the public in the United States after the omission has been discovered" (§405(a)(2)). Note particularly that the two elements of cure are *conjunctive*. There is little legislative or judicial guidance as to the extent of the "reasonable efforts" required under this provision. Perhaps the best that can be of-

fered in the abstract is to suggest all efforts that can be accommodated by the surrounding economic, business or related restraints after taking into account the potential value of copyright preservation.

It should be added that even where one of the foregoing conditions is met, notice omissions may effect the remedies available against innocent infringers who are mislead thereby (see §405(b)).

Can copyright notices be deliberately omitted from published copies? The legislative reports accompanying the new Act suggest that a notice may be omitted intentionally without invalidating copyright (see S. Rep. No. 94-473, 94th Cong. 1st Sess. 130 (1976); H.R. Rep. No. 94-1476, 94th Cong. 2d Sess. 147 (1976)). However, it may be questioned whether the courts will so hold when notice is deliberately omitted from copies or phonorecords published in the United States and the curative provision is relied upon. Doubt arises because this provision refers to the "discovery" of the omission.[i]

Current Copyright Office practice is to examine the deposit of published works accompanying an application for the presence or absence of notice, and to: (1) refuse registration for works published before January 1, 1978, with notice omissions or defects that would have thrown the work into the public domain under the prior law; but (2) make registration (with a possible "warning letter") for works published after that date with defective or omitted notices. In view of the five-year registration requirement in the statutory provision for cures, this practice may change somewhat after January 1, 1983, to permit refusals of registration for some works published after January 1, 1978, without notice.

CONCLUSION

Adoption of the principle of "automatic copyright" marks a welcome movement in the United States law toward recognition of proprietary rights as a natural attribute of creative effort. It also brings our law closer to that of many other countries, and may enhance our participation in world councils of intellectual property. But conditions pertaining to registration, notice, recordation, and place of manufacture in some cases remain as significant elements of full protection and must be considered from the viewpoints of both general client practice and specific issues. The wide range of subject matter covered by the new Copyright Act, and the effect of that Act on other systems of protection, commend a basic understanding of these matters to the general Bar.[13]

Footnotes

1. "Publication is defined in Section 101 of the Act, and is discussed below.

2. The deposit accompanying applications for registration of computer programs (and some data bases) need not comprise more than the first and last twenty-five pages or equivalent units. See 37 C.F.R. §202.20(c)(2)(vii). Thus, at least in the case of lengthy programs, crucial portions may be kept off the record. Programs also may be deposited in source code and (subject to recent Copyright Office hesitancy) object code format, thus making meaningful perusal of the deposit somewhat more difficult than in more conventional cases.

3. The validity of the secure test regulation was upheld in *National Conference of Bar Examiners* v. *Multistate Legal Studies, Inc.*, CCH Copr. L. Rep. Para. 25, 201 (N.D. Ills. 1981).[j]

4. The nature of the deposit required to accompany an application for registration—including the required number of copies or phonorecords, the possibility or requirement of identifying material in lieu of actual copies or supplemental material in some cases, questions of physical condition, priorities among different formats or "editions" of the same work, the possibility of petitioning for waivers of the usual rules ("special relief"), and other matters—is subject to detailed Copyright Office regulations and Library of Congress acquisition policy statements. See generally, 37 C.F.R. §202.20, 21 and C.O. Circ. R7b. (The library's acquisition policies are pertinent because, after examination, the deposits are available for accession to the library's collections.)

Deposit for registration is only one of two forms of deposit governed by the Copyright Act. The second form—so-called "Mandatory Deposit" under Section 407 of the Act and detailed implementing regulations (37 C.F.R. §202.19)—is not related to registration; it requires timely deposit of copies of all works, unless exempted by Copyright Office regulations, that are first or subsequently published with notice of copyright in the United States, whether or not registration is sought. The deposit is to be made in the Copyright Office "for the use or disposition of the Library of Congress" (§407(b)). Mandatory deposit thus serves as a means of supplying and enriching the collections of the national library. It is not a condition of copyright and a failure to make the required deposit does not affect copyright protection (§407(a)). However, substantial monetary penalties may be imposed for a failure to comply with a formal Copyright Office "demand" for deposit under this section. No fee, form, application or other document need accompany a deposit made under §407.

Several categories of works are exempt from mandatory deposit by specific Copyright Office regulation. See 37 C.F.R. §202.19. Exemptions for additional works or categories, or variations from the usual requirements, may be requested under procedures for "Special Relief" (see 37 C.F.R. §202.19(e)).

In the case of both deposit for registration and mandatory deposit, published "motion pictures" (including theatrical and nontheatrical film, television programs, video cassette and disc productions and the like) may be deposited under a "Motion Picture Agreement" with the Library of Congress that provides for return of the deposit to the remitter, but subject to recall and only under certain conditions (see 37 C.F.R. §§202.19(d)(2)(ii), 202.20(c)(2)).

5. The fundamental requirement of copyright is originality — that is, independent creation by the author rather than copying. Except to the extent that certain *de minimis* levels must be exceeded, "originality" is generally not subject to Copyright Office examination.

6. For example, where the deposit is a photograph of a sculpture, or a film or videotape of a dance performance, does the registration pertain to the photographic or sculptural, or cinematographic or choreographic, work, or both?. Aspects of this issue have recently arisen in litigation and administrative proceedings involving the registration of electronic games on the basis of videotape deposits.

7. Section 205(d) provides that "no person claiming by virtue of a transfer to be the owner of copyright or of any exclusive right under a copyright is entitled to institute an infringement action . . . until the instrument of transfer under which such person claims has been recorded in the Copyright Office, but suit may be instituted after such recordation or a cause of action that arose before recordation." (Copyright "transfers" include exclusive licenses as well as assignments (see §101).) This section raises a number of questions, including: its general applicability to transfers made before January 1, 1978; its pertinence to suits under the new law by parties who trace their rights to informal (unwritten) transfers of "common law copyright" made before that date; whether it requires recordation of only the plaintiff's link in the chain of title, or of all prior links as well; and the sufficiency of recording "short-form" transfers in order to avoid spreading all aspects of commercial dealings in the public record.

8. *Nova Stylings, Inc.* v. *Ringer*, CV79-3798-TJH (C.D. Calif., Aug. 12, 1980) (appeal filed).[k]

9. Certain works published before January 1, 1978, were subject to detailed statutory requirements as to the specific *place* of notice. A failure to comply with those specific requirements *before* January 1, 1978, may have thrown the work into the public domain; in that case, the new law does not reinstate protection.

10. In considering the application of this definition to the sale or offering of "one of a kind" art works, *compare* Cong. Rec., Sept. 22, 1976 at H. 10874-75 *with* Brenner, *Copyrighting the Fine Arts*, 24 Bull. Cr. Soc. 85, 111 (1976).

11. However, © notices referring to the recorded work are sometimes used for *in terrorem* effect, or to avoid possible judicial confusion. Note that if the music, words, lyrics, etc. of the recorded work also appear in visually perceivable form, as on an accompanying jacket, liner, script or the like, the © notice *should* be used on that material.

12. Errors in the name appearing in the notice will not forfeit copyright, but may provide defenses to "innocent infringers" who deal with the person named in the notice (§405(b)). *Omission* of any name (or date, where required) is, however, equivalent to the complete omission of notice (see §405(c)).

13. The focus of this article on copyright "formalities" and conditions should not obscure the significance of provisions of the new Act that govern such matters as ownership of copyright and the nature and scope of protected rights. In several cases these provisions materially change the rules in effect prior to January 1, 1978.

J. A. Baumgarten

ADDENDA

[*Editors' Note:* The author requested that the following comments be added to this reprinting.]

a Since June 1, 1982 the Copyright Office has imposed a fee of $120 (in addition to the basic registration fee of $10) on requests for special handling. *Fed. Reg.,* May 4, 1982 at 19254.

b Proposed regulations issued, *Fed. Reg.,* July 7, 1983 at 31245.

c Under recent regulations, a first term registration is not a condition to renewal of certain foreign works. (But a substitute "affidavit" pertaining to the first term, and the renewal itself, is required of such works.) See 37 C.F.R. §202.17(d).

d For further discussion of, and recent developments with respect to, the issue of deposits and confidentiality, see Baumgarten, *Copyright and Computer Software (Including Data Bases and Chip Technology).*

e Ibid.

f Ibid.

g Final regulations issued December 1, 1983. 37 C.F.R. §201.20.

h For further discussion, see Baumgarten, *Copyright and Computer Software (Including Data Bases and Chip Technology).*

i Compare *O'Neill Developments Inc.* v. *Galen Kilburn, Inc.,* 524 F. Supp. 710 (N.D. Ga. 1981) with *Beacon Loomis, Inc.* v. *S. Luchtenberg & Co.,* 552 F. Supp. 1305 (S.D.N.Y. 1982).

j Affirmed, 692 F.2d 478 (9 Cir. 1982), petition for cert. filed.

k Affirmed, *Nova Stylings, Inc.* v. *Ladd,* 695 F.2d 1179 (9 Cir. 1983) (*but* adding that in the absence of infringement, review of a refusal to register under the Administrative Procedures Act *is* available).

II: CREATORS AND OWNERS

Papers 5 Through 14: Commentary

Copyright inherently involves—protects—the works of creators, but these creators are not always the final owners. Rewards from their creations usually require synergistic, value-added marketing—historically, publishing with all that it entails. The partnerships involved are often not simple ones. This section of our book is thus a challenging one.

AUTHORS

According to Section 201 of the Copyright Statute, "Copyright in a work protected by this title vests initially in the author or authors of the work. The authors of a joint work are coowners of copyright in the work." Although copyright ownership is a topic that is of direct interest to authors, it is largely covered in the Overview and Basics section of this book. The types of articles covered here are those that deal with particular confusions with the law.

The first paper here (Paper 5) is "Copyright in Government Employee Authored Works," by John O. Tresansky. Works of the U.S. Government are covered under two sections of the Copyright Statute. In Section 101, a "work of the United States Government . . . [is] . . . a work prepared by an officer or employee of the United States Government as part of that person's official duties." Section 105 provides that "copyright protection under this title is not available for any work of the United States Government, but the United States Government is not precluded from receiving or holding copyrights transferred to it by assignment, bequest, or otherwise."

Tresansky mentions difficulties with the words "official duties" and presents case law and the legislative history on the statutory prohibition of copyright in works authored by U.S. Government employees. He cautions us to not interpret Sections 101 and 105 "more broadly than is clearly required to carry out its underlying public purpose . . ."; this would hinder government employees' incentives to prepare intellectual, creative works.

In Paper 6, "The Ownership of Contributions to Collective Works Under the New Copyright Law," Kurt D. Steele explains first how contributions to collective works were handled under the Copyright Statute of 1909. Under the old law, the question of who owned a contribution was based on an understanding between publisher and author: no written transfer was necessary for the publisher to gain

37

ownership. Steele points out that, under the new law, publishers are required to obtain explicit (written) transfers of copyright if they wish to own a contribution to a collective work, such as a journal or proceedings. Another way for a publisher to own the copyright to a contribution is to commission or order a work as a *work made for hire.* (This subject is also covered in Part I, and Papers 43 and 44 in Part V of this book.)

PUBLISHERS

Allan Wittman presented "Copyright: Kill the Goose or Protect the Golden Egg?" (Paper 7) at the 1981 Fall National Meeting of the American Chemical Society. He talked about the importance of copyright protection and copyright transfer to publishers; these insure maximum dissemination of intellectual and creative writings. He also talked about photocopying abuse and stressed, "There is no free lunch. Someone must pay for the cost of putting material into the system." Copyright does not restrict the dissemination of information. On the contrary, it promotes it by insuring that creators and copyright owners have the exclusive right to their writings; thus, investment in the creation and dissemination of information is encouraged.

Wittman said that users should not abuse copyright or contribute to the demise of a journal by being part of a "systematic" photocopying service that doesn't pay royalty fees due to publishers. By all means, he urged, don't stop copying, but do pay appropriate royalties for that right.

In Paper 8, "Copyright from a Permissions Person's Point of View," by Barbara A. Friedman (now Barbara Friedman Polansky), we are told what it is like to handle copyright questions and permissions on a daily basis. The American Chemical Society's copyright transfer form and permissions policy are described. Helpful hints are given to those who need to write to a publisher for permission. For instance, do not send your permissions request to the editor or to the author of a work unless specifically asked to do so by the copyright owner, usually the publisher. "Keep in mind that if you are not sure whether or not you need to obtain reprint permission, it's a good idea to ask the copyright owner. It is also a good idea to know the basics of the U.S. Copyright Law, for ignorance of the law is no excuse for innocent infringement."

The third article in this subsection, Paper 9, is entitled "Ownership of Copyright," by Patricia H. Penick. This is a witty paper on the importance of authors transferring copyright to publishers. When publishers require copyright assignment for everything they publish, this not only makes it easier for them to know they own the rights to all articles, but it also makes it easier for users to obtain permissions from one source, the publisher; then, users don't have to track down individual authors for their permissions. The copyright permissions policy, copyright transfer form, and functions of the copyright office within the Institute of Electrical and Electronics Engineers, Inc., are presented at some length. The Copyright Clearance Center, Inc., and its services are also described. Throughout the paper, Penick supports the opening sentence of her abstract: "Papers published in technical journals are more useful when their copyrights are owned by the journal publisher."

The next item in this subsection, Paper 10, is an editorial from *Folio* magazine, "Electronic Media and Copyrights: No Major Problems Foreseen." The article describes some problems that publishers are finding with the new copyright law. For one, some publishers' copyright agreements are inadequate because they do not include the right to disseminate information in electronic media. This omission means that they must go back to the author(s) to try to get such a right if they wish to own it. The article presents comments, suggestions, and helpful hints from both freelancers and publishers; some publishers say that they hold all rights by requiring freelancers to sign a works-made-for-hire contract; others feel that such contracts alienate too many artists and writers, so they are willing to go back to the authors to pay more money for additional rights beyond first-publication rights.

In his article "Copyright Infringement", Paper 11, Stephen H. Gross takes us through a hypothetical situation to show what a publisher can do when faced with a copyright lawsuit. While there are a number of steps that can be taken, the first is to seek legal advice. Gross suggests that publishers could possibly claim fair use, write a letter of apology to the original author, offer to give due attribution in the next available issue, or, if necessary, resort to payment. To guard against being forced to make payment to an author whose work has been infringed upon by a freelancer, the publisher should see that freelancers' contracts are properly drawn: "A freelancer should not only represent to the magazine that the entire contents of his contributed articles are original, he should also indemnify the magazine if that representation (or any other) proves to be false."

OTHER OWNERS

In Paper 12, Jack C. Goldstein briefly reviews the basics of musical copyright and describes the three music licensing organizations: American Society of Composers, Authors & Publishers (ASCAP) Broadcast Music, Inc. (BMI), and Society of European Stage Authors & Composers (SESAC). The content of the article is revealed to us in the article's title: "Questions and Answers About the Performance of Music Under the New Copyright Law." Goldstein's posed questions and concise answers cover such performance issues as private vs. public, for-profit vs. not-for-profit, "live," jukeboxes, sheet music, recordings, and liability of the owners of a place of business in which music is performed. He concludes by saying that "the copyright system is the legal mechanism which enables the songwriter to make a living out of his or her creativity and genius." Music is not free, and users must "pay the songwriter as well as the piper."

In Paper 13, "The Copyright Law and Dance," Nicholas Arcomano reviews the early history of copyright and how dance has been affected. He points out, through an example of an 1892 lawsuit, that under the 1909 Copyright Act, choreography was not the proper subject matter

39

for copyright protection. "Fortunately, the situation changed for choreographers with the 1976 law." Dance can be protected as long as it is fixed in a tangible medium of expression. To satisfy this requirement, choreographers are "fixing" their works on videotape. Arcomano believes that choreographers should give every consideration to "registering them with the Copyright Office so that they may secure the maximum protection of the new law."

Peter Hoffmann has written an interesting news item (Paper 14), "Judge Rules that Copyright Law Protects Architects," which appeared in *Architectural Record.* "In a decision of national significance, a Nebraska Federal District Court has ruled that engineers and architects enjoy copyright protection of their drawings. . . ." The judge ruled that "such drawings normally may not be reproduced by a client for use in building a second structure based on the original plans." The architectural structures themselves, though, are not subject to protection, but copying a plan from a plan is an infringement. Other issues were raised, such as works made for hire and coauthorship, but no rulings were made pending further testimony.

BIBLIOGRAPHY

Authors

Butler, T. L., 1982, Can a Computer Be an Author? Copyright Aspects of Artificial Intelligence, *Comm/Ent Law Jour.* **4**:707-747.

Crawford, T., 1978, Contributions to Collective Works Under the New Copyright Law, Part 1, *Copr. Manage.* **1**(6):3-5.

Crawford, T., 1978, Contributions to Collective Works Under the New Copyright Law, Part 2, *Copr. Manage.* **1**(7):3-5.

Hartnick, A. J., 1982, Government and Copyright: Merely a Matter of Administrative Discretion, *Commun. and the Law* **4**(2):3-16.

See, H., 1982, Copyright Ownership of Joint Works and Termination of Transfers, *Univ. Kansas Law Rev.* **30**:517-531.

Zegas, A. L., 1980, Personal Letters: A Dilemma for Copyright and Privacy Law, *Rutgers Law Rev.* **33**:134-164.

Publishers

Ellingson, C. A., 1983. The Derivative Work Exception: Uses Permitted, *ASCAP Copr. Law Symp.* **29**:83-135.

Goldstein, P., 1983, Derivative Rights and Derivative Works in Copyright, *Copr. Soc. U.S.A. J.* **30**:209-252.

Hunter, K. A., 1984, Publishing in the 1980s and 1990s: New Technology and Copyright, *STM Innovations Bulletin 6*, Amsterdam, The Netherlands.

Wade, S. K., 1980, Derivative Works and the Protection of Ideas, *Ga. Law Rev.* **14**:794-812.

Other Owners

Brohaugh, W., 1980, Photography and the Law, *Rangefinder* **29**(4): 59-61.

Gross, K., 1980 (May–June), The New Copyright Law and the Art Community, *Prof. Arts Guide,* pp. 23-29.

Hamlin, S., 1984 (August 29), Recipe Copyright Suit Settled, *The Daily News* **66**(567):6.

Hayes, H. C., 1982, Performance Rights in Sound Recordings: How Far to the Horizon, *ASCAP Copr. Law Symp.* **27**:113-153.

Livingston, K., 1980, Photographing Armageddon, *Am. Photog.* **4**(1):34-39.

5: COPYRIGHT IN GOVERNMENT EMPLOYEE AUTHORED WORKS*

John O. Tresansky**

The Copyright Act of 1976[1] continues the prohibition enunciated in the Copyright Act of 1909 against allowing copyright protection for certain works which the Congress believes to serve the public interest best by being placed in the public domain.[2] Section 105 of the current copyright statute states, in part, that "[c]opyright protection under this title is not available for any work of the United States Government."[3] The pertinent part of its antecedent, section 8, read: "No copyright shall subsist . . . in any publication of the United States Government, or any reprint, in whole or in part, thereof."[4]

Although the language of these statutory prohibitions may appear to be clear, diverse interpretations of the extent of the prohibition have been continually voiced. As one court stated with reference to section 8: "The precise scope of the phrase 'publication of the United States Government,' has long been a source of conflict and concern, as a result of which many

---

* The views expressed herein are those of the author and not necessarily those of his agency.

** B.E.E., Catholic University 1950; L.L.B. Georgetown University 1954; Patent Counsel, Goddard Space Flight Center; Distinguished Lecturer on Patent, Copyright and Trademark Law, Catholic University; Secretary, American Patent Law Association.

1. Pub. L. No. 94-553, 90 Stat. 2541 (codified in scattered sections of 17 U.S.C. (Supp. III 1979)).

2. Ch. 320, § 7, 35 Stat. 1077 (1909).

3. 17 U.S.C. § 105 (Supp. III 1979). The entire provision states: "Copyright protection under this title is not available for any work of the United States Government, but the United States Government is not precluded from receiving and holding copyrights transferred to it by assignment, bequest, or otherwise."

4. Ch. 320, § 7, 35 Stat. 1077 (1909). The 1909 Act provided:

> 7. That no copyright shall subsist in the original text of any work which is in the public domain, or in any work which was published in this country or any foreign country prior to the going into effect of this Act and has not been already copyrighted in the United States, or in any publication of the United States Government, or any reprint, in whole or in part, thereof: *Provided, however*, That the publication or republication by the Government, either separately or in a public document, of any material in which copyright is subsisting shall not be taken to cause any abridgement or annulment of the copyright or to authorize any use or appropriation of such copyright material without the consent of the copyright proprietor.

definitions and criteria have been suggested for categorizing various works as within or without the prohibition of the section."[5]

The language and legislative history of section 105 resolved many of the uncertainties which arose in connection with section 8 of the prior act.[6] The statutory definition of the expression "work of the United States Government" provided in section 101 of the current statute explicitly limits the expression to a "work prepared by an officer or employee of the United States Government as part of that person's official duties."[7] Difficulties arise, however, in interpreting the scope of the term "official duties" of government personnel in specific situations. A situation in which this difficulty frequently occurs is when a government employee, requested by a publisher to write an article for a commercial periodical on some facet of his assigned duties, writes the article during working hours.

Whether such an article is a "work of the United States Government" is of great importance to the publisher of the commercial periodical. Under section 201(c), the "[c]opyright in each separate contribution to a collective work is distinct from copyright in the collective work as a whole, and vests initially in the author of the contribution."[8] Absent an express transfer of the copyright in the individual contribution by its author, the publisher's copyright in the collective work extends only to the right of reproducing and distributing copies of the contribution as part of the collective work and not of the contribution alone.[9] Thus, publishers desiring to acquire the right to reproduce and distribute copies of individual articles apart from the collective work must require each author of an article to execute an assignment of the copyright therein to the publisher.[10] Where the arti-

---

5. Scherr v. Universal Match Corp., 297 F. Supp. 107, 110 (S.D.N.Y. 1967).

6. *See* Tresansky, *Impact of the Copyright Act of 1976 on the Government*, 27 FED. B. J. 22 (1978).

7. 17 U.S.C. § 101 (Supp. III 1979).

8. 17 U.S.C. § 201(c) (Supp. III 1979).

9. *Id.*

10. Assignment is only one way of transferring copyright ownership. *See* 17 U.S.C. § 101 (Supp. III 1979). The assignment must be contained in an instrument of conveyance, note, or memorandum of transfer, which is signed by the owner of the interests conveyed or an authorized agent. 17 U.S.C. § 204(a) (Supp. III 1979). A transfer of copyright ownership need not be acknowledged or notarized, but such a certificate of acknowledgment can be *prima facie* evidence of the execution of such a transfer. 17 U.S.C. § 204(b) (Supp. III 1979). If the transfer occurs in the United States, the acknowledgment is only *prima facie* evidence if issued by a notary or someone authorized to administer oaths in the United States. 17 U.S.C. § 204(b)(1) (Supp. III 1979). When execution is in a foreign country, however, the certificate must be issued by a diplomatic or consular officer of the United States, or by a person authorized to administer oaths whose authority is proved by a certificate of such diplomatic or consular officer, in order to be considered *prima facie* evidence of a transfer. 17 U.S.C. § 204(b)(2) (Supp. III 1979).

cle is a "work of the United States Government," however, an assignment of copyright by the author is inappropriate because under section 105, the article itself is not subject to a United States copyright. In addition, publishers of periodicals consisting preponderately of one or more works of the United States government are required by section 403 to include in the periodical's notice of copyright a statement identifying those portions of the periodical in which copyright is claimed or, alternatively, unclaimed.[11] The purpose of such statement is to serve notice to the public of those portions of the periodical which are in the public domain and, therefore, free for use.

The difference in emphasis between the section 101 definition of a "work of the United States Government" and the legislative history of section 105, as well as that of its predecessor, section 8, renders the applicability of the copyright prohibition of section 105 more difficult. The statutory definition of the phrase emphasizes the scope of the author's employment, while the legislative history of section 105 places the emphasis on the end product. The House Judiciary Committee's discussion of the scope of the prohibition of this section begins with the statement: "The basic premise of section 105 of the bill is the same as that of section 8 of the present law—that works produced for the U.S. Government by its officers and employees should not be subject to copyright."[12] The emphasis here is clearly on the entity for whom the work was written, and not on the circumstances of writing. The House Report further notes in its discussion of section 105 that, under the section 101 definition of a government work, "a Government official or employee would not be prevented from securing copyright in a work written at that person's own volition and outside his or her duties, even though the subject matter involves the Government work or professional field of the official or employee."[13]

The congressional emphasis on the entity for whom the work was authored is in accord with the legislative history of the copyright prohibition in government publications. Section 8 of the Copyright Act of 1909 contained the first legal prohibition in the copyright law against copyright in a

---

11. 17 U.S.C. § 403 (Supp. III 1979). Section 403 states:

> Whenever a work is published in copies or phonorecords consisting preponderantly of one or more works of the United States Government, the notice of copyright provided by sections 401 or 402 shall also include a statement identifying, either affirmatively or negatively, those portions of the copies or phonorecords embodying any work or works protected under this title.

12. H.R. REP. NO. 1476, 94th Cong., 2d Sess. 58 (1976), *reprinted in* [1976] U.S. CODE CONG. & AD. NEWS 5659, 5671.

13. *Id., reprinted in* [1976] U.S. CODE CONG. & AD. NEWS at 5672.

government publication.[14] Preliminary drafts of the bill purported to incorporate in this provision the common law prohibition of copyright in laws and judicial decisions, as well as the prohibition of copyright in government publications in the Printing Law of 1895.[15] Neither the hearings[16] nor the legislative reports[17] on the Copyright Act of 1909 defines a publication of the United States government.[18] The copyright prohibition of the Printing Law of 1895—the first such statutory prohibition—suggests, however, that the prohibition was intended to apply to any matter prepared for the government. The Printing Law authorized the sale by the Public Printer of "duplicate stereotype or electrotype plates from which any Government publication is printed."[19] To preclude private persons from asserting copyright in republication of government documents from the plates, the prohibition was added that "no publication reprinted from such stereotype or electrotype plates shall be copyrighted."[20] The Senate Committee on Printing, in reviewing the applicability of the prohibition to a congressman who attempted to republish a government publication, entitled "Messages and Papers of the Presidents of the United States," from such plates with a copyright notice in his name, stated:

> [T]he prohibition contained in the Printing Act was intended to cover every publication authorized by Congress in all possible forms. . . .
>
> Your committee thinks that copyright should not have been issued in behalf of the Messages, and that the law as it stands is sufficient to deny copyright to any and every work once issued as a government publication. If the services of any author or compiler employed by the Government require to be compensated, payment should be made in money, frankly and properly appropriated for that purpose, and the resulting book or other publication in whole and as to any part should be always at the free use of the people, and this, without doubt, was what Congress intended.[21]

---

14. Ch. 320, § 7, 35 Stat. 1077 (1909). The title on printing and documents, 44 U.S.C. § 505 (1976), previously contained the prohibition against copyrighting government publications. The 1978 amendment of this section deleted the copyright provision.

15. Ch. 23, § 52, 28 Stat. 608 (1895).

16. *Hearings Before Joint Committee on Patents on S. 6330 and H.R. 19853*, 59th Cong., 1st Sess. 133-35 (1906).

17. S. REP. No. 1108, 60th Cong., 2d Sess. (1909); H.R. REP. No. 2222, 60th Cong., 2d Sess. (1909), *reprinted in* S. ROTHENBERG, COPYRIGHT LAW—BASIC AND RELATED MATERIALS (1956).

18. Ch. 23, § 52, 28 Stat. 608 (1895).

19. *Id.*

20. *Id.*

21. S. REP. No. 1473, 56th Cong., 1st Sess. (1900), *reprinted in* Study No. 33, *Copyrights*

If, therefore, the Printing Act of 1895 is considered to be a statute *in pari materia* with the Copyright Act of 1909, the history of the former statute may be properly viewed as indicating that the legislative intent of the prohibition in the latter statute was to preclude a copyright in any work prepared for printing by the United States government.

Section 105 of the Transitional and Supplementary provisions of the Copyright Act of 1976 deleted the codification of the copyright prohibition of the Printing Act.[22] The commentary in the House Report on amendments to other statutes states the intent thereof to be the repeal of the "vestigial provision of the Printing Act dealing with the same subject" as section 105 of the Copyright Act of 1976.[23] It appears reasonable to conclude, therefore, that Congress viewed the copyright prohibition in the copyright and printing statutes as being directed to works prepared for the government.

The 1961[24] and 1965[25] Reports of the Register of Copyrights on studies aimed at the general revision of the copyright law further emphasized the importance of the entity for whom a work is prepared in determining whether the prohibition against copyright protection applies. These studies were undertaken by the Copyright Office under the authorization of Congress. The 1961 Report recommended retention of the prohibition of copyright in "publications of the U.S. Government."[26] Moreover, the Report recommended that this expression be defined as "works produced for the Government by its officers or employees."[27]

---

in Government Publications by Caruthers Berger (Oct. 1959), prepared for the Subcommittee on Patents, Trademarks and Copyrights, Committee on the Judiciary, U.S. Senate, 30.

22. 44 U.S.C. § 505 (1976).

23. House Report, *supra* note 12, at 5796.

24. HOUSE COMM. ON THE JUDICIARY, 87TH CONG., 1ST SESS., COPYRIGHT LAW REVISION: REPORT OF THE REGISTER OF COPYRIGHTS ON THE GENERAL REVISION OF THE U.S. COPYRIGHT LAW (Comm. Print 1961).

25. HOUSE COMM. ON THE JUDICIARY, 89TH CONG., 1ST SESS., COPYRIGHT LAW REVISION, PART 6: SUPPLEMENTARY REPORT OF THE REGISTER OF COPYRIGHTS ON THE GENERAL REVISION OF THE UNITED STATES COPYRIGHT LAW (Comm. Print 1965).

26. *See* note 24, *supra*, at 133.

27. *Id.* The Report presented the following rationale for the copyright prohibition: The legislative history of the initial prohibition in the Printing Law of 1895 indicates that it was aimed at precluding copyright claims by private persons in their reprints of Government publications. It was apparently assumed, without discussion, that the Government itself would have no occasion to secure copyright in its publications. Most Government publications at that time consisted of official documents of an authoritative nature. When the copyright laws were consolidated in the Act of 1909, the same provision in substance was incorporated in that act. . . .

The Federal Government today issues a great variety and quantity of information material—technical manuals, educational guides, research reports, historical reviews, maps, motion pictures, etc. The basic argument against permitting these

The 1961 Report also acknowledged that much uncertainty existed about the nature of a "publication of the U.S. Government." The Report identified four possible meanings:

> (a) It may refer to the work itself. In this sense a "Government publication" would be any work produced by the Government—that is, produced for the Government by its employees—regardless of who published it.
>
> (b) It may refer to the act of publishing copies of a work. In this sense a "Government publication" would be any work published by the Government, regardless of who produced it. . . .
>
> (c) Any work which has either been produced or published by the Government. . . .
>
> (d) Only a work which has both been produced and published by the Government. . . .[28]

The Report proceeds to make the observation that "[t]he courts have expressed various opinions, but the weight of authority seems to point to the first meaning: a work produced by the Government."[29]

The 1965 Report was a commentary on the copyright revision bill introduced in the 89th Congress.[30] The Report noted that in section 105 the bill included the 1961 Report's recommendation to retain the copyright prohibition in government publications and furthermore extended it to any work of the United States government.[31] The Report also pointed out that the 1961 Report proposed to include "published works produced for the Government by its officers or employees" within the scope of the prohibition. Further, it stated that section 105 defined a "work of the United States Government" as a "work prepared by an officer or employee of the United States Government within the scope of his official duties or employment."[32] The Report observed that under this definition:

> [A] Government official or employee would not be prohibited from obtaining copyright protection for any work he produces in his private capacity outside the scope of his official duties. The use of Government time, material, or facilities would not, of itself, determine whether something is a "work of the United

---

publications to be copyrighted is that any material produced and issued by the Government should be freely available to the public and open to the widest possible reproduction and dissemination.
Id. at 130.

28. *Id.* at 130-31.

29. *Id.* at 131.

30. H.R. 4347, 89th Cong., 1st Sess., 111 CONG. REC.1285 (1965). The Senate bill on the same matter was S. 1006, 89th Cong., 1st Sess., 111 CONG. REC. 1226 (1965).

31. *Supra* note 25, at 8-9.

32. *Id.* at 9.

States Government," but the Government would then have the privilege of using the work in any event (28 U.S.C. § 1498(b)), and the unauthorized use of Government time, material, or facility could, of course, subject an employee to disciplinary action.[33]

From the foregoing it appears that the Register of Copyrights interpreted the statutory copyright prohibition to apply to works authored by government personnel for use by the United States government and not to works authored for use by the private sector or to works with minor governmental contribution to their preparation.

Prior to the enactment of legislation by Congress prohibiting copyright in government works, the issue of whether copyrights could exist in judicial decisions had been decided by the Supreme Court. In *Wheaton v. Peters*[34] the issue was whether a reporter of court decisions, appointed under an act of Congress, could assert a copyright in his published reports against another who later published a book containing some of the reported decisions. The Court determined that whatever copyright existed in the reports was statutory and remanded the case for a determination of whether compliance with the statutory provisions requisite to a valid copyright existed.[35] The opinion concluded with the statement: "It may be proper to remark that the court are unanimously of opinion, that no reporter has or can have any copyright in the written opinions delivered by this court; and that the judges thereof cannot confer on any reporter any such right."[36] If the Supreme Court had been of the opinion that no copyright could exist in the reports of the decisions, the remand would have been without purpose. Thus, it may be assumed that the Court viewed material contributed by the reporter, such as headnotes, statements of facts, and arguments of counsel, as lawful subjects of copyright protection. Subsequently, in *Banks v. Manchester*[37] and *Callaghan v. Myers*,[38] the Court extended the prohibition against copyright to opinions of state courts. In *Callaghan*, the Court held that the reporter was nevertheless entitled to a copyright for his contribution to judicial opinions unless copyright was prohibited by statute. The Court reasoned that:

> [T]here is no ground of public policy on which a reporter who prepares a volume of law reports, of the character of those in this case, can, in the absence of a prohibitory statute, be debarred

---

33. *Id.*
34. 33 U.S. 591 (1834).
35. *Id.* at 667-68.
36. *Id.* at 668.
37. 128 U.S. 244 (1888).
38. 128 U.S. 617 (1888).

from obtaining a copyright for the volume, which will cover the matter which is the result of his intellectual labor.[39]

In all of these cases, the reports were prepared by individuals appointed to their positions pursuant to legislative authority. The fact that reporting of decisions constituted the official duty of the plaintiffs does not appear to have influenced the Court.

The earliest case clearly involving the issue of whether a work prepared by a government employee could be copyrighted is *Heine v. Appleton*.[40] Heine, a professional artist, had been a member of the crew that accompanied Admiral Perry to Japan and the China Seas. Although he was hired as a master's mate, his chief duty was to make sketches and drawings for the government. It was understood from the outset that all such works would be the exclusive property of the government. Upon completion of the expedition, the plaintiff's works were included in the official report on the expedition. Later, Heine obtained a certificate of copyright in his sketches and drawings. The court denied the plaintiff's right to copyright, stating, "The sketches and drawings were made for the government, to be at their disposal; and congress, by ordering the report, which contained those sketches and drawings, to be published for the benefit of the public at large, has thereby given them to the public."[41] While there was an explicit understanding that the plaintiff's works were to be the exclusive property of the government, this understanding arguably may have been directed to the physical embodiment of the works and not to the individual works contained in the report. The court's decision, however, was based primarily on the consideration that the works were made for, and published by, the government.

The first case to involve the applicability of the statutory copyright prohibition in the Copyright Act of 1909 was *Sherrill v. Grieves*[42] where the plaintiff, an army captain, was assigned to teach a subject in an army school. Because a suitable textbook for the course was not available, he wrote one during his off-duty time. At the request of the army, he consented to the incorporation of a considerable part of the material in a pamphlet which the army printed and distributed to students at the school. The pamphlets bore a notice of copyright in the plaintiff's name. Subsequently, the material contained in the pamphlet was included in the book that the plaintiff had been writing and which he also copyrighted. It was the book that plaintiff alleged was infringed by the defendant's book. The defendant contended that the plaintiff's copyrights were invalid because

---

39. *Id.* at 647.
40. 11 F. Cas. 1031 (S.D.N.Y. 1857) (No. 6324).
41. *Id.* at 1033.
42. 57 Wash. L. Rep. 286 (D.C. Sup. Ct. 1929).

the material was a publication of the United States government.[43] In holding for the plaintiff, the court stated, *inter alia*, that the pamphlet "was not a publication of the United States Government in the sense in which that phrase is used in the statute."[44] The court rejected defendant's argument that, although writing the subject material was not part of plaintiff's duties, it was plaintiff's duty to provide the best possible treatment of the subject. Thus, when he used the pamphlet to teach the class, it had to be assumed that his superiors consented to the discharge of his duty in this manner.[45] The court reasoned:

> The plaintiff at the time was employed to give instruction just as a professor in an institution of learning is employed. The court does not know of any authority holding that such a professor is obliged to reduce his lectures to writing or if he does so that they become the property of the institution employing him.[46]

The court also stated that printing of the pamphlet by the army did not put it in the "public domain," and that, even should the army's printing of the pamphlet have been proper, it did not follow that the pamphlet became a government document.[47] The circumstances of printing and use of the plaintiff's writing by the government did not persuade the court to conclude that the statute prohibited copyrighting of the plaintiff's pamphlet.

More recently, in *Sawyer v. Crowell Publishing Co.*,[48] the plaintiff, Executive Assistant to the Secretary of the Interior, asserted copyright in a map of Alaska. Upon returning from an official trip to Alaska, the plaintiff directed a subordinate to assist him in preparing the map. The map was prepared on government time using government materials and facilities as well as information on file in the Department. The map was printed and engraved by the Department bearing a copyright notice in plaintiff's name. The map was later republished by the Department as an official publication with additional information and containing the copyright notice from the original map.

The Court of Appeals for the Second Circuit affirmed the holding of the United States District Court for the Southern District of New York that "[t]he map was prepared as a result of and relating to the plaintiff's work in Alaska in the course of his official duties."[49] The district court observed

---

43. *Id.* at 287.
44. *Id.* at 290.
45. *Id.*
46. *Id.*
47. *Id.* at 290-91.
48. 46 F. Supp. 471 (S.D.N.Y. 1942), *aff'd*, 142 F.2d 497 (2d Cir.), *cert. denied*, 323 U.S. 735 (1944).
49. 142 F.2d at 498.

that persuasive evidence existed to indicate that the map had been drawn
to stress Alaska's importance and the need for its development. This, the
court found, related directly to the subject matter of the plaintiff's work.
The court noted the large governmental contribution to the preparation of
the map, the initial intention for the map to be part of an official report,
and the government's publication of the map as an official document. The
plaintiff's consent to the government's publication of the map as an official
document as well as his failure to make any commercial use of the map
were also considered significant.[50] In denying the plaintiff's right to a
copyright, the district court stated:

> It is true that the mere fact that one has created or invented
> something while in the employ of the government does not trans-
> fer to it any title to or interest in it. But it is equally true that
> when an employee creates something in connection with his du-
> ties under his employment, the thing created is the property of
> the employer and any copyright obtained thereon by the em-
> ployee is deemed held in trust for the employer. . . . The evi-
> dence is persuasive that this map was drawn to stress the
> importance of Alaska, as well as the need for its development,
> and this relates directly to the subject matter of the plaintiff's
> work.[51]

The most recent case to address the issue of whether a work authored by
a government employee is barred from copyright on the grounds that the
work is a publication of the United States government is *Public Affairs
Associates, Inc. v. Rickover*,[52] decided by the United States District Court
for the District of Columbia on remand from the United States Supreme
Court.[53] In *Public Affairs Associates*, a navy admiral asserted copyrights in
speeches on education and on an experimental atomic power station which
he prepared and delivered to private organizations at their request. During that time, the admiral had technical responsibilities in nuclear propul-
sion plants for naval vessels and reactors, including the experimental
atomic power station which was the topic of one speech. The court evaluated the question whether the speeches could be copyrighted as requiring a
resolution of the issue of whether they fell within the purview of the admiral's official duties.[54] Speechmaking, as the court noted, was not enumerated among the author's official duties nor was he directed to make them.[55]

---

50. 46 F. Supp. at 473.
51. *Id.* (citations omitted).
52. 268 F. Supp. 444 (D.D.C. 1967).
53. 369 U.S. 111 (1962) (per curiam).
54. 268 F. Supp. at 448, 456.
55. *Id.* at 448.

The court reasoned, however, that this was not dispositive of the copyright question because a high official has authority to act in a variety of ways not enumerated in his formal position description. In this context, the duties of a high government official should not be narrowly construed.[56] The court found that the preparation and delivery of the speeches was done outside of working time[57] and that the speeches were made in response to a direct invitation to the admiral as a private individual.[58] The final drafts, however, were typed and reproduced by government personnel using government material and time, and, in the case of one of the speeches, also served an official purpose.[59] The court determined that the subject matter of both speeches was far removed from the author's official duties.[60] The court concluded that the speeches were not a part of the admiral's official duties and, therefore, were not "publications of the United States government."[61] The copyrights in the speeches were upheld.

The principle of these cases is that a work authored by a government employee for the use of the government cannot be the subject of a United States copyright. A work, therefore, authored by a government employee which can be considered as an assigned or expected duty cannot be protected by copyright. A work voluntarily authored by a government employee and not intended for use by the government, however, can be protected by copyright. Thus, a copyright would exist in an article authored by a government employee at the direct request of a publisher or editor of a private publication, even though the article was written on government time and its content related to the author's official duties. In turn, a copyright would not subsist in an article on a government agency's activities authored by the agency's public affairs officer and published in a commercial periodical or in a work assigned by a superior to a government employee which the employee prepared outside of working hours.

A narrow interpretation of the scope of the copyright prohibition is consistent with the decisions of the United States Supreme Court on ownership of inventions made by government personnel. In one Supreme Court case, *United States v. Dubilier Condenser Corp.*,[62] the government sued for a declaration of government ownership of patents granted to two physicists

---

56. *Id.* at 448-49.
57. *Id.* at 449, 452.
58. *Id.*
59. *Id.* at 447.
60. *Id.* at 449. The atomic power plant speech was so viewed because its contents were aimed at administrators and not scientists.
61. *Id.* at 456.
62. 289 U.S. 178 (1933).

employed in the radio division of the National Bureau of Standards. The physicists belonged to a group engaged in research and testing of radios for aircraft. The patented inventions related to the use of alternating current to operate a radio receiver and a power amplifier for a dynamic type speaker. The evidence established that these projects were not involved in the projects assigned to the group, but rather were voluntarily assumed by the inventors.[63] In addition, the projects were pursued during working hours using government material and equipment with permission of their superiors.[64] In holding that the inventions were owned by the employees because they were not made as part of their employment, the Court stated:

> One employed to make an invention, who succeeds, during his term of service, in accomplishing that task, is bound to assign to his employer any patent obtained. The reason is that he has only produced that which he was employed to invent. His invention is the precise subject of the contract of employment. A term of the agreement necessarily is that what he is paid to produce belongs to his paymaster. On the other hand, if the employment be general, albeit it cover a field of labor and effort in the performance of which the employee conceived the invention for which he obtained a patent, the contract is not so broadly construed as to require an assignment of the patent.[65]

One must acknowledge that the ultimate results differ greatly between a determination that an invention made by a government employee is a part of the employee's official duties and a determination that work authored by a government employee is within the scope of the employee's official duties. In the former, title to the invention belongs to the government. In the latter, the work is in the public domain. The analogy between inventions and written works, however, is appropriate because of the common constitutional genesis of patent and copyright law.[66] Such analogies were considered by the courts in *Sawyer*[67] and in the initial decision in *Public*

---

63. *Id.* at 184-85.

64. *Id.* at 185.

65. *Id.* at 187 (citations omitted). In Hapgood v. Hewitt, 119 U.S. 226 (1886), the Court held that an employee under contract to devise improvements in plows for his employer, a manufacturer of plows, was not a trustee of a patent for his employer. Similarly, in Standard Parts Co. v. Peck, 264 U.S. 52 (1924), the court reasoned that where one was employed to develop machines, and was compensated for such services, the improvements developed by the employee properly belonged to his employer.

66. U.S. CONST. art. I, § 8, cl. 8 reads: "The Congress shall have Power . . . to promote the Progress of Science and useful Arts, by securing for limited Times to Authors and Inventors the exclusive Right to their respective Writings and Discoveries."

67. 142 F.2d at 499.

Affairs Associates,[68] although the former case adopted the principles of ownership of employee invention stated in *Dubilier Condenser*.[69]

The plain language of the Copyright Act of 1976 does not clarify fully the ambiguities of earlier court decisions. The House Report's commentary on section 105 includes a statement which contributes to the uncertainty about the scope of the copyright prohibition. The Report states: "Although the wording of the definition of 'work of the United States Government' differs somewhat from that of the definition of 'work made for hire,' the concepts are intended to be construed in the same way."[70]

A literal interpretation of this statement would lead to conflicts between the various statutory provisions governing these kinds of works. Initially, while section 105 provides that a copyright cannot exist in a work of the United States government,[71] section 201(b) provides that the author of a work made for hire is the employer, or other person for whom the work is prepared, and section 201(a) provides that the copyright in a work initially vests in the author.[72] Secondly, section 201(b) provides that this "statutory authorship" may be avoided by the parties' express written agreement to the contrary.[73] No such "exemption" is provided for the copyright prohibition in a work of the United States government. Finally, the definitions of "work of the United States Government"[74] and "work made for hire"[75]

---

68. 177 F. Supp. 601, 603 (D.D.C. 1959), *rev'd*, 284 F.2d 262 (D.C. Cir. 1960), *vacated and remanded*, 369 U.S. 111 (1962), *opinion on remand*, 268 F. Supp. 444 (D.D.C. 1967).

69. *See* note 62 and accompanying text *supra*.

70. *Supra* note 12, at 58, *reprinted in* [1976] U.S. Code Cong. & Ad. News at 5672.

71. *See* note 3 and accompanying text *supra*.

72. 17 U.S.C. § 201(a) & (b) (Supp. III 1979). The two provisions state:

(a) Initial ownership

Copyright in a work protected under this title vests initially in the author or authors of the work. The authors of a joint work are coowners of copyright in the work.

(b) Works made for hire

In the case of a work made for hire, the employer or other person for whom the work was prepared is considered the author for purposes of this title, and, unless the parties have expressly agreed otherwise in a written instrument signed by them, owns all of the rights comprised in the copyright.

73. *See* note 72 *supra*.

74. Section 101 states in pertinent part: "A 'work of the United States Government' is a work prepared by an officer or employee of the United States Government as part of that person's official duties." 17 U.S.C. § 101 (Supp. III 1979).

75. Section 101 defines "work made for hire" as:

(1) a work prepared by an employee within the scope of his or her employment; or

(2) a work specially ordered or commissioned for use as a contribution to a collective work, as a part of a motion picture or other audiovisual work, as a translation, as a supplementary work, as a compilation, as an instructional text, as a test, as answer material for a test, or as an atlas, if the parties expressly agree in a

set forth in section 101 differ significantly because the former expression is limited to government personnel while the latter expression includes both employees and independent contractors on special order or commission. It would seem evident from the foregoing that the full significance of the analogy is unclear.

In *Scherr v. Universal Match Corp.*,[76] decided under the prior copyright statute, the "work made for hire" concept was applied to a work authored by government personnel. In this case two ex-servicemen asserted a copyright in a statue which they had sculptured while in the army. The district court rejected the defense that the work was not copyrightable because it was a publication of the government on the rationale that "there seems to be unanimous, albeit tacit, agreement that 'publications of the United States Government' refers to printed works."[77] The district court held for the defendant, however, on the ground that whatever copyright existed in the work belonged to, or inured to the benefit of, the government because the statue was a work for hire.[78] In affirming the judgment of the District Court for the Southern District of New York, but explicitly leaving undecided the ruling that the statue was not a government publication, the Court of Appeals for the Second Circuit identified the factors which it considered determinative of whether the "work for hire" doctrine applied:

> The essential factor in determining whether an employee created his work of art within the scope of his employment as part of his employment duties is whether the employer possessed the right to direct and to supervise the manner in which the work was being performed. Other pertinent, but non-essential, considerations, are those indicating at whose insistence, expense, time and facilities the work was created. Additionally, the nature and amount of compensation or the absence of any payment received by the employee for his work may be considered; but when com-

---

written instrument signed by them that the work shall be considered a work made for hire. For the purpose of the foregoing sentence, a "supplementary work" is a work prepared for publication as a secondary adjunct to a work by another author for the purpose of introducing, concluding, illustrating, explaining, revising, commenting upon, or assisting in the use of the other work, such as forewords, afterwords, pictorial illustrations, maps, charts, tables, editorial notes, musical arrangements, answer material for tests, bibliographies, appendixes, and indexes, and an "instructional text" is a literary, pictorial, or graphic work prepared for publication and with the purpose of use in systematic instructional activities.
17 U.S.C. § 101 (Supp. III 1979).

76. 297 F. Supp. 107 (S.D.N.Y. 1967), *aff'd*, 417 F.2d 497 (2d Cir. 1969), *cert. denied*, 397 U.S. 936 (1970).

77. 297 F. Supp. at 110.

78. *Id.* at 112.

pared with the above factors it is of minor relevance.[79]
Under this test, the court concluded that an employer-employee relationship existed between the government and the servicemen, and any ownership of copyright in the statue belonged to the government.[80] The court
noted such factors as the army's power to supervise the servicemen on the
project, appropriation of government funds, time and facilities to the project as well as the fact that the statue was created pursuant to a formal
government-commissioned project.[81] No conflict was considered to exist
between the legislative history of the prohibition or the test applied in the
determination of a "work made for hire" in this case and the tests applied
in the prior cases to determine whether the statutory copyright prohibition
applied to a work prepared by government personnel because it was part
of their official duties.[82]

Finally, the House Report's commentary on the "works made for hire"
provision of section 201 noted that this approach was adopted rather than
the "shop right" approach of patent law under which the employee keeps
title to his work but the employer generally acquires the right to use the
employee's work to the extent needed for purposes of the employer's regular business.[83] As the reasoning for this choice, the Report explained:

> The pesumption [*sic*] that initial ownership rights vest in the em-
> ployer for hire is well established in American copyright law, and
> to exchange that for the uncertainties of the shop right doctrine
> would not only be of dubious value to employers and employees
> alike, but might also reopen a number of other issues.[84]

This statement may be viewed as casting a cloud on the "Government
shop right" provision.[85] Under this statute, a copyright owner may sue the
government for an infringement of a copyright which had been authorized
and consented to by the government. This right to sue the government
explicitly applies to employees of the government except where an employee is in a position to order, influence, or induce the government's use
of the copyrighted work.[86] However, this right to sue the government is
expressly denied by the statute to

> any copyright owner or any assignee of such owner with respect

---

79. 417 F.2d at 500-01 (citations omitted).

80. *Id.* at 501.

81. *Id.*

82. *Id.*

83. *See* note 12, *supra* at 121, *reprinted in* [1976] U.S. CODE CONG. & AD. NEWS at
5736-37.

84. *Id., reprinted in* [1976] U.S. CODE CONG. & AD. NEWS at 5737.

85. 28 U.S.C. § 1498(b) (Supp. III 1979).

86. *Id.*

to any copyrighted work prepared by a person while in the employment or service of the United States, where the copyrighted work was prepared as a part of the official functions of the employee, or in the preparation of which Government time, material, or facilities were used.[87]

The latter portion, "or in the preparation of which Government time, material, or facilities were used," is considered to create a "Government shop right" in works authored by government personnel outside of their official duties but with a contribution by the government.[88] This "Government shop right" exists despite the comment to the contrary in the House Judiciary Committee's discussion of section 201.[89] Supportive of this view is the statement in the 1965 Copyright Register's Report: "The use of Government time, material, or facilities would not, of itself, determine whether something is a 'work of the United States Government,' but the Government would then have the privilege of using the work in any event (28 U.S.C. § 1498(b))."[90] Also supportive of this view is section 105(c) of the Transitional and Supplementary provisions of the Copyright Act of 1976 which merely changed a cross reference in section 1498(b) without altering the operative provision of section 1498(b), the "Government shop right" provision.[91]

In sum, neither the case law nor the legislative history of the statutory prohibition of a copyright in works authored by government personnel warrants a broad interpretation of section 105. To interpret this provision more broadly than is clearly required to carry out its underlying public purpose would unnecessarily vitiate the government officer's and employee's incentive to intellectual creativity provided by Congress in the Copyright Law pursuant to the intent of the framers of the Constitution.

---

87. *Id.*
88. *See* notes 83-84 and accompanying text *supra*.
89. *Supra* note 25, at 9.
90. *Id.*
91. *See* note 85 and accompanying text *supra*.

6: THE OWNERSHIP OF CONTRIBUTIONS TO COLLECTIVE WORKS UNDER THE NEW COPYRIGHT LAW

Kurt D. Steele

Assistant General Counsel
McGraw-Hill, Inc.

Most publishers of collective works such as magazines, encyclopedias, anthologies, and handbooks now realize that their right to use contributions that are not prepared by employees has been significantly restricted by the new copyright law in effect since January 1, 1978. The point has not escaped the attention of contributors. Many of them now also realize that they are much more able to control publishers' use of their work.

With six months' experience under the new copyright law, this is a good time to review the question of who owns a contribution to a collective work. How does the new copyright law affect the ownership of a contribution? What must a publisher do to acquire the right to use a contribution? Has the new copyright law created any truly irreconcilable problems between publishers and contributors over the ownership of contributions?

Old Law

To understand the impact of the new copyright law on the ownership of a contribution, it is necessary to look at what the copyright law was before January 1, 1978. Throughout this article, "contribution" will mean a separate work, such as an article, assembled with a number of other contributions to form a collective work. A "collective work" is a work in which a number of contributions are assembled into a collective whole.

Employees Under the old copyright law, a contribution prepared by an employee of a publisher within the scope of that employee's employment was a "work made for hire." This meant that the publisher was considered the author of the contribution and owned all exclusive rights to it. No written agreement was necessary to establish this ownership.

The new copyright law does not treat the ownership of this type of contribution differently, but two problems still exist. There was and still is an issue as to whether the contributor is a bona fide employee. What is an "employee"? Evidence of employee status includes a publisher withholding tax from an individual's salary, making premium payments for unemployment and workmen's compensation insurance, and providing customary employee benefits such as vacations and medical insurance.

Even if employee status is assumed, there was and still is the issue of whether the contribution was prepared within the scope of the employee's employment. For example, if a staff photographer writes an article on photography, it would probably not fall within that employee's scope of employment.

If there is any question as to whether a contribution was prepared by a bona fide employee, or whether the work falls within the scope of that employee's employment, it is advisable for the publisher to treat the author-employee as an outside contributor.

Outside Contributors In general, an "outside contributor" is a freelancer or other nonemployee who prepares contributions. The contribution may be "over the transom" (unsolicited) work or "commissioned" work. An outside contributor may also be a correspondent or a stringer who, although not an employee, prepares material for a publisher on some type of continuous basis under either an oral or a written contract.

Under the old copyright law, the question of who owned a contribution prepared by an outside contributor was based on the understanding between the contributor and the publisher. There was no need for this understanding to be reduced to an agreement signed by the contributor.

Publishable unsolicited contributions were frequently accepted by a friendly letter that thanked the contributor for the contribution but did not specify in any detail the publisher's right to use the contribution. Perhaps less frequently, publishers also commissioned contributions by letter without specifying in any detail the publisher's right to use the contribution.

Where there was no clear written or oral understanding between the publisher and the contributor as to the use the publisher could make of the contribution, the extent of the publisher's ownership was inferred by the publisher from the type of contribution and trade customs. In the case of both solicited and unsolicited contributions, publishers sometimes implied they possessed broad rights, not just first-time publication rights, but also, for example, the right to reprint, excerpt, revise, and include the contribution in other works (such as a book if it originally appeared in a magazine). The situation was even more informal in many cases where stringers were used. Some publishers freely used stringers' material without any clear written or oral understanding.

Present Law

It should be no surprise that one significant change in the new copyright law was intended to restrict greatly the informal practices that often existed between publishers and outside contributors over the ownership of contributions. Under the new copyright law, a publisher can no longer imply ownership of any exclusive rights to a contribution prepared by an outside contributor. The publisher possesses these rights only if the contributor has transferred them to the publisher in writing.

Presumed Rights If there is no written transfer of exclusive rights, the publisher is presumed to have, under the new copyright law, only the very limited right to include the contribution in a particular collective work, in any revision of that work, and in any later collective work in the same series.

With respect to magazines, the right to include the contribution in any revision would appear to be of little value to the publisher. On the other hand, the right to include the contribution in any later collective work in the same series may be of value if a magazine publisher wants to reprint an article in some later issue of that magazine. The publisher of a collective work in book form can include a contribution in a revision of the book, or in a later collective work that is part of the same series (such as an encyclopedia yearbook).

Without a written transfer of exclusive rights from the contributor, however, what are some of the more important ways a publisher is prohibited from using the contribution? The contribution cannot be included in another collective work—in a book, for example—if it first appeared in a magazine. The contribution cannot be revised in any way, which means that although it could be included in a revised edition of the collective work in which it originally appeared, the contribution itself could not be revised. The contribution cannot be separately reprinted either in whole or in part, and permission cannot be given to a third party for reprinting.

Theoretically, the oral grant of nonexclusive rights to a publisher is not prohibited by the new copyright law either. Since a publisher would have a hard time proving this grant in court, however, it would be prudent to reduce such a grant to a written agreement signed by the contributor.

Exclusive Rights Suppose a publisher needs or wants exclusive rights to use a contribution in ways other than those permitted under the new copyright law without a written agreement from an outside contributor. In this case, the publisher must ask the contributor to grant those rights to the publisher in a written agreement signed by the contributor.

All Rights Although it is easy to understand this new requirement of a written agreement signed by the outside contributor where a transfer of exclusive rights is to be made, the actual articulation of the specific exclusive rights to be transferred is not so easy. In some cases, depending upon the subject matter of the contribution and the type of publisher and publication involved, the publisher may desire to own all exclusive rights to the contribution. Assuming the contributor is willing, there are two ways to accomplish this.

First, if the contribution is one that the publisher is soliciting or ordering as a special assignment, it can be commissioned as a work made for hire. In order to accomplish this, both the publisher and the contributor must enter into a written agreement that should refer to the contribution being prepared by the contributor for the publisher as a work made for hire. Given such an agreement, the publisher is legally considered the author of the contribution and therefore the owner of all exclusive rights to it. This is similar to the situation previously discussed where all contributions prepared by an employee within that employee's scope of employment are also considered works made for hire (but in that case no written agreement is necessary in order to achieve that result).

One special application of a work made for hire agreement could occur where a publisher uses freelance stringers and correspondents regularly. Like all outside contributors, freelancers and correspondents own all exclusive rights to their material unless they agree otherwise in writing. Although it would be theoretically possible for the publisher to enter into a separate agreement for each story filed, it would be easier to enter into an agreement with each stringer and correspondent who files stories regularly. This agreement should provide that until the agreement is terminated each future story filed with the publisher shall be considered a work made for hire.

Such an agreement also provides an opportunity to indicate (for reasons unrelated to copyright) that the stringer or correspondent is not an employee for purposes of tax withholding or workmen's compensation and unemployment insurance and that this person has no authority to make any commitments on behalf of the publisher. The agreement can also specify any fees to be paid and any credit line to be given for material submitted and accepted by the publisher.

One uncertainty with respect to work made for hire agreements, however, should be noted. At the present time it is not clear whether it would be permissible under the new copyright law for a publisher to enter into a work made for hire agreement with a contributor for a contribution that has already been prepared and comes to the publisher over the transom. Since technically speaking the copyright to a pre-existing article has already become vested in its creator and the new copyright law speaks in terms of "commissioning" a work made for hire, it would be prudent to enter into work made for hire agreements only for contributions to be prepared and not for those which have already been prepared.

An alternative way a publisher may become the owner of all exclusive rights to a contribution is for the contributor to assign to the publisher, without any reservation of rights, the contributor's copyright (which means all exclusive rights to the contribution). (The same result can be achieved by the contributor "granting to the publisher all exclusive rights to the contribution.") This assignment must also be in writing and signed by the contributor, but it may be made either before or after the contribution has been prepared, assuming the contributor has not previously assigned some rights to the contribution elsewhere.

There are only two practical differences in the rights vested in the publisher under a work made for hire agreement and under a copyright assignment: First, the term of copyright for any new contribution not prepared as a work made for hire is the contributor's life plus 50 years. The copyright term for any new contribution prepared as a work made for hire is 75 years. Second, where the copyright is assigned the contributor generally has the right to demand the termination of the assignment and the reversion of the rights the contributor granted to the publisher at any time between the thirty-fifth and fortieth year from the date of the publication of the contribution, or between the fortieth and forty-fifth year from the date of the copyright assignment to the publisher, whichever period ends earlier. As a practical matter, these differences are probably relevant to only a few types of contributions, such as poetry and fiction.

Limited Rights In some cases, the publisher may not want, or the outside contributor may not be willing to transfer, all exclusive rights to a contribution, at least not for a fee the publisher considers reasonable. The alternative is an agreement in which only some specified or limited exclusive rights are transferred to the publisher.

In order for such a transfer of limited exclusive rights to be effective, it must also be made in a written agreement signed by the contributor. The fundamental problem with a "limited rights" agreement from a publisher's perspective is the difficulty of articulating the specific exclusive rights desired.

A publisher when articulating such limited exclusive rights must always be aware of both future publishing possibilities and future technology that may allow use of the contribution in ways not now readily discernible. For example, a grant of only worldwide exclusive periodical rights clearly would not permit the publisher to use the contribution in book form. If exclusive book rights are also desired, they must also be granted to the publisher by the contributor in writing. But what about the magazine publisher who thinks ahead and does get book rights, but later finds that the contribution can also be used in a computer database information service? These variations and the problems they pose when articulating the exclusive limited rights to be transferred to the publisher are endless.

Other Problems The administrative burden on the publisher entering into written agreements

60

of whatever type with outside contributors will often be substantial. A considerable amount of thought must be given by the publisher both to the type of exclusive rights needed and to the development of standard contributor agreements that reflect these needs and treat contributors fairly.

Some author groups have recently said that the publishers' use of standard contributor agreements where all exclusive rights to a contribution are granted to or vested in the publisher is unfair. Although there may well be some standard contributor agreements now in use that are unfair, the concept of a contributor transferring all exclusive rights to a publisher, or vesting in the publisher all exclusive rights to a contribution prepared as a work made for hire, is not per se unfair. A publisher may seek all exclusive rights from contributors in a variety of situations in order to have maximum flexibility to use contributions in a number of ways without having to constantly seek additional permissions from a multitude of contributors for different uses of their contributions.

The real issues with respect to all-rights standard contributor agreements are whether the contributor, where appropriate, can retain the right to reuse a contribution in specified situations and whether, where appropriate, with respect to at least some uses by the publisher, the contributor is paid extra for those uses. One particularly helpful technique with respect to reuse is to provide in the all-rights contributor agreement, if the contributor is not going to reserve certain specified rights, that the publisher's permission for any future reuse by the contributor will not be unreasonably withheld.

It should be noted that although the general discussion of all-rights standard contributor agreements are also applicable to photographs as a matter of trade custom, few publishers purchase all rights to photographs. In addition, no attempt has been made in this article to discuss musical compositions that may be included in a collective work.

A publisher may also want to consider the inclusion of still other provisions in its standard contributor agreements. Several were mentioned previously with respect to agreements with freelance stringers and correspondents. Such provisions as the details relating to the preparation, content, and delivery date for contributions being commissioned, any fee being paid to the contributor, the credit line (if any), and a warranty by the contributor regarding such matters as libel, privacy, and copyright infringement may also be appropriate in certain types of contributor agreements.

Two final points must be made with respect to contributor agreements. First, their value is completely lost if there is no efficient record-keeping system to identify easily the exclusive rights owned by the publisher when future uses are considered. Second, the possibility of recording with the U.S. Copyright Office the grant to the publisher of exclusive rights to a contribution should be considered. The detailed consideration of this step is beyond the scope of this article.

Transitional Problems

If a contributor has not granted any exclusive rights in writing to a publisher, there are several "transitional problems" that can affect a contribution. In particular, what use can be made now by a publisher of a contribution originally published prior to 1978? In this situation, the old copyright law probably applies. This means, as previously discussed, that the publisher must review the scope of any oral grant of rights, or if there were none, decide what rights may be reasonably inferred as having been granted to the publisher by the contributor. If there is doubt about the rights that are actually owned or that may be reasonably inferred by the publisher, the publisher can always, of course, seek the contributor's written permission for any future use.

What use can be made of a contribution by a publisher initially published in 1978 or after, but which was either arranged for or delivered to the publisher prior to 1978? Although the old copyright law may apply, it would be prudent to obtain a written agreement from the contributor specifying the exclusive rights to be owned by the publisher.

There are many technicalities that affect contributions under the new copyright law. The important ones have been discussed generally in this article. Nevertheless, where appropriate, copyright counsel should be obtained to resolve specific problems.

7: COPYRIGHT: KILL THE GOOSE OR PROTECT THE GOLDEN EGG?[†]

Allan Wittman

John Wiley & Sons, Inc.
New York, N.Y. 10158

Copyright protects the rights of scientists and scholars as authors who wish to achieve the widest possible dissemination of their work and as researchers who require access to information. The founding fathers of the United States acknowledged the need for copyright protection. Two centuries later, Congress reiterated the concept that copyright assures wide dissemination of valuable information. Chemists and other scientists depend on the existence of publications with narrow constituencies in which specialized knowledge is distilled. The uncontrolled practice of photocopying without payment to the owner will surely spell the demise of science's most important medium for the exchange of current knowledge at the forefront of advancing research.

INTRODUCTION

The papers which follow explore the legal, moral, and practical issue relating to adherence to, and respect for, the copyright law. The points of view come from persons in different sectors, and they may appear adversarial. But they are not. Publishers and librarians, for example, have uncovered areas of disagreement stemming from different interpretations of the new law. However, we are all part of a continuing chain. At one end of this chain is the scientist/author conveying information to a colleague at the other end of the chain, a scientist/reader who returns the favor with his own subsequent contribution. We are simply the middlemen, the brokers in this chain, and we function as catalysts for stimulating development at the forefront of chemistry.

THE ISSUES

The Constitution of the United States says, in Article I, Section 8, "The Congress shall have power to promote the progress of science and useful arts, by securing for limited times to authors and inventors, the exclusive right to their respective writings and discoveries".

Most of you have contributed papers to journals. Many of you have contributed a chapter to a book. Some of you are authors of books. Many of you have worked on a development for which a patent was subsequently obtained, either by yourself or your company. Your right to protect your "respective writings and discoveries" is a basic constitutional right embedded in the original Articles. It is not a new idea. Chemists respect the patent and proprietary rights of others. Do they always respect the intellectual rights of fellow authors to their writings? I leave it to the reader to examine his conscience and to answer this question for himself.

Just as you transfer patent rights to your employer for the development and dissemination of the practical values in a discovery, you transfer your copyright to a publisher to ensure maximum dissemination of the ideas in your writings. When a fellow researcher photocopies your article or a chapter from your book without permission to do so or without compensation

[†] Presented at the 182nd National Meeting of the American Chemical Society, New York, NY, 1981.

for the use of the information, he is stealing from you. When you make unauthorized copies of copyrighted material, or your library does it for you, you may be stealing from your colleagues. You may also be destroying the foundations of the distribution system for scientific literature.

There is no free lunch. Someone must pay for the cost of putting material into the system. Congress recognized this economic fact of life when it created the copyright law. It explained that copyright does not restrict dissemination of information; on the contrary, copyright promotes such dissemination. It does so by encouraging investment in the creation and distribution of the publication. Whether the publisher is a professional society such as the American Chemical Society (ACS), a commercial publisher such as John Wiley & Sons, or a university press such as MIT Press, the publisher weighs carefully the prospect of a return on his investment through the sale of enough copies of a book, enough subscriptions to a journal, enough reprints, enough microfiche, or enough uses in an electronic delivery system. The legislative history details in several places that copyright is meant to encourage such dissemination by protecting the investment from unlicensed use.[1]

Where does the abuse come from? What is the danger? In a word, the answer is republishing. Original publishing requires more than simply printing and binding. The process includes evaluating the quality of the ideas and the presentation, which in our field requires the peer review process. It means editing manuscripts for clarity. It means designing a format to improve legibility. In short, there is value added by the publisher initially, which he hopes to recoup through the distribution process. When the printed page is then photocopied and "republished" without compensation, the original publisher cannot recover his investment. The result is that a journal such as this one may very well be terminated, even though there is a wide (albeit illicit) audience for its papers. This is the journal you write for, the journal you read to keep abreast of developments. Its very existence is currently threatened by copying without permission and payment. Without respect for copyright, the system will offer less material of value or, worse, material of lesser value.

Why does a publisher need to administer copyright in a manuscript? Under the current law the author owns the rights to the manuscript at the moment it is created and exists in tangible form. When you transfer your rights to the ACS or Wiley, you enable your publisher not only to publish and distribute the work but also to license others to redistribute it, to sell reprints and photocopies of it, to share it with abstracting and indexing services, to include it in electronic data bases, and to create new forms of it such as microfilm.

Do not make the mistake of thinking your single, occasional use of the company Xerox machine is always trivial. Sometimes it is, and sometimes it comes under fair use. But if you work for a large chemical, petroleum, or pharmaceutical company, for example, your trip to the photocopy machine is being repeated elsewhere in your company by others like you, and, as Congress said,[2] these so-called trivial abuses, in the aggregate, can deal a mortal blow to an important journal serving a narrow, specialized subset of a discipline.

Of the thousands of journals being published today, many number their subscribers in the hundreds and not in the thousands. It does not require many photocopies to put such journals out of business. That ultimate result runs contrary to your best interests. Taking advantage of the publisher will reduce your opportunities for places to publish. If you or your company or school library are making photocopies of copyright material, the use should be reported conscientiously through the Copyright Clearance Center (CCC) so that payment can be made in support of the publication. The code appearing at the bottom of the first page of most articles in ACS journals announces the fee to be paid through the CCC. It is not designed to delay or restrict copying. It provides instant, on-the-spot permission to copy, provided the copying is paid for.

You are the authors. You are the readers. You are the users. These are your publications, and you have a vested interest in their health. Protect them by using your influence inside your companies. Express your views to the librarians and the management so that they understand you and your colleagues need to ensure the system. Urge your libraries or other photocopying facilities to secure licenses or permission to copy where necessary or else to register as users of the CCC. If you teach, please do not order multiple copies of book chapters or periodical articles without making sure your fellow authors and their publishers are compensated.

If you are an author, think about how you feel when cheated out of a royalty. If you publish in highly specialized, state-of-the-art, advanced journals, think about how you feel when such journals fold. Every two years an estimated 8000 journals cease to exist.[3] As science expands, the exchange of information about discoveries must keep pace. The charge of "proliferation of journals" is misleading in implying that the rate of growth is excessive. It is science which is expanding and the need for documentation and dissemination of information is accelerating to keep pace.

All who depend upon the system of exchanging information through publishing must honor that system by ensuring that photocopying in the library or academic institution is paid for by license or through the CCC. Do not stop copying. Do try to provide your share of the sustenance needed to maintain the goose that lays that golden egg. If not, all that will remain of the egg will be the odor of hydrogen sulfide.

REFERENCES AND NOTES

(1) "Copyright Law Revision"; Study 33: Studies Prepared for the Subcommittee on Patents, Trademarks and Copyrights of the Committee on the Judiciary, United States Senate; Washington, DC; U.S. Government Printing Office: Washington, DC, 1961; p 35.
(2) "Copyright Law Revision"; House Report No. 83; U.S. Government Printing Office: Washington, DC, 1967; pp 35–6.
(3) "Ulrich's International Periodicals Directory", 15th ed.; R. R. Bowker Co.: New York; 1973–1974; 16th ed., 1975–1976.

8: COPYRIGHT FROM A PERMISSION PERSON'S POINT OF VIEW†

B. A. Friedman

American Chemical Society
Washington, D.C. 20036

In order for publishers to effectively and efficiently handle permission requests for further dissemination of information, it is necessary for them to have copyright to the material they publish. Some publishers require that, to the extent possible, copyright be transferred to them. In return, certain rights are generally returned to authors or their employers in the case of works made for hire.

A copyright owner is not the only one who is concerned with copyright. As copyright administrator for the American Chemical Society Books and Journals Division, I get telephone calls, letters, and telegrams from authors, editors, librarians, publishers, lawyers, educators, and users of information. One of the main concerns of a permissions person is to respond to requests for copyright information and reprint permission in a timely manner. Another concern is to ensure that copyright transfer forms are properly signed.

It goes without saying that you must be the copyright owner of requested material in order to be able to grant reprint permissions. Because copyright transfer and ownership is germane to granting reprint permissions, and because we feel that our owning copyrights to works we publish is a service rather than a deterrent to information dissemination, the ACS Books and Journals Division requires authors to transfer their copyright to ACS, except in those cases where a work is in the public domain because authors of a paper are employees of the U.S. Government and have prepared a paper as part of their official duties.

The rights we return to authors, employers, and the U.S. Government appear on the ACS copyright transfer form which is printed every year in the first issue of each of our research journals. We state directly on our form that copyright transfer

becomes effective if and when a work is accepted for publication by ACS. At the top of the ACS form is the statement, "This manuscript will be considered with the understanding you have submitted it on an exclusive basis". If we discover that another publisher is also reviewing a paper that was submitted to an ACS publication, all production on the paper is stopped. We then alert the author to the statement on the ACS form and ask that we be notified in writing of the author's intention as to where the paper is to be published. This is important because it is our policy not to publish any paper in our research journals that has been published elsewhere.

Section A of the ACS copyright form states that authors retain the right to revise, adapt, prepare derivative works, present orally, or distribute their work provided that all such use is for their personal, noncommercial benefit. Section B states that "in all instances where the work is prepared as a 'work made for hire', the employer . . . retains the right to revise, adapt, prepare derivative works, publish, reprint, reproduce, and distribute the work provided that all such use is for the promotion of its business enterprise and does not imply the endorsement of the American Chemical Society". Section E, which for some reason is the most overlooked section, provides that for "works prepared under U.S. Government contract, the American Chemical Society recognizes the Government's prior nonexclusive, royalty-free license to publish, translate, reproduce, use, or dispose of the published form of the work or allow others to do so for U.S. Government purposes". For those authors who receive ACS copyright

†Presented (in part) before the Divisions of Chemical Education and Chemical Information, Symposium on "The Copyright Law", 182nd National Meeting of the American Chemical Society, New York, NY, Aug 27, 1981.

forms from either the editors' offices or the ACS office, there is an attachment at the bottom of the form entitled, "Dear Author". This section describes what is and what is not acceptable as far as signing our form. The most important general rules for signing the ACS copyright form are as follows:

> Substitute forms or changes to the ACS form are not acceptable.
>
> Any addition or changes made to the form will delay the processing of a paper for publication.
>
> Only one section of the copyright form should be signed.
>
> If one or more authors are *not* U.S. Government employees, the top section of the copyright form should be signed by a non-U.S. Government author.
>
> An original signature must be on the form; photocopied signatures are not acceptable.

These provisions are required so that we can efficiently handle the more than 10 000 copyright forms we receive each year. Most of our editorial assistants, who initially receive and process the copyright forms for our 21 primary publications, are not located at ACS headquarters; they are located throughout the United States. Their primary concern is editing and processing papers for publication. Although our editorial assistants know that we require copyright transfers from authors, they are not familiar with copyright to the extent that they would know what phrases would be acceptable to the Society. Therefore, it is efficient and effective for us to tell them that we only accept the ACS form signed as is, without changes. If an editorial office receives an unacceptable form, they are instructed to either ask the author to submit another ACS copyright form or request that I obtain a correct form from the author. Production on a paper may continue; however, if a paper is ready for publication and we do not have a correctly signed form, the paper will be delayed until an acceptable form is received. Of course, there are exceptions. Sometimes an unacceptable form slips through and a paper is still published. However, even after publication, a thorough check is made of all copyright forms and authors are asked to submit correctly signed forms when necessary.

The American Chemical Society feels that copyright transfer is intrinsic to disseminating scientific information through books, journals, magazines, reprints, photocopies, and other means. We feel that our owning copyright is a service to requestors of information, for they can easily locate us to obtain necessary reprint permission. Also, you can be assured that we handle permission requests within a reasonable amount of time. This is a timesaver for requestors; just imagine if you had to obtain reprint permission from an author who is the copyright owner of a work and who prepared it while attending an academic institution; since that time the individual copyright owner has had several employment positions in various organizations throughout the country. How many telephone calls or letters would it take to locate an individual to obtain copyright permission? The American Chemical Society as well as other organizations who require copyright transfer from their authors take responsibility to respond to permission requests, for they are mostly reliable organizations which can be quickly and easily located.

We feel that quick turnaround time for granting permissions is important. I do not know what the turnaround time is in other permission offices, but we strive to respond to permission requests within 3 working days of receipt for figures and graphs and within 1 week for full articles. Of course, there are exceptions: if someone's request is received by special delivery or by telex, we will respond in the same manner, within reason. If requestors wish to have verbal permission, they may have it as long as their written request is received by us. We then follow up the verbal permission with written permission, usually within 1 week. This is a precaution so that our material is not misused by individuals who say that they received verbal permission when in fact they did not.

Granting reprint requests is not a small operation for the ACS Books and Journals Division. We handle an average of 20 permission requests for full articles per week; this does not include granting the 200 or so requests for permission to reuse excerpts, tables, graphs, and other illustrations, which is done on a routine basis by rubber stamping a requestor's letter with "permission granted" and the required ACS credit line.

As I mentioned previously, the ACS copyright form specifies rights that are granted to authors, employers, and the U.S. Government. This is only a skeleton guideline for us to use in handling requests for reprint permission. Such requests which are received at ACS are handled in accordance with an 11-page set of working guidelines which was prepared in 1980, 2 years after the Copyright Law went into effect. The guidelines for the reproduction and use of ACS copyrighted material include various types of requests and how to handle them. Of course, with the advancement of technology, new and different types of requests continually arise. Therefore, we made our working guidelines general enough to cover such requests.

We believe that the ACS permissions policy is lenient relative to that of some commercial publishers. Requests to reprint or republish specific tables, figures, and illustrations are usually granted without a royalty charge and without our requesting that the author's permission also be obtained. In the 2 years that I have been with ACS, there has only been one time that a royalty fee was levied for permission to reprint figures and tables. In this case, the illustrations comprised more than one-half the entire article; a token royalty fee was charged, and we required that the requestor also obtain the author's permission.[1]

With regard to obtaining reprint permissions in general, the address to which you should send a written request will usually be printed in the front of a publication; look for a section entitled "permissions" or "copyright". On the inside front cover or within the first few pages of most ACS journals, we direct requestors to write to the Copyright Administrator at the ACS Washington address. As a general rule, if you are unable to locate this type of information, direct your request to the publisher and mark it to the attention of the Copyright or Permissions Office. This will expedite your request which might otherwise sit in a mailroom for a day or two until someone reads your letter and determines where to forward your request. I also suggest that you do not send your permission requests to the editor or author of a work unless this is requested by the copyright owner.

Requests for reprint permission should include complete bibliographic information including the title of the publication, year, volume number, issue number, inclusive page numbers of the article if you are copying a full article, authors' names, and the exact information you wish to see, for example, Figures 3, 4, and 8, Table 7, etc. Also, please specify how you intend to use the requested material, for example, to modify a figure, to publish the material in a book, to present the material in a talk which will be published in a proceedings book to be circulated to 500 attendees free of charge, to include it in a specified journal, and so forth. If the material you wish to reuse is cited as a second or third source, I suggest you carefully check to make sure than the information you request is complete and accurate. Also, ensure that you forward your request for reprint permission to the copyright owner. Keep in mind that the more information you provide, the quicker we can handle your request.

I do not know whether I speak for other societies or publishers, but it would make our job easier if your requests for various figures and tables from several ACS publications were listed on one page.

Besides handling reprint permission requests and making sure that the ACS copyright transfer form is signed correctly, I also draft copyright licensing agreements for final approval by our general counsel. I also serve as a copyright information specialist to those people who call or write to me to find out what rights they have or permissions they need.

A good source of information is the U.S. Copyright Office. Circular R1 (Copyright Basics) is a succinct primer for copyright. Other U.S. Copyright Office circulars which I believe are valuable, quick-reference sources of information, are Circulars R2 (Publications of the Copyright Office), R21 (Reproduction of Copyrighted Works by Educators and Librarians), and R22 (How to Investigate the Copyright Status of a Work).[2] Please note that these and other publications of the U.S. Copyright Office are available free of charge. If you have any questions about copyright registration, or if you are not sure about copyright in general, you may call the U.S. Copyright Office public information office from 8:30 a.m. to 5:00 p.m. at (202) 287-8700. Their public information specialists are quite helpful; however, note that U.S. Copyright Office personnel may only state facts and inform you what the copyright law says; they will not offer any interpretation of the law nor will they express any opinion as to the legal significance or effect of any facts that they may provide.

For questions about copyright in general, call or write to the U.S. Copyright Office or contact your organization's reprint permissions person or general counsel or the publisher to whom you submitted your work for consideration of publication. If you have any copyright questions concerning a paper that you submitted to, or material that you wish to use from, an ACS publication, do not hesitate to call us. Keep in mind that if you are not sure whether or not you need to obtain reprint permission, it is a good idea to ask the copyright owner. It is also a good idea to know the basics of the U.S. Copyright Law, for ignorance of the law is no excuse for innocent infringement.

REFERENCES AND NOTES

(1) Friedman, B. A. "Copyright Permissions", presented at the CESSE Meeting, Boston, MA, July 16, 1981.
(2) U.S. Copyright Office Circulars, Copyright Office, Library of Congress, Washington, DC.

9: OWNERSHIP OF COPYRIGHT

Patricia H. Penick

Manager, Publication Administrative Services
The Institute of Electrical and Electronics Engineers, Inc.

This paper was delivered on September 17, 1981 at the 1981 IEEE Professional Communications Society Conference. It was part of a session entitled Self-Protection in which the other speakers were patent attorneys.

ABSTRACT: Papers published in technical journals are most useful when their copyrights are owned by the journal publisher. Under the new Copyright Law, copyrights must be transferred to the publisher in order for the publisher to fulfill its traditional role of protecting copyright on its own behalf and on behalf of its authors and their employers. By holding copyright to all copyrightable material it publishes, the publisher can ensure consistent reprint and republication policies, can enable legitimate copying which the new law would otherwise prohibit and can collect and set copying fees when appropriate.

Copyright law is not the same as patent law. Copyright doesn't protect inventions; it doesn't protect titles or symbols. Those are the province respectively of patent law and trademark law. Furthermore, copyright can't protect facts or ideas, although it does protect the author's particular expression of them. What copyright law does do, in the words of the statute is to protect ". . . original works of authorship fixed in any tangible medium of expression, now known or later developed, from which they can be perceived, reproduced, or otherwise communicated, either directly or with the aid of a machine or device."

You'll be relieved to know that that will be my only quotation from the law! I'm not an attorney. I'm a member of the IEEE Headquarters Publishing Services staff and, as such, am responsible for, among other things, the administration of copyrights and permissions for IEEE. All of my comments, therefore, will be in the context of copyright as it relates to IEEE's publishing program. As many of you realize, IEEE is not only the world's largest professional society with an international membership of over 200,000 engineers and scientists, IEEE is also a major publisher. In its journals and conference records alone, IEEE publishes over 15,000 papers annually. This output represents about 15% of the world's literature in electrical and electronics engineering.

Once upon a time, holding copyright to this vast amount of material was relatively easy. Under the old law, copyright arose when a paper appeared in a journal which was itself copyrighted. It has always been an unquestioned tradition that a professional society had the right to hold copyright to all original, non-Government material submitted to it and, indeed, authors submitted their material for publication with this clear understanding.

By holding copyright to what is known legally as the "work as a whole," IEEE and its predecessor societies automatically held copyright not only to each of its publications but also to the individual papers in those publications. Holding all copyrights made it possible for IEEE, in turn, to be the central point for handling requests for reprint and republication permission and to see that permissions policies were handled consistently and fairly.

All that changed radically with the new copyright law which went into effect in January, 1978. For a publisher like IEEE, two elements of the new law were of particular importance. First, the new law says that copyright arises at the moment a work is in tangible form. Second, the law now specifically prohibits systematic copying. The importance of each, how they are linked, and what IEEE does to cope with both will, I hope, be clear in what follows.

It comes as a surprise to most people -- although perhaps not to people attending an IEEE Professional Communication Society meeting! -- that now copyright may exist from the moment of creation. For instance, when you jot down, say, a poem on the back of your cocktail napkin, you immediately own copyright to that poem without doing another thing. If, instead of a poem, you write a technical paper as an employee of a company, that paper is legally considered a "work made for hire" and it is normally the company, not you, which immediately holds the copyright regardless of whether or not the work is ever published. If you do submit the poem or the paper to a publisher, the copyright still resides with the copyright owner until or unless the copyright - or more precisely - the copyrights are transferred.

Unlike the situation under the old law, copyright is now divisible. When you deal with a publisher for your poem, for instance, you may want to transfer only publication rights and reserve performing rights, the right to translate the poem into Serbo-Croatian and other important subsidiary rights. When it comes to publishing your technical paper, it might occur to you -- or more likely to your company's patent attorney -- that the thing to do is to give the publisher permission to publish, but to re-

tain all the copyrights for the company. After all, your paper on fast Fourier transforms might be a real box office hit as a movie! In the real world of technical publishing, though, having copyrights scattered to the four winds is usually viewed as conterproductive. Worse, it makes handling reprint and republication requests a hopeless administrative quagmire.

Can you imagine what handling thousands of permissions requests would be like if the publisher had to check first to see who owned what rights? Even with the microcomputer my department expects to have soon, the two people handling copyrights and permissions would certainly have to be cloned and we'd probably need an in-house attorney. Many commercial publishers do, in fact, have large staffs doing nothing but handling permissions and subsidiary rights. However, IEEE and most other not-for-profit and non-profit professional societies do not operate this way. They not only don't, they can't. They are publishers to be sure, but they are first of all membership societies and have, as a major responsibility, the task of serving the information needs of their members and the greater scientific and engineering community. Unlike the poets on one hand and the rather different community of poetry readers on the other, those who use IEEE material and those who create it are from the same, or at least a largely overlapping, community. Therefore, in order to serve the needs of the information users and to protect its own and its authors' rights -- and, of course, to cut down on the quagmire effect -- IEEE, like most major professional societies, needs to hold all copyrights. We therefore require copyright transfer as a condition of publication.

The importance of copyright and who owns it can best been seen when you think of yourself as one of those information users. Suppose, for the moment, that you are no longer relaxing in the cocktail lounge (where you do your poetry writing); you're now back at the office and about to launch into a major project involving gromet technology - an obscure field you know little about. You rootle around in whatever indexes you have handy hoping to find a few gromet references, you check the company library and, if you're fortunate enough to have a good librarian, you throw yourself on his or her mercy. Finally, you realize, or your librarian suggests, that what you need is the help of a sophisticated search system like Lockheed's DIALOG. (If you don't have easy access to a DIALOG system, the Engineering Societies Library in New York has one.) You eventually come up with a bibliography far more extensive than you were prepared for and you realize that it will be important for you to read the full texts of at least a dozen papers. The DIALOG system includes a document delivery service, but, since the copyright law prohibits systematic copying and, since everyone agrees that the copying resulting from a search system is indeed systematic, the system may only be able to point you in the right direction, rather than efficiently providing the copies you need. What makes the difference is who has the copyright and whether the owner of copyright has made provisions to permit this kind of copying.

Before I explain how publishers like IEEE permit rather than prohibit certain kinds of copying, a word or two on copying in general might be in order. First of all, copying is a fact of life and one publishers ignore at their peril. On one hand, it is now technically possible for a publisher - or anyone else for that matter - to prepare just one copy of something, perhaps in machine readable form, and have that same material disseminated all over the world. In the information community, by the way, many see this process as someday replacing traditional hard-copy publishing. Some publishers claim to recognize a direct link between declining subscriptions and known or suspected copying of their publications.

IEEE doesn't make such a claim because subscriptions haven't gone down and we have no way of knowing whether there would be more subscriptions if all copying magically came to a halt. On the other hand and aside from any real or imagined peril, it is clear that the need for information is legitimate, and that thwarting that need by totally prohibiting copying not only won't work, it simply promotes defiance of the law.

At the time the new copyright law was framed, it was recognized that publishers and users of published material, especially in the science and engineering fields, would need to work out some legally acceptable mechanism for handling the copying problem. The result was the formation of a non-profit organization called the Copyright Clearance Center. This organization does not provide actual copies of anything and it does not grant permissions on behalf of publishers. The way it works is that users of copyrighted material and publishers may join simply by agreeing to certain guidelines. The publishers use a special numerical code at the bottom of the first page of each paper and include in it the copying fee they have established. IEEE has a modest copying fee of $0.75 per copy and announces in a masthead statement in each of its publications that it participates in the CCC. Users belonging to CCC are then free to do whatever amount of systematic copying they wish by paying the publisher's fee (identified by code number) via the CCC. The CCC then distributes the money back to the publisher (after deducting 25¢ per item). In IEEE's case, money that comes in from the CCC is disbursed back to the Society sponsoring the copied material (after deducting a 25% administrative charge which reimburses my department). In spite of the fact that the CCC is still having growing pains, that the number of users in the system is still skimpy and that all publishers in the system are still relinquishing a percentage of their copying income to help support CCC, nonetheless, IEEE received over $6000 in copying fees for 1980. Our Computer Society alone got $1800 of that money - money which would not have been collected any other way.

Not only is it important for U.S. publishers and copiers to have a system like CCC, it permits a collection point for copying fees which other countries now want to give U.S. publishers. The CCC is presently working out arrangements with at least two countries which have collected money for U.S. copyrighted material. You might also be interested in knowing that the British Library Lending Division is in the throes of considering (in conjunction with Elsevier Science Publishers, Pergamon and Springer-Verlag) a massive document delivery service covering the world's scientific literature. Fees will be paid back to copyright owners, although not necessarily via CCC.

The point here isn't to overwhelm with detail, but simply to emphasize that the information business is big business and growing as fast as a kudzu vine. It can only work, however, if a publisher participates in the system and the publisher can only participate by being owner of the necessary copyrights.

Thanks to my boss, Woody Gannett, who is Staff Director of Publishing Services and who, himself, is one of the big honchos in the information handling field, IEEE was well prepared when the new copyright law came into effect. On the recommendation of our Publications Board, our Executive Committee and Board of Directors blessed as policy the requirement that IEEE obtain individual copyright transfers as a condition of publication for all original, non-Government papers. With that as a basis, we were then able to establish administrative procedures to make the policy work.

We sent out mailings to our volunteer Editors and publication committee people and we rewrote guidelines. We joined the Copyright Clearance Center and registered all of our publications with them -- and keep registering as new ones spring up and old ones change their names. We obtained International Standard Serial Numbers (ISSNs) for each of our publications in order to set up individual CCC paper codes for each using the ISSNs. We explained what was going on to our printers and compositors and, for the same reason, held meetings within our Publishing Services staff and with key people in other departments. We explained to our 1,400 library subscribers that we had joined the CCC and that this would permit them to do legal systematic copying for a reasonable fee. My former Administrative Assistant was promoted to become Administrator of Copyrights and Permissions and she now has an Administrative Assistant of her own. And, as I mentioned, we will soon have a microcomputer to help tidy up the incredible amount of complexity spawned by our new procedures. We're still copyrighting each issue as a "work as a whole" in addition to obtaining individual copyrights from each author. And, this, of course describes only a fraction of the effort.

IEEE is not only huge, it has an extremely complex structure -- something like a millipede crossed with a giant squid! What was and is hard is getting the word passed along to the hundreds of hard-working IEEE volunteers who suddenly have dumped on them primary responsibility for obtaining and pursuing individual copyright documents for each paper in the publications they handle. Guidelines help, but an ongoing teaching and explaining job will probably always be essential. Many of you, I'm sure know IEEE's past General Manager Dr. Richard Emberson and may remember his classic description of dealing with the ever-changing cast of Society volunteers. He said talking to them was like trying to give a speech to a parade!

A key feature of our new system was, of course, the document by which copyrights may be transferred to IEEE. We spent a good deal of time and energy designing one. What we came up with was a two-part document which can serve either as a transfer form or as certification that a paper is wholly written by employees of the U.S. Government and therefore not subject to U.S. copyright protection. In the transfer portion, we took great pains to return to our authors and their employers the rights we had become convinced they needed as much as we needed to hold copyright. Mainly in response to feedback from company patent attorneys, our form clearly states that we recognize that all proprietary rights, such as patent rights are retained. Our form also tries to make clear the important difference between work which is wholly the work of the U.S. Government, that is, performed by an employee of the Government as a part of his official duties and work which is simply done under U.S. Government contract or grant. The former isn't subject to U.S. copyright protection; the latter most assuredly is. We do, however, recognize all the retained rights required under the terms of such contracts or grants. Although our copyright form has been the subject of praise and commendation (I have fan mail to prove it!) even by Government attorneys, a few points can be made clearer still and we plan, in the next few months, to issue a slightly revised version.

Our major effort was and is the matter of getting the forms signed. Our authors usually were willing; the attorneys - usually patent attorneys - at their companies often were not. Nothing had prepared us for the exhaustive and exhausting dialogue needed to persuade these attorneys - folks we'd literally never heard from before - that we weren't trying to steal something from them. We pointed out that, under the old law, we had responsibly held copyright on their behalf as well as our own for close to one hundred years. When they insisted that they now wanted to retain the copyright which the new law gave them we firmly said no and pointed out that our transfer form explicitly returned rights to them which before would have required formal permission. When they agreed to transfer copyright, but only on their own forms and stating their own terms, we again said no and explained that we were a a business operation, too, and that it would be irresponsible for a professional society to spend the time and money required to assure that 15,000 or so different company forms gave us the rights we needed both to publish and grant permissions. Our best argument went like this: Under your company's other hat -- as a user of information -- you should be glad that a publisher behaves in a responsible fashion, holds all copyrights so that permissions can be centralized and, by virtue of holding copyright, is able to participate in the CCC and thereby provides a legal way for your company to do the copying you may need to do! Needless to say, these attorneys were as astonished by our ferocity as we were offended by their arrogance.

I'm happy to say we have prevailed. For the major companies we deal with, virtually all riots have been quelled and mutual respect, cooperation and even friendship have replaced the former barbs and bristles.

Although the title of this Session is "Self-Protection," I hope the above is a convincing arguement that the best protection for technical information is the kind that provides not only protection for individuals and their employers, but also assures appropriate access to others. IEEE insists on holding copyright in order to do both.

10: ELECTRONIC MEDIA AND COPYRIGHTS: NO MAJOR PROBLEMS FORESEEN

As more and more magazine publishing companies become involved in the new electronic media, publishers are finding that copyright implications are one of the many areas in which complications may arise.

Although most publishing companies involved in these rapidly growing new media have made provisions for, and say they do not expect any major problems in, handling copyright agreements, some publishers are now finding that their copyright agreements are inadequate.

"Copyright matters are certainly an issue to be dealt with, but I don't think the issues will be any different from those that exist already in traditional publishing," says Kurt Steele, associate general counsel for McGraw-Hill, Inc. "That is, I don't think copyrights will pose much of a practical problem for publishers, as long as they honestly ask for those rights they believe they need, and compensate the author or photographer fairly for those rights."

"As far as copyright goes, we basically do not anticipate a problem in relation to the new electronic media, because the fact that they are new media does not change the presumption of ownership of the copyright on the part of the author under the Copyright Revision Act of 1976," agrees free-lance writer Norman Schreiber, who is current chairman of the electronic media committee of the American Society of Journalists and Authors (ASJA) and the former chairman of ASJA's copyrights committee.

"At this point, every good, professional writer is very aware of the fact that copyright matters are negotiable, give-and-take situations," he adds. "There will be instances in which a writer will want to sell rights beyond first North American publication rights to a company interested in republishing an article through a database service, or through cable television, or whatever. But we're talking about selling—there is no instance in which a writer should give such secondary rights away."

Phil Leonian, chairman of the copyright committee of the American Society of Magazine Photographers (ASMP), expresses similar feelings on the subject.

"The standard agreement between photographers and magazines is that the magazine is sold the first-time publication rights. This is because publishers want, in general, to pay the least possible amount of money for copyrights, and do not want to have to pay for additional, secondary rights," Leonian says. "So people in the magazine publishing industry are very used to—and comfortable with—renegotiating with photographers when they want to obtain secondary rights for use of photographs in a book or in other traditional print media. I see no reason why the same won't happen in electronic media negotiations."

Some publishing companies, however, have already experienced problems with copyrights in regard to the new electronic media, according to publishing attorney Faustin Jehle.

"Some publishers—even old-line publishers—are being tripped up on this," Jehle says. "They're discovering now that they don't have the necessary rights on some material they have that could be used for the new electronic media. So now they have to go back to the author and try to get those rights, which is not only a hassle, but is likely to cost them more than they would have paid had they obtained those rights in the first place."

Jehle says he advises his clients to obtain, whenever possible, all rights to an article through a proprietorship of a work-for-hire agreement. Such an agreement must be made before an article is written, because once it is on paper, all rights to the article are immediately vested in the author, he explains.

"If you haven't secured such an agreement before an article is written, you must then go back and try to get the author to assign to you, on paper, all rights. If you don't get all the rights, you are limited to use of the article in only those media to which you have secured rights, and you may not be able to foresee some uses that may crop up in the future."

Several magazine publishing companies contacted by FOLIO report that they have made it a practice to secure all rights, and are therefore covered in using editorial material in their electronic ventures.

"We are one of those maverick publishing companies who insist on getting a proprietorship of a work-for-hire in all cases," says Neil Kuehnl, editor in chief of the Meredith Corporation's magazines. "So we anticipate no problems in the future. We've always done this, but since the new copyright act, some writers and photographers have taken more militant stands on these matters. Some of them just won't work for us. But that's the way it is."

"Call it foresight or just luck, but we began securing all rights, whenever possible, about eight years ago," says Arthur Hettich, editor of Family Circle Inc. publications. "Not on items that we knew would become dated, but on the things we knew were nuggets that would last, such as beauty tips and decorating ideas. On those articles for which we do not have all rights, nothing is different in dealing in electronic publishing than if we wanted to reprint the article in a cookbook. We simply go back to the author and negotiate. We have always been willing to pay more money for additional rights beyond first publication rights."

Hubert Luckett, editorial director of Times Mirror publications, reports that Times Mirror found that trying to secure all rights through work-for-hire alienated too many writers.

"We experimented with that for a few months after the new copyright law went into effect, but found it just wasn't worth it," he says. "We then went to a standard agreement in which we have the first North American serial rights and rights beyond that without having to pay additional compensation—but the author has non-exclusive rights, with the exception of the first serial rights, to sell his article anywhere he wants."

"Very early on, we started to secure broader rights up front," says Steele of McGraw-Hill. In addition to obtaining all rights through a work-for-hire agreement or through an author's agreement to assign over all rights after a work is written, Steele notes, publishers have the option of using a "grocery list" approach.

"There are many instances in which a publisher can and should enumerate only a few rights that he needs and negotiate fair payment for each one with the writer," Steele says. "Every case is different, depending on the publisher's needs. If he thinks he will need only a small set of specific rights, it's probably easier and cheaper to wait until he needs those rights and go back and negotiate with the writer."

Steele and most others interviewed acknowledged that, although no insurmountable copyright problems are likely in regard to new electronic media, negotiations are likely to be a cumbersome and extensive process in some instances—for example, if authors of articles in back issues must be contacted because a magazine wants to input articles for which it does not have the rights into a database.

It is also difficult to negotiate now about an article whose value in the future for the new media is uncertain, they note.

"It is a guessing game, to some extent," says Steele. "If you should decide to get only the first serial rights—and you guess wrong—you may be out of luck."

11: COPYRIGHT INFRINGEMENT

Stephen H. Gross

Partner
Krause, Hirsch & Gross

In the field of copyright infringement, early communication with counsel can usually avert or minimize troublesome situations. Let's examine a hypothetical situation to see what steps can be taken when a publisher is faced with a copyright lawsuit.

Assume that a magazine commissions a free-lance writer to prepare a nonfiction article on the survival rate of koala bears in U.S. zoos. The publisher, being prudent, obtains a written warranty from the writer that all of the material in the article to be submitted will be both wholly original and prepared solely and exclusively by the writer.

Three months after the article is published, a letter arrives from a prominent Australian law firm, informing the publisher that three entire paragraphs of the 15-page article constitute a direct, verbatim quote from its client's previously published treatise, *Koalas Around The World*, and that he should consider himself placed on notice that pleadings for a million dollar lawsuit are being prepared by the Australian firm.

The publisher, although duly impressed by the number of zeroes in the threatened litigation, decides that the lawyer's action is merely a bluff, a thinly-veiled threat to extract money from your magazine. He therefore deposits the letter in his crank correspondence file and forgets it. When a follow-up certified letter from a local lawyer arrives shortly thereafter, advising that he has been retained by the Australian author for the purpose of instituting suit against his magazine for copyright infringement, he hurriedly forwards both letters to his own attorney.

Immediate action possible

Assuming that the free-lancer did, in fact, "borrow" three paragraphs from the Australian author, there are a number of things the publisher's lawyer could have done as soon as the first letter arrived.

A. *Fair Use*—If the American publisher's magazine were read primarily by scholars of zoology, curators of zoos, or other individuals engaged principally in educational endeavors, then the publisher's attorney might have suggested that the magazine may have a valid legal defense to an infringement suit. If the Australian work itself ran to many hundreds of pages, and if only three paragraphs of that work were copied in a 10-page article, so insubstantial a portion may support a "fair use" defense to the infringement suit, particularly if it can be demonstrated that publication of the article in the U.S. will have minimal impact on the future sales of the original Australian work.

Despite the availability of this "fair use" defense to a lawsuit, however, early consultation with the attorney might have made the following alternatives more viable.

B. *Apology*—Frequently an author whose work has been infringed has actually suffered a greater wound to his ego than to his pocketbook. In such a situation, a personal letter from the publisher or the editor expressing amazement and surprise that such a terrible thing as the unauthorized borrowing could have occurred may sufficiently assuage the infringed author's feelings and induce him to drop the lawsuit.

Since it is rare that an editor will

have knowingly consented to the infringement of a third party's copyright, a sincere apology frequently has the desired result of terminating further threat of litigation. The publisher should have his attorney review the letter of apology to make certain there is no language in the letter which might imply either that the magazine was terribly negligent or that the magazine acquiesced in the unauthorized copying.

C. *Attribution*—If a letter of apology alone does not suffice, the publisher may offer to include a printed statement in the next available issue of the magazine, attributing the proper source of the infringing material to the aggrieved author. In this situation, the editor should prepare the note of attribution, specifying the original author's name, the title and publisher of the first work, and a reference to the material copied.

The publisher should also get the infringed author's written consent to the publication's printing a proper attribution of source in the forthcoming issue. This consent must be obtained prior to publication since the infringed author may take exception to the size of the type, the location in the issue, or the absence of an appropriately abject note of contrition.

To further forestall litigation, the publisher's attorney should prepare a letter of settlement to be signed by the infringed author. Such a letter will constitute a full release of all future claims and demands against the magazine, subject to the magazine's printing the attribution.

D. *Payment*—If both the offer of an apology and the publication of a proper attribution fail to deter the threatened lawsuit, the publisher may still resort to payment to the original author. Unfortunately, since our hypothetical situation involved letters from an Australian lawyer and a local lawyer, the sum which might have been accepted initially may now have been increased by virtue of legal fees.

In this case, the publisher should offer a flat sum to the author, based perhaps on a percentage that the infringing material bears to the maga-

zine article as a whole. Any payment which is contingent upon the number of copies of the issue sold or distributed brings with it all the problems of verification. No publisher wants to be bothered with the original author's auditor scrutinizing single-copy sales and active subscription files to ascertain that the payment was correct.

Watch for multiple claimants

A true story about a publisher forced to pay off an author whose work had been infringed involves a magazine in the sports field. After paying a fairly substantial sum to a professional athlete who claimed his published biography had been copied without permission, the publisher filed the general release with the cancelled check. A number of months later, he was quite surprised when he received a claim from the author of the biography, informing him that the copyrighted material was his, not the athlete's, and that as author, he insisted upon compensation for the unauthorized use of his literary creation. A second payment was made, but not before the publisher's attorney had verified that the supply of possible claimants with a legal right to payment had been exhausted.

A publisher forced to make payment to an author whose copyrighted work is infringed may have insurance to cover such a contingency. Since this is typically not the case, a publisher should be sure his attorney prepares adequate contracts for acquiring publishing rights. A free-lancer should not only represent to the magazine that the entire contents of his contributed article are original, he should also indemnify the magazine if that representation (or any other) proves to be false.

If such a contract is properly drawn, it will indemnify the magazine against claims, not merely judgments requiring the payment of damages. A publisher, then, can sue a free-lancer for breach of the warranty of originality.

There is, of course, a world of difference between being able to sue and being able to collect. However, the publisher should certainly have the opportunity to obtain reimbursement from the free-lancer for sums the magazine was forced to pay to the original author, as well as legal fees incurred.

A concluding word of caution: Once you, as publisher, have had to dispose of a claim made by an infringed author, make certain that all editors and those charged with acquiring articles are apprised of the name of the individual from whom you purchased the infringing article. Perhaps of equal importance, do not sell reprints or otherwise license rights in that article unless the material borrowed from the original author is fully deleted.

Stephen H. Gross is an attorney specializing in publishing law. A partner in the New York law firm of Krause, Hirsch & Gross, he has represented publishers of more than 200 magazines in the past 15 years. He is also the author of Single Copy (Newsstand) Distribution Agreements.

12: QUESTIONS AND ANSWERS ABOUT THE PERFORMANCE OF MUSIC UNDER THE NEW COPYRIGHT LAW

Jack C. Goldstein

INTRODUCTION

After more than twenty years of study, public hearings, and debate,[1] a new federal copyright law was enacted in 1976[2] and became effective on January 1, 1978.[3] The 1976 Act was the first general revision of the United States copyright law since the Copyright Act of 1909.[4] Long before it was superseded, the 1909 Act had become outmoded as a result of numerous technological advances which had had a profound impact upon various classes of copyrighted works, including musical compositions.

Many developments and refinements—such as those in the recording, jukebox, radio, and television industries—had spawned vast new enterprises which not only thrived on the use of copyrighted music but also shifted the songwriter's economic interests. **Even before 1976, royalties based upon the public performance of music had become the major source of income for the songwriter;**[5] royalties on recordings had remained limited because of statutory compulsory licensing at 2 cents per recording;[6] and royalties on the sale of sheet music had dwindled with the decline of the sheet music industry.[7]

The nondramatic performing rights in essentially all copyrighted music have been in the past, and are today, licensed in the United States through three organizations, each of which offers a different collection of music. The oldest of these licensing organizations, the American Society of Composers, Authors & Publishers, known by the acronym "ASCAP," was formed in 1914. Broadcast Music, Inc., known by its initials, "BMI," was not formed until 1939-40 but is today the largest of the three licensing organizations, at least insofar as the popularity of its repertoire is concerned. BMI and ASCAP are nonprofit organizations in that all of the license fees which they receive, less operating expenses and reserve,

are distributed to affiliated songwriters and music publishers. The third organization, SESAC, Inc., formerly the Society of European Stage Authors & Composers, licenses a smaller, more specialized collection of music compared with the collections licensed by either BMI or ASCAP. The copyright statute expressly recognizes ASCAP, BMI, and SESAC as organizations which license the nondramatic public performance of musical works.[8]

Since BMI's and ASCAP's vast repertoires include **inter alia** around 65% and 35%, respectively, of the top 100 songs in recent years according to the musical trade publications such as **Billboard**, most establishments must be licensed by both BMI and ASCAP to avoid wholesale copyright infringement. BMI and ASCAP grant nondiscriminatory licenses at modest fees which depend on such things as the licensee's annual entertainment costs, the room capacity, the number of days (or nights) per week that the establishment is open, and whether there is a cover charge. The typical BMI or ASCAP license provides that, upon the payment of an annual fee, the licensee is given permission to make an unlimited number of nondramatic performances of all of the licensing organization's music, without the licensee's having to keep any records as to the actual music used. Thus, BMI and ASCAP serve as conduits between the masses of songwriters and music users for the exchange of performing rights and license fees. The licensing organizations are clearinghouses which make it feasible not only for the typical music user to obtain permission to perform all of the copyrighted music he or she actually uses but also for the typical songwriter to deal with the multitude of places where his or her music is being used.

If a music user refuses to take a license from either BMI or ASCAP, the music user will be "logged," or monitored, to garner reliable, accessible,

and admissible evidence that infringing performances are occurring. An infringing music user may be sued in federal court[9] and subjected to substantial liability in the form of statutory damages,[10] which may be far greater than the license fees would have been.[11] BMI's and ASCAP's vigorous copyright policing and enforcement procedures provide an additional, compelling incentive for music users to become licensed instead of permitting unlicensed, infringing performances to continue.

It is by this system that the typical songwriter makes the major portion of his or her living from performance royalties—and has done so for many years. Cognizant of this practice, Congress passed the 1976 Act, which expanded the copyright owner's public performance right with respect to copyrighted music in the following three ways:

(1) by expressly defining "perform" and "perform publicly" more broadly than those terms had previously been construed by the courts,[12]

(2) by eliminating the limitation that an infringing public performance must be "for profit,"[13] and

(3) by eliminating the so-called "jukebox exemption."[14]

In addition, the duration of copyright protection was enlarged from (a) a 28-year initial term plus a 28-year renewal term to (b) life of the author plus 50 years as a general rule.[15]

Particularly in view of the new copyright law, the following questions and answers may be helpful to music users and to attorneys who represent music users. In some instances, the questions and answers relate to unchanged aspects of the old copyright law of which such persons may not be fully aware.

IN WHAT KINDS OF PLACES DOES THE PERFORMANCE OF COPYRIGHTED MUSIC, WITHOUT THE COPYRIGHT OWNER'S PERMISSION, CONSTITUTE AN INFRINGEMENT?

Under the 1909 Act, the owner of the copyright in a musical composition was granted the **exclusive** right to perform the musical composition "publicly for profit."[16] In other words, under the old law, the public performance for profit of copyrighted music—if done without a license (that is, without the copyright owner's permission)—constituted an infringement. However, since the 1909 Act did not expressly define "for profit," the courts frequently had to construe that limitation in deciding what was, and what was not, a copyright infringement under the old law.

In 1917, two cases involving the unlicensed performance of copyrighted music were simultaneously decided in a single opinion by the Supreme Court.[17] Live musical performances in those cases took place in a restaurant and in a hotel dining room. The proprietors of the restaurant and hotel argued that the performances were not "for profit" because there had been no charge for admission to hear the music. The Supreme Court rejected that argument, noting that the music was part of a total price which the public paid through increased prices of the food, and that the proprietors' **purpose** in employing the music was profit.

Subsequent to the restaurant and hotel dining room cases, copyright infringement suits were successfully maintained on the basis of musical performances at theaters,[18] dance pavilions,[19] dance halls,[20] roller skating rinks,[21] night clubs,[22] cabarets,[23] and raceways.[24] Eventually, it became well established, even under the old law, that the unlicensed performance of copyrighted music at virtually any kind of place of business constituted an infringement.

Because Congress was aware that the line between commercial and nonprofit organizations was becoming increasingly difficult to draw and that many nonprofit organizations were being highly subsidized and were capable of paying royalties,[25] the 1976 Act eliminated the "for profit" limitation in favor of a limited list of exempt performances.[26] Thus, **under the new law, any public performance of copyrighted music, except one that has been either specifically exempted by the statute or licensed, constitutes an infringement;** and, as will be explained below, "public" really means "semipublic."

ARE "PRIVATE" CLUBS AND OTHER PLACES WHICH ARE NOT OPEN TO THE PUBLIC AT LARGE EXEMPT FROM THE COPYRIGHT LAW?

No, semipublic places are **not** exempt from the copyright law. To the contrary, the new law is perfectly clear that **performances at clubs, lodges, factories, summer camps, schools, and the like are clearly subject to copyright control.**

As previously mentioned, the 1909 Act granted the exclusive right to perform copyrighted music "publicly for profit."[27] Since the term "publicly," like "for profit," was not expressly defined in the 1909 Act, the courts also had to construe that term in the context of copyright infringement cases.

With respect to so-called "private" clubs, the courts uniformly held that musical performances in a club might be "public" performances **insofar as the federal copyright law was concerned** even though the club was considered "private" for other purposes, such as state liquor laws. Thus, even under the 1909 Act, "public" performances of copyrighted music were held to have occurred in so-called "private" clubs in Massachusetts,[28] Texas,[29] Minnesota,[30] and Oklahoma.[31]

A significantly broader scope of protection exists under the 1976 Act—which grants to the copyright owner the exclusive right to perform copyrighted music publicly[32]—because an express definition in the statute makes it clear that a performance is considered to be "public" for purposes of the copyright law if the performance occurs "at a place open to the public or **at any place where a substantial number of persons outside of a normal circle of a family and its social acquaintances is gathered.**"[33] Moreover, the relevant legislative history of the 1976 Act is expressed in both the Senate and House reports as follows: "One of the principal purposes of the definition was to make [it] clear that. . . performances in 'semipublic' places, such as clubs, lodges, factories, summer camps and schools, are 'public performances' subject to copyright control."[34] Thus, **the 1976 Act extends to musical performances at some places which may have been outside the 1909 Act.**[35]

(**Editor's Note:** We normally will not publish legal articles of the length of "Questions and Answers About the Performance of Music under the New Copyright Law" by Author Jack C. Goldstein. However, in view of the article's excellence and novelty, readers should find it most interesting. If a case of its nature comes into one's office, the article will provide a law review type of research and reference. Also, our Regular Feature contributor Robert Keegan is moving his office and was unable to furnish the copy of his "Advising Innovators" column for this issue.)

Mr. Goldstein is a member of the Arnold, White & Durkee law firm of Houston. He specializes in practice before the U.S. Patent and Trade Office. He is member: Advisory Board, **Patent, Trademark and Copyright** Journal; Board of Trustees, Copyright Society of the U.S.A.; American Patent Law Association; Houston Patent Law Association (President-Elect, 1978-); and various bar associations.)

CAN COPYRIGHTED MUSIC BE INFRINGED IF IT IS NOT PERFORMED LIVE? IF SO, WHAT MANNER OF PERFORMANCE WILL CONSTITUTE AN INFRINGEMENT?

The early cases **did** involve only live performances, but that was because recorded music was of such poor quality that it was not used commercially and because jukeboxes, radios, and televisions were not then in existence.

As various mechanical means for performing music came into widespread commercial use, copyright infringement suits were successfully maintained under the old law on the basis of unlicensed musical performances by means of player pianos,[36] phonographs,[37] master radio sets for receiving and retransmitting radio broadcasts through amplifiers and multiple loudspeakers,[38] music services provided over telephone wires,[39] and jukeboxes.[40]

The 1976 Act includes the following all-encompassing definition: "To 'perform' a work means to recite, render, play, dance, or act it, either directly or by means of any device or process. . ."[41] Thus, **the public performance of copyrighted music by virtually any means is subject to the new copyright law.**[42]

AREN'T JUKE BOXES EXEMPT FROM THE COPYRIGHT LAW?

No. Jukeboxes were never **wholly** exempt from the copyright law, even under the old law. In any event, the limited "jukebox exemption" of the 1909 Act was eliminated by the 1976 Act.

In 1909, there were no jukeboxes as we know them today. However, some penny arcades used to provide earphones through which patrons might, by inserting coins in slots, hear something that resembled music. Since that practice was more of a novelty than a viable commercial use of music, the copyright owners of the 1909 era were not concerned that the 1909 Act included a limited exemption for the rendition of music by means of "coin-operated machines."[43] It was not until later, when the jukebox became a significant factor in the music industry, that that provision became known as the "jukebox exemption" and became controversial. Even under the old law, the "jukebox exemption" was limited: it was inapplicable if the jukebox (1) was located in a place where an admission fee was charged[44] or (2) was wired to be activated without the use of a coin.[45]

Thus, the 1976 Copyright Act merely rectified a historical accident by eliminating the limited "jukebox exemption." For **most** circumstances, however, the new law provides for an inexpensive compulsory license which the jukebox operator may obtain through the Copyright Office.[46] Nevertheless, if one does not obtain either a compulsory license through the Copyright Office or licenses from the licensing organizations (or directly from copyright owners), the public performance of copyrighted music by means of a jukebox constitutes an infringement under the new law.[47]

Some jukebox performances must be licensed through the performing rights licensing organizations (or through the copyright owners) to avoid infringement. Under any one or more of the following circumstances, the statutory compulsory license for jukeboxes is of no avail:[48]

(1) the jukebox is not activated by the insertion of coins, currency, or other monetary units,

(2) a direct or indirect admission charge is made,

(3) a list of the music is not affixed to the jukebox or posted where the list can be readily examined by the public, or

(4) the patrons are not permitted to make the choices as to the music to be played.

In any event, **jukeboxes are no longer exempt from the copyright law; and a public performance of copyrighted music by means of a jukebox, if not licensed or exempted, constitutes an infringement.**

IF THE MUSICIANS ARE INDEPENDENT CONTRACTORS OVER WHOM THE PROPRIETOR HAS NO CONTROL, IS THE PROPRIETOR OF THE PLACE OF BUSINESS NEVERTHELESS LIABLE FOR THE MUSICIANS' PERFORMANCE OF COPYRIGHTED MUSIC?

Yes. The proprietor of a place of business must bear the legal responsibility for the unlicensed performance of copyrighted music by musicians hired by the proprietor, **even if the musicians are independent contractors over whom the proprietor has no control.**[49] The legislative history of the 1976 Act, as expressed in both the Senate and House reports, makes it clear that Congress intended that that rule be continued under the new copyright law:

> The committee has actively considered **and rejected** an amendment. . . intended to exempt the proprietors of an establishment, such as a ballroom or night club, from liability for copyright infringement committed by an independent contractor, such as an orchestra leader.[50] [Emphasis added.]

In addition, when the proprietor of an establishment rents the establishment with knowledge that music is to be played, the proprietor is liable for the unlicensed performance of copyrighted music by musicians **hired by the renter**—if the proprietor has a financial interest, direct or indirect, which is related to, or contingent upon, the event at which the music is played. In one recent case, a catering hall and night club proprietor had (1) rented its ballroom with knowledge that it was to be used for a dinner dance and show featuring music and (2) supplied the food and liquor which was served by the proprietor's employees.[51] Based upon those facts, the proprietor was held liable for copyright infringement arising from the unlicensed performance of copyrighted music by musicians hired by the renter. In another, older case, a corporation which had merely rented its premises for a **fixed** amount was held not liable for the unlicensed performance of copyrighted music by the renter's musician; however, the court indicated that the situation would have been quite different if the corporation had received or derived a profit from the performance.[52]

IF THE PROPRIETOR OF A PLACE OF BUSINESS INSTRUCTS THE MUSICIANS NOT TO PLAY CERTAIN MUSIC, IS THE PROPRIETOR LIABLE IF THE MUSICIANS NEVERTHELESS PLAY THE MUSIC?

Yes. The proprietor of a place of business may be held liable for copyright infringement even though the musicians performed the copyrighted music against the proprietor's orders.[53] In one old case, the proprietor of a night club in Louisiana had written contracts with orchestra leaders who had agreed, at the proprietor's request, not to play certain music.[54] Moreover, the proprietor had prominently posted notices stating that he objected to certain music being played. In another, more recent case, suit was brought against the proprietors of a South Carolina night club; similarly, the band had been instructed not to play certain music.[55] In both of those cases, the proprietors were held liable for copyright infringement when the musicians played the copyrighted songs against the proprietors' orders.

IF THE PROPRIETOR OF THE PLACE OF BUSINESS DOES NOT PAY THE MUSICIANS, BUT RATHER MERELY ALLOWS THE MUSICIANS TO COME IN, PLAY, AND COLLECT TIPS, IS THE PROPRIETOR NEVERTHELESS LIABLE?

Yes. Several cases have held the proprietor of a place of business liable for copyright infringement even though the proprietor did not pay the musicians, but merely allowed them to come in, play, and collect tips.[56]

In the first reported case (which later cases followed), the proprietor of a barbecue stand in Missouri was sued for infringement; and the proprietor's defense was that the musicians had not been employed or paid by the proprietor, although he **had** permitted the musicians to come to his place of business, furnished them with a place to play, and permitted them to collect tips from his customers.[57] The court rejected the defense, concluding (1) that the proprietor had allowed the musicians to play with the view that the performance would be of benefit to his business, (2) that the performance had been advantageous to the proprietor, and (3) that the proprietor had paid the musicians **indirectly** by furnishing them space in his place of business.

IF MUSICIANS PLAY FROM SHEET MUSIC ON WHICH A ROYALTY HAS BEEN PAID OR IF MUSIC IS PERFORMED BY MEANS OF A RECORDING ON WHICH A ROYALTY HAS BEEN PAID, DOESN'T SUCH A ROYALTY PAYMENT EXHAUST THE COPYRIGHT OWNER'S RIGHT?

No. As applied to musical composition copyrights, the law grants different kinds of protection in three separate and distinct areas, namely: (1) sheet music, (2) recordings, and (3) public performances. When one purchases sheet music or a recording, the purchaser certainly may use the sheet music or recording to render either a performance which is not public[58] or a public performance which is specifically exempted under the new law.[59] However, the portion of the very modest sheet music royalty or statutory recording royalty (i.e., now 2-3/4 cents per recording[60]) which may ultimately find its way from the purchaser to the songwriter does not entitle the purchaser to render an otherwise infringing public performance.[61]

WHAT SANCTIONS MAY BE IMPOSED AGAINST A COPYRIGHT INFRINGER?

A copyright infringer is subject to a civil action in federal court[62] for an injunction[63] and the copyright owner's actual damages,[64] the infringer's profits,[65] or statutory damages[66]—plus court costs[67] and attorney's fees.[68]

In copyright infringement cases involving the performance of music, the copyright owner will generally obtain a judgment for statutory damages, rather than actual damages or profits. Statutory damages ordinarily will not be less than $250 or more than $10,000[69] for **each** copyrighted song performed publicly without a license.[70] The 1976 Act doubled the maximum statutory damages from the $5,000 upper limit of the 1909 Act.[71]

Damages for copyright infringement are **not** measured by the modest amount which the infringer might have paid under a performing rights license.[72] A copyright infringement suit simply is not a suit for breach of a license agreement which the copyright infringer refused to accept when it was offered. If the license fees were the sole measure of damages for copyright infringement, there would be little or no financial incentive for any music user to take a license since it would not cost any more to infringe than to take a license.

In addition to civil liability for copyright infringement, the copyright law also includes the following **criminal** sanctions: "Any person who infringes a copyright willfully and for purposes of commercial advantage or private financial gain shall be fined not more than $10,000 or imprisoned for not more than one year, or both. . ."[73]

MAY AN INDIVIDUAL WHO CONTROLS THE AFFAIRS OF A CORPORATION BE HELD PERSONALLY LIABLE FOR COPYRIGHT INFRINGEMENTS OCCURRING AT A PLACE OF BUSINESS OWNED AND OPERATED BY THAT CORPORATION?

Yes, the individual may be held personally liable. There are many circumstances under which an individual will not be shielded from personal liability by the existence of a corporation which the individual controls, manages, and operates. For example, if an officer, di-

rector, or stockholder of a corporation participates in the actual infringement of a copyright, then that person is subject to liability along with the corporation.[74] Similarly, a corporate officer and principal stockholder, who is the dominant influence in and who determines the policy of the corporation, is equally liable with the corporation for its infringements.[75]

CONCLUSION

Our forefathers regarded the encouragement of the work of authors to be so important that the original Constitution specifically provided for copyrights.[76] Indeed, as stated by the Supreme Court:

The economic philosophy behind the [constitutional] clause empowering Congress to grant patents and copyrights is the conviction that encouragement of individual effort by personal gain is the best way to advance public welfare through the talents of authors and inventors. . . Sacrificial days devoted to such creative activities deserve rewards commensurate with the services rendered.[77]

The songwriter must eat, as well as make music. The copyright system is the legal mechanism which enables the songwriter to make a living out of his or her creativity and genius. Music is not "free as the air." To the contrary, music users must pay for their use of the songwriter's only product, music. When music is played publicly, one must pay the songwriter, as well as the piper.

FOOTNOTES

[1]**See** Goldstein. **Outline of the Legislative History of Copyright Law Revision from 1955 to 1976**, 6 Am. Pat. L.A.Q.J. 74 (1978).

[2]Act of Oct. 19, 1976, Pub. L. No. 94-553, § 101, 90 Stat. 2541, which amended 17 U.S.C. in its entirety. The new copyright code, which appears as an appendix immediately after the old copyright code in the 1976 edition of the official United States Code, will be cited hereinafter as "17 U.S.C. app. § _____ (1976)." The new copyright code also appears in 17 U.S.C.A. (1977).

[3]Act of Oct. 19, 1976. Pub. L. No. 94-553, § 102, 90 Stat. 2541, 2598-99.

[4]Act of Mar. 4, 1909, ch. 320, 35 Stat. 1075 (as amended, codified in 17 U.S.C., which was enacted into positive law by Act of July 30, 1947, ch. 391. § 1, 61 Stat. 652). The old copyright code, which appears in the 1976 edition of the official United States Code, will be cited hereinafter as "17 U.S.C. § _____ (1976)." The old copyright code also appears as an appendix in the pocket part of 17 U.S.C.A. (1977 & Supp. 1979).

[5]Shemel & Krasilovsky, **This Business of Music** 135 (rev. ed. 1971).

[6]17 U.S.C. § 1(e) (1976). Thus, under the old law the statutory royalties paid on a "million seller" recording was $20,000. Of that, by custom in the trade, half went to the publisher, who served as a promoter. The other half often had to be divided between or among two or more songwriters, particularly since the composers who supply the music are often different from the authors who supply the lyrics.

[7]Shemel & Krasilovsky, **This Business of Music** 124 (rev. ed. 1971).

[8]17 U.S.C. app. § 116(a) (3) (1976).

[9]28 U.S.C. §§ 1338(a), 1400(a) (1976).

[10]**Compare** 17 U.S.C. § 101(b) (1976) **with** 17 U.S.C. app. § 504(c) (1976). **See also** Jewell-LaSalle Realty Co. v. Buck, 283 U.S. 202 (1931).

[11]Widenski v. Shapiro, Bernstein & Co., 147 F.2d 909 (1st Cir. 1945).

[12]17 U.S.C. app. § 101 (1976).

[13]**Compare** 17 U.S.C. § 1(e) (1976) **with** 17 U.S.C. app. § 106(4) (1976). **But see** 17 U.S.C. app. § § 110. 111(a) (1976).

[14]17 U.S.C. § 1(e) (1976).

[15]**Compare** 17 U.S.C. § 24 (1976) **with** 17 U.S.C. app. § 302(a) (1977).

[16]17 U.S.C. § 1(e) (1976).

[17]Herbert v. Shanley Co., 242 U.S.C. 591 (1917).

[18]**M. Witmark & Sons v. Pastime Amusement Co.,** 298 F. 470, 472 (E.D.S.C.), **aff'd,** 2 F.2d 1020 (4th Cir. 1924) (live musical accompaniment during silent movies).

[19]Irving Berlin, Inc. v. Daigle, 31 F.2d 832 (5th Cir. 1929).

[20]Dreamland Ball Room, Inc. v. Shapiro, Bernstein & Co., 36 F.2d 354 (7th Cir. 1929).

[21]Remick Music Corp. v. Interstate Hotel Co., 58 F. Supp. 523, 533 (D. Neb. 1944), aff'd, 157 F.2d 744 (8th Cir. 1946). cert. denied, 329 U.S. 809 (1947).

[22]Edwin H. Morris & Co. v. Burton, 201 F. Supp. 36 (E.D. La. 1961).

[23]MCA, Inc. v. Wilson, 425 F. Supp. 443, 446 (S.D.N.Y. 1976).

[24]Famous Music Corp. v. Bay State Harness Horse Racing & Breeding Association, 554 F.2d 1213 (1st Cir. 1977).

[25]S. Rep. No. 94-473, 94th Cong. 1st Sess. 59 (1975); H.R. Rep. No. 94-1476, 94th Cong., 2d Sess. 62 (1976). **See** Associated Music Publishers, Inc. v. Debs Memorial Radio Fund, Inc., 141 F.2d 852 (2d Cir.), cert. denied, 323

U.S. 766 (1944), in which the court practically wrote the "for profit" limitation out of the 1909 Act.

[26]**Compare** 17 U.S.C. § 1(e) (1976) **with** 17 U.S.C. app. §§ 106(4), 110, 111(a) (1976). Pursuant to 17 U.S.C. app. § 110 (1976), the musical performances exempted by the statute are those made in the course of (1) face-to-face teaching activities of a nonprofit educational institution, (2) certain systematic instructional broadcasting or telecasting activities of a governmental body or a nonprofit educational institution, (3) religious services, (4) certain nonprofit performances as to which the performers, promoters and organizers are not compensated, (5) the mere public reception of a broadcast or telecast on a home-type receiver, (6) agricultural or horticultural fairs (insofar as any governmental body or nonprofit agricultural or horticultural organization is concerned), and (7) the mere promotion of retail sales of recordings of the music. Certain secondary transmissions in hotels, apartments, or similar establishments are also exempted, pursuant to 17 U.S.C. app. § 111(a) (1976).

[27]17 U.S.C. § 1(e) (1976).

[28]**Lerner v. Club Wander In, Inc.,** 174 F. Supp. 731 (D. Mass. 1959); **M. Witmark & Sons v. Tremont Social & Athletic Club,** 188 F. Supp. 787 (D. Mass. 1960).

[29]**Porter v. Marriott Motor Hotels, Inc.,** 137 U.S.P.Q. 473 (N.D. Tex. 1962).

[30]**Lerner v. Schectman,** 228 F. Supp. 354 (D. Minn. 1964).

[31]**Broadcast Music, Inc. v. Walters,** 181 U.S.P.Q. 327 (N.D. Okla. 1973).

[32]17 U.S.C. app. § 106(4) (1976).

[33]17 U.S.C. app. § 101 (1976) (emphasis added).

[34]S. Rep. No. 94-473, 94th Cong., 1st Sess. 60 (1975); H.R. Rep. No. 94-1476, 94th Cong., 2d Sess. 64 (1976).

[35]For example, the first copyright infringement suit against a college or university based upon the unlicensed performance of copyrighted music has been filed by BMI. **Broadcast Music, Inc. v. President & Fellows of Harvard College** d/b/a/ Harvard University, Civil No. 79-467-G (D. Mass. filed Mar. 8, 1979) (dismissed by stipulation filed July 25, 1979, pursuant to the parties' settlement which included Harvard's taking a BMI license).

[36]**M. Witmark & Sons v. Calloway,** 22 F.2d 412 (E.D. Tenn. 1927); **Buck v. Lester,** 24 F.2d 877 (E.D.S.C. 1928).

[37]**Buck v. Heretis,** 24 F.2d 876 (E.D.S.C. 1928).

[38]**Buck v. Jewell-LaSalle Realty Co.,** 283 U.S. 191 (1931). **But see Fortnightly Corp. v. United Artists Television, Inc.,** 392 U.S. 390 (1968); **Teleprompter Corp. v. Columbia Broadcasting System, Inc.,** 415 U.S. 394 (1974); and **Twentieth Century Music Corp. v. Aiken,** 422 U.S. 151 (1975), which all but overruled much of **Buck v. Jewell-LaSalle.** However, the broad definition of "perform" in the new law, 17 U.S.C. app. § 101 (1976), overrules the **Fortnightly, Teleprompter,** and **Aiken** cases; but 17 U.S.C. app. § 110(5) (1976) exempts certain receptions "on a single receiving apparatus of a kind commonly used in private homes," and 17 U.S.C. app. § 111(a) (1976) exempts certain secondary transmissions in a hotel, apartment, or similar establishment.

[39]**Harms, Inc. v. Sansom House Enterprises, Inc.,** 162 F. Supp. 129 (E.D. Pa. 1958), aff'd per curiam sub nom., **Leo Feist, Inc. v. Lew Tendler Tavern, Inc.,** 267 F.2d 494 (3rd Cir. 1959).

[40]**Quackenbush Music, Ltd. v. Wood,** 381 F. Supp. 904 (M.D. Tenn. 1974); **Warner Bros.,**

Inc. v. O'Keefe, 468 F. Supp. 16, 20 (S.D. Iowa 1978).

⁴¹17 U.S.C. app. § 101 (1976).

⁴²There are, however, exemptions for the *mere* public reception of a broadcast or telecast "on a single receiving apparatus of a kind commonly used in private homes" provided that there is no direct charge to see or hear the broadcast or telecast, 17 U.S.C. app. § 110(5) (1976), and for certain secondary transmissions in hotels, apartments, or similar establishments. 17 U.S.C. app. § 111(a) (1976).

⁴³17 U.S.C. § 1(e) (1976).

⁴⁴17 U.S.C. § 1(e) (1976); **Quackenbush Music, Ltd. v. Wood,** 381 F. Supp. 904 (M.D. Tenn. 1974); **Warner Bros., Inc., v. O'Keefe,** 468 F. Supp. 16, 20 (S.D. Iowa 1978).

⁴⁵**Buck v. Kelly,** 7 U.S.P.Q. 164 (D. Mass. 1930) (dictum).

⁴⁶17 U.S.C. app. §§ 116(a)(2), 116(b)(1) (1976).

⁴⁷17 U.S.C. app. § 116(b)(2) (1976). ASCAP and BMI have begun to bring copyright infringement suits under the new law alleging unlicensed public performances of copyrighted music by means of jukeboxes. **Senor Music v. Paramount Automatic Machines Corp.** Civil No. 78 Civ. 3449 (S.D.N.Y. filed July 29, 1978); **Broadcast Music, Inc. v. Mark IV Club,** Civil No. H-79-306 (S.D. Tex. filed Feb. 20, 1979).

⁴⁸17 U.S.C. app. § 116(e)(1) (1976).

⁴⁹**M. Witmark & Sons v. Pastime Amusement Co.,** 298 F. 470, 475 (E.D.S.C.), aff'd, 2 F.2d 1020 (4th Cir. 1924); **Irving Berlin, Inc. v. Daigle,** 26 F.2d 149 (E.D. La. 1928), **modified as to the amount of damages only,** 31 F.2d 832 (5th Cir. 1929); **Dreamland Ball Room, Inc. v. Shapiro, Bernstein & Co.,** 36 F.2d 354 (7th Cir. 1929); **Remick Music Corp. v. Interstate Hotel Co.,** 58 F. Supp. 523, 533 (D. Neb. 1944), aff'd, 157 F.2d 744 (8th Cir. 1946), **cert. denied,** 329 U.S. 809 (1947); **Famous Music Corp. v. Bay State Harness Horse Racing & Breeding Association,** 554 F.2d 1213, 1215 (1st Cir. 1977).

⁵⁰ S. Rep. No. 94-473, 94th Cong., 1st Sess. 141 (1975); H.R. Rep. No. 94-1476, 94th Cong., 2d Sess. 159 (1976).

⁵¹**Italian Book Corp. v. Palms Sheepshead Country Club, Inc.,** 186 U.S.P.Q. 326 (E.D.N.Y. 1975). **See also MCA, Inc. v. Wilson,** 425 F. Supp. 443, 456 (S.D.N.Y. 1976); **Buck v. Crescent Gardens Operating Co.,** 28 F. Supp. 576, 577-78 (D. Mass. 1939).

⁵²**Fromont v. Aeolian Co.,** 254 F. 592, 593, (S.D.N.Y. 1918).

⁵³**See Buck v. Cecere,** 45 F. Supp. 441 (W.D.N.Y. 1942); **Famous Music Corp. v. Bay State Harness Horse Racing & Breeding Association,** 554 F.2d 1213 (1st Cir. 1977); **KECA Music, Inc. v. Dingus McGee's Co.,** 432 F. Supp. 72 (W.D. Mo. 1977); **Warner Bros., Inc. v. O'Keefe,** 468 F. Supp. 16, 19-20 (S.D. Iowa 1978).

⁵⁴**Shapiro, Bernstein & Co. v. Veltin,** 47 F. Supp. 648 (W.D. La. 1942).

⁵⁵**Bourne v. Fouche,** 238 F. Supp. 745 (E.D.S.C. 1965).

⁵⁶**Buck v. Rogers,** 17 U.S.P.Q. 434 (E.D. Mo. 1933); **Donaldson, Douglas & Gumble, Inc. v. Terris,** 37 U.S.P.Q. 39 (M.D. Pa. 1938); **Buck v. Pettijohn,** 34 F. Supp. 968 (E.D. Tenn. 1940).

⁵⁷**Buck v. Rogers,** 17 U.S.P.Q. 434 (E.D. Mo. 1933).

⁵⁸**See** text accompanying n.32, *supra.*

⁵⁹**See** n.25, *supra.*

⁶⁰17 U.S.C. app. § 115(c)(2) (1976).

⁶¹**Remick Music Corp. v. Interstate Hotel Co.,** 58 F. Supp. 523, 534-35 (D. Neb. 1944), aff'd, 157 F.2d 744 (8th Cir. 1946). **cert. denied,** 329 U.S. 809 (1947); **Irving Berlin, Inc. v. Daigle,** 31 F.2d 832, 834-35 (5th Cir. 1929).

⁶²28 U.S.C. §§ 1338(a), 1400(a) (1976).

⁶³17 U.S.C. app. § 502(a) (1976). **See M. Witmark & Sons v. Calloway,** 22 F.2d 412, 414 (E.D. Tenn. 1927).

⁶⁴17 U.S.C. app. § 504(b) (1976).

⁶⁵17 U.S.C. app. § 504(b) (1976).

⁶⁶17 U.S.C. app. § 504(c) (1976).

⁶⁷17 U.S.C. app. § 505 (1976).

⁶⁸17 U.S.C. app. § 505 (1976). **See Alfred Bell & Co. v. Catalda Fine Arts, Inc.,** 75 U.S.P.Q. 283 (S.D.N.Y. 1947) (awarding attorney's fees to the prevailing plaintiff, notwithstanding the defendants' good-faith belief in the existence of a valid defense); **Warner Bros., Inc. v. O'Keefe,** 468 F. Supp. 16, 21 (S.D. Iowa 1978) (awarding attorney's fees to the prevailing plaintiffs, in an amount greater than the statutory damages awarded).

⁶⁹17 U.S.C. app. § 504(c) (1) (1976).

⁷⁰**Jewell-LaSalle Realty Co. v. Buck ,** 283 U.S. 202 (1931).

⁷¹17 U.S.C. app. § 101(b) (1976). **See Douglas v. Cunningham,** 294 U.S. 207 (1935); **F.W. Woolworth Co. v. Contemporary Arts, Inc.,** 344 U.S. 228 (1952).

⁷²**Widenski v. Shapiro, Bernstein & Co.,** 147 F.2d 909 (1st Cir. 1945).

⁷³17 U.S.C. app. § 506(a) (1976).

⁷⁴**Warner Bros.-Seven Arts, Inc. v. Kalantzakis,** 326 F. Supp. 80, 82 (S.D. Tex. 1971). **See also Buck v. Crescent Gardens Operating Co.,** 28 F. Supp. 576, 577-78 (D. Mass. 1939).

⁷⁵**Tempo Music, Inc. v. International Good Music, Inc.,** 143 U.S.P.Q. 67, 69 (W.D. Wash. 1964) aff'd sub nom., **K-91, Inc. v. Gershwin Publishing Corp.,** 372 F.2d 1 (9th Cir. 1967), cert. denied, 389 U.S. 1045 (1968); **Warner Bros., Inc. v. O'Keefe,** 468 F. Supp. 16, 20 (S.D. Iowa 1978).

⁷⁶U.S. Const. art. I, § 8, cl. 8.

⁷⁷**Mazer v. Stein,** 347 U.S. 201, 219 (1954).

13: THE COPYRIGHT LAW AND DANCE

Nicholas Arcomano

Choreography finally came of legal age with the passage of the revised Copyright Act of 1976. Choreographic works together with pantomimes were for the first time named as one of the categories of copyrightable subject matter in the United States.

Until the new law went into effect on Jan. 1, 1978 (after a revision process that lasted more than 20 years), the only way a choreographer could obtain protection against unauthorized performances of a dance work was to attempt to register it as a "dramatic composition." This was an unrealistic and narrow approach.

An 1892 lawsuit involving the celebrated dancer Loie Fuller highlights the inadequate treatment. Fuller, one of the "mothers" of American modern dance, brought an action against another dancer, Minnie Bemis, for the unauthorized performance of her innovative "Serpentine Dance."

"La Loie" had performed the work with success at Madison Square Theater in New York and also had registered it with the Copyright Office accompanied by a detailed description of her choreography. But Fuller lost the suit. The court ruled that

> "a stage dance illustrating the poetry of motion by a series of graceful movements combined with an attractive arrangement of drapery, lights, and shadows, but telling no story, portraying no character and depicting no emotion is not a dramatic composition within the meaning of the Copyright Act."

The first copyright law in the United States was enacted in 1790 and protected only maps, books, and charts. Through the years, other areas of creativity were added—musical compositions in 1831, photographs in 1865, and paintings, drawings, and sculpture in 1870, but choreography remained a stepchild of the arts.

The Copyright Act of 1909 was also deficient in its treatment of choreography. According to the Copyright Office at that time, ballet had to "tell a story, develop a character or express a theme or emotion by means of specific dance movements and physical actions." How would this requirement relate to abstract ballets, such as Balanchine's "Agon" or to modern and experimental dances? It didn't, in any satisfactory way. Such works lacked official recognition by the Copyright Office unless they could find their way into the category of dramatic works.

A vigorous advocate of copyright reform in this area, Agnes de Mille

Nicholas Arcomano, counsel for SESAC, Inc., is a member of the American Bar Association and chairman of a subcommittee on problems of choreographic works. He contributes to Dance Magazine.

put it succinctly in a comment submitted to the Copyright Office in 1959: "Choreography is neither drama nor storytelling. It is a separate art. It is an arrangement in time-space, using human bodies as a unit design. It may or may not be dramatic or tell a story."

The Copyright Office's position, however, gradually became less restrictive. In 1952, Hanya Holm had submitted a microfilm copy of a Laban score (a system of dance notation) of her choreography for the musical "Kiss Me Kate" for registration as a dramatic work. It was accepted by the Copyright Office, although the dances did not tell a story, in and of themselves. This was also reported to be the first time dance notation was accepted. It was an historical event for choreographers and, I believe, a turning point for the Copyright Office.

But a solution to the problem was still a long way off. Most choreographers had only the protection of what is known as the "common law." However, this would not apply if the work were commercially exploited — that is, if copies of the choreography were to be made generally available to the public by sale or distribution.

Fortunately, the situation changed for choreographers with the 1976 law. The legal door was open to grant full protection to "original" choreographic works that are "fixed." Ballet and modern dance vocabularies to contain basic movements which can be used by anyone and incorporated into an original choreographic work, but it is the unique combination of dance steps that determine "originality."

"Fixed" means that the dance work must be so that it can be "perceived, reproduced or otherwise communicated for a period of more than transitory duration." Fixing the dance work is of vital importance. The new law protects the choreography *instantaneously* upon its creation, but legally it is not considered "created" until it is fixed. So when Mr. Balanchine is, in fact, creating one of his ballets during rehearsal — trying and revising steps and a series of movements while working directly with the dancers — his dance work is not legally created until it is fixed.

Are choreographers taking advantage of the new law? George Balanchine, Martha Graham, Alwin Nikolais, and Fokine's heirs are. Mr. Balanchine submitted his first application for registration in January of last year for "Square Dance" together with a videotape of the work. Barbara Horgan, his assistant, has registered at least 30 more of his works.

In addition to registering her works Miss Graham is also placing copyright notices on performance programs. Fokine's heirs have secured registration for his best known works through the submission of videotapes and films. Alwin Nikolais, who often creates not only the choreography but also the sound scores, costumes, and the lighting designs for his works, can make his claim to each of the individual elements he has created through the deposit of one videotape with the Copyright Office.

Although the law does not require that a work be registered with the Copyright Office to secure protection, it makes good legal sense to register the choreography (Form PA), pay the required fee ($10), and make the necessary deposit of copies (notation, film, videotape, or whatever) of the work all at the same time. Registration is recommended because it provides advantages in enforcing the protection of the rights granted under the law.

And just what are those rights? There are five, and permission must be granted by the choreographer before they can be exercised by anyone else: 1) The right to reproduce or make a copy of the dance work (videotape, film and so forth). 2) The right to prepare derivative works such as adaptations or new versions as in a motion picture. 3) The right to distribute copies to the public by sale or other transfer of ownership; or by rental, lease or lending. 4) The right to perform the work publicly. 5) The right to display a copy of the dance by means of a film or slide or television image. There are certain limited "fair use" situations for purposes such as criticism, teaching, scholarship, or research which may not require prior authorizations.

Legal protection lasts the life of the choreographer and for 50 years after his death. This was one of the major changes in the new law and is in line with the length of protection other countries grant to original works. It can't last forever because the framers of the Constitution, from which our copyright law is derived, were primarily interested in encouraging the creation of intellectual works for the *public* good, although they recognized that creators should have for "limited times" exclusive rights in their works and the economic benefits resulting from their use. When the "life plus 50" term is over, the public is then considered the owner of the choreography.

All choreographic works that were fixed in a copy for the first time on or after Jan. 1, 1978 are entitled to the protection for the "life plus fifty" term. If the choreography was created before that date (and had not been published or registered for copyright under the 1909 law to the extent that this was possible) it will also be considered created as of Jan. 1, 1978.

The marketplace for choreography—one of the richest expressions of man's creativity—is expanding rapidly on both the domestic and international levels. In view of this, all choreographers should give every consideration to fixing their works and registering them with the Copyright Office so that they may secure the maximum protection of the new law.

14: JUDGE RULES THAT COPYRIGHT LAW PROTECTS ARCHITECTS

Peter Hoffman

World News
Washington, D.C.

In a decision of national significance, a Nebraska Federal District Court has ruled that engineers and architects enjoy copyright protection of their drawings under the Copyright Act of 1976. In one of the first such cases under the Act, Judge Warren K. Urbom ruled that such drawings normally may not be reproduced by a client for use in building a second structure based on the original plans.

The decision came in a suit for copyright infringement brought by the architecture/engineering firm of Aitken, Hazen, Hoffman, Miller, against the Belmont Construction Co., both of Lincoln.

The firm, in 1977, had designed an apartment building for Belmont, which was completed in 1979. Later, Belmont used the same plans for the construction of a similar apartment building in 1980 without the firm's permission, and the firm filed suit.

Because of the case's potential impact on future interpretation of the Copyright Act, the American Institute of Architects (AIA) and the National Society of Professional Engineers (NSPE) joined the Nebraska Society of Architects as "friends of the court" supporting the plaintiff's position.

Judge Urbom ruled that copyright protection for design plans extends only to the copying of such plans, as opposed to the structure itself. Citing from a legal reference, Judge Urbom wrote, "Where the alleged infringer has copied a plan from a plan, the copying has been held to be an infringement." He also said that the law indicates that architectural structures themselves may not be subject to copyright.

Another issue that arose in the case was whether the architect/engineer had an employee relationship with the construction client, or was acting as an independent contractor. The copyright law provides that an employer owns the copyright to work that is prepared by employees as part of their employment or specially ordered or commissioned as part of a collective project.

Judge Urbom ruled that the plans and drawings in the case before him are, "not a commissioned work . . . because there is no written agreement between the parties that the plans should be considered a work made for hire." But he put off until further hearings a ruling on whether the architecture/engineering firm could be legally considered an employee of the construction company.

In another aspect of the case, the construction company claimed that its suggestions to the firm during the design development were significant enough to make it a co-author of the plans, and, therefore, free to reuse them with immunity from copyright infringement. The architecture/ engineering firm countered that the client's contribution was minor. Judge Urbom declined to rule on this issue pending more testimony. The firm also argued that its client could not be considered a co-author of the plans in any case because it is not licensed to practice architecture or engineering in Nebraska. Judge Urbom said that argument is attractive and has considerable policy strength, but again he declined to make a ruling, pending further testimony.

III: USERS

Papers 15 Through 29: Commentary

Authors do not write simply to get their ideas and facts down on paper. Artists do not always create simply to express themselves. Publishers and other synergistic marketers of copyrighted works do not operate in a vacuum. In the minds of all of these are the ultimate users of their creations, those who will buy or otherwise use them in one way or another to satisfy needs and desires.

However, the needs and desires of users are often no longer satisfiable simply through the creation and marketing of printed books and periodicals because of economic stringencies and the "temptations of technology." This point is amplified in later sections of this book, if it does not become crystal clear from the papers included in this section. Most of these deal with photocopying, which was one of the first technological issues to cause concern with copyright proprietors. Photocopying is likely to continue, as is the controversy about what is and what is not permitted.

EDUCATORS

In revising the Copyright Statute, Congress gave special consideration to the importance of the educational function, that is, to the ability of educators to copy copyrighted works "freely," at least to a reasonable extent, for educational purposes. In Section 107 of the Statute, the fair use of copyrighted works, "including such use by reproduction of copies for purposes such as . . . [for] teaching (including copies for classroom use) . . . is not an infringement of copyright." In enacting the Statute, the House of Representatives also included in its report classroom guidelines for such additional copying; these were reaffirmed as "the sense of Congress" in the Conference Report of the House and Senate committees.

By 1976, of course, photocopying had long been a common practice among and for educators, including some photocopying by libraries for library-reserve use. Despite (or perhaps because of) the new statute and all the debates preceding it, much controversy and uncertainty seem to have continued regarding how far educators and those working in their behalf may go without charge, or at least without the express permission of the copyright owners. Litigation by publishers has resulted against both commercial copying centers, many of which are located near educational sites, and educational institutions themselves.

In response to this unrest, Mary Hutchings, counsel for the American Library Association, prepared the "Model Policy Concerning College and University Photocopying for Classroom Research and Library Reserve Use"; this guide, distributed in 1982, is included as Paper 15 in this volume.

In 1981, reiterating the publishers' point of view, Carol A. Risher prepared a "Copyright Primer for Chemical Educators" (Paper 16). This article contains guidelines, definitions, prohibitions, and permission-request instructions and examples.

Publishers have not been happy about the beyond-the-law educational photocopying they believed was taking place. In attempts to bring this under control in the early 1980s, specific publishers under the aegis of the Association of American Publishers filed a number of suits, first against some commercial "quick printers" operating near university campuses and then against New York University (NYU) and nine of its professors.

The significance of the settlement of the first suit against a quick printer (Gnomon) is discussed in Paper 17 by Henry Kaufman. Some of the photocopying guidelines that resulted from the settlement of the NYU suit are summarized in Paper 18 by Daniel Wise. We have also included the full NYU guidelines, as Paper 19.

Barbara Rystrom reports in Paper 20 that groups in the university and library communities felt that the Section 107–based guidelines, on which the NYU settlement was based, are too restrictive in the college and university context because they were negotiated only by secondary-school educators. Accordingly, her Association of College and Research Libraries (ACRL) Copyright Committee felt that colleges and universities need not conform to the guidelines as set forth in the NYU settlement.

More agreement seems to exist regarding the off-the-air recording, retention, and use of television programs in classrooms. Paper 21 by Eileen Cooke reports some 1981 guidelines developed by a committee appointed by Representative Kastenmeier; these guidelines were inserted by him in the *Congressional Record.*

Educators are also confronted with copyright-based restrictions on copying computer software. Lauren T. Letellier's article entitled "Copying Software: Crime in the Classroom?" (Paper 22) deals with teacher and software-producer viewpoints on making copies of computer programs that are useful in the classroom. After buying many units of expensive hardware, one educator was quoted as saying that "schools are not in a position to buy [software] in multiples . . . I would never purchase software that didn't allow for copying, at least for archival purposes." In talking about ethics, this same educator went on to say "It's unethical to copy, but it's also unethical to develop these materials for use with the hardware —in which so much money has been invested—and then turn around and make it unavailable to the users."

LIBRARIES

The debate over what photocopying is legally permitted by and in libraries goes on unabated, despite all the efforts that led to Section 108 in the 1976 Copyright Statute, studies by the National Commission on New Technological Uses of Copyrighted Works (CONTU) (see Paper 45 in this volume), and the Register of Copyrights' Five-Year (1983) Section 108(i) Report (see Paper 26).

Shortly after the passage of the 1976 Statute, Lewis I. Flacks of the U.S. Copyright Office wrote "Living in the Gap of Ambiguity; An Attorney's Advice to Librarians on the Copyright Law" (Paper 23). This paper included answers to specific questions often asked by librarians. Some of the questions and answers are now out of date, but the article and its illustrations still constitute an apt introduction to the subject.

Late in 1983, Charles H. Lieb summarized what amounts to the publishers' position on photocopying in "Document Supply in the United States"; Paper 24 deals with the "out-of-house delivery of copies of copyrighted materials by library and document-delivery houses." Among other pronouncements, it states: "Central source libraries, i.e., libraries that exist for the principal purpose of supplying copies to others, by their very nature make and supply these copies systematically . . . [hence] gain no safe harbor either from [Sections] 108 or 107 and are infringers [if they do not pay]."

Laura N. Gasaway has published two articles on special-library copyright aspects of nonprint works and audiovisual materials. The first of these, on nonprint works, is included in this volume as Paper 25; the second is referenced in the Bibliography at the end of this section. Her papers are particularly interesting because she is basically sound on legal facts, but interprets them quite liberally from the viewpoint of librarian needs.

Section 108(i) of the 1976 Copyright Statute calls for the Register of Copyrights to report to Congress every five years after 1978 on the effectiveness of the statutory balance as to "the rights of creators and the needs of users." Copyright owners, library users, and librarians are to be consulted, and were consulted by the Register through extensive hearings in preparation for his 1983 report. Also, an extensive statistical study—another "King report" (see Bibliography under Libraries)—was again made on library photocopying.

The Register's report (Paper 26) is summarized in an *Information Hotline* article. Generally, the Register reported that a balance exists, but with some anomalies and confusions. For example, about a quarter of the photocopying transactions in libraries are for two or more copies, although Section 108 permits only single photocopies. Many of the other findings are equally interesting, but the Register recommended

91

only five statutory changes: permitting conditional library reproduction of out-of-print musical works, passing the "Umbrella Statute," "clarifying" the Section 108(a)(3) notice requirement to specify "the" notice of copyright (instead of "a" notice), specifying in paragraphs (d) and (e) of Section 108 that unpublished works are excluded from the copying privileges, and changing the reporting months for the Register's five-year 108(i) reports from January to March. Seven nonstatutory recommendations were also included.

However, the last article in this section, from *American Libraries* (Paper 27), states:

> The Copyright Office report sent to Congress early in January [1983] by Register David Ladd [has] added fresh sparks to the continuing dispute between librarians and publishers over [library] photocopying. . . . The library community believes that the desired balance between the rights of the creators and the needs of users is being achieved, and recommended no legislative changes except on musical works.

(Publishers, on the other hand, believe that the intended balance is not being met.)

IN-HOUSE COPYING

Photocopying, whether it is done in an in-house library, by an outside service or other library, or by individuals for themselves, is very important to the work of employees in most organizations. Most of the papers included in the next section of this volume, entitled Intermediaries/Information Services, also pertain to the subject of supplying photocopies to libraries and individuals, but here we have included or cited several that deal specifically with in-house copying.

In Paper 28, one of us (Weil) has described the copyright-compliance principles, practices, and problems of one industrial organization at hearings conducted in 1982 by the Register of Copyrights. Permission payments are preferably first made through the Copyright Clearance Center's transactional program, then through negotiation of bilateral licenses with other pertinent publishers. However, it was felt that "there is a legitimate need for statutory relief in those instances where a user has exerted reasonable effort to obtain permissions from publishers but the publishers have not responded." The "Umbrella Statute" amendment, dealt with in Part VII of this book, was deemed desirable in oral testimony.

Some of the lawsuits filed by publishers against specific industrial organizations that were accused of photocopying the publishers' works beyond statutory limits are covered by Michael C. Elmer and John F. Hornick in Paper 29. The authors discuss the rationale and significance of these lawsuits and the resultant out-of-court settlements. Their interpretations of how the Copyright Statute applies to industrial organizations are widely held, but readers of Paper 24 by Charles H. Lieb will note that the Association of American Publishers, whom Lieb represents, has a more rigorous viewpoint, as does the Register of Copyrights in his five-year Section 108 report (see Paper 26).

BIBLIOGRAPHY

Educators

Association for Educational Communications and Association of Media Producers, 1977, *Copyright and Educational Media: A Guide to Fair Use and Permissions Procedures,* Washington, D.C.

Association of Research Libraries, 1983, *Reproduction of Copyrighted Materials for Classroom Use: A Briefing Paper for Teaching Faculty and Administrators,* Washington, D.C.

Butler, M., 1978, Copyright and Reserve Books—What Libraries Are Doing, *Coll. Res. Lib. News* **39**(5):125-129.

Fields, H., 1983, NYU Suit Lists 13 Counts of Copying Violations, *Publ. Wkly.* **223**(2):16.

Friedman, B., 1983, Register's 5-year Report to Congress, *Soc. for Schol. Pub. Lett.* **5**(1):6-7.

Harer, J. B., and Huber, C. E., 1982, Copyright Policies in Virginia Academic Library Reserve Rooms, *Coll. Res. Lib.* **43**(3):233-241.

Harris, R. W., 1981, Memorandum: Introductory Guide to Academic Risks of Copyright Infringement, *Coll. Univ. Law J.* **7**(3):329-345.

Mawdsley, R. D., and Permuth, S., 1981. Multiple Photocopying in Educational Institutions, *Nolpe School Law Jour.* **10**(Winter):18-29.

NACUBO, 1980, Copyrights at Colleges and Universities, *Admin. Ser./Suppl.* **2**:4:3:1-7.

"NYU Case" Photocopy Center to Require Written Permission from Customers, 1983, *Information Hotline* **15**(8):1, 9, 14.

NYU Issues Photocopying Policy Statement, 1983, *Adv. Technol. Libs.* **12**(10):4-5.

Polansky, B. F., Multiple Copies for Library Reserve Rooms: Fair Use?, 1984, *Soc. for Schol. Pub. Lett.* **6**(3):12.

Snyder, Fritz, 1980, Copyright and the Library Reserve Room, *Law Libr. J.* **73**(3):702-714.

Troost, F. W., 1983, A Practical Guide to Dealing with Copyright Problems Related to Emerging Video Technologies in Schools and Colleges, *Libr. Trends* **32**(2):211-221.

Libraries

Billings, R. D., Jr., 1983, Fair Use Under the 1976 Copyright Act: The Legacy of Williams & Wilkins for Librarians, *Libr. Trends* **32**(2):183-199.

Copyright Office, 1977, Announcement—Final Regulation, Warning of Copyright [Notice] for Use by Libraries and Archives, *Fed. Regist.* **42**(221):59264-59265.

Demas, S., 1985, Microcomputer Software Collections, *Spec. Lib.* **76**(1):17-23.

Duemmler, E. L., 1981, Library Photocopying: An International Perspective, *ASCAP Copyr. Law Symp.* **26**:151–196.

Fields, H., 1983, Copyright Report to Congress Supports Key Publisher Views, *Publ. Wkly.* **223**(3):16, 26, 28.

Gasaway, L. N., 1983, Audiovisual Material and Copyright in Special Libraries, *Spec. Lib.* **74**(3):222–229.

Hattery, L. H., 1983, Library Photocopying—Legal or Illegal, More or Less!?, *Inf. Retr. Lib. Autom.* **18**(9):1–3.

Hunter, C. O., 1983, Library Reproduction of Musical Works: A Review of Revision, *Libr. Trends* **32**(2):241–248.

Lieb, C. H., 1975, Some Reflections on the Williams and Wilkins Case, *Copr. Bull. 6,* STM, Amsterdam, The Netherlands.

Lieb, C. H., 1977, Library Photocopying Under the 1976 Copyright Law, Proceedings, [ABA] Section of Patent, Trademark and Copyright Law, pp. 226–232.

Matthews, L. M., 1983, Copyright and the Duplication of Personal Papers in Archival Repositories, *Libr. Trends* **32**(2):223–240.

Sinofsky, E. R., 1985, *Off-Air Videotaping in Education,* R. R. Bowker Co., Ann Arbor, Michigan, 163p.

Steuben, J., 1979, Interlibrary Loan of Photocopies of Articles Under the New Copyright Law, *Spec. Libr.* **70**(5/6):227–232.

Study of Libraries, Publishers, and Photocopying [by King Research, Inc.], 1982, *Inf. Hotline* **14**(10):1, 5–8.

In-House Copying

Artigliere, R., 1978, The Impact of the New Copyright Act on Photocopying by Law Firms, *Fla. Bar Jour.* **52**(7):528–535.

Oxton, J. G., 1980, Copyright Compliance Program [IBM], *Jour. Libr. Auto.* **13**(1):45–49.

Prewitt, B. G., 1980, *Testimony to the Register of Copyrights at the Houston ACS Meeting,* Rohm and Haas Co., Bristol, PA.

Stanton, R. D., 1978, Bellpay—Bell Laboratories Library Network [Photocopying] Royalty Accounting System, *Am. Soc. Inf. Sci. Proceedings* **15**:326–329.

Wagner, S., 1978, AAP, Authors, Set Guidelines for Corporate Library Photocopying [later revoked by AAP], *Publ. Wkly.* **213**(3):27–28.

Other-User Aspects

Brait, S., 1980, Alas. All That Lovely Music Is Not Free, *Today's Spirit* **107**(240):11.

Walch, D. B., 1979, Slide Duplication and the New Law: A Survey of Publishers, *Audiovisual Instruction,* March 1979, pp. 64–65.

Weil, B. H., 1982, Why Should Chemists Care About Copyright?, *J. Chem. Inf. Comput. Sci.* **22**(2):61–63.

15: MODEL POLICY CONCERNING COLLEGE AND UNIVERSITY PHOTOCOPYING FOR CLASSROOM, RESEARCH AND LIBRARY RESERVE USE

Mary Hutchings

Editor's Note: This model policy was prepared by Mary Hutchings, ALA's legal counsel, in March, 1982.

I. THE COPYRIGHT ACT AND PHOTOCOPYING

From time to time, the faculty and staff of this University [College] may use photocopied materials to supplement research and teaching. In many cases, photocopying can facilitate the University's [College's] mission; that is, the development and transmission of information. However, the photocopying of copyrighted materials is a right granted under the copyright law's doctrine of "fair use" which must not be abused. This report will explain the University's [College's] policy concerning the photocopying of copyrighted materials by faculty and library staff. Please note that this policy does not address other library photocopying which may be permitted under other sections of the copyright law, e.g., 17 U.S.C. §108.

Copyright is a constitutionally conceived property right which is designed to promote the progress of science and the useful arts by securing for an author the benefits of his or her original work of authorship for a limited time. U.S. Constitution, Art. I, Sec. 8. The Copyright statute, 17 U.S.C. §101 *et seq.*, implements this policy by balancing the author's interest against the public interest in the dissemination of information affecting areas of universal concern, such as art, science, history and business. The grand design of this delicate balance is to foster the creation and dissemination of intellectual works for the general public.

The Copyright Act defines the rights of a copyright holder and how they may be enforced against an infringer. Included within the Copyright Act is the "fair use" doctrine which allows, under certain conditions, the copying of copyrighted material. While the Act lists general factors under the heading of "fair use" it provides little in the way of specific directions for what constitutes fair use. The law states:

17 U.S.C. §107. Limitations on exclusive rights: Fair use.
Notwithstanding the provisions of section 106, the fair use of a copyrighted work, *including such use by reproduction in copies* or phonorecords or by any other means specified by that section, for purposes such as criticism, comment, news reporting, *teaching (including multiple copies for classroom use), scholarship, or research,* is not

an infringement of copyright. In determining whether the use made of a work in any particular case is a fair use the factors to be considered shall include—
(1) the purpose and character of the use, including whether such use is of a commercial nature or is for nonprofit educational purposes;
(2) the nature of the copyrighted work;
(3) the amount and substantiality of the portion used in relation to the copyrighted work as a whole; and
(4) the effect of the use upon the potential market for or value of the copyrighted work. *(Emphasis added.)*

The purpose of this report is to provide you, the faculty and staff of this University [College], with an explanation of when the photocopying of copyrighted material in our opinion is permitted under the fair use doctrine. Where possible, common examples of research, classroom, and library reserve photocopying have been included to illustrate what we believe to be the reach and limits of fair use.

Please note that the copyright law applies to all forms of photocopying, whether it is undertaken at a commercial copying center, at the University's [College's] central or departmental copying facilities or at a self-service machine. While you are free to use the services of a commercial establishment, you should be prepared to provide documentation of permission from the publisher (if such permission is necessary under this policy), since many commercial copiers will require such proof.

We hope this report will give you an appreciation of the factors which weigh in favor of fair use and those factors which weigh against fair use, but faculty members must determine for themselves which works will be photocopied. This University [College] does not condone a policy of photocopying instead of purchasing copyrighted works where such photocopying would constitute an infringement under the Copyright law, but it does encourage faculty members to exercise good judgment in serving the best interests of students in an efficient manner. This University [College] and its faculty and staff will make a conscientious effort to comply with these guidelines.

Instructions for securing permission to photocopy copyrighted works when such copying is beyond the limits of fair use appear at the end of this report. It is the policy of this University that the user (faculty, staff or librarian) secure such permission whenever it is legally necessary.

II. Unrestricted Photocopying

A. Uncopyrighted Published Works

Writings published before January 1, 1978, which have never been copyrighted may be photocopied without restriction. Copies of works protected by copyright must bear a copyright notice, which consists of the letter "c" in a circle, or the word "Copyright", or the abbreviation "Copr.", plus the year of first publication, plus the name of the copyright owner. 17 U.S.C. §401. As to works published before January 1, 1978, in the case of a book, the notice must be placed on the title page or the reverse side of the title page. In the case of a periodical the notice must be placed either on the title page, the first page of text, or in the masthead. A pre-1978 failure to comply with the notice requirements resulted in the work being injected into the public domain, i.e., unprotected. Copyright notice requirements have been relaxed since 1978, so that the absence of notice on copies of a work published after January 1, 1978, does not necessarily mean the work is in the public domain. 17 U.S.C. §405 (a) and (c). However, you will not be liable for damages for copyright infringement of works published after that date, if, after normal inspection, you photocopy a work on which you cannot find a copyright symbol and you have not received actual notice of the fact the work is copyrighted. 17 U.S.C. §405(b). However, a copyright owner who found out about your photocopying would have the right to prevent further distribution of the copies if in fact the work were copyrighted and the copies are infringing. 17 U.S.C. §405(b).

B. Published Works With Expired Copyrights

Writings with expired copyrights may be photocopied without restriction. All copyrights prior to 1906 have expired. 17 U.S.C. §304(b). Copyrights granted after 1906 may have been renewed; however the writing will probably not contain notice of the renewal. Therefore, it should be assumed all writings dated 1906 or later are covered by a valid copyright, unless information to the contrary is obtained from the owner or the U.S. Copyright Office (see Copyright Office Circular 15t).

Copyright Office Circular R22 explains how to investigate the copyright status of a work. One way is to use the *Catalog of Copyright Entries* published by the Copyright Office and available in [the University Library] many libraries. Alternatively you may request the Copyright Office to conduct a search of its registration and/or assignment records. The Office charges an hourly fee for this service. You will need to submit as much information as you have concerning the work in which you are interested, such as the title, author, approximate date of publication, the type of work or any available copyright data. The Copyright Office does caution that its searches

are not conclusive; for instance, if a work obtained copyright less than 28 years ago, it may be fully protected although there has been no registration or deposit.

C. Unpublished Works

Unpublished works, such as theses and dissertations, may be protected by copyright. If such a work was created before January 1, 1978, and has not been copyrighted or published without copyright notice, the work is protected under the new Act for the life of the author plus fifty years, 17 U.S.C. §303, but in no case earlier than December 31, 2002. If such a work is published on or before that date, the copyright will not expire before December 31, 2027. Works created after January 1, 1978, and not published enjoy copyright protection for the life of the author plus fifty years. 17 U.S.C. §302.

D. U.S. Government Publications

All U.S. Government publications with the possible exception of some National Technical Information Service Publications less than 5 years old may be photocopied without restrictions, except to the extent they contain copyrighted materials from other sources. 17 U.S.C. §105. U.S. Government publications are documents prepared by an official or employee of the government in an official capacity. 17 U.S.C. §101. Government publications include the opinions of courts in legal cases, Congressional Reports on proposed bills, testimony offered at Congressional hearings and the works of government employees in their official capacities. Works prepared by outside authors on contract to the government may or may not be protected by copyright, depending on the specifics of the contract. In the absence of copyright notice on such works, it would be reasonable to assume they are government works in the public domain. It should be noted that state government works may be protected by copyright. See, 17 U.S.C. §105. However, the opinions of state courts are not protected.

III. Permissible Photocopying of Copyrighted Works

The Copyright Act allows anyone to photocopy copyrighted works without securing permission from the copyright owner when the photocopying amounts to a "fair use" of the material. 17 U.S.C. §107. The guidelines in this report discuss the boundaries for fair use of photocopied material used in research or the classroom or in a library reserve operation. Fair use cannot always be expressed in numbers—either the number of pages copied or the number of copies distributed. Therefore, you should weigh the various factors listed in the Act and judge whether the intended use of photocopied, copyrighted material is within the spirit of the fair use doctrine. Any serious questions concerning whether a particular photocopying constitutes fair use should be directed to University [College] counsel.

A. Research Uses

At the very least, instructors may make a single copy of any of the following for scholarly research or use in teaching or preparing to teach a class:

1. a chapter from a book;
2. an article from a periodical or newspaper;
3. a short story, short essay, or short poem, whether or not from a collective work;
4. a chart, diagram, graph, drawing, cartoon or picture from a book, periodical, or newspaper.

These examples reflect the most conservative guidelines for fair use. They do not represent inviolate ceilings for the amount of copyrighted material which can be photocopied within the boundaries of fair use. When exceeding these minimum levels, however, you again should consider the four factors listed in Section 107 of the Copyright Act to make sure that any additional photocopying is justified. The following demonstrate situations where increased levels of photocopying would continue to remain within the ambit of fair use:

1. the inability to obtain another copy of the work because it is not available from another library or source or cannot be obtained within your time constraints;
2. the intention to photocopy the material only once and not to distribute the material to others;
3. the ability to keep the amount of material photocopied within a reasonable proportion to the entire work (the larger the work, the greater amount of material which may be photocopied).

Most single-copy photocopying for your personal use in research—even when it involves a substantial portion of a work—may well constitute fair use.

B. Classroom Uses

Primary and secondary school educators have, with publishers, developed the following guidelines, which allow a teacher to distribute photocopied material to students in a class without the publisher's prior permission, under the following conditions:

1. the distribution of the same photocopied material does not occur every semester;
2. only one copy is distributed for each student which copy must become the student's property;
3. the material includes a copyright notice on the first page of the portion of material photocopied;
4. the students are not assessed any fee beyond the actual cost of the photocopying.

In addition, the educators agreed that the amount of material distributed should not exceed certain brevity standards. Under those guidelines, a prose work may be reproduced in its entirety if it is less than 2500 words in length. If the work exceeds such length, the excerpt reproduced may not exceed 1000 words, or 10% of the work, whichever is less. In the case of poetry, 250 words is the maximum permitted.

These minimum standards normally would not be realistic in the University setting. Faculty members needing to exceed these limits for college education should not feel hampered by these guidelines, although they should attempt a "selective and sparing" use of photocopied, copyrighted material.

The photocopying practices of an instructor should not have a significant detrimental impact on the market for the copyrighted work. 17 U.S.C. §107(4). To guard against this effect, you usually should restrict use of an item of photocopied material to one course and you should not repeatedly photocopy excerpts from one periodical or author without the permission of the copyright owner.

C. Library Reserve Uses

At the request of a faculty member, a library may photocopy and place on reserve excerpts from copyrighted works in its collection in accordance with guidelines similar to those governing formal classroom distribution for face to face teaching discussed above. This University [College] believes that these guidelines apply to the library reserve shelf to the extent it functions as an extension of classroom readings or reflects an individual student's right to photocopy for his personal scholastic use under the doctrine of fair use. In general, librarians may photocopy materials for reserve room use for the convenience of students both in preparing class assignments and in pursuing informal educational activities which higher education require, such as advanced independent study and research.

If the request calls for only *one* copy to be placed on reserve, the library may photocopy an entire article, or an entire chapter from a book, or an entire poem. Requests for *multiple* copies on reserve should meet the following guidelines:

1. the amount of material should be reasonable in relation to the total amount of material assigned for one term of a course taking into account the nature of the course, its subject matter and level, 17 U.S.C. §107(1) and (3);
2. the number of copies should be reasonable in light of the number of students enrolled, the difficulty and timing of assignments, and the number of other courses which may assign the same material, 17 U.S.C. §107(1) and (3);
3. the material should contain a notice of copyright, *see*, 17 U.S.C. §401;
4. the effect of photocopying the material should not be detrimental to the market for the work. (In general, the library should own at least one copy of the work.) 17 U.S.C. §107(4).

For example, a professor may place on reserve as a supplement to the course textbook a reasonable number of copies of articles from academic journals or chapters from trade books. A reasonable number of copies will in most instances be less than six, but factors such as the length or difficulty of the assignment, the number of enrolled students and the length of time allowed for completion of the assignment may permit more in unusual circumstances.

In addition, a faculty member may also request that multiple copies of photocopied, copyrighted material be placed on the reserve shelf if there is insufficient time to obtain permission from the copyright owner. For example, a professor may place on reserve several photocopies of an entire article from a recent issue of *Time* magazine or the *New York Times* in lieu of distributing a copy to each member of the class. If you are in doubt as to whether a particular instance of photocopying is fair use in the reserve reading room, you should seek the publisher's permission. Most publishers will be cooperative and will waive any fee for such a use.

D. Uses of Photocopied Material Requiring Permission

1. *Repetitive copying:* The classroom or reserve use of photocopied materials in multiple courses or successive years will normally require advance permission from the owner of the copyright, 17 U.S.C. §107(3).

2. *Copying for profit:* Faculty should not charge students more than the actual cost of photocopying the material, 17 U.S.C. §107(1).

3. *Consumable works:* The duplication of works that are consumed in the classroom, such as standardized tests, exercises, and workbooks, normally requires permission from the copyright owner, 17 U.S.C. §107(4).

4. *Creation of anthologies as basic text material for a course:* Creation of a collective work or anthology by photocopying a number of copyrighted articles and excerpts to be purchased and used together as the basic text for a course will in most instances require the permission of the copyright owners. Such photocopying is more likely to be considered as a substitute for purchase of a book and thus less likely to be deemed fair use, 17 U.S.C. §107(4).

E. How to Obtain Permission

When a use of photocopied material requires that you request permission, you should communicate complete and accurate information to the copyright owner. The American Association of Publishers suggests that the following information be included in a permission request letter in order to expedite the process:

1. Title, author and/or editor, and edition of materials to be duplicated.
2. Exact material to be used, giving amount, page numbers, chapters and, if possible, a photocopy of the material.
3. Number of copies to be made.
4. Use to be made of duplicated materials.
5. Form of distribution (classroom, newsletter, etc.).
6. Whether or not the material is to be sold.

7. Type of reprint (ditto, photography, offset, typeset).

The request should be sent, together with a self-addressed return envelope, to the permissions department of the publisher in question. If the address of the publisher does not appear at the front of the material, it may be readily obtained in a publication entitled *The Literary Marketplace,* published by the R. R. Bowker Company and available in all libraries.

The process of granting permission requires time for the publisher to check the status of the copyright and to evaluate the nature of the request. It is advisable, therefore, to allow enough lead time to obtain permission before the materials are needed. In some instances, the publisher may assess a fee for the permission. It is not inappropriate to pass this fee on to the students who receive copies of the photocopied material.

The Copyright Clearance Center also has the right to grant permission and collect fees for photocopying rights for certain publications. Libraries may copy from any journal which is registered with the CCC and report the copying beyond fair use to CCC and pay the set fee. A list of publications for which the CCC handles fees and permissions is available from the CCC, 310 Madison Avenue, New York, N.Y. 10017.

Sample Letter To Copyright Owner (Publisher) Requesting Permission To Copy

March 1, 1982

Material Permissions Department
Hypothetical Book Company
500 East Avenue
Chicago, Illinois 60601

Dear Sir or Madam:

I would like permission to copy the following for continued use in my classes in future semesters:

Title: Learning is Good, Second Edition
Copyright: Hypothetical Book Co., 1965, 1971
Author: Frank Jones
Material to be duplicated: Chapters 10, 11 and 14 (photocopy enclosed).
Number of copies: 500
Distribution: The material will be distributed to students in my classes and they will pay only the cost of the photocopying.
Type of reprint: Photocopy
Use: The chapter will be used as supplementary teaching materials.

I have enclosed a self-addressed envelope for your convenience in replying to this request.

Sincerely,
Faculty Member

F. Infringement

Courts and legal scholars alike have commented that the fair use provisions in the Copyright Act are among the most vague and difficult that can be found anywhere in the law. In amending the Copyright Act in 1976, Congress anticipated the problem this would pose for users of copyrighted materials who wished to stay under the umbrella of protection offered by fair use. For this reason, the Copyright Act contains specific provisions which grant additional rights to libraries and insulate employees of a non-profit educational institution, library, or archives from statutory damages for infringement where the infringer believed or had reasonable grounds to believe the photocopying was a fair use of the material. 17 U.S.C. §504(c)(2).

Normally, an infringer is liable to the copyright owner for the actual losses sustained because of the photocopying and any additional profits of the infringer. 17 U.S.C. §504(a)(1) and (b). Where the monetary losses are nominal, the copyright owner usually will claim statutory damages instead of the actual losses. 17 U.S.C. §504(a)(2) and (c). The statutory damages may reach as high as $10,000 (or up to $50,000 if the infringement is willful). In addition to suing for money damages, a copyright owner can usually prevent future infringement through a court injunction. 17 U.S.C. §502.

The Copyright Act specifically exempts from statutory damages any employee of a non-profit educational institution, library, or archives, who "believed and had reasonable grounds for believing that his or her use of the copyrighted work was a fair use under Section 107." 17 U.S.C. §504(c)(2). While the fair use provisions are admittedly ambiguous, any employee who attempts to stay within the guidelines contained in this report should have an adequate good faith defense in the case of an innocently committed infringement.

If the criteria contained in this report are followed, it is our view that no copyright infringement will occur and that there will be no adverse affect on the market for copyrighted works.

(Many educational institutions will provide their employees legal counsel without charge if an infringement suit is brought against the employee for photocopying performed in the course of employment. If so, this should be noted here.)

[*Editors' Note:* The Editors' Note at the beginning of the article appeared in the original 1982 publication.]

16: COPYRIGHT PRIMER FOR CHEMICAL EDUCATORS†

Carol A. Risher

Director—Copyright and New Technology
Association of American Publishers

Copyright is the sine qua non of authorship and publishing. Without it, the publishing industry as we know it would not exist. The basis for the U.S. copyright law is found in Article I, Section 8 of the Constitution:

> "Congress shall have the power to promote the progress of science and the useful arts by securing for limited time to authors and inventors the exclusive right to their writings and discoveries."

In order to encourage creativity and hence "promote [public] progress," Congress has passed a series of copyright laws. The most recent was enacted in 1976 and took effect in 1978. I will today focus on its impact on those of you who are active in the field of chemical education, both as users of copyrighted material and as authors.

Copyright protection begins at creation — that is, upon the "fixation" of a work. Section 102 of the law provides that "protection subsists . . . in original works of authorship fixed in any tangible medium of expression now known or later developed from which they can be perceived, reproduced or otherwise communicated either directly or with the aid of a machine or device . . ." Section 101 defines "fixed" as when its embodiment is sufficiently permanent or stable [for example, on paper, film, or tape] to permit it to be perceived, reproduced or otherwise communicated for a period of more than transitory duration."

The term of protection for a work created after January 1, 1978, is the life of the author plus 50 years. For anonymous or pseudonymous works, or works-made-for-hire, (where the copyright holder is the employer) the term of protection is generally 75 years from publication or 100 years from creation, whichever first expires.

The copyright law provides the copyright holder with the exclusive right to do and to authorize others to do the following:

* to reproduce in copies
* to prepare derivative works
* to distribute copies to the public either by sale, rental or lending
* to perform the work
* to display the work

The law also recognizes limits on these rights. The most well known is Section 107, the "Fair Use" provision, which permits certain limited and reasonable uses of copyrighted material without permission of the copyright holder. There are generally four criteria to consider when determining if a particular use of copyrighted material is "fair." These four criteria are: the nature of the work, the nature of the use, the portion used as it relates to the work as a whole, and the effect of the use upon the market for or

† Presented (in part) before the Divisions of Chemical Education and Chemical Information, Symposium on "The Copyright Law," 182d National Meeting of the American Chemical Society, New York, NY, August 27, 1981.

value of the copyrighted material. Because the fair use doctrine is what is known in law as an "equitable rule of reason" and each case must be decided on an ad hoc basis, the Judiciary Committee of the House of Representatives urged that the publishers, authors, and representatives of the educational community reach an agreement on guidelines that would assist teachers in determining what Section 107 means when it relates to the classroom environment. The guidelines that were agreed to are reprinted below.

GUIDELINES

I. SINGLE COPYING FOR TEACHERS:

A single copy may be made of any of the following by or for a teacher at his or her individual request for his or her scholarly research or use in teaching or preparation to teach a class:

A. A chapter from a book;

B. An article from a periodical or newspaper;

C. A short story, short essay or short poem, whether or not from a collective work;

D. A chart, graph, diagram, drawing, cartoon or picture from a book, periodical, or newspaper.

II. MULTIPLE COPIES FOR CLASSROOM USE:

Multiple copies (not to exceed in any event more than one copy per pupil in a course) may be made by or for the teacher giving the course for classroom use or discussion, PROVIDED THAT:

A. The copying meets the tests of brevity and spontaneity as defined below; and

B. Meets the cumulative effect test as defined below; and

C. Each copy includes a notice of copyright.

DEFINITIONS:

Brevity:

i. Poetry: (a) A complete poem if less than 250 words and if printed on not more than two pages or (b) from a longer poem, an excerpt of not more than 250 words.

ii. Prose: (a) Either a complete article, story or essay of less than 2,500 words, or (b) an excerpt from any prose work of not more than 1,000 words or 10% of the work, whichever is less, but in any event a minimum of 500 words.

[Each of the numerical limits stated in "i" and "ii" above may be expanded to permit the completion of an unfinished line of a poem or of an unfinished prose paragraph.]

iii. Illustration: One chart, graph, diagram, drawing, cartoon or picture per book or per periodical issue.

iv. "Special" works: Certain works in poetry, prose or in "poetic prose" which often combine language with illustrations and which are intended sometimes for children and at other times for a more general audience and fall short of 2,500 words in their entirety. Paragraph "ii" above notwithstanding such "special works" may not be reproduced in their entirety; however, an excerpt comprising not more than two of the published pages of such special work and containing not more than 10% of the words found in the text thereof, may be reproduced.

Spontaneity:

i. The copying is at the instance and inspiration of the individual teacher, and

ii. The inspiration and decision to use the work and the moment of its use for maximum teaching effectiveness are so close in time that it would be unreasonable to expect a timely reply to a request for permission.

Cumulative Effect:

i. The copying of the material is for only one course in the school in which the copies are made.

ii. Not more than one short poem, article, story, essay or two excerpts may be copied from the same author, nor more than three from the same collective work or periodical volume during one class term.

iii. There shall not be more than nine instances of such multiple copying for one course during one class term.

[The limitations sTated in "ii" and "iii" above shall not apply to current news periodicals and newspapers and current news sections of other periodicals.]

I. PROHIBITIONS AS TO I AND II ABOVE;

Notwithstanding any of the above, the following shall be prohibited:

A. Copying shall not be used to create or to replace or substitute for anthologies, compilations or collective works. Such replacement or substitution may occur whether copies of various works or excerpts therefrom are accumulated or are reproduced and used separately.

B. There shall be no copying of or from works intended to be "consumable" in the course of study or of teaching. These include workbooks, exercises, standardized tests and test booklets and answer sheets and like consumable material.

C. Copying shall not:

a. substitute for the purchase of books, publisher's reprints, or periodicals;

b. be directed by higher authority;

c. be repeated with respect to the same item by the same teacher from term to term.

D. No charge shall be made to the student beyond the actual cost of the photocopying.

AGREED

March 19, 1976

| AD HOC COMMITTEE ON COPYRIGHT LAW REVISION By Sheldon Elliott Steinbach | AUTHOR-PUBLISHER GROUP AUTHORS LEAGUE OF AMERICA By Irwin Karp, Counsel ASSOCIATION OF AMERICAN PUBLISHERS, INC. By Alexander C. Hoffman, Chairman. Copyright Committee |

In commenting on these guidelines, the House Committee noted that the American Association of University Professors and the Association of American Law Schools criticized them as being too restrictive. However, the conclusion finally reached is clearly stated:

"The Committee believes the guidelines are a reasonable interpretation of the minimum standards of fair use. Teachers will know that copying within the guidelines is fair use. Thus, the guidelines serve the purpose of fulfilling the need for greater certainty and protection for teachers." (from House Rep. No. 94-1476)

You will note that the Classroom Guidelines specifically prohibit the unauthorized creation of anthologies. Based in part on this prohibition, seven publishers sued the Gnomon Corporation in February 1980. Gnomon is representative of several copy shops that solicit professors to select material from a variety of books and journals that will be photocopied and sold to students. This is frequently done without requesting permission from copyright holders and with no regard for the copyright law. The Gnomon lawsuit, and a similar one against Tyco Corporation, resulted in court-ordered consent decrees that require the shops to comply with the copyright law and obtain assurance from teachers that multiple copying requested is done with express permission of the copyright holder or is within the Classroom Guidelines.

The law also attempts to deal with the proliferation of Xerox machines and similar photocopying equipment and their extensive use in libraries. It does this in a special section, 108. The language of this section caused some contention between librarians and publishers before the passage of the law and remains an area of dispute today. I will not dwell on the debate but will simply mention that there are still some points of question. Copying is permitted without permission under this section for certain interlibrary loan arrangements so long as these are not "in such aggregate quantities as to substitute for a subscription to or purchase of the copyrighted material." This language was sufficiently vague to warrant another set of guidelines negotiated by the librarians, publishers, and authors with the assistance of the National Commission on New Technological Uses of Copyrighted Works (CONTU). These have become known as the CONTU guidelines and permit a library to request from another library up to 5 articles per year from a given journal title for periodicals published within five years prior to the date of the request. These Guidelines do not cover copying from periodicals older than 5 years or copying done by a library of material to which it does subscribe, socalled "intralibrary" copying. AAP and the Authors League have issued a booklet entitled "Photocopying by Academic, Public and Nonprofit Research Libraries" which gives the copyright proprietors' viewpoints on these issues. The booklet is available for $2.00 prepaid from: Association of American Publishers, 2005 Massachusetts Ave., NW, Washington, DC 20036.

Because compliance with the copyright law is so important to the Association of American Publishers, we prepared a booklet to assist educators in obtaining permission to make photocopies beyond those permitted by the copyright law. The booklet is incorporated as Appendix E of the previously mentioned "Photocopying by Academic, Public and Nonprofit Research Libraries."

Attached to this article is a reprint from that booklet. I encourage any of you who are having difficulty locating a copyright holder to call my office and ask for assistance. When copying is in excess of that permissible under the law, it is required that you ask for permission. In many cases, publishers will grant it readily and speedily. But be sure to ask.

Many of you, in addition to being users of copyrighted material, are also authors. For that reason, I will say a few words about ownership and transfer of copyright. As I indicated earlier, initial copyright ownership rests with the author upon creation, except in the case of a work-made-for-hire and certain works made on commission.

Copyright ownership may be transferred in whole or in part, which means that an author may assign, for example, the North American serial rights to someone, and to someone else the movie rights, and to someone else the translation rights, and to someone else the exclusive distribution rights for various countries, states, cities and locales. The owner of any particular exclusive right is entitled, to the extent of that right, to all of the protection and remedies accorded to the copyright owner by the U. S. copyright law.

Some of you have done research under grants from the United States Government and have wondered if the work is eligible for copyright protection because of Section 105 of the copyright law. Section 105 says: "Copyright protection . . . is not available for any work of the U. S. Government," which is defined as "work prepared by an officer or employee of the U. S. Government as part of that person's official duties." This does not relate to works merely funded by the U. S. Government. Thus, works prepared under Federal grant or contract *are* eligible for copyright protection unless the terms of the grant or contract specify otherwise.

Compliance with the copyright law is important to all of us on today's panel. I hope after hearing us, you will all share our belief in its importance.

APPENDIX E

(This is excerpted from "Explaining the New Copyright Law," published by AAP.)

How To Obtain Permissions

For uses which go beyond "fair use," permission must be granted by the copyright owner.

Under U.S. copyright law, there is a requirement for the copyright notice, which consists of the year of publication, the name of the copyright owner and, in general, any acknowledgments of other copyrighted material used in the book. In this context, the word "acknowledgment" indicates that some materials were originally published elsewhere, and that the copyright for these materials remains with the original owner. It is wise to check ... when requesting permission to duplicate, since the material in question may be the property of an author or publisher other than that of the material you are using. The page with the copyright notice is also useful in determining the actual copyright holder (particularly in the case of paperback editions, reprints, etc.) because the material is, unless marked "original edition," probably still the property of the first edition publisher. In the case of audiovisual materials, this notice is printed on the label. Some materials, graphs, charts, or photographs may not be the property of the immediate publisher or author, and thus permission to duplicate cannot be granted by that publishing house.

After checking to determine who owns the copyright on the material, the next step is to request permission to duplicate. One of the most frequent reasons cited by permissions departments for delays in answering requests of this nature is incomplete or inaccurate information contained in requests. A survey of permissions professionals conducted by the AAP determined that the following facts are necessary in order to authorize duplication of copyrighted materials.

1. Title, author and/or editor, and edition of materials to be duplicated
2. Exact material to be used, giving amount, page numbers, chapters and, if possible, a photocopy of the material
3. Number of copies to be made
4. Use to be made of duplicated materials
5. Form of distribution (classroom, newsletter, etc.)
6. Whether or not the material is to be sold
7. Type of reprint (ditto, photocopy, offset, typeset).

The request should be sent, together with a self-addressed return envelope, to the permissions department of the publisher in question. If the address of the publisher does not appear at the front of the material, it may be readily obtained in publications entitled THE LITERARY MARKETPLACE (for books) or ULRICH'S INTERNATIONAL PERIODICALS (for journals) published by the R. R. Bowker Company and available in all libraries.

Because each request must be checked closely by the publisher, it is advisable to allow enough lead time to obtain the permission before the materials are needed. Granting of a permission to duplicate is not simply a "yes" or "no" matter. (Although many publishers have a minimum or no-charge policy for such uses by noncommercial organizations, they must first review the status of the copyright to see if the power to grant duplication rights of this nature is within their scope or province.) Each such request requires a careful checking of the status of the copyright, determination of exact materials to be duplicated (which sometimes involves ordering a copy of the material from a warehouse), and assignment of author's royalties if fees are involved. Some helpful hints from those involved daily in the processing of permission include:

1. Request all permissions for a specific project at the same time
2. Don't ask for a blanket permission—it cannot, in most cases, be granted
3. Send a photocopy of the copyright page and the page or pages on which permission is requested
4. Make sure to include a return address in your request.

Sample Request for Permission

GORDON SCHOOL DISTRICT
ALPINE, TEXAS

February 6, 1975

Permissions Department
Harvey Book Company
3 West Road
Baltimore, Maryland 21214

Gentlemen:

I would like permission to duplicate the following for use in next semester's class:

Title: *Helping the School Librarian*, Second Edition
Copyright: Harvey Book Company, 1965, 1971
Author: Sara Howes and Don Johnson
Material to be duplicated: Pages 23, 24 and 57 (photocopies enclosed), all in Chapter One
Number of copies: 25
Distribution: Continuing education classroom; the material will be distributed gratis to students
Type of reprint: photocopy.

The checklists contained on the pages listed above will be used as supplementary materials for a training class.

A self-addressed envelope is enclosed for your convenience.

Please let us know what your fee will be for this permission.

Sincerely,

John Craig, Director
Continuing Education Department

MOST IMPORTANT: Check and doublecheck to make sure that all your information is complete; the more accurate the request, the more rapid the response.

17: GNOMON COPYRIGHT CASE REVISITED

Henry R. Kaufman

Ed. note: "On My Mind" regularly provides a forum in support of ALA policy 10.2, which states, in part: "Columns of American Libraries shall be kept scrupulously and faithfully open to expression of all viewpoints of interest and concern to the profession."

[*Editors' Note:* Material has been omitted at this point.]

A brief description of the copyright abuses challenged by publishers in the *Gnomon* case (and never seriously contested by Gnomon) will serve to place the legal action in its proper perspective. Gnomon is a for-profit "copy mill" with branches near several major university campuses in the Northeast. Before the publishers sued Gnomon, it was aggressively marketing a "Micro-Publishing" service that mass-produced "anthologies" of copyrighted works, without permission of the copyright owner, for resale to the public.

Gnomon's "Micro-Publishing" activities resulted in repeated copyright infringement on a massive scale. Thus, AAP readily obtained from Gnomon's shops more than 9,000 pages of materials, from 300 separate books and journals, almost all of it photocopied from published copyrighted works not in the public domain. Two of the largest anthologies (three-hole punched in the left-hand margin for convenient binding!) each contained more than 1,000 pages, primarily entire periodical articles and chapters or series of chapters from books. And Gnomon was not making just one or even a few copies of such huge "micro-published" anthologies—it made a minimum of 10 to 30 copies and in many instances made 50 to 100 copies or more.

In AAP's view, these for-profit "publishing" activities, undertaken with no effort whatsoever to secure permission from the copyright holder, amounted to a most flagrant form of copyright infringement. We find it hard to believe that any responsible group, whatever its fundamental point of view concerning copyright and fair use, would condone these extreme practices.

The *Gnomon* case was terminated with the entry of a court-ordered decree consented to by the parties. Although Gnomon issued a press release suggesting that it settled simply because it could not afford to fight the suit, in reality one must attribute the settlement to recognition of the

Henry R. Kaufman is counsel to the firm of Lankenau Kovner & Bickford in New York City. He was vice president-general counsel of the Association of American Publishers when the *Gnomon* case was prosecuted.

overwhelming evidence of copyright infringement and the futility of
contesting such a suit.

[*Editors' Note:* Material has been omitted at this point.]

It is important to remember that the case involved photocopying by a
commercial firm. Obviously, there are significant distinctions between such
a for-profit operation and the photocopying that may be done in or by a non-
profit educational institution or library. The *Gnomon* settlement does *not*
purport to state "the law" regarding nonprofit library photocopying or the
scope of "fair use" in other contexts, and AAP has never claimed that it does.
What the *Gnomon* decree does seek to secure is the cessation by
Gnomon—and other commercial photocpiers like Gnomon—of indefensible
photocopying practices. To that end, the judgment prohibits Gnomon from
making multiple copies of copyrighted published works except in carefully
defined circumstances. . . . Multiple copies *may* be reproduced when either
Gnomon itself, or its customer, has permission (specifically from the
copyright owner or through automatic permissions mechanisms like the
Copyright Clearance Center) to make the requested copies. In addition,
multiple copying may be done without such permission when it comes
within the so-called "classroom copying" guidelines incorporated in the
legislative reports accompanying the new copyright act.

[*Editors' Note:* Material has been omitted at this point.]

. . . The decree clearly applies—and is intended to apply—*only* to
works in copyright. . . . [W]ith regard to photocopying on unsupervised
floor machines[,] [t]here is specific language in the legislative history of
the copyright act that distinguishes bona fide nonsystematic individual
patron use of floor machines in not-for-profit libraries open to the public
from the installation of machines by for-profit corporations for the use of
their employees in the course of their employment. The provisions of the
Gnomon decree applicable to coin-operated machines in commercial copy
shops do *not* in any way ignore or overrule this important distinction or
change the rules regarding the use of unsupervised floor machines in
not-for-profit libraries.

[*Editors' Note:* Material has been omitted at this point. The Editor's Note at
the beginning of the article appeared in the original 1980 publication.]

18: GUIDELINES SET FOR PHOTOCOPYING MATERIAL: PUBLISHERS SETTLE WITH N.Y.U. IN COPYRIGHT VIOLATION SUIT

Daniel Wise

The settlement of a lawsuit underwritten by a publishing trade association against New York University and nine of its professors alleging copyright violations in the photocopying of materials for curriculum use was announced yesterday.

The settlement establishes a set of guidelines for the photocopying of materials for classroom use in an effort to accommodate the educational needs of the university with the publishers' rights under the Copyright Act. Lawyers for both sides said that the extent to which the "fair use" doctrine protects classroom copying is unclear.

PUBLISHERS' STATEMENT

Townsend Hoopes, president of the Association of American Publishers, the organization that financed the litigation, stated, "We are hopeful that this agreement will serve as a basis for administrative responsibility and faculty compliance at other colleges and universities."

The settlement resolves the publisher's claim of copyright infringement against N.Y.U. and its professors in *Addison-Wesley Publishing Co., Inc. et al.* v. *New York University et al.* (82 Civ. 8333), filed in the U.S. District Court for the Southern District of New York. The plaintiffs' claims against the Unique Copy Center, Inc. are still outstanding.

LEGISLATIVE HISTORY

Under the terms of the agreement, the publishers are withdrawing their lawsuit in exchange for N.Y.U.'s agreement to adopt, implement and enforce the guidelines for classroom copying incorporated in the report of the U.S. House of Representatives, accompanying the Copyright Act of 1976. According to S. Andrew Schaffer, general counsel for N.Y.U., both Yale and Johns Hopkins Universities have adopted similar guidelines, declined to speculate as to the amount of fee that would be required in any specific situation.

Among the limitations incorporated into the agreement are the following requirements:

- Complete poems of more than 250 words may not be photocopied.
- Complete prose passages of more than 2,500 words may not be photocopied.

- Excerpted prose passages of over 1,000 words or 10 percent of the total work, whichever is less, may not be photocopied.
- Material may be copied for only one course in the school.
- No more than one short poem, article, story, essay or two excerpts from the same author may be photocopied during one class term.

A University policy statement incorporated by the agreement also establishes a procedure professors may use to secure permission to photocopy materials that exceed the established limits. Jon A. Baumgarten of the firm Paskus, Gordon & Hyman, representing the plaintiffs, said publishers may or may not require a fee when permission to distribute works is granted. He declined to speculate as to the amount of fee that would be required in any specific situation.

NEW OBLIGATION

Mr. Baumgarten said that while the guidelines had existed since the passage of the Copyright Act in 1976, "to his knowledge" the obligations imposed under the agreement requiring N.Y.U. to implement and enforce the restrictions on photocopying are "new."

Under the agreement, N.Y.U. is required to take "appropriate action" against professors who fail to adhere to the limitations placed on photocopying and it is prohibited from providing a defense or indemnifying professors charged with violating the new rules. The University will nevertheless defend a professor where its general counsel's office approves the photocopying in the face of a denial from a publishing house, Mr. Schaffer said.

Prior to the commencement of the lawsuit, Mr. Baumgarten said that violations of the Copyright Act at N.Y.U. and other campuses across the country were "widespread." He added that he was hopeful that the agreement with N.Y.U. will serve as a model and "change that situation."

Mr. Schaffer acknowledged that the new rules will require that permission be obtained from the publisher "in many instances in which photocopying was done before."

The new procedures need not result in increased educational costs to students, he said, because they could read the materials in the school library. He also noted that nothing in the agreement prohibited students from making photocopies of the material for their own use.

The nine publishers who were plaintiffs in the action were Addison-Wesley Publishing Co., Alfred A. Knopf, Inc., Basic Books, Inc., Houghton Mifflin Co., Little, Brown and Company, Inc., Macmillan Publishing Co., Inc., National Association of Social Workers, Inc., Random House, Inc., and Simon and Schuster.

19: POLICY STATMENT ON PHOTOCOPYING OF COPYRIGHTED MATERIALS FOR CLASSROOM AND RESEARCH USE APPROVED BY THE BOARD OF TRUSTEES, MAY 9, 1983

New York University
Association of American Publishers

In December, 1982, nine publishers commenced a lawsuit against the University and nine members of the faculty (as well as an off-campus copy shop) alleging that the photocopying and distribution of certain course materials, without the permission of the copyright owners of the materials, violated the Copyright Act (17 U.S.C. §§101 et. seq., 90 Stat. 2541, Pub. L. 94-553). It has become increasingly clear that the subject of photocopying for classroom and research purposes is of significant concern to the faculty, who have inquired about issues such as when photocopying may be done without the consent of the copyright owner; when and how permission to photocopy should be obtained; how exposure to liability may be reduced; and under what circumstances the University will defend them against claims of copyright infringement arising out of photocopying for classroom and research use. To assist the faculty in resolving these issues, to facilitate compliance with the copyright laws, and as part of the settlement of the publishers' lawsuit, the University is issuing this Policy Statement.*

1. The principles of the copyright law are designed to promote the creation, publication, and use of works of the intellect. These principles include both the exclusive rights of copyright owners to determine certain uses of their works (in not-for-profit as well as commercial contexts), and certain exceptions including the doctrine of "fair use".

---

* This Policy Statement supersedes the document entitled "Interim Guidelines Concerning Photocopying for Classroom Research and Library Use" which was distributed on January 18, 1983.

These precepts are in the mutual interest of the university, author, and publisher communities and of the public.

2.   Under the copyright laws, certain photocopying of copyrighted works for educational purposes may take place without the permission of the copyright owner under the doctrine of "fair use" (presently set forth in Section 107 of the Copyright Act). This principle is subject to limitations, but neither the statute nor judicial decisions give specific practical guidance on what photocopying falls within fair use. To achieve for faculty greater certainty of procedure, to reduce risks of infringement or allegations thereof, and to maintain a desirable flexibility to accommodate specific needs, the following policies have been adopted by the University for use through December 31, 1985 (and thereafter, unless modified). On or before December 31, 1985 the University will review these policies to determine their effect and whether modifications, based on our experience, might be needed. If members of the faculty experience any problems or have suggestions, they are asked to communicate them to the Office of Legal Counsel.

A.   The Guidelines set forth in Appendix I are to be used to determine whether or not the prior permission of the copyright owner is to be sought for photocopying for research and classroom use.* If the proposed photocopying is not permitted under the Guidelines in Appendix I, permission to copy is to be sought. An explanation of how permissions may be sought and a procedure for furnishing to the administration information concerning the responses by copyright owners to requests for permission is set forth in Appendix II. After permission has been sought, copying should be undertaken only if permission has been granted, and in accordance with the terms of the permission, except as provided in the next paragraph.

B.   The doctrine of fair use may now or hereafter permit specific photocopying in certain situations, within limitations, beyond those specified in the Guidelines* or

---

*   To minimize intrusiveness and over-centralization, the respon-
    sibility for making this determination will continue to reside
    with the individual faculty member.   In making this
    determination, the faculty member should carefully consider
    all sections of the attached Guidelines.

*   The Guidelines contained in Appendix I were negotiated by
    education, author, and publishing representatives in 1976
    and were incorporated in the House of Representatives report
    accompanying the Copyright Act of 1976. The introductory
    explanation of the Guidelines in the House Report describes
    their relationship to the doctrine of fair use as follows:

those that might be agreed to by the copyright owner. In order to preserve the ability of individual faculty members to utilize the doctrine of fair use in appropriate circumstances without incurring the risk of having personally to defend an action by a copyright owner who may disagree as to the limits of fair use, a faculty member who has sought permission to photocopy and has not received such permission (or has received permission contingent upon conditions that the faculty member considers inappropriate) may request a review of the matter by General Counsel of the University. If upon review the General Counsel determines that some or all of the proposed photocopying is permitted by the copyright law, the General Counsel will so advise the faculty member. In that event, should any such photocopying by the faculty member thereafter give rise to a claim of copyright infringement, the University will defend and indemnify the faculty member against any such claim in accordance with the provisions of the Board of Trustees policy on Legal Protection of Faculty (Faculty Handbook [1982 ed.] pp. 109-112).

C. In the absence of the determination and advice by the General Counsel referred to in paragraph B, or in the event that permission has not been first requested by the faculty member as provided in paragraph A, no defense or indemnification by the University shall be provided to a faculty member whose photocopying gives rise to a claim of copyright infringement.

Agreement on Guidelines for Classroom Copying in Not-for-Profit Educational Institutions

With Respect to Books and Periodicals

The purpose of the following guidelines is to state the minimum standards of educational fair use under Section 107 of H.R. 2223. The parties agree that the conditions determining the extent of permissible copying for educational purposes may change in the future; that certain types of copying permitted under these guidelines may not be permissible in the future; and conversely that in the future other types of copying not permitted under these guidelines may be permissible under revised guidelines.

Moreover, the following statement of guidelines is not intended to limit the types of copying permitted under the standards of fair use under judicial decision and which are stated in Section 107 of the Copyright Revision Bill. There may be instances in which copying which does not fall within the guidelines stated below may nonetheless be permitted under the criteria of fair use.

[*Editors' Note:* Appendix I and the sample letter in Appendix II have been omitted here.]

APPENDIX II
PERMISSIONS

A.   How to Obtain Permission

When a proposed use of photocopied material requires a faculty member to request permission, communication of complete and accurate information to the copyright owner will facilitate the request. The Association of American Publishers suggests that the following information be included to expedite the process.

1.   Title, author and/or editor, and edition of materials to be duplicated.

2.   Exact material to be used, giving amount, page numbers, chapters and, if possible, a photocopy of the material.

3.   Number of copies to be made.

4.   Use to be made of duplicated materials.

5.   Form of distribution (classroom, newsletter, etc.).

6.   Whether or not the material is to be sold.

7.   Type of reprint (ditto, photocopy, offset, typeset).

The request should be sent,* together with a self-addressed return envelope, to the permissions department of the publisher in question. If the address of the publisher does not appear at the front of the material, it may be obtained from The Literary Marketplace (for books) or Ulrich's International Periodicals (for journals), both published by the R. R. Bowker Company. For purposes of proof, and to define the scope of the permission, it is important that the permission be in writing.

The process of considering permission requests requires time for the publisher to check the status and ownership of rights and related matters and to evaluate the request. It is advisable, therefore, to allow sufficient lead time. In some instances the publisher may assess a fee for permission, which may be passed on to students who receive copies of the photo-copied material.

B.   Gathering Data on Responses to Requests for Permission to Photocopy

In order to help assess the effect of this Policy Statement upon the faculty it will be useful for the administration to compile data on responses by copyright owners. Each member of the faculty is therefore requested to forward a dated copy of each request for permission and a dated copy of each response to the Office of Legal Counsel, Bobst Library, 11th Floor, 70 Washington Square South, New York, New York 10012.

20: COPYRIGHT: AN ACRL RESOLUTION

Prepared by the ACRL Copyright Committee
Barbara Rystrom, Chair

In June 1983 the Association of American Publishers (AAP) sent a letter to college and university administrators urging them to adopt as their copyright compliance policy the agreement which New York University (NYU) accepted as part of the May 9, 1983, out-of-court settlement of the copyright infringement lawsuit brought against it by a group of publishers and coordinated by the AAP.[1] Out-of-court settlements in lawsuits are not imposed by the courts and do not set legal precedents; therefore, such settlements are not necessarily appropriate models for entities not a party to the settlement.

The NYU policy states that faculty can expect the University to defend and indemnify them in the event of a claim of copyright infringement only if the faculty member has followed the guidelines incorporated in the policy, gotten permission from the copyright owner, or cleared the copying with the General Counsel of the University. The guidelines incorporated in the policy are familiar to copyright observers, because they are from the Agreement on Guidelines for Classroom Copying in Not-for-Profit Educational Institutions with Respect to Books and Periodicals (hereafter referred to as the Classroom Guidelines). Designed to clarify the principle of fair use as it applies to copying for classroom instruction, and to provide "greater certainty and protection for teachers," the Classroom Guidelines were negotiated by primary and secondary school educators with authors and publishers, and were incorporated into the House Report on the copyright law.[2] The American Associa-

[1]*Chronicle of Higher Education*, April 20, 1983, pp.1, 22.

[2]U.S. House of Representatives. Committee on the Judiciary. *Report on Copyright Law Revision*, H.R. 94-1476, September 3, 1976, pp.68–70, with corrections in the *Congressional Record*, September 21, 1976, pp. H10727–28.

tion of University Professors and the Association of American Law Schools were not parties to the agreement, which they felt was too restrictive in the college and university context. The Association of Research Libraries has described the Classroom Guidelines as "unsuitable in the context of postsecondary education," and the American Library Association has stated that the Classroom Guidelines "normally would not be realistic in the University setting."[3]

Though the Classroom Guidelines clearly state the purpose is "to state the minimum and not the maximum standards of educational fair use," experience shows that such guidelines are often referred to as if they provided outer limits; for example, the NYU policy says that permission is required for copying "not permitted under the (Classroom) Guidelines." And those Guidelines are truly limiting. Among other details, the Cumulative Effect section indicates that a given item can be copied "for only one course in the school in which the copies are made," and that "not more than one short poem, article, story, essay or two excerpts may be copied from the same author, nor more than three from the same collective work or periodical volume during one class term." The Brevity section limits copying of poetry to "a complete poem if less than 250 words" or "from a longer poem, an excerpt of not more than 250 words," and copying of prose to less than 2,500 words. It is clear that these stipulations are unworkable in a postsecondary setting.

The ACRL Copyright Committee shares the opinion that the Classroom Guidelines are not appropriate for colleges and universities and that, therefore, the NYU policy, which incorporates them, is not an appropriate model. The ALA Model Policy Concerning College and University Photocopying for Classroom, Research and Library Reserve Use, reprinted in *C&RL News*, April 1982, pp. 127–31, offers a much more pertinent interpretation of fair use. In addition, several institutions have devised copyright compliance policies which are appropriate for colleges and universities. Therefore, at its Midwinter 1984 meetings, the Committee drafted the following resolution, which was adopted by the ACRL Board at its meeting at the end of the conference.

The ACRL Copyright Committee would welcome comment on this and any other copyright related issue, and urges college and university librarians to keep it informed about local developments and problems in copyright at their institutions. Please contact the chair at the University of Georgia Libraries, Athens, GA 30602; (404) 542-3274.

---

[3]Association of Research Libraries, "Reproduction of Copyrighted Materials for Classroom Use: A Briefing Paper for Teaching Faculty and Administrators," July 1983, available from ARL; "Model Policy Concerning College and University Photocopying for Classroom, Research and Library Reserve Use," *C&RL News*, April 1982, pp.127, 129.

The resolution

Whereas, the 1982 lawsuit settlement between New York University (NYU) and nine publishers calls for NYU to adopt campus wide guidelines on photocopying instructional materials which duplicate almost verbatim the copying standards set forth in the Agreement on Guidelines for Classroom Copying in Not for Profit Educational Institutions with Respect to Books and Periodicals;

Whereas, the Agreement on Guidelines for Classroom Copying, developed by primary and secondary school educators and publishers, was criticized by the American Association of University Professors and the American Association of Law Schools as too restrictive for classroom application at the university level;

Whereas, the Association of American Publishers has openly and aggressively encouraged the NYU guidelines be adopted by all colleges and universities;

Whereas, the American Library Association's Model Policy Concerning College and University Photocopying for Classroom, Research and Library Reserve Use, which is more appropriate to academic institutions and their libraries, offers a legitimate and less restrictive interpretation of Fair Use than the NYU guidelines;

Whereas, other academic institutions have adopted acceptable and legitimate copyright guidelines other than those resulting from the NYU settlement. Now, therefore be it resolved,

That colleges and universities and their libraries should continue to interpret the Copyright Act in a manner that is in the spirit of the law and consistent with the rights and needs of both copyright proprietors and the academic community, and need not conform to the guidelines as set forth in the NYU settlement.

21: OFF-AIR COPYING UPDATE: GUIDELINES, ADVICE TO EDUCATORS

Eileen Cooke

Director, ALA Washington Office

"Safe-harbor" guidelines for off-air taping of copyrighted programs were officially recognized Oct. 14 when House copyright subcommittee chair Robert Kastenmeier inserted them in the *Congressional Record* (see box).

Voicing his congratulations and pleasure in announcing that agreement had finally been reached by the negotiating committee of copyright owners and educators, he said he shared their view "that these guidelines reach an appropriate balance between proprietary rights of copyright owners and the instructional needs of educational institutions."

Along with the nine-point fair-use guidelines, Kastenmeier also put into the record a transmittal letter from the committee co-chairs, Eileen Cooke of ALA and Leonard Wasser of Writers Guild of America, East, and two letters reflecting disparate views from the Motion Picture Association of America and the Association of Media Producers.

After having paddled around in the murky waters of copyright for over two years and finally anchoring on these compromise guidelines, negotiators now see fog ahead. On Oct. 19, the 9th U.S. Circuit Court of Appeals in San Francisco overturned a Dec. 1979 court decision in the controversial Betamax case.* The lower-court decision, favoring off-air taping, was one of the factors that sparked various groups into action on the off-air taping issue.

Four bills have already been introduced to exempt home use or private noncommercial recording of copyrighted works on video recorders from copyright infringement.

Meanwhile, the Washington-based, education community's Ad Hoc Committee on Copyright Law has issued the following advisory statement on the off-air recording guidelines. They urge the educational community to live up to the spirit of the copyright law and to assume responsibility for monitoring educational practices. At the same time, the Ad Hoc Committee asks all members to be on the alert and to report any instances in which a copyright proprietor tries to restrict the application of these fair-use guidelines.

Ed. note. An Oct. 31 press release from the Library of Congress reported that: "Register of Copyrights David Ladd has called for 'thought, reflection, and care' in responding to a recent U.S. Court of Appeals decision holding that . . . users of home video recorders are liable for damages if they use the recorders to tape copyrighted television programs off the air. . . . Mr. Ladd said that if the U.S. Supreme Court takes the case on appeal, as is expected, a final decision is more than a year away. In the meantime, there is time to frame legislation that would balance the need for public access to video programs with the need to compensate the creators of such programs."

Guidelines for off-air recording of broadcast programming for educational purposes

In March 1979 Rep. Robert Kastenmeier (D-Wis), chair of the House Subcommittee on Courts, Civil Liberties, and Administration of Justice, appointed a negotiating committee of 19 educational users and copyright proprietors to write guidelines applying the "fair use" provision of the copyright law to the recording, retention, and use of television programs in classrooms (*AL*, July/August, pp. 413 and 426).

Chaired by Eileen Cooke of ALA and Leonard Wasser of the Writers Guild of America, the committee agreed on these guidelines and transmitted them to Kastenmeier Sept. 28. They were published in the Oct. 14 *Congressional Record*, pp. E4750–E4752.

1. The guidelines were developed to apply only to off-air recording by non-profit educational institutions.

2. A broadcast program may be recorded off-air simultaneously with broadcast transmission (including simultaneous cable re-transmission) and retained by a non-profit educational institution for a period not to exceed the first forty-five (45) consecutive calendar days after date of recording. Upon conclusion of such retention period, all off-air recordings must be erased or destroyed immediately. "Broadcast programs" are television programs transmitted by television stations for reception by the general public without charge.

3. Off-air recordings may be used once by individual teachers in the course of relevant teaching activities, and repeated once only when instructional reinforcement is necessary, in classrooms and similar places devoted to instruction within a single building, cluster or campus, as well as in the homes of students receiving formalized home instruction, during the first ten (10) consecutive school days in the forty-five (45) day calendar day retention period. "School days" are school session days—not counting weekends, holidays, vacations, examination periods, or other scheduled interruptions—within the forty-five (45) calendar day retention period.

4. Off-air recordings may be made only at the request of and used by individual teachers, and may not be regularly recorded in anticipation of requests. No broadcast program may be recorded off-air more than once at the request of the same teacher, regardless of the number of times the program may be broadcast.

5. A limited number of copies may be reproduced from each off-air recording to meet the legitimate needs of teachers under these guidelines. Each such additional copy shall be subject to all provisions governing the original recording.

6. After the first ten (10) consecutive school days, off-air recordings may be used up to the end of the forty-five (45) calendar day retention period only for teacher evaluation purposes, *i.e.*, to determine whether or not to include the broadcast program in the teaching curriculum, and may not be used in the recording institution for student exhibition or any other non-evaluation purpose without authorization.

7. Off-air recordings need not be used in their entirety, but the recorded programs may not be altered from their original content. Off-air recordings may not be physically or electronically combined or merged to constitute teaching anthologies or compilations.

8. All copies of off-air recordings must include the copyright notice on the broadcast program as recorded.

9. Educational institutions are expected to establish appropriate control procedures to maintain the integrity of these guidelines.

Advisory Statement
on Off-Air Recording Guidelines

"The Ad Hoc Committee on Copyright Law is pleased to announce that an agreement has been reached on guidelines for off-air recordings of television programs for educational use.

"Wide divergence of views on the proper application of the copyright law to off-the-air recording of television broadcasts characterized the period of development of the Copyright Act of 1976. Congressman Robert C. Kastenmeier of the House Subcommittee on Courts, Civil Liberties and Administration of Justice appointed a negotiating group consisting of representatives of some 25 organizations with off-air taping interests. The organizations are diverse in nature, ranging from producers of copyright materials, creative guilds, and owners of copyright materials to those representing all of education. The guidelines reflect the consensus of the committee members on an effective and acceptable application of 'fair use' to off-air recording and use in schools of broadcast television programs for educational purposes. It must be noted, however, that not all of the representatives of copyright proprietors agreed to the new guidelines, and that some educational representatives expressed reservations about their scope.

"In accepting this agreement, copyright owner representatives have agreed that copying and use of broadcasts that conform with the agreed guidelines should not be the subject of claims of infringement by copyright owners. The representatives of the education community have agreed that the education community must live up to the spirit of the law, and that we must be responsible in a major way for monitoring educational practices.

"The committee negotiators of this agreement cannot, of course, change the copyright law as enacted by Congress or bind any court to a particular interpretation of that law. Their joint issuance of these guidelines, however, reflects their carefully considered view of how the law can be satisfactorily applied in the mutual interest of the proprietors, the disseminators, the teachers, and the students. From the point of view of educators generally, it is recognized that there are likely to be instances in which adherence to the letter of these guidelines would interfere with legitimate needs of educational procedures. In pursuit of those needs, particular educators may deem uses beyond the guidelines to be appropriate, fair, and within the law. It must also be recognized, however, that individual copyright owners, for their part, are not constrained by these guidelines to refrain from a claim of infringement in what they consider to be unfair application of the agreed upon guidelines.

"It must be emphasized that even though these guidelines are now law, the courts will look with great deference to them in any infringement action. Courts will always look to the state of the art and common business practice when interpreting an unclear legal matter. Therefore, the guidelines are especially important.

"The Ad Hoc Committee alerts its membership that the guidelines contained in the agreement *only* apply to copyright materials. Programs that are not copyrighted do not enjoy the protection of the guidelines. They may be copied in toto and kept literally forever.

"Similarly, the Ad Hoc Committee urges all of its members to be on the alert and to report any instances where a copyright proprietor tries to restrict the application of these guidelines." ☐

[*Editors' Note:* The Editor's Note at the beginning of the article appeared in the original 1981 publication.]

22: COPYING SOFTWARE: CRIME IN THE CLASSROOM?

Lauren T. Letellier

I T IS A BOON TO EDU-
CATORS WHO WANT TO MAKE GOOD QUAL-
ITY SOFTWARE AVAILABLE THROUGHOUT
THEIR SCHOOL OR DISTRICT. IT IS A RELIEF
FOR ADMINISTRATORS PLAGUED BY SHRINK-
ING BUDGETS AND CHRONIC FINANCIAL
WORRIES. IT IS EASY; IT IS ACCEPTED.
AND IT IS VERY CLEARLY AGAINST THE LAW.

The reproducing of copyrighted microcomputer software has become one of the
most controversial and difficult topics of the electronic age, and nowhere is the
question debated more heatedly than in educational circles. On the one hand are
teachers who believe that because they are acting in the public interest, they
should have the right to copy educational programs. On the other hand are the
producers of those programs, who feel they are not being compensated for their
efforts. In this special report, *EL* takes a look at the arguments raised by both
sides—and at the law that's designed to settle the issue.

*Lauren Letellier, a former teacher and journalist, now
works for a legal book publisher in New York City.
This is her first article for* Electronic Learning.

THE EDUCATORS' ■ SIDE ■

TEACHERS AND ADMINISTRA-tors who are in the habit of copying software cite the following points as justification for the practice.

● **The Scarcity of Quality Programs**

"Let's face it," says Jack Turner, a computer-using teacher in Eugene, Oregon, "the vast majority of programs are junk. Three out of four programs from mail houses, for example, are pedagogically worthless, or not what they claim to be. If teachers can get their hands on a good program, they are naturally going to copy it."

● **The "Public Interest"**

"The fact that it's happening in a school," Turner explains, "tends to soothe the violators. On the teachers' side is the conviction that what they're doing is not for personal gain. Schools are non-profit institutions and when teachers act on behalf of their students, they view the action as altruistic." He hesitates, then continues, "The question of conscience then is not so difficult. I've known many teachers who copy software for exactly these reasons. They've put their conscience on idle for three minutes to benefit their students."

In some cases, the question of conscience does not even arise. Greg Smith, Director of Educational Marketing for Apple, remembers hearing the teacher of one of his children proudly tell a Parents' Night audience that she was saving the taxpayers' dollars by copying software. "School people," he says, "just don't perceive the software protection laws as pertaining to them."

● **Software Abuse**

Teachers also plead that the nature of software use in the classroom absolutely requires available backup copies and accuse manufacturers of insensitivity to these special problems. Inexperienced students, a stray smear of mustard from the lunchroom, a kid with a magnet in his pocket—all of these play havoc with the fragile cassette or diskette.

● **Cost**

But for many teachers, the real crux of the issue is a matter of simple economics. "Say you have 76 stations in a school," hypothesizes Stan Silverman, President of the National Institute for Microbased Learning. "Schools are not in a position to buy in multiples of 76. We are hardware intensive, and when it costs so much for hardware, you can't ask a school board to come back and buy this exceedingly expensive software. I would never purchase software that didn't allow for copying, at least for archival purposes.

"We all understand the problems of software producers," he acknowledges. "But there are two ethical considerations in this situation. It's unethical to copy, but it's also unethical to develop these materials for use with the hardware—in which so much money has already been invested—and then turn around and make it unavailable to the users."

THE PRODUCERS' ■ SIDE ■

THE WRITERS AND MARKET-ers of these programs, meanwhile, don't think they're being unethical at all. What they *are* thinking about is the difficulty of getting a financial return on their investment.

In the May 1, 1981, *Wall Street Journal*, it was estimated that illegal copying of microcomputer courseware costs the software industry between $12 and $36 million annually, or roughly 6–18% of total annual sales. While opinions vary on how much of the "pirating" is actually being done in schools, industry sources certainly concur on its effects. "The level and quality of software is determined by income," asserts George Blank, Editorial Director of Creative Computing in Morris Plains, New Jersey. "And we cannot afford to invest more than we can recover from it. The sooner the public realizes this, the sooner better quality software will be available. Basically, because of the copying problem, I have to decide how much money I can afford to lose each year, and then I produce that much educational software."

In order to protect their investment, software manufacturers and publishers have resorted to a variety of marketing strategies. Some, such as Addison-Wesley, attempt to price back-up copies so low—almost at the price it would cost to reproduce—that there is no incentive to copy. Others, including Radio Shack, have developed a technique of implanting a transparent device in the program that limits the number of copies one can make out of their software. Charles Phillips, Radio Shack's Senior Vice President of Special Markets, takes a hard line on copying. "We acknowledge that it's a problem—that's why we've introduced this method of limiting the number of back-up copies one can make. Our philosophy of software," he continues, "is to price it reasonably, realistically, and trust in this fairness and our reputation to sell the product." Phillips is scornful of proposals for *licensing* software, such as the one suggested by a group called Computer Using Educators (CUE) in San Mateo, CA. (*See box.*) "I only have two words for them—good luck. Let's face it. We're living in the Age of the Pirate. People are using everything from tape recorders to satellite transmissions to steal. We're in this business to make profits—we owe it to a great many people. It is not fair to stand by and watch people take what you've developed."

In spite of what Phillips says, one major

software producer—Science Research Associates (SRA)—has foregone all technical protection strategies, and is applying a licensing agreement to its software. The company claims that this policy has been a successful deterrent to illegal copying. SRA Legal Counsel Thomas Karle explains the agreement as follows: "Essentially, the license gives the user possession and use of the courseware. A school system would sign the agreement only once, and all other purchases in that system would apply under the original agreement. The school agrees not to copy the material, but they can do anything else with it that they want."

In terms of enforcement, Karle admits that this is a cumbersome way of doing business. The SRA licensing agreement, he says, is effective only as a psychological disincentive—it draws attention to the observation of the copyright laws. What he would really prefer, he continues, would be a further refinement of those software copyright laws by Congress.

But that, unfortunately, is more easily said than done.

L AWMAKERS WHO'VE ATtempted to address the controversy over software copyrights have been faced with a peculiar dilemma: the technology moves faster than they do. As a result, up until a year ago Congress could do little more than preserve the status quo, applying general copyright law to the new programs and programmers. The 1976 Copyright Reform Act promised that as soon as the issues and problems of the new technology became "sufficiently developed," a "definitive legislative solution" would be formulated and enacted.

That solution, it has quickly become apparent, will come neither quickly nor easily. A first step, nevertheless, has been taken in the form of Public Law 96-517, which Congress passed in December of 1980. It amends common copyright law to grant the owner of a particular computer program the right to copy it *if and only if* (1) such a copy is "an essential step in the utilization of the program in conjunction with a machine," or (2) the copy is for archival purposes only, i.e., to serve as a back-up in case the original is lost or destroyed. Together, these exemptions are known as the "fair use" doctrine.

Some copying, then, is perfectly legal; the law as it now stands adequately responds to educators' claims that they require back-up copies simply to protect their investment. That, however, is where the line is drawn. In a brief prepared for the National Audio-Visual Association, Inc. (NAVA), lawyer and copyright specialist Thomas M. Gould states: "In practical terms, a school *cannot* purchase one microcomputer program copy or one course program and reproduce it in quantity for use with several microcomputer hardware systems.... The economics of this practice are understandable, but the practice is absolutely a violation of law against which 'fair use' defense will, and should, fail."

T HE LAW CERTAINLY SEEMS clear enough. Why shouldn't it settle the issue once and for all? Part of the explanation lies in the fact that copying software is so technically easy. If it weren't, the temptation might not be so powerful—and the law easier to enforce. In addition, some observers suggest, the casual use of the photocopying machine in schools and businesses may have made the "innocent" crime of software-copying an easy one for teachers to accept. Concedes Delores Radtke, National Consultant for Electronic Publishing at McGraw-Hill: "Teachers are in such a habit of reproducing workbook pages that it's an easy matter for them to take a cassette and make a copy without thinking of the illegality of doing so." Finally, New York Teacher Center Coordinator Ann Spindel suggests plain ignorance might also play a part. If teachers were simply "re-alerted" to the existence of copyright laws, she maintains, enforcement would not be such a problem.

The facts are, however, that right now enforcement *is* a problem; that teachers often cannot afford to buy what little good-quality software is available to them; and that the commercial producers of educational software often do not recoup their original investment. Therein lies the real hazard of the present situation; for if the profits in writing and marketing educational software dry up, some producers warn, so may the supply of software. It will be a challenge—and a responsibility—for both educators and producers to find a satisfactory solution before that happens.

23: LIVING IN THE GAP OF AMBIGUITY; AN ATTORNEY'S ADVICE TO LIBRARIANS ON THE COPYRIGHT LAW

Lewis I. Flacks

In a short and thoughtful book, former Attorney General Edward Levi observed that, in a sense, all law tends to be unclear; further, that if the law was completely certain, organized society might well become impossible. The "gap of ambiguity," he asserted, is a necessary condition which enables us to confront and resolve our differences, short of force or other disorder. Much of this philosophy affects the treatment of library and archival reproductions under the new copyright law.

In the six months since the bill for the general revision of the copyright law became an act, there have been scores of symposia, conferences, and published articles attempting to prepare dozens of constituencies for the magic day, January 1, 1978, when PL 94-553 finally becomes effective. Among all the groups concerned with copyright, libraries have probably been the most active and closest students of the new law.

The provisions in the copyright act bearing on library services, particularly interlibrary loan arrangements, were hammered out in long and difficult negotiations. The resulting compromise evoked considerable concern in some segments of the library community, not to mention author and publisher groups.

If the old cliché is to be believed—that the hallmark of a successful com-

promise is widespread dissatisfaction—then perhaps Sections 107 and 108 are a success. But in this case, I believe, the dissatisfaction I have encountered tends to arise out of misplaced expectations about what the law would do, rather than criticism of what it actually achieved.

For more than a year I have been talking with library groups about the bill, now law. I rarely encounter the kind of hostility I expected after witnessing the negotiations leading to Section 108 and the guidelines. By and large, most librarians now seem anxious to live within the letter of the law, if the letter can only be explained to them.

Having spent my whole professional life with the Copyright Office as an attorney and not a librarian, I was used to dealing exclusively with the internal logic of the law. But, as Charles Black says, law does not deal with law any more than a knife deals with other knives; a knife deals with cutting. Applying the new copyright to the everyday life of American libraries and archives turned out to be more difficult than I had expected.

This brief article is an effort to share with a wider audience part of the experience of my talks with librarians. I have selected nine frequently encountered questions which, much to my discomfort, I have had to answer. Some are relatively simple and permit clear answers; others are more general and go to the heart of the carefully calculated ambiguity of the law. In these areas, the answers are neither simple nor necessarily helpful—at least not for day-to-day business. But they may help librarians to think about the copyright law and accept the task of working out the future in concert with copyright proprietors and authors.

Roadmap to Section 108

Before turning to the specific questions, it may be useful to make a few observations about how to approach Section 108 of the copyright law. Confronted for the first time, it appears to some librarians as an impenetrable maze. Actually, it is a neatly ordered provision. Without going into analytic detail, I'd like to provide a sort of roadmap.

First, Subsection (a) sets out the requirements for determining what kind of libraries and archives are eligible to claim the benefits of the rights of reproduction and distribution set out in the rest of Section 108;

Second, Subsections (a) and (b) concern the extent to which libraries and archives may reproduce unpublished and published works respectively, for internal purposes of maintaining the collection (i.e., not reproductions for library users);

Third, Subsections (d) and (e) concern the extent to which libraries and archives may reproduce copies of works for users. Subsection (d) covers the reproduction and distribution of contributions to periodicals and small parts of other works, and (e) covers similar activities with respect to entire works;

Fourth, Subsection (f) is a four-part "laundry list" of miscellaneous but important items. The list includes questions of liability of libraries or users in connection with the unsupervised use of reproducing equipment, reproduction and distribution rights with respect to audiovisual news programs, contractual restrictions, and "fair use";

Fifth, Subsection (g) puts a general lid on the exercise of reproduction and distribution rights set out earlier;

Lewis I. Flacks is an attorney on the staff of the U.S. Copyright Office. The views expressed in this article are personal and do not necessarily reflect the opinions or policies of the Copyright Office or the Library of Congress. Copyright is not claimed in this article.

Reprinted from *Am. Libr.* **8**:252-257(1977); cartoons reproduced by permission of Bion Smalley.

Sixth, Subsection (h) sets out types of works which are generally excluded from the rights of reproduction and distribution granted by 108(d) and (e); and,

Seventh, Subsection (i) provides for a review of the entire section five years after the effective date of the law.

Having set out the framework of the section, let's turn to some specific questions of interpretation which have arisen.

1. Are libraries and librarians responsible for the potentially illegal use of coin-operated photocopying machines by readers or users of the library?

In general, they are not. Section 108 (f) (1) establishes the rule that a library and its employees are exempt from liability arising out of the unsupervised use of reproducing equipment located on its premises, provided the equipment displays a cautionary notice with respect to possible copyright liability arising out of the machine's use. Though the legislative history of this provision is actually somewhat scanty, common sense is probably the best guide to interpretation.

The key element in this subsection of the law is not really the cautionary notice; rather, it is the word "unsupervised." The notice required by the section is not a talismanic device for avoiding liability for all uses of repro-

ducing equipment, only unsupervised uses.

Perhaps one should keep in mind the fact that "unsupervised" is a potentially elastic word. On the one extreme, it can mean comprehensive "supervision"—actually regulating physical access to and uses of reproducing equipment: At the other end, it might well include less extensive, but discretionary, controls—an institutional decision to specifically refer users from its copying centers to the self-service machines when the request is clearly an infringement of copyright.

2. Can replacement copies of one or two issues of a periodical be obtained under Section 108, when back issues are available only in bound volumes?

Section 108 (c) allows the reproduction of a published, copyrighted, work solely for the purposes of replacing a damaged, deteriorating, lost or stolen copy, if, after a reasonable investigation, the library determines that "an unused replacement cannot be obtained at a fair price."

The legislative history is silent on the precise question, and the issue reduces itself down to what is a "fair price"—for what you are seeking and not necessarily for what is being sold. Thirty-five hundred dollars is a fair price for some auto-

mobiles, but rather high if one is only interested in buying a new tire. Similarly, the unavailability of a replacement issue of a periodical, except as a part of an entire back-ordered volume, may mean that the issue is not available at a fair price.

3. Are restrictions imposed on manuscript materials in deeds of gift rendered ineffective by the reproduction rights accorded to libraries under Section 108 (b)?

No. While Section 108 (b) allows the facsimile reproduction of unpublished works solely for purposes of preservation, security, or research deposit with another library, Section 108 (f) provides that nothing in Section 108, "in any way affects . . . any contractual obligation assumed at any time by the library or archives when it obtained a copy or phonorecord of a work in its collections."

Somewhat to my surprise, a fair number of questions involving contractual restrictions affecting donated materials continue to arise. What does the law allow a library or archive to do with tapes of speeches, lectures, and unpublished dissertations which are deposited by graduate students? What all these issues seem to have in common is the acquisition by a library of unpublished materials without any guidance as to what uses the donor, or the author, would regard as acceptable. Classically, everyone in a position to know is dead or otherwise hopelessly out of touch.

Some talented copyright lawyers have pointed out that, in this kind of "classical" situation, all rights of reproduction and distribution which would ordinarily apply to a particular type of work would continue to apply, since there is no agreement to the contrary. But the problem with this answer—an answer I am inclined to accept—is that, in fact, there may have been understandings limiting access to or use of donated materials. The ill will of a donor or an author can be as significant to an archive as outright illegality under the copyright laws.

If the truth be known, the copyright law rarely, if ever, addresses such questions with any great specificity. It is not intended to provide a comprehensive listing of answers to every conceivable question. Like most property law, it establishes a general regime, with some desirable presumptions and outright prohibitions. Within its boundaries, we are left to sort things out pretty much on our own. The real answer to the problem of what to do with unpublished materials, in the absence of express restrictions, is to seek to resolve those issues at the time the materials are created, as in oral history programs, or

"So, at last we've caught up with you, Fritz! May we reproduce your 1941 'Letter to the Fuehrer' in a library exhibition catalog?"

acquired, as in the case of dissertations and the like.

4. What are the consequences of exceeding the copying limitations of the CONTU Guidelines for the Proviso of Subsection 108 (g) (2)?

A straightforward question that may not have an easy, single answer. Much of the difficulty lies in understanding the place of the guidelines under the new law. The Conference Report on the new law, which prints the guidlelines, notes:

. . . the guidelines are not intended as, and cannot be considered, explicit rules or directions governing any and all cases, now or in the future. It is recognized that their pur-

pose is to provide guidance in the most commonly encountered interlibrary photocopying situations, that they are not intended to be limiting or determinative in themselves or with respect to other situations, and that they deal with an evolving situation that will undoubtedly require their continuous reevaluation and adjustment. With these qualifications, the conference committee agrees that the guidelines are a reasonable interpretation of the proviso of Section 108(g)(2) in the most common situations to which they apply today.

These are all significant qualifications, and to me, at least, they support the notion that the purpose of the guidelines was not to mark out a sharp boundary between legality and illegality, but

rather to provide a limited area of predictability in an evolving field of the law which had been intentionally left ambiguous.

The much-maligned guidelines are not *the answer* libraries and publishers had been struggling to reach for well over a decade. In 1964, the preliminary draft for a revised copyright law contained a brief provision governing library reproductions, loosely related to the new law's Sections 108(a), (d), and (e). It drew considerable heat, and the Register of Copyrights noted:

Opposition to the provision was equally strong on both sides but for exactly opposite reasons, with one side arguing that the provision would permit things that are illegal now and the other side maintaining that it would prevent things that are legal now. Both agreed on one thing: that the section should be dropped.

Some touch of this earlier conundrum survives in Section 108 and the guidelines. Given the broad and uncertain reach of Section 108 (g) (2), a minimal agreement on interlibrary loan was required, but such an agreement had to be somewhat open-ended.

5. Is the doctrine of "fair use" relevant to library photocopying, or does Section 108 regulate the area exclusively? And, by the way, whatever happened to the Williams and Wilkins case?

Section 108 (f) (4) provides that nothing in Section 108 "in any way affects the right of fair use as provided by Section 107 . . . ." If, as the House Report says, "Section 107 is intended to restate the present judicial doctrine of fair use, not to change, narrow or enlarge it in any way," then it would seem that Williams and Wilkins is alive and as well as it can be, under the existing law of fair use.

Of course, there is considerable debate over exactly how much vitality Williams and Wilkins has. It has been observed that the Supreme Court's 4–4 affirmance of the Court of Claims decision, under other rulings considering the effect of such a split, robs the case of any value as precedent for the future. This is very interesting, but considering the narrowness of the Court of Claims decision, it is doubtful whether such a highly technical argument is terribly important in the long run. Regardless of how hard one hacks away at Williams and Wilkins, it's still there in the morning.

The real significance of the case, in any event, is not in the force of its holding, but in the demonstration of its logic: the reproduction and distribution of

"What is 'fair use'?"

resources will necessarily be diverted to new administrative burdens. I am not sure how realistic this concern is. The ordinary interlibrary loan transaction routinely generates some paperwork, quite probably in enough detail to identify the material requested, as well as the institutions involved, to satisfy the record-keeping requirement. Since no set form is required, it may be possible for libraries subject to the guidelines simply to retain existing forms for the prescribed period.

7. *When will the Copyright Office publish its regulations governing library photocopying? When will the Copyright Office publish regulations governing the required "copyright warnings" and notice under Section 108(a), (d), and (e)?*

This question surprised me, insofar as the general photocopying and 108(a) issues are concerned, because the Copyright Office has not been authorized by the statute to set rules and regulations with respect to either of these subjects. Still, the impression persists that the Copyright Office has a major regulatory role to play in the implementation of Section 108. This is erroneous; indeed, it would probably be contrary to the philosophy of Section 108, which looks toward voluntary, direct negotiations between the affected interests for resolution of areas of uncertainty. In no area of the law does the Copyright Office exercise regulatory authority affecting relationships between copyright proprietors and users.

The Register of Copyrights is, however, charged with two specific functions touching on library photocopying: 1) to set requirements for a warning of copyright for use at copying counters and on order forms in connection with transactions covered by 108(d) and (e); 2) to report to the Congress, five years after the effective date of the new law (Jan. 1, 1978), the extent to which Section 108 effectively balanced the interests of creators' and users' rights. This report will be submitted after consultation with a wide range of proprietary, library, and public representatives. The report should present, if warranted, specific recommendations for legislative or other action.

As to the copyright warnings under Section 108(d) and (e), the Copyright Office published an Advance Notice of Proposed Rulemaking in the *Federal Register*, March 30, pp. 16838-39. It invited people to comment and make suggestions about the content and use of the warnings by May 6. These comments may be inspected and copied at the Copyright Office; replies to the initial

large numbers of articles taken from copyrighted periodicals can be considered, in the light of reasonable restrictions and a valid public interest, to be a "fair use."

It is, nonetheless, rather difficult to predict just how the law of fair use might be applied in light of Section 108's detailed regulation of library and archival reproductions. Conceivably, a challenge to a given library practice might be resolved by a complex process of determining:

1) whether the practice is specifically sanctioned under Section 108;

2) whether it is prohibited under an interpretation of Section 108 (g), taking the guidelines into consideration;

3) if prohibited under 108, as a whole, whether or not it satisfies the tests for determining whether a use is "fair" or not.

Not only is this process elusive, it is highly speculative. The continuing relevancy of "fair use" to library reproductions and distribution of copyrighted material does more to maintain the state

of flux in the law than to provide detailed rights. One hopes that the vast amount of room which has been left for argument and negotiations will produce serious agreements on voluntary licensing or more comprehensive guidelines.

6. *What kind of records must be kept by "requesting entities" under the interlibrary loan guidelines?*

Section 4 of the CONTU Guidelines for the Proviso of Subsection 108(g)(2) simply states that "the requesting entity shall maintain records of all requests made by it for copies or phonorecords of any materials to which these guidelines apply" and further requires that such records be kept for a period of three years from the date of such requests. No specific form of record is prescribed and no special retention practice is established, apart from the three-year period.

The record-keeping requirement seems to have generated a good deal of anxiety and annoyance among librarians, who are concerned that already overtaxed

"I . . . I couldn't afford another subscription!
I had six hungry subject divisions to feed . . ."

I will only raise an even more difficult question: can library reproductions made in conformity with the educational guidelines be distributed through interlibrary loan arrangements, notwithstanding the ILL guidelines? And how do we count them?

9. To what extent can libraries tape television programs off-the-air either for a videotape collection or on behalf of teachers for use in face-to-face teaching activities?

Nothing in Section 108 authorizes libraries and archives generally to tape television programming off-the-air. Even more, Section 108(h) excludes virtually all motion pictures and audiovisual works from the rights of reproduction and distribution accorded under the section. Motion pictures and audiovisual works may be reproduced for the limited purposes set out in 108(b) and (c), but not for library users under (d) and (e).

A limited exception to this rule is made for audiovisual news programs. Section 108(f)(3), read with Section 108(h), provides that nothing in Section 108 is intended to preclude the reproduction and distribution by lending of a limited number of copies and excerpts of an audiovisual news program. Just what an "audiovisual news program" is appeared to have stirred up some disagreement. The House Judiciary Committee report noted that the exemption applied to "daily newscasts of the national television networks," but did not apply to documentary or "magazine-format or other public affairs broadcasts dealing with subjects of general interest to the viewing public." This formulation was too restrictive, and the Conference Committee report added this controlling modification:

> . . . a library or archives qualifying under Section 108(a) would be free, without regard to the archival activities of the Library of Congress or any other organization, to reproduce, on videotape or any other medium of fixation or reproduction, local, regional or network newscasts, interviews concerning current news events, and on-the-spot coverage of news events and to distribute a limited number of reproductions of such a program on a loan basis.

Although educators sought a limited exception to permit off-the-air taping of television programming for use in classroom teaching, the statute does not expressly provide such a right. Additionally, an effort was undertaken to negotiate voluntary guidelines for off-the-air educational tapings, but it proved too difficult to secure. The House Report recognized the difficulties and observed that ". . . the fair use doctrine has some

comments must be received by May 23.

8. What is the relationship between the classroom reproduction guidelines interpreting Section 107 (fair use) and Section 108?

This is perhaps one of the most interesting questions flowing out of any consideration of the "open-ended" character of Sections 107 and 108. In considering the requests of educational organizations for a limited exception to allow certain reproductions of copyrighted works (including multiple copying) in connection with face-to-face teaching activities, the Congress rejected the relatively specific approach of Section 108 in favor of considering the subject under "fair use." To provide some certainty and predictability in the application of "fair use," the legislative reports go into detail and include two sets of voluntarily negotiated guidelines covering classroom reproductions of books, periodicals, and music. These guidelines are more detailed and less ambiguous than those dealing with interlibrary loan.

The basic question seems to be whether or not multiple reproductions of copyrighted works which may be barred under Section 108(g) are permissible when the requester is a teacher acting in conformity with the educational guidelines. The issue may also involve not only multiple copying of works subject to Section 108, but any copying of works excluded from 108, if allowed under the educational guidelines (e.g., pictorial illustrations, music).

The guidelines covering books and periodicals state that copies "may be made by or for the teacher." The probability is that the party who will make copies for the teacher is the librarian or library assistant. The educational guidelines interpret "fair use" in specific situations. Section 108(f)(4) establishes the rule that nothing in 108 "in any way affects the right of fair use as provided by Section 107" (a double-edged provision: not everything in Section 108 is per se a "fair use," and, on the other hand, the doctrine may sanction library reproductions not treated in Section 108).

The result may be that a library making 35 copies of an article (under 2,500 words) for Lewis Flacks could find itself in violation of 108(g). If the same service was provided to a teacher for the use of his or her pupils in class the library might be in the clear. Neither the guidelines nor the legislative history address the question.

limited application in this area . . . Nothing in section 107 or elsewhere in the bill is intended to change or prejudge the law on the point."

The committee—it is probably fair to say the Congress—urged the various interests to continue actively discussing the issue, possibly under the leadership of the Register of Copyrights.

That no one really knows the answers to the questions growing out of the new copyright law is an awkward truth. A goodly number of answers are, in fact, in the copyright law, or they can be readily deduced by any reasonable person reading its terms, in light of the relevant legislative history. Actually, catalogers in particular are rather adept at it.

In some situations, however, the law is noticeably silent or ambiguous. For interlibrary loan arrangements, "fair use" and similarly volatile issues, "silence" and "ambiguous" are frequently encountered words. The entire process of determining how to live within the letter of the law is difficult, when so much is left unresolved or committed to future resolution. It is doubly difficult for bureaucratic organizations, such as libraries and educational institutions, where maximum effectiveness requires clear and calculable rules and predictable legal impact. Perhaps after all, in the words of a distinguished jurist, "it is more important that the law be settled than that it be settled right."

Clear-cut rules do not characterize the new copyright law. Perhaps more than in other areas, library and educational uses of protected works are treated in a way that encourages the affected interests to reach accommodations through active discussions pursued in a constructive spirit. A number of vehicles exist to carry forward this process of "private law-making":

1) The professional and trade organizations that negotiated both the library and educational guidelines. Congress hopes that the process initiated with those agreements will continue in a constructive spirit.

2) The Commission on New Technological Uses of Copyrighted Works. CONTU is now studying the photocopying problem in considerable detail, along with the closely related issue of computer uses of copyrighted works. Its report and recommendations will surely carry great weight with Congress.

3) Over a five-year period, beginning on January 1, 1978, the Register of Copyrights will be considering ways in which to prepare a congressionally mandated report on the problems and successes of Section 108, including legislative recommendations, if warranted.

Of course, there are also the various pieces of recurring legislation under which Congress supports the development of library services, such as the Medical Libraries Act. These can serve as forums in which the problems of integrating national library and copyright policies might be confronted.

In short, the treatment of library reproductions under the new law should not be seen as the end of a process. If Congress could have seen the future of libraries and publishing with any degree of certainty, then that certainty would have appeared in the law. It did not, it could not. However, confronted with the need to legislate with respect to an "evolving situation," Congress wisely chose a flexible course. That flexibility makes our lives a bit more complicated, but it has the virtue of leaving the shape of the future to our own imagination and good sense. □

"It's the new Copyright Compliance Center. We used to call it a library."

24: DOCUMENT SUPPLY IN THE UNITED STATES

Charles H. Lieb*

I will briefly summarize our new United States copyright law
insofar as it affects out-of-the house delivery of copies of copyrighted material by libraries and document delivery houses. I first
must make clear, however, that the sections of the law to which I
will refer are new and in the main untested, and that it will be years
before they have been authoritatively interpreted. Also, although I
believe the discussion that follows is even-handed, you should know
that I have been a spokesman for publishers and that my views and
those of some of those who speak for library and document delivery
houses have at times differed sharply.

Under the new law, 90 Stat.2541, October 19, 1976, Title 17
United States Code, copyright protection is afforded from the date
of creation to original works of authorship "fixed in any tangible
medium of expression, now known or later developed, from which they
can be perceived, reproduced, or otherwise communicated, either
directly or with the aid of a machine or device". Thus it makes no
difference what the form, manner or medium of fixation may be, --
whether in words, numbers, graphic or symbolic indicia; whether
embodied in written, printed, punched, or magnetic form, or whether
capable of perception directly or by means of a machine or device --
the work will be in copyright from the time that it is first reduced

----

* Paskus, Gordon & Hyman
  New York, New York and Washington, D.C., and
  Editor, STM Copyright Bulletin

to tangible form.

In the discussion that follows I will limit my remarks to the reproduction and out-of-house distribution of published "literary works", a term which connotes no criterion of literary merit, and includes such works, among others, as directories, compilations of data, and tables.

Nor will I discuss the delivery of "U. S. Government Works" which are defined as works prepared by an officer or employee of the United States government as part of that person's official duties and which are not eligible for copyright protection in the United States. U. S. Government Works do not encompass works prepared by others under government contract or grant, which may or may not be in copyright depending on the terms of the contract or grant.

Within this context the relevant sections of the copyright law which require review are §106 which enumerates the exclusive rights which belong to the owner of copyright; §107 which codifies the fair use limitation on those rights, and §108 which grants limited reproduction rights to qualifying libraries and archives. Two other sections are also relevant, §504 which protects teachers and other employees of non-profit educational institutions from statutory damages for unwitting infringement within the scope of their employment, and §602 which makes the unauthorized importation of copies lawfully made outside the United States an infringement of the copyright owner's exclusive rights in the United States.

Section 106 provides that subject to sections 107 and 108 the copyright owner has the exclusive right "to reproduce" the copyrighted work in copies.

Section 107 states that notwithstanding the provisions of §106, the fair use of a copyrighted work, including reproduction in copies "for purposes such as criticism, comment, news reporting, teaching (including multiple copies for classroom use), scholarship or research" is not an infringement of copyright". Further, that in determining whether the use in any particular case is a fair use, the factors to be considered shall include (1) the purpose and character of the use, including whether it is of a commercial nature or is for nonprofit educational purposes; (2) the nature of the copyrighted work; (3) the amount and substantiality of the portion used; and (4) the effect of the use upon the potential market for or value of the copyrighted work.

The legislative history makes clear that §107 is intended to restate the existing judicial doctrine of fair use and not to change it in any way, and that the reference to "multiple copies for classroom use" is merely a recognition that the doctrine will be applicable under appropriate circumstances of fairness in a classroom environment. A specific exemption for copying for non-profit educational purposes, as requested by educators, was deemed "not justified" and was denied.

If the illustrations of fair use as contained in the "for purposes such as" portion of the first sentence of §107 were to be taken as a standard, library copying would not seem to fall within the fair use exemption. A library does not make a copy so that it, the library, may use it for criticism or comment or any of the other purposes specifically enumerated in §107. Rather, it makes a copy either so that it may use it for archival preservation, or it makes copies for the use of library patrons so that they may use it for their own study.

Nevertheless, no matter how remote library copying may be from classic fair use, it is clear that a library today does have some §107 fair use rights to make copies for its own or another library's users. To determine in advance the outer limits of these rights is difficult, but it is fair to say that another section, to wit §108, was enacted to make lawful some types of copying that exceed fair use.

Section 108 therefore requires close scrutiny. The relevant portions thereof are set out below, with key words and phrases *in italics*.

§108. Limitation on exclusive rights: Reproduction by libraries
and archives

(a) Notwithstanding the provisions of section 106, it is not an infringement of copyright for a library or archives, or any of its employees acting within the scope of their employment, to reproduce *no more than one copy or phonorecord* of a work, or to distribute such a copy or phonorecord, under the conditions specified by this section, if --

(1) the reproduction or distribution is made *without any purpose of direct or indirect commercial advantage;*

(2) the collections of the library or archives are (i) *open to the public*, or (ii) *available not only to researchers affiliated with the library* or archives or with the institution of which it is a part, but *also to other persons doing research in a specialized field;* and

(3) the reproduction or distribution of the work includes a notice of copyright.

[*Author's Note:* Material has been omitted at this point.]

(d) The rights of reproduction and distribution under this section apply to a copy, made from the collection of a library or archives where the user makes his or her request   or from that of another library or archives of *no more than one article or other contribution* to a copyrighted collection or periodical issue, or to a copy or phonorecord of a *small part* of any other copyrighted work, if --

   (1) the copy of phonorecord becomes the *property of the user*, and the library or archives has had no notice that the copy or phonorecord would be used for any purpose other than *private study, scholarship, or research;* and

   (2) the library or archives displays prominently, at the place where orders are accepted, and includes on its order form, a *warning of copyright* in accordance with requirements that the Register of Copyrights shall prescribe by regulation.

(e) The rights of reproduction and distribution under this section apply to the *entire work,* or *to a substantial part of it,* made from the collection of a library or archives where the user makes his or her request or from that of another library or archives, if the library or archives has first determined, on the basis of a reasonable investigation, that a copy or phonorecord of the copyrighted work *cannot be obtained at a fair price,* if -

   (1) the copy or phonorecord becomes the *property of the user*, and the library or archives has had no notice that the copy or phonorecord would be used for any purpose other than *private study, scholarship, or research;* and

   (2) the library or archives displays prominently, at the place where orders are accepted, and includes on its order form, a *warning of copyright* in accordance with requirements that the Register of Copyrights shall prescribe by regulation.

(f) Nothing in this section -

(1) shall be construed to impose liability for copyright infringement upon a library or archives or its employees for the *unsupervised* use of reproducing equipment located on its premises: *provided*, that such equipment displays a notice that the making of a copy may be subject to the copyright law;

- - - - - - - - - - - - - - - - - -

[*Author's Note:* Material has been omitted at this point.]

(4) in any way affects the right of fair use as provided by section 107, or any contractual obligation assumed at any time by the library or archives when it obtained a copy or phonorecord of a work in its collections.

(g) The rights of reproduction and distribution under this section extend to the *isolated and unrelated* reproduction or distribution of a single copy or phonorecord of the same material on separate occasions, but do not extend to cases where the library or archives, or its employee --

(1) is aware or has substantial reason to believe that it is engaging in the *related or concerted reproduction or distribution of multiple copies* or phonorecords of the same material, whether made on one occasion or over a period of time, and whether intended for aggregate use by one or more individuals or for separate use by the individual members of a group; or

(2) engages in the *systematic reproduction or distribution of single or multiple copies or phonorecords of material described in subsection (d): Provided,* That nothing in this clause prevents a library or archives from participating in interlibrary arrangements that do not have, as their purpose or effect, that the library or archives receiving such copies or phonorecords for distribution does so in such *aggregate quantities as to substitute* for a subscription to or purchase of such work.

It will be noted that §108 rights are not available to all libraries, but only to those meeting the criteria stated in §108(a); principally that the collections of the library be open to the public or available to all researchers including those affiliated with competitors (availability solely through interlibrary loan will not be sufficient), and that the library supplying the copy does so "without any purpose of direct or indirect commercial advantage".

The 1975 Report of the U.S. Senate Committee on the Judiciary (a part of the law's legislative history) flatly states that the "direct or indirect commercial advantage" phrase in §108(a)(1) "is intended to preclude a library in a profit-making organization from providing photocopies of copyrighted materials to employees engaged in furtherance of the organization's commercial enterprise, unless such copying qualifies as a fair use, or the organization has obtained the necessary copyright licenses".

On the other hand, the 1976 Report of the House of Representatives Committee on the Judiciary (also part of the legislative history) says that "the 'advantage' referred to in this subsection must attach to the immediate commercial motivation behind the reproduction or distribution itself, rather than to the ultimate profit-making motivation behind the enterprise in which the library is located", and therefore "that isolated, spontaneous making of single copies by such a library, without any systematic effort to substitute photocopies for subscriptions, would be exempt under §108 even though the copies are furnished to employees for use in their work".

The two statements are obviously contradictory, but as the Register of Copyrights suggests in his Report to Congress* the explanation of the

*Report of the Register of Copyrights: Library Reproduction of Copyrighted Works (17 U.S.C.108), January 1983

Senate Committee which was responsible for the original drafting of
this portion of the section should be more authoritative than that of
the House Committee which made no change in the language adopted by
the Senate.

Moreover, although there is ambiguity in the legislative history
with respect to the §108(a)(1) proscription of unauthorized photocopying "for direct or indirect commercial advantage", that identical
phrase as used in §110(4)(dealing with performances in non-profit educational institutions) is fully explained in the legislative history
of that section. In discussing §110(4) both the Senate and the House
Reports state that the "direct or indirect commercial advantage"
clause expressly adopts the principle established by earlier court
decisions, namely, that public performances given or sponsored "in
connection with any commercial or profit-making enterprises" are protected by copyright and require the consent of the copyright owner,
notwithstanding that the public is not charged for attending the performances. It is at least likely, therefore, that the same language
in §108 has largely the same meaning, namely, that as the Senate Committee stated, it is intended to preclude a library in a commercial
or profit-making enterprise from copying copyrighted material without the
consent of the copyright owner.

If a library, whether or not connected with a profit-making enterprise, does qualify for §108 exemption, -- it will then be free to make
for its own users or users of another qualifying library, without permission of the copyright owner, not more than one copy of copyrighted material
at a time, under circumstances described in §108(d) and (e). (A work will

133

be considered available "at a fair price under §108(e) if it is available through normal trade channels). But as stated in §108(g), these exemptions extend only to the "isolated and unrelated" copying of the same material on separate occasions, and do not extend to cases where the library has reason to believe that it is engaging in related or concerted copying of the same material on one occasion or over a period of time, or to the "systematic reproduction of single or multiple copies of journal articles and other material referred to in §108(d).

"Systematic" reproduction, as the word connotes, carries an implication of a common plan, or an organized or established procedure. As the Register's Report states, "the greater the commonality of a plan, the more regular the interaction, the more organized the network or procedure, then the more likely it is that the copying done is 'systematic'".

Three examples of systematic copying are stated in the Senate Report: (1) a library with a specialized collection informs other libraries that it will make copies available to them on request. Accordingly, the other libraries fulfill their patron's request by obtaining copies from the source library, and not by purchase or subscription; (2) A research center subscribes to one or two copies of needed periodicals and by reproducing copies, is able to make the material available to its staff in the same manner which otherwise would have required multiple subscriptions, and (3) several branches of a library system agree that one branch will subscribe to particular journals in lieu of each branch purchasing its own subscriptions, and the one subscribing branch will reproduce copies for users of the other branches.

The only exception to the ban on unauthorized systematic copying is found in the addition to §108(g)(2) (subsequent to the issuance of the Senate Report) of the so-called "interlibrary proviso", namely, that nothing in §108(g)(2) should prevent a library from participating in "interlibrary arrangements" (which otherwise would be one type of systematic copying) if such arrangements do not have, as their purpose or effect, that the library receiving such copies does so "in such aggregate quantities as to substitute for a subscription to or purchase of such work".

As the Register comments, the proviso in no way affects the scope of "systematic"; it simply permits one type of systematic photocopying -- limited interlibrary photocopying -- to be carried out, the preceding portion of §108(g)(2) notwithstanding.

The so-called CONTU*Interlibrary Arrangements Guidelines, insofar as here relevant, permit the supply through interlibrary arrangement in any calendar year of not more than five copies in the aggregate of an article or articles published in any particular periodical within five years prior to the date of the request. Thus, in any one year, the requesting library may receive one copy each of each of five different articles published for example in *Interlending & Document Supply* during the previous five years, or five copies of one of such articles, or three of one and two of another, so long as the total number of copies of articles from that periodical published during the five-year period does not exceed five. The Guidelines are not applicable, however, to institutions, public or private, which exist for the specific purpose of providing a central source for photocopies.

---

* National Commission on New Technological Uses of Copyrighted Works

And finally §108(f) provides that nothing in §108 should be construed to impose liability on a library "for the unsupervised use" of reproducing equipment located on its premises if the equipment displays a prescribed cautionary notice, notwithstanding that the individual who makes use of the equipment (or who requests the library to make a copy for him under §108(d))will be liable for infringement if the copying or later use of the copy exceeds fair use.

In a way, therefore, (at least with respect to on-the-premises photo-copying) it is moot whether a library in a for-profit organization can qualify for exemption under the "direct or indirect commercial advantage" clause. Copying done by corporate employees within the scope of their employment if authorized neither by §107 nor §108 nor by the copyright owner would be infringing, and therefore under established common law and copyright doctrine, the employee's employer, - the company - would similarly be liable*.

What conclusions can we draw from the limitations inherent in the fair use doctrine as incorporated in §107 and from the complex set of rules set forth in §108?

---

* Four major corporations, American Cyanamid, Squibb Corporation, Pfizer, Inc. and Texaco, Inc., have either agreed after commencement of infringement suits or have voluntarily adopted as corporate policy that copying of material entered in the Copyright Clearance Center will either be reported and accounted for through the Copyright Clearance Center or will otherwise be cleared with the copyright owner. These agreements cover not only copies made through or provided by the corporate library but copies made by employees on unsupervised "floor machines" as well.

(1) First, it must be understood that United States copyright law applies only within the United States. Copying and distribution of copyrighted material outside the United States is governed by the laws of the country in which those events take place and not by the laws of the United States. However, under §602(a) importation into the United States of copyrighted material without the consent of the copyright owner will be an infringement of the copyright owner's exclusive right to distribute copies in the United States, with certain exceptions which would require separate discussion but which are not relevant here. Therefore, in my view at least, copies forwarded, for example, by a central library outside the United States to corporate users in the United States without permission of the copyright owner would be infringing copies, and the forwarding library, and the United States document supply house through which the order may have been placed, as well as the user itself, would each be liable for the infringement.

(2) Participation by libraries in interlibrary arrangements or in networks or consortia involves the library in "systematic reproduction" or distribution. Therefore, unless the copying is cleared either directly with the copyright owner or in some other manner, as for example through the Copyright Clearance Center, it will constitute infringement unless engaged in by libraries qualified under §108(a) and done within the limits established by the §108(g)(2) proviso and the CONTU Guidelines. The guidelines speak only to material which was published during the five-year period immediately prior to the interlibrary request, but it seems reasonable to believe that if and when the question should come before the courts, it would be held that they would apply to older material as well.

If libraries connected with for-profit establishments do not qualify for §108 exemption, then it would follow that their participation in interlibrary arrangements would not be exempt under the §108(g)(2) proviso.

(3) Central source libraries, i.e. libraries which exist for the principal purpose of supplying copies to others, by their very nature, make and supply those copies systematically. Thus, whether with respect to §108(d) materials (journal articles or small parts of other works, whether or not in print) or §108(e) materials (works not obtainable through normal trade channels), they gain no safe harbor either from §108 or from §107 and are infringers.

(4) Commercial copyshops and commercial information brokers and document supply houses have only the most limited §107 fair use rights and have no §108 rights at all. This is because in conducting their business they act as principals for their own account and not as agents for their customers who may or may not have fair use rights, and because of the "commercial nature" of their business and the "commercial advantage" which they draw therefrom.

(5) Finally and again to paraphrase from the Register's Report, as new modes of access are created, as by CRT display of full text stored in computerized data bases or optical disks, there should be no limitation on copyright owners' rights and full copyright liability should attach to any unauthorized reproduction or distribution.

25: NONPRINT WORKS AND COPYRIGHT IN SPECIAL LIBRARIES

Laura N. Gasaway

Law and Library Faculty
University of Oklahoma

■ This is the first of two articles on copyright issues and nonprint and audiovisual materials in special libraries and information centers. Focusing on nonprint materials, the first article includes a general overview of copyright, as well as detailed analyses of particular problems of copyright, computer programs, databases, and electronic publishing. The unique copyright aspects for each of these formats is analyzed and explained. The second article will be published in the July issue of *Special Libraries* and will cover audiovisual, pictorial, and graphic works.

THE Copyright Revision Act of 1976(1) recognizes the special relationship that exists between libraries and copyright owners. Libraries are major purchasers of copyrighted materials and make them available to their users. Libraries thus act as intermediaries in gathering, storing, and indexing copyrighted books and materials for the ultimate consumer, the library user. Library organizations were instrumental in the passage of the 1976 Copyright Revision Act. Special Libraries Association, as well as other library and information societies, testified in congressional hearings and recommended amendments to pending copyright legislation and later guidelines under various sections of the Act. These activities were directed at striking a balance between the needs of library users and the rights of copyright holders.

During this period, librarians and publishers were myopically concerned with the issue of library photocopying of printed copyrighted materials. Despite the obvious importance of this issue to libraries and information centers, other vital areas of interest failed to receive the same degree of concern. Nonprint materials comprise large portions of many library collections, and issues relative to their use and copyright protection have become increasingly problematic as technological developments have made materials in various formats more readily available. The same concerns persist for the use of copyrighted nonprint works as exist for printed materials. Many of the questions concerning the photocopying of

Copyright © 1983 by Special Libraries Association; reprinted from *Spec. Libr.* 74(2): 156-170 (1983).

139

printed works have been answered, and librarians now are directing their attention to nonprint media in an attempt to find answers to questions about the use and duplication of this material by libraries.

Special library collections increasingly are comprised of nonprint materials such as computer programs and machine-readable databases. Electronically published material, i.e., those published and stored in electronic format rather than in hard copy, will be significant in most special libraries. Special librarians, generally, are asked to supply information, and the format or storage medium for that information is immaterial to the user. This article focuses on how the Copyright Act protects nonprint works along with the issues of use and duplication of such material in special libraries and information centers.

Nonprint works are not defined in the Act, but for purposes of this article the term will be used to describe computer programs, machine-readable databases, and electronically published materials. Microforms will be discussed only briefly since they are simple reductions of traditional print, pictorial, or graphic materials. Under most circumstances, the reproduction of a microform constitutes copyright infringement if copying the underlying work is an infringement.

Library Practices

Special libraries and information centers play a unique role among libraries. While making copyrighted materials available to users is standard practice for all types of libraries, special librarians often are asked to provide the information required and not just a citation to where the information may be located. Other types of libraries are far more likely to locate resource materials for users rather than analyze the information and provide exact answers to specific questions.

Library education long has stressed the desirability of selective dissemination of information to users. Librarians are taught that any good librarian should ascertain the research interests of users and be vigilant in calling the attention of users to newly published articles, books, and nonprint works pertinent to the users' subject interests. This is touted not only as good librarianship but aggressive librarianship sure to make the librarian a vital part of any research effort conducted by the institution or organization.

Prior to the availability of low-cost copy machines, fiche duplicators, and so forth, selective dissemination of information meant either routing the original to an interested researcher or citing the reference along with some notation that the material dealt with a specific research interest. Since the advent of photocopying, however, it has become standard practice for librarians in their mission as disseminators of information to copy the material and route the photocopy to the researcher without any specific request for the individual item from the researcher (2).

With the development of fiche-to-fiche duplicators, some libraries have the technology to duplicate fiche for users. Reproduced fiche can be used to satisfy interlibrary loan requests and to produce copies for users in the same way as photocopies are used. Libraries also participate in extensive interlibrary loan systems. Before the advent of low-cost photocopying, libraries hesitated to loan bound journal volumes and other difficult to replace material. The ability to meet user needs through the exchange of photocopies dramatically increased the scale of interlibrary loan, actually making it "interlibrary exchange." Original copies of nonprint works sometimes were loaned, but, in all likelihood, some duplicated copies also were furnished to satisfy interlibrary loan requests.

Commercial databases now are available which offer outstanding collections of information through computer technology. Libraries subscribe to these services and perform searches for users; some libraries have created their own in-house databases, also. A few libraries have had permission from database proprietors to download selected information from a commercial database into their in-house computers to provide for quicker and cheaper access to selected information from the database.

The new Act specifically addresses some of these library practices relating to nonprint works, while others are mentioned not at all. Library photocopying and interlibrary loan practices are treated in the Act and have received a great deal of attention in the literature. On the other hand, the duplication of nonprint materials largely has been ignored. In order to apply basic copyright principles to library copying of nonprint media it is necessary to review some general sections of the Act.

Overview of General Copyright Protection

In order to obtain copyright protection for a work, the author, producer, or creator of the work must meet two statutory requirements. The work must be original with the creator (3), i.e., not copied from the work of someone else, and the work must be "fixed" (4). There are seven categories of works susceptible to copyright protection: 1) literary works, 2) musical works including lyrics, 3) dramatic works including musical scores, 4) pantomimes and choreographic works, 5) pictorial, graphic, and sculptural works, 6) motion pictures and other audiovisual works, and 7) sound recordings (5).

Upon "fixing" the copyrighted work, the owner obtains a bundle of exclusive rights to do or authorize any of the following: 1) reproduce the work in copies or phonorecords, 2) distribute to the public the copies or phonorecords so reproduced through sale, rental, lending, or lease, 3) prepare adaptations or derivative works based on the original, 4) perform the work publicly, and 5) display the works publicly (6). On the other hand, the purchaser of a legitimate copy of a copyrighted work is the outright owner of that copy and may use it and dispose of it in any way desired (7). It is important to note, however, that the right to use a copyrighted work does not necessarily include the right to reproduce the work. Sections 107-118 of the Act detail specific exceptions to the exclusive rights of copyright holders. The two sections most important to librarians are sections 107 and 108.

Section 107

Through the years, as copyrights were infringed and litigation ensued to determine liability for infringement, the judiciary developed a so-called safety valve on the owner's exclusive rights known as the fair use doctrine. Under the fair use doctrine, conduct that normally would constitute an infringement of a copyrighted work may be excused as such if use of the work constitutes fair use (8). The Act defines fair use as . . . "including such use by reproduction in copies or phonorecords or by any other means specified by that section, for purposes such as criticism, comment, news reporting, teaching (including multiple copies for classroom use), scholarship, or research . . ." (9). Guidelines for § 107 on multiple copying for classroom use in nonprofit educational institutions were published in the House Report which accompanied the Act. The Act then lists the factors a court should consider in determining whether a use constitutes fair use: 1) the purpose and character of the use, 2) the nature of the copyrighted work, 3) the amount and substantiality of the portion used in relation to the copyrighted work as a whole, and 4) the effect of the use upon the potential market for or value of the work (10).

Section 108

In addition to § 107, libraries and archives are governed by § 108 entitled, "Limitation on Exclusive Rights: Reproduction by Libraries and Archives." Libraries and their employees acting within the scope of their employment may make one copy or phonorecord of a work and distribute the same if: 1) the copy is made and distributed without any direct or indirect commercial advantage, 2) the library's collection is either open to the public or available not only to researchers associated with the institution but also to persons doing research in specialized fields, and 3) copies made include a copyright notice (11).

The Act then identifies several situations in which works may be copied, such as to preserve an unpublished work or for deposit in another library or archives (12) and for replacing lost, stolen, damaged, or deteriorating material when a replacement cannot be obtained at a fair price (13). The rights of reproduction and distribution provided in § 108 apply when certain conditions are met, such as the user (or the library in an interlibrary loan transaction) requests no more than one article or other contribution in a periodical issue or collected work (14). The copy must become the property of the user, and the library should have no notice that the copy will be used for non-fair use purposes (15). Additionally, the library must prominently display a warning of copyright on its order form for copies and at the location where orders are placed for copies (16). To relieve the library from liability for copies made on unsupervised copy machines, the library must display a warning of copyright (17).

If a copy is made of a complete work or a substantial portion thereof, the library first must have determined on the basis of a reasonable investigation that a copy is not available at a fair price. Also, the copy must become the property of the user, and the library must have no notice that the copies being made do not qualify for the § 108 exemption (18).

Interlibrary loan arrangements are recognized throughout § 108, and the Act specifically says that nothing in this section shall prevent a library from participating in interlibrary arrangements which do not have as their purpose or effect the providing of copies in such aggregate quantities as to substitute for the purchase or subscription to such a work (19). Separately negotiated guidelines, referred to as the CONTU guidelines, were promulgated to clarify what constitutes "such aggregate quantities as to substitute for subscription to or purchase of such a work" for periodicals less than five years old (20).

The "direct or indirect commercial advantage" statement contained in § 108(a)(1) caused much confusion during the legislative process. The House Report settled the issue by making it clear that libraries in for-profit organizations did not lose all rights under § 108. Rather, if such libraries comply with the criteria and requirements of § 108, then an isolated, spontaneous making of a single copy without any commercial motivation would be permitted under the Act. Likewise, such libraries may participate in interlibrary arrangements (21).

Audiovisual and Nonprint Materials under §§ 107–108

Section 108 appears to eliminate the possibility of copying most audiovisual and some nonprint works. "The rights of reproduction and distribution under this section do not apply to a musical work, a pictorial, graphic or sculptural work, or a motion picture or other audiovisual work other than an audiovisual work dealing with news " (22) There are three specific exceptions: 1) pictorial and graphic works published as illustrations, diagrams, and so on, to accompany other works (23), 2) copying an unpublished audiovisual work for purposes of preservation, security or deposit in another library (24), and 3) copying to replace damaged or lost copies or phonorecords (25).

The most common practices involving the copying of nonprint materials are not detailed in these three exceptions, however. Certainly, the rights conferred under § 107 apply to the copying of nonprint media, but there are no clear guidelines such as those dealing with interlibrary loan (26). Perhaps the rule of reason should apply. If librarians recognize the rights afforded copyright holders and apply the fair use test to the best of their abilities, then the individual librarian should be able to determine whether the copying of a nonprint work qualifies as a fair use. Clearly, just having a good or beneficial purpose for copying is not enough to relieve a librarian from liability for copyright infringement.

Perhaps the starting point should be this; fair use seldom envisions copying an entire work. Specific examples of fair use are found in the legislative history, such as reproduction of a small portion

§ 107 to copying outside of education and academia. The Court applied each of the criteria in reaching its decision that home videotaping from copyrighted television programs is an infringement of copyright (32).

General Library Practices and Copyright

There are numerous books and articles devoted to interlibrary loan, photocopying, and copyright. The exchange of photocopies to satisfy interlibrary loan requests for printed matter is outside the scope of this article, but the interlibrary loan of copyrighted nonprint materials is within its purview.

If librarians recognize the rights afforded copyright holders and apply the fair use test to the best of their abilities, then the individual librarian should be able to determine whether the copying of a nonprint work qualifies as a fair use. Clearly, just having a good or beneficial purpose for copying is not enough to relieve a librarian from liability for copyright infringement.

---

of a work to illustrate a lesson (27), but most of the examples relate to copying for classroom use in a nonprofit educational institution. In fact, each of the four fair use considerations are explained in the Senate Report with reference to classroom situations (28). The four fair use criteria, however, do have applicability to the duplication of nonprint works outside of the educational setting.

In a recent case, *Universal Studios Inc., v. Sony Corporation of America* (29), the Ninth Circuit examined home off-the-air videotaping and applied the four-pronged fair use test (30). Although currently on appeal to the U.S. Supreme Court (31), the Ninth Circuit's application of the fair use factors to audiovisual copying indicates to applicability of

Few libraries actually participate in interlibrary loan arrangements for nonprint material. Because of the potential damage nonprint works could suffer from mailing and handling, libraries seldom actually loan them to other libraries. While the § 108(g)(2) CONTU guidelines provide suggestions for photocopying periodical articles, there is no provision directly relating to the copying of nonprint media for interlibrary loan (33). In fact, the interlibrary loan guidelines do not apply to audiovisual and some nonprint works (34); it also is difficult to formulate what sort of copying for interlibrary loan would be permissible under under § 107 fair use. It would seem logical, however, that a library which purchases copyrighted computer software and finds that the program has been damaged could replace it through an interlibrary loan transaction under § 108(c).

In-house copying, including the selective dissemination of information, is covered by the Act. Clearly, some intra-library copying is within fair use. The Act, however, neither specifies any numerical criteria nor defines systematic copying. The House Report outlines three practices that would constitute copyright infringement; two of these relate to in-house copying in libraries in for-profit organizations.

> Under § 108, a library in a profit-making organization would not be authorized to: (a) use a single subscription or copy to supply its employees with multiple copies of material relevant to their work; or (b) use a single subscription or copy to supply its employees, on request, with single copies of material relevant to their work, where the arrangement is "systematic" in the sense of deliberately substituting photocopying for subscription or purchase; or (c) use "interlibrary loan arrangements for obtaining photocopies in such aggregate quantities as to substitute for subscription or purchase of materials needed by employees in their work (35).

Isolated, spontaneous photocopying of single copies is covered by § 108 even though the copy is made for employees within the course of their work (36). A library may not avoid its liability by installing unsupervised photocopy equipment on company premises outside the library (37). The Association of American Publishers (AAP) early expressed its desire to quantify the number of in-house copies that could be made before reaching a level of copying that is systematic. AAP later changed its position, apparently believing that its earlier numerical guidelines were overly generous (38). Electronic publishing of journals may interface with all of this since the ability to make a printed copy may accompany a subscription.

The duplication of microforms by libraries has become a possibility with the development of fiche-to-fiche du-

plication equipment. Although the equipment is still relatively expensive, many libraries do own fiche duplicators. Whether copying a fiche for a user or for the library's own collection is permissible depends on the nature of the underlying work. If the fiche is a Senate report, for example, then duplicating the fiche is not an infringement of copyright. Government publications are public domain material and may be freely copied by anyone (39). On the other hand, if the work is a commercially published monograph, copying the work via fiche is equivalent to copying any other literary work by means of a photocopier.

If photocopying the underlying printed work is permissible under § 108, then duplicating the fiche copy also is permissible. The Act refers to "reproduction in copies or phonorecords" (40) and does not specify the form in which a copy may be made.

It appears, therefore, that copying in any form is treated as if the work were photocopied. Moreover, fiche generally represent an entire work, and the statute does not envision copying an entire work.

Some librarians have duplicated both print and nonprint copyrighted material for addition to the library's verticle files. Such duplication is not exempted from copyright infringement under § 108. Unpublished material might be so preserved for the vertical files (41), but published material does not receive the same exemption. Section 107 fair use may be applicable.

Copyright, Libraries and Nonprint Material

There are many reasons why a librarian might wish to reproduce copyrighted nonprint works. Some librarians may feel that in order to preserve certain nonprint works they should be duplicated for archival purposes, especially when such materials are no longer available on the open market. On the other hand, libraries may simply be responding to user demand by reproducing a copyrighted nonprint work.

Another possible reason for a library to duplicate nonprint works is in order to respond to an interlibrary loan request. Thus, the motives for such copying are as varied as are the techniques and technology used to produce the copy (42).

There are ways of reproducing nonprint material legally, either by asking permission and/or by paying royalties for the privilege of duplicating the materials (43). This applies to libraries, as well as individuals. A § 107 fair use claim also might exempt some copying.

The Act allows nonprint material to be reproduced by a library only under narrow circumstances. Unpublished works may be duplicated for preservation purposes (44), and when the library's copy of a published audiovisual work is damaged, deteriorating, lost or stolen, the library may reproduce the work after making a reasonable effort to find an unused replacement copy at a fair price (45). When illustrations accompany a printed work, they may be copied along with articles in accordance with §§ 108 (d) and (e) (46). This applies to all formats of material and will not be discussed for each individual type of nonprint work.

Computer Programs

Software for computers is included in the literary works category and is subject to copyright protection. Computer programs are governed under § 117 of the Act, which was amended in late 1980 (47). The Act now defines computer programs as "... a set of instructions to be used directly or indirectly in a computer in order to bring about a certain result (48). The new provision specifically describes the conditions under which the lawful owner of a copy of a copyrighted program may make additional copies of the program or adapt it.

The first condition relates to the use of the program by the owner of the

copy. If making the copy is an essential step in the use of the program with the existing hardware, a copy or adaptation may be made, for example, the translation of a software package from one computer language to another. The copy made under this provision may be used for no other purposes (49).

The second condition relates to making a copy for archival purposes. The owner of the copy must destroy archival copies in the event the possession of the program should cease to be rightful (50). A common example of a change in the legality of the possession would be the termination of a licensing agreement. At the end of the license period, the licensee must destroy the copy made under § 117.

Section 107 provides a fair use exemption for multiple copying for classroom use, but it is not likely that it would . . . apply to multiple copying of software, even for classroom use.

Libraries may be involved in using commercially produced software through lease or purchase or in the development of their own software. Libraries which use programs developed and copyrighted by others are subject to the provisions of § 117. Whether libraries may copy programs for users requires a close examination of §§ 107 and 108. Programs are considered to be literary works (51) and are not mentioned as nonprint material deserving special consideration under the provisions of § 108 as are audiovisual, pictorial, and graphic works. The assumption, therefore, is that duplicating a portion of a purchased copyrighted program for a user would not be an infringement of copyright provided that the other requirements of § 108 are met.

Duplicating multiple copies for a library's collection would be equated with making multiple copies of novels, and normally would be an infringement of copyright. Duplication of software in multiple copies for courses in computer programming and the like probably is an infringement. Software developers will sell programs in multiple copies, or at least sell the right to duplicate copies in excess of the exemption provided by § 117.

Section 107 provides a fair use exemption for multiple copying for classroom use, but it is not likely that it would be interpreted to apply to multiple copying of software, even for classroom use.

As with other works, determining the copyright status of computer software presents an additional problem for librarians. Although the Act specifies that notice should be placed on copies of a work in a manner to give reasonable notice of a claim of copyright (52), one cannot presume that a program is within the public domain if it lacks a copyright notice. The Act treats several reasons for notice omission as exceptions to the general notice requirements. An omitted notice will not invalidate the copyright if the notice is omitted from no more than a few copies, or if registration for the work has been made before or within five years of publication without notice and, after the omission is discovered, a reasonable effort is made to correct the lack of notice on all publicly distributed copies within the United States. Likewise, omission of the notice will not defeat the copyright if the notice was omitted in violation of an express written requirement for notice as a condition of the author's authorization of public distribution of copies (53).

The Copyright Office regulations specify the placement of the notice on machine readable copies. It may be embodied in machine readable form so it appears on any printouts, either with or near the title or at the end of the work. On the other hand, it might be continuously displayed on terminal display. The most common location for placement of the notice for programs probably is on the container, i.e., box, reel, disc, cartridge and so on (54).

Perhaps the safest course of conduct for a librarian wishing to duplicate software is to assume that it is protected by copyright. Should the copying be outside the provisions of §§ 107,108, or 117, the offer to pay royalties should be made.

Computer Databases

Computer databases may consist of several types of material. A database may be a previously copyrighted work now stored electronically. In that case, the protection given the underlying work also extends to the electronic copy. The fact that a work exists in a computer database does not change its copyright characteristics. On the other hand, a database may be an original compilation, i.e., "...a work formed by the collection and assembling of preexisting material or of data that are selected, coordinated, or arranged in such a way that the resulting work as a whole constitutes an original work of authorship" (55).

The technically correct term for both types of databases is "machine-readable database." The vast majority of existing databases are not in machine-readable form but are traditional compilations such as dictionaries, directories, citators, and so on. Compilations are noted not for their artistic and literary merit but for their commercial and practical value (56). Compilations are subject to copyright protection under the literary works category; their originality lies in the collection and organization of the data.

Section 103 provides that compilations can be protected, but the copyright in such works does not extend to any preexisting material that may be used in the compilation. The copyright, therefore, does not relate to each entry in a compilation but to the original elements of the work as a whole.

A machine-readable database derives its value from the organization of the material and the sophistication of the program which dictates the searching and retrieval of the information. The skill of the person performing the search also contributes to the value based on his or her skill in articulating requests in the process of interacting with the database (57).

A particularly difficult question arose early in the history of copyright protection for databases. Should copyright liability attach at the input or the output stage? In other words, is the copy made at the time the work is input into the computer memory unit in machine-readable form or when the search is made of data existing in the computer's memory (58)? The input/output consideration is not an idle theoretical question but deals with user patterns and determination of the stage at which royalties should be paid. There could be instances in which royalties should be paid at input and others at the output stage. If the work is never to be printed or reproduced in its entirety, then if royalties are due, they should be paid at the input stage. On the other hand, requiring royalty payment at the input

only on a screen and never is transferred to any hard copy (60). The answer to the question may be affirmative if one analogizes to video games. Recent court decisions have held that the audiovisual display in a video game caused by the repetition from game to game of images and sounds on the screen constitutes sufficient fixation for copyright purposes to qualify the game for copyright protection as an audiovisual work (61). If this repetition constitutes fixation, then repetition logically can be considered a copy for copyright purposes. The Act defines copy as:

> ...material objects, other than phonorecords, in which a work is fixed...from which the work may be perceived, reproduced, or otherwise communicated, either directly or with the aid of a machine or device. The term 'copies' include the material object, other than a phonorecord in which the work is first fixed. (62).

> **A particularly difficult question arose early in the history of copyright protection for databases. Should copyright liability attach at the input or the output stage? In other words, is the copy made at the time the work is input into the computer memory unit in machine-readable form or when the search is made of data existing in the computer's memory?**

stage could serve to inhibit the development of useful databases, especially if, at the initial stage, the developer considers the material to be marginal. It also might be easier to control the payment of royalties at the input stage (59).

At the output stage there is frequently a problem in defining what activities constitute output. Certainly, the printing of material from a database constitutes output. It is less clear whether merely scanning the database and seeing data displayed on a viewing device constitutes output. The display certainly is ephemeral when it appears

If the repetition on the screen is sufficient to "fix" a video game display, then the ability to repeat the display may be sufficient to qualify as a copy for output purposes.

The National Commission of the New Technological Uses of Copyrighted Works answered the input/output question in its subsequently enacted proposal for a new § 117 (63). The copyright owner has the exclusive right to store copyrighted works in machine-readable form.

The unauthorized storage of a copyrighted work constitutes infringement of the owner's reproduction right. The making of a copy of the entire work normally would be within the owner's exclusive rights subject to some possible fair use exceptions. The fact that only one copy is made, or that the owner of the database intends to exact no fee, would not insulate the copier from liability from infringement (64).

Database proprietors are likely to be concerned about two kinds of unauthorized use: 1) the misappropriation of database information for purposes of duplicating the information or for compiling a subsequent work based on the data, and 2) unauthorized searching of the database to use the information contained therein without compensation to the proprietor (65).

The unauthorized practice of downloading proprietary databases into a library's own internal computer's memory doubtless causes the owner to suffer economic harm. The owner is no longer compensated for searches and the entire database, or at least entire portions of interest to that user, have been appropriated. Both the general laws of unfair competition (66), as well as copyright laws, prohibit such unauthorized taking or copying.

Despite the fact that only a small portion of the database may be retrieved, infringement still occurs if the search is unauthorized (67). One seldom copies an entire database; rather the very nature of databases dictates that only data relevant to a particular search will be retrieved at any one time. Any unauthorized search deprives the proprietor of revenue no matter how small the amount of material actually retrieved may be.

Even if the data retrieved and used are public domain materials, the unauthorized search is still an infringement. The organization of the data and the ability to retrieve them in response to a request provides the element of originality in a computerized database; therefore, public domain material may not be free to all when it is retrieved from a database (68).

Since libraries also may create in-house databases, some attention should be given to the protection of these works. Since many of the formalities of copyright such as notice and deposit relate only to published works, whether the creation of a database constitutes publication presents an interesting question. Section 101 defines publication as "... the distribution of copies or phonorecords of a work to the public by sale or other transfer of ownership, or by rental, lease, or lending." Certainly, the distribution of hard copy or portions of a database would constitute publication, but what about databases where no hard copy is created? It seems logical that the sale of access to the database constitutes publication. Thus, if a library creates and "publishes" a database, the portions of the Act relating to protecting published works apply.

Determining the copyright status of computer software presents an additional problem for librarians. Although the Act specifies that notice should be placed on copies of a work in a manner to give reasonable notice of a claim of copyright, one cannot presume that a program is within the public domain if it lacks a copyright notice.

Elaborate security precautions will not stop the unscrupulous, unauthorized user but copyright notice will stop the honest person who gains access to a database by mistake. Notice of copyright should appear on the initial display for each search (69). Copyright notice consists of three essential elements: the name of the copyright owner, the year of first publication, and the symbol© or the word "Copyright" or the abbreviation "Copr" (70).

The registration and deposit of copyrighted works are not conditions precedent to the ownership of copyright. Registration is, however, essential for initiating a copyright infringement action in federal court (71). Since the deposit requirement is triggered by publication, an unpublished database would not be required to meet the deposit requirement (72). Database registration and deposit have some inherent problems since any useful database must be continually updated. Having to deposit copies of the database after each updating would be impractical. Fortunately, the Register of Copyrights has authority under the Act to modify the deposit requirements and may exempt any category of material by regulation (73). It seems likely that databases would be a category for exemption.

There also has been some concern that, because of the fluidity of databases and the updating performed, a database potentially could receive copyright protection for longer than the statutory 75 years. This problem, according to CONTU, is not unique. Just as each new edition of a telephone directory is separately copyrighted, the same is true of databases (74). Only the new information and its arrangement would be protected in subsequent updates; therefore, copyright protection is not extended for longer than the statutory period.

The problem of unauthorized use has been addressed by a recent bill introduced in Congress (75). The bill would expand the criminal provisions of the Act (76) which prohibit piracy of and counterfeit labels for phonorecords, tapes, and audiovisual works by including computer programs and databases. The bill would amend existing § 506(a), which currently states that anyone who willfully infringes a copyright for "purposes of commercial advantage or private financial gain shall be punished as provided in section 2319 of title 18" (77). Libraries in the for-profit sector would have difficulty establishing that any internal unauthorized use was for purposes other than commercial gain. Any library that downloaded specific information from a database in order to avoid the assessment of fees for each search is engaged in unauthorized use for commercial gain.

As more and more information becomes available through databases, libraries must become increasingly aware of the nature of the rights afforded to the proprietor of such databases. Libraries that subscribe to databases should be free to use the information for the intended purpose, but the unauthorized copying of any substantial portions of these databases probably infringes the rights of the database proprietor.

The development of optical scanners capable of rapid conversion of printed material to machine readable form may rival the invention of the photocopier relative to its effect on copyright. Not only can libraries and information centers convert copies of literary works with accompanying illustrations into machine-readable form for in-house use, but data may be transferred from one library to another in this fashion (78). These devices have the capacity to be more valuable than the telecopier for interlibrary exchange. Such transmission of copyrighted materials presents a whole new area of concern.

With traditional telecopiers, the supplying entity, in response to a request, photocopies the item to be transmitted and then sends the copy via a telecopier to a requesting library. Presumably the copy made by the lending library is destroyed. The copy received by the requesting entity is treated as any photocopy received through interlibrary loan and is governed by the guidelines. A copy converted to machine readable form by an optical scanner can be transmitted over the lower cost data transmission lines thereby reducing the overall costs of the transaction and potentially increasing the number of transactions. The requesting library receives the machine readable copy which it may store in its computer and/or print out a copy for the user making the request.

If the transaction is a pure interlibrary loan, the machine readable copy received by the requesting library should be destroyed and not stored electronically. If a copy is needed for the library's collection, it should be obtained through normal trade channels or through § 108 provisions. Sections 108(a) and 108(e) specifically state that a copy made for a user must become the property of that user whether the copy is received through interlibrary loan or made on the premises. Any retention of copyrighted material received through electronic data transfer other than as permitted under §§ 108(b) or 108(c) is an infringement of copyright.

electronic pages. Naturally, they will expect a reasonable return on their investments by selling the data for per-page or per-minute charges. Their business will depend on the security of the systems and protection against unauthorized copying and resale (79). Will the interlibrary loan of copies of journal articles printed by a subscribing library and furnished to a requesting library constitute unauthorized use? Although supporting arguments can be made for both sides, publishers of electronic journals surely will claim that such ar-

---

The new technology makes it easy . . . to download copyrighted material from the publisher's system into the subscriber's own computer system. Protection for the owner consists of breach of contract and copyright infringement if the unauthorized copying is detected.

Technological capabilities frequently are developed faster than the law can accommodate them. The apparatus to convert printed works to machine readable form is a prime example of technology moving ahead of the law.

Electronic Publishing

The electronic publishing of journals in lieu of publication in hard copy or microform currently is being considered as an alternative publication form by publishers of scholarly, scientific, and technical journals. As journal publishers move into the realm of electronic publishing, libraries and information centers must deal with the material and handle copyright problems as they arise. Because such publication is still in its infancy, the problems of copyright protection for these materials is still somewhat speculative.

Some electronic publishers will be expending large amounts of capital in order to obtain rights to publish material electronically and to design

rangements infringe their reproduction and distribution rights.

Unauthorized reproduction will constitute copyright infringement regardless of whether the reproduction is on paper or transferred to the memory of another computer (80). The application of traditional fair use analysis is imprecise for materials stored in traditional formats; fair use may be even less precise for electronic publications. For example, it might be fair use for a videotext subscriber to record portions of the material on a home computer where pages could be retrieved for later personal use (81). Would the same apply to libraries or would the personal use exemption constitute an equivalent to the home use exemption for audio recordings of music made off-the-air (82)? This issue is yet unanswered. Certainly, copyright infringement will be difficult to detect. The new technology makes it easy for a subscriber to videotext or teletext to download copyrighted material from the publisher's system into the subscriber's own computer system (83). To date, protection for the owner consists of breach of contract and copyright infringement if the unauthorized copying is detected. Perhaps, in the future, criminal penalties might be added for unauthorized reproduction from electronically published journals as has been recommended for computer programs and databases (*84*).

Subscriptions to electronic journals will provide the subscriber with rights print works. Eventually, free access could lead to no access (*86*). On the other hand, since libraries now pay high subscription costs, including the cost of interlibrary loan transactions, already there is no free access.

Answers to these problems should come from agreement between librarians and copyright proprietors (*87*).

Future technology should enable librarians to copy material even more conveniently and inexpensively. The very tools which have enabled libraries to create their information base could destroy the dissemination of information. If all libraries and library users wish to copy information and no one wants to pay for it, there will be no resources available to the commercial developer for the creation of new nonprint works. Eventually, free access could lead to no access.

---

to certain kinds of uses, and should include copying for some uses. The subscription contract should specify what these uses are and under what conditions copies may be made.

Conclusion

Libraries have available to them not only the provisions of § 108 but those of § 107, the fair use exception. Even the application of traditional fair use principle may fail to answer questions about specific library practices and the use and reproduction of nonprint and audiovisual material. The technological era has raised serious questions on the applicability of traditional fair use principles (*85*).

Future technology should enable librarians to copy material even more conveniently and inexpensively. The very tools which have enabled libraries to create their information base could destroy the dissemination of information. If all libraries and library users wish to copy information and no one wants to pay for it, there will be no resources available to the commercial developer for the creation of new non-

The recently negotiated guidelines for off-the-air videotaping for nonprofit educational institutions (*88*) are an excellent example of such consensus. Both interest groups, publishers and librarians have presented logical arguments for their respective positions. Publishers argue that library copying practices continue to have serious economic consequences for publishers of journals with small circulations (*89*). The King Report, however, fails to support this position (*90*).

During the hearings conducted by the Copyright Office on § 108, questions were posed by the Register concerning the CONTU interlibrary loan guidelines; a question concerning interlibrary loan of nonprint works was included. The Register's Report, however, did not include any recommendations to alter those guidelines (*91*).

The library community repeatedly has recommended no change in the Act at the present time. Perhaps the answer for nonprint materials lies in further guidance from library associations recommending compliance methods for specific practices and types of materials (*92*).

Literature Cited

1. 17 U.S.C. § 101, *et seq*. (1976).
2. *See* National Commission on Libraries and Information Science, *Library Photocopying in the United States* (1977) for a report on library photocopying practices before the effective date of the Act.
3. 17 U.S.C. § 102(a) (1976).
4. "A work is fixed when it is embodied in a copy or phonorecord in a permanent or stable form sufficient to permit it to be perceived, reproduced or otherwise communicated for a period of more than transitory duration." *Id*. at § 101.
5. *Id*.
6. *Id*. at § 106.
7. *Id*. at § 109.
8. See 3 M. Nimmer, *Copyright* § 13.05 (1982) for a detailed discussion of the fair use defense.
9. 17 U.S.C. § 107 (1976).
10. *Id*.
11. *Id*. at § 108(a).
12. *Id*. at § 108(b).
13. *Id*. at § 108(c).
14. *Id*. at § 108(d).
15. *Id*. at § 108(d)(1).
16. *Id*. at § 108(d)(2); the specific wording for the warning was promulgated by the Register of Copyrights on November 16, 1977, 42 *Fed. Reg*. 59,264 (1977).
17. *Id*. at § 108(f)(1) (1976); no specific wording is required on the warning sign according to the Register of Copyrights; *see* 42 *Fed. Reg*. 59,265 (1977).
18. *Id*. at § 108(e)(1).
19. *Id*. at § 108(g)(2).
20. The guidelines were negotiated by various library associations and publishers' group and were adopted by CONTU (the National Commission on New Technological Uses of Copyrighted Works) and were published in the Conference Report. H.R. Conf. Rep. No. 1733, 94th Cong., 2d Sess. (1976), *Reprinted in* 17 *Omnibus Copyright Revision Legislative History, 1976*, at 72–73 (1976). [Hereinafter cited as Conference Report].
21. H.R. Rep. No. 1476, 94th Cong., 2d Sess. (1976), *Reprinted in* 17 *Omnibus Copyright Revision Legislative History, 1976*, at 74–75 (1976). [Hereinafter cited as House Report].
22. 17 U.S.C. § 108(h) (1976).
23. *Id*.
24. *Id*. at § 108(b).
25. *Id*. at § 108(c).
26. *See* text at notes 20–21.
27. S. Rep. No. 473, 94th Cong., 1st Sess. (1975), *Reprinted in* 13 *Omnibus Copyright Revision Legislative History, 1974-1975*, at 61 (1975). [Hereinafter cited as Senate Report].
28. *Id*.
29. 659 F.2d 963 (9th Cir. 1981).
30. *Id*. at 969–74.
31. *Cert. granted*, 102 S.Ct. 2926 (1982).
32. 659 F.2d 963 (9th Cir. 1981).
33. Conference Report, *supra* note 20.
34. 17 U.S.C. § 108(h) (1976).
35. House Report, *supra* note 21, at 74–75.
36. *Id*. at 75.
37. *Id*.
38. Association of American Publishers, *Photocopying by Academic, Public and Nonprofit Libraries* 12–13 (1978); Association of American Publishers, *Final Comments for the Register's Report to Congress in Accordance with 17 USC 108(i) as Requested May 26, 1982*, 32 (1982).
39. 17 U.S.C. § 105 (1976).
40. *See id*. at §§ 107–108(a).
41. *Id*. at § 108(b).
42. *See contra*, Golub, "Not By Books Alone: Library Copying of Nonprint Copyrighted Material," 70 *L. Libr. J*. 153, 153 (1977).
43. Magnuson, "Duplicating AV Materials Legally," 13 *Media & Methods* 52 (1977).
44. 17 U.S.C. § 108(b) (1976).
45. *Id*. at § 108(c).
46. *Id*. at § 108(h).
47. 17 U.S.C. § 117 (1976), as amended by Pub. L. No. 96–517, Dec. 12, 1980, 94 Stat. 3028, codified as amended at 17 U.S.C. § 117 (Supp. V, 1981).
48. *Id*. at § 101.
49. *Id*. at § 117(1) (Supp. V, 1981).
50. *Id*. at § 117(2).
51. *See* National Commission on New Technological Uses of Copyrighted Works, *Final Report*, 26–27 (1979) for a criticism of the inclusion of programs as a type of literary work. [Hereinafter cited as CONTU].
52. 17 U.S.C. § 401 (1976).
53. *Id*. at § 405(a).
54. 46 *Fed. Reg*. 58,307 (1981).
55. 17 U.S.C. § 101 (1976).
56. Squires, "Copyright and Compilations in the Computer Era: Old Wine in New Bottles," in G. Bush & R. Dreyfuss, *Technology and Copyright* at 205, 206, 212–15 (1979). [Hereinafter cited as Squires].
57. CONTU, *supra* note 51, at 41.

58. *Id.* at 39.
59. Henderson, "Copyright Impacts of Future Technology," 16 *J. of Chemical Information & Computer Sci.* 72 (1976), *reprinted in* G. Bush & R. Dreyfuss, *Technology and Copyright*, 343, 352 (1979).
60. Levy, "Copyright Law and Computerized Legal Research," 20 *Bull. of the Copyright Soc'y* 159, 170 (1973).
61. *See* Stern Electronics v. Kaufman, 660 F.2d 852 (2d Cir. 1982) and Atari v. North American Phillips, 672 F.2d 607 (7th Cir. 1982).
62. 17 U.S.C. § 101 (1976).
63. CONTU, *supra* note 51, at 39–40.
64. *Id.*
65. Squires, *supra* note 56, at 229.
66. *See* International News Service v. Associated Press, 248 U.S. 215 (1918) for a discussion of misappropriation, an unfair competition cause of action.
67. Squires, *supra* note 56, at 232.
68. *Id.*
69. CONTU, *supra* note 51, at 39.
70. 17 U.S.C. § 401(b) (1976).
71. *Id.* at §§ 407–12.
72. *Id.* at 407(a).
.73. *Id.* at § 407(c).
74. CONTU, *supra* note 51, at 41–42.
75. H.R. 6420, 97th Cong., 2d Sess. (1982).
76. 17 U.S.C. § 506 (1976).
77. H.R. 6420, *supra* note 75.
78. The IBM Scanmaster I is an example of a machine with such capability.
79. R. Neustadt, *The Birth of Electronic Publishing* 119 (1982). [Hereinafter cited as Neustadt].
80. *Id.* at 120.
81. *Id.* at 121.
82. *See* H.R.Rep., No. 487, 92nd Cong., 1st Sess. 7 (1971). The so-called home use exemption for home recording of music was not mentioned in subsequent legislative history.
83. Neustadt, *supra* note 78, at 122.
84. *See* text at notes 77–78.
85. Timberg, "A Modernized Fair Use Code for the Electronic as well as the Gutenberg Age," 75 Nw.U.L.Rev. 193, 198 (1980).
86. Callison, "Fair Payment for Fair Use in Future Information Technology Systems," *Educ. Tech.* Jan., 1981 at 24.
87. Golub, *supra* note 42, at 169.
88. 127 *Cong. Rec.* E4750-52 (daily ed. Oct. 14, 1981).
89. *See* Association of American Publishers, *Final Comments for the Register's Report to Congress in Accordance with 17 U.S.C. 108(i) as Requested May 26, 1982.* (1982).
90. King Research, *Libraries, Publishers, and Photocopying: Final Report of Surveys Conducted for the United States Copyright Office*, at 4–14 (1982).
91. *Report of the Register of Copyrights: Library Reproduction of Copyrighted Works*, 358–63 (1983).
92. *See* American Library Association, *Model Policy on College and University Photocopying for Classroom, Research and Library Reserve Use* (1982).

Laura N. Gasaway is director,
Law Library, and law professor,
University of Oklahoma, Norman,
Okla.

26: COPYRIGHT OFFICE REPORTS TO CONGRESS ON PHOTOCOPYING ISSUE: UPHOLDS SECTION 108 AS WORKABLE

The first 5-year report on the copying practices of libraries and their clients concludes that the photocopying provisions in the copyright law "provide a workable framework for obtaining a balance between creators' rights and users' needs." In those instances where a balance has not been achieved, the Copyright Office concludes that it is either because the intent of Congress has not been carried out fully or because that intent is not clear to those who "behavior is within the ambit of the law." The report treats "balance" as meaning that section 108 "allows users to use — by photocopying — works protected by copyright in a way both consistent with traditional principles of copyright law and library practice and not exceeding a minimal encroachment upon the rights of authors and copyright owners."

That a balance exists is supported by evidence showing that between 1976 and 1980 library acquisition expenditures increased faster than the rate of inflation; that, during the same period, the ratio of serial "births" to serial "deaths" was 3.4 to 1; that some types of photocopying in certain classes of libraries have increased

"very slowly" or even decreased; and that serial publishers increased their revenues.

That there "might be an imbalance" relies on information that substantial quantities of the photocopies prepared by and for library patrons are made for job-related reasons, rather than for research or scholarship, and that in roughly one-quarter of the library photocopying transactions, two or more copies are made. Section 108 permits only a single copy.

According to the report, there appears to be significant confusion among many librarians about how the copyright law works and why its enforcement is frequently their responsibility. Furthermore, publishers contend that the present system is seriously imbalanced, and some of them have asserted their views in print and by bringing lawsuits. [See *Information Hotline*, Vol. 15, No. 2.]

After five years of "consulting with representatives of authors, book and periodical publishers, and with other owners of copyrighted materials, and with representatives of library users and librarians," the Copyright Office has submitted recommendations to Congress that include the encouragement of voluntary guidelines and of collective photocopying licensing agreements, studies of possible surcharges on photocopying equipment and of compensation systems based on sampling techniques, and the encouragement of agreements concerning archival preservation issues. Other recommendations relate to revisions of specific provisions in the copyright law.

Congress, recognizing that section 108 was bound to become controversial because it was such a radical departure from prior law, mandated that the Copyright Office submit a report every five years, giving its findings and recommendations. Briefly summarized, section 108 permits copying not authorized by section 107 (the "fair use" provision), but that fair use is not available on a broad and recurring basis once section 108's complying limits have been reached. The types of transactions authorized are: preservation copying of unpublished works; replacement copying under certain conditions of published works; "reserve" copying; and various types of copying for and by library users. Section 108 bans "related or concerted photocopying" and all "systematic" photocopying except within certain interlibrary transactions, unless, in each case, authorized by the copyright owner. Thus the section places certain limitations on the broad and exclusive rights granted to copyright owners in section 106, permitting otherwise unauthorized copying to occur. Copying by libraries not permitted by section 108 must be authorized by the copyright owner or it is an infringement of copyright.

Reprinted below are the executive summary as well as the full text of Chapter IX: Copyright Office Recommendations.

Report of the Register of Copyrights

**LIBRARY REPRODUCTION
OF COPYRIGHTED WORKS
(17 U.S.C. 108)
January 1983**

EXECUTIVE SUMMARY

Chapter One — Introduction

The introduction identifies the focus of the report: photocopying in libraries. The Copyright Office believes that §108 of the Copyright Act of 1976 provides a workable structural framework for obtaining a balance between creators' rights and users' needs, but that, in certain instances, the balance has not been achieved in practice, either because the intent of Congress has not been carried out fully or because the intent is not clear.

This report treats "balance" as meaning that §108 allows users to use — by photocopying — works protected by copyright in a way both consistent with traditional principles of copyright law and library practice and not exceeding a minimal encroachment upon the rights of authors and copyright owners.

Some of the evidence supports a conclusion that a balance now exists; other evidence calls that conclusion into doubt. Several organizations and individuals proposed statutory changes of various types, and the Copyright Office makes (in chapter nine) several statutory and nonstatutory recommendations.

The introduction next discusses the importance of information in today's world, and a philosophical clash between libraries and publishers about how to pursue the goal of efficient widespread dissemination of information. These are followed by a brief note on the importance of precision in the use of language and the nature of the conclusions reached in this report. Finally, the introduction discusses the difficulty of trying to forecast technological developments and the disappointing lack of successful discussions among the

155

parties concerned with a variety of copyright-photocopying issues.

Chapter Two — Background and Legislative History

Debates, drafts, and discussions about photocopying and copyright spanned the twenty-five year period in which the US Copyright Law was revised. Technological changes and the *Williams & Wilkins* case required Congress to address a variety of important issues concerning both fair use and library photocopying.

Before 1965 a library copying provision had been added to — and then deleted from — various proposals to revise the copyright law. A fair use provision was in all revision bills. As the *Williams & Wilkins* case — concerning large-scale photocopying in government libraries — progressed through the courts, specific changes regarding photocopying were proposed, which ultimately resulted in §108. Various organizations, both formal and informal, held meetings and hearings to try to accommodate the disparate views of the proprietary and library communities. Some progress resulted, such as the promulgation of the CONTU guidelines, but for the most part, the major accomplishment was the airing of adverse views, until the current Act was passed in late 1976.

The first version of §108 appeared in 1969, but was significantly different from what is now the law. The hearings and proposals addressing it reflected developments in the *Williams & Wilkins* case. Over time, provisions concerning what copyright information should be included on photocopies, distinctions between copying small portions and complete works, and limits to "108" copying were added. Finally, an exception to one of those limits, so as to permit interlibrary transfers of photocopies in lieu of interlibrary loan, was added in 1976.

During the same time, Congress rejected a general not-for-profit exemption, and encouraged the parties in interest to reach voluntary agreements concerning matters about which they disagreed. The "classroom" and "music" guidelines were adopted as a result of such agreements. Shortly thereafter, the CONTU guidelines, designed to quantify certain terms in one subsection of §108, were completed.

One of the final additions to §108 was subsection (i), which mandated this report. In preparing it, the Register of Copyrights appointed a committee of representatives of the interested parties and, on their advice, the Copyright Office held a series of regional hearings on photocopying-copyright issues and let a contract under which a substantial statistical survey was performed.

Chapter Three — Balance: Eligibility for §108 Treatment

This chapter addresses the criteria that govern libraries' eligibility for §108 photocopying privileges and the types of works to which those privileges apply. The fundamental rule in subsection (a) is that all copying permitted by §108 involves the preparation of no more than one copy at a time. There is empirical evidence that in roughly one-quarter of the library photocopying transactions in which library materials bearing a copyright notice are copied by library employees, two or more copies are made.

Another requirement is that copies prepared under §108 bear "a notice of copyright." There is a long-standing division of opinion between the library and proprietary communities about the meaning of this requirement. Librarians generally believe that a warning that copyright may protect the material is sufficient; proprietors urge that the formal copyright notice set out in §§401-403 of the law is required. The statute itself, like the legislative history, is ambiguous, but appears to support the latter position. Ideally, the parties should reach an accommodation which satisfies the proprietors' needs without placing undue clerical burdens on the libraries.

Several rules from §108 combine to suggest that §108 privileges are rather limited for special libraries in for-profit

entities. They include: (1) the extent to which the library is open to competitors' employees; (2) the meaning of the phrase "indirect commercial advantage"; (3) the extent to which employees, acting within the scope of their employment, should be said to be "supervised" when they prepare photocopies; (4) the extent to which certain transactions are "related or concerted"; and (5) the extent to which the copying done is "systematic."

As to types of works copyable under §108, the broadest privileges apply to literary works. Copying privileges are greatly reduced with respect to musical works, pictorial, graphic, or sculptural works, motion pictures, and non-news audiovisual works. The Music Library Association and the Music Publishers' Association of the United States have proposed a statutory change, which the Copyright Office endorses, to permit, after certain steps are taken, slightly more copying of musical works — for study, not performance — under §108.

Foreign works should generally be treated just as are works created and published in the United States.

Chapter Four — Balance: Copying and Other Issues

The question of balance requires an examination of what is occurring in practice as well as a determination of what the law intends. This chapter addresses both topics.

It begins by noting that §108 permits copying not authorized by §107 (the fair use provision) and that fair use is thus not available on a broad and recurring basis once §108 copying limits have been reached. Basically, in examining copying "beyond" §108, one must determine whether the transaction is of a type which could be fair use and, if so, consider, in the fair use calculus, the copying already done under §108. The record suggests substantial confusion about the relationship between these important sections.

The report next addresses the various types of transactions authorized and forbidden under §108. These include preservation copying of unpublished works under subsection 108(b), replacement copying, under certain conditions, of published works under subsection 108(c), "reserve" copying (a fair use issue not strictly within the scope of §108), and various types of copying for and by library users.

Subsection 108(g), which places two different but related "caps" on §108 photocopying, then receives substantial attention. Its bans on "related or concerted" photocopying of which libraries are aware and all "systematic" photocopying except certain interlibrary transactions (unless, in each case, authorized by the copyright owner) — appear to be a major source of confusion and disagreement. Its history is linked to the *Williams & Wilkins* case, and its provisions are the subject of similar debate. An important point, which does not appear to be well-understood, is that libraries do not necessarily obtain fair use privileges from their users. That is, copying which may be fair use, if done by a user, may be "related or concerted" if done by the library: the library may not do the photocopying without permission from the copyright owner.

That §108(g)'s terms are limits on §108 copying is also not completely understood. The structure of the law is clear: §106 grants broad and exclusive rights to copyright owners; §108 places certain limitations on those rights by permitting certain otherwise unauthorized copying to occur. Copying by libraries not permitted by §108 must generally be authorized by the copyright owner or it is an infringement of copyright.

The ban on most systematic photocopying is also less than perfectly understood. The proviso permitting certain interlibrary photocopying has been frequently considered by all concerned, but the general prohibition has not. The CONTU guidelines provide a quantitative rule for some interlibrary transactions, but the overall meaning of "systematic" remains an ideal subject for agreement among the parties.

Users, who obtain no copying privileges for themselves

under §108 (all of theirs deriving from §107), are liable for copyright infringement for their photocopying beyond fair use. The library in which infringing copies are made may be liable for its patrons' infringements <u>unless</u>: the copying is unsupervised <u>and</u> it occurs on a machine which bears the required warning.

Although §108 is directed exclusively to copying in libraries and archives, much copying which occurs elsewhere bears on the balance issue. The report discusses copying shops, commercial information brokers, and libraries not eligible for §108 privileges.

The next part of chapter four discusses issues about copyright proprietors — both authors and publishers. Much of the record and many of the copyright-photocopying controversies concern scholarly, scientific, and technical (SST) journals. The authors of the articles which appear in such journals may be less concerned with royalties than "traditional" authors, but the publishers must, of course, be concerned with at least recovering their costs. And of course, publishers do not always require payment for photocopying, but desire to keep some control over their works by requiring clear requests for permission to photocopy.

Since 1978 the Copyright Clearance Center has been in operation. Its publisher members authorize it to grant, in advance, transaction-by-transaction or larger-scale photocopy permissions to library and other members who, in turn, pay periodic fees for photocopying not permitted by §§107-108 according to a publisher-fixed scale. Although publisher and library membership has increased, it is still below original expectations.

Chapter Five — King Report

To augment the record created by the hearings and comment letters, the Copyright Office let a contract for the performance of several statistical surveys. King Research, Inc., performed three surveys of libraries, one of publishers, and two of library patrons. Its report contained a wealth of data concerning several types of photocopying transactions, publisher information, and user experiences.

The complete King Report is Appendix I to this report. The Copyright Office's analysis thereof is chapter five. We do not here summarize its findings, on the ground that any short summary necessarily shapes the reader's impressions. We commend the full King Report, and our analysis, to anyone concerned with copyright-photocopying issues.

Chapter Six — New Technology

The photocopy machine has introduced stress into the traditional copyright system by diluting the copyright proprietor's ability to control the reproduction of works in traditional print media. The copyright issues that have arisen have been complex and hard to resolve; but, no matter how difficult these have been, the widespread use of new technological media will raise even harder problems. To aid in understanding the magnitude and scope of these problems this chapter surveys the impact of the emerging technologies on librarians, publishers, and the copyright law.

Use of computers has revolutionized the reference functions of libraries and provided new entrepreneurial opportunities for commercial ventures. Document delivery services, however, have not progressed rapidly enough to keep pace with the speed with which bibliographic information may be retrieved. The data base industry supplies two generic products: source and bibliographic data bases. Source data bases supply the user with the data itself, whereas, bibliographic data bases serve the same function as a library and catalog. The widespread availability of these systems has caused librarians to question whether the costs of services of this kind should be passed on to library users. Government information policies also affect this market.

The application of these technologies has led to the growth of library networks which may lead to greater resource sharing and interlibrary loan activity.

In the publishing and information dissemination communities, the new technologies are creating new products and markets. Teletext, videotext, electrooptical discs and other new media present both opportunities for and threats to publishers and librarians. The inability of copyright proprietors to control further duplication of works in machine-readable media has caused and will continue to cause stress for the copyright community, and librarians will face increasing concerns over paying for the costs of access and copying.

The chapter ends by calling for serious discussions of how all the parties — users, librarians, authors, and publishers — can take full advantage of the opportunities for improved information dissemination provided by the new technologies.

Chapter Seven — Library Reproduction Abroad:
An Overview of Recent Developments

The copyright problems which arise out of library photocopying are not unique to the USA. They arise in all countries, but most acutely in economically advanced nations, which, like the USA, are members of international copyright conventions. Neither of the two principal conventions, the Universal Copyright Convention — to which the USA belongs — nor the Berne Convention expressly regulates the domestic treatment of library photocopying. But both conventions, posited upon the principle of treating foreign authors equally with national authors, tend to reinforce practical interdependence and have served as arenas for elaboration of informed international opinion on the matter of library photocopying.

At the intergovernmental level, there is general recognition that the legitimate interests of authors require that domestic law make provision for the payment of a fair remuneration for the reprographic reproduction of protected works, but beyond this general position, no uniform solution at the international level has been found.

At the nongovernmental level, international organizations representing publishers continue intensive study and consultations looking toward the development of comprehensive, easy-to-use collective licensing arrangements. Librarians, too, have international nongovernmental organizations to represent their collective concerns. The International Federation of Library Associations and Institutions (IFLA) has asserted strongly the view that nonprofit reproduction of works for teaching, scholarship and research is a right libraries must be able to perform for their users and that national copyright laws should so provide.

The national laws on photocopying in a number of important states are in a transitional period. Canada is in the process of generally revising its 1924 Copyright Act and is faced with the problem of whether to leave library photocopying to the unelaborated law of "fair dealing" or to adopt a more specific, statutory regime. The situation in the United Kingdom is similar to that of Canada, with the significant difference being that the UK copyright statute contains a specific provision covering nonprofit library reproduction of single copies or periodical articles in addition to a "fair dealing" provision.

Governmental studies and reports in the UK have pointed in two not incompatible directions: recommending establishment of a negotiated blanket licensing system, and possibly tightening the single-copying privilege in the statute. The latter would ensure that copying is restricted to purposes of "research and private studying," specifically excluding "research" carried out for the business ends of a commercial enterprise.

The approach to photocopying and copyright problems taken by Japan is somewhat unique. Japanese copyright law expressly recognizes a right of "personal" reproduction, for oneself, and the right of libraries to reproduce protected works under specific circumstances. Governmental study of the relationship of these two, very different sorts of exemptions produced the view that: the former right did not permit unauthorized copying for users by copying services, nor by coin-operated machines; and, as to the latter, that no change in the law was required.

A number of other states have taken steps to deal more fully with library (and educational) photocopying. Thus, Sweden has had since 1973 a blanket licensing scheme governing copying in educational establishments; so does Denmark, which is considering in a preliminary way possible extension of the system to noneducational institutions. Although the Federal Republic of Germany is quite advanced in developing mechanisms to remunerate copyright owners for a variety of personal reproductions of copyrighted works, its law on library photocopying is still unclear. Implicit in personal and library copying privileges are rather low aggregate quantitative limits, even for single copying.

Legislation is now pending in the FRG which would provide for the payment by the operator of a photocopying machine of compensation for copies made for private or other personal use. The amount of the payment would be based on sampling criteria.

Chapter Eight – Legislative Proposals

Chapter eight is a summary and analysis of the various legislative proposals placed in the record during the preparation of this report, and is not further summarized here.

Chapter nine is reprinted below in its entirety.

CHAPTER IX.
COPYRIGHT OFFICE RECOMMENDATIONS

This chapter summarizes the nonstatutory and statutory recommendations of the Copyright Office as requested by Congress in title 17 of the U.S. Code, §108(i). Most have been discussed in detail earlier in this report. They reflect our best judgment about possible solutions to the copyright issues relating to library reproduction of copyrighted works based upon

1) consultation with representatives of authors, book and periodical publishers, and other owners of copyrighted materials, and with representatives of library users and librarians about their understandings of, and experience under, the Copyright Act, and their proposed solutions, if any;

2) the surveys of library reproduction of works, of publishers, and of users reported by King Research, Inc., under contract with the Copyright Office (*Libraries, Publishers and Photocopying: Final Report of Surveys Conducted for the United States Copyright Office*);

3) a review of library reproduction abroad and of the technological developments affecting library reproduction of works; and

4) a review of the text and legislative history of the pertinent sections of the Copyright Act.

A. Nonstatutory Recommendations.

1. Collective licensing arrangements encouraged.

All parties affected by library reproduction of copyrighted works are encouraged to participate in existing collective licensing arrangements, and to develop new collective arrangements to facilitate compensated copying of copyrighted works.

2. Voluntary guidelines encouraged.

Representatives of authors, publishers, librarians, and users should engage in serious discussions with a view to clarification of terms and development of guidelines, both with respect to present photocopying practices and the impact of new technological developments on library use of

copyrighted works. The Office recommends that the respective Congressional copyright committees or subcommittees again urge the parties to engage in serious negotiations and report back to them by a certain date.

3. Study of surcharge on equipment.

In the next five-year review, a copyright compensation scheme based upon a surcharge on photocopying equipment used at certain locations and in certain types of institutions or organizations should be studied, taking into account experience with such systems in other countries.

4. Study of compensation systems based on sampling techniques.

In the next five-year review, various systems for copyright compensation based on a percentage of the photocopying impressions made on machines located at certain places in certain types of institutions or organizations, as determined by sampling techniques, should be studied.

5. Further study of new technology issues.

In the next five-year review, issues relating to the impact of new technological developments on library use of copyrighted works should be studied.

6. Archival preservation.

Representatives of authors, publishers, users, and librarians should meet to review fully new preservation techniques and their copyright implications and should seek to develop a common position for legislative action by Congress, taking into account the respective interests of libraries and their patrons and of authors and publishers.

7. Adequate funding for library services.

Proper recognition of the cost of creating and disseminating protected works in our society requires concomitant understanding at all levels of government of the need for adequate funding of publicly owned libraries to enable them to pay their share of creation-dissemination costs.

B. Statutory recommendations.[1]

1. Reproduction of out-of-print musical works.

The Copyright Office recommends enactment of the proposal submitted by the Music Library Association and the Music Publishers' Association,[2] either by amendment of §108, with consequential amendment of paragraph (h). If enacted, the amendment would permit library reproduction of an entire musical work (or substantial parts thereof) for private study, scholarship, or research following an unsuccessful, diligent search for the name and address of the copyright proprietor of the musical work.

2. "Umbrella statute."

The Copyright Office recommends favorable action by Congress on legislation embodying the principle of the so-called "umbrella statute," a proposal developed by an *ad hoc* task force of librarians and publishers and submitted by the Association of American Publishers.[3] The proposal would add a new section 511 to the Copyright Act limiting copyright owners to a single remedy — a reasonable copying fee — for copyright infringement of their scientific, technical, medical, or business periodicals or proceedings, if certain conditions are met by the user of the work, including membership in a collective licensing arrangement, unless the work was entered in a qualified licensing system or qualified licensing program. The purpose of the "umbrella statute" is to encourage publisher and user participation in collective

---

[1] All of the following recommendations concern proposed amendments to the Copyright Law of the United States, title 17 U.S.C. §§101 *et seq.*

[2] See, text *supra*, VIII, K.

[3] The proposal and accompanying documents are set out in App. VII at 41-61.

licensing arrangements. The Copyright Office further recommends that Congress require recordation with the Office of a document setting forth the basic terms and conditions of any qualified licensing program or qualified licensing system.

3. Clarification of the "108(a)(3) notice."

The Copyright Office recommends enactment of a clarifying amendment to §108(a)(3) as follows:

> "(3) the reproduction or distribution of the work includes the notice of copyright as provided in sections 401 and 402 of this title, if such notice appears on the copy or phonorecord in a position authorized by sections 401(c) and 402(c), respectively, of this title."

Publishers have generally interpreted the present Copyright Act as requiring libraries to use the statutory copyright notice on photocopies as a condition of the §108 copying privileges. Librarians have generally disagreed, maintaining that a warning that the work may be in copyright complies with the Act.[4] The amendment would accept the publishers' interpretation.

4. Clarification that unpublished works are excluded from paragraphs (d) and (e) of section 108.

The Copyright Office recommends an amendment to paragraphs (d) and (e) of §108 to make clear that unpublished works are not within the copying privileges granted therein.[5] Section 108(d) governs single copying of a small part of a work or one article of a periodical; section 108(e) establishes the conditions under which out-of-print works may be copied – either the entire work or a substantial part thereof. In the case of paragraph (d), the term "published" should be inserted in lieu of the word "copyrighted" each time the latter appears. In the case of paragraph (e), the term "published" should be inserted between "entire" and "work" and should be inserted in lieu of the word "copyrighted."

5. Change in reporting month for the section 108(i) report.

The Copyright Office recommends amendment of paragraph (i) of §108 to permit the filing of the periodic five-year report on or about March 1 of a given year in place of the present January reporting date. This change in the filing date is requested because of the staffing and administrative support problems inherent in preparing a major report during the year-end holiday period.

For further information or copies of the Executive Summary of the report, *Library Reproduction of Copyrighted Works (17 U.S.C. 108)*, Contact Craig D'Ooge, Library of Congress, Washington, DC 20540; 202-287-5108.

---

[4]These positions are discussed at III A(3), *supra*.

[5]These issues are discussed at IV A(4)(a) and (c).

27: LIBRARIANS OPPOSE REGISTER ON COPYRIGHT REPORT

The Copyright Office report sent to Congress early in January by Register David Ladd has added fresh sparks to the continuing dispute between librarians and publishers over photocopying.

The five-year review of the Copyright Act of 1976 asked Congress to press for a better balance between creators' rights and users' needs for access to copyrighted materials.

Section 108 on library photocopying provides a "workable structural framework" for such a balance, the Copyright Office maintains, but it has not been achieved in practice because Congress's intent has not been carried out fully or because that intent is not clear.

"Substantial quantities of the photocopies prepared by and for library patrons are made for job-related reasons, rather than for the type of private scholarship, study, or research most favored by the law," the report states. It adds that there seems to be significant confusion among many librarians about how the copyright law works and why its enforcement is frequently their responsibility.

Statutory recommendations.

To rectify what the Copyright Office sees as shortcomings in the law, Ladd asked Congress to amend it to:

1. Permit the reproduction of out-of-print musical works as proposed by the Music Library Association and the Music Publishers Association.

2. Endorse the "umbrella statute" proposed by the Association of American Publishers, limiting remedies for copyright infringement to a "reasonable copying fee in an amount fixed by the Court" if specific conditions are met by the users of scientific periodicals.

3. Require libraries to supply the statutory notice of copyright on all photocopies.

4. "Make clear" that unpublished works are not included in the rights granted in sections 108 (d) and (e).

The report also made nonstatutory recommendations encouraging the copyright community to agree on voluntary guidelines, collective photocopying licensing, surcharges on photocopying equipment, and compensation systems based on sampling techniques.

Contradictory reactions

At an AAP workshop later in January, copyright counsel Jon Baumgarten noted that the report was "generally supportive of publishers." He suggested that librarians had not presented the Copyright Office with their position, preferring to "stonewall" the issues by denying a problem exists.

Librarians and educators were angry and distressed. "It's not the disinterested, objective report of the situation we would have liked to have seen," said Shirley Echelman, executive director of the Association of Research Libraries.

The library community believes the desired balance between the rights of the creators and the needs of the users is being achieved, and recommended no legislative changes except on musical works. That opinion was based on the solid statistical data of the King report and the testimony at copyright hearings, said Nancy Marshall, chair of the ALA Legislation Committee copyright subcommittee.

In view of the tone and recommendations of the Copyright Office report, Marshall suggested it would be difficult to recapture the "spirit of '76" which resulted in hard-fought and hard-gained compromises. She expressed some doubt that Congress would be willing to tackle copyright issues after a respite of only five years.

A copy of the executive summary of the review is available free from the Information and Publicity Section, Copyright Office LM-455, Library of Congress, Washington, DC 20559.

The 365-page report and its seven appendices may be ordered at $100 from the National Technical Information Service, U.S. Department of Commerce, 5285 Port Royal Rd., Springfield, VA 22161 (PB 83148239, set). The report alone is $17.50 (PB 83148247).

The ALA Washington Office is preparing a special issue analyzing the report to be available this month.

28: TESTIMONY BEFORE THE PUBLIC HEARING ON THE REPORT OF THE REGISTER OF COPYRIGHTS ON THE EFFECTS OF 17 U.S.C. 108 ON THE RIGHTS OF CREATORS AND THE NEEDS OF USERS OF WORKS REPRODUCED BY CERTAIN LIBRARIES AND ARCHIVES (Wednesday, January 28, 1981, New York, N.Y.)

Ben H. Weil

The notice for this Public Hearing included an invitation for participation "not only of organizational representatives, but also of any individual whose informed opinion may contribute to the preparation of the report (of the Copyright Office) and the possible recommendation of changes in the copyright law." My remarks, today, hopefully fall within these categories: they are derived from considerable experience in attempting to satisfy the needs of certain corporate users for photocopies.

THE EXXON COPYRIGHT-COMPLIANCE PROGRAM

Exxon Corporation and its various U.S. subsidiaries maintain numerous libraries to help individuals to focus information on their work and to improve their expertise. Within these companies, divisions and individuals also subscribe directly to numerous journals and magazines. When their studies or assignments require it, individuals also have occasional need for individual copies of specific copyrighted articles. When an article is at hand, an individual will sometimes make his or her own single photocopy. Otherwise, he or she turns to in-house libraries or related reproduction centers to make or to obtain the copies needed. This is today a common situation, consonant with work efficiency.

After the passage of the new copyright law in 1976, the Trademarks and Copyrights part of the Law Department of Exxon Corporation studied the impact of the law on photocopying practices in the Corporation and its subsidiaries. It was joined in these studies by the law departments of several of these subsidiaries, some of whom also involved the staffs of their information centers and libraries. The basic goal of these studies was the design of an updated copyright-compliance program which would give due credence to the Corporation's ethical principle of strictly complying with laws, would not create unreasonable barriers to the flow of needed information, would be reasonably understandable, would be as efficient as possible, and would support publications maximally.

Original manuscript submitted as testimony, which also appears in *Library Reproduction of Copyrighted Works (17 U.S.C. 108),* Appendix VI, Part 1: New York Hearings Transcripts, Report of the Register of Copyrights, January 1983.

From these studies came our present copyright-compliance program, which has the following elements:

1. Every employee receives an Exxon Corporation booklet on "Brief Guide-lines for the Photocopying of Copyrighted Materials."

2. A "Notice Concerning Copyright" is posted at all unattended photocopy-ing machines. This Notice permits individuals to make only a single copy of a copyrighted document for their own research or scholarship; for multiple copies they must go to a designated Company library or authorized reproduction center (where express service is available if needed).

3. These Company libraries and authorized reproduction centers record their photocopying of copyrighted documents, including both single copies and multiple copies. Libraries also record photocopies obtain-ed outside the Company for which copyright fees have not been paid by the providing library or vendor.

4. Company libraries each report their copyrighted-document photocopying directly to the Copyright Clearance Center, Inc. (CCC) for copying from serials registered with the CCC, and to the Copyright Unit of Exxon Research and Engineering Company (ER&E) for their photocopying from non-CCC serials and other copyrighted sources. Authorized repro-duction centers report their copyrighted-document copying to the ER&E Copyright Unit.

5. The ER&E Copyright Unit centrally handles for Exxon Corporation and its U.S. subsidiaries the obtaining of royalty-free permissions or Photocopying Agreements (bilateral licenses) from publishers not reg-istered with the CCC. It also keeps the requisite records and handles yments.

Implementing this copyright-compliance program requires a very consider-able, ongoing effort. Because Exxon Corporation has many U.S. subsidiaries that operate at many locations, several variations in our photocopy-reporting systems have had to be developed to allow for differences in library and administrative-services operations, in addition to special needs. The com-plexities of our record keeping have inevitably required the development of a computer-based system. We have continued to work with the Copyright Clear-ance Center to make maximum use of its capabilities. And in our bilateral-licensing work we have found it necessary to contact hundreds of publishers repeatedly, first of all to attempt to obtain responses to our requests, and thereafter to explain their validity in a variety of ways to certain publish-ers who did not seem fully aware of the unique utility of photocopies.

POSSIBLE NEEDS FOR STATUTORY CHANGES

Significant problems have arisen in implementing and operating our copyright-compliance program, of course, but we are reasonably able to handle most of them. A few, however, do not seem fully solvable without some statutory relief. I will concentrate, here, on our principal problem, our inability to obtain responses of any kind from a significant percentage of the publishers from whom we seek photocopying permissions or Photocopying Agreements, even after a very considerable level of effort--repeated series of follow-ups. This no-response problem has been encountered by almost every seeker for photocopying permissions, even those of us expressing a willingness to make reasonable payments and to restrict distribution to a specific audience. It is not a trivial matter; the consequences could be serious disruptions in the flow of needed information.

It is not easy to give exact statistics on the magnitude of the problem that results from the absence of responses from many of the publishers approached: licensing programs are not static, so that additional publishers are regularly being added to the list of those contacted. The following data should suffice, however.

- A year after we had identified from our 1978 records that there were 125 publishers from whom we needed licenses because they were not registered with the CCC, and had sent each of them a photocopying-permission letter accompanied by our proposed Photocopying Agreement, 27 (19.2%) had not replied at all, despite three follow-up letters sent at intervals of about three months.

- Eight months after we had identified from our 1979 records that there were an additional 122 publishers from whom we needed licenses because they were not registered with the CCC, had sent each of them a photocopying-permission letter accompanied by our Photocopying Agreement, and had sent a single follow-up letter, 47 (37.6%) had not replied.

- Over-all, we have received responses of some sort from only 63.2% (254) of the 402 non-CCC publishers contacted. The best that we expect to be able to achieve, with multiple follow-ups, will probably not greatly exceed an 80% response.

We should make it clear, here, that we do not simply have an intermittent permission-requests program. We add very regularly to our list. Our Copyright Unit now regularly screens, weekly, the reports of photocopying that it receives in order to identify those "new" serials from which any copies have been made to date in the current year, and it promptly applies to them for permission to make photocopies when it appears that more than a few photocopies may be requested by the end of the year.

Troublesome though they may be, our response results are better than average, from all that I have been able to determine. So--what, then, are libraries and others to do--legally and realistically--to serve the legitimate needs of their users for photocopies from the significant percentage of journals from which they cannot obtain even a response? It will be years, if ever, before a library can obtain permission-paid photocopies from a National Periodicals Center. Existing and near-future licensed services will be able

to supply only part of the demand. And until the day of licensed, electronically delivered copies, neither an NPC or other services can equal in utility
the ability of organizational (internal) libraries to supply photocopies
quickly from their own specialized collections. If making these copies is
permissible.

We believe that there is a legitimate need for statutory relief
in those instances where a user has exerted reasonable efforts to obtain
permissions from publishers but the publishers have not responded.

There are a few other problems to which we would like at least to call
your attention. Some publishers report that they cannot give photocopying
permissions because they do not seek/obtain copyright transfers from their
authors; there is certainly no way, now, for anyone to obtain advance permissions from authors whose identities cannot even be predicted. A few publishers tell us that the copyright law requires them to insist on having specific,
lengthy credit lines added to all photocopies made under license, a requirement that might well double our operating costs if it became universal.

We make no assertions that our problems are common to all libraries. Our
program is Exxon's own best reading of what is reasonably required of a large
corporation that seeks to provide service to individuals when they need photocopies. We know that at your earlier hearings not many libraries reported a
need for changes in the law. However, we believe that we have demonstrated
that libraries such as ours have a legitimate need to gain the right to do
some above-present-statute photocopying. If the Copyright Act of 1976 is to
be adequately responsive to the reasonable photocopying needs of libraries
such as ours, in behalf of users, some statutory changes seem to be indicated.

We would appreciate your careful consideration of our problems, and will
be glad to attempt to answer questions, now or later.

29: IN-HOUSE PHOTOCOPYING SUBJECT TO NEW CHALLENGES

Michael C. Elmer

John F. Hornick

Mr. Elmer is a partner and Mr. Hornick is a law clerk at Washington, D.C.'s Finnegan, Henderson, Farabow, Garrett & Dunner.

Until recently, most profit-making organizations with large research and development departments probably thought that the last thing with which they needed to be concerned was the impact of the copyright laws on their in-house photocopying practices. Everyone knew that scientific and technical journals are protected by copyright, but the possibility that routine photocopying of such journals violates the copyright laws seems not to have been given much consideration. Then came *Harper & Row Pub., Inc. v. American Cyanamid Co.*,[1] in which a group of publishers of copyrighted scientific and technical journals brought suit against American Cyanamid, a major pharmaceutical manufacturer, for copyright infringement because of its in-house photocopying practices. Subsequently, another group of publishers brought suit in the same court against the Squibb Corporation, another major pharmaceutical manufacturer, for the same reason.[2] The plaintiffs in each of these cases sought to enjoin the pharmaceutical manufacturers from infringing their copyrights and to compel the manufacturers to register as users with the Copyright Clearance Center, the new "ASCAP" of the literary publishing world. Both American Cyanamid and Squibb settled their suits before trial, consented to register with the CCC, and thereby set the stage for the publishers to receive royalties on a continuing basis.

The American Cyanamid and Squibb lawsuits may just be the first of a series of attacks against profit-making corporations with in-house libraries and associated photocopying services for their employees. In an article in The New York Times, Charles Lieb, attorney for the plaintiffs in *American Cyanamid* and *Squibb*, stated:

> We chose companies in the pharmaceutical industry as our first target because they, of all large research-oriented companies, are the worst about observing the copyright laws. We assume they can't be in compliance unless they register with the Copyright Clearance Center, which happens to be the only game in town. Our hope is that the large companies don't deliberately violate the law but that they really don't know their obligations.[3]

These cases have heightened awareness and concern about the potential for similar actions against other corporations. There are many areas in which the question can arise as to whether such organizations need the permission of a copyright owner to photocopy material from a copyrighted work. For example, corporate library personnel may wish to make single photocopies from the library collection for the personal use of individual researchers, to reproduce articles about the corporation's products to send to customers, or to copy articles for submission to government agencies. Moreover, affording employees access to unsupervised photocopying machines appears to be commonplace. The copyright law permits "fair use" of copyrighted works by anyone,[4] but does not provide a blanket exemption for practices of these types. There are, however, provisions of copyright law that deal with library photocopying, and now is the time for corporations with in-house libraries to gain a better understanding of what that law provides.

Some Photocopying Permissible

Under certain circumstances, apart from "fair use" copying, a library may copy all or part of a copyrighted work for the use of its patrons. Section 108 of Title 17 of the U.S. Code specifies that a single copy made by a library is not copyright infringement if three threshold requirements are satisfied. First, the copy must be made or distributed "without any purpose of direct or indirect commercial advantage."[5] The "no commercial advantage" requirement has been interpreted as relating to the act of copying itself (e.g., charging a fee for the copy), and not to the ultimate profit-making character of the organization as a whole. The legislative history of the Copyright Act of 1976 indicates that the isolated, spontaneous reproduction, without any commercial motivation, of single photocopies by a library in a profit-making organization would come within the scope of §108 and would not constitute infringement.[7]

The second requirement for the library copying exemption is that the collections of the library also either must be open to the public or available to persons outside of the organization who are doing research in a specialized field.[8] It does not appear that all researchers in a specialized field must be allowed access to the library. There is no express requirement of actual access by such researchers to a library's materials, as in the case of open-stack libraries. Rather, the library collec-

tions apparently need only be "available" to outside researchers. Thus, the library's response by mail to the research requests of a limited number of outside academic researchers or scholars, or their occasional admittance to the library, probably would satisfy this requirement.

The third and final requirement is that the reproduced or distributed copy must include a notice of copyright.[9] Some commentators believe that it is sufficient to mark each copy as follows:

> This material may be protected by copyright law (Title 17 U.S. Code)

Others, however, believe that the notice required is the notice that must be affixed to copies of copyrighted works under 17 U.S.C. §401(n), e.g., © Acme Corp. 1983. In fact, the Register of Copyrights has recently recommended amending §108(a)(3) expressly to require the notice required under §401(b).[10] Libraries attempting to comply with §108 probably either should photocopy the page of the work which bears the §401(b) notice of copyright or transcribe the notice manually onto the first page of the photocopy.

Display of Copyright Warning

In addition to the three threshold requirements of §108(a), the statute imposes several additional conditions that a library must satisfy. That is, a warning of copyright must be "display[ed] prominently at the place where orders are accepted, and include[d] on [the library's] order form"[11] if such forms are used.[12] That warning must be a verbatim reproduction of the following notice:

NOTICE
WARNING CONCERNING
COPYRIGHT
RESTRICTIONS

The copyright law of the United States (Title 17, United States Code) governs the making of photocopies or other reproductions of copyrighted material.

Under certain conditions specified in the law, libraries and archives are authorized to furnish a photocopy or other reproduction. One of these specified conditions is that the photocopy or reproduction is not to be "used for any purpose other than private study, scholarship, or research." If a user makes a request for, or later uses, a photocopy or reproduction for purposes in excess of "fair use," that user may be liable for copyright infringement.

This institution reserves the right to refuse to accept a copying order if, in its judgment, fulfillment of the order would involve violation of copyright law.[13]

Moreover, a library may not distribute a copy to a user after receiving actual notice that the user will use the copy improperly.[14] However, a library is not required to make an affirmative effort to seek any information concerning the identity, status, or affiliation of the user, or to make any judgments as to the user's intent regarding the copy which he orders.

The right of reproduction and distribution granted by §108(a) of the statute is limited to a single copy of a copyrighted work, as opposed to systematic reproduction or distribution of multiple copies.[15] The Senate Report on §108 gave the following example of systematic copying of periodicals that is not exempted by this provision of the statute:

(2) A research center employing a number of scientists and technicians subscribes to one or two copies of needed periodicals. By reproducing photocopies of articles the center is able to make the material in these periodicals available to its staff in the same manner which otherwise would have required multiple subscriptions.[16]

Moreover, a library in a profit-making organization cannot evade these obligations by installing reproducing equipment on its premises for unsupervised use by the organization's staff.[17]

Although the scope and meaning of "systematic" photocopying under §108(g) is not fully clear, it does seem that under §108 a library has no right to make several copies of the same article at the same time, or as part of a related, ongoing operation. This represents an important limitation on the applicability of the statutory exception to copyright infringement which is accorded to libraries.

Considering all of the requirements of the statute for library exemption, an in-house corporate library should meet the following conditions in its single-copy photocopying practice:

(1) the library collections must be:

(a) open to the public, *or*

(b) made available in some way at least to academic researchers outside of the corporation (if this option is selected, then a record should be kept of the names of outside researchers who are allowed access to the library collections and the dates of such access);

(2) a fee must not be charged for copies made on supervised machines by library or photocopy staff members;

(3) a notice of copyright must appear on each copy, preferably including the following information:

(a) ©, the word "Copyright," or the abbreviation "Copr.";

(b) name of copyright claimant;

(c) year of copyright;

(4) the copy must become the

167

property of the user;

(5) the library must have no actual notice that the copy will be used for any purpose other than private study, scholarship, or research;

(6) the library must display prominently, at the place where photocopy orders are accepted, a warning of copyright as quoted *supra*;

(7) *if* photocopy order forms are used, such forms must display the notice specified in No. 6 above (see discussion, *supra*);

(8) *if* the photocopying request or order is for a copy of an entire work or a substantial portion thereof, the library must determine, on the basis of a reasonable investigation, that a copy of the copyrighted work cannot be obtained at a fair price; *and*

(9) the library must not use a single subscription or interlibrary loan arrangement to supply its employees with copies of a copyrighted work where such practice is a deliberate substitution of the photocopies for subscription to or purchase of multiple copies of the work.

The use of unsupervised photocopying machines in libraries—whether the library is nonprofit or part of a profit-making organization—poses a separate issue. The statute requires libraries to display a notice adjacent to such machines which states that photocopying may be subject to the copyright law.[18] However, under the statute,[19] the use of an unsupervised machine does not excuse liability for copyright infringement or for any subsequent infringing use of the copy if such use exceeds "fair use" as provided by 17 U.S.C. §107.

Fair Use Determined

In order for a user to justify the making of a copy as an instance of fair use, the user must show that the copy will be used for such purposes as criticism, comment, news reporting, teaching, scholarship, or research. In determining whether a use is a fair use, the factors to be considered include:

(1) the purpose and character of the use, including whether such use is of a commercial nature or is for nonprofit educational purposes;

(2) the nature of the copyrighted work;

(3) the amount and substantiality of the portion used in relation to the copyrighted work as a whole; and

(4) the effect of the use upon the potential market for or value of the copyrighted work.[20]

Fair use is a general exception to culpable copying under the copyright law. While the statutory provision relating to unsupervised photocopying machines permits the in-house corporate library to protect itself to some extent by displaying a warning notice adjacent to an unsupervised machine, if all machines are left unsupervised, the library might be viewed as merely attempting to evade its obligation to comply with copyright law. The risk of court challenge by copyright owners would increase under those circumstances.

The primary aim of the litigants who brought suit against American Cyanamid and Squibb appears to have been to compel those companies to register as users with the CCC. By registering with the CCC, a corporation is certain not to infringe the copyrights of materials published by members of the CCC and is protected from suits for copyright infringement by publishers whose periodicals are listed with the CCC.

On the other hand, additional recordkeeping is required in order to make the required reports to the CCC and an additional expense is incurred by the corporation. The expense factor is particularly significant where the corporation elects, for the sake of recordkeeping simplicity, to pay royalties to the CCC for all photocopies, including those which fall within fair use or §108 library exemptions.[21]

It is clear that noninfringing in-house photocopying may be conducted in profit-making organizations if the requirements of the copyright law are met. However, compliance with these requirements will not necessarily insulate such organizations from copyright infringement suits. Moreover, where in-house photocopying does not fall within fair use or the §108 exemption, the possibility of being charged with copyright infringement is of even greater concern.

Registration as a user with the Copyright Clearance Center is a means by which copyright infringement suits may be avoided. Soliciting licenses to photocopy from the publisher of each journal that a profit-making organization wishes to copy is another means of avoiding such suits. It may be that neither of those approaches will be considered practical, however, and we might see many more actions such as were brought against American Cyanamid and Squibb.

It should be noted that in the Squibb case, Squibb's answer to the complaint indicated that Squibb contemplated charging the plaintiffs with improperly using their rights under the copyright laws to coerce licensing through the Copyright Clearance Center. In the area of profit-making corporations having in-house libraries, potential challenges by publishers eventually could give rise to a battle that includes not only pure copyright issues, but also antitrust questions.

There can be no doubt that the suits brought by publishers who own copyrights in journals that frequently are found in corporate libraries have sparked a new and serious interest in the interplay between copyright law and photocopying practices that long have been taken for granted. For instance, The Washington Post and The New York Times reported the April 14, 1983, settlement of a suit brought by publishers against New York University as a test case against allegedly large-scale university photocopying.[22] Although the NYU case involved somewhat different copyright infringement issues and requested relief, it illustrates the current trend in copyright enforcement by publishers against corporate and institutional users of copyrighted materials.

[1] Harper & Row Pub., Inc. v. American Cyanamid Co., No. 81 Civ. 7813 (S.D.N.Y. March 17, 1982).
[2] Harper & Row Pub., Inc. v. E.R. Squibb & Sons, Inc., No. 82 Civ. 2363 (S.D.N.Y. Nov. 19, 1982).
[3] The New York Times, June 29, 1982, at D2.
[4] 17 U.S.C. §107.
[5] 17 U.S.C. §108(a)(1).
[6] H.R. Rep. No. 94-1476 at 74-79.
[7] H.R. Rep. No. 94-1733 at 70-74.
[8] 17 U.S.C. §108(a)(2).
[9] 17 U.S.C. §108(a)(3).
[10] The Register's Report of January 1983, entitled "Library Reproduction of Copyrighted Works," also recommends enactment of an amendment to subsections 108(d) and (e) to make clear that unpublished works are not within the scope of those subsections.
[11] 17 U.S.C. §§108(d)(2) and 108(e)(2).
[12] This is not to say that such forms are required. Nor must such forms be retained if used. The requirement is only that if used, such forms must bear the warning. *See* Treece, "Library Photocopying," 25 UCLA L. Rev. 5 & 6, 1050 (1977).
[13] 37 C.F.R. §201.14(b).
[14] 17 U.S.C. §§108(d)(1) and 108(e)(1).
[15] *See* 17 U.S.C. §108(g).
[16] S. Rep. No. 94-473 at 70 n. 35. *See also* the House Report on §108. H.R. Rep. No. 94-1476 at 75.
[17] H.R. Rep. No. 94-1476 at 75.
[18] 17 U.S.C. §108(f)(1).
[19] 17 U.S.C. §108(f)(2).
[20] 17 U.S.C. §107 (1981).
[21] The Association of American Publishers has proposed the enactment of an "umbrella statute" that would award an infringement plaintiff, who is not a member of the CCC, only the cost of infringing copies. Such a statute would serve the dual purpose of encouraging publishers to list with the CCC while reducing the number of non-CCC publishers from whom a profit-making organization would be forced to obtain individual licenses to copy or who might scrutinize the corporation's photocopying practices with an eye toward bringing an infringement suit.
[22] The Washington Post, April 15, 1983, p. D16; The New York Times, April 15, 1983, p. A1. ∎

IV: INTERMEDIARIES/
INFORMATION
SERVICES

Papers 30 Through 34: Commentary

In the communications chain, intermediaries are individuals or organizations that are useful or needed to focus information products in terms of the requirements of direct users. Actually, publishers, educators, and libraries are all encompassed by such a definition, but we have already treated them separately. What we have not yet discussed in terms of copyright are such intermediaries as the information services —those that access or deliver information or information products— with value-added efforts for at least the bibliographic services.

DOCUMENT-DELIVERY SERVICES

Traditionally, document suppliers have been the publishers, booksellers, subscription agencies, and, often, the libraries. This chain is still largely intact, but in the past one or two decades—as we have seen—users have looked to document-delivery services to provide single copies (usually photocopies) of pertinent documents rather than borrowing or purchasing entire works (books and periodicals).

In the past, photocopies could be obtained only from libraries having both the correct collections and interlibrary-loan services (including photocopying); this is still largely true today. However, in recent years there has been a sizable increase in the number of commercial document-delivery services that have emerged in response to users' special needs. From these services, users may order copies of specific documents through the mail, telecommunication channels, or online through database providers.

Until recently, little had been published about these commercial document-delivery services other than in their own circulars. However, a

1983 report on "Document Delivery in the United States," prepared for the Council on Library Resources (see the Bibliography), discusses them as well as interlibrary-loan and large library services. In this report, practically no mention is made of copyright royalty fees. But information on "Copyright Compliance," if any, is one of the information parameters listed for 184 "Document Retrieval Sources & Services" (all types, including some library services) in a 1982 directory with that title (new edition in 1985). Some 52 of the 184 sources provide a copyright-compliance service; most others say: "Responsibility of customer."

In this section we have included a paper by James L. Wood that describes the unique "Chemical Abstracts Service Document Delivery Sevice" (Paper 30). Photocopies are supplied where appropriate copyright-royalty fees can be paid through the CCC for those publications registered with it, or are paid directly to publishers through bilateral agreements. Where such fee payments cannot be arranged, the original documents are loaned to requesters. The Chemical Abstracts Service receives a vast array of documents, and the chemical community is large indeed, so initiation of this copyright-observing service in 1980, after experimentation, was welcomed by users and publishers alike.

We will comment later on the potential uses for document delivery, including online delivery, of optical/video discs. Suffice it to say here that "single-copy publishing" by or with the cooperation of the copyright owners has a real potential for service.

PERMISSION-PAYMENT CLEARINGHOUSES

The development of the Copyright Clearance Center, in which one of us (Weil) served as the system designer and implementor, is chronicled in two 1977 references listed in our Bibliography. The papers on the CCC that appear in this volume include a 1981 article, "Expanding Use of the Copyright Clearance Center" (Paper 31) which deals with the CCC's transactional system, and a 1984 update on its industrial-licensing program, "CCC Status Report" (Paper 32). Both of these papers were authored by the late David P. Waite, first president of the CCC; the second was coauthored by Joseph S. Alen. Since the 1984 update was published, the CCC's Board has authorized application of statistical modeling to effect the "copy-data-gathering simplification" mentioned at the end of the update.

Through the CCC, user organizations can either report bibliographic details of their copying transactions (the "transactional system"), or—at least for large industrial organizations—they can now sign an agreement under which their copying is sampled and statistically projected (the "annual authorizations service"). Publishers individually set unit fees for copying from their publications (largely periodicals and proceedings, at present). The CCC then processes and/or projects user data, bills the users, and periodically reimburses publishers for the copying reported and paid for from their publications.

We also cover the well-known clearinghouses for payments for performing musical compositions—payments made to some 50,000 composers and 16,000 music publishers. We had considerable difficulty in deciding between two excellent articles for inclusion in this book. We chose the one by Jeffrey E. Jacobson, "American Performing Rights" (Paper 33), but we also recommend the 1983 article by Becker and Petrowitz cited in our Bibliography.

Jacobson's article concentrates on the performing rights, but Becker and Petrowitz point out that composers and music publishers also sell a "synchronization right" for later "package" use of their music (if a composer has not been hired to write new music), usually through a broker such as the Harry Fox Agency, Inc. To broadcast the music, packaged or live, networks and local stations must get a performance license.

Jacobson reviews in detail the development of the blanket-licensing groups that provide performance rights. The two major organizations are the American Society of Composers, Authors and Publishers (ASCAP) and Broadcast Music, Inc. (BMI). Their licensees are entitled to use any of their millions of compositions during the term of the license. ASCAP and BMI distribute the resultant fees, minus their charges, to the copyright owners, based on surveys taken to estimate the use of the compositions. Jacobson also reviews the other types of organizations that need performance licences.

The clearinghouse concept typified by ASCAP and BMI has repeatedly run afoul of antitrust litigation. It was the subject of consent decrees in 1950; it recently won a Supreme Court decision versus CBS; and while it lost a District Court decision re Buffalo Broadcasting, an independent station, this decision was reversed by a Court of Appeals in September 1984, subsequent to Jacobson's article. The earlier ruling was that the blanket-licensing methods are unreasonable restraints when applied to independent television stations.

The antitrust problems of the music-performance clearinghouses were kept in mind when the CCC was designed. Participating publishers not only set their own fees, but they also remain free to continue to grant their own permissions and/or to engage in other licensing arrangements. Also, the CCC has no enforcement responsibilities. Indeed, the CCC's design and operations have several times been described to the Department of Justice to help keep them clear of antitrust complications.

BIBLIOGRAPHIC SERVICES

As we pointed out in Paper 1 in this compendium:

> There seems to be general agreement that the elements of bibliographic references, including titles, are not copyrightable, but that copyright protection extends to *compilations* (such as directories and, by inference, bibliographic databases) that contain such data in meaningful arrangements.

What we discuss here, uniquely, are copyright aspects pertaining to machine-readable bibliographic databases where the rights of a large number of contributors and others are involved. Readers are also referred

173

to the subsections Abstracts and Compilations/Databases in Part V, Basic Issues.

Paper 34, an International Federation of Library Associations (IFLA) study conducted by King Research, Inc., and summarized in *Information Hotline,* concludes that, instead of copyright law, "the most feasible methods at the present time for governing exchanges [of bibliographic data] are detailed bilateral agreements that specify the rights and responsibilities of exchange partners." Copyright was not deemed irrelevant:

> . . . but it was found that only a small number of agencies seek copyright protection for the systems of bibliographic records which they produce. . . . [and] there is some reason to question whether copyright will ever be clarified sufficiently or in such a manner to answer completely questions which arise concerning the international exchange of bibliographic data.

We deem it pertinent to mention here the recent library-community opposition to an application for copyright of its participative bibliographic database by OCLC Online Computer Library Center, Inc., although we did not locate a sufficiently comprehensive article on it to include in this book. Inputs to this database come in large part from its users.

BIBLIOGRAPHY

Document-Delivery Services

Champany, B. W., and Holz, S. M., 1982, *Document Retrieval Sources & Services,* The Information Store, San Francisco, CA.

Information System Consultants, Inc., 1983, *Document Delivery in the United States,* Council on Library Resources, Washington, D.C. Copying-charge data updated in *Log On* 7(4):2–3, July/August 1984.

Weil, B. H., 1978, Authorized Services for Supplying Photocopies and for Collection of Payments for In-House Photocopying Under the New Copyright Law, in *The Bowker Annual of Library & Book Trade Information,* 23rd ed., R.R. Bowker Co., New York, NY, pp. 33–41.

Clearinghouses

Association of American Publishers, 1977, Copyright Clearance Center, *IEEE Trans. Prof. Commun.* **PC-20**(3):174–176.

Becker, W. W., and Petrowitz, H. C., 1983, Play It Again, Sam, But Don't Forget to Pay the Fee. Broadcast Music: Copyrights and Price Fixing, *Fed. Bar News J.* **30**(1):29–36.

Brait, S., 1980, Alas! All That Lovely Music Is Not Free, *Today's Spirit* **107**(240):11.

Deitch, J., 1984, How Publishers Can Get Paid for Photocopying [through the CCC's licensing plan], *Publ. Wkly* **225**(22):28–30.

Ladd, D., 1983, *The CCC Blanket License: Loosening the Bonds,*

Remarks to the American Bar Association, Section of Patent, Trademark and Copyright Law, Atlanta, Georgia.

Lewin, T., 1984 (October 6), G. E. Copyright Accord [CCC blanket license] Covers Use of Copiers, *New York Times* **134**(46,189):29, 39.

Rowson, R. C., 1981, The Television Licensing Center: A Boon to Students, Teachers, and Researchers, *Videodisc/Teletext* **1**(2):104-107.

Weil, B. H., 1977, Copying Access Mechanisms, *IEEE Trans. Prof. Commun.* **PC-20**(3):171-173.

Bibliographic Services

McDonald, D. D., Rodgers, E. J., and Squires, J. L., 1983, Findings of the IFLA International Study on the Copyright of Bibliographic Records in Machine-Readable Form, *IFLA J.* **9**(3):205-211.

No Copyright on RLIN Database, 1983, *Amer. Libr.* **14**:511.

OCLC Copyright Debate Takes Toll, 1984, *Amer. Libr.* **15**:102.

OCLC Issues Major Statement on Database Copyright, 1985, *Amer. Libr.* **16**:109-191.

Polansky, B. F., 1983, Copyright News: Opposition to OCLC Registering Its Database for Copyright Protection, *Soc. Schol. Publ. Lett.* **5**(6):7.

Webster, D. E., and Maruyama, L., 1981, The Care and Feeding of Bibliographic Data, *Am. Soc. Inf. Sci. Bull.* **7**(6):24-27.

30: THE CHEMICAL ABSTRACTS SERVICE DOCUMENT DELIVERY SERVICE

James L. Wood

Chemical Abstracts Service
Columbus, Ohio 43210

The Chemical Abstracts Service Document Delivery Service received nearly 25 000 document copy requests from over 1300 organizations and individuals during the first 10 months of its operation. By combining photocopying with interlibrary lending, almost 80% of these requests were filled. User acceptance of this new service as indicated by its growth has justified its establishment.

On Sept 2, 1980, the Chemical Abstracts Service, acting with ACS Board of Directors and ACS legal counsel approval, established the CAS Document Delivery Service (CAS DDS). Planning for the CAS DDS began in early 1980 when the ACS Board created a special task force to study how the Chemical Abstracts Service could provide a document delivery service that would not be dependent upon exemptions to photocopying that had been incorporated into *United States Code Title 17—Copyrights*, *Section 107*. *Limitations on exclusive rights*: *Fair Use* and *Section 108*. *Limitations on exclusive rights*: *Reproduction by libraries and archives*.

In designing CAS DDS, specific design criteria were determined to be mandatory. The service was to be user friendly. Customers were to be provided a range of options for ordering, specifying delivery, and making payments. The service was not to infringe upon the rights of any copyright owners. It was to be as responsive as possible, providing customers with a high degree of assurance that their orders would be promptly processed and filled, if at all possible. The service was to be competitively priced and was to operate on a cost-recovery basis. A team of CAS staff members representing the Bibliographic Operations, Business Administration, and Marketing Divisions, following the design criteria, developed the new service. Customers would be able to order documents via mail, telephone, TWX or Telex, or electronically via the System Development Corporation's Electronic Mail Drop, Dialog Information Retrieval Service's Dialorder, OCLC's Interlibrary Loan Subsystem, CAS ONLINE, or the European Space Agency's PrimorDial. Delivery of filled orders would be by surface mail in North America and by air mail elsewhere. However, customers could specify delivery by United Parcel Service, Federal Express, or other air courier. Customers would be able to maintain deposit accounts for payments or could pay be credit card, check, outstanding prepaid CAS coupons, or be invoiced.

In order to have a service that was not dependent upon exemptions to the copyright law, and one that would recognize the rights of copyright owners, the CAS DDS was to combine photocopying with interlibrary lending. If a required document was copyrighted and CAS had neither royalty-free permission

to copy nor a mechanism for paying copying fees, the request would be filled by lending the customer CAS's copy of the original. Requests for documents in the public domain, registered with the Copyright Clearance Center, Inc., or covered by agreements CAS has with copyright owners would be filled with photocopies.

The team reviewed other document delivery services' practices of providing different classes of service based on processing time, such as RUSH and REGULAR. They decided against having classes of services and instead set as a goal full CAS DDS processing within 24 h after receipt of the request. They helped to establish new rules governing the circulation and disposition of CAS library receipts in order to assure the rapid availability of requested documents.

Pricing policies of other document delivery services were obtained and analyzed. CAS DDS cost studies were made, and a pricing structure was established that would assure price competitiveness as well as full cost recovery.

Because of the need to be able to collect copy fee information, to identify publishers with which CAS might need to negotiate right-to-copy agreements, and to monitor the system's performance, a computer-based management information system, the Document Service Management System (DSMS) was designed and installed. DSMS consists of a data base containing records for each document request received. Each record consists of data relevant to the request (i.e., what was requested, when, and by whom), fulfillment information, copyright status, and characteristics of the requested document, such as type of publication, age, number of pages, and country of publication.

During the first 10 months of operation over 1300 customers used CAS DDS. Collectively they ordered 24 492 documents. Table I shows the disposition of these requests. Of the 19 520 filled requests, 11 594 (59.4%) were filled with photocopies, and 7925 (40.6%) with loans of CAS's originals. When the decision was made to lend originals, it was recognized that some losses were bound to occur. To minimize the impact of this, about 85% of the originals loaned are pages cut from issues of journals or conference proceedings, and in only about 15% of the cases of lending is an entire issue or a nonserial volume loaned. As of the end of June 1981, 23 sets of cut pages and 23 whole issues had been lost, less than 0.6% of the total items loaned.

---

† Presented at the ACS Copyright Symposium, 182nd National Meeting of the American Chemical Society, New York, Aug 27, 1981.

Table I. Disposition of CAS Document Delivery Service Requests Received during Sept 1980–June 1981

disposition	no.	%
filled	19 520	79.7
not filled	4 972	20.3
total	24 492	100.0

Table II. Analysis of CAS Document Delivery Service Requests Received During September 1980–June 1981 That Were Not Filled

reason for nonfulfillment	no.	%
document cited but not received	1127	4.6
CAS original on loan	857	3.5
document not covered by CAS	833	3.4
document no longer at CAS	808	3.3
loan not wanted	416	1.7
CAS copy lost	392	1.6
invalid citation	196	0.8
translation wanted	147	0.6
other	196	0.8
total	4972	20.3

Table III. CAS Document Delivery Service Customers by Category with Number of Requests by Customer Category, Sept 1980–June Sept 1980–June 1981

	customers		requests	
category	no.	%	no.	%
manufacturing	671	50.4	19 324	78.9
academic library	155	11.6	784	3.2
government	137	10.3	1 714	7.0
research laboratory	102	7.7	1 151	4.7
individual	29	2.2	74	0.3
consultant	17	1.3	294	1.2
public library	16	1.2	220	0.9
information broker	11	0.8	318	1.3
hospital	7	0.5	25	0.1
other	186	14.0	588	2.4
total	1331	100.0	24 492	100.0

Table IV. CAS Document Delivery Service Method of Transmittal of Request Received Sept–Dec 1980 Compared to Jan–July 1981

	% of requests	
method of transmittal	Sept 1980–Dec 1980	Jan–July 1981
mail	89.8	82.2
telephone	7.9	5.8
TWX-Telex	2.3	0.9
electronic mail drop		0.8
dialorder		10.2
OCLC/ILL		0.1
total	100.0	100.0

While concerned about the possibility of losses, CAS is even more concerned about the 20.3% of the requests that have gone unfilled. Records for these were reviewed to identify the reasons for this nonfulfillment. The results of this review are given in Table II.

For each order received, the identification number of the customer and an organization-type code are included in the information entered into DSMS. An analysis of the CAS DDS customer records made after 10 months of operation is presented in Table III.

The CAS DDS customers are taking advantage of the ordering, delivery, and method of payment options offered by the Service. As shown in Table IV, the majority of the orders are being received by mail, although some shift to electronic delivery is beginning.

Table V. CAS Document Delivery Service Copyright Status of Documents Used To Fill Requists, Jan–June 1981

copyright status	% of filled requests	
copyrighted		61.4
registered with CCC	20.8	
CAS agreement with publisher	16.2	
no payment mechanism	24.4	
not copyrighted		38.6
total	61.4	100.0

Table VI. Country of Publication of Documents Requested from the Document Delivery Service, Jan–June 1981

country of publication	% of total filled requests
USA	26.2
USSR	15.6
UK	12.0
Germany (E. and W.)	9.9
Japan	9.3
Netherlands	6.0
France	4.1
all others	16.9
total	100.0

The Systems Development Corporations's Electronic Mail Drop and the Dialog Information Retrieval Service's Dialorder capabilities have been available since January 1981. Ordering documents via the OCLC Interlibrary Loan Subsystem was not available until late June 1981. Two other electronic ordering capabilities are in contract stages.

Of the copies and originals sent to customers, 69% was by first-class mail, 9.4% by air mail, 20.5% by United Parcel Service, and 0.6% by air courier, such as Federal Express.

CAS DDS customers are using the full range of payment options offered by the Service. Of the filled requests, 69% required invoicing while payments for 24% were debited against customers' deposit accounts. A much promoted method of payment, Mastercard and Visa, has not been popular, with less than one-tenth of 1% of the payments being received in that form. Almost 2% of the orders are received accompanied by check and slightly over 5% accompanied by Document Copy Service coupons sold by CAS prior to September 1980.

Prior to fulfillment of a request, the copyright status of the requested document is determined by examining the journal issue, conference proceedings, or other document. If the request is for an article from a journal bearing the Copyright Clearance Center (CCC) strip on each page, or some other evidence of CCC registration, the article will be photocopied. It is also photocopied if no evidence of copyright can be found. All other copyrighted publications are checked against an authority file of CCC registrations and CAS direct permissions to determine whether copying is permissible. Table V presents the copyright status of the documents used to fill the requests processed between January and June 1981.

Although most major publishers of journals cited by CAS have registered their journals with the CCC, many smaller publishers have not. Also, the CCC has not yet begun to register nonjournal publications. For those reasons, CAS has had to seek right-to-copy agreements with the publishers of these nonregistered materials. This program, only recently begun, has met with only modest success, with a single exception of the agreement CAS was able to reach and Vsesoyuznoe Agentstro po Avtorskim Pravam (VAAP), the Copyright Agency of the USSR. To date, 20% of the publishers contacted have signed agreements with CAS, 17.3% have denied CAS permission to copy their publications, and 62.7% have not responded. CAS is continuing to seek agreements with publishers in order to reduce the number of document requests that must currently be filled by lending.

The DSMS also provides information about certain characteristics of the documents being requested. For example, 74.7% of the requests are for journal articles, 18.6% for conference papers, 4.5% for patents, and the remaining 2.2% for technical reports, dissertations, and books. Documents published during the past 3 years account for 63.7% of the requested documents, while those published during the past 5 years constitute 83.9% of the requests. Of the requests, 67% are for documents ranging from 1 to 10 pages in length, 25% for documents of 11–25 pages, and 6% for 26–50 pages. Only 2% of the requests are for documents of over 50 pages. An analysis of the filled requests by country of document publication revealed the findings shown in Table VI.

During the first four months of CAS DDS operation, requests were received at an average rate of 85 per day. By the third quarter of 1981, this rate had increased to 196 per day. Such rates are modest indeed when compared to those experienced by institutions such as the British Library Lending Division, the National Library of Medicine, and many academic libraries in the United States. However, processing nearly 200 document requests per day has helped some 1300 organizations and individuals satisfy, in part at least, their needs to gain physical access to the documents cited by CAS.

The CAS DDS has received a positive reception from the community it serves, and CAS staff are pleased with its operation. By closely monitoring its performance, areas in need of improvement have been observed, and changes have been introduced in an effort to increase the fill rate and to reduce the time required to process requests. It is CAS's intention to continue to provide a Document Delivery Service that is reliable, economical, and responsive to our customers' needs.

31: EXPANDING USE OF THE COPYRIGHT CLEARANCE CENTER

David P. Waite

Copyright Clearance Center, Inc.
Salem, Massachusetts 01983

Not only is it important for organizations to comply with the newly revised copyright law, it is important that they recognize why it is ultimately in their own best interest to compensate the outside information sources used by paying authorization fees whenever secondary uses are made of copyrighted publications by making photocopies. The Copyright Clearance Center can help organizations do that with speed, convenience, and low cost.

Each of you as users of chemical information need continuing access to a flow of reliable information. You may never give it a conscious thought, but most of you make use of several "outside" sources of published information in carrying out your jobs. Anything threatening the sources of supply or the long-term welfare of "outside" producers of information could ultimately become a threat to the success of your businesses as well as your own professional career activities. If a large number of scientific and professional journals were discontinued as a result of economic failure, this would soon become a matter of serious concern to everyone engaged in research or development.

In addition to the basic need of access to outside information sources, nearly everyone's organization needs the right to make secondary uses of the publications they purchase. Though these publications, for the most part, are protected by copyright, many articles and other information items contained therein must often be photocopied and distributed internally to you and your colleagues. In some situations, photocopies must be acquired from outside document delivery supply houses on a price-per-copy basis to get the information you need.

Because there are limits set by copyright law as to the conditions under which reproduction, distribution, and/or resale of copyrighted materials can be done without authorization from copyright owners, there needs to be a means of your getting these authorizations, when needed, with the least expenditure of time and cost. This is the purpose for which the Copyright Clearance Center (CCC) was established. Our intent is to provide your organization with a convenient centralized service where permissions to photocopy can be obtained at prices established individually and independently by copyright owners.

USER NEEDS

There are counterparts to CCC in the music business.

† Presented (in part) before the Divisions of Chemical Information and Chemical Education, Symposium on "The Copyright Law", 182nd National Meeting of the American Chemical Society, New York, Aug 27, 1981.

ASCAP and BMI are two organizations that license places of business, broadcast networks, and others, who find it advantageous to replay music performances. Playing music helps to make businesses "go". It is the mainstay of many radio stations and an important ingredient for creating the desired atmosphere in most restaurants. Your own firm may be using it in manufacturing plants or to keep customers happy while waiting on the telephone line.

Notice that none of these users are making reproduction copies for sale in a bootleg-copy market. Users of these licenses simply need to use cassette tapes, phonograph records, or whatever the purchased items are for more than individual personal use. Broadcast networks, hotels, restaurants, and the like find their need to replay copyrighted music performances as important an ingredient, today, as bricks, mortar, food and beverage supplies, air conditioning, heat, light, and the other goods and services being used to make their businesses successful. Without the use of these music performance replay licenses, any one of these establishments would consider themselves disadvantaged in doing business.

Let us look at what every information user organization in industry does and needs to do with copyrighted publications. It need not be explained that engineers, scientists, managers, attorneys, executives, marketers, and salesman, in fact, people in all job areas, need to utilize reliable information in order to make their firm's businesses go. Manpower, money, machines, methods, materials, markets and management are all basic ingredients required by a functioning enterprise. The added vital activity that connects these together into a functioning fabric or whole is information flow. Three of the better-known types of important information are scientific and technical, economic and financial, and marketing.

Essential information flow, in some cases, comes from outside sources that use copyrighted publications as their media for reaching users. Reports of outside scientific research, for example, mainly flow through scholarly journals. Fast-moving economic and financial information are provided via a variety of copyrighted publications. A vigorous and healthy source of supply for each of these and other information sources is required to support the well-being of nearly every firm in industry. No less, I might add, are these needs shared by government agencies and educational institutions, especially universities and colleges.

If we look inside a typical modern organization, one with goods or services that have a high research and development content, for example, we find one or more of the following everyday activities engaged in to communicate incoming information in order to assure its utilization to the greatest possible value.

(1) Spontaneous exchange of copyrighted textual information occurs among colleagues, among managers and their subordinates, between home office marketing and field offices, among executives and the board of directors—in short, in nearly every active working relationship in the organization. Today the most widely used method for communicating copyrighted items is by photocopy.

(2) Systematic scanning of published literature by information specialists to identify those items of current or potential interest to individual workers, project groups, and established departments with on-demand photocopies made available through selective dissemination of information (SDI) procedures.

(3) Organizers of workshops and classroom instruction for in-house staff and/or customers and clients need to distribute photocopies of copyrighted materials.

(4) At conferences and symposia participated in by professional employees and colleagues outside the organization, distribution and use of photocopies of copyrighted articles occur.

(5) A great deal of copyrighted published information is used in sales work to support the needs of clients, customers, and sales personnel in their field sales and application work.

Nearly every organization in existence makes use of photocopies of copyrighted materials in several of these ways in order to operate their businesses.

Are the rights to make these copies and distribute them acquired by an organization when it pays the subscription price for a scientific journal or the purchase price of a reference book? Clearly not. No more than a plant manager acquires the rights in a music store if he purchases a reel of taped music and proceeds to bring it to his place of business to use as background music for his production workers. Management is fully aware of its further legal obligation to compensate copyright owners through payment of fees to either ASCAP or BMI, the appropriate licensing agency for this type of music use.

Similarly the recently revised U.S. Copyright Law now contains language requiring those making copies and distributing copyrighted literary works to obtain authorization from copyright owners. Under certain conditions, there are exemptions provided in the law that refer to fair use, as well as limited interlibrary loan uses of photocopies. However, there are attorneys well informed on copyright matters who believe that the bulk of all photocopying of copyrighted works done on behalf of an industrial firm requires authorization.

NEED FOR THE COPYRIGHT CLEARANCE CENTER

Since photocopying of copyrighted publications to further the success of business and all professional efforts is necessary and can be done legitimately recognizing copyright owner interests, a way is needed to convey authorizations in a convenient and rapid manner. (Video and electronic publishing technologies are also beginning to require similar attention.) The ease of photocopying has added substantially to the speed and effectiveness of communications throughout industry and the practice must not be in any way hampered. Rather, it must be facilitated by making authorizations from copyright owners as accessible as possible.

The Copyright Clearance Center, established in 1977, first focused its efforts on making available permissions to photocopy from scientific and professional journals, along with certain other serial publications.

Operationally, CCC has two functions. The first is to eliminate the time-consuming and laborious task of conveying copyright-owner authorizations generally referred to as "permissions to photocopy" from hundreds of the diverse types of publishing houses as requested by thousands of photocopy users of varying types. Generally, permissions to photocopy are made available for per-copy royalty fees established by copyright owners. The second function of the Center is to collect these fees for subsequent distribution to copyright owners. Without this central system through which both permissions and royalty collections now flow, users would have to individually contact hundreds of publishers. Such a burden would be totally unacceptable in light of the photocopying volume and timely service needs users have today.

CCC's approach to the authorization problem is also concerned with meeting the permissions needs of outside sources furnishing photocopies on a service basis such as document delivery supply houses and library networks. The former always require copyright-owner authorization and the latter, depending on the purpose and nature of network activities, sometimes require copyright-owner authorizations to furnish photocopies to requestors.

CCC'S START-UP EXPERIENCE

Photocopying in the U.S. is big business. A King Research Study in 1978, subsequently analyzed by CONTU, showed that of the fifty-four million copies of copyrighted materials reproduced in 1976, at least fifteen million would, in their estimation, have required authorization of the copyright owners. However, with the new law containing difficult language describing certain exemptions, full compliance with the new law is proceeding at a slow pace. Genuine lack of understanding about the law's intent combined with suspicions and bewilderment as to why publishers now have to begin collecting photocopying fees from tightly funded libraries after all these years of not doing so has resulted in an environment of mixed emotions—one not totally hospitable to starting up CCC's new service operation.

While some photocopy users still consider the questions of "does she or doesn't she" need to get photocopying authorization, publishers of scientific journals in particular continue to lose income from a dropoff in reprint sales and enjoy less than the full growth potential of reaching the expanding body of readers through subscription sales.

With a staff of 10 people plus a minicomputer, CCC has for the past 3 years been demonstrating that authorizations to photocopy and the collection of royalties can be handled on an instantaneous "pay as you use" transactional basis. This is all done by the Center at less than 25¢ a copy processing cost. I must hasten to point out, however, that we have taken on a considerable overhead expense each year to educate and promote awareness of the new law for both publishers and photocopy users. There are many in both groups who still have neither knowledge nor understanding of the requirements of the new law. Until they have this basic information, they simply cannot understand the service function of CCC. We often have to begin by pointing out that CCC does not produce and furnish photocopies.

The scope of CCC's operating activities can be identified best by describing our four overall program commitments:

(1) to implement effective comprehensive clearance mechanisms responsive to current needs

(2) to provide application assistance to both copyright owners and to photocopy user organizations
(3) to foster full compliance with the intent of the law by both photocopy users and copyright owners
(4) to build a viable service organization capable of meeting both present and future clearance mechanism needs as new technology develops

EFFECTIVE COMPREHENSIVE CLEARANCE MECHANISMS

The permissions service presently available from CCC comes under the heading of *Precoded Permissions Service*. Also, there are two other types of service CCC believes will be necessary for it to undertake, and possibly a fourth, in order to provide a truly comprehensive solution to the needs of both users and copyright owners. All of these service needs are the result of the recent revisions of copyright legislation in the U.S. and in other countries in the western world.

Precoded permissions are being made available through the use of codes printed by publishers on pages in their published items. These unique identifier codes contain the ISSN or ISBN (standard numbers) followed by year of publication and a permissions fee figure. If the publication is a scholarly journal, an additional six digits are added to the code enabling identification of each individual article. This precoding method eliminates any need for a user to contact CCC (much less the copyright owner) until the end of each month when his photocopying transaction report is simply sent to us. The code is used by photocopy users to record their photocopy transactions on a CCC supplied log sheet. We, in turn, use this for billing the user organization the following month. When fee payments are received at CCC, they are credited to the accounts of the appropriate CCC participating publishers whose publications are registered with us. You will find these titles listed in CCC's catalog known as the quarterly updated *PPC* (Publishers Photo-Copy Fee Catalog).

A *Permissions-By-Request Service* is anticipated to handle permissions for photocopying from textbooks and other reference materials where permissions will be given by a publisher only under certain conditions of known user intent. There is a major challenge here, but it is hoped that permissions criteria can be sufficiently reduced to basic parameters that will allow CCC to put data into its computer, thus providing a central point for users to clear photocopying of this type of material. In this mode, CCC will be acting as an agent conveying permissions for publishers participating in this service. The possibility is under study at present but will not be described further until the concept is approved for operational use.

International agreements are already an operational part of CCC. The need for clearance mechanisms to facilitate authorized photocopying is a current problem being experienced in many countries throughout the western world. The Netherlands, Australia, Norway, and other countries have generally taken different approaches to the problem than we have in the U.S. because of differences in our copyright laws, but collecting societies in all of these countries are attempting to establish reciprocal arrangements with each other and with CCC. The collective effort may ultimately establish an international network for handling the conveying of photocopy permissions and royalty collections. CCC has completed negotiations with one and is currently negotiating agreements with two additional overseas collecting societies for this purpose.

The fourth dimension of permission service I alluded to would come under the category of *licensing*. Some foreign nations are ready to make authorized photocopying of works published in their respective countries available in the U.S. through CCC acting, in effect, as their agent. An added

Figure 1.

possibility for using a limited licensing concept lies within the family of U.S. publishers as a way of providing authorization to photocopy from a long list of publication titles that appear to not warrant the administrative expense of formal registration in CCC's transactional precoded system.

Keeping in mind that the only permission service that has been operating to date at CCC has been the Precoded Permissions Service, note the graphs (Figure 1) that show the growth achieved during the first 3.5 years of operations. Publication titles have grown from 1000 to 4500. The number of users registered has grown from 200 to 1300. The number of photocopies reported annually is now up to 250 000. The dollar amount of fees collected annually is approaching $400 000. In relative terms these are healthy growth curves, but considering careful estimates of the volume of photocopying being done in the United States for which authorization is required, it is apparent that the present transaction level being reported to CCC is no more than 5% of what it should be for a fully comprehensive system and a national community of photocopy users fully complying with the new law.

CCC USE INSTRUCTIONS AVAILABLE

Following the initial surge to register technical journals by scientific publishers most concerned with unauthorized photocopying, the registration of additional serial titles in the CCC system has proceeded at a slower pace. CCC has since found it necessary to promote an awareness of the need for publishers to take action that will make permissions immediately available to photocopy users. The mechanics of registration as well as establishing and affixing codes to publications are described in printed publications.

Similarly, descriptive publications have been prepared for users with added assitance provided through individual contact and the use of seminars and workshops.

FOSTER FULL COMPLIANCE

Realizing the new law requires authorizations to photocopy, CCC believes a truly comprehensive service must be available to the user community. In the aggregate, users can eventually be expected to photocopy from nearly every copyrighted publication. Accordingly, CCC pursues the publishing industry by working with publisher associations such as the Association of American Publishers, the American Business Press, the Magazine Publishers Association, and others. We solicit their assistance in educating and motivating their members to make permissions-to-photocopy readily available through participation in the CCC program.

Fostering full compliance by photocopy users is a more difficult challenge for CCC. Though we believe full compliance by the photocopy-user community is important to maintaining a healthy information transfer chain from author to reader, CCC has no enforcement responsibility nor policing powers.

There is, however, one project expected to be operational this year called the CCC Document Delivery Awareness Program that is expected to markedly improve compliance by the document delivery service industry. This program will periodically distribute a listing of document delivery supply houses known to be using direct licenses and/or the CCC clearance mechanism to obtain permissions. Most photocopy user organizations that place orders on these services want some assurance that they are dealing with a photocopy supplier that is responsibly handling the authorization requirement, thereby keeping all parties out of trouble. Several document delivery service houses have applauded this Awareness Program. The desired result is that all document delivery supply houses will be operating on the same economic basis, charging and forwarding permissions fees.

For provision of another plus for the document delivery supply houses, the listing of participating suppliers will be given limited free space for advertising copy.

VIABLE SERVICE ORGANIZATION

Initially CCC, a nonprofit service organization, with no stockholders and no investment capital, had to meet operating expenses with gift monies alone. The volume of copies now being reported times the 25¢ per copy CCC charges publishers for service does not yet cover all CCC expenses. With the approval of consenting publishers, draws are made from permission fee collections to cover the deficit before remaining funds are distributed to the publishers. Last year, 45¢ on each dollar earned by the publishers was distributed to them. This was nearly a 50% increase in the distributed dollar amount as compared to the year before. This arrangement fully finances CCC's operating budget needs and still distributes a significant portion of permission fees that would otherwise not be possible to collect.

Though CCC has a long way to go to complete its task, it can now be said that CCC is an established and stable organization. Our commitments are, as I have described, to make voluntary photocopy authorizations obtainable from copyright owners and to make this work as an open, free-market system in the United States. If we were to fail, the inequities of alternative government administered compulsory licensing could become very real. The economic viability of publications that are particularly important to you require that

substitute revenues from photocopying permission fees (independently established by publishers) flow directly to them. Under compulsory licensing, ultimate consumers could easily end up paying for photocopying they do not do and receiving less from original outside source publications forced to trim to failing revenues. CCC's long range aim is to reduce burdensome record-keeping and reporting requirements for photocopying and distribution rights to a minimum.

RECOMMENDATIONS TO PHOTOCOPY USER ORGANIZATIONS

To Researchers and Other End Users

Find out what the official policy is in your organization on the new law's requirement for authorizations to photocopy and follow it.

If no official policy exists, bring this to the attention of your supervisor preferably in written memo form if you frequently make the photocopies of copyrighted works that need to be distributed to others.

To Librarians and Managers of Information Services

If top management has not already considered this subject and established an official policy, call the existence of the new law to their attention and point out the legal requirements found in sections 106–108 and the penalties for noncompliance in Sections 504 and 506.

Begin to include the expense of permission fees in your budget for purchased information items.

The average fee per photocopy users report to CCC is $1.70.

To R&D Managers and Executive Management

If you have not already done so, get competent legal advice regarding the impact of the new law on your organization's use of photocopies of copyrighted items. Note that many patent attorneys have little familiarity with copyright law.

Register your organization with CCC. It costs nothing to do so. The free information and experience we can provide can only help minimize the cost of complying with the new requirements.

Send one of your key people to a CCC User's Workshop. Speakers and attendees at these sessions tell how they are managing to work with the new copyright law in their organizations.

Establish an official policy for your organization and communicate it to all personnel that use photocopying machines. Most organizations assign responsibility to a specific individual for setting up and monitoring their internal systems and procedures on photocopying. That person is also usually named as the Contact Person in their registered account with CCC.

32: CCC STATUS REPORT

David P. Waite

Copyright Clearance Center, Inc.

Joseph S. Alen

Copyright Clearance Center, Inc.

Background

The Copyright Clearance Center (CCC), now 6 years old, has some 7500 titles and 750 copyright owners registered in its Transactional Reporting Service. That Service continues to enjoy modest growth and serves the significant needs of some 1500 organizational clients.

However, for some time it has been evident that the administrative processes necessary to record every photocopy act on a title-by-title basis are regarded as unnecessarily burdensome by certain segments of the User marketplace. CCC's new Annual Authorizations Service (AAS) now addresses the licensing needs of major US industrial/commercial corporations and is a direct effort to reduce substantially the administrative burdens of 100% transactional reporting. The evolution of the AAS has been a step-by-step, 2 year process, which has involved the direct participation of Users. In general, User response to the AAS, throughout all its developmental stages and to the present, has been characterized by good faith and support.

The 100% Transactional Reporting Service will continue to serve the needs of document delivery services and smaller organizations that make only occasional use of photocopies and/or service outside groups.

Scope of User License

Authority for CCC to conduct the AAS and grant licenses to photocopy results from an agreement between CCC and copyright owners creating a limited agency responsibility in CCC.

The license granted to a User corporation via the AAS consists of the following: a set of Basic Provisions which convey the authorization and specify its condi- tions; an attached Schedule A, which is a listing of all the titles registered in the AAS and for which authorizations are granted; an attached Schedule B, which is a listing of the various royalty fees set by individual copyright owners for each registered title relative to quantitative photocopy Survey data; and an attached Schedule C, which lists the User corporation premises included in the license.

The Basic Provisions essentially stipulate that:

- CCC, as a special agent of copyright owners, grants to User corporation a non-exclusive license to reproduce in any quantity, for its internal use only, limited portions of the works identified in Schedule A.

- Levels of Users' copying are determined by means of sampling Surveys at User corporations. (These are conducted for a limited time by attaching collection boxes and reporting labels to photocopy machines. Labels are completed and attached to an extra copy of the title page and are deposited for each copying act; then mailed to CCC for sorting and analysis.)

- The agreement term is 1 year, with an additional 1-year renewal option, price to be based on copyright owner fees then in effect. Amendments for additional title coverage are offered periodically.

- There is a contingent waiver by copyright owners regarding previous relevant infringement claims.

- CCC warrants strict confidentiality.

User Corporation Approach/Licensing Sequence

CCC's approach to an individual User corporation begins with a letter addressed to the Chief Executive Officer. This letter serves two purposes: a.) it sensitizes the organization to the issue of copyright at the highest level, and b.) it begins the delegation process for negotiating with CCC within the organization with appropriate accountability. The letter is followed-up by telephone calls and a series of face-to-face meetings ensue. The principal negotiating representative typically is the chief patent or trademark counsel. Much of the substance of the meetings revolves around amelioration of the User concerns regarding disruption to operations, questions of fair use, confidentiality, and the need for improving compliance levels. We have found that the potential cost of the license to the User, and the significance of the subject of copyright compliance, necessitate such in-person approaches to User corporations.

In most cases, after several meetings, the corporation agrees to conduct a brief Pre-Survey, usually within one of its research units or at its corporate headquarters. A Pre-Survey, conducted for 30 days, provides the corporation with insight regarding how the Survey would be run for the entire organization and its possible results. Its purpose is largely educational, but the data from it can be used as the initial part of a longer term 90 day Survey which is a principal basis for developing the cost of the License. In addition to copying data which result from the Surveys, additional information is requested from the User in order to assist in the License development -- such as listings of publications subscribed to by the User. After the cycle of publisher solicitation and License processing is completed, the License is presented for execution to the User corporation.

In order to adequately cover the entire United States with respect to User corporations, CCC has established four separate regions, each under the management of a regional sales manager. At the present time, the regional sales managers have two functions; 1.) development of negotiations with User corporations, and 2.) beginning the identification of independent account representatives to function under the managers' direction in order to begin broad scale interaction with User corporations.

Copyright Owner Solicitation/Sign-Up Cycle

CCC's initial strategy to persuade copyright owners to register their works in the Annual Authorizations Service was based upon a direct mail campaign initiated last Fall. Complete packages, containing detailed information, copies of a Publisher Agreement, the User License and various supporting documents, were mailed to two thousand publishers. Response to these broad mailings was disappointingly low. Consideration was given to the use of certified mail with return receipts for purposes of maintaining an open record of non-responsive copyright owners.

CCC's coverage of publications for any given User was too low to justify their entering into agreements with CCC. In order to meet this need, CCC began a process of telephone solicitation of copyright owners appearing on publication lists acquired from Users as well as focussing solicitation efforts on the results of titles copied in Pre-Surveys and Surveys. Copyright owner solicitation thus became tailored to individual User corporations. Of course, copyright owner registration, resulting from a particular User corporation's License development, nonetheless adds to the overall data base of authorizations for which CCC is authorized to act. Recently, CCC has begun utilization of a major telemarketing firm to augment our inhouse capability in telephone solicitation.

In order to increase available title coverage in the AAS with regard to foreign copyright owners, CCC has entered into bilateral discussions with the following reprographic rights organizations: VG WORT of the Federal Republic of Germany, the Copyright Licensing Agency from the UK, and KOPINOR in Norway. CCC has suggested that, if these organizations could provide en masse authorizations from their registered copyright owners, CCC, under the AAS, would collect royalties for photocopying within the USA and forward these to the appropriate reprographic rights organizations for further distribution to copyright owners. No consideration has been given to reciprocal collection in other nations for photocopying of US works there. CCC has had to delay somewhat the negotiation process of these several potential agreements because of complexities related to US antitrust law. It is, of course, critical that CCC navigate most carefully in these juristic waters. Because we are engaged in simultaneous discussions with three separate national reprographic rights organizations, each with unique characteristics particularly with respect to pricing approaches, the legal issues are especially intricate. Nevertheless, good progress is being made and resolutions of the delays are in sight.

Copy Data-Gathering Simplification

In conjunction with the activities described above, CCC has also undertaken, in a limited fashion, research on methods for reducing by one or more orders of magnitude the sampling procedures necessary to fairly determine the quantitative elements of a License. While efforts are still in early stages of development, nevertheless the results to date have been gratifying. CCC will have more to report on this topic in the future.

33: AMERICAN PERFORMING RIGHTS

Jeffrey E. Jacobson

An introduction to American performing rights requires a discussion of the implications of performing rights societies,[1] licensing and antitrust. There are three organisations in the United States which are performing rights societies: they are known as ASCAP, BMI and SESAC. ASCAP is a membership association run by its member publishers, composers and authors. BMI is a non-profit-making corporation with stock held by broadcasters. SESAC is a small profit-making corporation with stock held by a family.

The public performance of music was first recognised in 1791 in France,[2] and the Société des Auteurs, Compositeurs et Editeurs de Musique (SACEM) was formed in 1851 to license the non-dramatic public performance of music for France. The Copyright Act of 1909 created the performing right in America for the first time. In 1914, the Performing Right Society Limited (PRS) for Great Britain and the American Society of Composers, Authors and Publishers (ASCAP) for America were formed. The Society of European Stage Authors and Composers (now SESAC Inc.) was formed by Paul Heineke in 1931 in New York City. Subsequently, Broadcast Music Inc. (BMI) was formed by the American broadcasting industry in 1940.

ASCAP

Victor Herbert and a group of publishers and writers organised ASCAP in order to act collectively in the licensing of their non-dramatic performing rights in light of the Copyright Act of 1909. ASCAP was started by its first President, George Maxwell, the American representative of an Italian firm, and Nathan Burkan, its first Counsel, a copyright attorney. They decided that an association of publishers and writers was the only way to fight the hotel trade association. Victor Herbert, who had served as music director for the Pittsburgh Symphony Orchestra and composed concert pieces such as 'Babes in Toyland' and 'Sweethearts', was the music world leader for the writers and publishers to rally around. The first scheduled meeting of ASCAP in October 1913 was unsuccessful, but the second meeting in January 1914 was a success with over a hundred in attendance. For almost twenty years ASCAP was the only organisation engaged in licensing performing rights in America.

The first president of ASCAP, George Maxwell, served

Jeffrey E. Jacobson, member of the New York and District of Columbia Bar. The author is in the private practice of entertainment law with offices in New York City, and was formerly an attorney in the Legal Department of SESAC Inc.

1 'A performing rights society is an association or corporation that licenses the public performance of nondramatic musical works on behalf of the copyright owners, such as the American Society of Composers, Authors and Publishers, Broadcast Music Inc. and SESAC Inc.' 17 U.S.C. § 116(e)(3); 90 Stat. 2565; P.L. 94-553, 16 October 1976.
2 Stanley Rothenberg, *Copyright and Public Performance of Music*, Martinus Nijhoff, The Hague, Holland, 1954, at 27.

for ten years. He was followed by Gene Buck (who served from 1924 to 1941), Deems Taylor (1942–1948), Fred E. Ahlert (1948–1950), Otto A. Harbach (1950–1953), and Stanley Adams (1935–1956 and 1959–1980). The current president is Hal David of the famed Burt Bacharach/Hal David writing team. He was responsible for the lyrics to pieces such as 'Only Love Can Break Your Heart' and 'Raindrops Keep Fallin' on My Head'.

ASCAP as a membership association has about 30,000 writer and publisher members. ASCAP is governed by a Board of Directors elected annually by and from among its writer and publisher members, whereas BMI as a non-profit corporation is governed by a Board of Directors elected by the shareholders. Examples of ASCAP board members include: Leon Brettler, Executive Vice President of Shapiro Bernstein & Co; Sammy Cahn, publisher and author of musical compositions such as 'Let It Snow' and 'Day by Day'; Salvatore T. Chiantia, Chairman of the National Music Publishers Association and former President of MCA Music; Gerald Marks, composer and lecturer; Virgil Thomson, composer and conductor; and Irwin Z. Robinson, President of Chappell and Intersong Music Corporation.

ASCAP divides performance royalties equally between writers and publishers and pays half of its collections to the writer members and the other half to publisher members after deducting operating costs and setting aside monies for foreign societies. ASCAP conducts a 'scientifically designed survey' of performances on AM/FM radio, local/network television, public broadcasting, cable, airlines, Muzak, background music services, symphonies, concert halls, colleges and universities in order to determine distribution of monies collected. ASCAP collects more monies than any other society and surveys over 60,000 hours of radio programming a year.

The total royalties collected by ASCAP for 1982 was $186,975,000.00, which was a 10.7 per cent increase over the 1981 collection of $168,904,000.00. ASCAP collected $565,000.00 in dues for 1982 which was 1.6 per cent less than the previous year's collection of $574,000.00. ASCAP received $25,889,000.00 from foreign societies in 1982 as compared to $25,820,000.00 in 1981. Salaries, home office expenses, the cost for branches and overheads amounted to $35,251,000.00 for 1982, which was an 8 per cent increase from $32,464,000.00 for the previous year. When overheads are deducted from total domestic receipts, $125,835,000.00 remains for distribution to the membership for 1982; this is a 10 per cent increase over 1981's $110,620,000.00.[3]

ASCAP members have won 110 out of 134 Oscars and make up 88 per cent of all writers elected to the Songwriters Hall of Fame. This year 11 out of 13 Oscars Nominations went to ASCAP. Its writer members have won 74 per cent of the Grammys ever awarded for Song

3 'ASCAP Sets New High With Total '82 Receipts" *Billboard*, 5 March 1983, at 3.

of the Year and were very successful in this year's Grammy Awards.[4] ASCAP members have also won a great number of Tony awards for music in Broadway theatrical productions. These range from 'Kiss Me Kate', 'South Pacific', 'Guys and Dolls', and 'The King and I' to 'My Fair Lady', 'Annie', and 'Sweeney Todd'.

ASCAP maintains a headquarters across from Lincoln Center in New York City, 19 branch offices, three membership offices and a London office. ASCAP has relations with 42 foreign licensing societies, ranging from APRA in Australia and CAPAC in Canada to PRS in the United Kingdom and SOKOJ in Yugoslavia.

ASCAP has no initiation fee and usually deducts annual dues for writers ($10.00) and publishers ($50.00) from royalties, unless royalties collected for the writer and/or publisher seem to be too small to pay the dues, in which case, ASCAP bills the member for dues. BMI charges a one-time administrative fee of $50.00 to publishers to affiliate and makes no charge to writers.

In addition, ASCAP provides many grants and awards whereas BMI and SESAC generally only provide annual awards for serious classical composers. ASCAP has orchestra awards, scholarships, book prizes, a prize for the best article, prizes to law students for writing on copyright, young composer grants, radio station awards, standard and popular awards, as well as awards for serious music and for classical composers. Also, the ASCAP Foundation promotes and supports educational and charitable programmes in music and is a tax-deductible legal entity.

Over 40,000 establishments hold ASCAP licences. The ASCAP licence is generally more expensive than the licences of BMI and SESAC; for example, ASCAP's Private Club Licence runs $140.00 as the annual rate for a private club which has an annual expenditure for all entertainment at the premises of less than $4,999.99.

BMI

Broadcast Music Inc. is a non-profit-making body owned by 300 American broadcasters. It represents the rights for more writer and publisher affiliates than ASCAP and SESAC: it represents the rights of approximately 35,000 writers and 18,000 publishers. In 1940, about 600 enterprises, most of them principally engaged in broadcasting, formed BMI, with the sole purpose of creating a competitive source of music licensing in America. The original BMI organisers pledged 50 per cent of their 1937 ASCAP payments for funding. This came to $300,000.00 for stock and the $1,200,000.00 balance as initial licence fees. These original investments averaged about $500.00 per participant. No dividends have or are ever expected to be paid. BMI's current president is Edward Cramer. He was preceded by Carl Haverlin (1947–1964), Robert Burton (1964–1965), and Robert Sour (1966–1968).

About 1,000 new affiliates join BMI each year. Creators and copyright owners receive 82 to 83 per cent of the money received by BMI from the licences. The BMI repertory has over 1,150,000 licensed works with approximately 40,000 new works added annually.

BMI has a field staff of over 50 representatives in eight regional offices for licensing. ASCAP and BMI both get a percentage of broadcasters' advertising revenues in exchange for blanket performing rights licences.[5]

BMI logs approximately half a million hours of music which is submitted to it by radio, television networks, local television, AM and FM radio. Radio station logs which are required by Federal Communications Commission (FCC) rules are also submitted to BMI. It logs six times the amount of music logged by ASCAP and contends this results in a fairer distribution than either of its competitors.

BMI makes payments based on music performance on United States radio and television. By computerisation of logged reports in a scientifically chosen representative cross section of stations, performance royalty licence fees are divided. Performances are multiplied by a factor which reflects the ratio of station hours logged to the broadcast. BMI, as a non-profit licensing body, distributes all monies to affiliates after deducting operating expenses and retaining a necessary reserve. International performance income is distributed directly by BMI. BMI has reciprocal agreements with 39 licensing societies around the world ranging from SADAIC in Argentina and PRO in Canada to PRS in the United Kingdom and VAAP in the Soviet Union.

In 1940, when BMI was organised, there were three major American record companies and approximately 600 radio stations for the United States. ASCAP had about 1,100 writer members and less than 150 publisher members which shared all the performance licensing income. These distributions were made solely on the basis of national radio broadcasts which resulted in local regional music being virtually ignored. Today there are over 4,000 commercial American record labels, over 8,000 radio stations and approximately 750 television stations. BMI now claims to promote its 'open policy' of offering affiliation to any qualified writer or publisher.

BMI has licensed over one million musical compositions since its inception in 1940. As of 1980, out of this repertory, 392 have attained the status of one million or more performances. Examples of these compositions range from 'All Shook Up' written by Elvis Presley and Otis Blackwell (co-published by Unart Music Corporation and Elvis Presley Music Incorporated) to 'Your Song' composed by Elton John and Bernie Taupin (published by Dick James Music Incorporated). For 1977, BMI licensed 60 of the top 100 in *Broadcasting* magazine's playlist, 64 per cent of the *Cashbox* chart positions, 65 per cent of all *Billboard* chart positions, and 66 per cent of all *Record World* magazine charts.[6]

In television, during the 1977–78 season, out of 115 continuing series, 83 featured themes, scores and/or songs licensed by BMI. In the 1976–77 season, out of 90 continuing series, 73 had BMI works. In motion pictures, out of the top ten box office films for the same season, BMI licensed the music in eight films. It also licensed the scores, themes and/or songs featured in 25

---

4 *ASCAP in Action*, Spring 1981.

5 The administrative expenses deducted by ASCAP and BMI before they distribute the revenues collected usually run between 15 and 20 per cent.

6 BMI, *The Many Worlds of Music*, Issue 1, 1978.

of the top 40 films. Music in 73 per cent of the top thirty 1976 box office films were also licensed by BMI. Of the top thirty box office favourites of 1979 as listed by *Variety,* 24 motion pictures prominently featured scores, themes and/or songs by BMI affiliates. Of the top thirty all-time box office champions, 23 featured BMI music.

BMI actually publishes a payment schedule. This lists minimum royalty payments, such as six cents for the publisher and another six cents for the writers of a popular song performed on network AM radio. This is a minimum payment because BMI distributes all available income from all sources by a voluntary increase in payments. Another example of the payment schedule (effective as of June 1977, with no change as of July 1980) is twenty-four cents each for publisher and writer for a popular song performed on a local US television feature programme.

BMI, like ASCAP and SESAC, litigates to enforce its affiliates' rights. For example, since September 1982, BMI has filed 125 lawsuits on unlicensed jukeboxes. There have been out-of-court settlements in fifty and another fifty settled before commencement of the court action. Copyright infringement penalties, which range from $250.00 to $10,000.00 (and higher or lower based on circumstances for an innocent infringer), are the weapon used by the performing right societies in order to obtain compliance.

SESAC

Paul Heineke formed what became SESAC Inc. in 1931. At its inception, the repertory of SESAC consisted primarily of works published by European firms. It was instrumental in exposing the works of Arnold Schoenberg, Delius, Sibelius, Provost, and others to the American audience. From SESAC's beginning as a collector for European music, it became active in the fields of country and gospel music. This privately owned profit-making organisation has now expanded its activities into all areas of music.

SESAC only affiliated publishers (not writers) and was considered publisher-oriented until 1972, at which time a concentrated effort to sign writers directly was instituted.

The SESAC repertoire is significantly smaller than ASCAP and BMI 'and its administration costs far lower, since it does not conduct any regular survey of its users ... SESAC has recorded a substantial portion of its own repertoire in the form of transcription recordings which it then distributes to radio stations and other users in order to stimulate performance of its music'.[7] 'SESAC's spot checks of broadcasters to determine whether or not SESAC music is being used are generally made for the purpose of negotiating licences rather than for distribution of income.'[8]

Unlike ASCAP and BMI, SESAC licences synchronisation and mechanical rights in addition to performance rights. For example, SESAC issued a mechanical

7 Although this practice has been discontinued, a large transcribed library was made.
8 Allen Arrow, 'Performing Right Societies', *The Business and Law of Music,* Federal Legal Publications Inc., New York, N.Y., 1965, at 98.

licence to RCA Records in order for Elvis Presley to record affiliated publisher Ben Speer Music's 'I'll Walk Dem Golden Stairs'. Also, SESAC issued synchronisation licences in order for affiliated publisher J.M. Henson Music Company's 'From the Cradle To the Grave' to be used in the film 'Willie & Phil' and for affiliated publisher Kelman Music Company's 'I'm a Little Tea Pot' to be used in an 'I Love Lucy' television programme episode.

SESAC has agreements with approximately 35 foreign licensing firms (unlike ASCAP and BMI, for performance and/or mechanical rights) ranging from ACUM in Israel and CAPAC and G.V. Thompson in Canada to TONO in Norway and MCPS and PRS in the United Kingdom.

SESAC pays writers and publishers for music released on phonograms on the basis of 'Rate Cards' rather than surveys. This system involves averaging the highest chart position attained in *Billboard* and *Cashbox* for a 'bona fide national release'. For instance, a writer and a publisher would each receive $30,000.00 for a number one single on the pop charts under the SESAC Pop Rate Card effective 1 October 1981 or each would receive $25,000.00 for a number one single on the Country charts under the Country Rate Card. SESAC alleges that by avoiding the costs of an independent survey as that of BMI, it saves its affiliates a lot of money as royalties.

In addition to the charts, SESAC has an allocation committee composed of its officers which meets periodically to make royalty distributions. Six factors are used: total number of copyrights; diversity; growth of catalogue; seniority; promotional activity; and most important, performance. Release monies are also paid to writers and publishers for every composition included on a bona fide nationally distributed record label.

SESAC's fees for licences are basically lower than BMI and ASCAP, such as $75.00 for a Country and Private Club with up to 250 full-time, part-time and associate members. Broadcast licences are based on market population and highest one-minute spot rate as printed in the trade directory *Standard Rates and Data.* One example is an annual fee of $1,170.00 for a station with a rate under $2.49 in a market with a population over 2,000,000 people.

SESAC does not charge an initiation fee or any dues to its writer and publisher affiliates. Its publisher affiliation agreements usually run for five-year periods and the writer contracts are usually for three-year periods. Since SESAC does not operate under a consent decree, it is free to pick and choose applicants for affiliation. In the wake of the *Buffalo Broadcasting* case freezing of advances from ASCAP and BMI, SESAC seems to be the only American performing right organisation offering advances to prospective writer and publisher affiliates.

Licensing Areas

Licensing areas range from AM radio to local television. The performance right which the performing rights societies license is the exclusive right of the publisher and songwriter to permit a copyrighted work to be performed publicly. All American music users, unless they are within an express exemption in the Copyright Law, are required to pay for the performance of musical compositions. This includes radio and television stations, public broadcasters, discotheques, night clubs, country clubs, theatres, auditoriums, concert halls, background music users, skating rinks, restaurants, dance schools, and many other music users. Under the 1976 Copyright Law, for the first time, non-profit music users, such as colleges and universities, are also required to pay for performance rights. The blanket performance licences also cover the use of music in jingles and on commercials.

The 1976 Act also brought private clubs, dance schools, veterans' groups, colleges, universities and fraternal organisations into the 'public' category requiring performing rights licences. However, veterans' groups and fraternal organisations have been recently exempted by statutory amendments to the Copyright Law. The Copyright Act of 1976 has extensively expanded the area of American performing rights and the definitions of 'perform' and 'public performance' were expanded. The former 'for profit' limitation on payment was omitted. Cable television and public broadcasters were also new areas for performing rights licensing.

Jukeboxes, which had been exempted under the 1909 Act, were brought under a compulsory licence issued by the Copyright Office with fees established and distributed by the Copyright Royalty Tribunal (CRT). The performing rights annual fees were originally set at eight dollars per jukebox and were raised to twenty-five dollars per box effective 1 January 1982, fifty dollars effective 1 January 1984, and will be adjusted for inflation in January 1987 by the CRT.

Royalty rates were established by statute for cable. The CRT increased the originally set royalty by 21 per cent effective February 1981, and will review the fees again in 1985 and in each subsequent fifth calendar year. The CRT distributed $14 million for compulsory licensing of cable in the first collection in 1978. Of that sum, 4.5 per cent was allocated for music performing rights and split between these organisations. The CRT established a new rate structure effective 15 March 1983 which charges from 0.817 per cent to 1.416 per cent of gross basic revenue for the first distant signal imported by the cable company. The charge is 3.75 per cent of gross basic revenue for each distant signal over and above the Federal Communications Commission's former limits.

Public broadcasters are in a different situation. ASCAP, BMI and SESAC reached voluntary agreements in November 1982 with the Public Broadcasting Service (PBS) and National Public Radio (NPR) which established a schedule of fees for performing rights from 1983 to 1987. ASCAP will receive $11.5 million and SESAC will receive $300,000.00 over the five-year period from PBS and NPR, the large American educational public broadcasters. The BMI fee is confidential; however, it may safely be presumed to be about the same amount as ASCAP is receiving.

If a broadcaster is 'all-talk' and never uses music, performance licences are unnecessary. However, for the incidental use of music, a special 'Limited-Use' licence is available for the broadcasters.

ASCAP and BMI broadcast licences typically are between 1.4 per cent and 2 per cent of a station's gross income. The terms and fees of the broadcast licensing

agreements are the result of periodic negotiations between the societies and the 'All-Industry Radio Music Licensing Committee' and the 'All-Industry TV Music Licensing Committee'. These committees consist of owners and executives from television and radio broadcasters throughout the country. Under current antitrust decrees, the reasonableness of any ASCAP or BMI fee, in the event of there being no agreement between the parties, is to be determined by the judicial intervention of the United States District Court for the Southern District of New York. The broadcasting industry established these committees in order to negotiate with ASCAP and BMI and seek to minimise the rates and simplify the requisite book-keeping. ASCAP is subject to the '1950 Consent Decree' of USA v ASCAP and BMI is subject to the '1966 Consent Decree' of USA v BMI which restrains and enjoins their actions. The Consent Decrees also force ASCAP and BMI to accept any qualified writer or publisher as a member of ASCAP or as an affiliate of BMI. These decrees also make the courts available for review.

Anti-trust

CBS v ASCAP and BMI[9] held that the blanket licence was not a per se violation of the antitrust laws. On 2 March 1981 with the US Supreme Court determination to deny certiorari, the lengthy CBS v ASCAP and BMI antitrust lawsuit ended. Eleven years before in December 1969, the CBS Television Network sued ASCAP, BMI and their members (and affiliates) alleging that their blanket licences restrained competition in violation of the Sherman Antitrust Act in the United States District Court for the Southern District of New York. In April 1980, the Second Circuit Court of Appeals held unanimously that these blanket licences offered by ASCAP and BMI to the television networks were lawful and that CBS had failed to prove violation of the antitrust safeguards.

This case was ruled on by the Supreme Court twice. In April 1979, the US Supreme Court reversed a 1973 Court of Appeals' ruling that blanket licensing was per se illegal price-fixing and remanded the case for more detailed analysis under the 'rule of reason' in deciding the issue whether blanket licensing unreasonably restrained trade. The high court held that blanket licensing was not illegal price-fixing. On 13 April 1980, the Court of Appeals ruled for ASCAP and BMI. The Courts pointed out that a power such as the CBS Television Network could feasibly obtain individual performance licences from competing copyright owners. This is called 'licensing at the source' and is possible because ASCAP and BMI obtain non-exclusive rights to license public performance. Consequently, CBS could obtain authorisation to perform a non-dramatical musical composition from either the copyright proprietor (at the source) or from

9 CBS v ASCAP, 400 F.Supp. 737 (S.D.N.Y. 1975), rev'd and remanded 562 F.2d 130 (2d Cir. 1977), consol'd 439 U.S. 817 (1979); CBS v BMI, 421 F.Supp. 592 (S.D.N.Y. 1976); 424 F.Supp. 799 (S.D.N.Y. 1976), consol'd 439 U.S. 817 (1979), rev'd and remanded 441 U.S. 1 (1979), motion den'd 607 F.2d 543 (2d Cir. 1979), aff'd 620 F.2d 930 (1980), cert. den. 450 U.S. 970, reh. den. 450 U.S. 1050.

the performing rights society. The Court of Appeals expressly adopted trial court Judge Lasker's original 1975 finding, wherein he originally dismissed this CBS action which they had reversed in August 1977, that the blanket licence did not have the effect of compelling CBS to deal exclusively with ASCAP.

'Per piece' or 'per programme' licences are also available from the performing rights societies. Rather than a music user being compelled to obtain a blanket licence, the user may obtain non-dramatic public performance rights to a particular piece or groups of works by obtaining a 'per programme' licence from the society. These have not been available for long and are still in an experimental state. For example, BMI makes available a 'per programme' licence whereby broadcasters pay a higher licence rate than on the blanket licence but it is computed as based only on programmes utilising BMI licensed music. In this way, the music user does not pay for programmes which do not include BMI music. The ASCAP/BMI broadcast blanket licence bases the fee on all revenues whereas a 'per programme' licence is based on the revenue of one programme.

After the lawsuit, the settlement CBS made with ASCAP cost the network fifty-one million dollars over a five-year period. The payments were scheduled as $8,000,000.00 for 1981; $8,500,000.00 for 1982, $9,000,000.00 for 1983; $9,500,000.00 for 1984 and $9,800,000.00 for 1985. A supplemental $6,200,000.00 payment for the 1970 to 1980 period was included in the agreement.[10] Throughout this lengthy litigation, CBS paid an interim licence fee to ASCAP and BMI with the stipulation that it would be adjusted based on the lawsuits' settlement.

The most recent development is *Buffalo Broadcasting Company Inc. v ASCAP and BMI.*[11] This court action was instituted by the All-Industry Television Station Music Licence Committee in the US District Court for the Southern District of New York. Federal Court Judge Lee P. Gagliardi certified the case as a 'class' action. The Court ruled that the practice of requiring local television stations to obtain blanket performing right licences for the use of music in syndicated programmes is an unreasonable restraint of trade. The Court also held that there is no viable alternative to the local stations if they do not obtain the blanket licences. It was also pointed out that 'per programme' licences were not feasible due to their expense and the requisite reporting and record-keeping. This case was distinguished from the CBS suit on the basis of market power, that is local television stations have inadequate market power in order to make direct licensing an acceptable alternative. The societies and their members were enjoined from requiring local stations to obtain blanket licences.

In reaction to this ruling, ASCAP and BMI suspended their previous policy of cash advances to writers and publishers due to the financial questions raised by this ruling. Approximately eighty million dollars from seven hundred independent television stations is involved in this case.[12] However, despite the reduction in fees from local television, ASCAP projects that 1983 revenues from all sources will exceed revenues of 1982.

The decision is not effective until 1 February 1984 or completion of the appeal. Until that time, local television is paying fees at the 1980 level of $36.7 million rather than at the 1982 fees level of $44.4 million. This is seen as a loss of almost 18 per cent from local television. The appeal is scheduled for oral argument before the United States Court of Appeals for the Second Circuit in August 1983.

Conclusion

The issues in licensing, antitrust and the three performing rights societies make this an interesting area of intellectual property law. The future will surely be full of change due to the constant alterations involved in this field. Experimentation and shifts in power will clearly result in constant change in American performing rights. Who will win and what will happen?—Time will tell!

© Jeffrey E. Jacobson 1983

10 'CBS Settlement With ASCAP Will Cost TV Web $51,000,000', *Variety,* 8 July 1981, at 57; 'ASCAP, CBS Finalize TV License Agreement', *Cashbox,* 11 July 1981, at 6.
11 546 F.Supp. 274 (S.D.N.Y. 1982).

12 'ASCAP, BMI Freeze Advances', *Billboard,* 25 September 1982, at 1.

34: IFLA STUDY CITES COPYRIGHT LAW AS UNABLE TO GOVERN INTERNATIONAL EXCHANGE OF MACHINE-READABLE BIBLIOGRAPHIC DATA

IFLA STUDY CITES COPYRIGHT LAW AS UNABLE TO GOVERN INTERNATIONAL EXCHANGE OF MACHINE-READABLE BIBLIOGRAPHIC DATA and goes on to say that "The most feasible methods at the present time for governing exchanges are detailed bilateral exchange agreements which specify the rights and responsibilities of exchange partners; [that] economic uncertainties concerning the production and exchange of machine-readable bibliographic data, as well as producers' continuing desire to control the redistribution of their records, may lead to restrictions on international exchange; and [that] organizations such as IFLA (the International Federation of Library Associations and Institutions) must develop and promote mechanisms where economic, financial, and political differences can be openly discussed and analyzed."

This study to investigate copyright and international exchange of bibliographic records in machine-readable form was funded by IFLA through a grant from the Council on Library Resources. However, the project once undertaken by King Research, Inc. had to broaden its primary focus. "Copyright is not the only uncertainty which exists regarding the international exchange of bibliographic records. Neither is the question of 'record ownership,' which has been debated 'substantially' in the US, particularly regarding the sharing of bibliographic data by major bibliographic utilities." According to King Research, it found the greatest uncertainty to be a lack of appreciation of the economic realities involved in the production and exchange of bibliographic records in machine-readable form. It is King's perception that, based upon its activity in conducting the survey, that the exchange of bibliographic data in machine-readable form has developed as an outgrowth of librarians' traditional professional responsibility and preference for the development of mechanisms to support the "free flow" and exchange of information. This "flow," as facilitated by computer technology, has become an increasingly international business actively supported by organizations and programs such as IFLA and Universal Bibliographic Control. This exchange must be encouraged to continue, says the report. Yet financial pressures on the producing agencies will continue to increase as demand increases and as more agencies develop the capabilities for providing on-line access.

This is not to say that copyright is totally irrelevant. However, it was found that only a small number of agencies seek copyright protection for the systems of bibliographic records which they produce. While this may be due partly to a lack of clarity within various countries concerning copyright's applicability to bibliographic records, or even to the variation among different countries of their own copyright laws, the report says that there is some reason to question whether copyright will ever be clarified sufficiently or in such a manner to answer completely questions which arise concerning the international exchange of bibliographic data. The report urges support of programs, such as Unesco's, which seek to clarify guidelines for copyright's treatment of bibliographic records. The recommendation of the report is that continued reliance also be placed upon bilateral exchange agreements to govern bibliographic data exchange. However, the report says that it is "unrealistic to think that a universal, standardized exchange agreement will exist which can be entered into automatically by exchange partners." This is based on the following factors:

different agencies will have different reasons for entering into exchange agreements and will differ as to the interests they wish to protect;

agencies will differ to the degree they must (or wish to) recover costs of data base production and/or distribution;

agencies will differ as to the ratio of the total number of records distributed to the total number of records received and/or used;

agencies will differ as to the types of uses they wish to allow of the data which they supply;

national bibliographic agencies will differ as to the types of agencies to which they will be willing to release their records.

As noted above, a major uncertainty is a lack of appreciation or understanding of the economic realities on international data exchange, but the report points out that the value of such data, both in economic and noneconomic terms, "would be seriously underestimated if librarians focus too narrowly on the question of ownership of individual records." It is the opinion of King Research that the value of bibliographic data bases derives not only from the use or modification of individual records, but also in the overall availability of entire data bases which can be searched and used for a variety of purposes.

These issues would be simplified if bibliographic records were used solely for in-house cataloging purposes. However, the study reveals that now, or in the future, records also may be used as a basis for input to machine-readable data bases which are then redistributed to third parties whose use of such data eventually might compete with the product of the originating agency.

The report says that an ideal system for governing international exchange would be one which balances the universal availability with the varying economic and noneconomic interests of those agencies which produce such data. As noted, copyright is only one of the factors which must be considered for the protection of the moral and economic rights of authors. Other factors which should be balanced are the increasingly important questions concerning the international transmission by wire, satellite, or other means, of numeric and nonnumeric data and, also, the sharing of data among representatives of developing countries.

The report admits that the options of control via international consortia, blanket licenses, and compulsory licenses may not have been supported by survey respondents simply because it was not possible in the questionnaire to explain fully how such hypothetical mechanisms might operate. A key component of such mechanisms is that exchange partners relinquish some control over factors such as identification of customers, record use, and/or price setting. The study team says that "it feels confident in concluding that record producers are somewhat reluctant to relinquish control over reuse, selling, or modification of their records." This conclusion is based not only on survey responses, but also on knowing the general reluctance of any producer of intellectual property to relinquish total control over that property, no matter how efficient the licensing or distribution mechanism might be. As evidence, the report cites the existence in the US of past opposition to compulsory licensing in cable television as well as to the continued operation by many US publishers of their own photocopying and reprint permissions departments despite the existence of such organization as the Copyright Clearance Center. Furthermore, the report continues, the effort required to set up universal international licensing arrangements or consortia may be hampered by "substantial differences among various countries in their telecommunications, information, and import-export policies."

According to the report, there appears to be a potential conflict between the desire of record producers to control the exchange and use of their records, and the desire of the different organizations to share their data. The report says that it is clear that a balance must be developed between the needs of producers and needs of users. Such balancing, according to the report, can occur only "if parties with potential differences can communicate and compromise in an organized, cooperative fashion." Based on these conclusions and the study team's interpretation of the data and opinions collected, the report lists the following recommendations to IFLA:

- IFLA, or some other organization should advance the understanding of the economic issues surrounding the international exchange of bibliographic data, possibly through the performance or sponsorship of a cost-benefit study of such relationships among national bibliography agencies. At the least, the volume of exchange of bibliographic data should be monitored on a regular basis.

- IFLA should promote an understanding of the broader issues surrounding the exchange of data, possibly developing a consortium of international organizations involved or interested in data exchange.

- IFLA should attempt to determine why its members participate in international data exchange, possibly through an informal polling of its members; such an understanding might help to balance the interests of producers and users of bibliographic data.

- While copyright is only one of the issues which affects international data exchange, IFLA should assist its members in informing their national governments concerning data exchange.

- IFLA should establish a working group among its members to explore the future relationships between the copyright of bibliographic data and copyright of the documents which such data describes.

- IFLA should prepare a document for its member organizations which describes the different issues which might be included in bilateral exchange agreements.

V: BASIC ISSUES

Papers 35 Through 44: Commentary

Although the present Copyright Statute was enacted as recently as 1976, and although its development had been the subject of exhaustive studies and debate, it was too much to expect that even such an omnibus revision could or would resolve all existing issues to the satisfaction of opposing factions. Moreover, changes in social and economic structures have a way of unraveling compromises and of making problems in areas where none had apparently existed before. Finally, new issues continue to appear as new technologies emerge and are applied to communications media.

In addressing these areas in this compendium, it was not always easy to separate "basic issues" from other aspects of copyright; the subject is too complex, too integral. Also, issues affect people—authors and other creators, publishers and other intermediaries, and information users of all kinds. Issues call instinctively for solutions, some of them judicial clarifications, others of them legislative changes, all of them hard to obtain. Thus, readers will find many of the copyright issues treated in other sections of this volume where they relate more closely, more specifically.

Nevertheless, certain aspects of copyright—specific statutory principles and philosophies, and some business practices—are clearly "basic issues" in the real sense of that phrase, and have been identified as such in the copyright literature. Some of the key writings on these issues are therefore presented in this section.

FAIR USE

Possibly no other portion of the 1976 Copyright Statute has been subject to as much controversy and interpretation as has Section 107: "Limitations on exclusive rights: Fair use." In this section, Congress sought to make statutory law—without change—of what had previously been a judicial doctrine. In doing this, however, it opened a Pandora's box, even of judicial interpretation. So complex has the subject become, indeed, that for no other aspect of copyright did we as compilers have

195

as much difficulty in selecting a reasonable number of papers to cover the subject.

In the days when copyright was chiefly concerned with the creation and publication of printed works, the judicial concept of fair use was chiefly involved with considerations of how much of one author's work could be fairly used by another without securing the copyright holder's consent. This is still a major concern of authors, or at least publishers, as Carol E. Rinzler points out in Paper 35, "What's Fair About 'Fair Use'?" She singles out purpose and damage as the two fair-use tests that are most significant; however, "exploitation is not the same as commercial, and a desire for profit is by no means anathema. . . . Good faith—not even mentioned in the copyright act—may be the most important [factor] of all."

Rinzler says that the numerical cutoff set by book publishers for their own authors, "and the outside limit on the amount a house will pass as fair use when asked for consent— ranges typically between 50 and 100 words of prose and between zero and 10 lines of poetry. . . . The limits at most houses have dropped in recent years." In terms of what the courts might rule as fair, Rinzler believes that "publishers and authors often pay too much for too little" and cites examples. "Fees charged by publishers are negotiable, but they range generally from $15 to $100 per page of prose, from $5 to $25 per line of poetry, depending on the house and on the factors noted."

Former United States Register of Copyrights David Ladd goes far beyond one of the tests for fair use—"the effect of the use upon the potential market for or value of the copyrighted work"—in his eloquent 1983 Donald E. Brace Memorial lecture, "The Harm of the Concept of Harm in Copyright" (Paper 36). Ladd says that "the idea of harm [too much emphasis on it] . . . misconceives the end and purpose of copyright: to do justice by compensating justly . . . to protect, nourish, and celebrate our freedom and the world of wisdom, prophecy, and revelation which keeps us free."

According to Irving Louis Horowitz and Mary E. Curtis, the authors of Paper 37, the 1976 Copyright Statute has transformed the concept of fair use "from a rule of reason into a loophole, a rationale for free and virtually unrestricted use of copyrighted materials." Their contentions are based chiefly on aspects of library photocopying, but they conclude that "in the larger sense, the issue of fair use does not concern use at all, but ownership . . . fair return."

In Paper 38, "A New Definition of Fair Use," with emphasis on the Supreme Court's decision on the "Betamax case", Herbert Swartz points out that Congress, in writing the 1976 Copyright Statute, "gave the courts leeway to widen the definition of fair use far beyond any [previous] judicial doctrine," despite its intent not to. By permitting reproduction of *whole* copies for classroom and certain other uses, it departed from the previous concept that only *parts* of a work could be used in creating a second one. "The statutory language is descriptive but not prescriptive; . . . it now means anything a court says it means."

Another item that we have included on fair use, Paper 39, is an editorial from *Folio* that points out:

> Magazines will not be willing to pay as much as they have in the past for first rights to some copyrighted material, now that a federal appeals court has ruled that *The Nation* did not violate the copyright laws by publishing a story about the memoirs of former President Ford. . . . The major question raised . . . is whether it [the decision] gives magazines an expanded right to quote directly from copyrighted material written by important public officials under the "fair use" clause.

Our array of papers on fair use is admittedly one that is concerned with changes in its status. These and more traditional aspects are covered further in the papers listed in our Bibliography. In addition, there is much on fair use in the papers in this volume that pertain to photocopying, abstracts, databases, and home video recording. Fair use is indeed a basic copyright issue.

ABSTRACTS

As we reported in the first paper in this compendium, two studies on the copyright status of abstracts, the most recent of which is included here, have basically concluded that, beyond some limited fair use, the copyright of an *author abstract*—one that appears as a part of the document described—is probably the property of the copyright owner of the document, although its free use by a secondary journal has traditionally been permitted and even encouraged. These studies and the 1980 paper by Charles H. Lieb that is cited in the Bibliography also held that an *original abstract*—one prepared by someone other than the author and avoiding his or her phraseology—could normally be written without the permission of the copyright owner of the original work, and could be copyrighted itself, as long as it does not become a *derivative work*, that is, is not so long and so comprehensive that its use could be substituted for that of the original work.

The study included here as Paper 40 was published in two parts (the findings first) by the American Society for Information Science. We have placed the second article first in order to restore the original design of the study: to present definitions and issues before the reactions—positions—of the groups involved. Both parts were written by Ben H. Weil, Kurt D. Steele, Morton David Goldberg, M. Lynne Neufeld, and Lois W. Granick, acting as an ad hoc joint task force for the Information Industry Association (IIA) and the National Federation of Abstracting and Information Services (NFAIS).

In regard to original (nonauthor) abstracts, the IIA/NFAIS study differentiated between the typical 100- to 250-word abstracts of 5,000-to 8,000-word articles, which can seldom be derivative works because of their relative brevity, and very short "news" abstracts of newspaper and similar stories, which can sometimes contain all of the information in these stories, hence might be classed as permission-required derivative

197

works. However, for these short-item abstracts, attention was called to the fair-use privileges afforded to "news stories" in Section 107 of the Copyright Statute.

COMPILATIONS/DATABASES

Printed compilations of facts—directories, dictionaries, bibliographic (secondary) publications, and the like—whose preparation has required creative efforts to compile and to arrange, have long been held to be works of authorship, hence copyrightable, even though the individual elements might not be copyrightable. (Facts, as such, are not.) Because of this dichotomy, however, their copyright has sometimes been dubbed "thin," and exactly where their fair use ends and infringement begins occasionally evokes litigation.

A new factor in this situation, moreover, has been the use of modern technologies—computers and telecommunications—to make these compilations (now called *databases*) accessible far more quickly and conveniently. Stored in computers by their publishers or grouped together by database suppliers, the information in these compilations can now be viewed or printed out remotely, *online,* by users at terminals at the other ends of telecommunication channels.

There seems to be little doubt that copyright protection is afforded to bibliographic databases, even when they are made accessible via online computers. In addition to copyright protection, database information is usually further protected by use limitations that are spelled out in contracts between the database producers and the online suppliers (or vendors) and then between the latter and the online customers. Nevertheless, technology has put a strain on user compliance with both copyright and contract provisions. It is now possible for online users to easily *download* extensive portions of databases for later internal, payment-free use without detection by the database suppliers that anything other than printing out is going on. While some users have been asking for permission to download for printout editing, others have frankly admitted to what may amount to database misappropriaton.

Nevertheless, recent studies seem to indicate that unauthorized downloading is not as widespread as had been feared. Moreover, some of the major bibliographic-database services have announced licensing programs that permit such reuse. Continued attention to downloading seems warranted, however, because it adds to the economic impact of the online databases on hard-copy subscriptions and may thus affect the viability of the databases.

In Paper 41, however, Joseph H. Kuney states that "problems to date have been regarded by publishers and by users as minor and subject to ready solution," and that because of their cooperative attitudes, "the result is a growing business of database publishing and a growing clientele of users. Databases . . . are definitely a part of all of our futures . . . [and] point clearly toward the capability to provide a truly effective system of more selective dissemination. Our stake is to realize there are not threats—only opportunities."

On a less optimistic note, Christopher Burns points out in Paper 42:

> Even the copyright procedures for a database seem difficult and inappropriate, since the copyright seeks to protect the data set—which is ephemeral—not the rules that fashion it into something usable—which are the real genius of the publisher's effort. . . . We have developed elaborate leases and contracts that try to prevent subscribers from reselling database access or compilation products in any form, but since many of the individual *items* of information are freely available from other sources, it is often impossible to prove that the contract was broken.

He hopes, however—as does Joseph Kuney—that "we who are on all sides of this issue can get some lines painted on the track before the sound of crumpled fenders gets to be too much of a distraction."

There is more on this subject in the references listed in the Bibliography.

WORKS MADE FOR HIRE

Section 101 of the 1976 Copyright Statute says that a *work made for hire* is:

> (1) a work prepared by an employee within the scope of his or her employment; or
> (2) a work specially ordered or commissioned for use as a contribution to a collective work, as part of a motion picture or other audiovisual work, as a translation, as a supplementary work, as a compilation, as an instructional text, as answer material for a test, or as an atlas, if the parties expressly agree in a written instrument signed by them that the work shall be considered a work made for hire. For the purpose of the foregoing sentence, a "supplementary work" is a work prepared for publication as a secondary adjunct to a work by another author for the purpose of introducing, concluding, illustrating, explaining, revising, commenting upon, or assisting in the use of another work, such as forewords, afterwords, pictorial illustrations, maps, charts, tables, editorial notes, musical arrangements, answer material for tests, bibliographies, appendixes, and indexes, and an "instructional text" is a literary, pictorial, or graphic work prepared for publication and with the purpose of use in systematic instructional activities.

Further, Section 201(b) in Chapter 2 ("Copyright Ownership and Transfer") of the Statute goes on to say:

> In the case of a work made for hire, the employer or other person for whom the work was prepared is considered the author for purposes of this title [the Statute], and unless the parties have expressly agreed otherwise in a written instrument signed by them, owns all of the rights comprised in the copyright.

199

Clear? Was a fair balance achieved in the drafting of this statutory language? Should it be changed? The answers depend on who is talking or planning for action. Because a bill to amend the Statute has been introduced in Congress, we could have placed this discussion and papers in Part VII, Legislative and Judicial Issues, but the subject is basic to copyright, so we have included it here.

Howard Fields has reviewed the basic arguments of those involved in Paper 43, "Publishers and Authors Draw Lines for Work-for-Hire Battle," —the battle over a bill introduced in 1983 by Senator Thad Cochran. This bill would, "among other things, ban work-for-hire contracts for contributions to a collective work, supplementary work, or instructional text," making these "subject to the copyright law's provision for a limited rights transfer." According to Fields, freelancers claim that publishers now "always use work-for-hire and [do] not negotiate"—do not "make a distinction on a case-by-case scrutiny of the nature of the assignment and creativity."

At least one book publisher has said that if the bill is passed "publishers may have to retrench on their use of freelancers. . . . [We] might have to do more of our work in-house." The Association of American Publishers was quoted as saying:

> [The bill] would severely damage many of the industries we represent. . . . If publishers cannot specify, unambiguously and finally, in an agreement who owns the rights in a finished product, then they cannot market the product with confidence; they will be especially disadvantaged in those cases where a sale of rights is necessary to penetrate a new market—e.g., to publish the product in a foreign translation or to present it in a different medium.

No action was taken on this bill in 1984. Similar legislation will receive attention in the current session of Congress.

Edith and Phillip Leonian discuss the transfer of ownership to art and photography in Paper 44, "Copyright and Practices of the Trade." They detail the elements of a copyright license from the viewpoint of the artist and the photographer. In regard to work-for-hire contracts, they believe that publishers "are still unwilling to pay the much higher fees that go along with the purchase of extensive, or 'all' rights. . . . While some continue to offer them for signature, in most cases refusal to sign has had no effect on whether or not an author, photographer, or illustrator received an assignment."

BIBLIOGRAPHY

The following additional readings pertain to the Basic Issues covered.

Fair Use

Asser, P. N., 1980, Editorial: Fair Use Reproduction, *STM Newsletter* **51**:3-4.

Authors League Symposium on Copyright: January 27, 1982, *Copr. Soc. U.S.A. J.* **29**(6):611–646.

Boorstyn, N., 1984, The Doctrine of Fair Use: An Overview, *Copr. Law J.*, Special focus issue, pp. 2–5.

Copyright Office, 1977, *"Fair Use" of Copyrighted Work,* Library of Congress, Washington, D.C.

Gordon, W. J., 1983, Fair Use as Market Failure: A Structural and Economic Analysis of the Betamax Case and Its Predecessors, *Copr. Soc. U.S.A. J.* **30**(3):253–326.

Greenwood, V. D., 1980, Fair Use and Photocopy, *ASCAP Copr. Law Symp.* **24**:113–156. [Pertains to the 1909 statute]

Hart, W. M., 1981, The Conscientious Fair Users Guide to the Copyright Act of 1976: Video Recordation and Its Fair Use, *Univ. Pitt. Law. J.* **42**:317–374.

Jacobson, J. E., 1980, Fair Use: Considerations in Written Works, *Commun. and the Law* **2**(4):17–38.

Lawrence, M. S., 1982, Fair Use: Evidence of Change in a Traditional Doctrine, *ASCAP Copr. Law Symp.* **27**:71–112.

Mandelbaum, J., 1984, *The Nation*: Overprotection of the First Amendment in Fair Use Analysis, *Copr. Soc. U.S.A. J.* **32**(2):138–156.

Patry, W. F., 1985, *The Fair Use Privilege in Copyright Law,* BNA Books, Washington, D.C.

Timberg, S., 1980, A Modernized Fair Use Code for the Electronic as Well as the Gutenberg Age, *Northwestern Univ. Law Rev.* **75**(2):193–244.

Walker, W. C., Jr., 1983, Fair Use: The Adjustable Tool for Maintaining Copyright Equilibrium, *La. Law Rev.* **43**(3):735–757.

Abstracts

Lieb, C. H., 1980, Interactions and Tensions Between Primary and Secondary Scientific Publications, *Commun. and the Law* **2**(4):55–59.

Cambridge Research Institute, 1973, Periodicals, Abstracts, and Derivative Works, in *Omnibus Copyright Revision: Comparative Analysis of the Issues,* American Society for Information Science, Washington, D.C., 1973, pp. 161–166.

Compilations/Databases

Brandhorst, T., and Williams, M., 1978, Machine-Readable Data Bases: Copyright Status, *Am. Soc. Inf. Sci. Bull.* **4**(4):31.

Denicola, R. C., 1981, Copyright in Collections of Facts: A Theory for the Protection of Nonfiction Literary Works, *Columbia Law Rev.* **81**:516–544.

Gorman, R. A., 1983, Fact or Fancy? The Implications for Copyright, *Copr. Soc. U.S.A. J.* **29**:560–610.

Oberman, M. S., 1973, Copyright Protection for Computer-Produced Directories, *Fordham Law Rev.* **41**:767–806.

Tenopir, C., 1983, Full-text, Downloading, and Other Issues, *Libr. J.* **108**:1111-1113.

Williams, M. E., 1985, Electronic Databases, *Science* **228**(4698):445-456.

Wolfe, M., 1982, Copyright and Machine Readable Databases, *Online* **6**(4):52-55.

Works Made for Hire

Angel, D., and Tannenbaum, S. W., 1976, Works Made for Hire Under S. 22, *N.Y. Law School Law Rev.* **22**(2):202-239.

Butts, C. A., 1982, Work Hirer Responds, *Copr. Manage.* **5**:4-6.

Fields, H., 1984, Cochran Sponsors New Work-for-Hire Bill, *Publ. Wkly.* **225**(1):19.

Friedman, B., 1983, Copyright Can Reach Out and Touch You, *Soc. Sch. Publ. Lett.* **5**(3):3.

McMasters, T., 1982, Artists Implore Senators Plug Copyright Act Loophole, *Hollywood Rep.* **273**(42):1, 6.

O'Meara, W. O., 1981-1982, "Works Made for Hire" Under the Copyright Act of 1976—Two Interpretations, *Creighton Law Rev.* **15**(2): 523-543.

Publishers, Authors Spar in Works-for-Hire Testimony, 1982, *Publ. Wkly.* **222**(16):10-12.

Sadler, W. R., 1982, Free Lance Artists, Works for Hire, and the Copyright Act of 1976, *U.C. Davis Law Rev.* **15**:703-721.

"Work-for-Hire" Law Revision Sought, 1982, *Writ. Dig.* **62**(7):49.

35: WHAT'S FAIR ABOUT "FAIR USE"?

Carol E. Rinzler

ONCE when I was a book editor, I came across a 250-word quote in a manuscript I was editing, and that evening I buttonholed a lawyer at a party. "What's the story on fair use?" I asked. "Is it 300 words or what?" "Well," chuckled the lawyer, "it's really not that simple."

Fair use has been defined as the privilege of using copyrighted material in a reasonable manner without having to secure the copyright holder's consent. The policy underlying the fair use doctrine, judges have announced in many legal decisions, is that enabling others to build on prior works promotes intellectual progress and the public's access to information and ideas. But exactly what is "reasonable" has puzzled authors and publishers, as well as lawyers and judges, for years. Among authors and editors, the misconception exists that "reasonable" is determined by amount, and that someone, somewhere has a handy chart that sets out how much is too much.

In fact, the law supplies no absolute numbers or even rough percentage rules of thumb. Determining whether or not a use is fair involves applying a vague set of principles that has emerged from copyright infringement cases, for the question really being asked in any fair use inquiry is: How likely is it that the copyright holder will believe he or she could sue and win? Few of those cases have involved day-to-day publishing problems; the situations have been unusual or they have not involved publishing at all (television and film people tend to sue more often; the stakes are much higher).

The analytic process engaged in by judges who decide fair use cases consists of weighing four factors, which are now formally codified in the 1976 Copyright Act: 1) how large a portion of the copyrighted work was used; 2) the nature of the copyrighted material—whether it is heavily factual, e.g., an index, or redolent with expression, e.g., a poem; 3) the purpose of the allegedly infringing work—to contribute to scholarship, say, or to advertise the user's products; 4) did the allegedly infringing use financially damage the copyrighted work.

The first factor—how much you used—is not very helpful. As noted, there are no absolutes; it's all relative. Quoting 1000 words from a full-length book for a good purpose might be fair use; the same quote for the same purpose from a magazine might not be—although it might be if it were for an even better purpose. Does it help to know you can't engage in "substantial" or "wholesale

copying" or "take the essence" of a copyrighted work? The last definition does suggest that paraphrase is less of a safe way out than many people believe, although, just in case you were beginning to catch on, if it's just conveying the facts and the information, that's fine. The second factor—the nature of the copyrighted work—is not much more help. The cases are filled with language extolling "creative, imaginative and original" expression and suggesting that, all other factors being equal, you may use less of that sort of material than of heavily factual material; but most of those cases deal with special situations, e.g., how much may the compiler of a directory use of another directory? Cases concerning computer programs and databases as they burgeon may refine the usefulness of this factor.

Purpose and Damage Are Key Variables

The two factors the courts have relied on most in fair use analysis are the user's purpose and the economic effect on the copyrighted work. Some ends permit you more generous means; perhaps most favored is communicating information of "intense public interest." When Louis Nizer included over 3000 words from Julius and Ethel Rosenberg's letters in his book *The Implosion Conspiracy*, the court suggested the use might be fair because of "the continuing interest and importance of the celebrated Rosenberg case." John Keats, in his 1966 biography of Howard Hughes, quoted or closely paraphrased some 14% of a series of *Look* magazine articles about Hughes. The court, in deciding that the use was fair, found relevant the "privilege [that] the public have some information regarding important public figures." (It also helped that it was Hughes himself who had bought up the copyright in the articles and was trying to stop publication of the book altogether.) Compare the case in which the defendants televised a copyrighted silent movie without authorization. The court wrote: "It can scarcely be argued that the enduring fame of Rudolph Valentino or the intrinsic literary and historical merit of *Son of the Shiek* (whatever it may be) serves any public interest sufficient to endow these defendants with the privilege of fair use."

Interestingly, satire and parody are particularly "deserving of substantial freedom—both as entertainment and as a form of social and literary criticism." When *Mad* magazine was sued for parodying the lyrics of several popular songs, having copied the rhyme schemes and some of the lyrics verbatim, the court found the use fair, as did the court that passed on a "Saturday Night Live" parody of the song "I Love New York." You may take, say the courts, as much of a copyrighted work

---

Rinzler, formerly a book and magazine editor, and an author, is a lawyer with Cahill Gordon & Reindel, attorneys for the Nation *in the case referred to in the text.*

[*Author's Note:* The *Harper & Row v. The Nation* case mentioned later in this paper was subsequently reversed by the Second Circuit. At this writing (July, 1984), it is on appeal to the Supreme Court.]

as you need to "recall or conjure up the object" of your satire, so long as your work cannot substitute for the original. As for literary criticism, although the courts often mention that as the quintessentially perfect purpose, they've never actually decided such a case. The closest are cases in which the copyrighted material was used in order to refute it—a manufacturer combating a negative *Consumer Reports* article by sending the article, along with a retort, to its customers, for example. Of course, it's difficult to imagine a publisher suing a book reviewer (who easily may "take the essence" and who certainly can harm the work economically), but a more plausible problem—how much may a literary biographer or critic quote from the subject in a book-length work?—presents a harder question, one the courts have yet to tackle.

Judges respond least favorably to what they regard as exploitation. Using even a small amount of copyrighted material in an advertisement and arguing fair use rarely succeeds (quoting from a book review in an ad for a book, though, apparently has never been litigated). Crazy Eddie, for example, lost when he mocked up a Superman character in a TV commercial, as did Liggett & Myers some years ago when it quoted three sentences from a book in a pamphlet promoting cigarettes. But exploitative is not the same as commercial, and a desire for profit is by no means anathema. In the Howard Hughes case, the court went out of its way to note: "Whether an author or publisher reaps economic benefits . . . or whether [a book's] publication is motivated in part by a desire for commercial gain . . . has no bearing on whether a public benefit may be derived from such a work." Nonprofit motives, though, certainly don't hurt. The National Institutes of Health some years ago got away with extensive copying and circulation of entire scientific journal articles largely because the NIH's purpose was educational and nonprofit. The fact that home viewers recording TV shows don't make any money from their alleged infringement is one of the defendants' arguments in the Sony Betamax case, which the Supreme Court should decide this term. Nonprofit motives also will be at issue if and when the recently filed suit against New York University for reproducing copyrighted materials goes to trial.

The most likely of the four factors to defeat a fair use defense is economic harm to the copyrighted work. ABC, for example, was soundly trounced when it broadcast, without permission, brief portions of a copyrighted film about an Olympic athlete and the film's owners proved that ABC's use destroyed any possibility of marketing the film to network television. In practice, of course, economic harm rarely arises in a publishing context, assuming fair use is not a disingenuous defense. Using a minimal amount of a work almost never deprives the work of a market or decreases its sales; in fact it may even increase them. What, after all, is the market for even 1000 scattered words of most books or 20% of most poems? Occasionally, however, such a case does arise. In the recently decided *Harper & Row* v. *The Nation*, which is to be appealed, the publisher argued that the magazine's prepublication use of material from President Ford's autobiography, *A Time to Heal*, deprived it of $12,500 of the total proceeds from its previously negotiated first-serial sale to *Time* magazine. Even though it was Harper & Row that decided not to go ahead with the excerpt (*Time* merely wanted to advance publication by one week), the court weighed economic harm in deciding for the publisher.

A fifth factor in fair use analysis—good faith—is not even mentioned in the Copyright Act, but it may be the most important of all. People who have never heard of the four fair use factors or, for that matter, of copyright law, often can figure out who won a fair use case just by hearing the facts, applying a test that has its roots in life rather than law, and concluding that the use just

wasn't—well, fair. In the Olympic athlete case, for instance, it didn't help ABC that the owners of the film were able to prove that the network had copied it surreptitiously while assessing the film for possible purchase, and that ABC later denied having used the excerpt at all. Defendants who are offered copyrighted material, turn it down, then use it without paying, don't win fair use cases. And what the courts call "unjust enrichment" places an equitable limit on how much you can take, even where there's no economic harm. In other words, if fair use is a free lunch, it's not at Lutèce. Similarly, although there's not much in the cases concerning crediting a source for a brief verbatim use, I suspect that passing off someone else's words as one's own—a concept from unfair competition law—would go, and has gone, against users.

But good faith works both ways. The courts are unresponsive, for example, to copyright holders, like Howard Hughes, who simply won't let go. The author of a 1967 book about the Kennedy assassination, *Six Seconds in Dallas,* after having been denied consent, included copies of significant frames from the *Life* magazine-owned Zapruder film of the shooting. That *Life* had refused to grant permission at virtually any price (the publisher of the book, Bernard Geis, had offered all of its profits from the book) influenced the court in accepting the fair use defense.

Fair Use in the Real World

So much for fair use in the courtroom and the law books. How do publishing houses respond to requests to use small portions of books they publish, and at what point do they require their authors to secure consent from copyright holders for material they want to use in their own books?

Unlike judges, book publishers generally play by the numbers, beginning by establishing a numerical cut-off that varies from house to house but ranges typically between 100 and 500 words of prose and between zero and 10 lines of poetry. That cut-off sets the point at which a house ordinarily requires its own authors to secure permission, and the outside limit on the amount a house will pass as fair use when asked for consent. The limits at most houses have dropped in recent years. Those who field requests take several additional factors into account in deciding whether to tell the person making the request that the use is a fair use that doesn't require consent, or that they will give formal permission for free, or that the use does require a permissions fee. One calculation permissions departments typically engage in is a sort of what-the-traffic-will-bear test. If Plato and Aristotle both want to use 400 words of Socrates's prose in their biographies of Socrates, Plato, who is being published by a university press, may be told his use requires no consent or be given formal permission for free; Aristotle, whose effort is a trade book with a large first printing, may be charged for permission. Most houses also take into account the value of the material requested. When Mickey asks to quote 500 of Donald's words from a book that was remaindered, he may be told he requires no consent or be given permission for free; 200 of Minnie's Pulitzer Prize-winning words may cost Mickey $200.

Different purposes merit different treatment, according to publishers. Demosthenes, who wants 300 words from Socrates's work for his muckraking biography, and Sappho, who wants to use 200 words in her dirty novel, might be charged fees or even be denied permission altogether. Permissions people often weigh how important the material is to the person requesting its use or to that person's book. A house that charges Scarlett nothing for using eight lines of a poem in the body of her novel may charge her a permissions fee if she wants to use two lines of that poem as an epigraph, a chapter head or as the caption of a picture. "Anything that is set off," is where fair use ends at one house. Those who take this position feel that the purpose of such a use is commercial or exploitative.

Assuming for the moment that at least some requests need not have been made in the first place because the use was fair and thus required no consent, what is such caution costing authors? Fees charged by publishers are negotiable, but they range generally from $15 to $100 per page of prose, from $5 to $25 per line of poetry, depending on the house and on the factors noted above. Permissions people are in general agreement that fewer requests are being granted for free these days and that prices have risen in recent years. As transaction costs rise, the lower end of the price range is becoming a money-losing proposition (publishers typically receive 50% of a permissions fee). Some publishers have raised minimum fees or are contemplating setting them; some are starting to charge for uses they admit clearly fall under the fair use exception. At these latter houses, you may say, fair use stops when you ask.

Are Copyright Owners Fair?

Would the courts sanction the practices described? Here a distinction must be made between the author who requests consent and the author who uses material without seeking consent in the good faith belief that the use is fair. Assuming the latter and the positive purpose of that author's work, some uses for which publishers are charging fees—for instance, quoting several lines from a long poem in an epigraph—strike me as unlikely to stand up in court. The absence of economic harm—could a subsidiary rights director auction the epigraph rights?—probably would impress a judge or jury. If an author actually were quoted a permissions fee, though, and subsequently decided to use those lines without paying, the good faith factor might well shift the balance in the publisher's favor. How a court would react to a publisher who refused permission absolutely and an author who went ahead without it probably would depend on an assessment of the other factors.

Is all this academic because publishers and authors seldom sue? (With good reason; assuming no economic harm and the user's good faith, the most a copyright holder probably would recover, if he won the case at all, is the minimum amount of statutory damages, $250 or less.) Should an author be advised to bypass a permissions department simply because he or she probably won't get sued? Not necessarily. For one thing, one never knows when a copyright holder may sue on principle or to establish a precedent that might help out in future cases where the stakes are higher. For another thing, many authors don't have that choice; publishers increasingly are requiring authors to secure permissions for increasingly minimal uses. This trend toward greater courtesy or caution generates some distressing results, as in a recent case in which the author of a forthcoming book on the Vietnam War was instructed to secure permissions for brief (mostly 10- to 15-word) quotes from magazine articles. Most of the excerpts were themselves quotes from public figures to be used as chapter heads. Three of the magazines gave permission for free; a fourth charged $50 for a 12-word quote used as a chapter head; the fifth, two of whose lengthy articles reporting on the war in its early stages were being quoted at greater length and criticized in the text of the book, refused permission for those uses altogether—18 years later, the quotes were embarrassing. The publisher advised the author to paraphrase the passages in question instead. It would take a rare, and perhaps a foolhardy, publisher to advise otherwise and risk a lawsuit, even though the original decision

to require consent probably was in error, and the magazine probably would lose in court. "I was just being safe," says the editor involved. "It's a good thing the quotes weren't that important," the author mutters, like many authors when it's not prohibitions but permissions fees. Paying $25 or $100 for a permission or two is probably something most authors will shoulder, but an author faced with permissions so hefty they begin to eat into an advance may forego all but the most essential—to the detriment, at least some of the time, of the work and of the public.

Consider the case of song lyrics. The prevailing belief in the publishing industry is that there's no fair use in a song lyric at all. Despite several decisions, including the *Mad* magazine and "Saturday Night Live" cases already cited that go the other way, authors are almost invariably advised by their publishers to get permission to quote even a single line, and music publishers as routinely oblige them with a permission fee. (The pervasive terror of music publishers is odd; there appears to be no case in which holders of a copyright in a song lyric sued someone for using a small portion of the lyric and won. Perhaps it's the plethora of cases in which using part of the melody, usually in another, theoretically competing, song, was found not to be fair use that has everyone running scared.) So, much of the time, authors shrug and leave out the snatch of lyric, not only because fees are high but because procedures can often be complex. A call to ASCAP or BMI, which do not themselves handle book permissions, may or may not turn up the copyright holder, who in turn may or may not hold all the rights in a song, and who almost certainly will require additional payments if the book is bought by a book club or a paperback publisher or merely goes into a second printing. Suppose you use four lines of a song as a chapter head, say, without seeking consent, and you are sued. Would a court agree with one music publisher that "each word is magic" and find you liable? How much would it matter that a subsidiary market for song lyrics—selling single lines to cowed authors—apparently exists? I suspect you would win, but who wants to go through a lawsuit to find out for sure? Ultimately, paying for uses the courts might well find fair may amount to nothing more than legal insurance. Under the law, or if a case were litigated, an author might not need consent; but if he wants it, perhaps he should pay.

But where the use, under a good faith reading of the law, would be found fair, should an author pay more than a handling fee? And if it's the publisher who is insisting that permissions be secured, and the fee is high, should the publisher pay? Of course, some houses do wind up paying by advancing the fee against royalties and then finding themselves unable to collect from an author because the book didn't earn out.

A frequent publisher justification for charging permissions fees is similar to the music publishers'—every word is valuable, and if you want to borrow even a teaspoon of art, you must pay. Sometimes the pressure comes from the authors themselves, who may have a clause in their contract requiring that every request be cleared by them, and who may deny permission altogether or charge a high price. In a way, the argument that every word is valuable views unjust enrichment as starting right above zero; nothing in the law supports that position; nor does it support many of the decisions publishers are making to require consent or to deny fair use or to charge a high permissions fee, when at most a handling fee to defray the expense of sending out a letter is appropriate. The copyright monopoly granted to an author is no more limited in control than it is in duration. Current industry practices seem to be drifting toward a simple—but simply wrong—answer to the question: how much is too much? □

36: THE HARM OF THE CONCEPT OF HARM IN COPYRIGHT: THE THIRTEENTH DONALD C. BRACE MEMORIAL LECTURE*

David Ladd**

Copyright is today under stress. It is also under attack.

The stress arises primarily from the rapid succession of marvelous new machines, miraculous enough to delight Jules Verne, for copying and, in new ways, enjoying protected works. They are for that reason a boon.

By the same token, unauthorized copying of print, sound, and cinematographic works has become epidemic; copyright owners' control has weakened; and the domestic and international traffic in piratical copies of films and records has risen to floodtide.[1]

As new technologies of use appear, they create their own commercial interests, constituencies, and pressure groups whose fortunes are furthered by maximum public use of copyrighted works, whether compensated or not. There are likewise non-commercial groups who see copyright as hobbling their mission by placing unacceptable strains on their budgets, or complicating their work. These groups have often resisted the historic trend of extending and expanding copyright to new technologies, under pleas of special needs. Such resistance is never claimed to be justified in terms of self-interest, but of consumer interests in maximum distribution of goods and services at the lowest cost.

If the source of the stress lies in rapidly changing technology and if the political force of the attack draws from commercial or non-commercial self-interest, then the assault weapon is the notion that some proof of "harm" is a necessary condition for protecting a class of creative

---

*This lecture was delivered on April 13, 1983 at the Tishman Auditorium of the New York University Law Center, New York, New York.
**Mr. Ladd is the United States Register of Copyrights.

[1] Aside from controlling unauthorized copying of traditional works, another major problem, of course, is the crucial task of accommodating copyright to computer-related works. In this case, the problem is to adapt copyright to altogether new kinds of works of authorship rather than perfecting or completing protection for new uses of traditional works.

Reprinted from *Copr. Soc. U.S.A. J.* **30**(5):421-432 (1983).

works or a particular creative work, or a class of copyright owners, or a particular owner. This notion, an unhistoric interloper,[2] presents the primary doctrinal strain in copyright today.

What I call "the harm argument" is shorthand for a number of related justifications for exemption from copyright controls: that copyright proprietors are well-off enough that enhanced protection will only mean windfall profits; that only certain uses—large scale competitive ones—should be subject to control; that investments ought to be recouped only in these areas; and that the potential impediments which copyright clearances would impose on education and research would produce a harm outweighing any economic benefits copyright controls would produce. Explicitly or implicitly, however, the advocates of economic necessity as the test of copyright protection ultimately rest their case on an interpretation that the copyright clause of the Constitution is more a limitation than an empowerment, and, further, is itself hemmed in by the First Amendment.

The Constitution authorizes copyright "To promote the Progress of Science." From that phrase, the exponents of harm declare that where the imperatives of maximum distribution clash with property rights, the latter must yield; and that copyright should extend no further than to what is financially indispensable to motivate creation and publication. In more extended form, copyright is argued to be in opposition to other constitutional rights, including the right to the free flow of information and the public's right to know, both rooted in the First Amendment.

Copyright is *not* inimical to the First Amendment and the hallowed values it harbors. It is indeed of a piece, *in pari materia,* with the First Amendment and indispensable to it. That is the central idea of this lecture. The notion of economic "harm" as a prerequisite for copyright protection is mischievous because it disserves the basic constitutional design which embraces both copyright and the First Amendment. Proponents of the "harm" argument demand that we view publishers, motion picture and record companies, the information industries, and broadcasters as business interests undifferentiated from other businesses instead of what they are—instruments of free speech.

The harm argument should be rejected because it is amorphous and practically impossible to define or to apply consistently and fairly. That should be a full and sufficient reason for its rejection. More, it threatens

---

[2] The substantial legislation and jurisprudence concerning the availability of a preliminary injunction in copyright cases even without "a detailed showing of irreparable harm," (NIMMER ON COPYRIGHT §14.06[A]) and the availability of statutory damages, in lieu of actual damages, show that harm is an untraditional component of copyright infringement analysis.

to warp the universe of both authors and publishers[3]—a universe characterized by freedom, pluralism, dispersal of power and useful disorder; responsive to public taste, yet uncontrolled by any part of it. "Harm" as a basis for policy, substitutes, to borrow a phrase from welfare legislation, a means test for the historic and honorable principle of just compensation measured solely by what the public chooses to pay. It subserves indirect government control—an influence as chilling and corrosive to creative spirit and public discourse as the mechanisms of censorship outlawed by the First Amendment.

The general copyright revision of 1976 represented a towering achievement: the first total recodification and modernization of copyright in sixty-seven years, which culminated more than twenty years of study, debate, and drafting. The 1976 Act tamed, without quite domesticating, "killer" issues such as cable and photocopying. Beyond the hard compromises, the Act's basic purpose was to brace the development of copyright law to withstand and breast the predictable shocks of new machines, new uses, and new politics.

The Act's bracing is structural: its architecture is a framework of sweeping, broad, exclusive rights, limited only by express limitations, and a fair use doctrine declared to be no enlargement of that theretofore shaped in decisional precedent. The statute was fashioned with the purpose of guarding against "confining the scope of an author's rights on the basis of present technology so that, as the years go by, [the] copyright loses much of its value because of unforeseen technical advances."[4]

But the general revision has not given respite. The future has come too swiftly. Every session of Congress since 1976 has been vexed with copyright issues of great moment, often with political strife of unprecedented scope and intensity.

Of course, in one sense these issues are but latter-day versions of the perennial problem of extending and conforming copyright to new uses of works of authorship—an endeavor which has always characterized copyright, especially in the twentieth century in dealing with motion pictures, radio, and television. But those media did not develop at a

---

[3] The term *publisher*, along with words derived therefrom, is used as a term of art in a broad sense in this lecture to refer to any entrepreneur whose efforts lead to the public dissemination, performance, or display of works of authorship. In this extended definition, recording enterprises and motion picture producers, for example, are also "publishers."

[4] The quotation is from the 1965 SUPPLEMENTARY REPORT OF THE REGISTER OF COPYRIGHTS, at 14. The argument of the architecture of the Act, and its purpose, is elaborated in Ladd, *"Home Recording and Reproduction of Protected Works,* 68 A.B.A.J. 42 (January, 1982).

tempo as quick as that for tape recorders, photocopiers, videorecorders, computers, and satellites. Nor did they scatter widely among the public the instruments of copying, displaying, and performing.

There is yet a deeper difference today: works of authorship—copyrighted works—have moved to a more central place in our lives. We are now entering a post-industrial or information age. Increased wealth, higher education levels, more leisure, the growth of high technology (*i.e.,* information-fueled) industries, and rising tastes have vastly expanded the public need and appetite for "information." And "information" includes copyrighted works—books, motion pictures, sound recordings, and computer programs—for work, education, and entertainment.

Paradoxically, the growing importance of copyrighted works in professional and personal life has not led to a deeper appreciation and respect for authorship and copyright law. The steady resolve to extend and expand the incentives for authorship which has characterized copyright during much of this century now falters. Curiously, the argument now appears, and swells in volume, that precisely because works of authorship are so fundamentally important—not because they are trivial—barriers to their dissemination, including copyright payments to authors and publishers, must be overridden in the interest of maximum distribution and enjoyment.

The argument goes that copyright necessarily constrains the free flow of information, and to the extent that it does so, it contravenes its constitutional purpose and must be curtailed.[5] This contention—that proprietary control and the flow of money to creators and copyright owners are constraints on "information" dissemination—is aimed at the very principle of copyright. It throws into question the long accepted truth, declared by Justice Reed:

> The economic philosophy behind the clause empowering Congress to grant patents and copyrights is the conviction that encouragement of individual effort by personal gain is the best way to advance public welfare through the talents of authors and inventors. . . .[6]

---

[5] On the question of possible use of copyright to suppress information, *see* Professor Nimmer's thoughtful analysis. NIMMER ON COPYRIGHT (1980) §1.10 [D], *et seq.* That commercial exploitation of copyrighted works is subject to antitrust regulation is long established. *See, e.g.,* Straus v. American Publishers Assoc., 231 U.S. 222 (1913); U.S. v. Paramount Pictures Corp., 334 U.S. 131 (1948).

[6] Mazer v. Stein, 347 U.S. 201, 219 (1954).

The twenty-seven words in Art. I, §8, which give Congress the power to legislate copyrights and patents are plain and straightforward (and, incidentally, contain the only use of the word *right* in the entire main body of the Constitution):

> To promote the Progress of Science and Useful Arts, by securing for limited Times to Authors and Inventors the exclusive Right to their respective Writings and Discoveries.

How is the "exclusive right" intended "to promote the progress of science"? Is this a general declaration of purpose, and an authority for a general design? Or is it some sort of limitation of the class of "rights" thereby provided for, and upon each individual "right" authorized for each particular work? Is the constitutional goal of promoting "science" (resounding with its Latin origin and eighteenth-century meaning of *knowledge*) to be served by the creation of a private-property-based milieu in which authors' rewards are determined by the public in the market-place? Or does it envision the evaluation of every class of work, every individual work, or every use, to ascertain whether the progress of science is promoted, before determining whether copyright protection should be accorded in any given case, and if so, how much and what kind?

Proponents of the harm argument insist that a showing of harm is virtually required as a constitutional limitation: if there is no harm to the copyright owner, there is no demonstrated need for rewards under copyright to motivate the creation and dissemination of the work, and thus "to promote the progress of science."[7] The argument is not only unhistoric, but specious. It paves the way for government interference with information, speech, and discourse which, however indirect, is quite as unlovely as prior restraint.

In truth, the fundamental claim of copyright is one of justice. In many countries, copyright is deemed a natural right, part of the natural law, a true extension of personality, consisting of economic and moral rights, *i.e.*, the right to forbid uses of a work which would discredit the author directly or through his work. The United States, inheriting English law, has not generally accepted this philosophical ground. American copyright legislation may not fit into the formal philosophical edifice of "natural law." It does, nevertheless, express a felt sense of what is right and just.

---

[7] Whatever arguments might be made in this respect on the standards of patentability (Graham v. John Deere Co., 383 U.S. 1 (1966)), patents are not freighted with the First Amendment values here discussed.

The framers of the Constitution were men to whom the right to hold property was enormously important. They were not far removed from Locke. His ideas pervaded their debates and decision. Property was seen not as opposed to liberty, but indispensable to it; for men with property would be independent of the power of the State, in that rough-and-tumble roiling of opinion and power which marks freedom.

Not surprisingly, the Bill of Rights provides, in one breath, that "No person shall be deprived . . .of life, liberty, or property, without due process of law; nor shall private property be taken for public use without just compensation." Like Locke, Thomas Paine, our most passionate democrat, insisted on property as a bedrock of freedom, particularly in the area of literary property:

> It may, with propriety, be remarked, that in all countries where literature is protected, (and it never can flourish where it is not), the works of an author are his legal property; and to treat letters in any other light than this, is to banish them from the country, or strangle them in the birth.[8]

That rights of the author are thus of a special kind, rooted both in utility and felt justice, has long been recognized in our country. This has rarely been recalled with greater eloquence than in a statement by Professor Nathaniel Shaler of Harvard, presented to Congress in 1936 by Thorvald Solberg, one of my predecessors in this office:

> When we come to weigh the rights of the several sorts of property which can be held by man, and in this judgment take into consideration only the absolute question of justice, leaving out the limitations of expediency and prejudice, it will be clearly seen that intellectual property is, after all, the only absolute possession in the world. . . . The man who brings out of the nothingness some child of his thought has rights therein which cannot belong to any other sort of property. . . . The inventor of a book or other contrivance of thought holds his property, as a god holds it, by right of creation. . . . Whatever tends to lower the protection given to intellectual property is so much taken from the forces which have been active in securing the advances of society during the last centuries.[9]

---

[8] Letter to the Abbé Reynal (1782), in 1 POLITICAL WORKS OF THOMAS PAINE 4-5 (1817), quoted in B. BUGBEE, EARLY AMERICAN LAW OF INTELLECTUAL PROPERTY (1960) at 251.

[9] Hearings before H. R. Comm. on Patents, 74th Cong., 2d Sess. (1936), at 735.

And that concluding phrase, "securing the advances of society" clearly echoes the Constitution's "To promote the Progress of Science."

Before Solberg, Ainsworth Spofford, one of the great Librarians of Congress, bottomed his defense of copyright in 1886 on felt justice:

> [T]here can be no higher aim to statesmanship than the endeavor to establish justice, for justice is the highest interest of all men. . . . Either we must hold that authorship is the only form of human labor that shall go unpaid, or we must grant a copyright that shall be paid *pro rata* by all who use the authors' work. . . . Beyond question, the just thing will be found in the long run to be the expedient thing, and the fact that we cannot do perfect justice should not deter us from doing as much justice as we may.[10]

In 1974 my immediate predecessor, Barbara Ringer, after a careful assessment of the purposes of copyright, its public psychology, and its "demonology," sounded again the theme of justice and linked copyright to freedom. She said:

> If the copyright law is to continue to function on the side of light against darkness, good against evil, truth against newspeak, it must broaden its base and its goals. Freedom of speech and freedom of the press are meaningless unless authors are able to create independently from control by anyone, and to find a way to put their works before the public.[11]

The purpose of copyright is to reward authors as a matter of justice, yes; but only as a beginning. Copyright also is intended to support a system, a macrocosm, in which authors and publishers compete for the attention and favor of the public, independent of the political will of the majority, the powerful, and above all the government, no matter how unorthodox, disturbing, or revolutionary their experience, views, or visions.

The argument for copyright here, to be sure, is an argument of utility—but not mere economic utility. Utility is found in the fostering of a pluralism of opinion, experience, vision, and utterance within the world of authors. Authors are our seers, prophets, and visionaries. Our

---

[10] Statement of Ainsworth Spofford, before the Comm. on Patents of the U.S. Senate, on S. 191, 49th Cong. 1st Sess (1886) at 128.

[11] B. Ringer, "The Demonology of Copyright" R. R. Bowker Memorial Lecture, Oct. 24, 1974 (Bowker: 1974), at 19.

freedom depends on theirs. More importantly, as we have learned form Milton and Mill, our freedom depends not only on freedom for a few, but also on variety, regardless of the ultimate commingling of truth and error. Copyright fosters that variety.

The marketplace of ideas which the First Amendment nurtures is, then, and must be more widely understood to be, essentially a *copyright* marketplace. Although Ms. Ringer spoke of the danger of control "by anyone," now, as in the eighteenth century, the greatest danger to authors' independence comes from the government and organizations fundamentally dependent on government. That, in this country, the state tries less often—or less notoriously—to engage in prior restraint should not mask the fact that other government intrusions, which can be styled here "subsequent restraints," are insidious and, in their own way, ultimately as threatening to independent authorship.

Finally, authorship, although often profoundly, even painfully, solitary, is fruitful and socially useful only when its works are disclosed.

The glory of copyright is that it sustains not only independent, idiosyncratic, and iconoclastic authors, but also fosters daring, innovative, and risk-taking publishers.[12] Without such publishers, authors are as mute as if they did not speak at all. Without them, authors do not, in fact, speak. Just as we are best served by many visions and visionaries speaking from and to the breadth of human experience, so also do we require a vibrant, heterogeneous, and dissonant community of publishers. The greater their number and variety, the more likely is any author to find a publisher. And while this is of special importance in the areas of thought and political opinion, it is likewise crucial in the fine arts. Joyce and Proust, Beethoven and Stravinsky were all at one time scorned for works for which they later became immortal, but each found the publisher he needed. Those who pioneer, and thereby often disturb, cannot be silenced by anyone if publishers are numerous and the mail delivers the royalty checks.

Copyright fosters variety and freedom among both authors and publishers. Upton Sinclair, Ayn Rand, I. F. Stone, Costa-Gavras, John Steinbeck, Sigmund Freud, Bob Dylan, Wilhelm Reich, Malcolm X, Ken Kesey, and Eldridge Cleaver likewise needed to find only one publisher,

---

[12] Donald C. Brace's life as a publisher was characterized by this willingness, as a nonetheless practical businessman, to take intellectual and economic risks with unfixed, unknown talents. It was Harcourt, Brace that picked up and published Vernon Parrington's first volume of *Main Currents of American Thought,* on the chance that the uncompleted second volume might have some value as a university text. Thanks to such courage, fifty years of debate over Parrington's controversial thesis enriched the teaching of American history and civilization.

and acquire only a few to listen in order to hold their ideas and visions before the public.

Copyright sustains both authors and publishers. More relevantly here, copyright supports a system, a milieu, a cultural marketplace which is important in and of itself. If the system's variety is injured, then so too is freedom.

Copyright, after all, merely allows justice. It does not "give" the author or the publisher anything. It cloaks in legal raiment the undoubted right. It does not gurarantee success, or audience, or power, or riches. It is not a warranty, but an invitation to risk. When the rewards are large, we should not resent or envy, but rejoice, and we should likewise cherish every miserable failure. For in the midst of that striving, success, and failure, where even remaindered titles expand choice and possibility, there occurs the winnowing from which emerges the excellent and the enduring. The public decides by how it responds and pays. No government is so wise nor should be allowed to try to be.

Quality does emerge from quantity. Virgil Thomson's recently quoted statement on opera in America illustrates the point. Mr. Thomson said:

> The chief hope [of American opera] is that with every composer in the country writing operas and every house, for pay or not, producing them, the mere volume of this effort will give rise to a "school." If this happens, quality will develop automatically; it always does.[13]

From this, the New York *Times* critic generalized:

> In other words, boost the operatic GNP high enough and the modern equivalent of Don Giovanni or at least La Boheme will inevitably appear.[14]

Copyright should boost the GNP of mind and feeling. That GNP will be large and abundant to the extent that authors are free and their publishers numerous. We in copyright are concerned not only with producing authors and myriad publishers to give them voice, but also publishers who themselves create, and are, subcultures of technique, tradition, and wisdom who midwife the author's creation. *E.T.* is not merely the creation of Spielberg's isolated genius: it is his inspiration

---

[13] D. Henahan, An American Opera to the Top of the List, New York Times, April 3, 1983, Section 2, p. 1.

[14] *Ibid.*

and conviction informed and realized through the possibilities available to him out of the cumulative lore and know-how of decades of scenarists, camera men, special-effects people, filmstock technologists, editors, producers, cinema schools, and financiers. Thomas Wolfe is in the literature through Maxwell Perkins; and American literature is richer because of the judgment, taste, and courage of men like Alfred Knopf and Donald Brace, and women such as Elizabeth Wolff.

Authors and publishers are sometimes adversaries. Ask the Authors League or any literary agent. But they and we are one in our stake in a numerous, diverse and—yes, let us say it: profitable—population of publishers.

This world of both creators and publishers should not be forced to exist at the margin, under the cloud of harm. And does not harm mean that we shall, or at least may, continue to invade income and profit until someone is hurt? This world must be a sacred preserve. It is a world in which the system is as important as its population or its content at any one time. Our freedom lives there. Because of that, government control within it, either direct or indirect, should be prohibited, or at least stubbornly resisted.

The First Amendment bans prior restraint nearly absolutely; and it has been sorely tested. [15] But any control, even indirect, over what is said, or profitable to say, and the persons and agencies through which it is said, are also not to be countenanced. Thus, within the last month, the Supreme Court struck down a tax on ink and newsprint, not because it constrained any particular utterance but because, in burdening a vehicle of authorship, the tax trespassed, however slightly, on First Amendment terrain.[16] When the government seeks to promote its own ends at authors' and publishers' expense or to limit the rewards which the marketplace (read: people) will grant, whether by compulsory licenses or special-interest exemptions, the government at least influences and conditions, if not controls, speech and expression, no less proximately than in the *Minneapolis Star* case.

I do not assert that copyright cannnot be subject to any reasonable limitation; nor do I believe that it is technically within the penumbra of the First Amendment. I do declare that, ultimately, the same values are at stake in each.

---

[15] See, *e.g.*, New York Times Co. v. United States, 403 U.S. 713 (1971). That copyright was not involved in the Pentagon Papers is not as important as the fact that one copyright-supported publisher—and only one was needed—took the risk to make them public. Copyright thus serves its constitutional sister, the First Amendment.

[16] Minneapolis Star & Tribune Co. v. Minnesota Comm'r of Revenue, 51 U.S.L.W. 4315 (U.S. March 29, 1983).

Whatever one thinks of the comparative merits of national economic planning and free markets, or of government as an instrument of wealth distribution, our government should abstain as much as possible from intervention in the copyright world, and willingly forebear from setting or affecting the value or price of works of authorship. Otherwise, the government skews the copyright world, and thus what the people will hear. Better to trust the sum of consumers' choices in what they will pay to see and hear. If the government does intervene, we are harmed in a more grievous way than in being denied a free copy or a cheap copy, and the instant gratification of maximum distribution. [17]

When government regards copyright as a mere license, not a solemn acknowledgment of right, decisions on copyright tend to be made in the bruising welter of entitlement politics. Libertarians should note that in the recent struggle over the compulsory license for cable, a leading cable spokesman advanced his reason why this preferment should continue: the motion picture industry makes "unwholesome" films. Nor should it escape notice that the license favors cable systems over all other media—cable origination networks, theaters, and broadcast television—by exempting cable from acquiring programs competitively in the marketplace. And it is ominous that in two landmark cases involving mass copying by new technological means, *Williams & Wilkins* and *BOCES*,[18] government-supported entities have been the defendants.

By limiting potential rewards in the copyright market—whether by capping them with a compulsory license, or barring them with a complete exemption, or refusing to extend copyright to new uses, or curtailing them in any way under arguments of "harm"—the entrepreneurial calculus which precedes risk-taking in authorship and publishing is shifted in the direction of not taking a chance, *i.e.*, not writing or publishing a "risky" work, whether ideologically or economically risky. Every limitation on copyright is a kind of rate-setting. And however high-minded, every person who thus sets rates applies a value-judgment: how much the author or publisher should receive. Whoever makes this judgment regulates— *i.e.*, controls—how successful a class of authors, works, or publishers shall be. This control of idea-laden copyrighted works is more wisely left with the people than vested in a government tribunal, a sta-

---

[17] As Barbara Ringer put it: "[I]n the long pull, it is more important for a particular generation to produce a handful of great creative works than to shower its schoolchildren with unauthorized photocopies. . . ." Ringer, *op. cit. supra*, n. 11 at 7.

[18] Williams & Wilkins Co. v. United States, 487 F. 2d 1345 (Ct.Cl. 1973), *aff'd by an equally divided court*, 420 U.S. 376 (1975); Encyclopaedia Britannica Educational Corp. v. Crooks, 542 F. Supp. 1156 (W.D.N.Y. 1982).

tutory license fee, or even a sincere judge searching a record for un-defined harm.

In the current debate, harm is undefined. No one knows what it is, or is willing to say.[19] However stridently the argument of "harm" is put, it is always presented as a conclusion, never as a canon. No one has enumerated the elements of proof which would show harm, or an absence of harm. It is presented on a basis of, "I know it when I see it," or "I can't tell you what it is, but I'll tell you when you get there." Sound policy, justice, and jurisprudence are not formed of such ephemera.

The idea of harm as the basis of copyright is novel. It represents a principle not of just compensation for use, but political apportionment of the value of what authors create and publishers realize. It misconceives the end and purpose of copyright: to do justice by compensating justly—that is, as the people decide; but more broadly to protect, nourish, and celebrate our freedom and the world of wisdom, prophecy, and revelation which keeps us free, and to do so by rewarding authors as generously as the people will. In that we may acquit our debt to those who see and teach. Above all, we in that way honor both their right and our interest, and enjoy the blessings of liberty flowing from both copyright and the First Amendment.

---

[19] The infirmity of the notion of harm in its lack of definition is considered in Ladd, "Economic Harm: A Trojan Horse in Copyright," A.B.A. Summary of Proceedings, Section of Patent, Trademark and Copyright Law at 158 (1982).

37: FAIR USE VERSUS FAIR RETURN: COPYRIGHT LEGISLATION AND ITS CONSEQUENCES

Irving Louis Horowitz

Department of Sociology and Transaction Publishers
Rutgers University, New Brunswick, N.J. 08903

M. E. Curtis

John Wiley & Sons, Inc.
605 Third Avenue, New York, N.Y. 10158

The purpose of this article is to examine the ramifications of legislative recognition of the concept of fair use in the Copyright Act of 1976. The fair use concept, while of small consequence in its normative origins, has turned out to be the foundation of the most perplexing and divisive issues in the new legislative guidelines governing copyright. Legislative recognition of the concept of fair use, coupled with enormous growth of a new technology—extending from xerography to on-line database systems—creates de facto exemptions to both the intent and content of new copyright guidelines. The issue is not one of limiting use or suppressing information, but of mechanisms for safeguarding the rights of copyright holders, be they authors or publishers, and insuring the free flow of information by providing a proper return on both intellectual creativity and capital expenditures. The authors argue that the elimination, or at least curtailment of fair use doctrine, coupled with an increase in technological approaches to reporting of secondary use of copyrighted material, will benefit all sections of the knowledge industry. Authors will receive proper royalties on use; publishers will be able to sell more books and journals at lower prices; and librarians will be liberated from extensive chores such as monitoring usage or determining fee schedules and transferences. The issue is one of fair return—an issue obscured and ultimately subverted by fair use.

Prior to the Copyright Act of 1976, the law had never given explicit statutory recognition to the concept of "fair use." The courts had recognized the concept in decisions extending back more than a century, but in practice fair use generally had to do with the brief quotation by a sec-

ond author of a first author's work. Insofar as fair use had any broader definition, that definition had emerged from litigation and legal precedent. When a copyright holder chose to challenge a use as improper, judicial "rule of reason" was employed, and a body of legal precedent thus developed that provided guidelines for both user and copyright holder in questionable situations. However, in no instance did fair use mean reproduction of a work to use it for its own sake.

The doctrine of fair use evolved from a wide variety of exceptional circumstances not related to intrinsic use of the work, ranging from quoting materials for review purposes to reproducing excerpts from books, magazines, and films for pedagogic purposes. Such uses simply could not easily be regulated or monitored. Those who sought secondary use of copyright materials usually asked permission for such uses. The decision about whether use fell within commonly accepted bounds of fair use was made by copyright owners, who usually granted permission without fee when the copyright owner believed the use was reasonable and would not infringe upon the bundle of rights comprised in copyright. If a user used material without seeking permission of a copyright owner, it was done with foreknowledge that the use might be challenged, and if so judicial rule of reason ("would the reasonable copyright owner have consented to such use?") would be applied.

Earlier periods of discussion concerning possible revision of the 1909 Copyright Law devoted much attention to the doctrine of fair use. Broadly, there were two schools of thought. One group argued for explicit recognition of the concept of fair use in the law, and wanted the law to list instances in which the fair use concept might limit copyright prerogatives. A second group argued, as it turned

Received August 15, 1983; revised October 21, 1983; accepted December 13, 1983 out without ultimate success, for general recognition of the concept, but wanted no specific mention of particular uses that constituted fair use. This group felt that any definition of fair use in the law would inevitably erode copyright prerogatives. "Any attempt by statute to define fair use or to classify it would probably expand its scope [1].

The 1976 Copyright Law revision gives specific recognition to fair use, and since then, the concept has been transformed from a rule of reason into a loophole, a rationale for free and virtually unrestricted use of copyright materials. The Report of the Register of Copyrights on Library Reproduction of Copyrighted Works, charged with assessing the extent to which an appropriate balance between creator's rights and users needs has been achieved, concludes that the balance has not been achieved. We agree with this interpretation, but believe that the problem resides with the attempt to define fair use legislatively. Using "fair use" to defend the loophole, and locating the odd event not explicitly covered by legislation, threatens to negate copyright as a whole. The judicial doctrine is being transformed into the injudicious doctrine of free use.

Allan Wittman, former chairman of the Association of American Publishers Copyright Committee, has underscored the unintended consequences of this broadened use of fair use. "The principle of fair use arose out of the legal concept that the law does not deal with trivia. When that doctrine was developed, small amounts of copying were trivia. However, modern technology changed all that. One work can be subjected to thousands of so-called "trivial" transactions and the result is no longer trivial [2, p. 106].

Prior to the 1976 Copyright Law, the copyright owner determined whether or not to require payment for a secondary use or reproduction of a copyrighted work. If a copier took the time and trouble to copy even an entire book by hand, no penalty was exacted because there was no way it could be known that a copy had been made. If a copier reproduced a hand-copied document, however, he probably would be discovered, and of course he would be liable. The 1976 Copyright Law exempts certain reproductions as instances of fair use; by extending the concept of fair use it rendered it ambiguous. It also restricted copyright holders from collecting payments for some reproductions the law defines as "fair uses."

One intention of the 1976 definition of fair use was to ease certain uses of copyrighted materials. The law permits a teacher to make and use a single copy without seeking permission, for example, under certain circumstances multiple copies if they do not exceed more than one copy per pupil for classroom use. Within this broad framework clear limits are put forth concerning the brevity of an abstract cited, the spontaneity of copying purposes, and the prevention of a cumulative effect so that such fair use is not employed to repress or inhibit the production of new anthologies, or collected works. In practice, pedagogic "fair use" has been extended, as argued by a group of publishers in the recent legal action against New York University. Certainly some interpretations of the notion of fair use by teachers have become so broad as to be eccentric, as indicated by the interpretation of the fair use doctrine "in terms of constructive teaching and the extent to which photocopying needs to be used [3, p. 27]. This statement, made by Robert A. Gorman, professor of law at the University of Pennsylvania and former president of the American Association of University Professors, reveals not simply a personal idiosyncratic view of fair use, but a widespread belief that it is the statute of exemption and entitlement rather than a judicial doctrine of reasonableness. Operationally, pedagogic copyright exemptions have not only inhibited anthologies and collections, but have seriously eroded use of whole journals or books. And because copyright holders have been slow to defend their rights, small infringements have simply passed into the realm of social norms—legal abuses have become social norms.

Nine commercial publishers, as members of the Association of American Publishers, brought suit in December 1982 against New York University and select members of its faculty, alleging that photocopying and distribution of course materials without permission of the copyright holders violated the Federal Copyright Act. The litigants reached a settlement in June 1983 under which the University agreed to adopt, implement, and honor the terms of an Agreement reached in March 1976 by the Ad Hoc Committee on Copyright Law Revision, representing the Association of American Publishers, the Authors League of America. The Agreement, which brought together author and publisher groups, covered a broad spectrum of issues ranging from single copying for teachers to multiple copying for classroom use. However, this Agreement is also noteworthy for the absence of any mechanism for each payment on photoduplication, and by the absence of librarian support for the document as a whole.

Copyright holders have little control over social practice. Users and their agents such as libraries have tended to interpret the guidelines contained in the 1976 law very broadly. Robert Wedgeworth of the American Library Association has forcefully stated this position: "The law permits a number of uses for photocopies without fees and the copyright owner *cannot demand payment* for these fair uses and *other possible uses* under Section 108 "[4, p. 61, (emphasis added)]. Just how broadly fair use has come to be viewed is reflected in another librarian's position that "one of the traditional foundations of librarianship is ownership of information sources in order to make them accessible to library patrons." The *auteur* of this position, Jeanne G. Howard, fearful of publishers direct transmission to users through computerized search services, goes on to argue that "another basic tenet of librarianship is the guardianship of informational sources for archival purposes "[5, p. X]. It is easy enough to see that underneath the question of fair use is nothing less than the proprietary claims to the published word itself—whatever its form.

There can no longer be any question that for one group, the Copyright Subcommittee of the American Library Association, fair use has become the essential vehicle with which to confound and confront the publishing and author associations demands for a fair return alike. The Copyright Clearance Center, which as its title suggests, is an independent entity aimed at providing a mechanism of payment for copyrighted materials, is opposed "for the most important reason of all ... only a small percentage of library copying falls outside the limits of fair use." But since a "model policy" for fair use may involved reproducing materials at the behest of a faculty member for reserve use, "a reasonable number of copies" which "will in most instances be less than six" the intent of the new copyright legislation is clearly and intentionally to be circumvented [6].

Clearly, the librarian leadership perceives itself as providing "balance" between the rights of creators and the needs of library patrons. Ignoring the presumption that such a balancing role is uniquely the charge of librarians, or whether they even welcome such a discretionary role, the fact is that it is the doctrine of fair use which provides the legitimizing role for insisting, contrary to the Register of Copyright, David Ladd, that a balance has been achieved between owners and users of information. Again, under the banner of rights of fair use granted under Section 107 of the 1976 Copyright legislation, the librarian would presume to be the unique interpreter of such legislation— and in so doing, thoroughly subvert the aims of the legislation to begin with.

This is not intended as a denial of a central role to librarians, nor a refutation of specific empirical points about the extent of copyright violations—not even research reports intended to resolve such an issue have satisfactorily done so. Indeed, not until a sense of vestedness exists whereby the library community properly shares in the proceeds from copyright use will the critical participation and support of that community be insured. But the point from our perspective is simply to note that the notion of fair use is increasingly being invoked, not to broaden the basis of library use, but to subvert the foundations of copyright itself; that is to hold *acquistion* by any means and without payment to the copyright holder no less than *access* to copyright materials as essential and legitimate functions of a librarian.

Some early critics of the 1976 law argued that it is fundamentally flawed because it tampers with copyright in a fundamental way. Because the notion of copyright itself balances the rights of creators and the needs of users, exemptions interfere with its internal workings. In his analysis of fair use in copyright, Leon Seltzer observed that the photocopying problem was dealt with in the 1976 law by creating exemptions to the copyright holder's exclusive right to make and sell copies. Although the exemptions are held not to disturb the essential dynamics of copyright, the distinctions outlined in the 1976 copyright law are difficult to make, unenforceable, and impossible to

administer. "It is unreasonable to expect a user to distinguish between what is fair use, what is exempted use, and what is neither. And when Congress itself has failed to do so with a precision in which it has much confidence, courts will not find it easy to bring a photocopying excess about which there is any doubt at all within the reach of the enforcement provisions of the liability clause, Section 504 [7, pp. 116–117]. Seltzer's predictions proved correct.

Writing in 1978, Seltzer pointed out that Congress had essentially two options: (1) to narrow the range of the author's exclusive rights by permitting the broadest range of photocopying, or (2) to require a full and complete accounting of photocopying. Choosing the first option would mean that Congress believed that the interests of users and producers could be balanced outside of the copyright scheme. The second option relies on the internal efficiency of copyright as it has traditionally existed, to balance these interests. Seltzer's analysis led him to favor the second option, but Congress attempted to chart an ambiguous middle course between the two in the 1976 revision.

Ambiguities in law are usually clarified through subsequent litigation. In the case of the 1976 Copyright Law, these clarifications have been slow to come, for a number of reasons. Those who argued for maximum liberalization of the copyright law have simply behaved as if the new law gives them all that they had demanded. Librarian groups, for example, issued explanations and clarifications of the law to their membership that go far beyond the limited guidelines given in the law. Technological developments carry their own momentum. Library automation and networking involving reproduction of copyrighted material has become widespread. As the Register's Report indicates, the role of libraries has been profoundly changed by the existence and use of photocopying. Some libraries have become relative efficient document delivery centers, competing with legitimate centers that compensate copyright holders. Because some believe any copying that takes place within a library to be exempt, they do not compensate copyright owners. Because interlibrary loans traditionally were made without compensation to copyright owners, libraries argue that "loans" that involve photocopying require no compensation.

Publishers, for their part, have been slow to respond to the implications of the revised law. Those engaged in kinds of publishing most vulnerable to any decline in unit sales by broadening the definition of fair use were those primarily serving small, segmented markets—scientific, scholarly, and medical publishers. These publishers were poorly oganized. In 1976, the Technical, Scientific, and Medical Publishing Division of the Association of American Publishers (AAP) was relatively small. Many publishers of specialized materials did not even participate in publishers' trade associations, and others were affiliated with professional societies and therefore had mixed allegiances. Many major scholarly and professional publishers were outside the United States—Elsevier, Pergamon, and Springer-Verlag, for example. With some notable exceptions, large U.S. publishers with major commitments to specialized publishing, such as McGraw-Hill, were divided on how and whether to act. Only as other categories of publishing, such as textbook publishing, began to suffer the impact of erosion of regard for copyright, did publishers begin to develop a united front in regard to unauthorized reproductions.

Publisher-initiated attempts to clarify ambiguities in the 1976 Copyright Law through litigation did not begin until the 1980s. It is interesting to speculate about what may have finally mobilized publishers to take legal action to defend further erosion of copyright. In part, it was undoubtedly awareness that other technological developments were, without any doubt, going to dramatically affect their role as primary disseminators of information, in ways they could not anticipate and could not control unless there was clear-cut certainty about their copyright prerogatives. In part, it was increasing segmentation and specialization in all of the markets served by publishers—educational and professional as well as scholarly. In part, it was growing awareness that new technological developments were having severe impact on other segments of the information industry: on movies, television, and record industries, for example. Some of these were responding to technological challenges to their own copyright prerogatives with aggressive legal action.

Demands by copyright owners for protection of their rights have almost uniformly been challenged by arguments that any such protection would erode "fair use." What was intended as a modest series of pragmatic exemptions is now itself highly inhibiting to resolution of issues of concern to copyright holders, because the concept of fair use has been broadened to signifiy limitations on the exclusivity of copyright holders' claims. Because the definition of circumstances in which use may constitute fair use (Section 107) has been codified, it has in effect been linked with Section 108, permitting reproduction by libraries and archives of copyrighted material from one publisher to another, and secondary transmission of the same copyrighted material. The American Library Association critique of the Register's Report explicitly argues for the interrelationship of these two sections, challenging the Register's interpretation of Congressional intent. The cumulative impact has been an erosion of copyright. Social practice is taking us a long distance beyond the narrow exemptions articulated in the 1976 law.

The 1976 Copyright Law does attempt to address the question of copying by individuals for activities connected with teaching and research, but as with the guidelines for photocopying by libraries, they are ambiguous and unenforceable. It does not even begin to address copying by an individual for his personal needs and convenience, which has been fundamentally transformed by photocopying technology. Copying by hand was time consuming and laborious. Machine photocopying is not, gives the copier physical possession of a personal copy, yet the copier pays a negligible amount for the privilege of ownership of a

photocopy, essentially only the cost of the copy. No record, no accounting, and no compensation to the copyright holder is made.

The economic aspect of the information user's decision about how he wants to receive his information is more complicated than it used to be, because the user now has multiple options [8]. Before the development of technological capabilities such as photocopying, the economic decision of the user boiled down to a choice between expenditure of time and effort (in copying by hand) versus money (to purchase the printed product). Consciously or not, the user now makes a more complex choice. Today the user may spend time scanning a document and order a copy, or make one personally. The user may first wish to scan a screen, but then prefer the convenience of a hard copy. He often would have to spend more time and money to purchase the original product, even if he could find it, than a photocopy [9]. Consequently, the economic decision is more heavily weighted in favor of machine copying than it was when hand copying was the sole option. Purchase of the entire journal or an entire book may even be economically unsound. Machine copying is fast and relatively inexpensive versus the per page price of a printed product. As interests have become more specialized, and personal storage space more limited, users may want only a portion of a journal or even a book. As library sharing becomes more sophisticated, the printed product may rarely be readily available even if the user wants to go directly to it or to buy a personal copy.

The economic issue, as defined in the fair use guidelines, is too narrowly stated. Congress could not foresee the rapid explosion of the body of scholarly knowledge coupled with the need for sophisticated technology to control and manage that body of literature. Thus, the question of whether making a machine copy substitutes for buying a subscription or a book is much too narrow. Library spokesmen assert that their collections are no longer title (journal or book) related, but article related. On-line electronic access to abstracting services has accelerated this shift. If access, control, and use of scholarly literature is no longer title related, what meaning do copyright guidelines have that assume a title basis of use?

Congress clearly did not intend to suppress or weaken the distribution system by which scholarly literature is made available to the public. Its concern was simply not to make it impossible or difficult for that user to access and use the literature. Congressional intent, coupled with advances in technology, has certainly protected the user. The originator of scholarly literature, the copyright holder, has fared less well. Despite dramatic growth in use of scholarly literature, and despite data that the number of journals and the total number of subscriptions to all journals has increased, subscriptions to individual journals have not increased in the United States. In recent years, under the pressure of library networking and resource sharing, subscriptions to established journals have declined by 2 or 3% a year [10].

Users are now confident that they can obtain any literature they require from libraries. They are frustrated by the escalating prices of books and journals, which have been accelerated by declines in unit sales, and they have cut back their personal subscriptions or purchases of books. Publishers are caught in a classic economic double-blind. They must increase prices to continue their publishing activities. Further price increases drive down unit sales and make individuals and libraries feel justified in obtaining photocopies from a central source. While Congress certainly did not intend to encourage this dynamic, it has been intensified by the post-1976 erosion of copyright. Even information centers or libraries that would like to maintain their physical collections have been forced, by escalating prices, to cut back. The only non-loser, the end user, may eventually suffer if economic factors force publishers to change the nature of their publishing programs, fundamentally eroding the delicate mechanism by which scholarship and other forms of specialized publishing are disseminated.

Most discussions of copyright and fair use have become hung up on the mechanism for a full and complete accounting at a reasonable cost. Initially, the problem was conceptualized as a licensing problem, and the debate was over whether licensing should be voluntary or compulsory. In cooperation with the Author's League and publisher's associations, the Copyright Clearance Center was formed as a voluntary licensing body similar to the American Society of Composers, Authors and Publishers (ASCAP). After that point, the problem shifted to accounting: how to provide a simple, cost effective mechanism for accounting for photocopying. As with off-the-air videotaping, the problem was made more complex by the widespread and uncontrollable amount of reproduction by individuals. While institutions, essentially libraries, complained about the expense and difficulty of record keeping and reporting required under the licensing scheme of the Copyright Clearance Center, no one even addressed the economic dilemma of unaccounted for photocopying by individuals.

It has become increasingly clear that licensing is not, after all, the key issue. The real problem is accounting for copying, including the large amount of copying by individuals for purposes ranging from teaching to research to convenience. It is unreasonable and unworkable to expect individuals to report on copying activity, or to expect that copying machines can be restricted only to those who participate in such accounting. Such restrictions would seem, properly, to be an erosion of individual rights to free access. However, if accounting could be achieved passively, without requiring an individual to take some action, but "automatically," the compensation problem would be more easily addressed. If, for example, a record was made of items photocopied, by means of an ISBN, ISSN, or a bar code such as is used on products sold in retail outlets, and if these records were used to report on reproduction by item (or even by publisher) to a central

body on a regular basis, compensation could be made according to reasonable terms. The issue is similar but not identical to the videotaping issue. Home videotaping takes place in a private, personal situation. Most photocopying, at present, takes place in an institutional context, but at unsupervised machines. If copying was passively recorded and subsequently recorded, publishers would have other problems. They would have to establish equitable procedures for sharing revenues from copying with authors. Institutions, particularly libraries which traditionally would not have charged fees for photocopying, would have to decide who should pay for secondary uses of materials they archive. Just as some libraries and institutions ask users to pay a portion of the costs of on-line bibliographic searches of data banks, they may decide to ask photocopiers to pay a surcharge for photocopying privileges. Alternatively, they might decide to absorb such costs in their materials budgets, although few have budgets that could absorb such costs.

Photocopying per se cannot and should not be constrained; the right to use photocopying machines has been established by technological development no less than by social precedents. The right to reproduce copyrighted material without compensation is not an unqualified right. Ambiguities and unwarranted exemptions in the 1976 law, above all the assertion of the concept of "fair use," has impeded recognition of this fact and impeded technological solutions to a technologically induced imbalance between the rights of copyright proprietors and the needs of users.

Another fundamental problem, one that was not properly understood by the publishing community at the time the 1976 statutes came into force, is that the fair use exemptions operationally turn out to mean exemption of the first copy, or the *right* to reproduce a single copy of a copyrighted work without compensation. But very often the first copy is the most important copy, if not the decisive copy. If there were a strict economic correlation between value and price, the first copy would be the most expensive and the tenth copy the least expensive, rather than the current situation in which the first copy is free to users, and succeeding copies are compensated for at the same amount. The fair use exemptions inhibit any possibility of compensation whereby the first copy produced is reimbursed as the first order of magnitude.

The notion of fair use is sufficiently ambiguous and confusing as to vitiate any protection provided by other clauses. For example, not only can copying of an extract, a chart, or a graph be considered fair use, but also a chapter from a book, an article from a periodical, a short story, or an essay. Who is to say how much material from a book or journal is fair use and how much is gratuitous use? That single article lifted from an anthology or a book may make the difference between a sale and a nonsale. Defacto the burden of proof that a use is *not* a fair use now rests with the copyright holder. To take one example, the clause of multiple copies, while presumably safeguarding publishers who insist on notice of copyright, leaves wide open the use of multiple copies in multiple classes. To take another, without an enforceable proviso on length, the core of a book may well be extracted to the detriment of the author and publisher. Ultimately, books and journals will not be published because a market contraction of such magnitude cannot readily sustain the costs of publication.

Publishers who have argued for a narrow interpretation of the fair use doctrine have ended up having to defend themselves by proving that economic harm has been brought about by the fair use doctrine. Economic analyses have concluded that publishers suffer no economic hardships as a consequence of photocopying exemptions—that they are still receiving an "adequate return," whatever that means. A CONTU-sponsored study by the Public Interest Economics Center reached this somewhat presumptuous conclusion, one which reflected the anti-business climate of the early 1970s, and one which certainly revealed little understanding of how business actually operates [11]. In any case, it is extremely difficult to demonstrate the existence of economic harm, and since publishers tend to increase prices to offset unit declines, fair use-driven corrective actions by publishers may have prejudiced the public against the copyright holder, as well as distorted the marketplace. The consequence has been public perception of copyright in an older and essentially illicit view, as mere privilege, as a favor to publishers rather than an instrument to encourage broad-scale production and distribution of creative works. This position is forcefully stated in the ALA's response to the Register's Report. As Nancy Marshall states the case: "The CONTU Guidelines are useful guides, but they do not carry the force of law [12, p. 9].

Copyright has never simply been a property right. Its underlying intent since the Act of Queen Anne of 1709 has been to encourage dissemination of literary, scientific, and artistic works [13]. It recognizes that a creator requires some period of exclusive control of that work and protection of that creation to enjoy sufficient fruits of his labor to permit him to continue to produce. This aspect of protection has been turned against copyright holders, who are now asked to demonstrate economic harm as a condition of protection of copyright prerogatives. This demand has occurred as a response to fair use guidelines, which stipulate that permission to copy is not intended to reduce purchases of primary materials [14]. It does not follow that copying is permissible when a copyright holder cannot prove economic harm, but that is essentially how those arguing for minimal protection have put the issue.

The fair use doctrine has divided the consumer from copyright holders. It has juxtaposed entrepreneurs, investors, artists, and shopkeepers against consumers and their agents, librarians. Fair use has served as an ideological vehicle to argue that the copyright holders want to restrain trade and information in seeking to protect their copyright. The publishing community has been characterized as restraining knowledge and information rather than simply claiming their right to protect their copyrights and derive some return from secondary uses. This position is a difficult one for publishers, for both historical and moral reasons.

Perhaps the most serious short-term consequence of the 1976 fair use doctrine is its effect on inhibiting development and use of technological and/or mechanical devices that could account for what is copied. Proponents of the 1976 fair use doctrines assert that exemptions preclude any use of present technology to record the number of reproductions. The available technology, such as mechanical devices activating a reproduction machine, calculate from the first copy forward. The argument goes that because the fair use doctrine inhibits chargeback from the first copy, no known technology is appropriate. While this does not have to be so, that is to say, while equipment could be designed in such a way as to accommodate these objections, there is no doubt that the 1976 fair use doctrine forestalls a universal form of payment for authors of copyrighted materials. Use of the new technology to resolve dilemmas in accounting for copying has been thwarted by legislative safeguards that have no real status in tradition and even less meaning in fact.

Recent landmark developments in the fair use exemptions concern the settlement reached between the Association of American Publishers and E. R. Squibb, the pharmaceutical giant. In an effort to keep the momentum going for some sort of *general* recognition of copyright prerogatives, certain *specific* exemptions have been registered. The pharmaceutical firm negotiated an arrangement whereby a 6% exclusion, in effect an exemption of payment for "fair uses" in this amount, was agreed upon. While this clause undoubtedly was agreed to reluctantly by the AAP, it does contravene the essential principle that *all* materials copyrighted by a publisher are protected, and not a percentage thereof. It establishes a contrary notion: that reproduction of entire articles and/or books may be permitted if it can be included in the permissible 6%. It should be noted that the Squibb agreement provides for an exemption of 6% of the material copied over and above material not subjected to copyright restraints, such as old material in which copyright has expired and government documents in the public domain.

The principle of fair return, i.e., of proprietary claim, may be critically weakened in the very act of securing compliance with established legislation. Quite apart from requiring consent to monitor photocopying, instead of encouraging manufacturer's installation of simple mechanical devices, the foundations of copyright prerogatives may become subject to endless bilateral bartering arrangements as to what amount of copying is permissible. If the judicial notion of fair use exemptions becomes operationally a percentage of total material photocopied, there is no reason to expect that a 6% guideline will not turn into a 7% solution, i.e., an opiate to the publishers.

Herein lies the great weakness of any wide-ranging notion of fair use exemptions from fair return on investments.

Fair use is legally significant, but only in severely restricted circumstances. It protects the owner of a physical text much more than the owner of the ideas. However, in so doing the fair use doctrine subverts one of the original purposes of copyright, which was to make widely known findings in the areas of science and humanities. We need to reach a point where copyright is protected not from the second copy forward, but from the first copy. Only in this way can serious objections raised by librarians and academics to the dangers of information control be appropriately met. Ambiguities of the present situation will be salvaged only by recognition that no use is fair use; and parenthetically, that no kind of mechanical reproduction of a copyrighted work is exempt. All copyright materials deserve protection from random forms of copying. No possible resolution of the copyright dilemma is feasible if the ambiguities inherent in the 1976 doctrine of fair use inhibit the use of technology to recognize problems created by the new information technology [15].

Fair use has been uncritically linked with democratic ideals as part of a free marketplace of ideas; whereas fair return has with equal casuistry been linked to bourgeois avarice. For some commentators, demands for copyright protection as such have come to be labeled a kind of conspiracy against democratic rights to access. In fact, the early termination of 1976 fair use doctrine would enhance, not detract, from free inquiry. As copyright traditionally acknowledged, the replication of data, charts, or tables, for example, like the duplication of films or television shows, can better be monitored in an environment which recognizes both originating and continuing costs, and does not make presumptions of exemptions. The right to live does not entail a denial of payment for food. By the same token, the right to knowledge does not entail a denial of payment for information. In this sense, an elimination of fair use exemptions would permit publishers to return to realistic prices for copyrighted works. Publishers can also afford to be liberal and generous in granting permission to reproduce materials for scholarly and educational use. But that generosity can only be forthcoming when 97% of reproductions of copyright material is acknowledged; and not as in present circumstances, where less than 3% of the reproductions of copyrighted materials is acknowledged—much less paid for.

The ambiguities of the 1976 fair use doctrine have led to legal confusion and moral ambiguity. They have also helped create middlemen operating on all sides who profit from this climate of confusion and ambiguity. Free inquiry can best be served by proprietary clarity. That is the burden of traditional copyright law. Beyond that, it also happens to be the essence of the Western political system and its checks and balances against abuses of trust and privilege.

In its larger sense, the issue of fair use does not concern use at all, but ownership. The 1976 law has been structured in such a way as to satisfy public requirements for access to information and ideas in an entirely unencumbered manner. And while those public requirements are entirely worthy and require societal protection, any method of insuring the public right to know that results in a frontal assault on the right to property or the proprietary claims of authors and publishers, is dangerous. To the extent that the struggle to enlarge the fair use concept into a blanket endorsement of free use, one might even argue that systemic considerations of "socialism" and "capitalism" are at stake. But to pursue such a line of reasoning would open a Pandora's box of ideology and postpone resolution of the issues within the context of the present social and legal order of western societies.

However, the passions with which the issue of fair use have been debated on all sides, in all manner of media from video to software to books, would indicate that these larger issues are indeed lurking in the near background. Perhaps as long as actual social-economic formations are increasingly "mixed" rather than "pure," the problems raised by fair use will remain with us. However, a more realistic approach would be to accept the mixed character of our political economy, one which acknowledges a fair return, and hence the need to accommodate specific author-publisher-user demands for information in such terms. This article has been an effort to address fair use within the parameters of fair return, and to do so so that the right to universal access to information is protected as are the proprietary claims of authors, publishers, and citizens.

References

1. Gibbon, R. Curtis Publishing Company. Comments and Views Submitted to the Copyright Office on Fair Use of Copyrighted Works, October 24, 1958, Studies prepared for the Subcommittee on Patents, Trademarks, and Copyrights of the Committee on the Judiciary, U.S. Senate, Eighty-Sixth Congress, Second Session. Washington, DC: U.S. Government Printing Office, 1960.
2. Wittman, A. Statement before the New York Hearings of the Library of Congress, Register of Copyrights. *Library Reproduction of Copyrighted Works* (17 U.S.C. 108). Appendix VI (delivered January 28, 1981). Released as *Report of the Register of Copyrights*, January 1981, pp. 95-106.
3. Palmer, S. E. "Copyright suit: What effect on professors." *The Chronicle of Higher Education*. XXV (17):16-27; January 5, 1983.
4. Wedgeworth, R. Executive Director, American Library Association. Public Hearing on the Report of the Register of Copyrights on the Effect of 17 U.S.C., 108 on the Rights of Creators and the Needs of Users of Works Reproduced by Certain Libraries and Archives, January 28, 1981, New York, New York. *Report of the Register of Copyrights*, Appendix VI, Part 1, p. 61.
5. Howard, J. G. "Electronic journals: Potential dangers" (letter). *The Chronicle of Higher Education*. July 27, 1983.
6. Marshall, N. H. "Comments of the American Library Association on the Report of the Register of Copyrights to Congress: Library Reproduction of Copyrighted Works (17 U.S.C. 108)." Released by the Washington, DC office of the American Library Association. June 1983.

7. Seltzer, L. F. *Exemptions and Fair Use in Copyright: The Exclusive Rights Tensions of the 1976 Copyright Act*. Cambridge, MA: Harvard University Press, 1978, pp. 116–117.

8. Testimony of the Information Industry Association before the Copyright Office, January 29, 1981. *Report of the Register of Copyrights*, Appendix VI, Part 2, p. 4.

9. Nadeski, K.; Pontius, J. "Developments in micrographics, 'fair use', and video technology." *Library Resources and Technical Services*. 27 (3), pp. 278–296; 1983.

10. Campbell, R. "Making sense of journal publishing." *Nature*. 299 (October 7):491–492; 1982.

11. See Summaries of Commission-Sponsored Studies, "An Analysis of Computer and Photocopying Issues from the Point of View of the General Public and the Ultimate Consumer, Public Interest Economics Center, Final Report of the *National Commission on New Technological Uses of Copyrighted Works*. July 31, 1978. Washington, DC: Library of Congress, 1979, p. 129.

12. Marshall, N. H. "Comments of the American Library Association on the Report of the Register of Copyrights to Congress: Library Reproduction of Copyrighted Works (17 U.S.C. 108)." Released by the Washington, DC office of the American library Association. June 1983, p. 9.

13. Bloom, H. S. "The copyright position in Britain," and Keyes, A. A., "Copyright and fair dealing in Canada." In J. S. Lawrence and B. Timberg, Eds., *Fair Use and Free Inquiry: Copyright Law and the New Media*. Norwood, NJ: Ablex Publishing Company, 1980, pp. 198–221.

14. Karp, I. (Ed.) "Authors league symposium on copyright-protection of non-fiction works and literary/dramatic characters." *Journal of Copyright Bulletin*. (August): 611–616; 1982.

15. Horowitz, I. L; Curtis, M. E. "The impact of technology on scholarly publishing." *Scholarly Publishing*. 13(3):211–228; 1982, and Horowitz, I. L. "New technology, scientific information, and democratic choices." *Information Age*. 5(2):67–73; 1983.

38: A NEW DEFINITION OF FAIR USE

Herbert Swartz

In 1976, for the fifth time since the signing of the Constitution, Congress passed a new copyright act. In the same year, the so-called "Betamax case" was filed in a California federal court.

In that case, Universal Studios and Walt Disney Productions sued Sony Corp. for copyright infringement and asked for an injunction because Sony was selling videotape recorders. Last January, in a five-person, 37-page majority opinion, the U.S. Supreme Court ruled against the plaintiffs. The Court stated that the recorder is "a staple article of commerce," and one of its major uses is "time shifting"—taping a television show for later viewing, watching the show and then erasing the tape. The Court ruled that time shifting constitutes "fair use" of a creator's original work.

If time shifting is fair use, wrote Justice John Paul Stevens for the majority, the limited copyright monopoly cannot be employed "to encompass control over an article of commerce that is not the subject of copyright protection." The copyright tail, he implied, could not be used to wag the commerce dog.

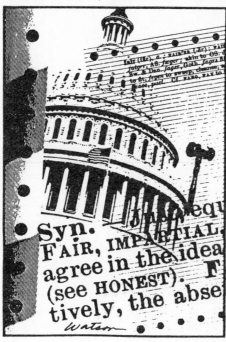

Because the actual lawsuit only involved the movie companies against Sony, the Court said it did not have to address the issue of persons who don't erase the tapes — who keep them in a library, sell or trade them or who don't have to buy or rent similar tapes later. Thus, having ruled that time shifting was a major use of a "staple article of commerce," the Court had nothing else to consider, sanctify or prohibit. But, in stating that time shifting constitutes fair use, the Court inflicted broad damage: the tone was set.

"If I were a law school professor, I would not give the [Supreme Court] opinion a passing grade," says Washington attorney William

A graduate of Harvard University Law School, Swartz practiced law for 10 years and now writes on computer law for a number of publications.

Patry, author of a forthcoming book on fair use.

Jon Baumgarten, partner in Paskus, Gordon & Hyman and former general counsel to the U.S. Copyright Office, agrees: the Supreme Court decision has changed copyright law. "Every defendant in a copyright-infringement suit henceforth will raise the case as a defense," he predicts. "Every copyright plaintiff will have to avoid [the Betamax case]."

By limiting copyright protection, the Betamax decision severely attenuates legal safeguards for the microcomputer industry. The alternatives to copyright law are usually not viable. Filing for a patent, for example, is expensive and dilatory, and patent law only rarely applies to software. Furthermore, the 1976 Copyright Act may have preempted trade-secret law, which at any rate is nebulous for microcomputer concerns.

Copyright is not a natural right. Rather, the Constitution empowers Congress to protect the "exclusive rights" of authors to their writings for the overall purpose of furthering knowledge. Give authors the incentive to create, the Constitution hypothesizes, and wisdom will increase. But the Constitution limits copyright "exclusiveness" to expression — and not to ideas or "staple articles of commerce" like videotape recorders. "Exclusiveness" implies a fixed standard, not "balancing" or "equitable rule of reason" — terms that allow standards to be translated into whatever the judges say they mean.

The concept of fair use was first defined in 1841 when a federal court in Massachusetts postulated it as a defense to copyright infringement. Describing this defense, that court stated: "We must often, in deciding [infringement] questions, look to the nature and objects of the selections made, the quantity and value of the material used and the degree in which the use may prejudice the sale, diminish the profits or supersede the objects of the original work." Thus, the Constitution's rule of copyright exclusiveness for the first time became subject to exceptions.

Lower federal courts had the fair-use issue entirely to themselves for more than a century. Congress did not define "fair use" until 1976, and the Supreme Court did not provide its version until last January, when it ruled on the Betamax case after 143 years of silence.

From 1841 to 1976, federal judges had defined "fair use" as "productive use"; that is, it allowed a scholar to copy part of a work to create a second work. This was intended to prevent duplication of research and spur creativity. With furthering knowledge as its goal, fair use required scholarship, not mere entertainment, and it required producing a second work. Fair use never implied "ordinary use," that is, copying a work for the original purpose for which it was intended. Under those narrow constraints, fair use was further limited to "copying in part." So, the fair-use defense allowed a scholar to go as far as "substantial taking" while limiting everyone else to "substantial similarity." Infringement, which amounted to exact duplication — including mimeographing, Xeroxing, videotape recording and using a microcomputer — had never been considered fair use.

The 1976 Copyright Act sets forth in section 106 an author's obligatory "exclusive" rights in five parts — reproduction (copying), distribution, display, performance and making derivative works. The act allows narrow exceptions to these rights in sections 108 through 117. A library, for example, can make one photocopy of an original work; an owner of a computer program can make one backup.

When Congress codified fair use (section 107) for the first time in 1976, it thought of using what New York University Law School Professor Alan Lipman calls "a paradigm of terseness": "The fair use of a copyrighted work is not an infringement of a copyrighted work." In any event, the House report on the 1976 act stressed that section 107 of the act "is intended to restate the present judicial doctrine of fair use, not to change, narrow or enlarge it in any way."

If the paradigm of terseness had been the statute, Congress would have left fair use with the courts, where it had always been, but with one slight change: fair use would thereafter become an exception by statute to the exclusive rights of copyright holders rather than a defense to copyright infringement. Such a change would have meant little in the marketplace.

However, Congress heard the siren call of technology. According to the House report, it wanted to provide for "the endless variety of situations and combinations of circumstances that can rise in particular cases" — far from a paradigm of terseness. The report continued: "The bill endorses the purpose and general scope of the judicial doctrine of fair use, but there is no disposition to freeze the doctrine in the statute, especially during a period of rapid technological change." In consequence, and despite its intention not to change the doctrine, Congress in section 107 gave the courts leeway to widen the definition of fair use far beyond any previous definition.

For under the act, fair use of copyrighted work includes "such use by reproduction of copies." Since "reproduction" is permissible "for purposes such as criticism, comment, news reporting, teaching (including multiple copies for classroom use), scholarship or research," the prohibitions against "ordinary use" and the requirement for a second work were severely wounded. As for "purposes" of copying a work, they now mean just about anything a court says they mean.

As a part of section 107, Congress did attempt to limit judicial power: "The factors to be considered [in determining fair use] shall include the purpose and character of the use, the nature of the copyrighted work, the amount and substantiality of the portion used and the effect of the use upon the potential market for the copyrighted work." But the act also defines "including" as "illustrative and not limitative." The statutory language is descriptive but not prescriptive; it circumvents Congress' intent not to change the doctrine.

Congress had unlocked a Pandora's box for the computer industry. Judges are now operating under a statutory adjuration to make policy, although lower federal court judges have so far resisted the invitation. The decision of the U.S. Court of Appeals for the 9th Circuit in the Betamax case was a model of traditional fair-use doctrine. But, since Congress had unlocked the box in the first place, the Supreme Court decided to lift the cover,

enabling people to copy original works until the copiers committed "unfair use," says New York attorney Walter Klasson of Brown, Raysman & Millstein. "In copyright law," continues Klasson, "'fair use' used to mean what you could do. Now, it means what you cannot do. That's a big difference, not just semantics. That's not two sides of the same coin, especially after lawyers and judges get through with it."

Now, a Supreme Court opinion says fair use encompasses ordinary use — for what else is home taping or even time shifting? A creator once had full control over his work, notwithstanding fair use, for the purposes for which the work was created or distributed. This is no longer so; fair use now also permits exact duplication.

Fair use also once required the production of a second work; now, the Court says a second work is not necessary. For example, said Justice Stevens, "a teacher who copies to prepare lecture notes is clearly productive. But so is a teacher who copies for the sake of broadening his understanding of his speciality." How does one define "scholarship" — the former boundary of fair use — if fair use now includes

entertainment use? And what about a computer executive who duplicates for library purposes?

Nor does the damage stop there. The Court posits a commercial/noncommercial distinction for fair use based on section 107. But the statute says: "The factors to be considered [for fair use] shall include the purpose and character of the use, including whether such use is of a commercial nature or is for non-profit, educational purposes." Says attorney Patry, "'Non-profit, educational purposes' do not mean anything and everything non-commercial, as the Court indicates." The Court's interpretation, he adds, "is the only way [time shifting] becomes a 'non-profit educational purpose.' The result doesn't make sense. [Time shifting] is just not educational."

The Court destroyed the whole tone of section 107 when it shifted to the copyright holder the burden of proving that copying an original work had caused harm. In effect, stated the Court, all uses are "fair" until proven "unfair," and all users are innocent until proven guilty. Comments Daniel Brooks, head of the Computer Law Association in Washington, "No harm, no foul. But that is not copyright law."

39: COPYRIGHT RULING MAY CAUSE DROP IN COST OF FIRST RIGHTS

Magazines will not be willing to pay as much as they have in the past for first rights to some copyrighted material, now that a federal appeals court has ruled that *The Nation* did not violate copyright laws by publishing a story about the memoirs of former President Ford, according to attorneys for a number of magazines.

The decision by the United States Court of Appeals for the Second Circuit means that magazines cannot be guaranteed exclusivity to copyrighted material on which they hold first rights, the attorneys said.

"If an editor feels another magazine or newspaper will be able to use substantial portions of copyrighted material, then it stands to reason that he will not be willing to pay that much for it," says Slade Metcalf, counsel for *New York Magazine* and other Murdoch publications.

"It will enable magazine publishers to bargain, assuming they even want to go with the material in the first place," adds Edward Smith, a publishing attorney who was formerly with *Newsweek.*

The attorneys said, however, that the scope of *The Nation* decision is limited, and that the media should not and will not use the ruling as an unlimited license to publish copyrighted material.

The suit was brought by Harper & Row, Inc. and Reader's Digest Association, Inc., publishers of Ford's "A Time to Heal." They had sold first rights to the book to *Time* for $25,000, but *Time* refused to pay the final $12,500 installment after *The Nation* published a 2,250-word story on the memoir in its April 1979 issue.

A federal district judge ruled that *The Nation* had violated copyright laws, and ordered the magazine to pay the book's publishers $12,500. A three-judge appeals panel reversed that decision.

The appeals court panel said the material used in *The Nation* article was not protected by copyright laws because it was either already a matter of public record, factual in nature and therefore unable to be copyrighted in the first place, or exempt from the law under its "fair use" clause. In essence, the court panel ruled that copyright laws protect how an author writes a piece, not what he or she writes about.

"Where information concerning important matters of state is accompanied by a minimal borrowing of expression ... the copyright holder's monopoly must not be permitted to prevail over a journalist's communication," Judge Irving Kaufman wrote in the majority opinion.

Harper & Row and Reader's Digest have appealed the decision to the full 11-member Court of Appeals for the Second Circuit.

Metcalf said *The Nation* decision should not affect the price of first rights to copyrighted materials by authors who are not major public officials. A copyrighted autobiography of a celebrity, for instance, will still be protected, he said. "In the case of a celebrity, much of the material might not be known by the public and more will be protected," the attorney says. "This decision focuses on a use of material by a public official in a matter of intense public interest."

"I don't think this means there's any wholesale emasculation of copyright law," adds Smith. "This situation is limited to a relatively small area: facts produced by public figures, mostly by politicians, where the book itself is news or what's in the book is news."

Attorney James Goodale, former vice chairman of *The New York Times,* who frequently represents Time-Life, Inc. magazines, said the major question raised by *The Nation* decision in terms of editorial content is whether it gives magazines and other media an expanded right to quote directly from copyrighted materials written by important public officials under the "fair use" clause.

"The open question is, 'Does it remove the limitation?'," Goodale says.

The attorney said he expects to see other cases that will test the extent of protection established by *The Nation* decision.

231

40A: PROPRIETARY ASPECTS OF ABSTRACTS

Ben H. Weil
Kurt D. Steele
Morton David Goldberg
M. Lynne Neufeld
Lois W. Granick

At the request of members of the Proprietary Rights Committee of the Information Industry Association, and of the copyright committee of the National Federation of Abstracting and Indexing Societies we are publishing a portion of the paper which the members prepared that was not included in the June issue's selection on positions of major players. The committee members believe that the work on definitions and issues is an important part of the total document. The material has been edited very slightly to conform to the Bulletin's *style requirements. Copies of the complete document are available from IIA, 316 Pennsylvania Ave., S.E., Suite 400, Washington, DC 20003.*

While everyone knows generally what abstracts are, and how they relate to the original works on which they are based, there is now a growing, significant need for clarification of proprietary aspects involved with their use. This paper has been prepared to summarize the available information and positions on this subject, in order that future deliberations may proceed with a clearer understanding.

What Are Abstracts?

According to American and international standards, an abstract is "an abbreviated, accurate representation of the contents of a document. . .For most [journal and proceeding] papers and portions of monographs, an abstract of fewer than 250 words will be adequate, . . .[while] for notes and short communications fewer than 100 words should suffice. . . .Brevity is especially important if the abstracts will be used in computer-manipulated databases in order to avoid wasting computer-storage capacity."

Abstracts are intended to serve one or both of two principal functions. If they are published as initial parts of original documents (papers, book chapters, patents), "author" abstracts can make the basic contents of these documents quickly and accurately identifiable to readers who want to know if they then need to *read* the full documents. The other function is closely related: when abstracts are made available by alerting sources, access ("secondary") journals, and/or computerized access ("bibliographic") databases, they enable searchers for pertinent documents to determine much more accurately whether or not they need to *obtain* the complete documents.

In the learned community, and especially in its scientific and technical (S&T) branches, the author abstracts published with the original documents have often been suitable or adaptable for reuse in alerting and access sources. For that reason, S&T journal publishers have increasingly heeded requests by the access community that they publish good author abstracts for this dual use. Two recent studies confirm these statements. In a major U.S. industrial research library, 76 percent of its current S&T journals (including foreign) that have been published continuously since 1950 now contain author abstracts, vs. only 46 percent in 1950 (3). Also, 84 percent of the 1,788 member-publisher journals recently surveyed by the International Group of Scientific, Technical, and Medical Publishers (STM) currently "permit royalty-free copying of abstracts of the articles in their issues."

Where author abstracts are not suitable or not available—the usual case for most of the other (non-S&T) publications—original abstracts are written by the alerting and access services. These abstracts are usually of the same type as author abstracts—100 to 250 words in length, at least descriptive of the contents of the original documents ("indicative abstracts"), and sometimes as information as is permitted by their prescribed brevity and by the nature and length of the original documents ("information abstracts").

S&T abstracts are thus 100–250-word abstracts of lengthy (5,000–7,000-word) articles and papers, or even 50–150-word abstracts of their 2,000-word synoptics (short versions) (5), hence are typically about 2–7 percent as long as the original documents. This is frequently not the case for abstracts of news items and stories in newspapers, trade magazines, and newsletters; here, the originals are usually much shorter, sometimes only a few paragraphs in length, so that their abstracts are usually a higher percentage of the length of the originals.

On occasion, users find abstracts to be of more use than "simply" for indicating which documents need to be read in full. Reading informative abstracts, brief though they may be, inevitably transfers a certain amount of information, and this is sometimes all that the readers require. The numerical data in some online business abstracts can even be used for statistical manipulation on computer terminals, and the online searching of the texts of abstracts can sometimes be substituted for the searching of indexes.

However, it is important to differentiate between abstracts as commonly defined and larger, more complete digests such as abridgements and condensations. These are inherently long enough to transfer most of the teachings of the original documents, hence to be generally substitutable for them. Popular examples of the latter include *Reader's Digest* and a variety of book condensations.

As noted, abstracts of all types are now finding increased use by individuals because of their availability in online, computerized databases. Printouts of abstracts produced by online searches of these databases, including regular searches of database updates ("selective dissemination of information," or "SDI") to alert readers to new references that deal with ongoing interests, are increasingly important to scientists, engineers, businessmen, and others, who can scan these printouts meaningfully to determine which documents they really need to obtain.

What are the Major Legal Issues?

To what extent can abstracts be *prepared* without the express permission of the copyright owners of the original works?

To what extent can abstracts be *used* without the express permission of: (1) the primary publications, and/or (2) the secondary (access) sources?

What are the applicable provisions of the U.S. Copyright Law?

We now have had a brief review of what abstracts are and how they are being used, and a statement of the major legal issues. Let us review some of the basic legal considerations involved. These are chiefly concerned with the U.S. Copyright Statute. Title 17 of the U.S. Code, the Copyright Statute enacted in 1976 and effective January 1, 1978, has a sizable number of provisions that pertain in abstracts.

What Is the Subject Matter of Copyright?

First of all, in listing the "Subject matter of copyright," Section 102(a) of the new statute includes "literary works" under the "original works of authorship" in which copyright protection subsists. The statute further states (Section 106) that:

Subject to Sections 107 ["Fair use"] through 118, the owner of copyright under this title has the exclusive right to do and to authorize any of the following: (1) to reproduce the copyrighted work in copies or phono records; (2) to prepare derivative works based upon the copyrighted work; etc.

However, the statute also makes it clear (Section 102(b)) that:

In no case does copyright protection for an original work of authorship extend to any idea, procedure, process, system, method of operation, concept, principle, or discovery, regardless of the form in which it is described, explained, illustrated, or embodied in such work.

What is a Derivative Work?

The statute (Section 101) defines a derivative work as:

A work based on one or more preexisting works, such as a translation, . . .abridgement, condensation, or any other form in which a work may be recast, transformed, or adapted. A work consisting of editorial revisions, annotations, elaborations, or other modifications which, as a whole, represent an original work of authorship, is a 'derivative work'.

Further as regards the "Subject matter of copyright: Compilations and derivative works" (Section 103), the statute states in Section 103(a) that:

The subject matter of copyright as specified by Section 102 includes compilations and derivative works, but protection for a work employing preexisting material does not extend to any part of a work in which such material has been used unlawfully. Meaningful, if the derivative work is to be copyrighted validly, that the consent of the owner of copyright in the preexisting work is needed, that it must be "fair use," that it is the work of the U.S. Government, or that the work is otherwise in the public domain.

Section 103(b) states that:

The copyright in a compilation or derivative work extends only to the material contributed by the author of such work, and does not imply any exclusive right in the preexisting material. The copyright in such work is independent of, and does not affect or enlarge the scope, duration, ownership, or subsistence of, any copyright protection in the preexisting material.

Who Owns What?

As regards "Initial ownership of copyright," the statute reaffirms in Section 201(a) that:

Copyright in a work protected under this title vests inistially in the author or authors of the work. The authors of a joint work are coowners of copyright in the work.

However, Section 201(c) introduces some very new concepts as regards "Contributions to Collective Works":

Copyright in each separate contribution to a collective work is distinct from copyright in the collective work as a whole, and vests initially in the author of the contribution. In the absence of express transfer of the copyright or of any rights under it, the owner of copyright in the collective work is presumed to have acquired only the privileges of reproducing and distributing the contribution as part of that particular collective work, any revision of that collective work, and any later collective work in the same series.

What Is Fair Use?

Finally, pertinent to some of the uses of abstracts is Section 107 ("Limitations on exclusive rights: Fair use"), which states that:

Notwithstanding the provisions of Section 106, the fair use of a copyrighted work, including such use by reproduction in copies or phonorecords or by any other means specified by that Section, for purposes such as criticism, comment, news reporting, teaching (including multiple copies for classroom use), scholarship, or research, is not an infringement of copyright.

In determining whether the use made of a work in any particular case is a fair use the factors to be considered shall include:

1. The purpose and character of the use, including whether such use is of a commercial nature or is for nonprofit educational purposes;
2. The nature of the copyrighted work;
3. The amount and substantiality of the portion used in relation to the copyrighted work as a whole; and
4. The effect of the use upon the potential market for or value of the copyrighted work.

What About Licenses and other Contracts?

The right to use certain access services is governed by licenses or other contracts that must be signed by their users. These are often specific as to what may or may not be done about such aspects as making multiple copies of the abstracts contained or making a digital record of the results of an online search. If these contracts are signed, their restrictions are binding on the users, regardless of copyright aspects, unless additional permissions are obtained.

40B: POSITIONS OF THE MAJOR PLAYERS ON ABSTRACTS

Ben H. Weil
Kurt D. Steele
Morton David Goldberg
M. Lynne Neufeld
Lois W. Granick

The Proprietary Rights Committee of Information Industry Association has prepared a paper defining the issues surrounding copyrighting abstracts and the positions of the major players. While not an official opinion paper, the document does pull together in one place, definitions, issues, legal questions and the positions of the different groups involved. The following is an excerpt from that paper, reprinted with the permission of the IIA.

We determined the following positions by circulating copies of a questionnaire quite broadly to concerned associations and federations in the areas of primary publications (journals, magazines, books, newspapers, and newsletters), access services, and (less extensively) users of abstracts. Many of these, in turn, sent copies to their members.

We allowed some months for the receipt of replies, and we followed up many of the contacts with conversations, especially where the parties did not deem it suitable to submit written positions, or when they reported themselves unable to arrive at unanimity among their members. In some of these cases we then heard directly from certain members. We thus heard at least indirectly from all concerned groups.

Journal and Magazine Publishers

According to a cover letter from the Association of American Publishers (AAP), its position "remains unchanged from the point of view outlined in Charles Lieb's recent paper on this subject" (*Communications and the Law*, Fall 1980). This recognizes the unique roles and interdependence of primary, secondary, and tertiary (question-answering) publishers, but states that (1) "authors' abstracts . . . are as much protected by the author's or the primary publisher's copyright as the text of the abstracted article itself," except where "the abstract is so brief and sparse that it merely states a bare principle or fact, articulatable for all practical purposes in no other way," and (2) "to the extent that the secondary publisher summarizes in his own words the facts or principles found in the work published by the primary publisher, the secondary publisher's abstract is itself an original work, which does not infringe the copyright of the primary work, and which itself is protected by copyright . . . [both] on the separate abstract which he (the secondary publisher) prepared (unless because of sparseness it is ineligible for protection) and on the collection of his abstracts which he publishes."

The AAP's position on primary-journal ownership of author's abstracts was echoed in responses from individual primary-journal publishers, including a few who are also associated with the publishing of access services; those concerned only with the latter disagree strongly, as we shall report later. Mr. Lieb

235

himself urged establishing guidelines and broadening the scope of the Copyright Clearance Center, Inc., "to accommodate the clearance and payment of publisher-prescribed fees for . . . abstracts first published in primary journals".

Literary magazine publishers are accustomed to payment for the right to prepare extensive digests of their articles. We did not receive any coordinated responses from magazine publishers in regard to abstracts, but some of the comments on the access-service abstracting of news items in **business** magazines were similar to those that we will report later about the abstracting of newspapers and newsletters.

Book Publishers

The only comments specifically received from book publishers were to the effect that books rarely contain author's abstracts and that access-service abstracting of books is a desirable form of publicity as well as retrieval.

Newspapers

No coordinated responses were received from newspaper publishers, but it was apparent from comments that some of the newspapers that are now marketing or licensing electronic-publishing (full-text) versions of their papers are at least uneasy about competition for these services from news-abstract databases. Most of the points that newspapers raise are similar to those brought forth by the publishers of newsletters, which we shall discuss next.

Newsletters

The Newsletter Association of America (NAA) submitted an extensive response on the position of the newsletter industry. It points out that newsletters consist "mainly of relatively short, brief, encapsulated news articles . . . that it would be extremely difficult to further condense or abstract further." It believes, therefore, that the information transmitted by abstracts of newsletter items "may be all that readers require," so that "any type of abstracting service that republishes copyrighted newsletter information in such a form that the reader then does not require a subscription to that publication is a clear violation of the fair-use guidelines of the Copyright Act. . . . NAA and its member publishers are particularly concerned about the potential for copyright abuse in 'abstracting,' especially in relation to royalty-based electronic [full-text] publishing services."

Much of the information supplied by NAA dealt with positions taken by some of its members on "indicative abstracts" of newsletter items that had been included in the now-discontinued *Key Issues Tracking* (KIT) service previously published by the New York Times Information Service. NAA maintains that the "indicative abstracts of information appearing in a number of copyrighted newsletters without permission or compensation to (copyright) holders constituted a violation of the fair-use portion of the Copyright Act" because "these 'indicative abstracts' could not be shown to qualify as fair use under each of the four criteria in Section 107:

"1. The nature of the use was commercial in character.
"2. The nature of the copyrighted work in question was proprietary; it was a business product of an entrepreneurial commercial venture.
"3. The amount and substantiality of the information used was especially considerable in relation to the total volume of the newsletters in question (which is considerably less than magazines or technical journals, etc.).
"4. Most especially, not only by providing the information from, for example, *The Energy Daily* in the 'indicative abstracts,' but by promoting in their marketing effort that the KIT-service subscriber received *The Energy Daily*, the potential for economic harm to the publisher from this reuse of his materials appears obvious."

NAA states that the exclusivity of newsletter arrangements with such full-text electronic publishing systems as NewsNet will pose a sharp legal conflict with any "further entity making 'indicative' abstracts."

The "new kid on the block" is clearly full-text electronic publishing.

Access Services

The access-service associations ultimately chose to leave responses to their members. Some of those that replied pointed to the "long history of 'fair use' of abstracts (copyrighted or not) by secondary services"; the continuing willingness of most primary publications to permit royalty-free use of author abstracts (primary publishers consider this "with the permission of the copyright owners," and some say "for the present"); the inordinate effort and expense that would be involved if permissions had to be requested from thousands of publications; etc.

None of the access services replying believes that it is necessary to request the permission of primary publications to prepare their own abstracts of copyrighted works because facts cannot be copyrighted, because of fair use, and because such abstracts are not derivative works; all but one believe that these original abstracts are copyrightable, as being "the products of substantial independent effort." All access services reporting believe that their compendia (both printed services and computerized "data bases") are also protected by copyright (and sometimes contracts) against unauthorized use, except for very limited fair use.

Repeated mention was made that access abstracts "are not published to replace the original documents, but rather to enable searchers for pertinent documents to determine whether or not they need to obtain the complete documents." Thus, the access services believe that their "citation of a work with an abstract will tend to increase, rather than decrease the demand for the original," and that the attention of primary publishers should be focused on obtaining revenues from the originals (subscriptions, copying royalties) rather than from the preparers of keys to them.

Some of the replies went into considerable detail. For example, on the subject of the right of access services to prepare original abstracts without the permission of the original copyrighted publications "within defined limits," and to deem that "these abstracts are themselves entitled to copyright protection," one IIA organization engaged in indexing/abstracting publications went on to say:

"When the essential purpose and effect of an original abstract is to describe the copyrighted work (thereby facilitating access to it and/or generating interest in it) rather than to serve as a functional substitute for it (thereby adversely affecting the market for it), the use is a fair one. Generally speaking, such an abstract should include no more of the substantive information contained in the copyrighted work than is necessary to accomplish the purpose of the abstract, and it should be relatively brief in comparison with the size of the work as a whole.

"An original abstract or collection of abstracts meeting certain basic criteria is itself entitled to protection under the copyright laws. Certainly, an abstract is protectable if it is the product of substantial independent effort, embodying an original expression that distinguishes it from the abstracted work or works, or from other abstracts. Such originality may be reflected in the selection and assembly of information to be included in the abstract, in the ordering and arrangement of that material, and in the editorial formulation of the expression comprising the abstract. Appropriation of any of these features of such a protected original abstract or collection of abstracts constitutes copyright infringement."

Another IIA member, a secondary publisher, commented that the "preparation of an abstract in itself does not constitute an infringement of the copyrighted work and that the use of an abstract published by a primary publisher in conjunction

with a copyrighted work is fair use well within the standards set forth in the Copyright Law." The publisher made the following observations regarding the four factors to be considered under Section 107 that were quoted earlier:

1. On "the purpose and character of the use, including whether such use is of a commercial nature or is for nonprofit educational purposes," the publisher notes that the fact that a defendant seeks to profit financially from its use does not necessarily preclude a finding of fair use, especially where the use can be characterized as furthering the public interest in the dissemination of information. Since publication of compilations of abstracts is designed to further the ends of teaching, scholarship, and research—purposes enumerated in Section 107 as most appropriate for a finding of fair use—the purpose and character of the use weigh heavily in favor of fair use.

2. In considering the second factor listed in the statute—"the nature of the copyrighted work"—this publisher notes that courts inquire whether the nature of the material is such that additional information on the subject of the first work would serve the public interest. Courts have been most receptive to the dissemination of educational, scientific, and historical work, and at least one court has stated that the scope of fair use is greater where the work copied is more one of diligence than of originality or creative effort.

3. In regard to "the amount and substantiality of the portion used in relation to the copyrighted work as a whole," this publisher believes that this third factor to be considered also supports a finding of fair use. In essence, an abstract is a key to the larger work; that its creation, in relation to the basics article, does not represent a substantial investment of labor, time, or money; and that it does not serve as a substitute for the entire article. As noted in the IIA draft paper, an abstract is typically only 2–7% as long as the article itself, so that its taking is insubstantial both qualitatively and quantitatively.

4. In regard to the fourth factor, "the effect of the use upon the potential market for or value of the copyrighted work," this publisher believes that the effect on the market is the most important of the fair-use factors, and that in the case of abstract compilations the use would increase rather than decrease the potential

market for the copyrighted work. It feels that such compilations serve to alert the professional community to the existence of articles and thus expand the audience for those articles, rather than being read in place of the articles. Moreover, given the plethora of journals and the limited time and funds available, it feels that it is unreasonable to believe that, in the absence of compilations, members of certain professions would purchase and plow through each journal to see if it contained any articles of interest.

The publisher points out that this point was recognized in an even more extreme case—the photocopying of entire articles—in the *Williams & Wilkins Co.* case, where the court reasoned that it was likely that certain readers who could not obtain articles through photocopying would do without them. Similarly, without access to abstracts, a researcher would either spend substantial time reading through individual issues of journals to locate a specific article of interest, or forgo a whole area of research. Thus, it feels that abstract compilations serve in effect as advertisements for journal articles that stimulate rather than detract from the market for the articles.

The New York Times Information Service has advised us that KIT was discontinued for economic reasons. It was originally established to track what was reported on a small number of national and international issues by 29 current journals, newspapers, and newsletters for the Executive Office of President —then Jimmy Carter. Its primary use was by governmental agencies and officers. It was discontinued when the Reagan administration terminated its funding.

"Indicative abstracts made and mounted in KIT were strictly facts or hard news. Section 102(b) of the Copyright Law expressly excludes copyright protection for any idea or principle embodied in a work, regardless of the form in which it is described. This is not only statutory but constitutional. The rubric that copyright protects the expression but not the idea is well-known. The concern of The Newsletter Association ignores the right to publish news, whether by an online database or in a printed newspaper. Reporting news from whatever source is a well-established right of the press under the First Amendment. This privilege even permits reporting the expression of a fact or idea if it can only be reported using essentially the same words. One need not call an 'earthquake' a 'ground tremor' to pass along a report.

"Assuming a report crosses the line into copying of expression, this copying is still not forbidden.

"Section 107 specifically provides that a use for 'news reporting' shall be included in fair use. An online database of public issues obviously would only look for a few leading facts. It would not set out to substitute its reports for the large number of subjects on the one topic of a specialized newsletter aimed at a small, interested audience. Complaints about including indicative abstracts of newsletter items in KIT never compared the minimal use of the material contained in KIT with the original sources. Also, attributing indicative abstracts of news items in a database is not unfair promotion; it is right and proper to credit a source. The New York Times Information Service, as an offshoot of the *New York Times,* is well aware that once an idea or fact is discovered and reported on at effort, cost, and expense, it is then nevertheless free for all to use."

What has been accomplished

The literature on the proprietary aspects of abstracts has hitherto been sparse, scattered, and not up to date. We hope, therefore, that the information collected in this paper will add to its completeness and clarity, and that, to quote our introduction, "further deliberations may proceed with a clearer understanding."

Our contacts with the abstracts-concerned communities have reconfirmed the major legal issues that we stated earlier: (1) to what extent can abstracts be prepared without the express permission of the copyright owners of the original works, and (2) to what extent can abstracts be used without the express permission of (a) the primary publications, and/or (b) the secondary (access) sources? While a few of those involved would still prefer that there be no discussion of these issues and their ramifications, we note that, in general, positions are much sharper than formerly, and that polarization is taking place.

Indeed, that is why we urge deliberations on the issues involved, deliberations undertaken with the firm intent of developing useful guidelines. These, we believe, would be preferable to litigation or additional legislation. Seeking the latter can well be a game of chance, and the technological situation is changing far too rapidly to be certain as to what would still be suitable tomorrow. Guidelines, on the other hand, can be much more flexible.

We have now brought up to date the information on the proprietary aspects of abstracts. The next step, for those involved, is to bring some order to the solution of the problems. ∎

41: OUR STAKE IN DATA BASE PROTECTION

Joseph H. Kuney

Informatics Inc.
Rockville, Maryland 20852

Data bases, whether scientific, technical, or personal, are definitely a part of the future for all who generate, distribute, and use information. The trends of technological development, coupled with growing user satisfaction, point clearly toward the ability to use data bases in a variety of new applications. These must be regarded as opportunities to vendors and users as a basis for working out use and pricing arrangements acceptable to both.

What have we learned these past 30 years in dealing with copyright problems that we can apply to the matter of data base protection? Certainly we have worked hard trying to solve the copyright problem:

We have sat through numerous mettings;

published equally numerous papers;

we have formed the Cosmos group, the Upstairs–Downstairs group, to name a few;

we conducted seemingly endless surveys on the basis of the premise if only we knew how many copies were being made we would be able to solve the problem—assuming, of course, that we could ever reach agreement on what the photocopying problem is;

we started the Copyright Clearance Center;

we spent some 15 years getting Congress to pass a bill to settle the problem;

now we are going to the Courts to resolve the matters we hoped were taken care of by the legislation.

Thus, I am concerned to see the matter of data base protection starting to heat up in much the same way the photocopy issue became a problem. Particularly I am concerned about the assumption that the problems of photocopying from printed products bear a direct relationship to the protection of data bases. The emotional issues may be similar but the practical aspects are different. From my experience to date, it appears that users and publishers have learned some lessons in the years of tilting at the windmills of copyright—lessons that are being applied in working out relationships that will enable both users

and publishers to maximize their respective benefits from automated data bases.

We should note also that the cast of characters involved in data base protection is somewhat different from that which took adversary positions on the photocopying issue. On the data base producer/vendor side the lead in making data bases available for computer search and retrieval was taken by individuals and organizations knowledgeable about computer technology rather than the publishers of print materials. The latter have since recognized the role of data base publishing in their respective futures, and they have acquired the necessary technological skills related to the building and dissemination of data bases.

On the user side of the photocopying issue, libraries played, and continue to play, the leading role. Libraries do have a special set of interests and problems that make it possible for libraries to present a unified position on photocopying. In the case of data bases, the users are more heterogeneous and do not perceive, as clearly as the libraries do, a special set of interests and problems. Even those users coming from a library culture tend to approach data base access differently from access to print products. Therefore, there is less likelihood that a common adversary position on data base access will develop.

As a result of their somewhat narrow interests and concerns, publishers and libraries both failed initially to recognize the significance of developing new technology. Thus the introduction of the Xerox machine was seen as a low-cost information option for users and a threat to the survival of their business by publishers. Only a few recognized this technology and the developing computer technology as an early step toward a solution to more effective and efficient access to information. Needs that were already becoming apparent as

† Presented (in part) before the Division of Chemical Information and Chemical Education, Symposium on "The Copyright Law", 182nd National Meeting of the American Chemical Society, New York, Aug 27, 1981.

rising costs began to erode the economic advantage of traditional printed products and specialization of interest began to create new information requirements.

Unfortunately and needlessly, the adversary relationship between library and publishers grew and continues to this date. There are thus far, despite all of the prophecies of doom on both sides, no reported casualties among users who have failed in their work because they were unreasonably denied access to copyrighted information. Neither are there any publishers who have—as yet—been forced out of business as a result of unauthorized photocopying.

How does data base protection differ from photocopying? For one thing, the uncertainty about the future of their business that bothered publishers so much with the onset of photocopying technology has been greatly reduced. As the ease and volume of photocopying steadily increased, publishers began to see that traditional methods of distribution would be challenged. But until fairly recently technology was not yet far enough advanced to demonstrate its potential in a measurable way, nor were users able to test the new systems. In this vacuum of information it was natural that publishers would seek to hold the line on copyright until such time as they could better determine the impact of the new technology on their business. Early on in the development users began to sense the potential for better access to information and were anxious to put the potential to use as rapidly as possible.

While publishers and librarians engaged in the battle over copyright protection, a new class of users and publishers were learning "to live with technology". They absorbed the lesson that technology is in itself neither good nor bad but succeeds only to the extent it meets a socioeconomic need. They learned also that technological progress is an evolutionary process. That is, change is the expected norm and yesterday's solutions may not solve today's problems. Even as this paper is being written, technology is being developed that will provide new capabilities to organize, transmit, store, process, and receive information—capabilities to be exploited by users as well as publishers.

About 20 years ago when the first efforts at computer-aided composition were being made, it was suggested that the resulting machine-readable record of the full text of papers would provide a means for direct access to scientific and technical papers via the computer. This suggestion was put down as impossible because in no way would the necessary computer storage capacity ever be available. But we did not have to be too alert to read the signs that computer processing costs were on a downward trend and computer storage capacities were on an equally sharp upward trend. Today it is clear that we have available the processing economics and the storage capacity to put us within a few years of easy access via the computer to full-text data bases.

The signs are even clearer that the impact of microprocessor chip technology is producing a somewhat astounding growth in the use of personal computers. Not only are prices dropping, but also capacity and capability are increasing rapidly. It is estimated that by 1985 you will be able to acquire a microcomputer system with mass storage and a printer for about $1500. Only those publishers completely out of touch with reality would seek to "protect" themselves against the obvious role these computers will have in the use of data bases. Fortunately, the evidence is strong that today's publisher sees the new markets being created and seeks to cooperate with his users in working out acceptable pricing arrangements.

Another technology-related lesson affecting data base protection is the awareness that the user has become highly sophisticated in the application of computer technology. Much of the technology used by today's publishers of data bases has been made available through the knowledge and skill of the users of data bases. In many cases—maybe in most cases—the

user works with computers at a sophisticated level of application far beyond what is required by data base producers. Effective communication technology, a key factor in making data base access an economic reality, is also the result of computer processing capability far beyond that required for data base publishing. It may have no relevance, but data base publishers appear to be continuing the tradition of their print technology predecessors in leaving research and development to others.

Still another lesson aiding the growing use of data bases is the acceptance of unit pricing—that is, payment for information on the basis of use rather than on the size of a fixed package, such as a book or journal. Before the advent of photocopying machines and computers, publishers had tried a variety of ways to charge users on the basis of use. None were successful. Some credit is due to the genius at Xerox who introduced the per copy concept for use of the machine. About the same time as photocopying was maturing into wide use, CA introduced a licensing concept for the use of its microfilm. Here the product was leased instead of outright sale as a means by which the publisher could be protected against unauthorized photocopying.

Still later we learned to pay for "hits", to charge for and to pay for connect time, to pay for printouts, and to pay royalties in fulfilling our needs for information. One of the problems of introducing a unit pricing scheme is how to keep track of who owes what. Computers can really do a job of who, what, and how many. It can even issue bills and send dunning letters.

More recently several major data base producers of data bases developed out of long-standing printed products have announced policies aimed at pricing data base use at full cost. In effect, users of many popularly used data bases have been subsidized in part by the print editions. As increasing use of automated access to data bases has reduced revenues from printed versions, publishers are finding it necessary to increase the price of data base access to include the cost of building the data base. Any price increase, particularly a sizeable one, stimulates the buyer to examine the need and/or to find alternatives.

Thus the message is clear for all to read who wish to do so. The technology points directly to an increasing ability to utilize the product of a data base in a variety of applications and higher prices provide stimulus to do so. Such usage might include

> holding data in storage for later use
> combining data base outputs to create a specialized data base for limited use
> repackaging for sale.

In effect, these are the photocopies of computer technology. Not as easily captured as a photocopy on a Xerox machine, but there is a Xerox equivalent. They are called "black boxes". A discussion of the technology of black boxes is outside the scope of this paper. It is sufficient to be aware of their effective role in capturing the content of data bases for subsequent reuse and to be aware that they are becoming increasingly available and versatile.

Thus, at the user level, the scene is set for using data bases for almost any use that can be conceived. Why then are the publishers of data bases not storming the halls of Congress demanding legislative relief or giving papers at meetings like this to protest the evil of copying from their data bases?

One reason is that today's publisher of data bases is highly sophisticated about the capability of computer-based systems, their reliability, and their economics. This sophistication permits a publisher to bring a data base to market with reasonable expectation of producing sufficient revenue to stay in business. In addition, the users role and capacity to purchase and use data bases has become well defined. As stated earlier, much of the data base application technology stems from users who are associated with organizations that make extensive use of computers. Thus a common interest focused on computer technology has tended to create a common bond between user and data base publisher—one which enables them to understand each other's needs and problems and therefore to cooperate in working out solutions.

None of this may sound very professional to those who might prefer to talk about data base protection in terms of right of access, need for a national policy, privacy, or the other emotional subjects that seem to come to the surface when we talk about copyright protection. Also, economic and cultural forces affecting our information requirements need to be analyzed in far greater depth than the hints given here. Rather, I have tried to present a sense of the results of those factors at work in a free market place and further to suggest that those forces have tended to produce a healthy marketplace for data base

publishing. What problems there have been to date have been regarded by publishers and by users as minor and subject to ready solution.

There is strong evidence that users recognize the rights of the data base producers and show a willingness to cooperate with publishers in working out arrangements acceptable to both. It appears to be working both ways, with publishers showing a similarly cooperative attitude.

The result is a growing business of data base publishing and a growing clientele of users. Data bases, whether scientific, technical, or personal, are definitely a part of all of our futures. There will be problems to solve. But the trends of technological development, coupled with growing user sophistication, point clearly toward the capability to provide a truly effective system of more selective dissemination.

Our stake is simply to recognize there are not threats—only opportunities.

42: COPYRIGHT AND THE INFORMATION INDUSTRY

Christopher Burns

The information industry consists of creators and distributors of information for scientists, economists, financial analysts, lawyers, credit managers, market researchers, and other professionals primarily through looseleaf publications, newsletters, special reports, and a variety of electronic information services. In 1983 the revenues for this sector of the economy were about $12.5 billion, larger than those for books or magazines, about the size of revenues for the whole television industry, half the size of those for the newspaper industry, and growing twice as fast as the economy.

Although the activity is an old one—Abraham Lincoln was a credit reporter for Dun & Bradstreet —it is the most modern of the media, the most aggressive in its use of new computer and communications technologies, and the perpetrator as well as the victim of much of today's copyright confusion.

We are the ones who, having successfully pried the expression free from traditional books and pamphlets so that it could be sold

Chris Burns made this statement on February 5, 1984, at a Copyright Office Symposium on the effects of new technologies.

more efficiently, are now learning to extract a pure idea from its original expression. And we wonder what laws, if any, will ultimately govern what we do.

We are caught, between a commitment to the free exchange of ideas—which is the flower of our civilization—and the business notion of secure property that makes that civilization prosper. The law no longer provides the unambiguous guidance that information companies need to avoid injuring each other during the rapid expansion period ahead, and we fear that the law may no longer be capable even of prescribing a fair remedy.

Consider how the industry derives and compiles new products and services from existing ones. An original report well researched and perceptively written often becomes, itself, an event to be reported. A Wall Street research report, for example, will create news and be quoted in a market newsletter and circulated by the clients who find the information valuable. Though all this is meant to enhance the distribution of important ideas, it often ends up eliminating exclusivity—the one advantage the author intended to provide his clients.

Meanwhile, an abstracting service writes a brief summary of the newspaper article and mails it to subscribers, even as an online financial wire service writes another abstract of the story and sends it out over the phone. Copies of the report go into private

libraries from which they freely circulate, and inevitably the full text makes its way into the hands of a competing research firm which then prepares a larger market study, using these findings as the keystone. None of these efforts quote very extensively from the original material—prose style is not the essence of its value—but all of them try mightily to capture the central ideas.

In due time a new publisher strips the market forecast numbers from the abstract of the original analysis and includes them in a data collection which is then sold to major corporations and other investment analysts. The wire service abstract is added to an online database which can be accessed more easily by future researchers. An enterprising subscriber to the database records his search onto a floppy disk for later reference (called "downloading") and in time he or she transfers the content of that disk to the company's central archive where others can retrieve it.

In this very real but much simplified description of the information industry a number of laws are imperfectly at work. In theory, all the products are copyrighted, but in practice they borrow liberally from each other without once paying license or royalty fees. The analyst gnaws glumly on the bones of notoriety, vowing next time to say something *really* provocative, while his or her employer swears to restrict future distribution even further. The

journals are emboldened to be more specific and more comprehensive in their covereage of such reports and the abstracters who feed on those journals resolve themselves to take even bigger bites next time. In fact, there is no protection.

A few years ago this subsidiary distribution took time—sometimes months—during which the original audience has an information advantage over those who were getting it second hand. But today's technology allows us to abstract *The New York Times*, for example, and make it electronically available for browsing or systematic searching by 8 a.m. the morning of publication. A market research study can be abstracted or summarized and stored in computer memory where anyone with a personal computer and a password can benefit from its insights.

The law says that derivative works require permission of the original author, but the definition of "derivative" is ambiguous in this context, leading us to believe that rigorous abstracts—like brief plot summaries—may not be among the author's exclusive rights.

And that old standby "fair use" now seems to cover a number of forms of *re-use*, even those that might erode the market for future sales. A family that can tape a movie off television is less likely to buy that tape in the future. If a subscriber to an online economic database retrieves the U.S Economic Model for the years 1972 through 1982 for all industries in a given two-digit SIC code, *recording that database as it is played over the line,* is that fair use?

Even the copyright procedures for a database seem difficult and inappropriate since the copyright seeks to protect the data set—which is ephemeral—not the rules that fashion it into something usable—which are the real genius of the publisher's effort.

We look for protection under the various unfair competition laws, and in fact there is case law (International News Service v. Associated Press) to discourage the systematic misappropriation of "hot news," but radio stations rip and read the press with impunity, and some online services use others as unidentified and unpaid sources.

We have developed elaborate leases and contracts that try to prevent subscribers from re-selling database access or compilation products in any form, but since many of the individual *items* of information are freely available from other sources, it is often impossible to prove that the contract was broken.

We watch use patterns and build software in the computer system to help identify the downloader, but as a matter of fact it is very difficult to write a contract that prevents the user from buying too much without appearing to contradict our own advertising.

Above all, the issue is how to

encourage a rapid evolution toward more effective distribution and access sytems, how to follow where the new technology beckons without the business damage and litigation that ambiguous laws seem inevitably to reap.

In the cases I have raised here we are concerned not with the artistic creation of a work or even the costly invention of a new chip or software package, but the commercial process of using new technology to increase access to ideas. I'm beginning to suspect that copyright law may *not* be the best legal tool for achieving the regulation we want; perhaps commercial concepts like misappropriation or unfair competition may offer us a sounder and simpler foundation.

In France, in Germany, and in Japan the governments are actively encouraging the development of new information access systems because they believe that these systems will improve health care and education, accelerate relevant scientific progress, and make industry more productive. We also believe that. But in our case we are not asking for interest-free loans, massive public investment, or a ministry for industrial growth. We are asking for laws that acknowledge a new technological reality, that strike a new balance between property and the public interest. And we are asking for laws that we can understand.

What *is* a derivative work?

What is it about a database that we are trying to protect—the data itself or the recipe that forms, maintains, and presents it?

What shall we agree are the customary first sale rights when it comes to information? And what is fair use?

There are other questions more mundane, more procedural, but just as knotty. In fact, there are too many questions. They can be resolved in legislation or they can be resolved in the courts—and we are resigned to a little of each. But we applaud and encourage a third alternative which the Library of Congress and the Copyright Office have begun here — the possibility that with your help and counsel we, who are on all sides of this issue, can get some lines painted on the track before the sound of crumpling fenders gets to be too much of a distraction.

Mr. Burns is President of Christopher Burns, Inc., a research and consulting firm that specializes in business development issues within the information industry. He was previously Senior Vice President and Associate Publisher of the Minneapolis Star and Tribune, Vice President Planning for the Washington Post Company, and a senior consultant at Arthur D. Little, Inc., where he directed much of that firm's research and consulting in the area of new technology and its impact on the media.

43: PUBLISHERS AND AUTHORS DRAW LINES FOR WORK-FOR-HIRE BATTLE

Howard Fields

Book publishers and authors, usually on the same side when it comes to fighting for or against policies in Washington, are donning armor to do battle with each other this year over the work-for-hire provision in the Copyright Act of 1976.

For some publishers, success by the freelance authors could mean an end to a long-standing method of doing business. And they suggest that the authors, if successful, could be cutting their own throats.

Freelance authors and graphic artists claim that publishers are abusing the intent of the Copyright Act by requiring work-for-hire contracts for works that are not commissioned by publishers, and by denying authors the secondary rights in violation of the Constitution.

Tad Crawford, legislative counsel for the Graphic Artists Guild and the American Society of Magazine Photographers, cites a survey the guild conducted among its members about their relations with the leading book publishers. Work-for-hire contracts in one or more of their divisions were being used, he says, by seven of the top 13 mass market publishers, seven of the top 10 elementary and high school publishers, and 8 of the top 11 hardcover publishers.

Armed with the survey and other examples, a number of organizations of freelancers got together and helped Sen. Thad Cochran (R., Miss.) write a bill last fall that would, among other things, ban work-for-hire contracts for contributions to a collective work, supplementary work or instructional texts. "These works would be subject to the copyright law's provision for a limited rights transfer," Cochran said upon introducing the bill. "Parties would be free to contract any rights to be purchased, but my bill proposes that each right to be purchased be enumerated in the contract with the consideration to be paid for each right stated."

That and the rest of the bill, S. 2138, publishers said in a February letter to Cochran, "would make radical changes in the assumptions underlying this carefully crafted compromise [the Copyright Act]." The AAP, which has formed a coalition of other industries that contract with freelancers, said in the letter over the signature of AAP president Townsend Hoopes that the changes "would severely damage many

of the industries we represent."

The Hoopes letter continued: "It is clearly understood between the contracting parties under work-for-hire that the original work products submitted by these people will often bear little resemblance to the version finally published; they will be rewritten, edited or otherwise changed by other freelancers, staff writers, illustrators and editors. But, if publishers cannot specify, unambiguously and finally, in an agreement who owns the rights in the finished product, then they cannot market the product with confidence; they will be especially disadvantaged in those cases where a sale of rights is

necessary to penetrate a new market— e.g., to publish the product in foreign translation or to present it in a different medium."

Representatives on the other side claim, however, that publishers have abused their position in the past and that authors and artists are merely trying to "put back into balance the inequity in bargaining position under which we see publishers paying for the limited use that they intend, but obtaining rights far in excess of that."

Ronald Schechter, who made that statement, is a member of Goldfarb, Singer & Austern, a Washington law firm representing Washington Independent Writers. He adds, "I think there has been an attempt to recognize the legitimate needs of encyclopedia publishers and textbook publishers," those considered to be affected most by any change in work-for-hire provisions.

Crawford, who is leading the effort behind the Cochran bill, is more concerned than Schechter about abuses by book publishers in the work-for-hire

area, especially publishers of textbooks.

"Our experience has been," he said, "that these companies tend to use work-for-hire on an across-the-board basis in those categories where it is possible to use it. They really don't make a distinction on a case-by-case scrutiny of the nature of the assignment and creativity." Therefore, he says, they have decided to "always use work-for-hire and not negotiate."

He adds, "We feel that freelancers really should not be treated as employees, and therefore there should be a clarification of what an employee is under the first part of the work-for-hire definition." And under the commissioned works section, he says, "certain works should be deleted and moved over to a category which would require the publishers to specifically enumerate the rights they want to use. There should be a linkage between the use the publisher intends to make of the material and the fee that is paid."

Schechter notes that although consideration was given in the Cochran measure for encyclopedia and textbook publishers, it is a much stronger and more sweeping bill than another version introduced two years ago.

In a Senate hearing on that bill, Robin Brickman, a member of the Graphic Artists Guild, told of her experiences with book publishers, citing Doubleday and Houghton Mifflin as major clients "that I can't afford to work for because of work-for-hire. When I worked for them, I gave up all future rights, never saw my original pieces again, and was paid some of the lowest rates in the text book industry, from $50 to $150, half the current rate."

Charles Butts of Houghton Mifflin, a past chairman of the AAP's copyright committee, believes his house is one of the best and fairest in the elementary and high school area where work-for-hire is most common. But because books in that area generally require a team of authors and their work is mixed throughout the book, he asks, "Where does authorship begin and end?"

Houghton Mifflin already provides some authors with royalties even though they are operating under work-for-hire contracts, Butts says. "In school textbook publishing, you don't have any possibility of other rights" being sold because the works are prepared for a specific market, Butts says, but there may be a future development, especially with today's technology explosion, that would open other markets.

If an unforeseen secondary use for a

How Work-for-Hire Is Defined

Following up on a provision in the U.S. Constitution giving power to Congress to secure "for limited times to authors and inventors the exclusive right to their respective writings and discoveries," the Copyright Act of 1976 defines work-for-hire as "a work prepared by an employee within the scope of his or her employment; or a work specially ordered or commissioned for use as…a supplementary work, as a compilation, as an instructional text, as a test, as answer material for a test, or as an atlas, if the parties expressly agree in a written instrument signed by them that the work shall be considered a work made for hire."

book had not been included in the "laundry list of rights" that would have to be enumerated under the proposed bill, he says, "we would not be able to market it, and this would be detrimental to our authors who are on a royalty basis."

Textbooks often have hundreds of contributors. In his own 1982 letter to Sen. Charles McC. Mathias (R., Md.), who conducted the hearing on the former bill, Butts said there were over 240 different agreements for a new program in language arts that Houghton Mifflin published for kindergarten through eight. "That's a lot of pieces of paper and that's a lot of people to have to track down if you need to go back to everyone at the time of revision or adaptation. So it becomes a very costly, time-consuming and prohibitive procedure on our part."

Butts suggests that if the bill is ever passed publishers may have to retrench

on their use of freelancers. "I know that we at Houghton Mifflin would have to rethink and reevaluate the numbers of artists that we use to supply materials and we might have to do more of our work in-house."

There have been suggestions that since a California law requires workman's compensation for freelancers, publishers have begun avoiding their use. Butts feels that efforts to change current practices are "detrimental to freelance artists at all levels. We pay more to an artist for an illustration in a school textbook if that work is paid under a work-for-hire, which gives us all rights, than we would pay to the same artist if our order was very specific, such as one illustration to be used on one chapter in one book."

Crawford scoffs at the differential that Butts cites: "That would be atypical in our experience. Generally, the rates in the field are so low that it would

be almost impossible to pay for a non-work-for-hire situation."

Whatever the truth, Butts says, "the copyright law is not the problem. It's a marketplace problem" and should be dealt with in that context.

Thus the lines are drawn. At least two publishers, Houghton Mifflin and McGraw-Hill, hired their own Washington attorney/lobbyists to look after their interests, but they, like other firms, are working through the coalition that AAP formed, since it represents both book and periodical publishers, and many houses are both.

Mathias has demonstrated little enthusiasm for S. 2138 and has not scheduled any hearings on it. Publishers are pressing members of Mathias's subcommittee to ignore the bill, while at the same time authors and graphic artists are pressing for spring hearings. At any rate, no one expects legislation to be pressed this year. HOWARD FIELDS

44: COPYRIGHT AND PRACTICE OF THE TRADE

Edith Leonian
Phillip Leonian

The stated intent of Congress in enacting the copyright law which took effect January 1st, 1978, was to foster "original works of authorship" and "new forms of creative expression" by vesting control of these works in the hands of their creators.

While there are basic conceptual changes in the new law, it was written with an eye to the "practice of the trade" which developed under the old law, so as far as the course of ordinary business is concerned, the effective changes have proved to be more of detail than substance.

Those few problems which have arisen have been due largely to lack of information on the part of the artists and their clients, or to misunderstandings, by both lawyers and laymen, as to how the new law does affect business practice.

This article is intended as a simplified look at those areas of the Copyright Act of 1976 (Public Law 94-553) which have proved to be of most concern to photographers, illustrators and their clients in the law's first year.

A caveat: while the law itself is straightforward and easy to understand, copyright disputes can become extremely complex. Answers are dependent on the specifics of each particular case. An experienced copyright attorney should be consulted on any problems, as most general attorneys lack the background to fully appreciate its ramifications.

First Ownership. Under the old law, work specially commissioned was considered "work made for hire," so the client owned the copyright in absence of agreement to the contrary. In practice, most photographers and illustrators limited the client's copyright by specifying permitted use in advertising, or one time reproduction in editorial work.

Under the new law, the photographers, illustrator or other author of an original work owns the copyright unless he signs an agreement to the contrary.

In other words, photographers and illustrators no longer have to negotiate for copyright. They own it from the instant of creation — "When it is fixed in a copy for the first time" — that is, the instant the film is exposed.

Transfer of Rights. The most single visible change in business practice caused by the new law is that any reproduction or derivative rights to a work must be transferred in writing[1]. In addition this transfer of rights, or license, must be signed by the creator or his or her authorized agent.

Copyright can no longer be legally transferred by verbal agreement. The new law supercedes common law copyright, and pre-empts any state law which deals with copyright matters.

Adding to the importance of the written transfer is the fact that under the new law, copyright is infinitely divisible — not one right, but a bundle of little rights which may be sold or assigned by the first owner (the photographer, illustrator or other author).

The concept is familiar in editorial work, but in advertising and other commercial work neither user nor supplier has been accustomed to spelling out what is being bought and what it being sold up front. Wording was loose, tacit understanding common. It worked, after a fashion. But it was also the cause of ninety percent of the misunderstandings between users of art and photography and their creative resources.

Now, under the new law, in order for buyers of art to be sure they have the rights they need in an assignment, it is impor-

tant for them to tell the photographer or other author what they are in advance, so that the author can grant those rights.

Since art directors or other buyers don't always know all the uses which will be made of a photograph in advance, the practice has continued to be for clients to buy only those rights they know they'll need. Then they either negotiate for additional rights as the need arises, or pre-negotiate fees so that they would know in advance the cost of any additional use.

Since abiding by these written agreements is now a matter of law rather than one of ethics, the effect thus far has been to reduce the number of after-the-fact disputes.

Therefore, since divisibility of rights has extensively enhanced the earning potential of a transparency or other artwork, "all rights" transactions, with their concomitantly higher fees, have been relatively rare.

Copyright Notice. Under the old law, if copyright notice failed to appear on a published work, even by accident, that work lost its copyright protection and entered the public domain.

The new law continues to call for notice on copies distributed to the public, but absence of notice, or error in notice, will not immediately result in loss of copyright.

Because of the provisions made for correction (§405 of the law), the need for notice has been played down and taken a bit too lightly in certain cases in the law's first year, which may yet result in a large body of work entering the public domain unless corrective steps are taken.

I. Improper Notice. Proper notice contains three elements:

A. The letter c in a circle — ©; the word "copyright" or the abbreviation "copr";

B. The year of the first publication of the work (or, in the case of previously unpublished work created prior to Jan. 1, 1978, the year 1978);

C. The name of the copyright owner.

If all three elements are not present, copyright protection does not ensue, and a correction must be filed. The most common error in notice has been the omission of the year date in credit lines for individual photographs.

II. Individual Notice for Advertisements. Advertisements are specifically mentioned only one time in the entire copyright law — and that mention is not only negative but parenthetical. §404 (1) provides that copyright notice for a "collective work" (such as a magazine, newspaper, or other periodical) does not protect advertisements inserted in that publication.

In other words, if an advertisement does not carry a copyright notice of its own, and subsequent corrective steps are not taken, it will enter the public domain. This means that it, or any of its elements, may be reproduced at will by anyone, for any purpose, whatever the wishes of the advertiser whose property the ad would otherwise be.

Leafing through the pages of any magazine during the past year or so, one will find many too many ads without copyright notice. As very few advertisers wish to dedicate these expensive pages to the good of the public, absence of notice can only result from ignorance or poor legal advice.

For this reason photographers and illustrators have been advised by their professional associations to include as a standard condition of sale on any of their licenses (invoices) that the user of the work shall provide copyright protection for it. This makes it possible for them to take advantage of corrective registration if necessary.

Even if a correction is filed, omission of notice can still provide a defense of "innocent infringement." And advertisers would keep in mind that Europeans, accustomed to American requirements for notice, routinely assume that any work published in the U.S.A. without a notice is in the public domain, and feel they can reproduce it at will.

An object Lesson: Each advertisement in the PAPA Directory carries individual copyright notice for the photographer placing the ad.

This does protect the advertisement as a whole, and its copyrightable elements, under the law.

This does not mean that the photographer necessarily owns all of the rights in each of the images he displays. The copyright in an original work like a photograph is separate or distinct from the copyright of a large work in which it is incorporated.

This sounds confusing, and often is. The best way to clarify ownership of individual images, ease registration and prevent disputes in such cases is for each individual illustration to carry separate notice.

III. Copyright Notice for the Photograph or Illustration. Photographers and illustrators have also been advised by their professional societies to make individual and adjacent copyright notice a standard condition of sale. Then, if the notice is "left off" an ad (where trade practice has not been to carry photographer credits), the Copyright Office can treat it as an error that is correctable by registration. Registration by the photographer saves the copyright of the photograph.

If the advertiser wishes to correct a notice deficiency, then he, she or it must use the alternate methods mentioned in §405 of the law.

In periodicals and other "collective works," the copyright notice of the magazine itself prevents the editorial contents from falling into the public domain. If the photographer's copyright notice appears adjacent to his or her work, she or he will enjoy the advantages of bulk registration (the best protection of a year's work for a single $10 fee) and protection against claims of innocent infringement.

Since copyright notice also serves as a credit line, it imposes no hardship on magazines where such credit has long been customary. Adjacent copyright notice in magazines is taking the place of the simple credit line as a hallmark of those photographers and other authors who value their work. Many go so far as to impose penalties of two or three times invoiced fees if specified adjacent notice is omitted editorially.

IV. Another New Notice Requirement: Foreign Publication. American work published abroad must be protected by copyright notice in its foreign publication, or its American copyright protection is abrogated. In other words, if a photograph or other work appears in another country without notice, it enters the public domain here. This change was made to conform to Universal Copyright Convention requirements.

Elements of a Proper Copyright License. The photographer, illustrator or other author and the client should agree up front on the rights being purchased, the fees and negotiable terms and conditions. It is recommended that the author list this informa-

tion on an unsigned assignment confirmation form, with a copy to the client. Then, upon delivery, the photographer's invoice will serve as transfer of stated reproduction rights, or the copyright license. This should include:

I. Description of the photograph, illustration or other work being licensed;
II. Rights being granted;
III. Fees and expenses;
IV. Standard duration of license is now generally one year from invoice date;
V. As a condition of sale: that the client copyright his product (magazine, ad, slide film, brochure, billboard, package, etc.);
VI. As a condition of sale: that the photographer, illustrator or other author receive adjacent copyright notice in legal form;
VII. Under 202 of the new law, purchase of reproduction rights is separate from purchase of the object (original transparency or other artwork), so terms and conditions for return of originals should be included, unless originals are separately purchased. (A bonus for buyers is that, at least in New York state, no sales tax is due if originals are returned undamaged and unchanged — a saving of 8% of the total of the invoice in New York);
VIII. Any other terms and conditions (payment terms, finance charges, model release requirements, etc.);
IX. Any restrictions important to the photographer or other author — for instance, "no cropping" for Henri Cartier-Bresson (to be agreed upon up front);
X. Last, but far from least, because without it the license is not sufficient under the new law: THE SIGNATURE OF THE PHOTOGRAPHER/ILLUSTRATOR/AUTHOR OR HIS OR HER AUTHORIZED AGENT.

Remember that the prime purpose of a properly drawn license with its clarity of terms is to facilitate business, prevent disputes and stay out of court.

Duration of Copyright. Under the new law, the creator's term of copyright on work created after Jan. 1, 1978, is his or her life plus fifty years. Work created before Jan. 1, 1978, but neither published nor in the public domain prior to that date, is protected for the creator's life plus fifty years.

Anonymous works, pseudonymous works or works made for hire receive copyright for a term of seventy-five years from the year of first publication, or one hundred years from year of creation, whichever expires first.

Which brings up a side issue.

Work Made for Hire. "Work made for hire" is the exception to the new law's rule that copyright vests in the creator. In 101 of the law, there are two definitions of "work made for hire" which allow an employer author status.

"(1) a work prepared by an employee within the scope of his or her employment; or

"(2) a work specially ordered or commissioned for use as a contribution to a collective work . . . if the parties expressly agree in a written instrument signed by them that work shall be considered a 'work made for hire.'"

"Collective work" as referred to in the law has a very specific meaning: "A collective work is a special kind of compilation; it must include a number of contributions, each of which must constitute 'separate and independent works in themselves,' and these individual parts must be assembled into a 'collective' as distinguished from a 'unitary' whole, thus leaving integrated works . . . outside the definition."[2]

Therefore, according to Barbara Ringer,[3] Register of Copyrights in the United States, very few advertisements involving individual contractors can qualify as "work made for hire." In fact it would be easier to list who is eligible to ask for it than who is not.

Magazines, newspapers, and other periodicals are eligible to ask for "work for hire," but only if the photographer or other author agrees to it in advance, in writing, in an instrument signed by both parties.

There is only one difference aside from the duration of copyright between a "work made for hire" and "all rights." On any license of copyright, the author has the right to terminate the grant of rights after thirty-five years. In a "work for hire," the author does not have that right.

This is rather remote, and the phrase "work made for hire" would be copyright curiosa if it had not been incorporated into some pre-employment contracts a few magazines sent to their contributors last year.

Editors for the most part found little need for the contracts once they found out what they meant. While some continue to offer them for signature, in most cases refusal to sign has had no effect on whether or not an author, photographer or illustrator received an assignment.

There are two reasons for this. Historically magazine publishers have bargained for the lowest possible rates in return for acquiring very limited rights, commonly one time reproduction rights. They are still unwilling to pay the much higher fees that go along with purchase of extensive, or "all," rights.

Second, serious legal questions have been raised concerning the validity of "blanket" pre-employment contracts for independent contractors, both on the grounds of the intent of Congress, and, interestingly, on anti-trust grounds.

To Know More. Space does not permit a full discussion of the copyright laws here. The Copyright Office has available its excellent *A General Guide to the Copyright Act of 1976* for the price of a stamp or phone call. You can also get copies of the law, as many of the commentaries as you can stomach, registration forms and instructions, and additional information on the formalities.

The address is: The Copyright Office
Library of Congress
Washington, DC 20559

The telephone number is 202/287-8700. They have added a 24 hour "hot line" to order registration forms: 202/287-9100.

The Copyright Office under Barbara Ringer[3] has the reputation of being efficient and responsive — a rarity among federal bureaucracies. If you call, you'll find the phone answered by an informed and helpful person who can either provide the information you seek or direct you to someone who can.

[1] The one exception is that work submitted to a periodical (magazine or newspaper) may be used in that publication without written license — but also without alteration, abridgement, cropping, etc.
[2] Marlene D. Morrisey, Special Assistant to the Register of Copyrights, in a 3M Co. supplement to Business Week.
[3] Barbara Ringer left the Copyright Office to write the definitive book on the new copyright law, and to practice law privately. The new Register is David Ladd.

VI: TECHNOLOGICAL ISSUES

Papers 45 Through 51: Commentary

Advances in technology that affect communications, hence copyright, are touched on in virtually every section of this book. Indeed, technological change is coming so fast that Congress finds it difficult to keep the Copyright Statute abreast of it, much less broad enough to anticipate it. This has happened in the past, but the media are no longer jukeboxes and player-piano rolls.

In this section, we include a number of copyright issues and studies in which specific technologies are the dominant factors.

CONTU

In 1974—two years before the passage of the present Copyright Statute—Congress passed a separate act creating a temporary National Commission on New Technological Uses of Copyrighted Works, known later as CONTU. Its creation had been pending for several years, during most of which time it was part of the omnibus copyright-revision bills. However, when enactment of the pending omnibus bill became unlikely in 1974, it was then decided to press ahead at long last with studies of the impact of technology even if they would not be completed in time to affect the pending copyright bill.

Robert W. Frase, who wrote part of CONTU's final report, has summarized the Commission's work and conclusions (including listing its meeting transcripts and studies) in a section from the *Encyclopedia of Library and Information Science* (Paper 45). Some of CONTU's work still has meaning, but *tempus fugit.* The passage of time and the technological ingenuity of man have created new problems and unraveled some of the previous solutions.

COMPUTER PROGRAMS

The use of computers and computer technology lies at the heart of this age of information, but protection for proprietary rights in these areas has not been easy to come by. The *hardware* can be protected by patents, but the *software*—programs to make the computers perform their magic—has been deemed protectable largely through copyrighting and/or as trade secrets. *Firmware*—computer programs combined with a medium, such as semiconductor computer chips—is covered in the early portion of Part VII.

Madeline M. Henderson has admirably condensed the basic information in "Protecting Computer Programs," an article from her *ASIS Bulletin* series (Paper 46). To condense it further here seems futile.

Because computer programs are not simply normal, eye-readable literary works, some of the requirements for depositing copies in the Copyright Office seem complex and "uncomfortable." The present requirements are set forth in Copyright Office Circular R61, which is reproduced in this book as Paper 47. The Copyright Office continues to listen to concerned groups regarding problems in this area.

Because the protection of computer programs is so important to the modern scene, we have also included here the copyright-related and background portions of Alan C. Rose's law-journal review, "Protection of Intellectual Property Rights in Computers and Computer Programs" (Paper 48). We particularly also urge readers to refer to Joseph Taphorn's 1979 paper, "New Developments in Copyright Protection of Computer Programs," along with others listed in the Bibliography.

CABLE TV

Arriving at equitable solutions to the proprietary problems involved in cable-TV-company pickup and carrying of off-the-air telecasts from local and remote TV stations delayed the passage of the present Copyright Statute for several years. Compulsory licensing with fees set by a Copyright Royalty Tribunal had to be incorporated in the Statute, but arguments continue. These have been thoroughly covered in Paper 49 by Dale N. Hatfield and Robert Alan Garrett.

OPTICAL/VIDEO DISCS

Micro methods/media for compacting large amounts of information and/or data for local lookup or copying, or—more recently—for online call-up and printout from remote locations, have long received much attention. Microforms—roll microfilm and sheet microfiche—continue to find commercial use, both in libraries and in semi-automated offices. As with other media, microforms are subject to problems when proprietors' copyrights are not observed.

While microforms can also be used for compact storage of digital information as well as text pages and other graphics, interest has shifted lately to image and data compaction on a new medium, the videodisc, and a variant, the optical disk. In Paper 1 in this volume we reviewed some recent developments concerning them—the ill-fated ADONIS Project and the plans of the Library of Congress to use the discs for preservation of materials and access to current periodicals.

Here we include a 1983 brochure (Paper 50) in which the Library of Congress gave some of the details of its disc project. The Library is consulting carefully with other libraries, publishers, and information businesses during the evolution and conduct of this study. The technical success of the project seems assured, but the proprietary implications could be staggering—namely, possible creation of de facto standards and possible government competition in the marketing of discs or the making of their contents accessible online. Photocopying may pale by comparison. [Incidentally, in negotiating publisher permissions for the project, the Library of Congress found that few publishers had acquired the "display rights" to advertising and other material that it wanted for screen viewings; therefore, some publishers felt that they could not enter their publications in the pilot program.]

OTHER TECHNOLOGICAL ISSUES

As mentioned, there are many other technological areas in which copyright issues abound, and some of these are touched on in other sections of this volume. However, one other area seemed too intriguing not to mention, so we have included in this volume an excerpt on copyright aspects from a paper by Reid G. Adler, "Biotechnology As An Intellectual Property" (Paper 51).

BIBLIOGRAPHY

CONTU

Final Report of the National Commission on New Technological Uses of Technological Works, 1978, U.S. Congress, CONTU, Bethesda, MD., ERIC Document Reproduction Service, ED 160 122, 1979.

Computer Programs

Aufrichtig, P. R., 1982, Copyright Protection for Computer Programs in Read Only Memory Chips, *Hofstra Law Rev.* **11**:329-370.

Boorstyn, N., and Fleisher, M. C., 1981, Copyright, Computers, and Confusion, *Calif. State Bar J.* **56**(4):149-159.

Cavaliere, K. F., 1982, Protection of Proprietary Rights in Computer *Programs: A "Basic" Formula for Debugging the System, St. John's Law Rev.* **57**:92-126.

Chandler, J. P., 1982, Proprietary Protection of Computer Software, *Univ. Baltimore Law Rev.* **11**(2):195-255.

Davidson, D. M., 1983, Protecting Computer Software: A Comprehensive Analysis, *Jurimetrics J.* **23**:337-425.

Franz, C. R., Wilkins, S. J., and Bower, J. C., 1981, A Critical Review of Proprietary Software Protection, *Inf. Manage.* **4**(2):55-69.

Hewitt, S., 1983, Protection of Works Created by the Use of Computers, *New Law J.* **33**:235-237.

Keplinger, M. S., 1981, Computer Software—Its Nature and Its Protection, *Emory Law J.* **30**:483-512.

Lechter, M. A., 1983, Protecting Software and Firmware Developments, *Computer* **16**(8):73-81.

McCutcheon, W. H., 1982, Copyright Protection for Computer Firmware in the World Market, *Houston J. Internat. Law* **4**:203-212.

Raysman, R., and Brown, P., 1983, Author–Publisher Software Contract, *N.Y. Law J.* **189**(70):1.

Squires, J., 1976, Copyright and Compilations in the Computer Era: Old Wine in New Bottles, *Copr. Soc. U.S.A. Bull.* **24**:18-46.

Taphorn, J. B., 1979, New Developments in Copyright Protection of Computer Programs, *Commun. and the Law.* **1**(3):29-44.

Taphorn, J. B., 1981, Protecting and Marketing Computer Programs, *A Practical Approach to Patents, Trademarks, and Copyrights* **2**(3): 179-187.

Ulmer, E., and Kille, G., 1983, Copyright Protection of Computer Programs, *Internat. Rev. Ind. Prop. and Copy. Law* **14**(2):159-189.

Warrick, T. S., 1984, Legal Aspects of Purchasing Microcompter Software, *Am. Soc. Inf. Sci. Bull.* **10**(6):9-12.

Cable TV

Berg, M., and Jacobs, S., 1984, Cable and Copyright Issues, *Broadcasting and Government Report: A Status Report,* National Association of Broadcasters, Washington, DC, pp. 360-408.

The Case Against Compulsory License, 1981, *Broadcasting* **101**:67.

Ladd, D., Schrader, D. M., Leibowitz, D. E., and Older, H. L., 1981, Copyright, Cable, the Compulsory License: A Second Chance, *Commun. and the Law* **3**(3):3-76.

Optical/Video Discs

Walter, G., 1983, The Optical Disc and Office Information Systems, *The Office* **98**(3):86, 88.

Other Technological Issues

Fantel, H., 1985, The Big-Dish Satellite Antenna Is Becoming a Best Seller, *The New York Times* **134**(46,372):H-26.

Hasper, D., 1982, Receive-Only Satellite Earth Stations and Piracy of the Airwaves, *Notre Dame Law Rev.* **58**:84-100.

Kayron, I., 1982, Copyright in Living Genetically-Engineered Works, *George Washington Law Rev.* **50**(2):191-219.

45: NATIONAL COMMISSION ON NEW TECHNOLOGICAL USES OF COPYRIGHTED WORKS (CONTU)*

Robert W. Frase

The temporary National Commission on New Technological Uses of Copyrighted Works (CONTU) was created by Congress as part of the effort to revise comprehensively the copyright laws of the United States. (This revision became PL 94-553 [1976], now codified as 17 USC Sec. 101 et seq.) Early in the congressional hearings on copyright law revision it became apparent that the use of the new technologies of photocopying and computers had effects on the authorship, distribution, and use of copyrighted works, and raised problems that were not dealt with by the pending revision bill. Because of the complexity of these problems, CONTU was created to provide the president and Congress with recommendations concerning those changes in copyright law or procedure needed both to assure public access to copyrighted works used in conjunction with computer and machine duplication systems and to respect the rights of owners of copyrights in such works, while considering the concerns of the general public and the consumer.

The act which created CONTU, approved on December 31, 1974, as Public Law 93-573, gave the commission 3 years to study and compile data and make recommendations on legislation or procedures concerning:

1. The reproduction and use of copyrighted works of authorship:
   a. in conjunction with automatic systems capable of storing, processing, retrieving, and transferring information.
   b. by various forms of machine reproduction, not including reproduction by or at the request of instructors for use in face-to-face teaching activities.
2. The creation of new works by the application or intervention of such automatic systems as machine reproduction.

*A large part of this article is taken from the *Final Report of the National Commission on New Technological Uses of Copyrighted Works*, dated July 31, 1978, and published by the Library of Congress in 1979 (U.S. Government Printing Office, Superintendent of Documents, Washington, D.C. 20402, Stock No. 030-022-00143-8). The author of this article wrote a considerable part of the *Final Report*.

On July 25, 1975, seven months after the bill was enacted, President Ford announced appointment of the following commissioners, according to the criteria set out in the legislation:

1. From authors and other copyright owners:
   John Hersey, president of the Authors League of America, Inc.
   Dan Lacy, senior vice-president, McGraw-Hill, Inc.
   E. Gabriel Perle, vice-president—law, Time, Inc.
   Hershel B. Sarbin, president, Ziff-Davis Publishing Company
2. From copyright users:
   William S. Dix, librarian emeritus, Princeton University (deceased February 22, 1978)
   Arthur R. Miller, professor of law, Harvard Law School
   Robert Wedgeworth, executive director, American Library Association
   Alice E. Wilcox, director, Minnesota Interlibrary Telecommunications Exchange
3. From the public:
   George D. Cary, retired register of copyrights
   Stanley H. Fuld, retired chief judge of the State of New York and the New York Court of Appeals
   Rhoda H. Karpatkin, executive director, Consumers Union
   Melville B. Nimmer, professor of law, University of California at Los Angeles Law School

The librarian of Congress and the register of copyrights were designated ex officio members of the commission; of these two, only the librarian had a vote in commission matters. Stanley H. Fuld and Melville B. Nimmer were designated chairman and vice-chairman of the commission, respectively.

At its initial meeting on October 8, 1975, the commission appointed Arthur J. Levine as executive director and authorized recruitment of a staff. The senior staff members subsequently appointed were Robert W. Frase, assistant executive director and economist; and Michael S. Keplinger, assistant executive director and senior attorney. The final meeting of the commission was held on July 31, 1978, and the commission was then dissolved.

The accomplishments of the commission fall into three categories:

1. Recommendations to the president and the Congress for legislation, and recommendations as to actions to be taken by government agencies and nongovernmental organizations
2. The development of the so-called CONTU Guidelines on Photocopying
3. The information collected in commissioned studies and in public hearings, much of which is summarized and analyzed in the *Final Report*

Recommendations of the Commission

COMPUTER LEGISLATION

Computer Programs

The new copyright law should be amended: (*a*) to make it explicit that computer programs, to the extent that they embody an author's original creation, are proper subject matter of copyright; (*b*) to apply to all computer uses of copyrighted programs, by the deletion of the present Section 117; and (*c*) to ensure that rightful possessors of copies of computer programs may use or adapt these copies for their use. (A bill, HR 6934, to carry out this recommendation was introduced on March 26, 1980, by Representative Robert W. Kastenmeier, chairman of the Subcommittee on Courts, Civil Liberties, and the Administration of Justice, Committee on the Judiciary, United States House of Representatives.)

Commissioner Hersey dissented as follows: The act of 1976 should be amended to make it explicit that copyright protection does not extend to a computer program in the form in which it is capable of being used to control computer operations.

Data Bases

The act of 1976 should be amended to apply to all computer uses of copyrighted data bases and other copyrighted works fixed in computer-sensible media, by the deletion of its present Section 117.

New Works

Works created by the use of computers should be afforded copyright protection if they are original works of authorship within the act of 1976. Consequently, no amendment is needed.

Computer Regulations

The register of copyrights should adopt appropriate regulations regarding the affixation of notice to and the registration and deposit of works of authorship used in conjunction with computers.

Congressional Action Concerning Computers

Any legislation enacted as a result of these recommendations should be subject to a periodic review to determine its adequacy in the light of continuing technological change. This review should especially consider the impact of such legislation on competition and consumer prices in the computer and information industries, and the effect on cultural values of including computer programs within the ambit of copyright.

PHOTOCOPYING LEGISLATION

The act of 1976 should be amended at this time only to provide specific guidance for situations in which photocopying is done by commercial organizations on demand and for profit.

Copyright Office and Photocopying

In conducting the 5-year review of photocopying practices required by Section 108(i) of the act of 1976, the register of copyrights should begin immediately to plan and implement a study of the overall impact of all photo duplication practices on both proprietors' rights and the public's access to published information.

Government and Nongovernment Agencies and Photocopying

Publishers, libraries, and government agencies should cooperate in making information about the copyright status of all published works, both current and older publications, more readily available to the public.

The CONTU Guidelines on Photocopying under Interlibrary Loan Arrangements

The CONTU Guidelines were developed to assist librarians and copyright proprietors in understanding the amount of photocopying for use in interlibrary loan arrangements permitted under the copyright law. In the spring of 1976 there was realistic expectation that a new copyright law, under consideration for nearly 20 years, would be enacted during that session of Congress. It had become apparent that the House subcommittee was giving serious consideration to modifying the language concerning "systematic reproduction" by libraries in Section 108(g)(2) of the Senate-passed bill to permit photocopying under interlibrary arrangements, unless such arrangements resulted in the borrowing libraries obtaining "such aggregate quantities as to substitute for a subscription to or purchase of" copyrighted works (94th Congress, 2nd Session, 1975, Senate Report 22).

At its meeting on April 2, 1976, the commission discussed this proposed amendment to the Senate bill. The commission felt that it might aid the House and Senate subcommittees by offering its good offices in bringing the principal parties together to see whether agreement could be reached on a definition of "such aggregate quantities." This offer was accepted by the House and Senate subcommittees and the interested parties, and much of the summer of 1976 was spent by the commission in working with the parties to secure agreements on "guidelines" interpreting what was to become the proviso in Section 108(g)(2) relating to "systematic reproduction" by libraries. The pertinent parts of that section follow, with the proviso added by the House emphasized:

> (g) The rights of reproduction and distribution under this section extend to the isolated and unrelated reproduction or distribution of a single copy or phonorecord of the same material on separate occasions, but do not extend to cases where the library or archives, or its employee . . .
>
> (2) engages in the systematic reproduction or distribution of single or multiple copies or phonorecords of material described in subsection (d): *Provided, That nothing in this clause prevents a library or archives from participating in inter-library arrangements that do not have, as their purpose or effect, that the library or archives receiving such copies or phonorecords for distribution does so in such aggregate quantities as to substitute for a subscription to or purchase of such work* (PL 94-553 [1976]).

Before enactment of the new copyright law, the principal library, publisher, and author organizations agreed to the following detailed guidelines defining what "aggregate quantities" would constitute the "systematic reproduction" that would exceed the statutory limitations on a library's photocopying activities.

Photocopying—Interlibrary Arrangements

Introduction

Subsection 108(g)(2) of the bill deals, among other things, with limits on interlibrary arrangements for photocopying. It prohibits systematic photocopying of copyrighted materials but permits interlibrary arrangements "that do not have, as their purpose or effect, that the library or archives receiving such copies or phonorecords for distribution does so in such aggregate quantities as to substitute for a subscription to or purchase of such work."

The National Commission on New Technological Uses of Copyrighted Works offered its good offices to the House and Senate subcommittees in bringing the interested parties together to see if agreement could be reached on what a realistic definition would be of "such aggregate quantities." The Commission consulted with the parties and suggested the interpretation which follows, on which there has been substantial agreement by the principal library, publisher, and author organizations. The Commission considers the guidelines which follow to be a workable and fair interpretation of the intent of the proviso portion of subsection 108(g)(2).

These guidelines are intended to provide guidance in the application of section 108 to the most frequently encountered interlibrary case: a library's obtaining from another library, in lieu of interlibrary loan, copies of articles from relatively recent issues of periodicals—those published within five years prior to the date of the request. The guidelines do not specify what aggregate quantity of copies of an article or articles published in a periodical, the issue date of which is more than five years prior to the date when the request for the copy thereof is made, constitutes a substitute for a subscription to such periodical. The meaning of the proviso to subsection 108(g)(2) in such case is left to future interpretation.

The point has been made that the present practice on interlibrary loans and use of photocopies in lieu of loans may be supplemented or even largely replaced by a system in which one or more agencies or institutions, public or private, exist for the specific purpose of providing a central source for photocopies. Of course, these guidelines would not apply to such a situation.

Guidelines for the Proviso of Subsection 108(g)(2)

1. As used in the proviso of subsection 108(g)(2), the words "... such aggregate quantities as to substitute for a subscription to or purchase of such work" shall mean:

(a) with respect to any given periodical (as opposed to any given issue of a periodical), filled requests of a library or archives (a "requesting entity") within any calendar year for a total of six or more copies of an article or articles published in such periodical within five years prior to the date of the request. These guidelines specifically shall not apply, directly or indirectly, to any request of a requesting entity for a copy or copies of an article or articles published in any issue of a periodical, the publication date of which is more than five years prior to the date when the request is made. These guidelines do not define the meaning, with respect to such a request, of " ... such aggregate quantities as to substitute for a subscription to such periodical."

(b) With respect to any other material described in subsection 108(d), (including fiction and poetry), filled requests of a requesting entity within any calendar year for a total of six or more copies or phonorecords of or from any given work (including a collective work) during the entire period when such material shall be protected by copyright.

2. In the event that a requesting entity:

(a) shall have in force or shall have entered an order for a subscription to a periodical, or

(b) has within its collection, or shall have entered an order for, a copy or phonorecord of any other copyrighted work, material from either category of which it desires to obtain by copy from another library or archives (the "supplying entity"), because the material to be copied is not reasonably available for use by the requesting entity itself, then the fulfillment of such request shall be treated as though the requesting entity made such copy from its own collection. A library or archives may request a copy or phonorecord from a supplying entity only under those circumstances where the requesting entity would have been able, under the other provisions of section 108, to supply such copy from materials in its own collection.

3. No request for a copy or phonorecord of any material to which these guidelines apply may be fulfilled by the supplying entity unless such request is accompanied by a representation by the requesting entity that the request was made in conformity with these guidelines.

4. The requesting entity shall maintain records of all requests made by it for copies or phonorecords of any materials to which these guidelines apply and shall maintain records of the fulfillment of such requests, which records shall be retained until the end of the third complete calendar year after the end of the calendar year in which the respective request shall have been made.

5. As part of the review provided for in subsection 108(i), these guidelines shall be reviewed not later than five years from the effective date of this bill.

These guidelines were accepted by the conference committee and were incorporated into its report on the new act (94th Congress, 2nd Session, House Report 1733, pp. 72–73).

The guidelines specifically left the status of periodical articles more than 5 years old to future determination. Moreover, institutions set up for the specific purpose of supplying photocopies of copyrighted material were excluded from coverage by the guidelines.

Commission Hearings and Studies

In the course of its existence the commission held 23 meetings, most of which consisted of public hearings at which witnesses were heard. For the first five meetings, only summaries exist. For the remaining meetings, full transcripts were prepared. The summaries and transcripts for all commission meetings were deposited with the National Technical Information Service (NTIS) of the U.S. Department of Commerce. They are listed in the Bibliography with the NTIS order numbers.

The commission let contracts with outside organizations for six studies. These studies were also deposited with NTIS, and they are listed with order numbers in the Bibliography.

BIBLIOGRAPHY

Final Report of the National Commission on New Technological Uses of Copyrighted Works, U.S. Government Printing Office, Superintendent of Documents, Washington, D.C., 1979.

Commission Meetings

Meetings 1 through 5, 1975, PB 253 757.
Summaries of the first five meetings of CONTU, held on October 17, November 19, and December 18–19, 1975, and February 11–13 and April 1–2, 1976. The first meeting was organizational; the second concerned photocopying, computers and data bases, and related topics; the third, computers, the Aus-

tralian copyright case, and the economics of the publishing industry; the fourth, information systems, the operations of the National Library of Medicine, and the economics of computerized information storage and retrieval systems; and the fifth, presentations by the Information Industry Association and the New York Times Information Bank, and the results of a study on future alternatives to present-day scientific and technical journals.

Transcript, CONTU Meeting No. 6, May 6–7, 1976, Arlington, Virginia, PB 254 765.
The major subject of the meeting was protection of computer software.

Transcript, CONTU Meeting No. 7, June 9–10, 1976, Arlington, Virginia, PB 254 766.
Verbatim transcript of hearings on protection of computer software and a discussion of photocopying guidelines.

Transcript, CONTU Meeting No. 8, September 16–17, 1976, Los Angeles, California, PB 259 749.
The meeting addressed copyright protection for data bases.

Transcript, CONTU Meeting No. 9, October 21–22, 1976, Arlington, Virginia, PB 261 947.
Transcript of hearings on photocopying, interlibrary loans, and library practices.

Transcript, CONTU Meeting No. 10, November 18–19, 1976, New York City, PB 261 946.
Testimony on the copyrightability of computer software was presented.

Transcript, CONTU Meeting No. 11, January 13–14, 1977, Arlington, Virginia, PB 263 160.
The commission heard testimony on library practices and other aspects of photocopying at the National Agricultural Library and Exxon, the technological capabilities of copying equipment, and a NTIS proposal for supplying authorized photocopies of journal articles. Other witnesses testifying on photocopying were representatives of the Association of American Publishers, the Information Industry Association, and the Authors League of America, Inc.

Transcript, CONTU Meeting No. 12, February 24–25, 1977, New York City, PB 265 765.
Matters under consideration were copyright protection for computer software and automated data bases, and possible approaches to check unauthorized photocopying of copyrighted materials. No testimony was presented at this meeting.

Transcript, CONTU Meeting No. 13, March 31 and April 1, 1977, New York City, PB 266 277.
Testimony included the following subjects: proposal for a copy payment center; the publishing and reprint sales activities of the American Institute of Physics; the sampling, licensing, and payment system of the American Society of Composers, Authors, and Publishers; the licensing, sampling, and payment system of Broadcast Music, Inc.; the problems of newsletter publishers vis-à-vis unauthorized photocopying; and an analysis of computer and photocopying issues from the point of view of the general public.

Transcript, CONTU Meeting No. 14, May 5, 1977, Arlington, Virginia, PB 267 332.
The commission discussed the CONTU subcommittee reports on copyright protection for computer software and automated data bases, made recommendations for amendments to the reports, and agreed to circulate them with dissenting and concurring opinions. The Photocopy Subcommittee discussed a request for additional guidelines to interpret further terms in Section 108 of the Copyright Act, and the commission agreed to offer its good offices to this end.

Transcript, CONTU Meeting No. 15, July 11–12, 1977, Washington, D.C., PB 271 326.
Testimony included the following subjects: the economics of property rights as applied to computer software and data bases; the economics of property rights; an analysis of computer and photocopying copyright issues from the point of view of the general public and ultimate consumer; a survey of publisher practices and present attitudes on authorized journal article copying and licensing; the costs of owning, borrowing, and disposing of periodical publications; and testimony on copyright for computer software and data bases.

Transcript, CONTU Meeting No. 16, September 15–16, 1977, Chicago, Illinois, PB 273 594.
Testimony on the commission subcommittee reports on computer software and data bases with additional comments was presented by the representatives of the computer industry. The commission also heard a report on a study on library photocopying in the United States and its implications for the development of a copyright royalty payment mechanism, and a description of the licensed photocopying activities of University Microfilms.

Transcript, CONTU Meeting No. 17, October 21, 1977, Washington, D.C., PB 275 786.
Testimony on photocopying was presented.

Transcript, CONTU Meeting No. 18, November 17–18, 1977, Cambridge, Massachusetts, PB 278 329.
The first day was a round-table discussion on the technologies which affect the present and future development of the collection, retention, organization, and delivery of information. On the second day, a study sponsored by CONTU, "Legal Protection of Computer Software: An Industrial Survey," was summarized.

Transcript, CONTU Meeting No. 19, January 12–13, 1978, Los Angeles, California, PB 280 052.
A witness testified on copyright protection for computer software; the commissioners heard summaries of current progress on subcommittee reports from members of the staff.

Transcript, CONTU Meeting No. 20, February 16–17, 1978, New York City, PB 283 876.
Witnesses spoke on copyright protection for computer software and the first 6 weeks of operation of the Copyright Clearance Center. The commission also adopted the report of the Data Base Subcommittee, discussed the report of the Software Subcommittee, and discussed a draft report of the Photocopy Subcommittee.

Transcript, CONTU Meeting No. 21, April 20–21, 1978, Washington, D.C., PB 281 710.
The witnesses presented testimony on the draft report of the Photocopy Subcommittee. The commission also discussed the reports of the New Works and Software Subcommittees. The majority of the commissioners voted to accept the report of the Software Subcommittee.

Transcript, CONTU Meeting No. 22, May 8, 1978, New York City.
This meeting transcript, dealing only with procedural matters concerning the printing of the final report, was also deposited with NTIS.

Transcript, CONTU Final Meeting, July 10, 1978, Washington, D.C., PB 284 178.
At this meeting, the commissioners discussed the final report, with the concurring and dissenting opinions, and voted unanimously to submit the report to the president and Congress. The commissioners also voted to have the final report printed for public distribution.

Commission-Sponsored Studies

An Analysis of Computer and Photocopying Issues from the Point of View of the General Public and the Ultimate Consumer, by Marc Breslow, Allen R. Ferguson, and Larry Haverkamp, Prepared under a CONTU contract with the Public Interest Economics Center, PB 283 416.

Costs of Owning, Borrowing, and Disposing of Periodical Publications, by Vernon E. Palmour, Marcia C. Bellassai, and Robert R. V. Wiederkehr, Prepared under a CONTU contract with the Public Research Institute, Center for Naval Analyses, PB 274 821.

Economics of Property Rights as Applied to Computer Software and Data Bases, by Yale M. Braunstein, Dietrich M. Fischer, Janusz A. Ordover, and William J. Baumol, Prepared under a CONTU contract with the New York University Economics Department, PB 268 787.

Legal Protection of Computer Software—An Industrial Survey, by Richard I. Miller, Clarence O'N. Brown, Francis J. Kelley, Deborah C. Notman, and Michael A. Walker, Prepared under a CONTU contract with Harbridge House, Inc., PB 283 876.

Library Photocopying in the United States, with Implications for the Development of a Royalty Payment Mechanism, by Donald W. King et al., Prepared under a CONTU contract with King Research Inc., PB 278 300. (Also available from the Superintendent of Documents, Government Printing Office, Stock No. 052-003-00443-7.)

Survey of Publisher Practices and Current Attitudes on Authorized Journal Article Copying and Licensing, by Bernard M. Fry, Herbert S. White, and Elizabeth L. Johnson, Prepared under a CONTU contract with the Research Center for Library and Information Science, Graduate Library School, Indiana University at Bloomington, PB 271 003.

46: PROTECTING COMPUTER PROGRAMS

Madeline M. Henderson

I recently asked a colleague, Jan Jancin, an attorney, to summarize the current status of protection for computer software. You may remember that the topic has been discussed in earlier "Copyright" columns in the *Bulletin* (August 1978, p. 27 and December 1979, p. 39) and in a news item in the February 1981 issue, p.5. Here is what Jan described:

Computer software can be an umbrella-type term to include machine-readable computer programs and human-readable documentation. Programs come in different languages and are available at different levels: a high-level language program is referred to as being in *source code* which is reducible to a machine-level *object code* by a compiler.

When the Copyright Office decided in 1964 to register its first computer program (deposited in source language in machine-readable form, with deposit of human-readable form required as well), it did so under the "Rule of Doubt" principle—i.e., since the office was uncertain as to whether the program's literary expression was copyrightable under the then applicable 1909 Copyright Act, the office gave the benefit of the doubt to the program proprietor with the note of caution that a court might later issue a verdict against the copyrightability of computer programs.

With the appearance of the new Copyright Act of 1976, it was generally agreed that the new law did encompass the copyrightability of computer programs even though the term per se did not appear anywhere in the act. To correct this, and following CONTU's studies in the topic area, Congress in 1980 enacted an amendment to the act which, among other things, provided a statutory definition for computer program as "a set of statements or instructions to be used directly or indirectly in a computer to bring about a certain result."

At the present time there is additional legislative effort to clarify as well as provide more protection for software, e.g., H.R. 6983, an amendment to the Copyright Law introduced in the 97th Congress by Rep. Kastenmeier, would revise definitions in the act to include "program descriptions" and other elements as expressly eligible for copyright protection, and would provide that confidential programs (and other materials) may receive "secure deposit" when registered. Kastenmeier is expected to reintroduce the legislation in the 98th Congress.

In addition, several computer program/copyright cases have been through the courts already and more are in the litigation process. e.g., the U.S. Court of Appeals for the Third Circuit ruled that a computer program's object code stored in the electronic memory of a video game is copyrightable. Such legal activity provides the "fine tuning" that eventually will afford a greater understanding about proprietary software rights under the copyright law.

As for patent law protection, the Patent Office early on took the position that computer programs were not patentable subject matter. An early Supreme Court decision seemed to verify this position. However, the complexity and growing importance of computer software, the tremendous financial investment in software, and the need for software innovators to protect such investment, helped to produce the situation which exists today, that computer program inventions may be patentable so long as certain patent law requirements are met. Further, questions were raised as to why hardware should be patentable and software not when problems could be solved equally well through hardware or software technologies. This is a complex area but the protection available under the patent law makes the possible rewards great.

Trade secret law is another means of protection: many computer programs are marketed today as confidential or trade secret packages. These are generally accompanied by contractual agreements between the software vendor and user specifying the rights and obligations of each party concerning the vendor's proprietary package. An interesting area of developing law is the notion of concurrent protection, as, for example, between copyright law and trade secret law.

These more important forms of intellectual property rights protection are in dynamic and important areas, affecting each and every one of us more and more as the computer moves from industry to business and into the home and almost every aspect of personal use. There is a greater need today than ever before for each of us to acquire an understanding of the basic applicable provisions to the ways of protecting computer software.

Henderson is an information management consultant in Bethesda, Md.

47: COPYRIGHT REGISTRATION FOR COMPUTER PROGRAMS

U.S. Copyright Office

DEFINITION

"A 'computer program' is a set of statements or instructions to be used directly or indirectly in a computer in order to bring about a certain result."

WHAT TO SEND

- A Completed Form TX
- A $10.00 Non-refundable Filing Fee Payable to the Register of Copyrights
- One Copy of Identifying Material (See Below)

EXTENT OF COPYRIGHT PROTECTION

Copyright protection extends to the literary or textual expression contained in the computer program. Copyright protection is not available for ideas, program logic, algorithms, systems, methods, concepts, or layouts.

DESCRIBING BASIS OF CLAIM ON FORM TX

- Space 2. In the "Author of" space identify the copyrightable authorship in the computer program for which registration is sought; for example, AUTHOR OF "Text of computer program," "Text of user's manual and computer program text," etc. (Do not include in the claim any reference to design, physical form, or hardware.)
- Space 6. Complete this space only if the computer program contains a substantial amount of previously published, registered, or public domain material (for example, subroutines, modules, or textual material).

DEPOSIT REQUIREMENTS

For published or unpublished computer programs, one copy of identifying portions of the program, (first 25 and last 25 pages), reproduced in a form visually perceptible without the aid of a machine or device, either on paper or in micro-

form, together with the page or equivalent unit containing the copyright notice, if any.

The Copyright Office believes that the best representation of the authorship in a computer program is a listing of the program in source code.

Where the applicant is unable or unwilling to deposit a source code listing, registration will proceed under our RULE OF DOUBT policy upon receipt of written assurance from the applicant that the work as deposited in object code contains copyrightable authorship.

If a published user's manual (or other printed documentation) accompanies the computer program, deposit two copies of the user's manual along with one copy of the identifying portion of the program.

DEPOSIT REQUIREMENTS
Section 202.20(c) (vii), 37 C.F.R.

(vii) *Machine-readable works.* In cases where an unpublished literary work is fixed or a published literary work is published only in the form of machine-readable copies (such as magnetic tapes or disks, punched cards, or the like) from which the work cannot ordinarily be perceived except with the aid of a machine or device,[4] the deposit shall consist of:

(A) for published or unpublished computer programs, one copy of identifying portions of the program, reproduced in a form visually perceptible without the aid of a machine or device, either on paper or in microform. For these purposes, "identifying portions" shall mean either the first and last 25 pages or equivalent units of the program if reproduced on paper, or at least the first and last 25 pages or equivalent units of the program if reproduced in microform, together with the page or equivalent unit containing the copyright notice, if any.

[4.1] Works published in a form requiring the use of a machine or device for purposes of optical enlargement (such as film, filmstrips, slide films, and works published in any variety of microform) and works published in visually perceptible form but used in connection with optical scanning devices, are not within this category.

Reprinted from *Circular R61*, Library of Congress, Washington, D.C., 1983, 2p.

LOCATION OF COPYRIGHT NOTICE
Section 201.20(g), 37 C.F.R.

(g) WORKS REPRODUCED IN MACHINE-READABLE COPIES.

For works reproduced in machine-readable copies (such as magnetic tapes or disks, punched cards, or the like, from which the work cannot ordinarily be visually perceived except with the aid of a machine or device,[1] each of the following constitute examples of acceptable methods of affixation and position of notice:

(1) A notice embodied in the copies in machine-readable form in such a manner that on visually perceptible printouts it appears either with or near the title, or at the end of the work;

(2) A notice that is displayed at the user's terminal at sign on;

(3) A notice that is continuously on terminal display; or

(4) A legible notice reproduced durably, so as to withstand normal use, on a gummed or other label securely affixed to the copies or to a box, reel, cartridge, cassette, or other container used as a permanent receptacle for the copies.

FORM OF COPYRIGHT NOTICE

Form of Notice for Visually Perceptible Copies

The notice for visually perceptible copies should contain all of the following three elements:

1. *The symbol* © (the letter C in a circle), or the word "Copyright," or the abbreviation "Copr."

2. *The year of first publication* of the work. In the case of compilations of derivative works incorporating previously published material, the year date of first publication of the compilation or derivative work is sufficient.

3. *The name of the owner of copyright* in the work, or an abbreviation by which the name can be recognized, or a generally known alternative designation of the owner.

Example: © 1983 John Doe

FURTHER QUESTIONS:

If you have general information questions and wish to talk to an information specialist, call 202-287-8700.

TO ORDER FORMS:

Write to Information and Publications Section, LM-455, Copyright Office, Library of Congress, Washington, D.C. 20559 or call 202-287-9100, the Forms Hotline.

Please note that a copyright registration is effective on the date of receipt in the Copyright Office of all the required elements in acceptable form, regardless of the length of time it takes thereafter to process the application and mail the certificate of registration. The length of time required by the Copyright Office to process an application varies from time to time, depending on the amount of material received and the personnel available to handle it. It must also be kept in mind that it may take a number of days for mailed material to reach the Copyright Office and for the certificate of registration to reach the recipient after being mailed by the Copyright Office.

If you are filing an application for copyright registration in the Copyright Office, you will not receive an acknowledgement that your application has been received (the Office receives more than 500,000 applications annually), but you can expect:

- A letter or telephone call from a copyright examiner if further information is needed;
- A certificate of registration to indicate the work has been registered, or if the application cannot be accepted, a letter explaining why it has been rejected.

You may not receive either of these until 90 days have passed.

If you want to know when the Copyright Office received your material, you should send it via registered or certified mail and request a return receipt.

48: PROTECTION OF INTELLECTUAL PROPERTY RIGHTS IN COMPUTERS AND COMPUTER PROGRAMS: RECENT DEVELOPMENTS

Alan C. Rose*

The following article examines the protection offered to computers and computer programs, under the various applicable patent, copyright, and trade secret laws. Concerning patent protection, the author discusses the history and current status of the patent laws, and analyzes in detail the landmark case of Diamond v. Diehr. Discussed also is an analysis of copyright protection for computer programs, offered by the 1980 amendments to section 117 of the 1976 Copyright Act; which paved the way for the increased protection.

[*Editors' Note:* Material has been omitted at this point.]

---

* B.S. Dartmouth College and Massachusetts Institute of Technology, 1948; J.D. George Washington University, 1951. Member: State Bar of California; American Bar Association; American Patent Law Association. Mr. Rose is a recognized author in the Patent, Licensing, and Copyright fields. He is currently in private practice in Los Angeles, California.

III.   STATUTORY CHANGES TO THE 1976 COPYRIGHT ACT

In order to fully understand the meaning of the December 12, 1980 statutory changes to the 1976 Copyright Act, a brief detour into the history of computer software copyright is necessary. Protection for computer programs under the earlier 1909 Copyright Act was uncertain. The uncertainty stemmed in part from a landmark copyright decision of the United States Supreme Court, *White-Smith Music Publishing Co. v. Apollo Co.*[56] This decision involved a player piano roll having a pattern of openings[57] which caused a piano to play a certain musical composition. The decision held that the player piano roll did not infringe a copyright on the original sheet music for the composition on the basis that the music on the piano roller could not be "read" or was not "eye readable."[58] Apparently, *White-Smith* was adopted into the 1909 Copyright Act implicitly.[59] The repercussions from *White-Smith* were felt even as late as 1973 when the Supreme Court stated in *Goldstein v. California*[60] that copyrighting sheet music would not prohibit unauthorized recording of the original compositions under the applicable 1909 Federal Statute. Taken together, these two cases imply that since computer programs represent tangible expressions of intellectual labor, they are copyrightable, but copyrights on source programs will not prevent the unauthorized duplication of the programs on punched cards or magnetic tapes because such machine copies would not be deemed as "infringing copies" upon the source programs.[61]

Even though there was confusion under the 1909 Act as to what protection a copyrighted program would be given, the Register of

---

56. 209 U.S. 1 (1908).
57. The paper roll in a player piano is analogous to programs which have often been implemented by punched cards.
58. Justice Day held in *White-Smith* that a musical composition "is not susceptible of being copied until it has been put in a form which others can see and read since a copy is " 'a reproduction or duplication of a thing which comes so near to the original as to give every person seeing it the idea created by the original.' " 209 U.S. at 17. In a reluctant concurring opinion Justice Holmes stated: "On principle anything that mechanically reproduces that collocation of sounds ought to be made a copy, or, if the statute is to narrow, ought to be made so by a further act. . . ." *Id.* at 20.
59. *See* 1 NIMMER, NIMMER ON COPYRIGHT § 2.03[B][1] (1981).
60. 412 U.S. 546 (1973).
61. *See* Pope and Pope, *supra* note 14, at 546.

Copyrights declared that software would be accepted for deposit and registration.[62] The Copyright Office allowed registration of software even though copyrightability was doubtful because of the Office's policy of resolving doubtful issues in favor of registration whenever possible.[63]

The situation that existed under the 1909 Act as to whether programs were copyrightable subject matter and the scope of protection afforded by such copyrights became an issue because of the impending enactment of the 1976 Copyright Act. It had been hoped that the 1976 Copyright Act would resolve the difficulties surrounding the copyrighting of computer programs and the scope of protection thus afforded. However, due to a disagreement between the House and the Senate,[64] section 117 was included in the Act. Section 117 of the 1976 Copyright Act, effective January 1, 1978, codified prior law with respect to computer programs.[65] In effect, Congress declared a moratorium on further legislative action regarding copyright status of computer programs and maintained the status quo of protection that had been available under the 1909 Act until further notice.

During this time, a special commission, the National Commission on New Technological Uses of Copyright Works (CONTU), was created in 1974 under the auspices of the Library of Congress to study the problem of protecting computer programs.[66] The CONTU Report recommended that section 117 be replaced with two provisions. These provisions were ultimately adopted on December 12, 1980.[67] In order to see how the CONTU recommendations changed the previous section 117, and thus the protection of

---

62. *See* Cary, *Copyright Registration for Computer Programs*, 11 COPYRIGHT SOC'Y U.S.A. BULL. 361 (1964).

63. *Id.*

64. The House clearly indicated an intent to protect computer programs through copyright. H.R. REP. NO. 1476, 94th Cong., 2d Sess. 54, *reprinted in* [1976] U.S. CODE CONG. & AD. NEWS 5659, 5667. The intent of the Senate at the time of the passage of the 1976 Copyright Act was unclear. S. REP. NO. 473, 94th Cong., 1st Sess. 54 (1975).

65. Section 117 was first introduced in the Copyright Revision Bill of 1969. S. 543, 91st Cong., 1st Sess., 115 CONG. REC. 1382 (1969). Section 117 was agreed upon by interested parties as a means of permitting passage of the revision bill without committing Congress to a position on the computer issue until more study could be undertaken. H.R. REP. NO. 1476, 94th Cong., 2d Sess. 116, *reprinted in* [1976] U.S. CODE CONG. & AD. NEWS 5659, 5661.

66. Act of Dec. 31, 1974, Pub. L. No. 93-573, § 201, 88 Stat. 1873 (1974).

67. It is important to note that a lengthy and forceful dissent was filed by Commissioner Hersey. CONTU, FINAL REPORT OF THE NATIONAL COMMISSION ON NEW TECHNOLOGICAL USES OF COPYRIGHTED WORKS 10 (1979). For a good synopsis

computer programs, the exact wording of each section is of considerable interest and will be set forth here, with the original wording appearing first: 117. *Scope of exclusive rights: Use in Conjunction with Computers and Similar Information Systems*

> Notwithstanding the provisions of section 106 through 116 and 118, this title does not afford to the owner of copyright in a work any *greater* or *lesser* rights with respect to the use of the work in conjunction with automatic systems capable of storing, processing, retrieving, or transferring information, or in conjunction with any similar device, machine, or process, than those afforded to works under the law, whether Title 17 or the common law or statutes of the State, in effect on December 31, 1977, as held applicable and construed by a court in an action brought under this title.[68]

Now, the new statute, identified as H.R. 6933, and effective in December, 1980, included the following relative to Title 17:

> SEC. 12 (a)   Section 101 of Title 17 of the United States Code is amended to add at the end thereof the following new language:
>
> A "computer program" is a set of statements or instructions to be used directly or indirectly in a computer in order to bring about a certain result.
>
> (b)   Section 117 of Title 17 of the United States Code is amended to read as follows:
>
> 117.   *Limitations on exclusive rights: Computer programs*
>
> Notwithstanding the provisions of section 106, it is not an infringement for the owner of a copy of a computer program to make or authorize the making of another copy or adaptation of that computer program provided:
>
> (1)   that such a new copy or adaptation is created as an essential step in the utilization of the computer program in conjuction with a machine and that it is used in no other manner, or
>
> (2)   that such new copy or adaptation is for archival purposes only and that all archival copies are destroyed in the event that continued possession of the computer program should cease to be rightful.
>
> Any exact copies prepared in accordance with the provisions of this section may be leased, sold, or otherwise transferred, along with the copy from which such copies were prepared, only as part of the lease, sale, or other transfer of all rights in the program. Adaptations so prepared may be transferred only with the authorization of the copyright owner.[69]

It can be seen that the original section 117 has been rewritten. It no longer merely preserves the status quo for computer program rights as available under the pre-1978 law. The new section 117 deals with an entirely different subject: the right of an owner of a computer program to make a copy of a computer program, with certain restrictions, apparently to permit normal use and archival protection to the program.

Apart from the specific provisions of the new section 117, the effect of the substitution is to make one important change in the law, and raise questions about a second. First, computer pro-

---

of Commissioner Hersey's views see Comment, *Copyright Protection for Computer Programs*, 47 TENN. L. REV. 809 (1980).

68. 17 U.S.C. § 117 (1976) (amended by 17 U.S.C. § 117 (1980)) (emphasis added).

69. *Id*.

grams are now clearly recognized as copyrightable subject matter by Congress and are specifically included in the 1976 Copyright Act. Second, cancellation of the original Section 117 might, in view of section 301 of the 1976 Act, the preemption statute, be construed as abrogating trade secret and unfair competition causes of action.

Returning to the first point, it may be noted that even though the House felt that some programs could be copyrighted,[70] nowhere in the original 1976 Copyright Act were programs mentioned. The Copyright Office did not, however, find any difficulty in determining that the 1976 Act included programs as copyrightable subject matter.[71] But now, with the new changes in section 117, programs are specifically mentioned.[72]

One effect of the amendment was to unequivocally overrule the out-dated *White-Smith Publishing Co. v. Apollo Co*.[73] decision as to computer programs. As noted above, this is the famous case in which the U.S. Supreme Court held that a piano roll did not infringe a sheet music copyright, although both would produce the same "collocation of sounds."[74] The *White-Smith* decision was based on the out-dated notion that there should be a significant difference in the treatment of eye-readable and non eye-readable material; thus it is a significant step that this archaic concept in the computer program infringement area has finally been eliminated.[75]

---

70. H. REP. NO. 1476, 94th Cong., 2nd Sess. 54 (1976) specifically states that computer programs are appropriate matter for copyright "to the extent that they incorporate authorship in the programmer's expression of original ideas as distinguished from the ideas themselves." *Id*.

71. Marybeth Peters, Senior Attorney Advisor in the Copyright Office, has written in her General Guide to the Copyright Act of 1976:

> *Computer programs*. Although they are not mentioned as copyrightable subject matter in section 102(a) and they are not referred to explicitly in the definition of "literary works" in Section 101, a careful reading of the new law with the legislative report makes it clear that computer programs are "software" is within the subject matter of copyright. The definition of "literary works" refers to work expressed in "words, number, or other verbal or numerical symbols or indicia." Cited in Bigelow, Copyrighting Programs-1978, 3 COMPUTER L. SERVICE REP. 4-3, art. 4, at 3.

72. 17 U.S.C. §§ 101, 117 (1976).

73. 209 U.S. 1 (1908).

74. *Id*. at 20.

75. It may be noted that the language of 17 U.S.C. § 102(a) states: "Copyright protection subsists, in accordance with this title, in original works of authorship fixed in any tangible medium or expression, now known or later developed, from which they can be perceived reproduced, or otherwise communicated, either directly or with the aid of a machine or device. . . ." This language would seem to

With respect to the second question regarding the effect of the cancellation of the original section 117, it may be noted that trade secret and unfair competition causes of action had clearly been preserved under the original section. There has been some concern that these possible causes of action for computer program subject matter might no longer be available in view of section 301 of the 1976 Act, the preemption section of the new copyright law.[76] This preemption section reads as follows:

17 USC Section 301 Preemption with Respect to Other Laws

(a) On and after January 1, 1978, all legal or equitable rights that are equivalent to any of the exclusive rights within the general scope of copyright as specified by section 105 in works of authorship that are fixed in a tangible medium of expression and come within the subject matter of copyright as specified by section 102 and 103, whether created before or after that date and whether published or unpublished, are governed exclusively by this title. Thereafter, no person is entitled to any such right or equivalent right in any such work under the common law or statutes of the State.

The scope of the preemption section set forth above is somewhat indefinite,[77] and a number of persons expressed concern that repeal of the prior section 117 might mean that unfair competition and trade secret rights might now be lost. However, the legislative history involving the repeal of the original section 117 is explicitly contra, with counsel for the cognizant legislative committee and counsel for the Copyright Office both stating that state remedies, such as those involving trade secrets or unfair competition, were not being limited or preempted by the change.

The *Goldstein* case[78] included a lengthy discussion of federal preemption under the pre-1978 copyright law, and its holding is of interest because the federal copyright law had *not* preempted a California criminal statute relating to record piracy. The moderately narrow view relative to federal preemption in the copyright field, as enunciated in *Goldstein*, supports the position that trade

---

overrule *White-Smith* in general but, as mentioned, there is now no doubt *White-Smith* has no validity regarding noneye-readable computer programs. H.R. REP. No. 94-1476, 94th Cong., 2d Sess. 52 (1976) states: "it makes no difference what form, manner, or medium of fixation may be whether it is words, numbers, notes, sounds, pictures, or any other graphic or symbolic indicia, whether embodied in a physical object written, printed, photographed, sculptural, punched, magnetic, or any other stable form, and whether it is capable of perception directly or by means of any machine or device "now known or later developed." *See* 1 NIMMER, NIMMER ON COPYRIGHT § 2.03[B] (1981).

76. For a detailed discussion of the application and the history of the federal preemption doctrine see Goldstein v. California, 412 U.S. 546, 552-60 (1972).

77. The intent of Congress in enacting section 301 is set forth in HOUSE COMM. ON THE JUDICIARY, COPYRIGHT LAW REVISION H.R. REP. No., 94th Cong., 2d Sess. 129-33 (1976). *See also* Allied Artists Picture Corp. v. Rhode, 496 F. Supp. 408 (1980), for a good discussion of section 301.

78. 412 U.S. 546 (1973).

secret and unfair competition relief has not been preempted as a result of the new changes.

IV. TRADE SECRET PROTECTION

Trade secret protection will only be mentioned to the extent necessary to point out that as an alternative method of protection for computer programs, it has retained its strength and viability. First, it is noted that the continued validity of trade Secret protection was confirmed in the recent past by a rare unanimous decision of the U.S. Supreme Court in *Aronson v. Quick Point Pencil Co.*[79] It is further noted that the 1976 Copyright Act states that copyrights arise or subsist upon creation and reduction to tangible form.[80] Therefore, publication, which might destroy the trade secret, with notice, is not necessary to establish copyright protection.

It is noted in passing that the definition of "publication" under section 101 of the 1976 Act includes "distribution of copies . . . by rental, lease or lending."[81] It would appear possible, therefore, that the leasing of computer programs, even with suitable confidentiality provisions included in the lease, could be considered to constitute a "publication," which might destroy trade secret rights.

V. REGISTRATION OF COPYRIGHTS

Copyright protection is invoked by notice, but certain statutory benefits, including the right to bring suit, accrue from the filing or the registration of a copyright in the U.S. Copyright Office. In computer program situations, the Copyright Office has indicated that it prefers to register the underlying "source code" and the "object code" rather than only the latter.[82] In this connection, it is

---

79. 440 U.S. 257 (1978).
80. 17 U.S.C. § 102 (1976).
81. 17 U.S.C. § 101 (1976).
82. Source code is typically the first encoded form of a program. A short example of source code is:
RD-MASTER
  READ GL-MASTER-IN AT END GO TO EOJ-MAS COMP-COM.
IF CC-NUMBER LESS THAN GL-COM PERFORM
  RD-COMP-CTRL GO TO COMP-COM.
IF CC-GLP15 = 0 GO TO RD-MASTER
MOVE CC-MO-END DATE TO SLASHED DATE
MOVE CORRESPONDING SLASHED DATE TO WRK-DATE6.
MOVE R-WRK DATE TO GL-BALDT.

noted that in order to use most computer programs without change, one would only need the object code; however, the source code indicates how the program is built up, and it is necessary for easy modification of the program. It is understood that the Copyright Office will give limited registration to an object code even if the source code cannot be made available.

Also, as of the present writing, it is understood that the Copyright Office has no procedure for maintaining computer programs in secrecy while proceeding to register the programs. Accordingly, at such time as formal copyright registration of a program is sought, trade secret protection may no longer be available. In some cases, however, where the program is lengthy, only selected portions are required or requested for deposit in the Copyright Office.

VI.   RECENT VIDEO GAME COPYRIGHT DECISIONS

There have not been many decisions under the new copyright act, as it only came into force on January 1, 1978, and it normally takes more than two or three years for a federal case to be tried. However, a preliminary injunction was granted in a copyright case involving an "audiovisual display" for an electronic or video game called "Scramble," despite the fact the underlying computer program was not copyrighted.[83]

In two other more recent similar cases, however, the plaintiffs

---

Object code is machine-generated code. The source code is read by the computer and compiled into object code, which may actually be used by the computer. A simplified description of the difference between source code and object code is that source code is "general" while object code is "specifically adapted" to the particular computer using the program. An example of the object code form of the source code is:

```
58 10 C 0D0
18 21
D2 02 2 021 C 059
58 FO 1 030
05 EF
50 10 D 1F8
58 80 D 1F8
58 50 C 024

07 F5
58 10 C 04C

07 F1
D7 D3 E 6D40309
```

See Comment, *supra* note 5, at 180.

83. Only a videotape of the output was copyrighted and registered with the Copyright Office. Since the underlying program itself was not copyrighted, extending protection from the output display to cover the underlying program becomes problematic. The Judge reasoned that the output display was an audiovisual work, and the program was like the film with the computer a projector. Stern Elec. v. Kaufman, 669 F.2d 852 (2d Cir. 1982).

were less successful, with their video games being considered valid but not infringed. More specifically in *Atari Inc. v. Amusement World Inc.*,[84] the court found that defendant's "Meteor" game did not infringe plaintiff's "Asteroids" game. In the case of *Atari, Inc. v. North American Philips Consumer Electronics, Corp.*,[85] the district court refused to grant a preliminary injunction based on plaintiff's copyrighted "Pac-Man" maze-chase game, based on the judge's opinion that plaintiffs were unlikely to prevail on the infringement issue involving defendants' "K. C. Munchkin" maze-chase game.

VII. COPYRIGHT PROTECTION FOR COMPUTER MEMORY CHIPS

As mentioned above, many computers now include digital program information in semi-conductor chips. These are often in the form of Programmable Read-Only Memory chips, or PROMS.

The following questions naturally arise: First, are these programs protectable by the copyright laws? And, secondly, if copyright protection is available, how would the manufacture of the computer invoke protection? These questions were considered by the Seventh Circuit in *Data Cash Systems, Inc. v. J.S. & A. Group, Inc.*,[86] and more recently in *Tandy Corporation v. Personal Micro Computers, Inc.*[87] In *Data Cash*,[88] the district court decision included dicta to the effect that such chips would not be protectable by the copyright laws; nevertheless, the Seventh Circuit held that the chips would be subject to copyright protection. However, the absence of a proper copyright notice barred recovery. In the *Tandy* case, the defendant's motion for summary judgment based on the proposition that copying a semiconductor chip is not a "copy" of the underlying copyrighted program was denied.

---

84. [1981] COPYRIGHT L. REP. (CCH) ¶ 25,347.

85. No. 81 C 6434 (N.D. Ill., filed Dec. 4 1981), reversed on appeal, No. 81-2920 (7th Cir., filed Mar. 2, 1982).
The Court of Appeals for the Seventh Circuit reviewed the decision of the district court, and held that because the test for copyright infringement was based on visual comparison, they were in as good a position to review the similarity of the games. They concentrated upon the overall similarity of the characters in the two games, rather than their specific differences, and felt that a preliminary injunction against defendant's game was warranted. They were careful to note, however, that this decision would not affect the decision on the merits.

86. 628 F.2d 1038 (C.C.P.A. 1980).

87. 524 F. Supp. 171 (N.D. Cal., 1981).

88. 480 F. Supp. 1063 (N.D. Ill. 1979).

In view of these cases, it would appear desirable to include a proper copyright notice on electronic equipment including permanent or read-only memory chips. In this way, copyright remedies are preserved, and if infringement occurs, the copyright may be registered and the infringer sued.

VIII.   PROTECTION POSSIBILITIES

Various possibilities for protecting proprietary rights in computers and computer programs have been outlined above, and the possible effect of recent judicial and legislative changes has been analyzed. It is clear that further case law development will occur. However, certain practical steps to protect proprietary rights in software and firmware include the following:

(1)   Invoking TRADE SECRET protection with a suitable confidentiality legend, before widespread distribution occurs;

(2)   Putting a COPYRIGHT NOTICE on a program and mentioning "unpublished work" when both trade secret and copyright protection are being invoked;

(3)   Having PROPRIETARY NOTICES (trade secret and/or copyright) printed out at the same time as the computer program prints out or as the results of the program are printed out.

(4)   Putting COPYRIGHTED NOTICES on Read Only Memories or electronic equipment labels;[89]

(5)   Not calling program licenses "LEASES", since the lease of a computer program may be construed as a publication which could destroy trade secret protection; and

(6)   In the patent area, the claims should emphasize the structure and the physical aspects of the particular system or the method. Any mathematics should be characterized as being a small part of the system, and claims should be presented so as to not wholly preempt a mathematical algorith. If control can be accomplished by a cam and a mechanical linkage, a "hard-wired" electrical circuit, or other similar structure, these alternatives should be mentioned in the patent specification.

IX.   CONCLUSION

In summary, the recent decisions of the Supreme Court and the amendment of section 117 of the Copyright Act of 1976 both appear to favor the protection of intellectual property rights in computers and computer programs. In the patent field, at least some types of subject matter involving computer programs are patentable, while in the copyright field, computer programs may be copyrighted, and even a noneye-readable computer program may constitute a copyright infringement. Through the judicious use of trade secret, copyright, and patent protection, appropriate protection for both computers and computer programs may be secured.

89. 628 F.2d 1038 (1980).

49: A REEXAMINATION OF CABLE TELEVISION'S COMPULSORY LICENSING ROYALTY RATES: THE COPYRIGHT ROYALTY TRIBUNAL AND THE MARKETPLACE

Dale N. Hatfield*
Robert Alan Garrett**

I. *BACKGROUND AND SUMMARY*

The royalties paid to copyright owners for the use of their works typically are established in the marketplace. The producers of information and entertainment maintain exclusive control of their product and attempt to negotiate the best possible price for it in the competitive marketplace. In the particular case of cable's retransmission of copyrighted television programs, Congress departed from this tradition. The Copyright Revision Act of 1976 (Act) affords cable systems a compulsory license to retransmit whatever television programming is permitted under the rules of the Federal Communications Commission (FCC); that is, cable operators may carry such programming without having to negotiate with copyright owners.[1] The Act also prescribes the royalty pay-

---

* Mr. Hatfield is currently an independent consultant and instructor in telecommunications policy at the University of Colorado. He has served as Deputy Assistant Secretary of Commerce for Communications and Information, United States Department of Commerce; Associate Administrator for Policy Analysis and Development, National Telecommunications and Information Administration; Chief, Office of Plans and Policy of the Federal Communications Commission; and Deputy Chief, Office of Studies and Analysis, Office of Telecommunications Policy, Executive Office of the President.

** Mr. Garrett is a partner in the law firm of Arnold & Porter in Washington, D.C. He represented the copyright owners of sports telecasts in the Tribunal rate adjustment proceeding.

The authors are indebted to Steven J. Hoffman and Marcia Cranberg, associates with Arnold & Porter, for their assistance in the preparation of this article.

[1] 17 U.S.C. § 111(c).

ments that cable operators must make for the use of this programming.[2]

The statutory fee schedule is essentially immutable insofar as it concerns the payment for programming carried pursuant to the FCC rules in effect on April 15, 1976.[3] However, the Copyright Royalty Tribunal (Tribunal), an independent agency within the legislative branch,[4] is empowered to adjust the rates for programming carried as a result of changes in certain of these rules.[5]

In 1980 the FCC voted to repeal two sets of cable rules. The first had restricted the number of television signals which certain cable systems could import from distant markets (distant signals); the other had required the blacking out of certain syndicated programming on distant signals.[6] After conducting an extensive evidentiary proceeding, the Tribunal in the fall of 1982 increased the statutory rates by as much as 1500 percent for programming which cable systems carry as a result of FCC deregulation.[7]

The Tribunal concluded: "We do not find in the compulsory license, as it exists today, any public policy justification for establishing royalty rates below reasonable marketplace expectations of the copyright own-

---

[2] 17 U.S.C. § 111(d) (2). Although the compulsory license extends to all television programming that the FCC permits cable systems to carry, the Act imposes royalties only for the carriage of the nonnetwork programming on television stations which are carried beyond their local service areas. The royalties are collected by the Copyright Office and then distributed to the copyright owners of the retransmitted television programming by the Copyright Royalty Tribunal. *See generally* National Ass'n of Broadcasters v. Copyright Royalty Tribunal, 675 F.2d 367 (D.C. Cir. 1982); National Cable Television Ass'n. v. Copyright Royalty Tribunal, 689 F.2d 1077 (D.C. Cir. 1982).

[3] The only exception is that the Copyright Royalty Tribunal may make certain limited adjustments to account for inflation. *See* 17 U.S.C. § 801(b) (2) (A); National Cable Television Ass'n. v. Copyright Royalty Tribunal, 689 F.2d 1077 (D.C. Cir. 1982).

[4] 17 U.S.C. § 801(a). For a more comprehensive description of the Tribunal and its various responsibilities under the Act, *see* Korman & Koenigsberg, *The First Proceeding Before the Copyright Royalty Tribunal: ASCAP and the Public Broadcasters*, 1 COMM. & THE LAW 15 (1979).

[5] *See* 17 U.S.C. § § 801(b) (2) (B) and (C).

[6] *See* Malrite TV of New York v. FCC, 652 F.2d 1140 (2d Cir. 1981), *cert. denied*, 454 U.S. 1143 (1982).

[7] The Tribunal's decision is published at 47 Fed. Reg. 52146 (1982).

The Tribunal determined that a cable system must pay 3.75 percent of its gross receipts from basic services for each "distant signal equivalent" that it was not permitted to carry under the former FCC rules. (*See* 17 U.S.C. § 111(f) for the definition of "distant signal equivalent".) The Tribunal also imposed a surcharge of between 0.089 and 0.599 percent on each distant signal equivalent that had been subject to the FCC's former syndicated exclusivity rules. By way of comparison, the statutory rates range from 0.2 percent to 0.675 percent for each distant signal equivalent.

The new rates do not apply to any cable system which has less than $214,000 in semi-annual gross receipts from basic services. There are also a number of other factors which might exempt any particular system from having to pay the new rates.

ers."[8] Accordingly, the Tribunal set rates which, on the basis of the record before it, reflect the marketplace value of distant signal television programming. In making this determination, the Tribunal focused upon evidence of the prices actually charged for programming in marketplaces analogous to the hypothetical distant signal marketplace. This evidence, in the Tribunal's judgment, made it clear that the statutory rates "could not be considered those that would result from full marketplace conditions if the compulsory license did not exist."[9]

The Tribunal's decision is one of the most significant and controversial ever affecting the Congressionally mandated marriage of copyright owners and cable operators. Its significance extends well beyond the fact that it will require the cable industry to pay an estimated $20 million in additional royalties each year.[10] Copyright owners have hailed the decision as recognizing that: (1) they should receive marketplace compensation from the cable industry and should not be forced to subsidize cable by providing their copyrighted programming at below-market rates; and (2) the statutory rates fall well short of adequate marketplace compensation. The cable industry, on the other hand, has attacked the new rates as excessive, claiming that most cable operators will drop distant signals rather than pay the increased royalties; therefore, they argue, the effect of the Tribunal's decision will be to reimpose the very restrictions which the FCC had eliminated.[11]

The National Cable Television Association (NCTA) has appealed the Tribunal's rate increases to the United States Court of Appeals for the District of Columbia Circuit.[12] It also has mounted a lobbying campaign to secure Congressional reversal of the Tribunal's decision. Cable's efforts failed in the 97th Congress, although it did secure a short postponement of the effective date of the rates for distant signals added as a result of FCC deregulation.[13] The cable forces have returned to the

---

[8] 47 Fed. Reg. at 52153.

[9] *Id.* at 52154.

[10] *The Washington Post,* March 6, 1983, at K13.

[11] The number of trade journal and newspaper articles that have been written concerning the Tribunal's decision is legion. For one relatively comprehensive account of industry reaction, *see* "Cable Operators Scramble in Distant Signal Crisis," *CableAge,* Jan. 31, 1983.

[12] National Cable Television Ass'n. v. Copyright Royalty Tribunal, No. 82-2389 (D.C. Cir., filed November 19, 1982). The parties involved in this appeal include several individual cable system operators; the States of New York and Connecticut; the Motion Picture Association of America; the National Association of Broadcasters; individual broadcasters; the music performing rights societies; various "common carriers" which retransmit distant signals to cable operators; the National Basketball Association; the National Hockey League; the North American Soccer League; the National Collegiate Athletic Association; and Major League Baseball.

[13] The effective date of the 3.75 percent rate was extended from January 1, 1983 to March 15, 1983. No change was made in the effective date of the Tribunal's syndicated exclusivity rate adjustment. *See generally* Fitzpatrick & Sherman, "97th Congress Reconciles Few Copyright Debates," *Legal Times,* Feb. 7, 1983, at 21.

Earlier during the 97th Congress, the NCTA, the Motion Picture As-

98th Congress in the hopes of obtaining legislation which will nullify or severely restrict the Tribunal's actions.[14]

The cable industry has raised several questions concerning the Tribunal's increase in rates for additional distant signals. The central issues, however, are (1) whether the Tribunal has exceeded its statutory authority by establishing rates which seek to replicate a free marketplace and which are well above those originally set forth in the Copyright Revision Act; and (2) whether, as a matter of policy, the Tribunal should have established such rates. The purpose of this article is to provide a framework within which the foregoing issues can be evaluated. The article does so by focusing upon the genesis of the statutory rate schedule and the Tribunal's rate adjustment authority, and upon the technological, market, regulatory and other changes that have occurred since passage of the Act. The conclusions to be drawn are that the Tribunal acted within the broad discretion granted to it by Congress, and that the Tribunal's adoption of a marketplace standard is fully justified as a matter of policy. Indeed, Congress itself should reexamine the rates applicable to all programming carried by cable systems in the same manner as the Tribunal has done.

[*Editors' Notes:* Parts II and III, and footnote 140, have been omitted here.]

---

sociation of America, and the National Association of Broadcasters had negotiated a compromise on issues affecting the cable compulsory license. The bill which reflected this compromise, H.R. 5949, retained the compulsory license but imposed certain restrictions on cable similar to the FCC's former syndicated exclusivity rules and its current rules which require the carriage of local television stations. *See generally* COPYRIGHT/CABLE TELEVISION: HEARINGS BEFORE THE SUBCOMM. ON COURTS, CIVIL LIBERTIES, AND THE ADMINISTRATION OF JUSTICE OF THE HOUSE COMM. ON THE JUDICIARY, 97th Cong., 1st and 2d Sess. (1982). The bill passed the House but died in the Senate during the final days of the 97th Congress, when, among other things, the NCTA attempted to amend the bill to overturn the Tribunal's rate increase. *See generally Cable Copyright and Signal Carriage Act of 1982: Joint Hearings on H.R. 5949 Before the Senate Comm. on Commerce, Science and Transportation and the Senate Comm. on the Judiciary,* 97th Cong., 2d Sess. (1983) [hereinafter cited as "1982 Joint Hearings"].

[14] *See, e.g.,* H.R. 2902, 98th Cong., 1st Sess. (exempting the first three distant independent television signals from the new rates); S. 1270, 98th Cong., 1st Sess. (exempting satellite-delivered "superstation" WTBS-TV from the new rates).

IV. *CONCLUSION*

The United States has now moved into the Information Age. Over 50 percent of our nation's labor effort currently is involved in the collection, processing and dissemination of information.[141] In other words, information activities have now surpassed the production of industrial goods just as industrial production once surpassed agricultural production as a percentage of our Gross National Product. Because of the increasingly dominant role of information in our society, it becomes more important than ever that the originators of such information—the producers of programs and software—be compensated fully and fairly for their creativity.

It is in this larger context that the royalty rates in the 1976 Act should be examined. These rates reflected a balancing between objectives based on the conditions extant at that time. The situation today, however, is entirely different. The policy concerns that originally may have justified a royalty schedule tied solely to cable's ability and willingness to pay are no longer applicable. Moreover, there are now strong policy reasons supporting rates that approximate those which the copyright owners would reasonably charge in a free marketplace.

The Tribunal's determination to adopt rates which, in its judgment, reflect such marketplace considerations is entirely consistent with the broad discretion with which it was vested by Congress in the Copyright Revision Act of 1976. Perhaps even more important, the Tribunal's approach represents sound policy. If the compulsory license is to be retained, Congress itself should be guided by the same approach in amending the statutory rates which apply to the vast majority of distant signal programming retransmitted by cable and which were unaffected by the Tribunal's decision.

_____

[141] J. NAISBITT, MEGATRENDS: TEN NEW DIRECTIONS TRANSFORMING OUR LIVES, ch. 2 (1982).

50: OPTICAL DISK PILOT PROGRAM

The Library of Congress

The Library of Congress has the largest collection of stored knowledge in the world. A significant number of its 80 million items are in an advanced state of deterioration. Most of the printed materials added to the Library's collections every year are on acidic paper; the acid in this paper causes the fibers to become very weak in 25 to 100 years. To preserve items in the original, the Library is developing deacidification technologies and trying to purchase materials printed on alkaline paper.

To provide secondary format preservation and timely public access to high-use material, and fragile or rare materials, the Library has embarked on a pilot program in image preservation and retrieval using optical disk technology. The three-year Optical Disk Pilot Program will evaluate the use of optical disk technology for information preservation and mangement, and determine the costs and benefits of such technology when used in a production setting.

In contrast to microforms, optical disk technology affords extremely high-density storage of information. A one-sided 12-inch digital disk can store between 10,000 and 20,000 pages of text depending on the resolution required. One side of an analog disk can store up to 54,000 images. This technology represents a potentially efficient and economical way to store and retrieve images. Optical storage also avoids wear resulting from continuous disk usage, since only a beam of light touches the medium during playback. In addition, information on the digital optical disk can be transferred to a new disk without any loss if changes are detected in the original disk. It is thus valuable as a preservation format. Together, these strengths make the disk a potentially ideal medium for on-demand retrieval of high-use items.

The pilot program was stimulated in part by the Library's use of optical technology in the Cataloging Distribution Service, where the images of catalog cards are captured on an optical disk which can then be used to print exact reproductions on demand. This and suggestions from researchers at the forefront of the technology caused the Deputy Librarian of Congress to initiate several preliminary investigations and to appoint an Optical Disk Storage Technology Committee. This group, using information gleaned from manufacturers, defined equipment and disk specifications and solicited bids. Two contracts resulted: one with Integrated Automation (formerly Teknekron Controls, Inc.) to supply an experimental digital disk system, and the other with SONY Video Communications Products Co. to supply experimental videodiscs and commercial players.

Reprinted from *Optical Disk Pilot Program,* The Library of Congress, Washington, D.C., 1983, 4p.

The Optical Disk Pilot Program, then, has two aspects. Print materials will be stored on digital optical disks. Non-print or image-based materials will be stored on analog optical discs, or, as they are commonly known, videodiscs. These two aspects of the program are different in nature, but involve related technologies, described below.

PRINT MATERIALS

High-use current periodicals will be given initial emphasis in the digital disk project. Up to 500,000 images per year can be captured, including: materials provided by the Congressional Research Service under its Selective Dissemination of Information (SDI) service (consisting of articles and government documents on public affairs topics); journals in science, technology, and business; German, Brazilian, Japanese, Thai, French, and Hebraic periodicals; government documents such as the Budget of the United States and the Congressional Record; and United States Agriculture Decisions and Social Security Rulings from 1960 to 1975. Also included will be selected maps, atlases, microforms, manuscripts, and sheet music.

Document preparation will be an assembly line process involving keyboarding, scanning, and writing to optical disks. At the document preparation station, information relating to the printed library materials will be entered by keyboarding via computer terminals into the Library of Congress Information System (LOCIS) database with a document number corresponding to a Library retrieval number. Documents will then be sent to the input station where they will be scanned and digitized at 300 lines per inch resolution by a high-speed scanner. This digitized information will then be transferred, by a laser writing process, onto the surface of an optical disc. To assure the accuracy of the keyboarding and the precision of the scanning, the information will be written on magnetic disk before being transferred to optical disk.

Because of the high resolution of the digital process, the disk will contain substantially all of the information contained in the original item. As a result, the digitized image will be capable of serving as a black-and-white secondary preservation format for the original item, much as microforms are now used. The image will be stored on the disk in much greater detail than is now capable of being displayed in currently available high-resolution terminals.

To recall the information, the user will type in the appropriate identification. The Library's computer will tie the request to the image coded on the disk, and display the black-and-white image on the terminal screen. The user stations, to be located in several Library reading rooms, will have a high-resolution terminal for requests and display of full pages of text, along with a medium-speed printer for single-page printout for which there may be a charge. Off-line batch printing will be available from a central facility which may also require a fee.

IMAGE MATERIALS

The analog videodisc is the most promising medium for storing the Library's image materials since up to 54,000 separate black-and-white or color images may be stored on one side of a 12-inch videodisc, and selectively viewed a frame at a time. Among the variety of materials in the Library's collections which are included in this phase of the program are: 58 large-format color photoprints that were originally made by adding color lithographically to black-and-white negatives; 5 albums of Detroit Publishing Company mounted photoprints of views of the United States and two foreign countries; 600 glass lantern slides; approximately 20,000 glass negatives and transparencies by the Detroit Publishing Company, mostly views and scenes of the United States; 32 paper-print motion pictures; and 91,000 motion picture stills. Several sound recordings will also be transferred to digital compact audio disks.

All of the images except for the motion pictures will be filmed on 35mm motion picture color film and transferred first to videotape, which will then be used to prepare a videodics. The Library will investigate the use of the disk in conjunction with a computer-generated captioning method. In this system, the caption identifying the image would be typed into a terminal connected to a microcomputer and stored on floppy disks. Users would be able to consult the machine-readable index thus created, determine the pictorial items to be viewed, and then command the images of the selected items to appear on the screen for viewing. Users would be able to view the image and the caption either simultaneously or separately.

The analog system, unlike the digital system, will use off-the-shelf technology. It will display items in color on standard television monitors. The disks will not replace the original items, but rather act as service copies. Every user does not need to handle the original item; in many cases only the images on the item need be reviewed. In these instances, the disks will allow significant use of the collection without resultant physical deterioration of the original items. The originals will be retained and used only by those with a specific need to study them.

The Library is conscious of its responsibilities under the copyright law. Since this program raises important copyright issues which will need to be resolved, the Library will be working with the publishing community to be sure that all proprietary interests are protected.

While preservation is initially the primary objective of the Optical Disk Pilot Program, the disks are also expected to solve the problem of availability of frequently used materials which are not on the shelf. They will also permit viewing of rare and historically important collections not now accessible to the researcher. The Library of Congress is carefully investigating this new technology in order to identify and evaluate different ways of organizing, servicing, and accessing important materials in the Library while also ensuring their long-term preservation.

51: BIOTECHNOLOGY AS AN INTELLECTUAL PROPERTY

Reid G. Adler

Summary. Recent advances in biotechnology have created many public policy and legal issues, one of the most significant of which is the treatment of biotechnological industrial products, particularly under the patent system. Patents represent one of several types of intellectual property; their ownership confers the right to exclude others from benefitting from the tangible products of a proprietary subject matter. Intellectual property law and its protections will play a major role in the rate at which biotechnology develops in the United States. In this article biotechnological intellectual property issues are reviewed in the context of their underlying legal requirements. The implications of other factors, such as international competition, research funding, and gene ownership, are also considered.

One of the most significant issues created by the emergence of modern biotechnology has been the legal characterization and treatment of biotechnological industrial products. Advances in most other technologies have been readily assimilated by the patent system and routinely licensed and marketed. Because of the tremendous potential impact of biotechnology on many diverse areas, however, it has received an unusual amount of attention and generated a variety of public policy issues and legal uncertainties. This article focuses on biotechnology as an intellectual property.

The term property is generally associated with physical objects, such as household goods or land for which ownership and associated rights are guaranteed and protected by the government. Intellectual property, on the other hand, is intangible. It includes patents, trade secrets, copyrights, and trademarks—rights (which can be bought, sold, or licensed) to exclude others from making, copying, or in some instances using or selling tangible embodiments of the proprietary subject matter.

Although microorganisms have been used for industrial purposes such as baking or fermenting for millennia (1), the recent use of restriction enzymes to create recombinant DNA has fueled interest in developing genetic engineering techniques and encouraged the creation of a host of new processes and products. The characterization of these research results as intellectual properties encourages industry to allocate labor, research and development, and funding to facilitate the production of commercially marketable items. As is similarly becoming evident in several other areas, including gene therapy (2) and environmental dissemination of organisms (3), biotechnology as an intellectual property has also challenged legal and public policies and will continue to catalyze change for several years.

Reid G. Adler is an attorney and is a technical law clerk to the Honorable Giles S. Rich, U.S. Court of Appeals for the Federal Circuit, Washington, D.C. He also teaches "Science and the Law: Biotechnology" at the Graduate School at the National Institutes of Health.

[*Editors' Note:* Material has been omitted at this point.]

Copyrights

A copyright protects the expressed form of an idea but not the idea itself. This differs from patent and trade secret protection, which can encompass the substance of the idea behind a particular object (*52*). The purpose of the copyright law is to secure public benefit by encouraging the efforts of those who create "original works of authorship" (section 102 in Table 1) (*53*). The copyright owner is granted the exclusive right to reproduce and distribute the work (*54*); however, the actual use of a copyrighted work is not protected. To be copyrightable, the work must be "fixed in a tangible medium of expression, now known or later developed," such as print, painting, or other media including those in which the work cannot be directly perceived by the human senses, such as film or videotape (*55*). Copyright has evolved with the growth of technology since the invention of movable type; for instance, Congress recently amended the copyright statute to explicitly recognize the copyrightability of computer software (*56*).

It has been suggested that copyright protection extends to original DNA sequences—works that arguably may embody creative, and indeed artistic, expression (*57*). This argument is made by analogy; a cell's DNA is a compilation of instructions to cellular machinery like the computer instructions embodied in software. The analogy does not fit precisely, however. Alternative computer programs can accomplish the same result through equivalent but different instructions. In contrast, the limited redundancy in the genetic code permits fewer ways to specify particular amino acids. This might preclude protection under copyright, since the judiciary is reluctant to protect works in which the underlying idea is capable of expression in only a few ways (*58*). Furthermore, the value of a copyrighted DNA sequence would be minimal. Once a gene has been disclosed, it would be a relatively simple matter to prepare an analog, without copying, to express the underlying idea by taking advantage of the code's wobble.

A work may also be denied copyright protection if its appearance has "an intrinsic utilitarian function" (*59*). Because particular codons may ultimately determine the higher order structure necessary for effective transfer RNA functioning during translation, DNA sequences may be inherently useful and noncopyrightable for this reason as well. Computer data bases, photomicrographs of DNA, or instruction manuals related to biotechnology can be copyrighted, as is this issue of *Science*. But again, copyright protection is limited. This issue of *Science* cannot be reproduced but all the ideas in it may be freely used (*60*).

[*Editors' Note:* Material has been omitted at this point.]

Choice of Intellectual Property Protection

Biotechnological products and processes are protectable by the various property rights discussed above. These properties can be bought, sold, and licensed like any other type of property. Their worth depends on what the market will bear and on the value placed on protection from competition by the property owner. Selection of the most appropriate mode of protection is a business judgment based on several factors that differ from case to case. These include the pace of technological development (if rapid, then a trade secret approach may be preferable to patenting), associated costs (the costs of secrecy may exceed those of obtaining a patent but perhaps not the costs of trying to enforce it), security considerations (it may be impossible to prevent disclosure of a trade secret or its reverse engineering), the need to show patents to investors or venture capitalists as a measure of success, or the basic, pioneering nature of a discovery (patents that grant broad rights may be more valuable). Also, the type of subject matter sought to be protected is a determining factor—for example, instruction manuals can be copyrighted and protected as a trade secret but are not patentable.

International Competition and Related Issues

An authoritative study recently issued by the Office of Technology Assessment (OTA) reports that, although the United States is the world leader in the basic science and commercial development of biotechnology, continued preeminence is not assured (62). In the face of mounting interest by foreign governments in their own biotechnology industries, OTA evaluated several factors that may be critical to our international competitiveness. It found that the most important factors are the availability of start-up financing and tax incentives for business, increases in federal funding of basic and applied research, and the continued availability of trained scientific and technical personnel. Factors of moderate importance are the ultimate regulatory umbrella of health, safety, and environmental laws; intellectual property law; and university-industry relations.

Several of these factors are interrelated. Thus, in this era of decreasing federal research subsidies, changes in the funding and licensing interactions of the federal government, private industry, and universities merit attention (63). Research strategies and directions may be affected as a result of these changes, in part because industry's research funding is increasing and because universities are assuming a more active and sophisticated role in establishing industry-university relations (64).

In addition, businesses of all nations operate in an increasingly competitive worldwide market. Some nations favor cooperation between native businesses; however, potential risks of antitrust liabilities for joint venture research and development programs may have impeded cooperative research efforts of domestic industries. This is partly due to vast potential civil liabilities and to doubts about the validity of patents obtained as a result of such efforts or certain licensing practices that may later be held to be illegal (65). Because patents provide a crucial incentive for research and innovation (66), as foreign competition increases, strong domestic and international protection of worthwhile research and licensing programs and of patents and trademarks will be important to the success of U.S. business in world markets (67).

The Reagan Administration responded to some of these issues in its bill, the National Productivity and Innovation Act (NPIA) of 1983 (68), which is designed to "create a legal environment that does not unreasonably discourage investment in new technologies and does not deter the efficient exploitation of these technologies'' (*69*). This goal would be achieved in part by eliminating costly punitive damages for antitrust violations for research and development joint ventures. The NPIA addresses another problem by making products of patented processes no longer importable into the United States without infringing the U.S. process patent. This would be a significant gain for the biotechnology industry. Several other bills affecting intellectual property laws also have been introduced.

Other factors will affect biotechnology as an intellectual property. For example, the creation of a new federal court of appeals on 1 October 1982—the Court of Appeals for the Federal Circuit (CAFC)—should bring a needed uniformity to patent infringement decisions (*70*). As part of its jurisdiction, this court now hears all patent infringement appeals from the nation's district courts, rather than the other courts of appeal, some of which had been notoriously anti-patent in philosophy. The CAFC will influence the proper scope and range of equivalents to be accorded claims for biotechnological inventions as well as the statutory subject matter and other infringement issues peculiar to this technology. Related bills are also appearing; the proposed patent term restoration acts would extend the term of chemical or pharmaceutical patents beyond their present 17 years to compensate for delays in obtaining EPA or FDA product approvals. The necessity of such an act is debatable (*71*); however, its proposal exemplifies a renewed interest in strengthening intellectual properties.

In addition to concerns over competitiveness and protectability, a recent lawsuit has sharply focused attention on another legal uncertainty, the ownership of cell lines and cellular components such as genes or plasmids. Hoffmann–La Roche and the University of California disputed the ownership of a bacterial strain that incorporated a human interferon gene copied from a human cell cultured by a University of California scientist (*72*). The real concern, of course, was that only the owner would earn royalties from the sale of interferon: does the cell donor, the culturing researcher, host institution, or commercializing business have a superior proprietary interest?

The case was settled for an undisclosed amount, leaving no judicial resolution as a precedent. It highlights the increasing complexity of cooperative research efforts. Unfortunately, the lesson learned by many from this dispute is that scientific material should not be shared without prior license agreements. This may have a chilling effect on the more collegial practice of informal sharing that has been the norm for biomedical researchers. The new protocol may in time become routine but should not unduly hamper technological development.

Conclusions

Intellectual property protection will play a major role in the rate at which biotechnology develops in the United States. Legal uncertainties, such as the standard for enabling disclosures in patent applications claiming multicellular organisms, may ultimately require congressional intervention. The courts will probably resolve many of the remaining patent, trade secret, copyright, and trademark issues. Proposed federal legislation in the funding, patent, antitrust, and technology transfer areas will enhance the development and competitiveness of the domestic industry. Finally, a better understanding of intellectual property by research scientists, businesspeople, and university administrators will increase the pace of technological development in biotechnology and other fields.

[*Editors' Note:* Only the references sited in the preceding excerpts have been reproduced here.]

References and Notes

1. A. L. Demain, *Science* **214**, 987 (1981).
2. H. Miller, *Biotechnology* **1**, 382 (1983).
3. F. McChesney and R. Adler, *Environ. Law Rep.* **13**, 10.366 (1983).
52. M. Nimmer, *Nimmer on Copyright* (Bender, New York, 1963, and annual updates). The duration of a copyright also differs—copyright protection exists from the time that a work is fixed in a tangible medium of expression to the end of its author's life plus 50 years [17 *U.S. Code*, sect. 302(a)]. The works of an employee endure for 100 years after creation or for 75 years after publication, whichever is shorter [*ibid.*, sect. 302(c)].
53. 17 *U.S. Code*, sect. 102(a). The requirement of "originality" means independently created and is less stringent than that of novelty for patentability. "Works of authorship" were purposely left undefined, but illustrative categories include literary, dramatic, and choreographic works; motion pictures; and sound recordings. The constitutional term "writings" in Article I, Section 8, Clause 8, which provides the congressional authority for the copyright law, has been broadly interpreted to include ". . . any physical rendering of the fruits of creative intellectual or aesthetic labor" [*Goldstein* v. *California*, 412 *U.S. Rep.* 561 (1973)].
54. 17 *U.S. Code*, sect. 106.
55. *Ibid.*, sect. 102(a).
56. *Ibid.*, sect. 117; *Williams Electronics, Inc.* v. *Artic International, Inc.*, 685 *Fed. Rep.* 2nd ser. 870 (Third Circuit Court, 1982).
57. I. Kayton, *George Wash. Law Rev.* **550**, 191 (1982).
58. *Morrissey* v. *Procter & Gamble*, 379 *Fed. Rep.* 2nd ser. 675 (First Circuit Court, 1967).
59. 17 *U.S. Code*, sect. 101; see also M. Nimmer (*52*, sect. 2.18).
60. 17 *U.S. Code*, sect. 102(b).
61. 15 *U.S. Code*, sect. 1127; see also J. McCarthy, *Trademarks and Unfair Competition* (Lawyers Co-operative, Rochester, N.Y., 1973, plus updates).
62. *Commercial Biotechnology: An International Analysis* (Office of Technology Assessment, Washington, D.C., 1984).
63. F. Press, *Science* **218**, 28 (1982); R. R. Nelson and R. N. Langlois, *ibid.* **219**, 814 (1983); A. B. Giamatti, *ibid.* **218**, 1278 (1982); R. Roy, *ibid.* **178**, 955 (1972).
64. B. J. Culliton, *ibid.* **216**, 155 (1982); G. A. Keyworth, II, *ibid.* **217**, 606 (1982).
65. E. Kessler and R. Adler, *Am. Pat. Law Assoc. Q. J.* **9**, 318 (1981).
66. *Ibid.* **10** (1982), entire issue.
67. G. J. Mossinghoff, *Pat. Trademark Copyright J.* **26**, 546 (1983); E. G. Jefferson, *Science* **222**, 243 (1983).
68. U.S. Congress, S. 1841 and H.R. 3878 (98th Congress, First Session, 1983).
69. R. B. Andewelt, *Pat. Trademark Copyright J.* **27**, 73 (1983).
70. L. Shapiro, *Dist. Lawyer* **7**, 29 (1983).
71. M. Sun, *Science* **222**, 593 (1983). "The term is now an historical accident. . . . If changed it would be just as arbitrary. [The term of 17 years was] a period arrived at by compromise between a former term of fourteen years, supposed to be the time required to train two apprentices in succession, and twenty-one years which was once allowed by a statute permitting a further extension of seven years" (*14*, p. 162).
72. B. J. Culliton, *Science* **219**, 372 (1983); M. Sun, *ibid.* **220**, 393 (1983).
73. The assistance of the following in reviewing the manuscript is gratefully acknowledged: Carolyn R. Adler, Esq.; Robert L. Price, Esq., Judge Giles S. Rich; Steven A. Soffen, Esq.; and John E. Tarcza.

VII: LEGISLATIVE AND JUDICIAL ISSUES

Papers 52 Through 67: Commentary

Under the title Legislative and Judicial Issues we have grouped a number of issues that, lacking this heading, would have otherwise have been placed under Basic Issues or Technological Issues. We have used this grouping because there have been recent, important legislation (some pending) and litigation in these areas. Admittedly, there are legislative or judicial issues in some of the other areas that we have covered previously; however, no classification system ever really permits perfect placement of subjects in only one category.

SEMICONDUCTOR CHIP ACT

As early as 1978, legislation was introduced in Congress to better protect proprietary rights in semiconductor computer chips, which are vital to modern computer technology. "Update on Software Publishers and Semiconductor Chip Legislation," Paper 52, was prepared in 1983 by Jon A. Baumgarten and William F. Patry. The authors mentioned print-publisher trepidations concerning how other copyright issues might be affected by the limitations that were incorporated in most of the chip bills, such as shorter terms of copyright and compulsory licensing.

Allen R. Grogan and Michael J. Kump authored Paper 53, "The Broader Meanings of Apple v. Franklin in the Development of Compatible Operating Systems and in Determining Standards for Injunctive Relief," in which they contend that some basic questions remain unsolved in the area of permissible computer compatibility.

L. Ray Patterson has traced some of the history of copyright that has led to dichotomies in the Copyright Statute in his congressional testimony on one of the semiconductor-chip protection bills (Paper 54). He believes that copyright "integrity"—"consistency"—would be harmed if semiconductor chips were to be protected by amendment of the present statute. He deplores "the lack of a sound conceptual basis for copyright", which, he claims, is a "schizophrenic legal concept." He points out:

> The copyright clause [in the Constitution] empowers Congress to secure to authors the exclusive right to their writing for limited times. One would assume from this language that copyright is intended to benefit authors. But the Supreme Court says that this is not so. Copyright is intended to benefit the public. Yet the Copyright Statute functions primarily to benefit the publisher or entrepreneur.

Finally, late in 1984, Congress passed legislation for semiconductor-chip protection that added a *sui generis* section to the Copyright Statute. The "mask works" that are needed to produce the chips are protected for a period of ten years. This section also has other unique features that neither depend on nor interact with the rest of the Statute. These are described in some detail in Paper 55 by Nadine Cohadas.

HOME VIDEO RECORDING ("BETAMAX")

The importance of copyright litigation in the area of home video recording has already been made crystal clear by the articles we have included under Section V–A, Fair Use. As we have seen, the impact on fair use of the Supreme Court's decision in the "Betamax case" has been immense.

As we pointed out in Paper 1, "this was a case in which a motion-picture studio sued a Japanese manufacturer of television videotape recorders, claiming that their sale (and home use of) for off-the-air taping of its copyrighted movies constituted contributory infringement of its copyrights. The Supreme Court disagreed," chiefly on the basis that "time shifting"—recording a program to view it later—was a fair use, but also because Congress had not legislated specifically otherwise. Legislation to reverse this decision, or perhaps "to levy a sales tax on recorders to compensate the copyright owners for compulsory use," has languished in Congress, chiefly, it is said, because Representative Kastenmeier sees no need for it; he is said to feel that what goes on within the home is sacred.

The full decision of the Supreme Court is too lengthy to include here, although it makes important reading, as does the minority opinion. However, we have included the Syllabus as Paper 56.

Before the case reached the Supreme Court, it had been acted on by two lower courts. In the first, the decision (as in the Supreme Court) went in favor of the Japanese manufacturer, provoking such profound reactions as that of former Register of Copyrights David Ladd in his article "Private Use, Public Policy: Copyright and Home Recording," Paper 57. Ladd opts for legislative action—says that "our response to the problems of home taping will test our resolve to enrich society, by rewarding and protecting authors, and our ingenuity in fashioning adaptations for copyrights as ingenious as the innovations in technology itself."

After this lower-court decision was reversed in favor of the motion-picture producer by a Court of Appeals—before the case moved to the Supreme Court—Charles H. Lieb, in Paper 58, was hopeful that the appeal court's action would be "a straw in the wind that such copying [including photocopying and the copying of musical scores] will be held lawless and controllable." While this was not to be, we have included both Ladd's and Lieb's papers as significant commentaries on this litigation and for their general teachings.

We again remind readers of the related papers in Part V.

UMBRELLA STATUTE AMENDMENT

In 1977, when the Copyright Clearance Center, Inc. (CCC) was still being discussed, the Association of American Publishers testified before the National Commission on New Technological Uses of Copyrighted Works (CONTU) in favor of amending the Copyright Statute to provide some assistance to libraries. It was clear that some libraries needed statutory relief to permit them to copy from the works of publishers that would neither participate in the prospective CCC nor offer their own copy-licensing systems.

In Paper 59, Carol Risher reviews the development of the Umbrella Statute amendment idea through the drafting of statutory language by a task force composed of industrial librarians/information managers and publishers. She reports that the resulting Umbrella Statute amendment was subsequently submitted to the Register of Copyrights, hopefully for inclusion in his 1983 report to Congress on library photocopying.

The Register did indeed recommend such legislation, but Congress has not yet held hearings on his report. There have recently been stirrings in its support, however, so we are including as Paper 60 an *Information Hotline* article that contains the full text of the proposed Umbrella Statute amendment and of the explanation of it prepared by the task force that drafted it.

FIRST-SALE DOCTRINE/RENTALS

Under the 1976 Copyright Statute, purchasers of copyrighted works can sell, rent, or otherwise dispose of them unless they have signed an agreement limiting such rights. Some of us may be old enough to remember book-rental libraries in the corner drugstores (and some bookstores) where one could rent the latest books for three to ten cents per day, long before they appeared on the shelves of the public libraries. The advent of inexpensive paperback books drove these rental libraries out of existence in the 1940s, but they were the forerunners of today's video-store rentals of prerecorded videocassettes. Also, they helped prompt Congressional consideration of legislation to provide some revenue from such rentals to the copyright owners of the (mainly) motion pictures in the cassettes.

However, no legislation on videocassette rentals was passed in 1984, and future prospects were said to be poor, for "public good" reasons ("home use"). Nancy B. Lewson has discussed the basics of this subject in considerable detail in her Paper, number 61, on "The Video-cassette Rental Controversy."

The first-sale/rental "problem" also extends to sound recordings and computer software. A "record-rental" protection law (S.32) was enacted late in 1984, stipulating (according to Senator Mathais) "that a person who wishes to rent out records on a commerical basis must get the permission of the copyright owner before doing so"; this area did not prove as controversial as videocassette-rental protection. Legislation was also introduced by Senator Mathais (S. 3074), but not enacted, "to protect copyrighted computer programs from illegal copying" based on unauthorized rentals.

PUBLIC LENDING RIGHT

Related to the rentals issue is the public lending right, which is a concept for compensating authors when their works are loaned in public libraries. Already in operation in Great Britain, West Germany, and at least eight other countries, this concept is again being talked about in the United States. Paper 62 tells us that Senator Charles Mathais introduced a bill in 1983 to establish a commission to study whether public lending rights would be in the public interest, would encourage authors to write, and could be funded without financial hardships to libraries.

John Y. Cole has summarized a 1983 Library of Congress symposium on the public lending right in Paper 63. "Will the money to pay for public lending rights be taken out of [present] library budgets? The answer must be no—and nobody is saying it should be."

Edith McCormick, in Paper 64, "PLR Could Cost Libraries Millions," reported "a mixed bag" on early results of the British system. Her subtitle reads: "Fussy System Promises Few Pence for Authors as British Lending Right Begins."

MANUFACTURING CLAUSE

In 1976, following enactment of the omnibus Copyright Statute, Charles H. Lieb enthusiastically wrote "The New United States 'Manu-facturing Clause,' or A Toronto Promise Fulfilled (With Good Measure)" (Paper 65). The previous Manufacturing Clause had provided that English-language books by American authors or foreign authors domiciled in the United States had to be printed and bound in the United States or would otherwise be denied U.S. copyright protection. Under the new 1976 Statute that Lieb was celebrating, this restriction was to end in 1982.

However, all this was changed in 1982 in a flurry of legislative and executive action in which Congress extended the expiration of the Manufacturing Clause until 1986 and then overrode President Reagan's veto of its action. These developments are related in an article from *Information Hotline,* Paper 66. Proponents of retaining the clause claimed at the time that hundreds of thousands of jobs would otherwise have been lost (although the statistical study on which this claim was based was later strongly challenged).

The Authors League has since sought judicial action to have the Manufacturing Clause declared unconstitutional as a violation of the First Amendment. One way or another, the demise or further extension of the Manufacturing Clause will soon come up again.

MORAL RIGHTS

Present studies on the possibilty of U.S. adherence to the Berne Convention may alter the U.S. status (nonstatus) of the "moral rights" of authors. Whatever, we felt it appropriate to report here on the lack of much U.S. statutory protection for authors "against subsequent distortions or misrepresentations."

In his brief article, "The Author and Moral Rights" (Paper 67), Michael F. Schwartz states that contracts with publishers usually result in authors relinquishing all creative control over their works because of the lack of statutory moral-rights protection. He points out that the European doctrine of moral rights, or *droit moral,* gives a creator:

> The absolute right to claim authorship of his work, to prevent his name from being used for a creation not his own, and to prevent others from being named the creator of his work [the "concept of paternity"]. Under the concept of integrity [the other European moral-rights concept], an author can prevent others from making changes that distort or mutilate his work.

Schwartz says that the only safe recourse that a writer now has is contractual limitations.

BIBLIOGRAPHY

Semiconductor Chip Act

Boorstyn, N., 1985, The Semiconductor Chip Protection Act of 1984, *Copr. Law J.* **1**(7):1-6.

Frank, R. J., 1984, Bill May Reduce Chip Copying, *The Institute (IEEE)* **8**(1):11.

Lechter, M. A., 1983, Protecting Software and Firmware Developments, *Computer* **16**(8):73-81.

McCutcheon, W. H., 1982, Copyright Protection for Computer Firmware in the World Market, *Houston J. Internat. Law* **4**:203-212.

Other pertinent references are included in the Bibliography for Part VI, Computer Programs.

Home Video Recording ("Betamax"), Including
Home Audio Recording

Copyright Office, 1980, *Copyright Registration for Motion Pictures Including Video Recordings,* Circular R45, Library of Congress, Washington, D.C.

Fields, H., 1984, Betamax Ruling Widens Fair-Use Interpretation, *Publ. Wkly.* **225**(5):290-291.

Foti, L., 1982, Home [Audio] Taping Issues Probed in EIA Study, *Billboard* **94**(39):1, 15.

Hart, W. M., 1981, The Conscientious Fair User's Guide to the Copyright Act of 1976: Video Recordation and Its Fair Use, *Univ. Pitt. Law Rev.* **42**:317-374.

Nimmer, M. B., 1982, Copyright Liability for Audio Home Recording: Dispelling the *Betamax* Myth, *Va. Law Rev.* **67**:1505-1534.

First Sale Doctrine/Rentals

Cohen, J., 1982, Record Renting: Is There A Problem? If So, Are the Solutions Worse? What Are the Radio Implications?, *Copr. Manage.* **5**(8):1-4.

Colby, R., 1984, The First Sale Doctrine—The Defense that Never Was?, *Copr. Soc. U.S.A. J.* **32**(2):77-108.

Holland, B., 1983, Full Senate Passes Record Rental Bill, *Billboard* **95**(28):6.

Video Rental Rooms Fought, 1984 (August 20), *New York Times* **133**(46, 142):D1, D5.

Zechowy, J., 1982, Cheaper by the Dozen: Unauthorized Rental of Motion Picture Videocassettes and Videodiscs, *Fed. Commun. Law J.* **34**(2):259-291.

Public Lending Rights

Brophy, B., 1984, *Guide to Public Lending Right,* Gower, Brookfield, VT.

Manufacturing Clause

Frase, R. W., 1980, Tariffs and Other Trade Barriers: The U.S. Experience, in *Encyclopedia of Library and Information Science,* A. Kent, ed., Dekker, New York, NY, vol. 30, pp. 119-127.

Reilly, J. B., The Manufacturing Clause of the U.S. Copyright Law: A Critical Appraisal of Some Recent Studies, *Copr. Soc. U.S.A. J.* **32**(2):109-137.

Moral Rights

Amarnick, P., 1983, American Recognition of the Moral Right: Issues and Opinions, *ASCAP Copr. Law Symp.* **29**:31-81.

52: UPDATE ON SOFTWARE PUBLISHERS AND SEMICONDUCTOR CHIP LEGISLATION

Jon A. Baumgarten

Paskus, Gordon & Hyman
Washington, D.C.

W. F. Patry

Paskus, Gordon & Hyman
Washington, D.C.

As computer technology approaches the dawn of the Fifth Generation, the efforts of innovative engineers to create ever more powerful microprocessor functions and to expand memory capabilities integrated onto a single semiconductor chip have increased manyfold. These efforts entail considerable skill, labor and investment, and have generated claims to protection from appropriation. Some publishers of applications software, perceiving a community of interest with chip designers in insuring that adequate legal safeguards for computer products are in place, have been supportive in principle of recent legislative attempts to expressly include chip design as a protected form of intellectual property under the copyright laws.[1] This community of interest has not, however, prevented these publishers from questioning certain aspects of proposed legislation that may, in their view, adversely affect the protection software presently enjoys under the Copyright Act.[2]

These concerns will be summarized after a short review of prior chip legislation, a review that will enable us to better appreciate why the pertinent provisions exist. Before proceeding, however, caution dictates a word of definition. In intellectual property contexts, references to "chips" and "chip protection" are all too often used indiscriminately to refer to a *variety* of independent works embodied or reflected in the same silicon carrier:[3]

● Schematic diagrams, layouts, and the like represented in paper, mylar sheets, photolithographic masks, and the like during the process of chip design and manufacture;
● Computer programs fixed in chips;[4]
● Audiovisual works, program-related, generated, or dependent, but generally found to be independently "fixed" in chips for some copyright purposes;[5] and
● The configuration, "topology," "architecture" or surface and sub-surface appearance or pattern of the chips themselves.

It is only the fourth (chip configuration) and, apparently, the first (layout, etc.) categories that are avowedly the subjects of the legislative efforts referred to in this report. Indeed, the premise of the publishers whose views are summarized herein is that the second (applications software) and third (audiovisual works) categories were intended to—and should—remain unaffected.[6]

H.R. 14293, H.R. 1007

In October 1978, Congressmen Edwards, McCloskey and Mineta of California introduced H.R. 14293, the first legislation to propose the extension of copyright protection to chip design. This bill would have accomplished its goal by simply amending the definition of "pictorial, graphic and sculptural works" in section 101 of the Copyright Act to include:

the photographic masks used to imprint patterns on integrated circuit chips and to include the im-

---

This article is based in part on testimony given by Mr. Baumgarten on behalf of conventional publishers and software publishers before the copyright subcommittees of the House and Senate Judiciary Committees in 1983.

1. See, e.g., Hearings on H.R. 1028 before the Subcommittee on Courts, Civil Liberties, and the Administration of Justice of the House Judiciary Committee, 98th Cong., 1st Sess., August 3, 1983 (statement of the Association of American Publishers); Hearings on S. 1201 before the Subcommittee on Patents, Copyrights and Trademarks of the Senate Judiciary Committee, 98th Cong., 1st Sess., May 9, 1983 (same).
2. See generally, Baumgarten, Copyright and Computer Software in Johnston (Chairman), Fourth Annual Computer Law Institute (Law & Business, Inc., 1983).

3. For a more detailed review of the separate treatment of these distinct works in Copyright Office practice, see Hearings on H.R. 1007 before the Subcommittee on Courts, Civil Liberties and the Administration of Justice of the House Judiciary Committee, 96th Cong., 1st Sess., April 16, 1979 at 6-8, 12-14. (statement of Jon Baumgarten, General Counsel, U.S. Copyright Office); and Hearings cited in fn. 1, supra (statements of Dorothy Schrader, General Counsel, U.S. Copyright Office.)
4. See generally, fn. 2, supra.
5. See generally, Patry, Electronic Audiovisual Games: Negotiating the Maze of Copyright, 31 J. Copr. Soc. No. 1 (October 1983).
6. This premise extends as well to other works that may come to be disseminated in chip form—e.g., books (see Remarks of Townsend Hoopes, President, Association of American Publishers, before the New York University Workshop on Book Publishing: The Electronic Revolution and the Future of the Book,

printed patterns themselves even though they are used in connection with the manufacture of, or incorporated in, a useful article.

This legislation was felt necessary in part because of the Copyright Office's refusal to register claims to copyright in integrated circuit devices as such, or to accept chips as published copies of copyrighted works.[7] No action was taken on this bill, which was reintroduced in January 1979 as H.R. 1007.

Hearings were held on H.R. 1007 on April 16, 1979, in San Jose, California.[8] Apparently unbeknownst to the Congressional subcommittee, there was a substantial division within the semiconductor industry over the bill,[9] a division that clearly manifested itself in opposing testimony. The result of this lack of unity was not only a failure to pass the bill, but a four-year delay in the convening of further hearings.

Although a variety of reasons was given for opposition to H.R. 1007, including lack of time for adequate consideration, substantive objections including assertions that competition within and entry into the industry would be hampered; that the bill would inhibit "legitimate" reverse engineering; and that there was inadequate provision for the interests of innocent vendors and purchasers of infringing chips and chip-based products.[10] Attempts to reconcile these differences are apparent in the currently proposed legislation.

H.R. 1028, S. 1201

It was not until 1983 that industry efforts to introduce a consensus bill were successful.[11] On February 24, 1983 Congressmen Edwards and Mineta introduced H.R. 1028 and on May 4, 1983 Senator Mathias introduced the substantially (but not wholly) identical S. 1201. Responding to the criticisms raised at the 1979

hearings, these bills differed substantially from their predecessors. For example, rather than including chip design as a species of "pictorial, graphic and sculptural" work, H.R. 1028 and S. 1201 create a new subject matter of copyright—a "mask work," defined as:[12]

a series of related images—(1) having the predetermined, three-dimensional pattern of metallic, insulating, or semiconductor material present or removed from the layers of a semiconductor chip product, and (2) in which series the relation of the images to one another is that each image has the pattern of the surface of one form of the semiconductor chip product.

Additionally, the copyright owners in such works would be given a number of specific exclusive rights, including the rights to embody the mask work in (and distribute) masks, to use a mask embodying the mask work to make a semiconductor chip product, to reproduce images of the mask work on semiconductor chip products, and to distribute and "use" a semiconductor chip product made or reproduced from the mask work.[13] In substantial departures from conventional copyright principles, mask works would have only a limited, ten-year term of copyright, and protection would be subject both to a "compulsory license" and to exclusions of liability, under specified circumstances, for certain "innocent infringers." In accordance with traditional copyright principles, to qualify for protection "mask works" would need only satisfy the minimal copyright standard of originality (as opposed to novelty or the like).

Hearings were held on S. 1201 on May 19, 1983, and on H.R. 1028 on August 3, 1983.[14] Unlike the situation in April 1979, the semiconductor industry presented a united front in support of the proposed legislation, due mainly to the legislative limitations and adjustments

---

January 22, 1982; Evans, The Micro Millenium 115-117 [1979]; U.S. News & World Report, May 9, 1983 at A-8).

7. See Intel Corp. v. Ringer, Civ. No. C-77-2848 RHS (N.D. Cal.). Complaint filed December 16, 1977 (mandamus action to compel acceptance of chip for deposit purposes) (Dismissed without prejudice).

8. See Hearings on H.R. 1007, supra fn. 3 (hereinafter, "1979 Hearings"). See generally, Redmond, Industrial Designs in High Technology in 1980 Patent Law Annual (Southwestern Legal Foundation, 1980); Oxman, Jurimetrics Journal, Summer 1980, at 34.

9. See fn. 8, supra; see also, e.g., Electronic News, April 23, 1979 at 1, 76; Electronic Engineering Times, May 14, 1979 at 1, 4; Northern California Electronic News, April 30, 1979 at 1, 25.

10. See generally, 1979 Hearings at 50-55, 55-69, 74-79. See also, testimony of F. Thomas Dunlap, Jr., Corporate Counsel and Secretary of Intel Corporation in Hearings

on H.R. 1028, supra fn. 1.

11. Following the divided 1979 Hearings, Congressman Edwards did reintroduce H.R. 1007 during the Second Session of the 97th Congress. Senator Mathias also introduced a companion bill in the Senate. S. 3117, but no hearings were held on these bills.

12. H.R. 1028 and S. 1201, 98th Cong., 1st Sess., sec. 2. The bills also define "mask" and "semiconductor chip product." Id.

13. H.R. 1028 and S. 1201, supra, sec. 4. During hearings, the addition of the right to "use" semiconductor chip products made or reproduced from the mask work drew considerable questioning from the Copyright Office and other witnesses as inconsistent with traditional copyright principles. This "use right" was subsequently eliminated from the Senate bill in a marked-up version favorably reported by the Senate Subcommittee on November 15, 1983.

14. See fn. 1., supra.

noted above and the increase of unauthorized chip duplication.[15] The principal reservations voiced at these hearings were from the Copyright Office and the Association of American Publishers (representing both conventional and software publisher members), essentially more as to matters of form, structure, and drafting detail than as to matters of the principle of "chip" protection. On November 15, 1983, the Senate bill was marked up and favorably reported by the Senate Subcommittee to its parent Judiciary Committee with a number of substantial changes. Action by the full Senate Judiciary Committee is anticipated in early 1984. On December 1, 1983, additional hearings were held on H.R. 1028 by the House Subcommittee. During these hearings, the testimony of the Copyright Office and Professor Lyman Patterson, responses to questioning by PTO Commissioner Mossinghoff (on behalf of the Cabinet Council on Commerce and Trade), and colloquy among the members present appeared to give considerable impetus in the House to the crafting of a specific design protection statute for chips, in lieu of the piecemeal amendments to the Copyright Act proposed in the current bills. However, the precise nature of further House action remains to be seen.

Software Publisher Concerns

During the 1983 hearings, and in informal discussion, a number of concerns over the impact of the proposed legislation have been raised by software publishing interests. For the most part, they may be summarized as follows:

• The bills would subject the owners of copyright in "mask works" to a number of potentially significant limitations on their rights and remedies for infringement. As noted earlier, these include a truncated term of protection and compulsory licensing and exemption from liability for certain innocent infringers. These limitations were presumably not intended to apply to infringement of computer programs (or audiovisual works) resulting from unauthorized chip reproduction or distribution. However, this lack of application is not

entirely free from doubt,[16] particularly in light of the complex definitional provisions in the bills and an anticipated lack of technological sophistication in the courts. Accordingly, it was urged that the bills be amended to expressly disclaim any impairment of existing copyright protection for programs and other works embodied in semiconductor chips or chip products. Recent revisions adopted by the Senate Subcommittee have sought to meet this concern by the addition of express "savings" clauses to the effect that "copyright in a mask work shall neither extend to nor affect, limit, or impair any other work of authorship . . .," and that the bill does not "add to or detract from existing rights of owners of copyright. . . ."

In a related vein, the bills specifically enumerate those references to the word "copy" in the current Act that would be considered to include semiconductor chip products. However, these references do not include the use of "copies" in section 106 or 101 (general definitions) of the Act. Thus, concern has been expressed that an unauthorized reproduction or distribution of computer programs (or other works)—whether originating in "paper," diskette, or other media—in chip form might be inadvertently immunized from infringement for lack of a "reproduc[tion] . . . in *copies*" or "distribut[ion] [of] *copies*" within the terms of section 106. Although this risk might be diminished somewhat by adoption of a savings provision as mentioned above and the breadth of the Act's current definitional provisions, recollection of *White-Smith v. Apollo*[17] is not easily purged from memory. In sum, publishers—joined by the Copyright Office[18]—find little reason to rely on a circuitous affirmation of their fundamental copyright privileges and seek more certain assurance of continued protection.

Going beyond specific drafting problems, software publishers have also raised broader questions relating to the possible precedential impact of the tactical adjustments made by the bills' proponents. For example, a memorandum introduced in the Congressional Record by the House sponsors and endorsed by the Senate sponsor sought to assuage prior fears among segments of the chip design industry that copyright would pre-

---

15. *See, e.g., testimony of F. Thomas Dunlap, Jr., fn. 10, supra.*
16. *Section 2 of S. 1201, as introduced, provided: "The copyright in a mask or mask work shall not extend to any other work of authorship embodied therein." (Emphasis added.) This provision, however, missed the publishers' point—namely, that the limits on the protection of mask works should not impair copyright in other works of authorship. Cf. 17 U.S.C. 114 (limitations on protection of sound recordings do "not limit or impair" performing rights in musical compositions fixed in same phonorecord); see also, 17*

U.S.C. 103(b) (copyright in compilations and derivative works does not "affect or enlarge" copyright in underlying works).
17. White-Smith Music Publishing Co. v. Apollo Co., 209 U.S. 1 (1908) (pianola roll not infringing "copy" of recorded musical composition).
18. See Statement of Dorothy Schrader, Associate Register for Legal Affairs, Copyright Office, in Hearings on H.R. 1028 Before the Subcommittee on Courts, Civil Liberties and the Administration of Justice of the House Judiciary Committee, 98th Cong., 1st Sess., December 1, 1983 at 27, 37.

clude reverse engineering of chips for competitive purposes.[19] The memorandum asserted that customary reverse engineering in the industry would be shielded from infringement by the fair use doctrine. Software publishers, however, suggested that applying fair use to widely varying conceptions of reverse engineering that have been described in oral testimony could well distort fair use principles in other contexts, and for other works.[20] (The Senate Subcommittee has moved toward allaying this concern by adoption of a specific reverse engineering exemption, rather than relying on fair use.) Similarly, publishers expressed concern with the potential impact of the bills' adoption of compulsory licensing in a computer context.[21] It is feared—with some recent justification in light of reports of foreign governmental considerations of compulsory licensing for software—that compulsory licensing may appear as a politically expedient answer to computer copyright issues, both in this country and abroad, and that "technical" distinctions between chips and embedded programs may be subordinated to the *principle* of compulsory licensing adopted in the proposed chip legislation.

53: THE BROADER MEANINGS OF APPLE v. FRANKLIN IN THE DEVELOPMENT OF COMPATIBLE OPERATING SYSTEMS AND IN DETERMINING STANDARDS FOR INJUNCTIVE RELIEF

Allen R. Grogan
Michael J. Kump

As has been widely reported in both the trade press and popular media, the Third Circuit Court of Appeals held in *Apple Computer, Inc. v. Franklin Computer Corporation*, 714 F.2d 1240 (3d Cir. 1983) that a computer program in object code form embedded in ROM (read only memory) is protectible under copyright law, and that systems software is not *per se* excluded from copyright protection. Despite coverage by some of the popular media suggesting that these were groundbreaking conclusions, other courts had reached the same conclusions on these issues previously. *See, e.g., Tandy Corp. v. Personal Micro Computers, Inc.*, 524 F. Supp. 171, 173 (N.D. Cal. 1981); *GCA Corp. v. Chance*, 217 U.S.P.Q. 718, 719-20 (N.D. Cal. 1982); *Apple Computer, Inc. v. Formula International, Inc.*, 562 F. Supp. 775, 779-81 (C.D. Cal. 1983). The Third Circuit opinion in *Franklin* was significant in that it overturned a poorly reasoned district court opinion, which had reached contrary conclusions on these issues, and because it provided extensive analysis of these issues for the first time by a court of appeals.

The opinion may also prove to be significant for other reasons. This article will focus on two aspects of the case which, though of substantial importance, have received considerably less attention.

First, how does one distinguish between ideas expressed in computer programs (which are unprotectible by copyright) and the expressions of those ideas in com-

puter programs (which are protectible by copyright)? Is the goal of achieving compatibility with another operating system an "idea" to which the idea/expression analysis should be applied in determining whether any copyright has been infringed? The proper standard for determining whether a compatible operating system is an infringement of the system it emulates is of considerable significance, since many companies have introduced or plan to introduce machines which are, to varying degrees, compatible with the IBM PC, and several companies in addition to Franklin are marketing or plan to market Apple-compatible machines. If a court were to determine that the similarities *required* to create an Apple compatible or an IBM compatible operating system are sufficient to constitute a copyright infringement, it would have devastating impact on a number of companies.

The second issue which will be addressed is the appropriate standard and the factors to be considered in determining whether a preliminary injunction should be issued in a copyright infringement action. Although the court in *Franklin* may have reached the right conclusion in reversing the district court's denial of a preliminary injunction against Franklin, the standard it enunciated for doing so is at variance with the standard applied by most courts.

Because Apple and Franklin recently settled their dispute, these issues apparently will not be further resolved or explored in this case. Both issues, however, are likely to arise in future disputes between other parties.

Franklin's "Development" of a Compatible Operating System

In *Franklin*, the defendant had copied Apple's operating system computer programs in order to manufacture an Apple compatible microcomputer. Operating systems programs are fundamental programs at the heart of a computer which manage the internal flow of data within the machine and allow the user to use additional programs known as applications programs, which perform specific tasks such as accounting, word processing, game playing, etc. The applications programs must interface with the operating systems software, and accordingly an application program which is compatible with and will run on a computer utilizing one operating system generally will not run on a computer utilizing another operating system. To take advantage of the availability in the marketplace of a substantial library of application programs which will run on the Apple computer, Franklin decided to market a computer which was intended to be capable of running all the applications programs which will run on the Apple computer.

To achieve this compatibility, Franklin simply copied Apple's operating systems software with a few minor variations (principally consisting of deleting from the programs any references to Apple and any copyright notices in Apple's name).

Idea/Expression Dichotomy

Among the defenses to copyright infringement raised by Franklin was its contention that there are a limited number of ways to write an operating system which will run most Apple compatible software. This defense has its foundation in a fundamental principle of copyright law: that copyright protection extends only to the "expression" of an idea, and not to the idea itself. *Mazer v. Stein*, 347 U.S. 201, 217, 74 S.Ct. 460, 470 (1954). The idea/expression dichotomy is now reflected in the Copyright Act itself, which states that "in no case does copyright protection for an original work of authorship extend to any idea, procedure, process, system, method of operation, concept, principle, or discovery, regardless of the form in which it is described, explained, illustrated or embodied in such work." 17 U.S.C. §102(b).

Courts and commentators have always had a difficult time defining where the line between idea and expression is properly drawn. Obviously, this question is of considerable significance in any copyright infringement action, since one of the elements a plaintiff must demonstrate in order to prove infringement is that the two works are substantially similar in their form of expression; mere similarity of ideas is not sufficient.

The distinction is also important for a related reason, which was the principal focus of the Third Circuit's discussion of the idea/expression dichotomy in *Franklin*.

A corollary to the concept that copyright protects only the expression of an idea is that if an idea nad the expression of that idea are indistinguishable, the copying of the expression of the idea will not constitute an infringement of copyright. If a particular idea can only be expressed in one way or in a very limited number of ways, protecting the expression of the idea would effectively grant the copyright owner a monopoly on the underlying idea itself. *See, e.g., Herbert Rosenthal Jewelry Corp. v. Kalpakian*, 446 F.2d 738, 742 (9th Cir. 1971) (idea and expression of idea of a jeweled bee pin indistinguishable where the similarities between pins created by plaintiff and defendant were no greater than was inevitable from the creation of a jewel encrusted bee).

Apple Compatibility—Idea, Expression or Neither?

Franklin apparently argued that due to what it characterized as *a limited number of ways to write an operating sysem which will run most Apple compatible software*, the idea of achieving Apple compatibility merged with the expression of that idea and was not subject to copyright protection. Although the Court of Appeals rejected this contention, the basis for the court's conclusion is far from clear.

In its opinion, the court adopted the analysis of *Dymow v. Bolton*, 11 F.2d 690, 691 (2d Cir. 1926), which stated that "if the same idea can be expressed in a plurality of totally different manners, a plurality of copyrights may result, and no infringement will exist." Starting from this premise, the court in *Franklin* proceeded with the following discussion:

> If other programs can be written or created which perform the same function as Apple's operating system program, then that program is an expression of the idea and hence copyrightable. In essence, this inquiry is no different than that made to determine whether the expression and idea have merged, which has been stated to occur when there are no or few other ways of expressing a particular idea. [Citations omitted]

The district court made no findings as to whether some or all of Apple's operating programs represent the only means of expression of the idea underlying them. Although there seems to be a concession by Franklin that at least some of the programs can be rewritten, we do not believe that the record on that issue is so clear that it can be decided at the appellate level. Therefore, if the issue is pressed on remand, the necessary finding can be made at that time.

303

Franklin claims that whether or not the programs can be rewritten, there are a limited 'number of ways to arrange operating systems to enable a computer to run the vast body of Apple-compatible software', Brief of Appellee at 20. This claim has no pertinence to either the idea/expression dichotomy or merger. The idea which may merge with the expression, thus making copyright unavailable, is the idea which is the subject of the expression. The idea of one of the operating systems programs is, for example, how to translate source code into object code. If other methods of expressing that idea are not foreclosed as a practical matter, then there is no merger. Franklin may wish to achieve total compatibility with independently developed application programs written for the Apple II, but that is a commercial and competitive objective which does not enter into the somewhat metaphysical issue of whether particular ideas and expressions have merged. [Emphasis added.]

Either the court's line of reasoning in this section of the opinion is circular and contradictory, or the court has failed to articulate what it believes to be the proper definition of an "idea". On the one hand, the court acknowledges that if a particular idea can only be expressed in a limited number of ways, the idea and expression may merge and not be subject to copyright protection. On the other hand, the court refuses even to apply the idea/expression dichotomy analysis to Franklin's contention that there are only a limited number of ways to express the idea of creating an Apple compatible operating system, dismissing that as a "commercial and competitive objective" which is somehow distinguishable from an "idea" as that term is used in applying the idea/expression dichotomy doctrine.

A district court opinion in another case brought by Apple against a similar defendant suggests that Franklin's claim that there were only a limited number of ways to rewrite the operating systems program to be Apple compatible may be without merit. In *Apple Computer, Inc. v. Formula International, Inc.*, 562 F. Supp. 775, 782 (C.D. Cal. 1983), the court made the following observations:

Plaintiff [Apple] has introduced evidence, which was not directly controverted by Defendant [Formula], that numerous methods exist for writing the programs involved here that would be 'ninety-eight percent compatible' with Apple computers, yet not so similar to plaintiff's particular sequence as to infringe its copyright. If there were only one or two ways to write a program to perform a particular function, then extending copyright protection to the program might in effect give its author a patent on the idea itself. But those facts do not exist in this case.

In *Franklin*, however, the court observed that the record of the trial court included no findings as to

whether the ideas expressed in Apple's operating systems can only be expressed in a limited numbr of ways. Thus, the court in *Franklin* was not rejecting Franklin's defense based on a finding that in fact there are a variety of ways to write Apple compatible operating systems. Rather, the court appeared to reject the contention that the "idea" of writing an Apple-compatible operating system is even an idea to which the idea/expression analysis should be applied. The court concluded, without explanation and without citing any previous authority, that individual functions performed by the operating system, such as converting source code into object code, are ideas for purposes of the idea/expression dichotomy, but that compatibility or incompatibility with applications programs is not an idea for purposes of the idea/expression dichotomy.

The implications of the court's refusal to apply the idea/expression dichotomy analysis to the issue of achieving compatibility are potentially quite significant. The court appears to have taken the position that even if Franklin could establish that there is no way to develop an Apple compatible operating system without appropriating the form of expression of Apple's operating system (or a portion thereof), the court would refuse to hold that the idea of Apple-compatibility merges with the expression of the idea. It therefore appears that even in the face of such a showing, the court would be willing to permit Apple to use the copyright law to maintain a complete monopoly on Apple compatible operating systems.

To understand what the court in *Franklin* may have been trying to articulate, an understanding of where the line is drawn between ideas and expressions of ideas in computer programs is obviously important. Unfortunately, an examination of existing case law on the idea/expression dichotomy sheds little light on the subject because the standards which have been applied to literary works, music, art, toys and other copyrighted works are not easily applied to computer programs.

For example, in a very influential opinion, Judge Learned Hand suggested an approach to distinguishing ideas from expressions of ideas which has since become known as the "abstractions test" and has been frequently cited and applied by other courts. Unfortunately, the famous passage provides little useful guidance to distinguish ideas from expressions in computer programs:

Upon any work, and especially upon a play, a great number of patterns of increasing generality will fit equally well, as more and more of the incident is left out. The last may perhaps be no more than the most general statement of what the play is about, and at times might consist only of its title; but there is a point in this series of abstractions where they are no longer protected, since otherwise the playwright could prevent the use of his "ideas" to which, apart from their expression, his property is never extended [citation omitted]. Nobody has ever been able to fix that boundary, and nobody ever can. In some cases the question has been treated as though it were analogous to lifting a portion out of the copyrighted work [citation omitted]; but the analogy is not a good one, because, though the skeleton is a part of the body, it pervades and supports the whole. In such cases we are rather concerned with the line between expression and what is expressed. As respects plays, the controversy chiefly centers upon the characters and sequence of incident, these being the substance. *Nichols v. Universal Pictures Corporation*, 45 F.2d 119, 121 (2d Cir. 1930).

In holdings and dicta in a variety of other cases, courts have attempted to distinguish idea from expression as applied to a variety of copyrighted works. *See, e.g., Sid and Marty Krofft Television v. McDonald's Corp.*, 562 F.2d 1157, 1168 (9th Cir. 1977) (in dicta, court observed that the idea of Michelangelo's David is simply a statue of a nude male, to which Michelangelo added much more in expressing that idea); *Hoehling v. Universal City Studios, Inc.*, 618 F.2d 972, 978 (2d Cir. 1980) (theory as to cause of Hindenburg disaster constituted unprotectible idea which a subsequent author was free to use so long as he did not bodily appropriate the expression of that idea in the original author's book); *Reyher v. Children's Television Workshop*, 553 F.2d 87 (2d Cir. 1976) ("the essence of infringement lies in taking not a general theme but a particular expression through similarities of treatments, details, scenes, events and characterizations").

An examination of the dozens of cases which have attempted to delineate the line between idea and expression shed little insight on where to draw that line with respect to computer programs. Although one may have an intuitive sense of the distinction between an unprotectible idea and the expression of that idea in a literary work, the corresponding elements of similarity or lack thereof in a computer program are far from self-evident. Are any aspects of a computer program analogous to plot, characterization, scenes, or other elements often cited in other copyright cases?

A further difficulty in determining what constitutes substantial similarity in the expression of ideas in computer programs for purposes of determining whether an infringement has occurred is that substantial similarity has generally been held to be properly determined by whether the average lay observer would recognize such substantial similarities as to lead him or her to conclude that the alleged copy must have been appropriated from the copyrighted work. *See, e.g., Herbert Rosenthal Jewelry Corp. v. Honora Jewelry Co.*, 509 F.2d 64, 65 (2d Cir. 1974). Obviously the average lay observer has no basis for making a rational judgment as to whether one line of computer code is substantially similar to another.

One of the few discussions of the idea/expression

dichotomy as applied to computer programs is contained in the final report of the National Commission on New Technological Uses of Copyrighted Works (the so-called "CONTU Report"):

In the computer context . . . [the idea/expression dichotomy] means that if one's specific instructions, even though previously copyrighted, are the only and essential means of accomplishing a given task, their later use by another will not amount to an infringement. . . . [C]opyright protection for programs does not threaten to block the use of ideas or of program language previously developed by others when that use is necessary to achieve a certain result. When other language *is* available, programmers are free to read copyrighted programs and use the ideas embodied in them in preparing their own works.

One possible explanation for the *Franklin* court's holding on the idea/expression issue is that, like the CONTU Commission, the court equated "idea" as applied to computer programs with the accomplishment of a given task or a given function, and that the court believed that such tasks or functions should be defined in a fairly narrow sense. The design of an Apple-compatible operating system involves the creation of a number of different interrelated programs performing thousands of functions. The *Franklin* court may have been trying to suggest that the idea of achieving Apple compatibility was simply too broad in scope for any meaningful application of the idea/expression dichotomy and that any analysis should properly be conducted on a program by program basis or even at a lower level, such as an examination of similarities in subroutines.

Clearly, a significant part of the problem in applying any previously enunciated standards to the question of determining where the idea ends and expression begins in computer programs is that there are fundamental differences in kind between most copyrighted works and computer programs. Computer programs are designed to perform specific tasks or functions and their design is dictated primarily by considerations of how to achieve these functions in the most efficient manner. Other types of copyrighted works, *e.g.*, paintings, sculptures, novels, music, motion pictures, etc., are designed to communicate ideas or to make aesthetic impressions on people, and their design is dictated more by artistic or aesthetic considerations than by functional considerations.

Thus, "idea" in a non-computer program context is rarely equated with the accomplishment of a task or function. The *Franklin* court's failure to articulate what it meant by an "idea" (except for its example of converting source code into object code) leaves us with no basis or standard for determinig what the court would view as an idea and what it would dismiss as something outside the scope of idea/expression analysis.

The closest analogy in existing case law to the

functional aspects of computer programs may be to cases involving the copyrightability of forms and documents used in business. As one court observed in a case involving alleged infringement of insurance company forms for bonds, affidavits of loss and indemnity agreements:

> In the fields of insurance and commerce the use of specific language in forms and documents may be so essential to accomplish a desired result and so integrated with the use of a legal or commercial conception that the proper standard of infringement is one which will protect as far as possible the copyrighted language and yet allow free use of the thought beneath the language. *Continental Casualty Company v. Beardsley*, 253 F.2d 702, 706 (2d Cir. 1958).

Thus, where a particular contract clause is intended to accomplish a particular result, *e.g.*, to require that any lawsuits arising under the agreement be filed in a particular forum, the clause is intended to serve largely dictates the form in which it is expressed, and the idea may merge with the expression, rendering the language of the clause unprotectible under copyright law. Similarly, since computer programs are designed to perform certain functions, the idea of performing a particular function may merge with its expression if there is only one way (or a very limited number of ways) to write code which will perform that function.

This still leaves open, however, the question of whether the court in *Franklin* should properly have viewed achieving Apple-compatibility as an "idea" and remanded for consideration by the trial court the question of whether that idea is capable of expression in more than one way. Part of the *Franklin* court's concern, though not articulated, may have been the conflicting results one might wish to achieve on public policy grounds depending on what the facts proved to be as to whether it is possible to design Apple compatible operating systems in a variety of different ways.

At the time the Apple operating systems software was originally designed, it was written primarily to perform a variety of functions within the Apple computer. Clearly, an Apple competitor designing another computer more or less simultaneously with Apple should be deemed to have infringed Apple's copyrights if it simply copied Apple's operating system software, since the competitor could, through its own independent efforts, design operating systems software to manipulate data within its own machine in a fashion functionally similar to the way that data is manipulated in the Apple without duplicating Apple's code.

During the period since the Apple computer was introduced, however, thousands of applications programs which are capable of interfacing with the Apple operating systems software have been created by unrelated third parties. Since one of the principal functions

performed by operating systems software is to interface with applications programs, the creation of these thousands of applications programs which are compatible with Apple's operating system has added a new dimension to creating an operating system which is functionally similar to Apple's, since functional similarity now includes compatibility with such applications programs. If in fact there is now only one way to write an operating system which will interface with most or all of these applications programs, it might be viewed as somewhat anomalous if what would have been an infringing act at the time Apple originally created its operating system software somehow becomes a noninfringing act because the intervening actions of independent third part software developers have made the idea of Apple compatibility merge with the expression of that idea.

On the other hand, if as Apple itself has apparently suggested, it is possible to design other operating systems that will run most or all of the Apple compatible applications programs, the *Franklin* court's refusal to consider the idea of achieving Apple compatibility as an "idea" to which the idea/expression dichotomy should be applied is difficult to understand.

The goal of achieving compatibility with applications programs configured for the most popular microcomputers has been pursued by a number of companies in various ways. For example, among the companies which either are marketing or have announced an intention to market computers which are to varying degrees compatible with IBM PC applications software are Compaq, Eagle, Corona, Seequa, ITT, Televideo, Visual, Otrona, Tava, Sanyo, Sperry, Panasonic and Hyperion. Manufacturers of Apple-compatible machines include, in addition to Franklin, Video Technology, Commuter Computer and W.T.I. Computer. It is generally believed that most of these companies have achieved compatibility not by simply copying Apple's or IBM's system programs but by writing such programs more or less independently within the confines imposed by their desire to achieve compatibility.

Franklin was, in a sense, a very easy case to decide, because Franklin apparently made no effort to develop independently an Apple compatible operating system; instead, it simply copied Apple's. A more interesting and difficult case would be presented if Apple or IBM were to sue the developer of a compatible operating system which was to a greater or lesser degree written independently. Depending on the degree of similarity between the systems in question, such a case could present very clearly the question of where ideas end and expressions of ideas begin under the copyright law as applied to computer programs.

The outcome of such a case is difficult to predict. Obviously the facts in any individual case would be critical: how the compatible system was developed, to what degree it was similar to the operating system it was designed to emulate, etc.

Compatibility as an Idea Under Synercom Technology

At least one court opinion may shed some light on how such a case might be decided, and the decision should be at odds with the approach to compatibility taken by the *Franklin* court. In *Synercom Technology, Inc. v. University Computing Company*, 462 F.Supp. 1003 (N.D. Tex. 1978), one of the defendants, EDI, designed a structural analysis engineering program which was compatible with Synercom's structural analysis engineering program in the sense that a user could input data in the same format and sequence for either program. The defendants' strategy, at least in part, was to lure away some of Synercom's customers who were already familiar with the operation of Synercom's system by offering a lower priced alternative that did not require the customer to reformat any of its data. If a customer knew how to format and input data for Synercom's program, it could format and input data for EDI's program.

To achieve compatibility with Synercom's input formats, EDI wrote a preprocessor program containing FORTRAN statements which the court described as "derived directly and precisely" from Synercom's copyrighted formats. 462 F.Supp. at 1012. The court concluded, however, that EDI did not infringe Synercom's copyrights because the arrangement, sequence and order of data reflected in the input formats and copied by EDI was merely an idea, not an expression of an idea, and therefore EDI only appropriated an idea, not an expression of an idea. The court further offered as an alternative holding that if the arrangement, sequence and order of data reflected in the input formats were deemed to constitute an expression of an idea, the formats were not copyrightable, because "the form, arrangement, and combination is itself the intellectual conception involved," *i.e.*, the idea and its expression are indistinguishable. 462 F.Supp. at 1014.

If someone were to attempt to create independently an operating system capable of running most or all Apple compatible applications programs, there are certain similarities to the Apple operating system programs that would have to be present, including various entry points and memory locations. For those unfamiliar with operating systems design, these entry points and memory locations are more or less arbitrarily picked numbers which designate where certain functions or information may be accessed. Other parts of the coding for such a project may be dictated by other aspects of the machine architecture of the computer for which the operating system is being developed, thus resulting in more similarities if the machine architecture were similar to that of the Apple. Substantial portions of the code, however, probably could be independently created and need not look much like the Apple code. The crucial question, obviously, would be whether whatever similarities were

incorporated in order to achieve compatibility would be sufficient *per se* to render the compatible operating system an infringement.

Applying the reasoning of the court in *Synercom*, a court might conclude that mere duplication of the entry points of an operating system in order to achieve compatibility would not constitute a copyright infringement, since the entry points arguably represent simply an arrangement, sequence or order of functions and data and not an expression of an idea. The refusal by the court in *Franklin* to consider the intention to achieve Apple-compatibility in light of the idea/expression analysis, however, has potentially troubling implications. If, for example, the court in *Synercom* had applied similar reasoning, it might have dismissed out of hand EDI's contention that there was only one way to achieve compatibility with Synercom's input formats as a "commercial and competitive objective" and held in Synercom's favor.

Because of the court's failure to articulate its standards for determining that achieving Apple compatibility is not an idea for purposes of the idea/expression dichotomy, the impact of the *Franklin* opinion in future cases involving compatibility and/or the distinction between ideas and expressions is difficult to assess. Certainly the court in *Franklin* contributed little to an understanding of where ideas end and expressions begin in computer programs.

A Rebuttable or Conclusive Presumption of Injunctive Relief For the Copyright Plaintiff?

Franklin will be very useful to the software owner alleging infringement at the preliminary injunction stage. The normal rule is that the showing of a reasonable likelihood of success on the merits raises a presumption of irreparable harm; but the presumption is rebuttable and the courts still consider the balance of hardships and the public interest. In *Franklin*, upon a showing of a reasonable likelihood of success on the merits and a showing that Apple had made a significant investment in its software, the court appeared to erect a conclusive presumption in favor of granting the preliminary injunction. The court of appeals admonished the district court for even considering the balance of hardships or the devastating impact on Franklin, and eliminated any consideration of the public interest by a simple citation to Congressional intent in enacting the copyright laws.

Apple's request for a preliminary injunction against Franklin, if granted, would undeniably have had a devastating impact upon Franklin. The district court in *Franklin*, in denying Apple's motion, determined that Apple "is better suited to withstand whatever injury it might sustain during litigation than is Franklin to withstand the effects of a preliminary injunction." 545 F.Supp. at 825. However, the Third Circuit Court of Appeals rejected consideration of the balance of hardships between Apple and Franklin.

> Nor can we accept the district court's explanation which stressed the 'devastating effect' of a preliminary injunction on Franklin's business. If that were the correct standard, then a knowing infringer would be permitted to construct its business around its infringement, a result we cannot condone. 714 F.2d 1255.

The appellate court gave no equitable weight to the fact that a preliminary injunction could put Franklin out of business. According to the Third Circuit in *Franklin*:

> A copyright plaintiff who makes out a prima facie case of infringement is entitled to a preliminary injunction without a detailed showing of irreparable harm. 714 F.2d at 1254.

Moreover, the court of appeals specifically distinguished an earlier case from the Third Circuit suggesting that the strength of the required showing of irreparable injury varies inversely with the strength of plaintiff's showing of a likelihood of success on the merits. As the court of appeals explained:

> Normally, . . . the public interest underlying the copyright law requires a presumption of irreparable harm, as long as there is, as here, adequate evidence of the expenditure of significant time, effort and money directed to the production of the copyrighted material.

Otherwise, the court said, the intent to protect creativity underlying the copyright law would be undermined.

Virtually every software copyright case will allow a showing of the expenditure of "significant time, effort and money" in the creation of the copyrighted software. The reasoning of *Franklin* supports a conclusive presumption in favor of preliminary injunctive relief in such a case, disregarding whether the preliminary injunction will put the defendant out of business without trial.

Traditionally, courts have balanced four separate criteria — *i.e.*, irreparable harm, probability of success, balance of hardships, and the public interest — in determining when injunctive relief should be granted. Courts do create a rebuttable presumption favoring injunctive relief upon a prima facie showing of infringement, but the presumption is not conclusive and evidence concerning the other equitable criteria — *i.e.*, irreparable injury, balance of hardships, and public interest — are still weighed before granting such extraordinary relief. *See, e.g., Atari, Inc., v. JS&A Group, Inc.*, No. 83-C-8333, (N.D. Ill., E.Div., Dec. 6, 1983) (district court granted Atari's motion for preliminary injunction on copyright infringement claim where court found: Atari was likely to prevail on merit; irreparable injury to Atari; that the balance of hardships tipped in Atari's

favor since it had invested hundreds of millions of dollars in its video games whereas defendant only invested $12,000 in inventory; and that public had interest in protecting Atari's copyrights thereby regarding creative expression); *Clark Equipment Co. v. Harlan Corp.*, 539 F.Supp. 561 (D. Kan. 1982) (where manufacturer and supplier of trucklift parts commenced action for copyright infringement, district court denied motion for preliminary injunction after presuming irreparable injury, finding lack of probability of success on merits, and finding that interference with defendants' business and loss of good will during period of temporary restraining order tipped hardships in favor of defendants); *Ideal Toy Corp. v. Kenner Products, etc.*, 443 F.Supp 291 (S.D.N.Y., 1977) (where toy manufacturer brought suit for declaration that sale of toys did not infringe rights in film *Star Wars* and defendant requested injunction for copyright infringement by plaintiff, district court denied injunctive request where defendant failed to show probable success and irreparable harm, since injunction would completely disrupt established promotional campaign and distribution and good will and would cause financial hardships); *see also Nimmer on Copyright* § 14.06[A], 14-48 & n.9 (collection of cases where courts have denied injunctive relief to copyright plaintiffs upon balancing the hardships between the parties).

The court of appeals in *Franklin* did not give any consideration to the traditional (even as employed in copyright cases) criteria for granting preliminary injunctive relief. The *Franklin* court erected a conclusive presumption in favor of injunctive relief upon a showing of probable success on the merits and showing an expenditure of "time, effort and money", the latter of which should virtually always be present in software copyright cases. The opinion in *Franklin* should serve as very strong support for the plaintiff seeking provisional relief in software copyright cases.

54: STATEMENT ON H.R. 1028, THE SEMICONDUCTOR CHIP PROTECTION ACT OF 1983

L. Ray Patterson

Emory University
December 1, 1983

Mr. Chairman and Members of the Subcommittee:

Having been a student of copyright law and its historical development for some twenty-five years, I appreciate this opportunity to appear before the Subcommittee to express some ideas resulting from my studies.

One of the advantages of not representing any particular constituent is the opportunity to view a problem in terms of general rather than particular issues. I wish to take advantage of the opportunity and view the problem of copyright protection for semiconductor chips in the context of copyright and new technology. Consequently, my approach is a conceptual one.

There are two reasons for examining the concept of copyright in light of the problems that new technology poses: First, copyright law as it presently exists does not have a sound conceptual basis. Secondly, until and unless there is agreement on a sound conceptual basis, the problem of the application of copyright to new technology will continue to be resolved on an *ad hoc* basis, in all probability with consequences that Congress neither contemplated nor intended.

The ultimate issue is the problem of integrity in the law of copyright. By integrity, I mean consistency in the principles which the law encompasses. While consistency for its own sake is a virtue of small consequence, consistent principles for a body of law are essential for integrity in the interpretation and administration of that law.

The conclusions to which I have come are two: (1) It would be unwise for Congress to provide copyright protection for semiconductor chips by amendment to the present statute. The basis for this conclusion is that the present copyright statute purports to provide for an author's copyright. (2) The appropriate solution to the problem of protection for semiconductor chips is the creation of an industrial copyright, separate and distinct from the author's copyright. The basis for this conclusion is that copyright protection for semiconductor chips under the present statute would be to create another fiction for copyright and contribute to the conceptual confusion that has plagued copyright law for over two and a half centuries.

The route to reach these conclusions is a circuitous one, with many by-ways which there is no time to explore here. But a good starting point is to recognize that Anglo-American copyright in origin was the product of new technology, the printing press, which William Caxton introduced into

Reproduced from *Testimony Presented Before the Subcommittee on Courts, Civil Liberties, and the Administration of Justice of the Committee on the Judiciary, House of Representatives,* Washington, D.C., December 1, 1983, 9p.

England in the 1470s. The interesting point is that copyright existed for three hundred years before it was applied to the product of other technology, the camera in 1865.

The 1865 Act notwithstanding, Congress traditionally has granted copyright protection for the products of new technology with considerable reluctance. It was not, for example, until 1972 that Congress provided copyright protection for sound recordings. And even in the current statute, copyright for phonorecords is the most limited of the copyrights available under the act in that copyright for sound recordings precludes duplication, not imitation.

The relevant question here is this: Why has Congress been reluctant to grant copyright protection to new technology? The answer, I think, is the lack of a sound conceptual basis for copyright law. If the fundamental principles are not agreed upon, there is no common ground for agreeing what to do, and no way of predicting what rules will emerge by way of judicial interpretation of ambiguous legislation. The most recent example is the *Apple Computer* case in which the Third Circuit gave an expansive reading to section 102(a) of the Copyright Act and in effect gave a judicial answer to the legislative question with which this subcommittee is now concerned. *Apple Computer, Inc.* v. *Franklin Computer Corporation,* 219 U.S.P.Q. 113 (3d Cir. 1983).

The fault here is not that of Congress, but history, as a result of which copyright can be characterized as a schizophrenic legal concept. The copyright clause empowers Congress to secure to authors the exclusive right to their writings for limited times. One would assume from this language that copyright is intended to benefit authors. But the Supreme Court says this is not so. Copyright is intended primarily to benefit the public. Yet the copyright statute functions primarily to benefit the publisher or entrepreneur. The contradiction in constitutional language, court decisions, and congressional action has an explanation in the tortuous story of copyright development, which is reflected in the major conceptual weakness of current copyright law. That weakness is a dichotomy between form and function: in form copyright is an author's right, in function it is a publisher's right.

This dichotomy has created and continues to support the basic controversy over the concept of copyright: Is it a regulatory or a proprietary concept? The Supreme Court has answered the question. Copyright is a regulatory, not a proprietary concept, a statutory monopoly granted in the interest of the public. Yet, the answer has never been wholly accepted because of the characterization of copyright as an author's right. It is one thing to say that copyright for a publisher is a statutory monopoly, quite another to say that copyright for an author is a statutory monopoly. A person's writings are uniquely his own, for as an ancient Irish king is supposed to have said in resolving a copyright dispute: "To every cow her calf."

The point here is simply that the concept of copyright does not have a sound conceptual base because it encompasses two contradictory and antithetical ideas: a statutory monopoly of one's own creations. Thus, despite the insistence of the Supreme Court that copyright is a regulatory concept, the notion that it is in fact a proprietary concept persists, and it is

310

this view of copyright that underlies the *Apple Computer* opinion. And it is this view that has been the basis for continually enlarging the statutory monopoly of copyright, on occasion unwittingly so.

One example will suffice to illustrate my point. In the 1790 Copyright Act, the exclusive rights given to the copyright owner were to print, reprint, publish, and vend the copyrighted works, books, maps, and charts. Until the 1909 Act, these remained the exclusive rights for literary works. In the 1870 Copyright Act, Congress provided copyright protection for, among other things, statuary and models of works of fine art. The exclusive right given in connection with these works was the right to copy. In the 1909 Copyright Act, the exclusive rights given to all copyright works were the rights to print, reprint, publish, *copy* and vend all copyrighted works.

House Report 2222 indicates that Congress was not cognizant of the implications of the change. But it is one thing to give the copyright owner the exclusive rights to print, reprint, publish and vend a book. It is quite another to give him in addition the exclusive right to copy the book. And except for the notion that copyright is an author's right, there would have been no reason for the change. The consequences of the change, of course, were not felt until the advent of new technology in the form of the Xerox, and paradoxically this change in the 1909 Act presented Congress with one of its most difficult problems in enacting the 1976 Copyright Act.

Despite its label as an author's right copyright is functionally a concept of statutory unfair competition based on the misappropriation rationale that serves the entrepreneur better than the author, a point demonstrated by the work-made-for-hire doctrine and the conferring of statutory benefits on the copyright owner rather than the author. Indeed, there is only one provision of the 1976 Copyright Act that is of unique benefit to the author, the termination right, the origin of which can be traced back to the Statute of Anne of 1710, the English copyright act which served as the model for the American Copyright Act of 1790. And there are few who would argue that the work-made-for-hire doctrine is of benefit to the author.

To provide copyright protection for semiconductor chips by amending the present statute will be to widen the gap between the form and the function of copyright. To say that copyright for semiconductor chips is an author's copyright is to stretch fiction beyond both its rational and functional limits. More important, perhaps, Congress is not here dealing only with semiconductor chips, it is dealing with the problem of copyright for the products of new technology, of which the semiconductor chip is only the beginning.

The semiconductor chip bill, then, is only the pilot project, and it is important to understand the essential difference between copyright protection for a book and a semiconductor chip. A book is a product, an end in itself. A semiconductor chip is both a product and a process, a means to an end. Copyright protection for the semiconductor chip in traditional terms can be analogized to a copyright for books that protects the printing press as well as the book.

My objection is not legal protection for semiconductor chips. My objection is protection for them in terms of an author's copyright. What I am suggesting is the creation of an industrial copyright designed for, and directed to, the problems that need to be resolved. To deal with these problems, an industrial copyright would have the characteristics of both copyright and patent, and would in effect be a quasi-patent right.

The essential problem to which the industrial copyright would be directed is industrial piracy. One of its major advantages would be that it would provide an opportunity to provide new remedies not appropriate for the author's copyright. An industrial copyright statute, for example, could create an action in the nature of the common law *qui tam* action authorizing an action on behalf of the copyright owner by United States Attorneys, with half of any recovery going to the United States. Precedent for the *qui tam* type action is found in the Copyright Act of 1790, which was based on the pure *qui tam* action in the Statute of Anne. Moreover, such a statute would provide an opportunity for considering the public interest, since the fair use doctrine, the major protection for the public interest in the present statute, has little meaning when applied to semiconductor chips.

My argument for an industrial copyright statute is twofold: First, it would provide more effective protection for industry because it would rest on an unadulterated predicate: statutory unfair competition based on the misappropriation rationale. A sound and generally accepted predicate would be protection against judicial misinterpretation resulting from a free choice of competing principles to govern a particular decision that the confused concept of copyright presently provides.

Secondly, such a statute would be a major step toward establishing a sound conceptual basis for the traditional author's copyright. It would provide a basis for cleansing the copyright law of provisions dealing with problems of no consequence to the creative author, but which serve to dilute his protection. I have always thought, for example, that the failure to give recognition to the moral right of the author is one of the major deficiencies of our copyright law. Authors and artists in a very real sense are the persons who teach us to appreciate beauty in which we find the values that give quality to life by creating the conscience which impels us to strive for justice and equality. They merit protection for their efforts, and the failure to provide better protection I attribute to the confused concept of copyright.

The conceptual basis for an author's copyright should be protection for the reputation as well as the profit of the author, predicated on the fact that creative works are an expression of the author's personality. The conceptual basis for an industrial copyright should be purely and simply unfair competition based upon the misappropriation rationale.

To round out the scheme, there should be an additional type of copyright, one to protect the entrepreneur who enables the author to secure his profit, that is the publisher, or one who produces works that have no one author, for example, television broadcasts, the exemplar of which is the work made for hire. This could be characterized as a commercial copyright.

The ultimate point, perhaps, is that copyright law must encompass and balance the interest of three groups: the creator, the entrepreneur, and the public. With increasingly sophisticated new technology, the balancing process is becoming increasingly complex and difficult. That is why we must return to fundamentals and establish a sound conceptual base for copyright law. To amend the present statute to provide protection for semiconductor chips would be to create an additional obstacle to the many that already stand in the way of needed reform.

55: COMPUTER CHIPS PROTECTED, TRADEMARK STATUTE CLARIFIED

Nadine Cohodas

Congress Oct. 9 cleared a legislative package (HR 6163) that gives new legal protection to makers of tiny computer chips, clarifies trademark laws, sharply reduces the civil cases entitled to speedy federal court consideration and creates a new institute to help state judicial systems.

The bill also modifies a 1980 patent law (PL 96-517) that was designed to establish a uniform policy for inventions arising from contracts between the government and small businesses or non-profit organizations, including universities. *(1980 Almanac p. 405)*

The vehicle for all this legislation was a federal court housekeeping bill that established new sites for holding sessions of selected federal courts.

Protection for Computer Chips

The most important part of the package was a section granting the makers of semiconductor chips, which lie at the heart of the microcomputer revolution, 10 years of legal protection from illegal copying of their chips.

Testimony before House and Senate committees showed that manufacturers of semiconductor chips are vulnerable to piracy by firms that photograph a chip, analyze and duplicate it. These "pirate" firms can then sell the chip more cheaply than the original maker because they have been spared the millions of dollars in research expenditures usually required to develop a chip. *(Background, Weekly Report pp. 135, 1436)*

Rep. Carlos J. Moorhead, R-Calif., noted one recent government study found that "the R&D costs for a single complex chip could reach $4 million, while the costs of copying such a chip could be less than $100,000."

Unless chip makers receive protection from copying, supporters of the bill said, innovation could be sti-

fled as companies become increasingly leery of committing resources to the development of new, more sophisticated chips only to see them copied and sold cheaply by pirate companies.

"This vote occurs not a minute too soon," said Rep. Don Edwards, D-Calif., who, with Rep. Norman Y. Mineta, D-Calif., first introduced the semiconductor chip bill in 1978.

"With this measure," Edwards continued, "innovating firms finally will be able to combat the unfair chip piracy that is sapping their strength and destroying their incentive to continue to invest in the crucial but very expensive creative endeavors necessary to maintain American leadership in this field."

The most troublesome issue surrounding chip protection was defining what a chip actually is and then fitting it into existing law.

A semiconductor chip is something like a scientific Dagwood sandwich. It is made up of a system of intricate layers of material with unique designs etched on them. The designs route electrical signals so they will perform specific tasks, and chips run computers and other products.

Under existing law, copyright protection is not available for the imprinted design patterns on the semiconductor chips, known as "mask works."

A bill (S 1201) passed May 16 by the Senate would have given copyright protection to semiconductor chips for 10 years. Both the House and the final bill took a slightly different approach.

As cleared, HR 6163 gives the mask works 10 years of what is essentially copyright protection, but it creates a new section of law specifically designed for the computer chips.

This approach, the brainchild of Rep. Robert W. Kastenmeier, D-Wis., does not attempt to fit chip protection into existing copyright law, which covers more traditional "writings" such as books and plays. "Quite clearly, a mask work is not a book," Kastenmeier said Oct. 9. "The measure ... therefore does not engage in the fatal flaw of treating books and mask works similarly."

Kastenmeier noted that the bill constituted "the first new intellectual property law in nearly 100 years."

The Senate's chip bill provided for criminal penalties for infringement, but the House bill and the final compromise version provided only civil remedies.

"It seems that every day we are creating a new penal statute of some sort with little thought given to investigative and evidentiary problems, to the burdens on judges and juries, and to the goals of and pressures on the

Congress has granted 10 years of copyright-style legal protection to makers of semiconductor chips, which lie at the heart of computer technology. The chip pictured above is sealed in a protective ceramic package.

correctional system," Kastenmeier said Oct. 9. "I am pleased we have not so erred in this act."

When the Senate approved the compromise Sept. 27, Sen. Charles McC. Mathias Jr., R-Md., said the Senate "with some reluctance" would yield to the House. Mathias said he believed that criminal sanctions do play "a limited but important role" in copyright enforcement, and added that he would seek to reopen the issue of criminal sanctions for mask work infringement if the civil remedies proved inadequate.

the House May 22, but it failed to get the two-thirds required under suspension of the House rules. *(Institute, Weekly Report p. 1228)*

The Senate had passed separate bills on computer chip protection (S 1201) and the creation of a state justice institute (S 384). *(Weekly Report pp. 1213, 1529)*

On Oct. 3, the Senate tacked all of the measures onto HR 6163, the court housekeeping bill. Final action on the package came Oct. 9, when the House by 363-0 agreed to the Senate's amendment. *(Vote 396, p. 2676)*

Final Provisions

As cleared by Congress, HR 6163 included these major provisions:

[*Editors' Note:* Material has been omitted at this point.]

[*Editors' Note:* Material has been omitted at this point.]

Legislative History

All but the patent and judicial institute sections of HR 6163 had been passed earlier by the House as separate measures.

The patent provisions were approved in a somewhat different form by the Science and Technology Committee (HR 5003 — H Rept 98-983).

The institute section received a 243-176 majority when it was considered as a separate bill (HR 4145) by

Computer Chips

● Created a new chapter of Title 17 of the U.S. Code (the copyright title) to protect semiconductor chips from unauthorized copying.

● Provided 10 years of copyright-style protection for "mask works fixed in a semiconductor chip."

● Defined a mask work as a series of related images fixed or encoded on a piece of semiconductor material, such as silicon, that are arranged in a pattern to perform a specific function.

● Provided that a mask work is considered "fixed" when it is part of an actual semiconductor chip product, such as a computer, not just a plan or drawing of such product. The definition is worded so that a mask work could also be considered to be fixed when it is put on a magnetic tape that could be reproduced.

● Allowed the owner of a mask work to apply to the Register of Copyrights for registration of a claim of protection, and directed the register to issue a certificate of registration if he determines that the mask work meets the specified requirements.

● Allowed an owner of a mask work to seek federal district court review of a refusal to register a mask work, provided the appeal is filed within 60 days of the refusal.

● Provided that a mask work is entitled to protection if the owner is a national or domiciliary of the United States, a national or domiciliary or sovereign authority of a foreign nation that is a party to a treaty affording protection to mask works to which the United States is also a party, or a stateless person, wherever that person is domiciled.

● Provided protection for a mask work that is first "commercially exploited" in the United States. "Commercially exploited" was defined to mean the distribution to the public of a semiconductor chip product embodying the mask work in question. The term covers an offer to sell or transfer such a product only when the offer is in writing and occurs after the mask work is "fixed" in the semiconductor chip product.

• Provided protection for mask works that come within the scope of a presidential proclamation covering protection afforded to mask works by foreign nations.

• Barred protection for mask works that are not original or consist of designs that are staple, commonplace, or familiar in the semiconductor industry, or that are combinations of designs in a manner not considered as a whole to be original.

• Provided the owner of a mask work protection for 10 years and provided further that protection would begin on the date on which the mask work is registered or first commercially exploited anywhere in the world, whichever occurs first.

• Granted the owner of a mask work exclusive rights to reproduce the mask work by optical, electronic or any other means, to import or distribute a semiconductor chip product embodying the mask work, and to have another person reproduce, import or distribute such product.

• Allowed "reverse engineering" of protected mask works, which covers the reproduction of the mask work "solely" for the purpose of teaching, analyzing or evaluating the concepts or techniques embodied in the mask work or its components.

• Protected an innocent purchaser of a pirated semiconductor chip product from liability for using the chip but required the user to pay a "reasonable royalty" on each unit of the infringing product that the purchaser imports or distributes after being notified that the mask work involved is protected.

• Made liable for infringement any person who violates any exclusive rights of the owner of a protected mask work.

• Entitled the owner of a registered mask work to file a civil action for infringement.

• Entitled the owner of a mask work that was denied protection to file a suit for infringement under specified circumstances and gave the Register of Copyrights the discretion to join the suit on the issue of whether the mask work is eligible for protection.

• Gave the secretary of the Treasury and the U.S. Postal Service authority to write regulations concerning the exclusion of products from the United States that may infringe on a protected mask work.

• Gave federal district courts the authority, in an infringement suit, to grant temporary restraining orders and permanent injunctions to restrain infringement of a mask work owner's exclusive rights.

• Allowed an owner who prevails in an infringement suit to be awarded actual damages and the infringer's profits attributable to the infringement under terms specified in the legislation.

• Allowed a prevailing mask work owner to elect to receive a flat damage award covering all infringements of one mask work instead of actual damages and profits. The award could not be greater than $250,000.

• Required any action for infringement to be initiated within three years after the claim arises.

• Authorized a judge, while an action is pending, to impound any products, drawings or tapes that are claimed to have been made, imported or used in violation of the mask work owner's exclusive rights.

• Authorized a judge, as part of a final judgment, to order the destruction of any infringing semiconductor chip products.

• Barred a civil action for infringement of a mask work until 60 days after enactment of the law.

• Provided protection for a mask work first commercially exploited on or after July 1, 1983, and before the date of enactment, if a claim of protection is registered with the Copyright Office before July 1, 1985.

• Authorized the secretary of commerce to provide protection for mask works of nationals, domiciliaries and sovereign authorities of a foreign nation under specified conditions set out in the legislation.

[*Editors' Note:* Material has been omitted at this point.]

56: SONY CORPORATION OF AMERICA ET AL. V. UNIVERSAL CITY STUDIOS, INC., ET AL. (SYLLABUS)

J. Stevens

SYLLABUS BY REPORTER OF DECISIONS

Petitioner Sony Corp. manufactures home video tape recorders (VTR's), and markets them through retail establishments, some of which are also petitioners. Respondents own the copyrights on some of the television programs that are broadcast on the public airwaves. Respondents brought an action against petitioners in Federal District Court, alleging that VTR consumers had been recording some of respondents' copyrighted works that had been exhibited on commercially sponsored television and thereby infringed respondents' copyrights, and further that petitioners were liable for such copyright infringement because of their marketing of the VTR's. Respondents sought money damages, an equitable accounting of profits, and an injunction against the manufacture and marketing of the VTR's. The District Court denied respondents all relief, holding that noncommercial home use recording of material broadcast over the public airwaves was a fair use of copyrighted works and did not constitute copyright infringement, and that petitioners could not be held liable as contributory infringers even if the home use of a VTR was considered an infringing use. The Court of Appeals reversed, holding petitioners liable for contributory infringement and ordering the District Court to fashion appropriate relief.

Held: The sale of the VTR's to the general public does not constitute contributory infringement of respondents' copyrights.

(a) The protection given to copyrights is wholly statutory, and, in a case like this, in which Congress has not plainly marked the course to be followed by the judiciary, this Court must be circumspect in construing the scope of rights created by a statute that never contemplated such a calculus of interests. Any individual may reproduce a copyrighted work for a "fair use"; the copyright owner does not possess the exclusive right to such a use.

Reprinted from pages 577-578 of *78L Ed 2d 574* (1984). (United States Supreme Court Reports, Lawyer's Edition, February 21, 1984.)

(b) Kalem Co. v Harper Brothers, 222 US 55, 56 L Ed 92, 32 S Ct 20, does not support respondents' novel theory that supplying the "means" to accomplish an infringing activity and encouraging that activity through advertisement are sufficient to establish liability for copyright infringement. This case does not fall in the category of those in which it is manifestly just to impose vicarious liability because the "contributory" infringer was in a position to control the use of copyrighted works by others and had authorized the use without permission from the copyright owner. Here, the only contact between petitioners and the users of the VTR's occurred at the moment of sale. And there is no precedent for imposing vicarious liability on the theory that petitioners sold the VTR's with constructive knowledge that their customers might use the equipment to make unauthorized copies of copyrighted material. The sale of copying equipment, like the sale of other articles of commerce, does not constitute contributory infringement if the product is widely used for legitimate, unobjectionable purposes, or, indeed, is merely capable of substantial noninfringing uses.

(c) The record and the District Court's findings show (1) that there is a significant likelihood that substantial numbers of copyright holders who license their works for broadcast on free television would not object to having their broadcast time-shifted by private viewers (i. e., recorded at a time when the VTR owner cannot view the broadcast so that it can be watched at a later time); and (2) that there is no likelihood that time-shifting would cause nonminimal harm to the potential market for, or the value of, respondents' copyrighted works. The VTR's are therefore capable of substantial noninfringing uses. Private, noncommercial time-shifting in the home satisfies this standard of noninfringing uses both because respondents have no right to prevent other copyright holders from authorizing such time-shifting for their programs, and because the District Court's findings reveal that even the unauthorized home time-shifting of respondents' programs is legitimate fair use.

659 F2d 963, reversed.

Stevens, J., delivered the opinion of the Court in which Burger, C. J., and Brennan, White, and O'Connor, JJ., joined. Blackmun, J., filed a dissenting opinion in which Marshall, Powell, and Rehnquist, JJ., joined.

57: PRIVATE USE, PUBLIC POLICY: COPYRIGHT AND HOME RECORDING

David Ladd

Nowadays, above all else, technology dictates the content of our copyright laws and plots their course into the future. In the last twenty years, more than ever, copyright specialists have been preoccupied with problems falling under the heading of "new technology." The problems arising from the relationship between copyright and new technologies are, however, not new.

Copyright originated in technological change —the printing press—and at each stage in the history of copyright law, technological innovation has been a central problem to policy makers. However new the computer may seem, however strange or exotic laser holography, the videodisc, and direct satellite broadcasting, the central questions they pose for authors, disseminators, and users have been with us a long time.

The contemporary attitude toward our generation's copyright problems with new technology is ambivalent: optimism over the prospects of new markets, new modes of education, and new sources of consumer satisfaction is tempered by anxiety over the dangers of irretrievable loss of control over copyrighted works because of that technology.

Videocassette recording technology is only a simple and clear example:. educators are eagerly and imaginatively exploiting this new tool, the prospect of large video sale and rental markets is excitingly attractive, yet the motion picture and television production industries sense that recording equipment can blight markets for rentals and sales to consumers, and even the broadcast market as well. In short, in the area of new technologies and elsewhere, domestically and internationally, copyright is pressed to keep pace with changes for the benefit of authors and proprietors; and, in some

---

David Ladd *is U.S. Register of Copyrights. This article is an adaptation of a speech delivered in September before the International Copyright Society in Toronto.*

quarters, questions are raised about whether copyright can keep pace at all.

This is unfortunate, because copyright, as the principal instrument for protection of author's rights, is widely accepted throughout the world. The principle is clearly stated in the preamble of the Universal Copyright Convention: that a universal copyright system "will ensure respect for the rights of the individual and encourage the development of literature, the sciences and the arts. . ."

And throughout the world, under the international conventions, copyright has extended and expanded to accommodate that principle to new kinds of works and to new uses of works. Whatever its basis anywhere—reward or incentive, privilege or natural right—the exclusive rights of the author have always been rooted in economic realities. Protection for the creations of authors may be based upon recognition of the special role of creative artists in shaping national or human culture. The nature of such protection, however, depends upon the marketplace in given societies. We may dwell in the sublime realms of Don Quixote's vision only if we also are properly mindful of Sancho Panza's more earthly concerns.

Adapting copyright to new technology
Applying this instrument of copyright to contemporary conditions has not always been easy. The adaptation of copyright rules to technology began with piano rolls and jukeboxes, then with motion pictures, broadcasting, sound recording, and television, and recently with computers, cable television, and photocopying machines.

The questions that arose were varied and difficult. The marvel is that the adaptation occurred in the United States as efficiently as it did, since it was largely accomplished by judicial decision. But courts can only go so far, particularly when they are forced to compromise conflicting interests when statutory guidance is absent or unclear. The marketplace of the 1920s and '30s was smaller and more amenable to gradual, judicial expansion of copyright. Today we may not have the luxury of assessing technological impact at our leisure.

Technology now presents copyright with especially troublesome problems of adaptation. The rate of technological change has accelerated, and accordingly, the strains on copyright have intensified. There has also emerged a new problem different in kind: how to control uses of copyrighted works that are not readily detectable and therefore not readily policeable. Until recently, nearly all infringements of copyrighted works were public and so visible at their source that enforcement of copyright presented no special problems, particularly after the appearance of collecting societies.

Take, for example, the cinema market of the 1930s. Replication was strictly controlled; distribution was only through a limited number of theaters, and filmmakers did not even part with ownership of their prints. Contrast this with the multitiered markets for motion pictures today: theaters, television, cable, MDS, cassettes, special educational, and 16mm markets. The same reproduction devices once used only by the copyright owner are now widely owned, and copyright owners are confronted with the problem of controlling unauthorized copying of protected works with these devices. Now, in these new problem areas, we must decide whether we can devise and use the equivalent of the theater-era box office to collect payments for use, or whether we must throw up our hands and accept all home copying as lawless but uncontrollable, or lawful because it is uncontrollable.

Current audio and video taping practices
Audio and video recording equipment are used by many different groups including unauthorized commercial "pirates," schools, libraries, archives and other nonprofit organizations, and private individuals. Each of these uses presents different concerns, interests, and potential dangers. While this article focuses on private home taping, a few words about each kind of taping may be useful.

● *Unauthorized commercial recording*—In recent years, there has been rapid growth in the unauthorized reproduction and distribution of copyrighted sound recordings and audiovisual works in copies or phonorecords. It poses a threat not only to the recording and motion picture industries, but to the public.

In fact, film and record piracy has become epidemic around the world, as participants at the World Intellectual Property Organization Forum on the Piracy of Sound and Audiovisual Recordings well know. In the United States, this form of unauthorized recording is clearly an infringement under section 106 of the copyright law. Sanctions, both civil and criminal, are available under chapter 5 of the law to deal with this situation. However, with the recent developments in technology, experience indicates that the present criminal sanctions, especially the length of the prison terms, should be increased in the hope of restraining those who illegally interfere with the legitimate market for sound recordings, motion pictures, and other protected works. Legislation to achieve that purpose is now pending before Congress.

● *Educational recording*—Educational uses of television and radio programming is *not* a subspecies of the larger issue of home taping. Educational off-air taping is not merely a matter of personal convenience. Film and video are so much a part of world culture and modern history that education without the moving image would be incomplete. Educational off-air taping can take several forms: spontaneous taping for a single use or collecting for repeated use, perhaps by several cooperating educational institutions. The materials taped off-air may be unavailable from authorized sources, or they may in fact be works specifically created for sale, rental, or broadcast to schools.

● *Private home recording*—Home recording by individuals for their own personal, private use has flourished in the United States. Its scope and growth have caused concern to copyright owners. While recording of both audio and audiovisual works represents potential harm to copyright owners, the varied reasons for recording and the possible legal response to different cases warrant separate analysis.

People record audio works at home primarily to build a library for repeated enjoyment. Audiovisual works, on the other hand, by their length and nature, have a limited reuse value.

This difference, when coupled with the current high cost of blank videotape (as opposed to blank audiotape), somewhat reduces the immediate prospects for extensive collecting of audiovisual works.

Why, then, is home video recording increasing? Two reasons have been mentioned in public discussions: people want to avoid commercial advertisements and to shift programming times. Commercial broadcast stations today charge advertising rates according to the popularity of their particular programming. And because copyright owners' royalties are tied to audience size, unmeasured time-shifting and commercial advertisement avoidance are important to the program supply industries. This looks merely technical, but it cuts to the very heart of our system for determining broadcast value of films and television programs. The price of freeing the viewer from the constraints of broadcast scheduling creates uncertainty in audience measurement by present sampling methods and also risks reduction of audience size for later broadcast reruns.

The legal response to copyright violations
How are all these diverse interests and activities treated under the 1976 Copyright Act? What structure does it provide to guide market evolution? Section 106 of our new law enumerates five fundamental and exclusive rights. Three of these rights—distribution of copies and phonorecords, performance, and display—are limited to public uses. No such limitations are present with respect to the right of reproduction and adaptation.

The statute sets forth these rights in broad terms, unlimited by general requirements of commerciality or profit, and then provides express and specific limitations, qualifications, and exemptions to these rights in the twelve sections that follow. The very architecture of the statute thus has compelling advantages in explicitly demarcating the legislature's balance between the rights of ownership and the rights of use.

By the same token, the statute avoids wholesale exceptions, such as "not-for-profit" uses, that entail too great a risk of eroding the copyright monopoly. Furthermore, it makes possible that claims for additional limitations, qualifications, or exemptions can be subjected

to the legislative process and there assessed upon the whole evidence from all interests, instead of a limited litigation record between a few private parties.

The structure of the statute is central to the home taping issue because of one obvious fact: none of the twelve sections *expressly* recognizes home taping as permissible. Instead, attempts to balance interests in this area center around section 107 and the doctrine of fair use of copyrighted works. Regardless of the context —commercial, noncommercial, educational, or private—the question in the United States so far has boiled down to two lines of inquiry: whether the use is "fair" or infringing, and whether the unqualified right of reproduction in section 106 is inherently limited to exclude private reproductions.

First, a few words about the doctrine of fair use in United States law.

"Fair Use" in U.S. copyright law
For 188 years, before the 1976 Copyright Act came into force, the principle of fair use was devised, applied, and elaborated by courts. Some see it as a policy-based defense, or waiver, for infringing use. Others view it as an inherent, in-dwelling limitation on the author's right, which, in a given case, bars a conclusion that infringement has occurred.

The absence of a statutory definition of fair use may have posed difficulties in applying it prospectively to certain activities; but, as a judicial instrument utilized in litigation, it was a flexible way of adjusting the reach of the copyright monopoly to fit the needs of justice in practical situations. Adding up particular holdings to reach a single definition of fair use was, however, a speculative business. It still is.

The new law sets out the principle of fair use in section 107, with four tests (here paraphrased) to guide its application in specific cases: (1) quantity—that is, how much of the protected work was taken; (2) the nature of the work; (3) the practical substitutability of the copied portions for the original work; and (4) the possibility or degree of risk that the copy poses to the market for the copyrighted original—that is, the impact of the copying on the potential market for or value of the work.

The tests were developed from commercial

litigation. From a canvass of this litigation as a whole, it appears that in ninety-nine percent of the reported cases, courts applied "fair use" to assure that the copyright monopoly in one work would not be so overreaching as to prevent a second, otherwise original work from becoming available to the public. Less than a half-dozen cases deal with noncommerical, educational uses, and only one deals with private, noncommercial reproduction. Yet, under our new law, "fair use" is the cockpit of conflict over educational and private copying privileges.

Legal responses to educational off-air taping
Scattered throughout the law are a number of limited exceptions to the exclusive rights of the copyright owner that involve noncommercial or classroom uses of protected works: for example, archival preservation of audiovisual news reporting and ephemeral recording of non-dramatic literary and musical works in educational broadcasting. But only the doctrine of fair use would appear to insulate educators from potential liability for the kinds of off-air recording activities they wish to routinely pursue.

On this question, the Congress, in enacting the 1976 revision, noted only that:

> The problem of off-the-air taping for nonprofit classroom use of copyrighted audiovisual works incorporated in radio and television broadcasts has proven difficult to resolve. The Committee believes that the fair use doctrine has some limited application in this area, but it appears that the development of detailed guidelines will require a more thorough exploration . . . of the needs and problems of a number of different interests affected and of the various legal problems presented. . . . [T]he Committee. . . . urges the representatives of the various interests, if possible under the leadership of the Register of Copyrights to continue their discussions actively. . . .

"Guidelines" are a curious U.S. invention: they raise the well-known "gentlemen's agreements" to a somewhat higher, publicly endorsed status. Standing somewhere between these "gentlemen's agreements" and law, they can symbolize consensus and enhance definition in the application of abstract principles like "fair use." They can exercise the kind of influence that one hopes good common sense always has; and they can be changed, as experience exposes their flaws, more readily than legislation can be amended.

In 1979, during the course of an oversight hearing, Congress selected a small number of individuals drawn from among educators, copyright owner interests, public broadcasting, and artists' guilds to negotiate guidelines on educational fair use of broadcast audiovisual works. After nearly three years of work, during which negotiations were stalemated and almost terminated, guidelines have been produced.

I will not belabor you with their details. I'll note only that the thrust of the guidelines is to give individual teachers the freedom to make tapes or to request that taping be done in more or less spontaneous fashion; that a fixed period for retention and classroom use is permitted, followed by a period during which the work recorded may be evaluated (previewed) for possible longer term retention and use; and express recognition that, for longer term use or retention, the permission of the copyright owner is required.

The negotiation of these guidelines may have been, in some degree, influenced by copyright litigation. In the case of *Encyclopaedia Britannica Educational Corp. v. Crooks* (known as the "BOCES" case), a preliminary injunction was issued on behalf of the plaintiffs, copyright owners of educational audiovisual works. The injunction enjoined a noncommercial educational media center from systematically videorecording copyrighted programs off-the-air and subsequently distributing the copies to schools in a number of districts. Two crucial facts should be noted: first, the copying was done at a copying center whenever it was determined that a program of educational value was broadcast on television, and the copies were then offered to the teachers in the various schools by use of listings in a catalog; and second, the copy center did not require that the copy be returned or erased after use.

The court stated: "The scope of BOCES' activities is difficult to reconcile with its claim of fair use. This case does not involve an isolated instance of a teacher copying copyrighted material for classroom use but concerns a highly organized and systematic program

for reproducing videotapes on a massive scale."
A final decision on the merits of this case is
expected soon.

Private home recording and the law

To consider the extent to which "fair use"
is applicable to the home recording of television
programming in the United States, one must
begin with already famous "Betamax" case of
*Universal Studios, et. al. v. Sony Corp. of
America, et. al.*

The case held that the noncommercial home
recording of copyrighted material broadcast
over the public airwaves, under the circumstances of the case, was not an infringement
and was permissible as fair use under the
Copyright Acts of 1909 and 1976. This decision is on appeal to the Court of Appeals for
the Ninth Circuit. [For update information on
the court's decision on the case, rendered on
October 19, see box below.]

Several points about the "Betamax" case
raise the question of whether litigation and
court decisions can satisfactorily resolve such
complex issues. It must be said, however, that
the court had to decide, because statutory
law may not have.

First, in finding an implied limitation of the

exclusive right of reproduction, the court gave
significant weight to the legislative history of
the Sound Recording Act of 1971, despite the
differences in the types of works involved and
the different commercial markets for them.

Second, in applying fair use, the court emphasized that the programming involved was
broadcast *freely* over the public airwaves, and
expressly refrained from addressing home recording from either pay or cable television.
Nor did it rule on the legality of either tape
swapping or tape duplication.

Third, the court found that the plaintiffs had
failed to establish any present or past harm
as a result of off-air taping, and that plaintiff's
allegations of potential harm were too speculative to provide a basis for relief.

The "Betamax" court gave vent to its feeling
that the problem was not well suited to judicial
resolution:

> The ramifications of this new technology
> are greater than the boundaries of this
> lawsuit. A court reviewing the limited claims
> of specified parties in a particular factual
> setting cannot and should not undertake
> the role of a government commission or
> legislative body exploring and evaluating
> all the uses and consequences of the video-
> tape recorder.

The limitations of judicial decisions

What does it mean when courts emphasize
how little law they are pronouncing, acknowledge how blunt a tool for policy-making litigation is, and glance pointedly at the national
legislature?

When law, and broad policy, are created
judicially—and make no mistake, in America
nowadays they undeniably are so made—policy
emerges piecemeal by small accretions of precedent; or, in an effort to achieve legislation-
like results, courts issue broad declarations
that really rest on the particular facts of the
given case. These shortcomings need to be
carefully considered, because the courts are
already moving to apply the test of fair use to
private taping and other copyright problems
created by new technologies. The result may
be the emergence of broad policies without any
clear legislative guidance.

A relatively small number of households
with videotaping equipment may not be enough

Unexpected decision in "Betamax" case

On October 19, 1981, a Federal appellate
court in San Francisco reversed the earlier
ruling in the "Betamax" case. The recent
decision, which came as a surprise to
many observers, holds that videotape
recording of copyrighted television programs, even if done at home for private
use, is an infringement of the right of
those who own the programs.

The decision, which applies only to
nine Western states, is seen as a major
blow to one of the most rapidly growing
segments of the consumer electronics
market: an estimated four percent of
American homes now have videotape recorders.

Sony Corporation, which has been in
litigation on the case since 1976, is
expected to petition the Supreme Court
for a review of the decision.

to create immediate palpable harm to copyright owners—whether one views markets broadly or narrowly. But a national viewing public that has integrated videocassette technology into its home entertainment habits is, cumulatively, quite another thing. A single family making a single copy of a free television program may not seem too much; but, as one observer remarked: "Babies are born one at a time, but can result in overpopulation."

International efforts to protect copyright

The international copyright community has recognized that legislation, not case-by-case adjudication, is necessary to deal with home video recording. Several agencies have called attention to global compensation systems that could provide revenue for all rights holders from both home audio and video recording. They have recommended legislation to prevent inevitable harm to creators, with emphasis on the idea of a levy upon either videotape hardware or blank cassettes. Whether or not one calls this a tax, levy, or fee, it must be recognized that its essence is a license.

Doubtlessly the interest over a levy—a global compensation system—is partly due to the tremendous difficulties of enforcing private rights in private homes. However, the fact that several states have, or are considering, this system raises hopes that experience will demonstrate its political feasibility and its justness to the public and creators. The jury is, however, still out.

The German Copyright Act, which was enacted September 9, 1965, and went into effect January 1, 1966, contains the first legislative provision that provides compensation to copyright owners for the private home audio and video taping of their protected works. As a pioneering effort, it has attracted great interest and considerable commentary. Already, on the basis of experience under the law, amendments to it have been proposed. There have also been proposed changes to Austrian copyright laws.

The British government recently published its "Green Paper" relating to copyright, designs, and performers' protection. Without drawing any final conclusions, the paper noted that the government "has still not received convincing evidence that the introduction of a levy on audio or video equipment or blank tape would provide an acceptable solution to the problems or potential problems." The document did suggest, however, that the industries continue research "aimed at finding a technological solution to the problem." It further offered to consider supporting legislation making illegal any anti-spoiler devices that might be developed to circumvent technological solutions. Although it may be possible for spoiler devices to discourage home taping in the short term, it appears likely that the only result of building a better mousetrap, in the form of spoiler devices, will be the education of smarter mice.

Legislation of the German and Austrian types has its defenders and detractors. Whatever their defects, the German and Austrian laws are grounded on a crucial premise: copyright owners need not demonstrate serious market damage *before* some form of protection or remuneration will be provided.

In the United States, there is not yet any congressional action on this question, but there is no doubt in my mind that academicians, copyright specialists, broadcasters, creators of television programs, and the professional unions are beginning to stir. In the United States, off-air educational taping absorbed our attentions first; the time to deal with home taping is fast approaching.

As I see it, in the United States we should move on the legislative front on home taping. I would rather heed our courts' calls for legislative solutions than attack their efforts to discharge their duty. There are even more severe tests ahead on our commitment to copyright and on our ability to adapt copyright to innovation of market change.

Consider the home communications center of the future, where data, images, and performances will all flood into the consumers' home entertainment and information center with all its capabilities. What then becomes of the bundle of rights? Where then is the box office? Our response to the problems of home taping will test our resolve to enrich society, by rewarding and protecting authors, and our ingenuity in fashioning adaptations for copyright as ingenious as the innovations in technology itself. And the experience will be needed in the tests to come.

58: THE SONY BETAMAX CASE — WINDS OF CHANGE?*

Charles H. Lieb

Charles H. Lieb is a partner in the
New York City law firm of Paskus,
Gordon & Hyman.

One of the most important copyright events that has occurred in many years is the recently announced decision by the United States Court of Appeals for the 9th Circuit in Universal City Studios and Walt Disney Productions against Sony Corporation and others.[1]

The Sony case, involved the home recording on Sony Betamax videotape recorders for subsequent home viewing of televised free television (as distinguished from cable television) broadcasts of copyrighted films.

The plaintiffs were the motion picture producers. The defendants were Sony, the Japanese manufacturer of Betamax, and its American distributor. Also named as defendants were four retail stores which had offered Betamax for sale; the advertising agency retained by Sony to advertise Betamax, which had been indemnified by Sony for any liability it might incur by reason of such activities, and a home owner and user of Betamax, William Griffiths, who consented to be a defendant on the plaintiffs' promise to waive damages or costs against him.

Griffiths, who admitted using Betamax to record the televised films, and the retail stores which recorded portions of broadcasts to

---

1. Nos. 79-3683, 79-3735, 79-3762, Oct 19, 1981.

*Adapted from an article prepared for publication in the Copyright Bulletin of the International Group of Scientific, Technical & Medical Publishers (STM).

demonstrate the machine to prospective customers were, of course, charged with direct infringement. So too were the Sony companies and the advertising agency, but probably to more effect they were also charged with contributory or vicarious infringement, that is, with knowingly participating in or making possible and encouraging the complained of infringements.

After three years of litigation and five weeks of trial, the Court in October of 1979 directed judgment in favor of all the defendants. In so deciding, it held that recording for home use from free as distinguished from cable television is not copyright infringement either under the old or the new 1976 copyright law, and that in any event Griffiths' home recording for his own subsequent use would be a fair use.

The Court of Appeals reversed, holding that home video recording does constitute infringement and is not excusable as fair use, and accordingly, that the home user, the manufacturer and its distributor and the advertising agency were guilty of infringement. The Court relieved the retail stores, on the ground of fair use, of liability for making demonstration recordings. Such use, the Court agreed, was narrow and limited; they had no intent to use or profit from the copyrighted works but only to demonstrate the machine.

The plaintiffs' principal target of course was the manufacturer, and the Court held that it knew and expected that Betamax's major use would be to record copyrighted programs off the air, and that it and its distributors and its advertising agency were together sufficiently engaged in the enterprise to be held accountable as contributors to the resulting infringement by the home user.

In so deciding and in remanding the case to the trial court for further consideration, the Court admitted that the fashioning of the relief to be accorded to the plaintiffs would present a complex problem; but that such difficulty should not dissuade it from granting whatever relief would be appropriate in the circumstances.

In an aside, the Court suggested that instead of permanently enjoining the manufacture and use of Betamax videotape recorders, it might award damages or indeed, that it might even require the payment of "a continuing royalty". In support of this suggestion, the Court quoted with approval from Professor Nimmer's work on Copyright with respect to photocopying that

> "The Courts might well conclude that photocopying practices for private use, *particularly in the area of scientific writings,* involve . . . such . . . a public interest . . . that a judicially created compulsory license

as a substitute for injunctive relief could be found appropriate." [Emphasis added.][2]

The defendants have petitioned for reargument *en banc,* that is to say, before the full 9th Circuit bench as compared with the three judge bench that decided the case.

If reargument is not granted, or if in reargument the decision is affirmed, the United States Supreme Court in the exercise of its discretion (appeal to the Supreme Court is not a matter of right) might then decide to hear the case, and what it would decide in that event is anybody's guess.

In finding Sony and the other parties liable for infringement, the Court refused to follow the 1973 decision of the Court of Claims in the Williams & Wilkins case which, it will be recalled, held that the National Institutes of Health and the National Library of Medicine were not guilty of infringement when they photocopied articles appearing in Williams & Wilkins journals.[3] The Sony Court distinguished the Williams & Wilkins case on its facts, criticized it as creating "doctrinal confusion", and in any event said that it is not binding in the 9th Circuit.

In my view, it should also have said that with respect to post-1977 copying, the Court Claims' decision has been supplanted by the 1976 Copyright Act prohibition against "systematic copying."[4] The Court of Claims' opinion was affirmed by a divided Supreme Court, four to four, with Justice Blackmun refraining from participation. What the Supreme Court would do now with a similar case or with the Sony case, with Justice Stewart off the bench and Justice Sandra O'Connor replacing him, and with Justice Blackmun participating is a matter for conjecture.

And Congress itself may decide to intervene. Already four bills have been introduced which would establish home recording as non-infinging and would thus remove the question from further litigation.

But whatever happens, either in further proceedings before the courts or in Congress, there is reason to hope that the winds may be changing, and that the permissiveness and the willingness to extend the fair use doctrine far beyond its traditional limits that characterized the reason-

2. Nimmer, sec. 13-05 [E][4][e]
3. Williams & Wilkins Co. v. United States, 487F.2d. 1345 (1973), affd. by an equally divided Court, 420 U.S. 376 (1975).
4. P.L. 94-553, Oct 19, 1976, sec 108(g)(2); Sen. Rep. 94-473, 94th Cong., 1st Ses. Nos. 1975, ab p 70.

ing of the Court of Claims in the Williams & Wilkins case may be coming to an end.

The return to orthodox fair use reasoning in the Sony decision is refreshing. And even if on the facts of the case the decision should be reversed on appeal, or if in effect it is annulled by legislation, the thrust of the 9th Circuit Court's reasoning should influence courts which deal with the fair use doctrine at a later date.

The statutory framework, the court said, is unambiguous. A bundle of exclusive rights are granted by statute to the copyright proprietor and are limited only by statutory exceptions. In deciding an infringement case therefore, the court should not ask itself whether the Congress intended to *afford* protection to copyright holders from a particular kind of use (in the Sony case, an off-the-air videorecording of a copyrighted film, — in another case, perhaps, the reprographic reproduction of a copyrighted journal article). Instead, the question the court should determine is whether the Congress intended to *withdraw* protection for that kind of use. Surely, one cannot quarrel with the Sony court on this basic approach.

The next question then is whether Section 107 of the copyright law, the section which codifies the fair use doctrine but does not change or narrow or extend it in any way, exempts from infringement the particular use that is complained of.

Here too the Sony court goes back to basic principles. Fair use, it said, has traditionally involved a *"productive"* use of the copyrighted work, — that is, a use by a second author or by a critic of the first author's work, — as contrasted with an *"intrinsic"* purpose, — that is, an "ordinary" use, the use for which the work was created.

Because the court found that the home recordings involved in the Sony case were used for the same purpose as the televised film, it held that a finding of fair use could not be justified. In my view, one might quarrel with the factual basis for this finding, but not with the statement of the principle.

Thus, for example, if to further its business an employer supplies its employees with unauthorized copies of journal articles or other reference material, or permits and encourages its employees to make the unauthorized copies for themselves, this should be an intrinsic use, the use for which the material was published, and the fair use doctrine should not excuse the copying.

Nor should convenience provide an excuse, the court noting that the fair use statute, Section 107, does not list "convenience" or "increased access" as purposes within the general scope of fair use. This would seem particularly true if the journal article or other material is entered in the Copyright Clearance Center apparatus. In such event not even convenience or lack of access could be offered as an excuse for unauthorized copying, the entry of the work in the CCC system providing both convenience and access.

And finally, the court made the penetrating statement that in a case where it is likely that the defendant's infringement may be representative of general infringement, the court should not confine its attention to the particular infringement before it, but should consider the cumulative effect of the proliferation of minor infringements by others on the rights of the copyright owner plaintiff.

In support of this conclusion, the court quoted the statement from the legislative history of the 1976 copyright act, that:

> "Isolated instances of minor infringement, when multiplied many times, become in the aggregate a major inroad on copyright that must be prevented."[5]

This, of course, has been the argument of publishers since the advent of high-speed xerography.

Recent statements by the Attorney General of the State of Kansas and by the Register of Copyrights may also be straws in the wind.

The Attorney General of the State of Kansas was asked whether music educators may duplicate music scores for distribution to judges in music competitions without infringing copyright laws. The music director of the school district who had asked for the opinion contended that the copying of musical scores for use by the judges should be regarded as copies made for the purpose of criticism and comment and therefore should be held to be fair use. The Attorney General refused to accept this reasoning, holding that the copies that were made without authorization of the copyright owner served as substitutes for the purchase of the scores and hence were clearly infringement. And in a pithy sentence reminiscent of the remark of the Sony Court, the Attorney General said that:

> "Certainly the demand for the original work would be decreased if *all* teachers could make copies for *all* judges in *all* music competitions. Because music

---

5.   Sen. Rep. 94-473, supra, at p 65.

teachers are obviously a major part of the potential
market for certain works of music, it is likely that the
market for those works would decrease if unauthorized copies could be made indiscriminately. This
potential loss of value to the copyright owner must
weight heavily in our consideration of 'fair use.' "
[Emphasis in original.][6]

David Ladd, the Register of Copyrights, in a recent talk in Toronto[7]
commented that until relatively recently, nearly all infringements of
copyrighted works were public and so visible at their source that enforcement of copyright presented no special problem. But now, he said,
the problem is how it will be possible to control uses of copyrighted
works which are not readily detectable and therefore not readily
policeable. In these new problem areas, he said, we must decide
whether we can devise and use the equivalent of the theater-box office
to collect payments for use or whether we will have to throw up our
hands and accept all home videocopying (and I will add all photocopying) as lawless but uncontrollable, or lawful because it is uncontrollable.

The Sony decision may be a straw in the wind that such copying will
be held lawless and controllable.

6. Atty. Gen. Op. No 81-202, Aug 25, 1981.
7. Sept. 23, 1981 Toronto meeting of International Copyright Society.

59: HOW PUBLISHERS AND LIBRARIANS CAN AGREE ON COPYRIGHT

Carol Risher

There has long been a myth that copyright is one area in which librarians and publishers can never agree. I have never accepted this myth as true. Publishers and librarians are natural allies. They share a common goal—to disseminate information. Publishers need librarians to buy books and subscribe to journals as a means to inform the user community; librarians need publishers to provide the information for the users. There is a common bond and a common interdependence. The copyright law provides authors and publishers with the incentive to create and distribute the information that is needed by the user community. Librarians recognize this fact and support the right of copyright holders to fair compensation and fair treatment.

During the years leading up to the Copyright Act of 1976, publishers heard librarians decry the difficulties they have in obtaining permissions in a timely fashion from journal publishers to make photocopies of articles urgently needed by their clientele. Congress also heard this message and urged publishers to facilitate photocopying permissions. Many copyright owners responded by participating in the Copyright Clearance Center, Inc., (CCC) a multi-copyright owner system that permits copying without advance permission.

Users register with the CCC at no charge and are assigned a user identification number. Publishers participate in CCC by printing a code at the bottom of the first page of each article in the journal or in the masthead of other types of periodical publications. The code signifies the amount of royalty required for each copy of the article. Users can copy materials from participating publications without delay. Copying is reported to the CCC, which bills the user and then collects the royalty fees and disseminates them to the publishers. Some publications, instead of or in addition to participating in CCC, offer their own advance licensing systems that, for a flat fee or some other arrangement, allow a user to copy from the publication.

Carol Risher *is Director of Copyright, Association of American Publishers, Washington, D.C.*

Members of the library community who have registered with the CCC find it useful for making copies from those periodicals that participate but are troubled by the fact that there are some publishers that neither participate in CCC nor offer their own advance licensing systems. As early as 1977, in testimony before the National Commission on New Technological Uses of Copyrighted Works (CONTU), the American Association of Publishers (AAP) suggested that the copyright law be amended to provide some assistance to libraries faced with this specific problem. The amendment was called "The Umbrella Statute" because, like an umbrella, it provides protection.

The Umbrella Statute is simple to understand. "Reasonable copying (not for public distribution) of technical, scientific and medical articles that do not bear the CCC code could be undertaken, subject only to the right of the non-participating . . . journal publisher to collect a reasonable copying fee."

AAP provided testimony at the hearing to support the proposed statute: "To approve the universality of the system [CCC], we would favorably consider what we call an umbrella statute which would protect users by permitting reasonable copying (not for public distribution) of journal articles published by publishers not in the system, provided that the copier would be subject to the obligation to pay a reasonable copying fee, but would be excused from the otherwise statutory obligation of an infringer to pay either statutory damages or attorney's fees."

The concept was easily understandable, but it required cooperation and coordination with the user community to hammer out the draft language for such a statutory amendment. At the end of 1980, Allan Wittman, chairman of the AAP Copyright Committee, convened a task force composed of four for-profit and not-for-profit journal publishers and four librarians and information managers from corporations that were registered users of the CCC.

The group set the goal of drafting an umbrella statute to balance the rights of copyright owners with the needs of users of specified works. The task force was particularly concerned with scientific, technical, medical, and business periodicals and proceedings for which immediate reproduction was necessary for purposes of research or study.

The eight-member task force met over an eighteen-month period and worked to draft a document that would limit action against a copier if certain conditions are met. The principal conditions are as follows:

• that the material reproduced was not available for reproduction without securing advance permission;

• that the reproduction is a facsimile copy and was made directly from the issue in which it appeared or from a copy that has been earlier made under the same conditions;

• that the reproduction was made and used for purposes of research and study and includes a notice of copyright; and

• that persons contributing to the making of the reproduction participate in the Copyright Clearance Center, Inc. or other multiple-copyright owner system that dispenses with advanced permission for photocopying or like reproduction of materials of similar nature.

If these conditions are met, the sole remedy that may be awarded for copyright infringement is an assessment of a reasonable copying fee under the circumstances as determined by the court; neither injunctive relief, actual damages or profits, statutory damages, costs, attorney's fees, nor impoundment are available against the infringer. If any one of the conditions is not met, the court may deal with the infringement as would otherwise be appropriate under the Copyright Act.

The Umbrella Statute applies only to infringement of copyright in contributions to scientific, technical, medical, or business periodicals and conference proceedings. Newspapers and newsletters have been specifically excluded from the section, because these publications derive their value from the immediacy of content or the serving of limited markets. AAP has explained that the "draft has no implications and establishes no precedent, whatsoever, for other works," and that the definition of those publications covered by the statute intends to connote that their content is exclusive. Works that to any substantial extent include social

"What about the copyrights?"

history or narrative, fiction, poetry, or belles lettres are excluded from and are not subject to the limitations of the draft.

The Umbrella Statute and AAP's letters of endorsement have been filed with the Register of Copyrights in preparation for the five-year review on library photocopying and the report to Congress due January 1, 1983. The Register might include the recommendation in his report to Congress, he might recommend changes in the draft amendment, or he might exclude mention of the statute in the final report.

Members of the AAP and the library community are currently awaiting the report of the Register of Copyrights. After the report is filed, Congress is expected to hold hearings on any recommended legislative changes. At that time the various parties will have another opportunity to comment, either in oral testimony or in writing, on the proposed statute and any other legislative changes. In the meantime, the existence of the draft statute, worked out with the mutual cooperation of librarians and publishers, proves that it is possible for publishers and librarians to cooperate in the area of copyright and to continue their healthy alliance as partners in the dissemination of information.

60: AAP URGES CHANGES IN COPYRIGHT LAW

AAP URGES CHANGES IN COPYRIGHT LAW "to balance the rights of copyright owners and needs of users of certain specified works — contributions to scientific, technical, medical, and business periodicals and proceedings — in particular circumstances, namely, reproduction for purposes of research or study where there is an immediate need for copies." The Association of American Publishers claims that the regulations and and guidelines intended to strike that balance are not working because

1. Huge amounts of copies of copyrighted material are made without permission by librarians on library controlled machines.

2. An uncountable but undoubtedly large number of copies are made on machines within walking distance of the library without permission.

3. Multiple copies are made without permission in a very large number of copying "transactions" — interlibrary as well as local.

4. Much of the unauthorized copying that is done by libraries and particularly by special-for-profit libraries is systematic.

5. Much of the unauthorized copying done for interlibrary arrangements is outside that permitted under Section 108.

6. Much of the unauthorized copying that is done exceeds fair use (fair use in most instances would permit making only some single copies).

7. Much of the unauthorized copying by government agencies exceeds the permissible limits.

8. Much of the unauthorized copying that is done for interlibrary use is of material older than five years.

9. Very little use is made of CCC facilities.

10. There is a lack of understanding in the user community of the meaning of the copyright notice and the implications.

11. Reserve room copying violates the law.

Other claims made by the AAP are: the volume of library photocopying reported by King Research is underestimated; mechanized systematic document delivery by libraries is an unanticipated problem that needs addressing and solution; the CONTU guidelines are not working.

The AAP recommends to the register of copyrights amending Section 108(a)(3) of the 1976 Copyright Law to read as follows:

Section 108(a)(3) is hereby amended to read:
"the reproduction or distribution of the work includes *the* notice of copyright *as provided* in Section 401(b) of this title."

The explanation given by the AAP is that the legislative history makes clear that this section was intended to mean that the statutory notice of copyright appear on any copies made or distributed under Section 108. Earlier drafts of the copyright act cite that copies should indicate both the source and the actual notice of copyright reproduced from the document.

The use of the indefinite article "a" rather than the definite article "the" caused confusion for more than five years, according to the AAP. In the face of this confusion, the American Library Association recommended that its membership stamp copies made under Section 108 "This may be in copyright." That meaningless phrase, says the AAP, also implies that "This article may not be in copyright." If both propositions are true, says the AAP, there is nothing to be gained by use of the stamp. Nothing in the statement causes users to refrain from making subsequent copies or assists users who desire to make subsequent copies in determining copyright status or copyright ownership. AAP thinks that its proposed amendment will make clear the legislative intent of Section 108(a)(3).

The AAP recommends changing the statutory damages specified in Section 504(c)(1) for three reasons: to reflect congressional intent by adjusting for unanticipated double-digit inflation; to serve as a deterrent to would-be infringers; and to make the effort of enforcement worth the time and money required by the copyright holder.

AAP recommends adding a new Section 511 to the copyright law. The draft statutory amendment and explanation appear below.

Sec. 1 Chapter 5 of title 17 of the United States Code is amended by inserting at the end thereof the following new section:

§511. Limitation on remedies for infringing reproduction of portions of particular works in certain cases.

(a) Notwithstanding sections 502 through 505, in the case of liability for infringement of copyright described in subsection (b) of this section the exclusive remedy of the copyright owner shall be the recovery of a reasonable copying fee in an amount fixed by the court.

(b) The limitation on remedies under subsection (a) shall, subject to subsection (c), apply to direct, contributory, or vicarious liability for the infringing facsimile reproduction of an article or other contribution, or portion thereof, published in an issue of a scientific, technical, medical, or business periodical or conference proceeding (as hereinafter defined and referred to as a "subject publication") if —

(1) the article or contribution was not entered in a qualified licensing program or qualified licensing system at the time the reproduction was made;

(2) the reproduction was made directly from the issue in which the article or contribution was published, from a lawfully made facsimile copy, or from a copy made under conditions that limit liability under this section;

(3) the reproduction was used solely for purposes of research or study (a) by the person who made the reproduction, or by anyone employed by or in a common employment relationship with that person if the reproduction was made and used in the course of that employment, or (b) by a person at whose request the reproduction was made, or by anyone employed by or in a common employment relationship with that person if the reproduction was requested and used in the course of that employment; and

(4) the reproduction includes a notice of copyright.

(c) The limitation on remedies under subsection (a) does not apply where —

(1) in any case, the person making the reproduction has not been registered as a user with a qualified licensing system; or

(2) in the case of reproductions made at the request of another, the requestor has not been registered as a user with a qualified licensing system; or

(3) within a period of three years preceding the date of infringement, the infringer has been held finally liable, after all appeals, for infringement of the right to reproduce any material that was, at the time of such prior infringement, entered in a qualified licensing program or qualified licensing system; or

(4) the reproduction was made, used, or requested for purposes of distribution or offering to the public, for advertising or promotional purposes, for stock or like purposes, for archival or similar deposit or collection, or for any purpose other than research or study by any person mentioned in paragraph (b)(3).

(d) As used in this section, the following terms and their variant forms mean the following:

A "scientific, technical, medical, or business periodical or conference proceeding" and a "subject publication" mean a periodical or conference proceeding that is (A) devoted to one or more branches of science, technology, medicine, or business; (B) designed, advertised, promoted, marketed, and distributed to serve these special fields of interest, rather than to or for the general public; and (C) published in a form that is generally visually perceptible and intelligible without the aid of a machine or device. An "issue" of a subject publication is any unit thereof published in such form at any particular time. For these purposes, a "periodical" is a published collective work issued at regular intervals, more frequently than annually, under the same title and bearing numerical or chronological designations; a "conference proceeding" is a published collective work comprising papers that have been prepared in connection with meetings or conferences; and "periodicals" and "conference proceedings" do not include newsletters or newspapers.

A "qualified licensing program" is a publicly announced policy established by the copyright owner of one or more subject publications that permits the facsimile reproduction of articles and other contributions published in issues of such subject publications on stated terms or conditions that eliminate the necessity of permission being requested or granted prior to such reproduction of such material. A work is "entered" in a qualified licensing program when it is available for such reproduction without such advance permission.

A "qualified licensing system" is a publicly announced system, such as the Copyright Clearance Center, Inc., participated in by several copyright owners of subject publications that permits the facsimile reproduction of articles and other contributions published in issues of such subject publications on stated terms or conditions that eliminate the necessity of permission being requested or granted prior to such reproduction of such material. A work is "entered" in a qualified licensing system when it is available for such reproduction without such advance permission. A person or entity is "registered as a user" with a qualified licensing system when it has taken such steps as are required to avail itself of such system. For the purposes of this section, an employee is considered so registered if his or her employer has so registered, with respect to reproductions made and requested in the course of such employment.

Sec. 2. Section 506(a) of Chapter 5 of title 17 of the United States Code is amended by inserting the parenthetical phrase "(except under the circumstances described in subsection (b) of section 511)" after the phrase "private financial gain."

Sec. 3. Supplementary and Transitional Provisions

(a) This Act becomes effective on its enactment.

(b) This Act shall not apply to any cause of action that arose prior to the effective date of this Act.

(c) The table of sections for Chapter 5 of title 17 of the United States Code is amended by inserting after the item relating to section 510, the following:

"§511. Limitation on remedies for infringing reproduction of portions of particular works in certain cases."

The purpose of the proposed AAP amendment is to balance the rights of copyright owners and needs of users of certain specified works — contributions to scientific, technical, medical, and business periodicals and proceedings — in particular circumstances, namely, reproduction for purposes of research or study where there is an immediate need for copies.

In earlier attempts to accommodate these needs and rights, the Congress urged copyright owners to facilitate photocopying permissions. Many copyright owners responded by participating in the Copyright Clearance Center, Inc., a multicopyright owner system that permits copying without the need to seek or secure permission in advance, subject to later payment of royalties. Others have established or are considering similar mechanisms for one or more of their own publications. The proposed amendment further encourages these efforts and the participation therein by the user community, and seeks to temper inhibitions on fulfilling needs for immediate reproduction of similar materials in which copyright is owned by entities that have not taken such steps. It does so by limiting the remedies that would otherwise be available against infringing reproduction, if certain conditions are met.

In summary, the principal conditions that will create the limitation are the following:

- that the material reproduced was not available for reproduction without securing advance permission;

- that the reproduction is a facsimile copy, and was made directly from the issue of subject publications in which it appeared, or from a lawfully made facsimile copy of that material,* or from a copy that had been earlier made under the same conditions;

---

*The condition that the earlier made copy be a "facsimile," and that the limitation applies only to "facsimile" reproductions, together with the definition of subject publications, is intended to restrict this section to those forms of photocopying, microform reproduction and the like, where the needs sought to be served have become apparent. The section would apply, for example, to microform reproduction from a full-size original, or from a lawful microform copy of a work that is also published in full-size format, as well as to photocopying. However, it is not intended to apply to computer input, storage and manipulation or the like, which raise other concerns and are not earmarked by similar considerations.

- that the reproduction was made and used for purposes of research and study and includes a notice of copyright**; and

- that persons contributing to the making of the reproduction (or their employer) participate in the Copyright Clearance Center, Inc. or other multiple-copyright owner system that dispenses with advance permission for photocopying or like reproduction of materials of similar nature.

If these conditions are met, the sole remedy that may be awarded for infringement is an assessment of a reasonable copying fee under the circumstances as determined by the court; neither injunctive relief, actual damages or profits, statutory damages, costs, attorneys' fees, or impoundment are available against the infringer. If any one of the conditions is not met, the court may award such relief as would otherwise be appropriate under the statute.

This section applies only to infringement of copyright in contributions to scientific, technical, medical, or business periodicals and conference proceedings. The latter category has been included because, for practical purposes, such proceedings are assimilated in purpose, nature, content and use to periodicals dealing with the same subject matter; and the definition of this category includes papers that have been "prepared" in connection with conferences, even if they have not been read or delivered at such meetings. Newspapers and newsletters, however, have been specifically excluded from the section because each of these forms of publication is characterized by special factors, such as the value derived from immediacy of content, or the serving of limited markets.

It must be emphasized that this section is designed to accommodate the needs and interests of all parties — authors, publishers, users — in circumstances unique to the contents and use of scientific, technical, medical, and business periodicals and proceedings. This section has no implications, and establishes no precedent, whatsoever for other works. In that connection, it may be noted that the term "devoted" in the definition of a subject publication is intended to connote a degree of virtual exclusivity of content. Thus, as examples only, works that to any substantial extent include social history or narrative, fiction, poetry, or *belles lettres* are excluded from and are not subject to the limitations of this section.

AAP again emphasizes the need for further guidelines for library photocopying under Section 108. In 1978 AAP and the Authors League of America prepared a booklet on photocopying which states in its introduction: "Library personnel cannot be expected to interpret Sections 107 and 108 (and their legislative history) each time they are asked to reproduce copyrighted materials or distribute a photocopy. It is in the common interest of libraries, authors and publishers that library personnel have specific, practical criteria to assist them in determining which photocopying transactions do, and do not, require copyright permission . . . Guidelines have not yet been developed for applying Section 108's limits on in-house photocopying, interlibrary photocopying of journal articles and contributions more than five years old, and other categories of library photocopying, although the AAP and Authors League have urged the library associations to work with us in developing them."

The AAP states that the confusion and other conditions causing those statements have not changed, and the association continues to urge the library community to work with it to negotiate guidelines for in-house copying, for journal articles more than five years old, and to define multiple and systematic copying. However, the AAP continues, "we believe, in retrospect, that our proposed interim guidances in 1978 were overly generous and we are no longer endorsing them. We feel that the user and proprietor communities will benefit by

---

**The phrase "notice of copyright" is intended to have the same meaning as in section 108(a)(3) of title 17.

clarifying these terms and we urge the assistance of the Register since the parties obviously cannot meaningfully resolve their differences over these terms. Five years have gone by and the library representatives are still unwilling to discuss negotiating additional guidelines."

The above comments and changes were sent to the Register of Copyrights to be included in the report from the Copyright Office to Congress in January 1983 on the effectiveness of the changes in the Copyright Act passed in 1976.

61: THE VIDEOCASSETTE RENTAL CONTROVERSY: THE FUTURE STATE OF THE LAW

Nancy B. Lewson*

PART I

ARTICLES

John Jones, a middle-income family man, has recently purchased a Video Cassette Recorder. He planned to buy a prerecorded cassette of "The Wizard of Oz" to show his family on Halloween Eve. When he went to the neighborhood Video Store, the salesman informed him that the tape was available on a rental plan for $8, to be returned within 48 hours. Mr. Jones thought to himself, "Fantastic! Instead of buying the tape for $60 I will rent it!" With the money Mr. Jones saved he also rented an adult film to enjoy privately with his wife, and took the family out for a Halloween dinner, after the show.

I. INTRODUCTION

The Video Cassette Recorder (VCR) entered the home commercial market in 1976.[1] By the end of that year approximately 50,000 VCR's had been purchased.[2] The market for VCR's has grown rapidly, and projections have been made that by 1985, thirteen to twenty million VCRs are expected to be in use.[3]

With the explosive growth of the videocassette recorder industry

---

* Ms. Lewson is a Walter J. Derenberg Fellow in Copyright Law at New York University School of Law. This article was awarded First Prize in New York University's Nathan Burkan Memorial Competition.

[1.] Note that for the purposes of this article, no distinction will be made between the Videocassette Recorder (VCR) and the Video Home System (VHS), though there are technical variations important to the consumer.

[2.] P. Nulty, *Matsushita Takes the Lead in Video Recorders*, FORTUNE (July 16, 1979).

[3.] 118 TIME 58 (Dec. 14, 1981). In addition, BUSINESS WEEK estimates that approximately 1,000,000 video disc players will be in use by 1984. 25 BUSINESS WEEK 72 (July 7, 1980). Video discs and disc players will not be treated in this article, but keep in mind that the discs are significantly less expensive than the cassettes, and therefore, are expected to have impact on the videocassette market.

has come a new emphasis on "software," the prerecorded tapes which became available in 1977 and are currently available through more than 5,000 retail outlets in the United States.[4] The programs that are placed on videocassettes are owned largely by the entertainment industry—the movie studios, record companies and T.V. networks.[5] The prerecorded motion picture films have had the most commercial impact. Therefore, only the software films owned by the movie studios will be discussed in this article.

The major motion picture studios have all formed divisions to handle the production, acquisition, licensing and distribution of their "software." By July 1980, Business Week reported that the movie industry had begun to tighten a grip on this market which it determined to be rightfully its own.[6]

Prerecorded videocassette films range in price from $40-$80 each, at retail. The feature films available range from x-rated "adult titles," to Hollywood hits such as "Close Encounters" or "M.A.S.H." The films can readily be purchased and filed on a shelf for viewing at any time.[7] The identical film can just as readily be rented at an average price of $5 per tape. Not surprisingly, the business of renting prerecorded cassettes is exploding. The average viewer does not want to view movies more than once or twice, and only a few film classics are deemed worth collecting, particularly by the new middle-income consumer.

The average video cassette may be rented twelve to twenty times before it is ultimately sold. Since a videocassette has a useful playing life in excess of 200 plays, twelve to twenty rentals would not detract significantly from the subsequent sales value of the cassette.[8] Industry executives estimate that there are anywhere from five to thirty rentals prior to each sale, and that rentals are estimated to account for at least half of the overall total revenues of the prerecorded video cassette business this year.[9]

According to Stephen Roberts, president of Twentieth Century Fox Telecommunications, the rental schemes have a "major negative effect

---

[4.] *Oversight of the Copyright Act of 1976: Hearings before the Committee on the Judiciary,* 97th Cong. 1st Sess. 317 (July 29, 1981) (prepared statement of Stephen Roberts, President, Twentieth Century Fox, Telecommunications Division) [hereinafter cited as *Testimony of Stephen Roberts*].

[5.] 25 BUSINESS WEEK 76 (July 7, 1980).

[6.] *Id.*

[7.] *Clearing Up the Confusion over Video Recorders,* 23 BUSINESS WEEK 126 (June 25, 1979).

[8.] Testimony of Stephen Roberts, *supra* note 4, at 318, citing 3M Company and TDK technical specifications.

[9.] A. Pollack, *A Battle Over Video Cassettes: Millions in Tape Rentals Are At Stake,* NEW YORK TIMES (December 11, 1981) at D1 [hereinafter cited as *A Battle*].

on the manufacturer-distributors, the copyright owners, and the individual members of the creative community."[10] Rental schemes result in the use of copyrighted works without additional compensation to the copyright owner (or to guild and union membership) and dilute the market for sales of copyrighted works.[11] Retailers, on the other hand, contend that they take an unmarketable product and make it marketable by renting for much less than the prohibitive sales cost. They also argue that growing demand for rentals lures customers into stores, which then leads to added sales.[12] Both sides concede that simple economics favor the rental market. Thus, as the New York Times stated,

> a bitter tug-of-war that could shape the future of the video-cassette industry is taking place over how the revenues from the booming business of renting prerecorded cassettes should be divided.[13]

The future shape of the copyright laws might also be at stake. Video-cassette recording technology presents the copyright laws with troublesome problems of adaptation and interpretation.[14]

In order to stop the rentals, the motion picture studios have looked

---

[10] Testimony of Stephen Roberts, *supra* note 4, at 318. Roberts provides the following statistical chart:

	Sale Only	Rental Plus Sale	
		Case #1[12]	Case #2[13]
Retail Sale Price	$60	$ 40	$ 29
Rental Price	—	$ 5	$ 6
Number of Rentals	0	12	20
Retail Rental Revenue	—	$ 60	$120
Gross Revenue to Retailer	$60	$100	$149
Wholesale Cost of Video Cassette Gross Revenue to Manufacturer-Distributor	$40	$ 40	$ 40
Gross Royalty Revenue to Copyright Owner	$ 8	$ 8	$ 8
Guild/Union Membership Participation	$ 1	$ 1	$ 1

[11] *Id.*

[12] L. Leff, *Firms Renting Videocassettes Worry Studios*, WALL STREET JOURNAL (March 27, 1981) section 2, p. 3E.

[13] *A Battle, supra* note 9, at D1.

[14] Note that this article addresses only the basic primary problem of rental and home viewing, as set forth in the John Jones hypothetical, *see* text, *supra* p. 1. Further complications arise from potential swapping schemes, rentals by remote vendees, and increased propensity of copying.

to the Copyright Act of 1976[15] for some form of protection. Alternatively, they seek a share of the profits, and have already begun to implement licensing and rental schemes of their own. The next few years hold prospects of turmoil in the videocassette industry unless substantial action is taken.

In this article, the author attempts to present some of the complicated issues and potential solutions to the video cassette controversy. The reader must keep in mind that due to limited data and a vacuum of substantial comprehensive studies in this area, the article is prospective in format, attempting to provide a starting point of reference for further academic and legislative analysis.

II. COPYRIGHT INFRINGEMENT

Are the exclusive rights of copyright owners of prerecorded videocassette tapes infringed when retail outlets rent those tapes to individual viewers? Under federal law, copyright protection is granted to all original works fixed in a tangible medium.[16] Within the categories of protected works of authorship, the statute includes "motion pictures and other audiovisual works."[17] According to the House Report accompanying the Copyright Act, videotape is included within the meaning of motion picture.[18] Prerecorded videotape, as a medium in which original works of authorship are fixed into a tangible form of expression, is therefore recognized as a protectible class of copyrightable matter in §102 of the Act.[19] As enumerated in §106,[20] the copyright owner has the right to exhibit, rent, sell, license, reproduce, make derivative works of or publicly perform his own creation.

The Distribution Right and the First-Sale Doctrine

In the videotape rental situation, the copyright owner is concerned with his right "to distribute copies . . . of the copyrighted work to the public by sale or other transfer of ownership, or by rental, lease, or lending,"[21] as provided in §106(3). This language supports the conten-

---

[15.] Copyright Revision Act of 1976, Pub.L.No. 94-553, 90 Stat. 2541, codified at 17 U.S.C. §§101-810 [hereinafter 17 U.S.C. §§ 101-810].

[16.] 17 U.S.C. §102(a).

[17.] 17 U.S.C. §102(a) (6).

[18.] H.R. Rep. No. 1476, 94th Cong., 2d Sess. 63 (1976), reprinted in [1976] U.S. CODE CONG. AND AD. NEWS 5659 [hereinafter H. Rep.].

[19.] 17 U.S.C. §102.

[20.] 17 U.S.C. §106.

[21.] 17 U.S.C. §106(3).

tion that a retailer of videocassettes can be prohibited from reselling or renting the copy without specific permission from the owner of copyright. However, the §106(3) distribution right is subject to §109(a) which states:

> Notwithstanding the provisions of section 106(3), the owner of a particular copy or phonorecord lawfully made under this title, or any person authorized by such owner, is entitled, without the authority of the copyright owner, to sell, or otherwise dispose of the possession of that copy or phonorecord.[22]

It is clear that in the purest situation, where the copyright owner authorizes the outright sale of a particular copy, he may not invoke the distribution right so as to prevent or restrict the resale of such a copy. In *United States v. Wise*,[23] the court explains,

> While the copyright laws protect the rights of the copyright proprietor to vend his work, that right is not absolute, but is subject to the "first sale doctrine" . . . [T]he doctrine provides that where a copyright owner parts with title to a particular copy of his copyrighted work, he divests himself of his exclusive right to vend that particular copy. While the proprietor's other rights remain unimpaired, the exclusive right to vend the transferred copy rests with the vendee, who is not restricted by statute from further transfers of that copy . . .[24]

According to the *Wise* court, this must be the result, because the copyright is distinct from the property which is copyrighted, and the sale of one does not constitute a transfer of the other.[25] This concept is given express statutory recognition in the 1976 Act, which provides:

> Ownership of a copyright, or of any of the exclusive rights under a copyright, is distinct from ownership of any material object in

---

[22.] 17 U.S.C. §109(a). Note that §109(a) is similar but not identical to the second clause of section 27 of the 1909 Copyright Act which provided that "nothing in this title shall be deemed to forbid, prevent or restrict the transfer of any copy of a copyrighted work, the possession of which has been lawfully obtained." But according to the House Report, "Section 109(a) restates and confirms the principle that . . . has long been established by the court decisions and section 27 of the present law." H. Rep., *supra* note 18 at 79.

[23.] 550 F.2d 1180 (9th Cir. 1977).

[24.] *Id.* at 1187.

[25.] *See id.* at 1187.

which the work is embodied.[26]

Once a first sale of a copy has occurred, not only is the resale of such copy immune from the charge of copy infringement. Any further transfer is likewise immunized. For example, a library which owns a copy of a work may lend such copy to its patrons without infringing the copyright owner's distribution right.[27] Rentals are similarly within the immunized domain.[28]

The 1976 statute speaks in terms of a lawful transfer of possession,[29] but the judicial gloss on the statute has always required a transfer of title, before a "first sale" can occur.[30] Only an initial distribution which constitutes a sale, gift or other transfer of title terminates further application of the distribution right. For example, in *Platt and Munk Co. v. Republic Graphics, Inc.,*[31] the Second Circuit Court of Appeals concluded that an unpaid manufacturer of copyrighted works, alleged to be defective by the copyright proprietor who has ordered them, may not sell the goods until valid title to them was determined by a court of law. Mere authorized possession of the copies did not trigger application of the predecessor of §109(a).

Unless title to the copy passes through a first sale by the copyright holder, subsequent sales or transfers do not confer good title.[32] Consequently, "even an unwitting purchaser who buys a copy in the secondary market can be held liable for infringement if the copy was not the subject of a first sale by the copyright holder."[33]

Therefore, whether a transfer of title has occurred is a crucial issue, particularly within the context of motion picture film. Motion picture companies rarely expressly sell or transfer title in theatrical prints of their films. The language used by the motion picture industry when

---

[26.] 17 U.S.C. §202.

[27.] H. Rep., *supra* note 18, at 79.

[28.] *Cf.,* Avco Embassy Pictures Corp. v. Korshnak (M.D. Pa. 1974) (unreported but set forth in Appendix B, American International Pictures Inc. v. Foreman, 400 F. Supp. 928 (S.D. Ala. 1975), *rev'd.,* 576 F.2d 661 (5th Cir. 1981)).

[29.] 17 U.S.C. §109(a); (c).

[30.] *See* U.S. v. Wise, 550 F.2d 1180, 1187 (9th Cir. 1977).

[31.] 515 F.2d 847 (2d Cir. 1963). The *Platt and Munk* court also held that the first sale which terminates the exclusive right to distribute need not be a truly voluntary one, but can consist of some reasonable and recognized form of compulsory transfer, such as judicial sale or court-compelled assignment. 315 F.2d at 854. *See also* Harrison v. Maynard, Merrill Co., 61 Fed. 689 (2d Cir. 1894).

[32.] *See* American International Pictures, Inc. v. Foreman, 576 F.2d 661 (5th Cir. 1978).

[33.] *Id.* at 664.

transferring possession of a copy is couched in terms of "license" rather than "sale."[34] Furthermore, motion picture prerecorded videocassettes are "sold" to retailers with restrictive agreements or printed legends restricting the use of the copy.[35] If there has been no "first sale," but merely a license, then restrictions on distribution will be controlled by the federal copyright law. All subsequent transferees will be bound by the same restrictions.

Litigation has proven that it is difficult to construe whether a first sale has been made in the motion picture context. The absence of an express transfer of title in print will not prevent the conclusion that a first sale has occurred.[36] Yet, mere failure to expressly reserve title does not require the finding of a first sale.[37] In *United States v. Bily*,[38] the district court noted that, "in each case, the court must analyze the arrangement at issue, and decide whether it should be considered a first sale."[39]

In *Hampton v. Paramount Pictures Corp.*,[40] a transfer of possession

---

[34.] 2 M. NIMMER, NIMMER ON COPYRIGHT §8.12[B] [1] (1979).

[35.] For example, Warner Brothers uses the following restrictive legend on its videocassettes:

The motion picture contained in this videocassette is protected under the copyright laws of the United States and other countries and the cassette is sold for home use only. Duplication, public exhibition, rental or any other commercial use, in whole or in part, is strictly prohibited. Any unauthorized use may subject the offender to civil liability and criminal prosecution under applicable federal and state law. This cassette contains an individual and traceable serial number as well as 'stop copy' protection.

The Paramount restrictive legend states: "Licensed only for non-commercial private exhibition in homes. Any public performance, other use, or copying is strictly prohibited. All rights under copyright reserved."

The legend also bears a so-called F.B.I. warning: "Federal law provides severe civil and criminal penalties for the unauthorized reproduction, distribution, or exhibition of copyrighted motion pictures and video tapes (Title 17, United States Code, Section 501 and 506). The Federal Bureau of Investigation investigates allegations of copyright infringement (Title 17, United States Code, Section 506)."

It is interesting to note that the Paramount restrictive legend was contained on the cassette itself but not on the protective cardboard container.

The MCA Distributing Corporation "Videocassette Dealer Agreement" while not couched in terms of license and which in fact uses language such as *purchase* and *sold* nonetheless contains a provision that the "Dealer shall not lease or rent the product."

[36.] U.S. v. Atherton, 561 F.2d 747 (9th Cir. 1977).

[37.] U.S. v. Wise, 550 F.2d 1180 (9th Cir. 1977).

[38.] 406 F. Supp. 726 (E.D. Pa. 1975).

[39.] *Id.* at 731.

[40.] 279 F.2d 100 (9th Cir. 1960), *cert. den.*, 364 U.S. 882, 81 S.Ct. 170, 5 L.Ed.2d 103 (1960).

agreement was determined to have been a license. That court set forth factors helpful in interpreting agreements including: lack of limitation as to time, flat lump-sum payment, and no requirement that the film be returned.[41] The *United States v. Wise*[42] court suggested that the "general tenor" of each individual agreement must be interpreted by examining purpose, language and terms.[43] These tests must be applied to prerecorded videocassette agreements and legends to determine whether transfer of possession constitutes a first sale.[44]

Enforcement of Restrictions Under Copyright Law

One who possesses a copy of a motion picture which has not been the subject of a first sale cannot exercise any right enumerated in §106,[45] including sale or rental, without permission of the copyright owner. One who lawfully possesses a copy due to an unrestricted first sale is free to sell or rent that copy for private viewing under §109(a).[46] When one possesses a copy sold with an agreement or legend restricting its uses, what is the effect of a violation of that agreement?

As previously noted, several motion picture companies will allow sale of their prerecorded videocassettes only to dealers who sign written restrictive agreements. Others sell video cassettes with restrictive legends or labels.[47] According to one author,

> To the extent the restriction attempts to prohibit one from renting

---

[41] *Id.* at 103.

[42] 550 F.2d 1180 (9th Cir. 1977).

[43] *Id.* at 1191.

[44] An important issue which has subsequently arisen and been the subject of much debate, is upon whom the burden of proof shall lie, when it must be determined whether a first sale has occurred. According to the House Report, H.R. Rep. No. 1476, 94th Cong. 2d Sess. 81 (1976), it now seems fairly clear that the burden lies with the defendant who is presumed to be better able to trace the origin and subsequent transfers of the particular copy. On appeal in American International Pictures, Inc. v. Foreman, *supra* note 32, the court confirmed this principle but noted that the rules in criminal cases might be different because of due process requirements. Other experts feel strongly that the burden should be upon the plaintiffs in civil cases, particularly within the videocassette rental controversy. *See* J.J. Beard, *The Sale, Rental and Reproduction of Motion Picture Videocassettes: Piracy or Privilege,* 15 NEW ENG. L. REV. 435 (1979-80), 3 M. NIMMER, NIMMER ON COPYRIGHT §12-78 (1979).

[45] 17 U.S.C. §106.

[46] 17 U.S.C. §109(a).

[47] *See* L. Leff, *Firms Renting Videocassettes Worry Studios,* WALL STREET JOURNAL (March 27, 1981), sec. 2, p. 31E.

to another for private home viewing, the owner goes beyond what is provided in the Copyright Act and attempts to limit the §109(a) rights of the owner of a copy.[48]

The issue of whether a sale of a copy in violation of a provision of a restrictive sale agreement constitutes copyright infringement arose as early as 1886. In *Henry Bill Publishing Co. v. Smythe,*[49] the court stated that when the owner of a copyright "sells a copy to another . . . the purchaser takes the copy with the ordinary incident of alienation belonging to all property; and *that* copy is no longer under the copyright law."[50]

In *Harrison v. Maynard, Merrill & Co.,*[51] the owner of a copyright attempted to restrain, by virtue of the copyright statutes, the sale of a copy of a book whose title had been transferred. The court stated that remedies for a breach of contract might be available,

> [b]ut the right to restrain the sale of a particular copy of the book by virtue of the copyright statutes has gone when the owner of the copyright and of that copy parted with all his title to it . . . although with an agreement for a restricted use.[52]

In *Bobbs-Merrill Co. v. Strauss,*[53] the Supreme Court addressed the issue of whether the sole right to vend (as granted by §4952 Rev. Stat., pre-1909 Act) gives the copyright owner the right ". . . after a sale of the book to a purchaser, to restrict future sales of the book at retail . . ."[54] In this case, the copyright owner tried to restrict future sales to a certain price per copy by a notice in the book that a sale at a different price would be treated as an infringement of copyright. Those undertaking to sell for less than the named sum had bought the books from a middleman, but they were aware of the restrictive legend. The court concluded that

---

[48.] J.J. Beard, *The Sale, Rental and Reproduction of Motion Picture Videocassettes: Piracy or Privilege?* 15 NEW ENG. L. REV. 436 (1979-80).

[49.] 27 Fed. 914 (C.C.S.D. Ohio 1886). In *Henry Bill,* the owner restricted sales of his book to individual subscribers and made clear that they were not to be resold. An agent then resold to non-subscribers.

[50.] *Id.* at 925.

[51.] 61 Fed. 689 (2d Cir. 1894). In *Harrison,* copyrighted books had been damaged in a fire. The copyright owner was willing to sell the paper for reuse, but did not want the whole books resold in their damaged state.

[52.] *Id.* at 691.

[53.] 210 U.S. 339 (1908).

[54.] *Id.* at 350.

the copyright statutes, while protecting the owner of the copyright in his right to multiply and sell his production, do not create the right to impose, by notice, such as is disclosed in this case, a limitation at which the book shall be sold at retail by future purchasers, with whom there is no privity of contract.[55]

It is not entirely clear whether the first buyer, who was in privity, would have been bound by the restriction under the copyright statutes. The Court's strong language does imply that any restrictions beyond to whom the first sale is made, and at what price, "would give a right not included in the terms of the statute, and . . . extend its operation by construction, beyond its meaning . . ."[56]

Under the 1909 Act,[57] a district court in New York reiterated the principle that the exclusive right to vend is limited, and exerts no restriction on the future sale of that copy.[58] Similarly in *Independent News Co. v. Williams*,[59] defendant purchased coverless copies of comic books from waste paper dealers who were restricted to sell the coverless comics as waste only. The plaintiff's exclusive right to vend was satisfied when the plaintiffs sold the magazines to their independent wholesalers. Defendant was not liable for copyright infringement.

The 1976 Act incorporates the historical judicial interpretation. A violation of a restrictive sale agreement would not be an infringement of the §106 rights of the copyright owner, under the Copyright Act. According to the House Report:

> Thus, for example, the outright sale of an authorized copy of a book frees it from any copyright control over its resale price *or other conditions of its future* disposition . . . This does not mean that conditions on the future disposition of copies or phonorecords, imposed by a contract between their buyer and seller would be

---

[55] *Id. See also* Burke and Van Heusen v. Arrow Drug, Inc., 233 F. Supp. 881 (E.D. Pa. 1964) at 884. "The fact that [non-privity] defendants knew of the restrictions which were part of the . . . agreement between plaintiff and Beechum neither binds defendant to a contract to which they were not parties, nor widens the scope of control granted by the Copyright Act."

[56] Bobbs-Merrill and Co. v. Strauss, 210 U.S. 339 at 351.

[57] The 1909 Copyright Act (Title 17 U.S.C., Revised to Dec. 31, 1977).

[58] Fawcett Publications, Inc. v. Elliott Publishing Co., 46 F. Supp. 717 (S.D.N.Y. 1942) at 718. Defendant publishing company purchased second-hand copies of a publication known as "Wow Comics, #2 Summer Edition", which was copyrighted by the plaintiff. Without removing the copyright notice, the publishing company bound them together with other second hand publications within one copyrighted cover of its own.

[59] 184 F. Supp. 877 (E.D.Pa. 1960), *aff'd.*, 293 F. 2d 510 (3d Cir. 1961).

unenforceable between the parties as a breach of contract, but it does mean that they could not be enforced by an action for infringement of copyright.[60]

Though there has always been a strong public policy against restraint on alienation (which most of the aforementioned cases addressed) there is no evidence that a restriction imposed on the right to rent a copy would not be treated as other restrictions imposed on future disposition of the copy under the Act. In conclusion, an agreement which attempts to limit the rental of a videocassette cannot be enforced under the copyright law. Secondly, renting in violation of the agreement would not be an infringement of the exclusive right to distribute, if a first sale/transfer of title has been proven.

The Public Performance Right

A first sale extinguishes the §106(3)[61] right to distribute, but does not extinguish the other rights of the copyright owner as enumerated in §106 of the Copyright Act. Section 109(a) merely authorizes "the owner of a particular copy . . . to sell or otherwise dispose of the possession of that copy . . ."[62] The section, by its terms, creates a respite "notwithstanding the provisions of §106(3),"[63] and does not address any other of the §106 rights.

The copyright owners' right to public performance granted by §106(4) extends to "literary, musical, dramatic, or choreographic works and sound recordings."[64] According to *Hampton v. Paramount Pictures Corp.*,[65] the owner of a copy of a film print does not by reason of such ownership have the right to use that print for the purpose of causing a public performance of the motion picture. Consequently, the owner of a videocassette tape could not rent to a customer knowing that the customer intended to publicly exhibit the films, unless permission of the owner of the copyright was obtained.[66]

Does the rental and/or subsequent home play of a video cassette infringe the exclusive public performance right of the copyright owner? Stephen Roberts, president of Twentieth Century Fox Telecommunications division, has argued that public performance infringement does

---

[60] H. Rep., *supra* note 17, at 79, emphasis added.
[61] 17 U.S.C. §106(3).
[62] 17 U.S.C. §109(a).
[63] *Id.*
[64] *Id.* at §106(4).
[65] 279 F.2d 100 (9th Cir. 1960).
[66] *See* Kalem Co. v. Harper Bros., 222 U.S. 55 (1911).

occur.[67] In order to determine whether infringement of the §106(4) right has occurred, two questions must be answered affirmatively: (1) was there a "performance?" and (2) was the performance "public?"

To perform a work is "in the case of a motion picture or other audiovisual work, to show its images in any sequence or to make the sounds accompanying it audible . . .,"[68] by any device or process. It is therefore clear that the use or play of a video cassette in a VCR constitutes a "performance" of the motion picture recorded on the tape.[69] However, only those performances which are rendered "publicly" are included in the performance right granted under the Copyright Act.[70]

The requirements of performing a work publicly, as defined in §101, concern:

a) the composition of the audience;
b) the geographical dispersion of the audience; and
c) the chronological dispersion of the audience.[71]

A) According to the 1976 Act, when a work is performed "at a place open to the public, or at any place where a substantial number of persons outside of a normal circle of a family and its social acquaintances is gathered . . .,"[72] it is public. This new definition reversed a line of cases, exemplified by *MGM Distributing Corp. v. Wyatt*,[73] which suggested that performances were not public when an audience was limited to a particular group. Under the 1976 Act, it is clear that when a substantial number of persons outside of a normal circle of family and social acquaintances attend the performance, it will be characterized as public, whether or not that group is limited by membership or access. Moreover, the fact that only an insubstantial number of persons actually attend a performance will not detract from its character as a public performance when the substantial number could have attended. In the videocassette situation, the total number of persons cumulatively capable of receiving the performances, as a result of renting a tape, collectively constitute a substantial number of persons outside of a normal circle of one family and its social acquaintances.

B) When a substantial or unrestricted number of persons are able to view a given performance, it is not necessary that the audience be assembled together in order for the performance to be public. Clause (2) of the definition of "to perform a work publicly" explicitly states that

---

[67.] Testimony of Stephen Roberts, *supra* note 4.
[68.] 17 U.S.C. §101 (definition of 'to perform a work publicly').
[69.] *See* H. Rep., *supra* note 18, at 62, 63.
[70.] 17 U.S.C. §106(4).
[71.] *See* 2 NIMMER, NIMMER ON COPYRIGHT, §8.14[C] (1979).
[72.] 17 U.S.C. §101.
[73.] 21 C.O. BULL. 203 (D. Md. 932).

the performance can be public "whether the members of the public capable of receiving the performance, . . . receive it in the same place or in separate places . . ."[74] The House Report confirms this principle by commenting that, under the Act,

> a performance made available by transmission to the public at large is 'public' even though the recipients are not gathered in a single place, and even if there is no proof that any of the potential recipients was operating his receiving apparatus at the time of transmission.[75]

Therefore, though each video cassette play may be rendered at a separate location, by separate individuals, the first two prongs of the public performance test are satisfied when several individuals rent a tape and each one performs it in his home.

C) The §101 definition goes on to provide that a work is performed publicly whether the performance is received "at the same time or at different times."[76] It is this language of the definition upon which this copyright infringement claim hinges. Stephen Roberts explains:

> [I]t seems clear that what must have been intended by that language was that *if the same copy* of a given work is repeatedly "performed" by different members of a public, albeit at different places and at different times, it constitutes a "public performance" within the meaning of the Copyright Act.[77]

Roberts provides an analogy to the old fashioned penny arcade, where no more than one person at a time views a given performance of a motion picture sequence, and concludes that "the single copy in the coin-operated device would give rise to numerous performances seen by the public each day"[78] and as such the performance is public. He also compares the videotape rental situation to a movie theater with only one person in attendance, as well as to a hypothetical future genre of theaters with separate screening rooms for each individual viewer. Roberts concludes that each such performance must be regarded as public.

Neither the Senate nor the House Report offers an explanation of "the same or different time" clause. The language is sufficiently broad

---

[74.] 17 U.S.C. §101.
[75.] H. Rep., *supra* note 18, at 65.
[76.] 17 U.S.C. §101.
[77.] Testimony of Stephen Roberts, *supra* note 4, at 321.
[78.] *Id.*

to support Stephen Roberts' contention. However, it is difficult to believe that the phrase was intended to be interpreted literally. As Professor Nimmer pointed out, such an interpretation would mean that one who buys a phonograph record of a song, and then plays it in the privacy of his home is "publicly" performing the song because other members of the public will be playing duplicate copies as well.[79] Any use of a video cassette would be subject to the same difficulty.

In response, a distinction can be made between the phonograph record hypothetical and the video cassette rental hypothetical. In the latter, the *same* copy of a given work is performed by each individual. There is no indication that the public performance right was aimed at the simultaneous private performance of several copies, each one private, but "public" when "added up" together. Thus, the distinction is theoretically plausible.

However, there is also no indication that the framers of the 1976 Act wanted to address the problem of individual viewers collectively performing the same copy sequentially. The legislative history implies, rather, that the public performance definition was struggled over and shaped in response to a controversy over cable retransmissions and multiple performances.[80] It is most likely that the actual intent of the "at the same or different time" clause, as Nimmer has suggested, was to make the point that a delayed rebroadcast (by reason of time differences in certain geographic areas, or for other reasons) is to be regarded as part of the same public performance as the original broadcast.[81]

There are several practical arguments against Roberts' construction of the public performance right. In the first instance, the consequences of each individual viewer's liability and the difficulties of enforcement are disproportionate to the harm of home viewing. For example, a court holding the home viewing to be public performance would promulgate a rule of law virtually unenforceable against a primary infringer. Additionally, any enforcement that did occur against a direct infringer would be selective and therefore would seem unjust. The constititutional right to privacy[82] might be endangered. Equally difficult would be to fashion an appropriate remedy. What is the actual harm? How would

---

[79.] 2 NIMMER, NIMMER ON COPYRIGHT, §8.14[C] [3] (1979).

[80.] *Cf.*, Buck v. Jewell-La Salle Realty Co., 283 U.S. 191 (1931); Fortnightly Corp. v. United Artists Television Inc., 392 U.S. 390 (1968); Teleprompter Corp. v. Columbia Broadcasting System, Inc., 415 U.S. 394 (1974); Twentieth Century Music Corp. v. Aiken, 422 U.S. 151 (1975); 17 U.S.C. §111(a) (1); H. Rep., *supra* note 18, at 91-92; A. LATMAN, R. GORMAN, COPYRIGHT FOR THE EIGHTIES, 431-448 (1981).

[81.] NIMMER, *supra* note 79.

[82.] Griswold v. Connecticut, 381 U.S. 479 (1965).

it be measured? Injunctive relief would cause tremendous hardship.[83] An analogous situation is home recording on VCR's which was attacked and addressed in the well-known *Betamax* cases.[84] Once again, the §107 "fair use" provision[85] would be prevailed upon in an attempt to exempt home viewers. And if, as in *Universal City Studios, Inc. v. Sony Corp. of America*,[86] the court concludes that the fair use exemption is inapplicable, consequent attempts would be made to amend the Copyright Act to provide a specific home use exemption.[87] Why would the drafters of the Copyright Act effectuate an obtuse interpretation of an otherwise clear provision, which would then necessitate disclaimers and exemptions? They would not.

Secondly, a similar controversy arose and was reported, first, in the Tentative Draft of the Report of the Register of Copyrights on General Revision of the Copyright Law, in 1961. Motion picture producers and distributors urged that the performance right in motion pictures should extend to clearly private performance behavior, including performances of leased or rented films given in private homes. They pointed to the now extinct *Patterson v. Century Productions, Inc.*[88] concept that exhibition is a form of "copying" for theoretical support of their proposition. The Register conceded that the argument might have theoretical plausibility, but maintained that for practical reasons, the extension would not be made. According to the Register:

a) Injury to the copyright owners from private performances would be minimal, and license fees or breach of contract damages were sufficient protection;

b) The unauthorized private performances could rarely be discovered or controlled;

c) Films or motion pictures were also sold for home use, and those purchasers should not be subjected to a risk of liability.[89]

[83.] *See Universal City Studios, Inc. v. Sony Corp.: Fair Use Looks Different on Videotape*, 66 VA. L. REV. 1005 (June 1980), at 1024, for an analysis of these questions in reference to home recording.

[84.] Universal City Studios, Inc. v. Sony Corp. of America, 480 F. Supp. 429 (C.D. Cal. 1979), *rev'd.*, 659 F.2d 963 (9th Cir. 1981).

[85.] 17 U.S.C. §107.

[86.] Universal City Studios, Inc. v. Sony Corp. of America, 659 F.2d 963 (9th Cir. 1981).

[87.] S.1758, 97th Cong. 2d Sess. (1981).

[88.] 93 F.2d 489 (2d Cir. 1937).

[89.] *Report of the Register of Copyrights on the General Revision of the U.S. Copyright Law, Report to House Committee on the Judiciary*, 87th Cong., 1st Sess. (1961).

The drafters followed the Register's recommendation that the statute simply provide explicitly that the copyright owner of any motion picture shall have the exclusive right to perform (or exhibit) it *in public*, though the definition of "in public" was yet to be fashioned.[90]

The third argument rests upon the economic reality of the video-cassette rental problem. It is actually the behavior of the commercial rental outlets that the motion picture companies want to curtail by imposing contributory liability. According to the House Report, the phrase "to do and to authorize" was used in conjunction with the rights granted in §106, in order to avoid any questions as to the potential liability of contributory infringers.[91] The House Report expressly states that a person who lawfully acquires an authorized copy of a motion picture would be an infringer if he or she engages in the business of renting it to others for purposes of unauthorized public performance.[92] It does not, however, make sense to attack only the secondary/contributory infringement when the primary infringement is deemed inconsequential by the attackers.

Promotion of Science and the Useful Arts.

Though there is no direct infringement of an exclusive right of copyright in the video cassette rental problem, the copyright law is not necessarily inapplicable. The "rights" of copyright owners are involved. It is a matter of interpretation whether the owners are being harmed in a manner which impedes the Constitutional goals to promote the useful arts and sciences.[93] The exclusive rights of the owner have always been rooted in economic realities.[94]

The 1976 copyright statute explicitly demarcates the legislature's balance between the rights of ownership and the rights of users. Yet, the videocassette user/owner conflict has arisen in light of new technology and therefore was not considered or addressed. David Ladd, the Register

---

[90]. *Id.*

[91]. H. Rep., *supra* note 18, at 61-62.

[92]. *Id.*

[93]. U.S. Const. Art. I, §8, cl. 8, provides that Congress is empowered "to promote the progress of science and useful arts, by securing for limited times to authors and inventors the exclusive right to their respective writings and discoveries."

[94]. Mazer v. Stein, 347 U.S. 201, 74 S.Ct. 460, 471, 98 L.Ed. 630 (1954). The Supreme Court stated, "The economic philosophy behind the clause empowering Congress to grant patents and copyrights is the conviction that encouragement of individual effort by personal gain is the best way to advance public welfare through the talents of authors and inventors in 'science and Useful Arts'."

of Copyrights, has pointed out that the architecture of the statute "makes possible that claims for additional limitations, qualifications or exemptions can be subjected to the legislative process, and there assessed upon the whole evidence from all parties . . ."[95] He added, "[C]opyright owners need not demonstrate serious market damage *before* some form of protection or renumeration will be provided."[96]

Upon examination, the 1976 copyright revisions, on the whole, tended towards strengthening the protection of copyright owners of motion pictures. Peter Nolan examined the impact of the new copyright act on motion pictures and pointed to "the longer term of protection, the extension of the performance right to all motion pictures, and the partial elimination of the renewal process" for "three of the more favorable changes."[97] Furthermore,

> the industry benefits most, however, where the new statute takes position on various troublesome issues that arose under the 1909 Act. The Wyatt cases [limiting the definition of public performance] [*MGM Distributing v. Wyatt*, 21 C.O.Bull. 304 (D. Md. 1932)] is specifically overruled, and protection for motion pictures embodied only on videotapes and for soundtracks is expressly confirmed.[98]

The drafters did not attempt to confront all of the copyright problems the motion picture industry might encounter through the remainder of the twentieth century. When the videocassette rental controversy is addressed, the legislature might be compelled to follow the trend of strengthening motion picture owners' protection. Additionally, when examining the issue on first impression, the burden should be on the "user", not the owner, to prove his right of access to the work.

III. BREACH OF CONTRACT

Even if there is no copyright infringement when a retailer rents a prerecorded videocassette in violation of a restrictive agreement or legend, the transfer of possession of a particular copy may give rise to a cause of action by the copyright owner for breach of contract. The House Report accompanying the copyright legislation determined that,

---

[95.] Remarks of David Ladd to the Internationale Gesellschaft fur Urheberrecht (INTERGO), Toronto, Canada (Sept. 23, 1981), at 17.

[96.] *Id.*

[97.] P. Nolan, *A Brighter Day for the Magic Lantern: Thoughts on the Impact of the New Copyright Act on Motion Pictures*, 11 Loy. L.A.L. Rev. (1977), at 44.

[98.] *Id.* at 44.

> [T]he outright sale of an authorized copy . . . frees it from any copyright control over . . . its future disposition . . . This does not mean that conditions on future disposition of copies . . . imposed by a contract between their buyer and seller would be unenforceable between the parties as a breach of contract . . .[99]

Validity of Restrictive Contracts.

In order to enforce their rights, parties must be subject to a *valid* contractual obligation preventing or restricting further disposition. The validity of each restrictive contract must be examined to determine whether it is binding. Contracts are held to be invalid when they place unreasonable restraints on trade, in violation of the antitrust laws. If action is taken against those who will not comply, the retailer can bring an action for violation of antitrust laws and consequently gain freedom from the restrictive agreement and/or equitable relief of treble damages.[100] Additionally, if a plaintiff in a copyright infringement action is himself guilty of a violation of the antitrust laws, that violation might constitute a valid defense.[101]

According to the Court of Appeals for the Second Circuit, a fun-

---

[99.] H. Rep., *supra* note 18, at 79. Note that the language is limited to "between the buyer and seller". The non-privity situation is not addressed, yet no difficulty or difference is suggested. The problem of non-privity relations occurs with remote vendees and private swapping. For a discussion of these issues, *see* J.J. Beard, *supra* note 48. Also note that 17 U.S.C. §301 preemption does not disturb the state law remedies for breach of contract governed by the Uniform Commercial Code.

[100.] Sherman Antitrust Act, 26 Stat. 209 (1809), as amended 15 U.S.C. §1. Mere announcement of a policy in advance, and a unilateral refusal to deal with those who reject the announced policy, does not run counter to the antitrust laws, but, where producer or supplier secures adherences to his suggested restrictions by means which go beyond mere refusal to sell to one who will not observe his announced policy, the antitrust laws are violated. *See* Sahm v. V-1 Oil Co., 402 F.2d 69 (10th Cir. 1968).

[101.] The theory is that one with "unclean hands" cannot bring an action in equity. In the main, those cases that have ruled on this question have held that no defense may be claimed. *See*, for example, Orth-O-Vision Inc. v. H.B.O., 474 F. Supp. 672 (S.D.N.Y. 1979); Peter Pan Fabrics, Inc. v. Candy Frocks, Inc., 187 F. Supp. 334 (S.D.N.Y. 1960). In Hoehn v. Crews, 144 F.2d 665 (10th Cir. 1944), *aff'd*, 324 U.S. 200 (1945), the court noted that it is not required that one who would seek equity must himself possess "spotless hands", and that it is not "every stain" that will bar one from equitable relief. The following language from Alfred Bell and Co. v. Catalda, 191 F.2d 99 (2d Cir. 1951) is appropriate,

> "We have here a conflict of policies: a) that of preventing piracy of copyrighted matter and b) that of enforcing the antitrust laws. We

damental purpose of the exclusive right of public performance is to protect copyright proprietors against dilution of the market for their works.[102] Though copyright grants certain exclusive rights and protections, it does not, however, confer an absolute market monopoly.[103] There is a point at which the policy favoring a copyright monopoly for authors gives way to the policy opposing restraints of trade and restraints on alienation.[104] It is clear that an agreement which is illegal, for example, because it suppresses competition is not any less so because the competitive article is copyrighted.[105]

A contract which limits in any way the right of either party to work or to do business, whether as to the character of the work or business, its place, the manner in which it is done, or the price to be demanded for it, is a contract in restraint of trade. Contracts in restraint of trade are regarded with disfavor by the courts, and will be strictly construed so as to limit the restrictions imposed. As a general rule, an agreement which is an unreasonable restraint of trade is illegal and void, while an agreement which is a reasonable restraint of trade is valid.[106]

The restrictive agreements imposed by the motion picture companies prohibiting retailers from renting videocassettes are "vertical" restraints. A vertical restraint is one imposed as part of a relationship between firms which perform functions at successive stages in the production and distribution of a product, and it can affect market competition in many diverse ways. In passing the Sherman Antitrust Act,[107] Congress was concerned with protecting the freedom of individual traders to make for themselves, free of coercion or compulsion, decisions about the markets they would enter, the prices they would charge, and in general, how they would compete.[108] According to the Sherman Antitrust Act,

> Every contract, combination in the form of trust or otherwise, or conspiracy in restraint of trade or commerce among the several

---

must balance the two, taking into account the comparative innocence or guilt of the parties, the moral character of their respective acts, the extent of the harm to the public interest, the penalty inflicted on the plaintiff, if we deny it relief." *Id.* at 291.

[102.] U.A.T.V. Inc. v. Fortnightly Corp., 377 F.2d 872 (2d Cir. 1967), rev'd. on other grounds, 392 U.S. 390, 88 S.Ct. 2084, 20 L.Ed. 2d 1176.

[103.] Schnadig Corp. v. Gaines Mfg. Co., Inc., 620 F.2d 1166 (6th Cir. 1980).

[104.] Blazon, Inc. v. Deluxe Game Corp., 268 F. Supp. 416 (S.D.N.Y. 1965).

[105.] Interstate Circuit v. U.S., 306 U.S. 467 (1939).

[106.] 17 C.J.S. CONTRACTS §238.

[107.] 26 Stat. 209 (1890), as amended 15 U.S.C. §1.

[108.] L. SULLIVAN, HANDBOOK OF THE LAW OF ANTITRUST, Arrangements Between Suppliers and Customers In Restraint of Trade, Ch. 5, §§130-175 (1979).

states, or with foreign nations, is declared to be illegal . . .[109]

An act in restraint of trade is one which

> hinders and prevents the selling and exchanging of personal prop-
> erty, or an article or commodity of trade that is in everyday use,
> and in this way a necessary and indispensable article of com-
> merce.[110]

Most unreasonable restraint of trade cases have addressed restrictions as to price, territory and/or persons. The restriction which deprives
an owner of a copy to whom title has passed, of his right to rent that
copy, is a restriction which limits the *means* of exchanging an article or
commodity of trade.[111] The videocassette restrictions are also set apart
in that they involve copyrighted works, to which a form of "monopoly"
automatically attaches.[112] There are no cases on record in which parties
have contracted to prohibit a retailer from renting the distributed product to his customers. Therefore, for the purpose of analysis, the prohibition on rentals can be compared to general and partial restrictions
on the right to resale. Restraints on rental and restraints on alienation
are both restrictions within the distribution process of a product. Both
involve public access to that product.

At common law, it was established at an early date, and has since
been recognized, that a general restriction on the alienation of chattels
is void. A seller of ordinary property cannot restrict its future use or
alienation, nor can he ordinarily fix the price at which it can be resold
by the buyer, even in the case of goods manufactured under secret
process.[113]

---

[109] 15 U.S.C. §1.

[110] *Id.*

[111] The restriction does not seem to be implemented in an attempt to prohibit
or limit sales of the product. On the contrary, the prohibition of rentals is
designed to encourage and promote sales. In the end, however, the important fact is, more or less, one of distribution and access. The agreements are
restraints on distribution.

[112] An attempt to extend the scope of this monopoly has, under certain circumstances, resulted in violation of the antitrust laws. Such violations have been
held to occur as a result of a number of copyright owners acting in combination (Strauss v. American Pub. Ass., 231 U.S. 222 (1913)), and where
particular copyright owners have refused to license certain of their more
desirable products unless "tied-in" with licenses of certain of their less desirable products (U.S. v. Loews, Inc., 371 U.S. 38 (1962), Interstate Circuit
v. U.S., 306 U.S. 467 (1939)). *See* NIMMER, *supra* note 79, at §13.09[A].

[113] *See* 17 C.J.S. CONTRACTS §253. For example, in W.H. Hill Co. v. Gray, 163
Mich. 12, 127 N.W. 803 (1910), an owner fixed the retail price of secret

An exception exists when a very special kind of property, such as an heirloom, is involved. For example, in *Meyer v. Estes*,[114] an agreement with the purchaser of electrotypes, to be used only for the purpose of illustrating works to be published by him, provided that he was "not to sell these electrotypes to any other parties, nor to multiply them for the purpose of selling them."[115] The court stated that the contract "is an agreement in restraint of trade, but in view of the nature of the property, is reasonable, [and] will be enforced between the parties to it.[116]

Partial restrictions on the right to *resell* are, as a general rule, upheld when there is a contract between the parties. In *Smith v. San Francisco and Northern Pacific Railroad Co.*,[117] a buyer-seller stock voting agreement was regarded as legal and not in restraint of trade. That court broadly stated,

> As the owner of property has the right to withhold it from sale, he can also, at the time of its sale, impose conditions upon its use without violating any rule of public policy and there is nothing inconsistent with public policy for two or more persons, who contemplate purchasing certain property, to agree with each other, as a condition of the purchase, that neither will dispose of his share within a limited period, or for less than a fixed sum, or except upon certain limitations . . .[118]

Such a liberal construction would not be upheld if the agreement had been a 'vertical' restraint on trade, as compared to an agreement between two stockholders. For example, today, under the Sherman An-

---

formula medicine through a system of contracts with wholesalers and retailers. The court held that the contract prevents competition; no exemption as to its secret formula since owner manufactured and sold the product in the first instance.

114. 164 Mass. 457, 41 N.E. 683 (1895).
115. *Id.* at 462.
116. *Id.*
117. 115 Cal. 584 (1897).
118. *Id.* at 587. *See also* Fowle v. Park, 131 U.S. 88, 9 S.Ct. 658, 33 L.Ed. 67, where a contract relating to a patent medicine which communicates its ingredients in confidence, and provides in substance that the parties shall enjoy a "monopoly" of the production and sale of it, each within a defined region in the U.S. and that it shall not be sold below a certain rate or price, is not unreasonable or invalid as in restraint of trade, and Gano v. Delmas, 140 Miss. 323, 105 So. 535 (1925), where contract provided that, if buyer sold cement purchased, or used any part of it in work other than that described, seller could decline to make further deliveries, the contract was held not to violate antitrust statute.

titrust Act,[119] resale price maintenance agreements are unlawful and void per se. The per se rule also governs restrictions imposed by a seller on the territories within which, or the customers to whom the buyer may resell.

Yet, there are exceptions even within the vertical restraint category. According to Lawrence Sullivan's treatise on antitrust, restrictions to control the quality of goods and services sold under a trademark license are generally reasonable restraints. Additionally, where a manufacturer sells to a dealer the manufacturer's own "brand name" products for resale, the manufacturer has an interest in seeing that his product is retailed in a way which will yield a high volume of sales. Thus, the manufacturer may impose rules respecting the type of showroom facilities or require certain displays. These "quality" conditions will be held unlawful only if in particular circumstances, they can be shown to injure competition.[120]

The Reasonableness Test

Many versions of a judicial test have been implemented to help determine which restrictions should be declared invalid. The common threshold is that in order to be valid and enforceable, the restriction must be "reasonable."[121] In *Fowle v. Park*,[122] the Supreme Court examined a restrictive contract on the distribution of a patented medicine. According to the Court,

> public welfare is first considered and if it be not involved, and the restraint upon one party is not greater than protection to the other requires, the contract may be sustained. The question is whether, under the particular circumstances of the case, and the nature of the particular contract involved in it, the contract is, or is not, unreasonable.[123]

It is particularly relevant to our inquiry that this court felt compelled to add:

---

[119] 15 U.S.C. §1.
[120] L. SULLIVAN, *supra* note 108, §172.
[121] For example, in Dunlop v. Gregory, 10 N.Y. 241 (1851), the court explained,
> The contract, to be upheld, must appear from special circumstances to be reasonable and useful, and the restraint of the covenantor must not be larger than is necessary for the protection of the covenantee in the enjoyment of his trade or business.

Id. at 243.
[122] 131 U.S. 88, 9 S.Ct. 658, 33 L.Ed. 67.
[123] *Id.* at 97.

> The policy of the law is to encourage useful discoveries by securing their fruits to those who made them. If the public found the balsam efficacious they were interested in not being deprived of its use, but by whom it was sold was unimportant.[124]

The tendency of modern authorities is to reject any fixed rules and to gauge the validity of a contract in restraint of trade by its reasonableness in light of the particular circumstances. A determination of the reasonableness of the contract must involve the weighing and balancing of the interests of the person protected, the person restrained and the general public.[125]

The Supreme Court has stated that they "would not expect that any market arrangement necessary to effecuate the rights granted to copyright owners would be deemed a *per se* violation" of the antitrust law.[126] When examining the reasonableness of the videocassette restrictive contracts, the special nature of the copyrighted works is particularly significant.

For example, the public welfare promoted by protecting copyright owners must be compared to the public utility of access to a desired product. The extent to which distribution would be curtailed without rentals, due to prohibitive sales prices, should be examined in light of the fact that copyright owners have the right to refrain from distributing their work entirely. Yet, on the other hand, the courts may be wary of extending market and competitive control to those who already have a limited "monopoly." Additionally, whether the restriction is a single isolated transaction or an industry-wide prohibition gains importance in light of the role of the Motion Picture Association of America. The largest distribution companies belong to the Association. As a group, these distributors' controlling power is more detrimental to the retailer

---

[124.] *Id.*

[125.] The RESTATEMENT OF CONTRACTS formulation of tests of reasonableness provides:

> A restraint of trade by contract is generally unreasonable if: First, it is greater than is required for the protection of the person for whose benefit the restriction is imposed; second, it imposes undue hardship on the person restricted; third, it tends to create a monopoly, or to control prices or to limit production artificially; fourth, it unreasonably restricts the alienation or use of anything that is a subject of property; fifth, it is based on a promise to refrain from competition and is not ancillary either to a contract for the transfer of good will or other subject of property or to an existing employment or contract of employment.

[126.] Broadcast Music v. Columbia Broadcasting System, 441 U.S. 1 (1979).

and to free market conditions.[127]

Without a particular contract to examine, and a particular set of facts for context, this issue cannot be concluded. Still, it is of consequence, not only in the realm of private litigation. The possibility that the restrictive agreement might be an invalid restraint of trade must be remembered when fashioning a proper remedy to the videocassette rental controversy.

III. POTENTIAL SOLUTIONS

There are numerous alternative solutions to the videocassette controversy, each one worthy of thought and discussion.

Laissez-faire

It is possible to conclude that the rental problem is purely economic and thus a matter of contractual relations between private commercial entities. Why should the film distributors and the retail outlets not work out their problems individually, without regulation? In fact, the industries have already begun to do just that, albeit as a temporary measure. By December of 1981, most of the movie studios had implemented rental plans of their own, initiating rentals to dealers so that control over their products would be assured. For example, the Metro Goldwyn Mayer/Columbia Broadcasting System plan specifies that one new title will be released each month which can be rented for a four-month period. Dealers may then purchase other films for resale or rental. The dealers cannot sell tapes which are in the rental phase; and the rental charge to dealers, per tape, is a $60 four-month royalty fee. Twentieth-Century Fox has separated its prerecorded films into sales and rental categories. Rental titles are leased for a six-month period with a $75 six-month royalty fee for the most popular movies, and $45 six-month royalty fee for other movies. Subsequently, the titles are released for sale or withdrawn from the market. Dealers cannot sell tapes while in the rental phase. Walt Disney's plan separates sales and rental programs but requires that separate inventories be kept for each title. Dealers may only sell "sales" tapes and rent "rental" tapes. The rental charge to dealer per tape is a $26 three-month royalty fee. The Warner Bros. program has received the highest amount of criticism from dealers, and has been

---

[127.] The issue of whether the participation of motion picture companies in the Motion Picture Association of America could constitute a violation of §2 of the Sherman Antitrust Act, 15 U.S.C. §2, which illegalizes attempts to and acts of monopoly, is not addressed in this article.

threatened with boycott. Warner retains ownership of all tapes. Dealers lease the tapes on a weekly basis and may only rent to customers. The weekly fees range from $4.40 per tape (for six or more weeks) to $8.25 per tape (for one week). Paramount, Inc., in contrast, has added a sur-charge onto all tape sales, based on the estimated number of rentals per title. The surcharge ranges from $1 to $10 per tape. The dealers can then sell or rent the tapes without restrictions. This solution seems the most plausible long-run choice.[128]

One problem inherent in a laissez-faire solution is the bookkeeping burden on the individual dealers. Each tape must be categorized, its agreement plan must be noted, its time chart must be kept. Tremendous expense is involved. If industry negotiations could lead to one plan for all, the system would be greatly simplified. For example, if a plan were negotiated among the major film studios, guidelines could be set so that popular new movies are rented only and older ones are sold. Yet com-plicated decisions would still have to be made as to when to release each film on videocassette, and how long to keep each film on a rental-only basis. Even general acceptance of a Paramount-type plan would require a much better understanding of the videocassette market. Some ques-tions that must be answered are: how much the rentals of videocassettes damage potential sales; how much early rentals of videocassettes damage theater receipts; how much in sales revenues will be lost if consumers are not allowed to buy a cassette when a movie is still at the height of its popularity; and what will the transference of extra costs to the retailer do to the consumer market?[129]

Within the Law of Copyright

Alternatively, the solution to the rental controversy should lie within the realm of copyright law (whether because the act is determined to be an infringement of the public performance right or simply because it is a problem affecting the intellectual property of copyright owners which arises within the Constitutional purpose to promote the useful arts and sciences).[130]

Would protection of the copyright owner's right against rentals pro-mote the creation and dissemination of artistic works? Some hold the view that compensating the copyright owners would not be aiding the

---

[128] A. Pollack, *A Battle Over Video Cassettes: Millions in Tape Rentals are at Stake,* NEW YORK TIMES (December 11, 1981) at D1, citing as source, Home Video Report.

[129] *Id.* Note, once again, the potential antitrust violations due to restraints of trade.

[130] U.S. CONST. art. I, §8, cl. 8. *See supra* note 93.

creation and dissemination of art, but merely putting money into an already rich motion picture industry. This argument must be confronted. It relies upon the reality that the large companies, and not the artists, are the copyright owners of most films. The theory that motion picture companies are "triple dippers" in the economic pot has been espoused by Jack Wayman, senior vice-president of the Consumer Electronics Group. He explains that the movie companies collect profits in three ways:

> 1) by the first release for showing in theaters. If the movie is a hit, the movie company makes tremendous profits;
> 2) by the release of the movie, in exchange for generous payments, to a manufacturer of prerecorded video tapes, or by themselves manufacturing and subsequently selling the tapes at retail from $50 to $100; and
> 3) by negotiated royalty arrangements to allow the movie to be shown on television.[131]

In response, I suggest that the "rich industry" argument ignores the importance of "royalties" to all artists. As one author points out,

> It is difficult to have much sympathy for such rich companies as Universal Studios, Inc., and Walt Disney Productions . . . But what about the individual writer, the producer, the director, the technician . . . The artist . . . sells the distribution rights for a pittance, hoping that royalties will save the day . . .[132]

If the videocassette market is hurt because of rentals, artists' royalties would be decreased. And, as noted above, their works would be in use without recompense.

An even more basic response to the "fat cat" argument is that the motion picture companies are entitled to get rich. They are entitled to make money and to take that money to make more motion pictures and more money. When one takes away from the motion picture companies money it deserves, whether it is "needed" or not, it is a harm that should be remedied. The Register of Copyright has stated,

> The public interest is paramount, to be sure. But the public is served quite as much by a respect for property—and copyright

---

[131.] *Testimony before the Senate Committee on S.1758,* Jack Wayman, senior vice-president of the Consumer Electronics Group (1981).

[132.] J. Saltzman, *Video Recorder Lawsuit is Battle that Likely Will Cost Consumer,* 1982.

is the highest kind of property—as by expropriating it from its creators and owners for mass, free use . . .

It is too often easy to convince people that the public interest is always served when someone else's property can be had for free. The more difficult task is to balance such impulses against the rights of our creative minority . . .[133]

Judicial Solution

It has been suggested that a solution to the problem should be effected by judicial decision, as soon as a case arises. Copyright adaptation has often been the result of court-made law. But example has shown that courts can only go so far, particularly where statutory guidance is absent or unclear. A recent example to be learned from are the "Betamax" cases,[134] where noncommercial home recording of copyrighted material broadcast over the public airwaves was ultimately declared infringement. Both the District Court and the Court of Appeals gave fully reasoned and important opinions in an attempt to resolve complex issues that the statutory law ignored. Yet the need has generally been recognized, and subsequent action has been taken, to bring the conflict to the legislature for ultimate solution. The Betamax court itself stated,

> The ramifications of this new technology are greater than the boundaries of this lawsuit. A court reviewing the limited claims of specified parties in a particular factual setting cannot and should not undertake the role of government commission or legislative body exploring and evaluating the uses and consequences of the videotape recorder.[135]

Like the photocopying issue discussed in Williams and Wilkins v. U.S.,[136] the videocassette issue is,

> preeminently a problem for Congress . . . Obviously, there is much to be said on all sides. The choices involve economic, social and policy factors which are far better sifted by a legislature. The

---

[133.] Remarks of David Ladd to the Internationale Gesellschaft for Urheberrecht (INTERGU), Toronto, Canada (Sept. 28, 1981) at 18.

[134.] Universal City Studios, Inc. v. Sony Corp. of America, 480 F. Supp. 429 (D.C. Cal. 1981) rev'd., 659 F.2d 963 (9th Cir. 1981).

[135.] 480 F. Supp., at 442.

[136.] 487 F.2d 1345 (1973), aff'd per curiam by an equally divided court, 420 U.S. 376 (1975).

possible intermediate solutions are also of the pragmatic kind legislatures, not courts, can and should fashion.[137]

Furthermore, David Ladd, Register of Copyrights, explained,

> When law and broad policy are created judicially ... policy emerges piecemeal, by small accretions of precedent; or, in an effort to achieve legislation-like results, courts issue broad declarations which really rest on the particular facts on the given case.[138]

An acceptable solution must reflect careful consideration of all conflicting interests and of the long-range consequences of any particular policy. The question requires legislative consideration.

Legislative Solution

Congress could approach the rental controversy in a variety of ways. If the legislature determines that the public interest in promoting the creation of artistic works requires protection of the copyright owners' rights against rentals, it could devise a scheme to compensate the owners, or it could restrict or prohibit videocassette rentals.

Compensation

A compensatory scheme can take numerous forms. For example, one potential solution is the imposition of levies on prerecorded videocassettes. Austria and the Federal Republic of Germany have addressed the "home taping" problem by imposing levies on video recorder hardware or blank tape, providing for distribution of proceeds to copyright owners. This solution has equal potential within the rental problem. In essence, the levy scheme is a statutory license, and the Copyright Royalty Tribunal could distribute the fees collected. The typical percentage of the price of a prerecorded videocassette attributable to copyright royalty would be low, yet the cumulative revenues could protect copyright owners and encourage creation of new motion pictures. Unfortunately, this solution does not tie the cost of the fee per tape to its actual rental volume and therefore could be over- or under-compensatory.

Alternatively, Congress could fashion a licensing arrangement in which retail outlets would pay into a central fund to be distributed as

---

[137.] *Id.* at 1360.
[138.] Remarks of David Ladd, *supra* note 133.

royalties to copyright owners. The payment could be linked to rental volume so as to avoid overbroad penalties. This scheme could be patterned upon the current licensing arrangement for American cable television systems.[139] An agreed-upon formula could be negotiated by which the Copyright Tribunal would distribute the money.

There are several advantages to this kind of licensing scheme. First, it works within a framework already provided in the 1976 Copyright Act. Second, the system is seemingly equitable since payment would directly attach to rental volume. Third, as in all licensing schemes, the system could be largely self-administered.[140]

However, there are obvious disadvantages to a licensing system. Congress presided over a series of hearings which focused on the cable television compulsory license system and acknowledged its flaws.[141] The cable industry has changed; it has grown tremendously. The compulsory license system no longer seems practical since the parties are better able to bargain and negotiate on their own. Similar growth and change is likely to occur in the videocassette industry.

Another more substantive disadvantage is the lack of guarantee that the amount collected and distributed will bear rational relation to the amount necessary to encourage production. This system may be economically inefficient.

A third alternative is to promulgate an arena for the development of voluntary guidelines, similar to the provisions of §118 of the Copyright Act.[142] Section 118 provides that

> the owners of copyright in nondramatic literary works and public broadcasting entities may, during the course of voluntary negotiations, agree among themselves, respectively, as to the terms and rates of royalty payments, without liability under the antitrust laws.[143]

Within two years, a report must be submitted to Congress setting forth the extent to which voluntary licensing arrangements have been reached and describing any problems that may have arisen, for legislative recommendation.[144] The owners of copyright in videocassettes could negotiate

---

[139.] 17 U.S.C. §111.
[140.] *See Universal City Studios, Inc. v. Sony Corp.: Fair Use Looks Different on Videotape,* 66 VA. L. REV. 1005 (June 1980).
[141.] *Oversight of the Copyright Act of 1976: Hearings before the Committee on the Judiciary,* 97th Cong. 1st Sess. (July 29, 1981).
[142.] 17 U.S.C. §118.
[143.] 17 U.S.C. §118(e) (1).
[144.] 17 U.S.C. §118(e) (2).

with representatives of commercial rental outlets within a modified free market system.

This system is advantageous because the agreements can be changed more readily than legislation can be amended, as the flaws become exposed. The scheme also provides a small but necessary degree of governmental involvement.

Two inherent problems however are: Who will represent the negotiating parties and how will equal bargaining power be achieved. Additionally, there is a potential for negotiation stalemate, and a general lack of uniformity when no law is made.

Restriction and Prohibition

The Motion Picture Association of America supports a solution which would restrict or prohibit rentals of videocassettes. A proposed amendment to the definition section of the Copyright Act has been introduced by Stephen Roberts, to the Senate Committee on the Judiciary Oversight Hearings on the Copyright Act of 1976.[145] The amendment confirms the Roberts interpretation of the "at different times" clause of the public performance definition, as explained in this text.[146] Renting and viewing a rented tape would explicitly be infringement of the public performance right. The proposed Amendment to 17 U.S.C. §101 provides:

> Section 101 of Title 17 of the United States Code is amended to add to the end of subparagraph (2) of the definition of "to perform or display a work 'publicly' " the following new language:
>
> > The reference to 'at different times' in the preceding sentence refers to those circumstances in which one particular copy or phonorecord of a work is employed to communicate two or more performances or displays of such work (whether such performances or displays occur in private homes or otherwise), provided: (i) the total number of persons cumulatively capable of receiving all such performances or displays collectively constitute a substantial number of persons outside of a normal circle of one family and its social acquaintances, and (ii) such particular copy or phonorecord was furnished or otherwise made available to com-

---

[145.] *Testimony of Stephen Roberts, supra* note 4, at 329.
[146.] *See supra* text accompanying notes 61-79.

municate such performances or displays in order to derive a direct or indirect commercial advantage.

Clause (ii) provides a safeguard against the private infringer by stipulating that the copy must have been furnished as "a direct or indirect commercial disadvantage," thus making it clear that it is only the renting entity and not the individual home user which is liable for infringement.

Why this interpretation should not prevail has been discussed above.[147] The commercial advantage language does not rectify the practical problems inherent in Roberts' solution.

Senator Mathias has proposed an alternative prohibitive amendment which addresses the §109(a) first sale doctrine.[148] The Mathias Amendment[149] is primarily an amendment to S.1758,[150] a bill introduced by Senators Di Concini and D'Amato in late 1981 to exempt home video recordings from copyright infringement liability, in response to the Ninth Circuit *Betamax* decision.[151] The Mathias Bill proposed a compulsory license for video recorder and video media manufacturers, importers and distributors as a method of providing royalties to copyright owners for the home video recording of their works. At the end of the Amendment, §4 introduces a provision that would make it illegal to dispose of the possession of a copy of a motion picture by rental, lease, or lending, for purposes of direct or indirect commercial advantage, unless authorized by the copyright owner. The text of §4 reads:

> SEC. 4. That §109(a) of chapter 1 of title 17 of the United States Code is amended by replacing the period at the end thereof with a colon and inserting thereafter the following: 'Provided, however, that the owner of a particular phonorecord of a sound recording, copy of a motion picture or other audiovisual work lawfully made under this title may not, unless authorized by the copyright owner, dispose of the possession of that phonorecord or copy by rental, lease, or lending, for purposes of direct or indirect commercial advantage.[152]

If one adheres to the proposition that rentals infringe the rights of

---

[147.] *See supra* text accompanying notes 82-92.
[148.] 17 U.S.C. §109(a). *See supra* text accompanying notes 21-44.
[149.] Amendment No. 1242, to S.1758, 97th Cong., 2d Sess. (1982), Cong. Rec. 12/16/81, p. S.15723.
[150.] S.1758 (H.R. 4608), 97th Cong., 2d Sess. (1982).
[151.] Universal City Studios, Inc. v. Sony Corp. of America, 659 F.2d 963 (9th Cir. 1981).
[152.] Amendment No. 1242, Cong. Rec. 12/16/81, p. S.15723.

copyright owners of motion pictures, this solution is both theoretically sound and practical. It promotes the goal of protecting copyright owners from the loss of profits and from others profiting from the unauthorized use of their works. It does not attempt to modify accepted definitional doctrine, such as the §101 public performance right.[153] The amendment would not necessarily contradict legislators' intent, since the problem of the videocassette rental controversy was not envisioned when formulating §109(a).[154]

The Mathias solution involves no time- and money-consuming governmental regulation. Rates do not have to be estimated; monies do not have to be distributed. No bookkeeping and inventory burdens are imposed upon retail outlets. There is no threat of unequal bargaining or forced negotiation.

Yet, §4 of the Mathias Amendment has two important flaws. The first is structural overbreadth. Prohibition is an extreme measure which should be rooted in direct evidence of the illegality of renting for commercial gain. There is no foundation for this finding in the Copyright Act. The prohibitive solution runs against the principles inherent in the comprehensive revision of the copyright laws. A broad prohibition simply limits access to the copyrighted works, to some degree. The legislative intent of the Copyright Act is to allow the public access to copyrighted works while securing compensation to producers, authors and other creative artists, according to use and enjoyment.

The second flaw is that §4 is a separate thought in an extremely important proposal for compulsory licensing for home video recording. The section was likely added as a "sweetener" provision, so that the Motion Picture Association would be more willing to support the bill. A drastic resolution such as §4 should be weighed and analyzed on its own. The videocassette rental controversy, like all revision problems, should not be resolved in undue haste. As the current Register of Copyrights has repeatedly emphasized, there is time. This particular question requires "the same fullness of debate, and technical input that culminated in the General Revision of 1976."[155] In the interim, the industry can and is adopting temporary plans. The rental problem does present an important, pressing issue, but the swiftest solution might not be the best.

IV. CONCLUSION

In this article, the author has attempted to provide a starting point

---

[153] 17 U.S.C. §101.
[154] 17 U.S.C. §109(a).
[155] Remarks of David Ladd, *supra* note 133.

for future scholarly and legislative analysis of the videocassette rental controversy. Only the surface of the complex problems and issues has been addressed. The additional damage accruing from potential swapping schemes, rentals by remote vendees and an increased propensity for copying must be examined. Rentals of prerecorded videocassette tapes that do not embody copyright works owned by the motion picture companies must be considered. Furthermore, the rental controversy must be examined within the context of a communications and entertainment technological revolution. It is not difficult to imagine a time when an advanced home computer/videocassette recorder system will be a common apparatus in every home.

In order to prevent years of turmoil, the legislature must take action; the copyright law must be adapted. Access to prerecorded videocassettes should not be limited to a sales-only basis; rentals should not be prohibited. On the other hand, it is vital that copyright owners are compensated for the use of and access to their creations. The best solution will analyze all of the conflicting interests, and provide for a workable system of compromise.

62: LEGISLATION IS INTRODUCED TO STUDY PUBLIC LENDING RIGHT

Legislation to establish a commission to study whether authors should be compensated when their books are borrowed from libraries was introduced by Senator Charles McC. Mathias of Maryland on November 18. A related article on this topic appears as an appendix to this issue of the LC *Information Bulletin* (pp. 427–32).

In introducing the legislation, Senator Mathias said, "The concept of compensating authors for public lending of their work is not new. At last count, 10 nations, including West Germany and Great Britain, have set up the system, popularly known as a 'public lending right,' to compensate authors. I believe the time is ripe to study the desirability and feasibility of compensating authors in this country."

The commission would consist of 11 members, including the Librarian of Congress and 10 others appointed by the President: two authors, two publishers, three librarians, and three public members. It would make a preliminary report after one year and a final report after two years.

Senator Mathias said the commission would examine whether a public lending right system would be in the public interest, whether it would encourage authors to write, and whether such a system could be funded without adding financial hardship to libraries or discouraging reading.

Reprinted from *LC Inf. Bull.* **42**:422 (1983).

63: PUBLIC LENDING RIGHT: A SYMPOSIUM AT THE LIBRARY OF CONGRESS

John Y. Cole

Executive Director
The Center for the Book

"Will the money to pay for public lending right be taken out of library budgets? The answer must be no — and nobody is saying it should be. If that would happen we would be working against readers, and working against readers is working against writers."
—William B. Goodman, September 29, 1983

Public lending right (PLR) is the notion that authors are entitled to be compensated for the multiple uses of their books in libraries. On September 29, the Center for the Book in the Library of Congress sponsored a symposium on Public Lending Right — what it is, how it works in the 10 countries in which it is in effect, and ways in which the concept might or might not be workable in the United States. The meeting, one in a series on contemporary issues in the book community, was organized by the Center for the Book to bring authors, librarians, and government officials together for an objective discussion before more formal consideration of the idea takes place in the United States. During the symposium, it was announced that Senator Charles McC. Mathias, Jr., of Maryland, chair of the U.S. Senate Subcommittee on Patents, Copyrights and Trademarks, plans to introduce a bill to create a commission to report to Congress on the merits and demerits of establishing a public lending right system in the United States. [*Editor's Note:* Such legislation was introduced on November 18.] In the United Kingdom, a bitter and protracted controversy between authors and librarians preceded the enactment of a public lending right system, which went into effect last year. The Center for the Book hopes that the objective, cordial atmosphere that characterized the serious discussions at its September 29 symposium will prevail as the public lending right idea is studied in the United States.

This article summarizes the remarks of the principal speakers and the discussions at the symposium. The Center for the Book's projects and programs are made possible by private contributions from individuals and organizations. It is grateful to the following for grants and contributions to support the Public Lending Right symposium: the Council on Library Resources, Inc., the Cultural Department of the British Embassy and the British Council, and Scandinavia Today.

Introduction

John Cole explained that the purpose of the symposium was to provide a deeper understanding of public lending right and to begin the education process about PLR that was needed among all parts of the book community. He cited the spring issue of *Library Trends,* which was devoted to PLR, as the stimulus for the meeting and welcomed four of the contributors to the issue: Perry D. Morrison, Dennis Hyatt, George Piternick, and Thomas Stave. Moderator Paul Goldstein, professor of law at Stanford University Law School, pointed out that the symposium had been structured to expose major issues concerning PLR, but that it was only the first step in exploring a topic that involved powerful and important questions of public policy.

A Brief History of the Idea

Thomas Stave outlined the history of public lending right, noting that it was not even suggested in print until 1920 nor enacted in any country until after World War II. In each of the 10 nations where it is now law, PLR was intended to accomplish three specific purposes, in varying degrees of emphasis: (1) to grant to authors what was perceived as their right to benefit from library loans of their books, (2) to provide a kind of social security for an underpaid group of writers, and (3) to assist in the survival of a national literature.

The first PLR system was established in Denmark in 1946. Other plans have been enacted into law in Norway (1947), Sweden (1954), Finland (1961, implemented in 1964), Iceland (1967), the Netherlands (1971), the Federal Republic of Germany (1972), New Zealand (1973), Australia (1974), and the United Kingdom (1979, implemented in 1982). PLR schemes vary widely. The only feature the 10 systems have in common is that payments to authors come from the government. In no case do library users pay a fee directly. In only one of the 10 countries, the Federal Republic of Germany, is the PLR statute part of the copyright law. Other variations include the amount and method of payment, the basis for computing the payment, and who receives the payment. In Norway and Finland, for example, no direct payment is made to individual authors. Payment instead goes to a writers' collective which determines the kinds of payments to be made to authors and other contributors to the book.

In conclusion, Mr. Stave noted that two conditions contributing to the success of public lending right abroad do not prevail in the United States. First, U.S. literature is in no way threatened by foreign book imports. Second, our political climate "is not receptive

Reprinted from *LC Inf. Bull.* **42**:427–432 (1983).

to the introduction of new forms of social welfare." Moreover, the United States does not have a strong tradition of government support for culture. For these reasons, he felt that the authors' strongest argument was the assertion that the public lending right was a natural right of authorship.

Legal Aspects in the United States

Dorothy Schrader, general counsel of the U.S. Copyright Office, explained that the Copyright Office has no position on the merits of a public lending right. No bill is pending in Congress. She did note, however, that technically there is "a public lending right of sorts" in the United States, as copyright owners have the exclusive right to lend copies of a work as long as the work is not sold. An effort is now under way in Congress to establish a commercial lending right for sound recordings. Her personal opinion is that if copyright is to be the vehicle of authors' compensation, "the establishment of a public lending right in the United States probably hinges on the outcome of the lending battles now being fought in the commercial arena between producers (who also represent creative artists), distributors, and retail specialty stores." Moreover, authors will have to become more energetic on the issue and enlist new allies, probably publishers, if they are to succeed. Finally, she raised a practical consideration "not related to the justice of the authors' claim." The "sheer size" of the United States and the decentralization of U.S. libraries and educational institutions will make it much more difficult to institute a PLR system here than in the smaller and more centralized nations of Europe.

Perspective of American Authors

Author Robert Caro, former president of the Authors Guild, announced that the Authors Guild Council, which represents 6,000 authors in America, has formally decided to campaign for the enactment of some form of public lending right in the United States. The justification is "fair payment for use," and the guild intends to mobilize and educate its members about the need for PLR and "the difference it could make in their lives." Ample evidence for the need, he explained, is in the results of a 1981 study of authors' incomes carried out by the Columbia University Center for Social Studies: the average American author — a contemporary writer who has had at least one book published — earns an annual income of less than $5,000 from writing. But the "simple justice of the case" was more important than the money. Authors should be paid for the use of their books, and this includes use through libraries. This argument was echoed by William Goodman, editorial director for David Godine, Publisher, who stated "the issue is the survival of

Robert A. Caro

culture. Culture does not survive, or flourish, if we are talking about books, unless writers flourish."

Mr. Caro deplored the mistrust between writers and librarians that developed in the United Kingdom over the PLR issue. "It would be quite a waste if we had to go through the same dreary scenario in the U.S. Moreover, we shouldn't be fighting at all. Books are threatened. We are all on the same side. We need to work together to develop a fair scheme for compensating authors for the multiple use of their copyrighted book in libraries." He felt that the lack of knowledge and experience in the United States regarding PLR might be a good thing, for "we can all start together."

John Sumsion, registrar for Public Lending Right in the United Kingdom, noted that in her new book, *A Guide to Public Lending Right* (1983), British author Bridget Brophy, a leader in the PLR movement, suggested the use of the term "authors lending right" instead of "public lending right." She feels "authors lending right" is more accurate and that it might be less controversial. U.S. author Anne Edwards, current president of the Authors Guild, endorsed this new name. She also reiterated Mr. Caro's remarks, explaining that while the Authors Guild did not yet have a specific plan in mind, it was committed to work "as long as it takes" to obtain a public lending right in the United States. First of all, authors need educating about PLR. But they also need to realize "that a scheme can be found that won't cut off what little government funding now exists for libraries and for writers." Barbara Tuchman could not see how PLR could harm libraries. She did, however, remind everyone that "libraries could not exist without authors."

Paul Goldstein and Anne Edwards

Robert Wedgeworth

Perspective of American Librarians

Robert Wedgeworth, executive director of the American Library Association, explained that it was extremely difficult to speak about a topic "which has elicited no serious discussion within the American library community and on which my association has taken no official position." He therefore offered his comments as personal observations. He first described the U.S. public library community, which consists of about 8,000 public libraries (excluding branches and other subdivisions). Half of these libraries serve populations of fewer than 50,000 persons. The "fragility of the public library enterprise" is especially obvious in its funding, which often is uncertain and inadequate. Approximately 85 percent of public library funding comes from local sources. This sum is supplemented by 10 to 12 percent from state governments and five to seven percent from the Federal Government.

Controversy about public lending right has occurred, he noted, because it has been very common for authors, in advancing the PLR concept, "to characterize the library and its lending service as inimical to their interest." This "understandable and highly emotional argument" has taken place "in the absence of any significant data on the role and influence of the library market on the sale of books." He pointed out that libraries support authorship in many different ways in addition to buying books, including the sponsorship of awards, public readings, and other programs that enhance the visibility of authorship and express its importance.

Mr. Wedgeworth felt that librarians would generally support almost any measure that is intended to bring benefits to the condition of authorship as long as library funding is not diminished. It is also reasonable to assume that librarians "will fight vigorously to defend

the principles, benefits, and operations of public libraries." He was pleased that this symposium was being held, for it gave the groups present an opportunity to frame the issues for public discussion. As PLR is explored, certain questions must be clearly answered. Why is PLR necessary and appropriate? Will the benefits go to those who need them, the "targeted beneficiaries?" Are there acceptable alternatives that would promote and enhance authorship? Finally, there were two conditions that, if met, "would be helpful in avoiding a major confrontation between librarians and authors." First, proposed PLR measures should not be construed as library programs at all. Instead the emphasis should be on enhancing authorship. Second, as a Federal program, PLR should be funded and administered separately from library programs.

Lester Asheim expressed doubt that library borrowing interfered with book sales, and agreed with others that a great deal more information is needed about the interplay between books and their readers and purchasers. Robert Wedgeworth noted that current research shows book borrowers to be heavy book purchasers. He also announced that the American Library Association had just signed a contract with the National Center for Educational Statistics to design a more effective data compilation system that would provide some of the needed information.

Toni Carbo Bearman suggested that there were two basic questions that symposium participants and others should focus on when discussing PLR: Is such a support system for authors "in the public interest"? And, if so, who will pay for such a system?

Agnes Griffin posed another question: Can PLR be applied to academic and research, school, and other libraries besides public libraries? Thomas Stave noted that in theory payments could come from the circulation of books in any kind of library depending, of course, on the type of PLR system adopted. In fact, the PLR system in Denmark includes both public and school libraries, and the greatest beneficiaries are the authors of school texts because their books circulate the most.

Public Lending Right in Continental Europe

Dennis Hyatt outlined how PLR works in Denmark, Norway, Sweden, Finland, Iceland, the Netherlands, and the Federal Republic of Germany, drawing on an article by Ole Koch, assistant director, State Inspection of Public Libraries, Copenhagen, Denmark, in the spring 1981 issue of *Library Trends* and on a September 12 letter from Mr. Koch to the Center for the Book. The various systems are diverse, and the administration of each is complicated, but each is workable. Furthermore, no one has ever suggested seriously that any of the schemes be repealed or that PLR is a "bad idea." But "do these schemes work for the purposes for which they were enacted?" Mr. Hyatt cited copyright protection, cultural encouragement, and author security as the basic purposes and asserted that their fulfillment "is still an open question." For example, "there is no evidence that any book has ever been written because of a PLR scheme, or that one has not been written because of the absence of such a scheme. Nor will any author become rich because of PLR."

Are the PLR schemes in continental Europe a model for the United States to follow? Mr. Hyatt thinks not. The United States is too much larger and culturally diverse than these countries for it to profit greatly from their experience. Another difference is that libraries in Europe are far fewer in number, more centralized, but more heavily used than in the United States. In his view, if the PLR idea is deemed to be in the public interest in the United States, it might be simpler to establish an "authors' recompense," an automatic grant to authors directly from the Federal Government. Libraries would not be involved at all.

Public Lending Right in the United Kingdom

John W. Sumsion described how the new British system worked, emphasizing its practical feasibility. Even though the scheme involves an approach which could be called "illogical, insular, and legally isolationist. . . it is gloriously workable." The system is based on loans from public libraries. Annual payments are made to authors and illustrators. Publishers, translators, and editors are excluded. There also are detailed rules for "eligible books," for example, at least 32 pages if chiefly of prose, 24 pages if mostly of poetry or drama. Payments are made from a separate government grant, which also supports administration of the system, including the costs of sampling loans in 16 major libraries. Modern computer technology and sampling techniques are used: "We now have a fully satisfactory way of calculating PLR remuneration in respect of books borrowed from public libraries. The objections to PLR as being infeasible or impractical have been completely overcome by using the latest available library computing technology."

The first payment under the British system will take place next February. Mr. Sumsion offered to assist interested parties in the United States in developing a plan for an American PLR scheme, pointing out that there are common problems to be faced in spite of the obvious cultural and governmental differences. In his view, the acrimony in Great Britain which preceded the enactment of PLR, and which occurred between authors' groups as well as between authors and librarians, was exacerbated by the lack of factual information and "political factors."

Alternatives to Public Lending Right

George Piternick explained that he was uncomfortable with two assumptions that many people at the symposium apparently shared. The first was the basic notion of a "right" to compensation. "Right" is a word and concept that he finds difficult to explain and translate into public policy. The second assumption, already mentioned by others, is that the effect of the circulation

John W. Sumsion

Barbara Tuchman

of books through libraries inevitably and invariably harms authors.

Mr. Piternick briefly described several "alternatives" to public lending right, other methods through which the importance of authorship could be recognized by libraries and by society. Libraries, for example, could pay augmented prices for books, or they might refrain from buying new books during their period of maximum sales, for example, the first year of publication. A more attractive idea was the exclusion, by the government, of authors' royalties and fees from income taxation, at least up to a specified amount. This plan, he emphasized, avoids "pointing the finger" at libraries and would allow all authors to benefit, not just the authors of bestsellers and trade books. It also would avoid sampling and all its inherent difficulties. Finally, there were two other methods which, while perhaps better suited to countries other than the United States, should at least be mentioned: government grants that would match an author's income from his or her earnings and fees and direct fellowships or grants-in-aid to authors from the government.

Harold Cannon of the National Endowment for the Humanities (NEH) offered several observations. He noted the limited but focused nature of the U.S. Government's support of the arts and humanities, pointing out the difference between merit-based programs, such as those administered by NEH and the National Endowment for the Arts, and the entitlement programs represented by PLR in other countries. He observed that in the United States the emphasis is on helping "beginners," or at least those creative artists in need of support who apply for assistance. One difficulty with certain PLR schemes now in effect, it seemed to him, was their prejudice in favor of well-established writers who no longer needed help.

Final Observations

Moderator Paul Goldstein put the day's discussions into a realistic perspective with several final comments. In spite of several obvious differences of opinion, he was impressed by the agreement of those present on one fundamental point: the need for society to encourage the greatest possible "production and consumption" of the written word. This is a "shared aim" of authors, librarians, copyright experts, publishers, and readers. Moreover, even though many caveats were raised, the answer of the assembled group to Toni Carbo Bearman's question whether PLR is in the public interest seemed to be yes. Yet it was probable that others in society would not see PLR as a priority item. Therefore, those favoring PLR must emphasize their "shared aims" in demonstrating to the nation that cultural goals are at least as important, in the long run, as other national goals. The availability of funds to support a PLR system depends on the development of such a "national consensus."

Mr. Goldstein also pointed out that more questions had been posed than answered, and that many of them stemmed from the empirical question, "Are authors properly compensated?" He agreed on the need for research on this and other topics discussed during the day, but also felt there were other useful ways of thinking about the topic that did not have to await the results of research studies.

For example, if the determination is made that some sort of a public lending right system is desirable in the United States, there are two extreme, hypothetical models that would help planners ascertain the consequences of choosing various methods. Under the "social insurance model," all professional writers would receive a specified subsidy, regardless of their "production." At the opposite pole, the "copyright model" compensates authors only for the use of their produced works. Each model has different advantages and disadvantages in the context of U.S. governmental and cultural traditions. But the model that is selected, which probably falls somewhere between the "social insurance" and the "copyright" extremes, will shape other important elements in the system. For example, which Congressional committee will have jurisdiction? Who pays—the Government or the consumer? How will the payment be made? Who collects—individual authors or societies representing all authors? Finally, the public policy dimension of PLR already is being affected by the new computer and video technologies that have made the

Eileen Cooke and Richard Kleeman

physical book, in certain circumstances, an "artificial distinction." There are now many libraries that contain no books, and the definition of "publication" is changing rapidly. When writers deposit their word-processed texts in data bases for publication on demand, a whole new method of royalty payments will have to be devised. In other words, the wider and most essential concern ahead of those concerned with the PLR concept is with the **use** of an author's words in all formats.

Participants

Guests
Lester Asheim, School of Library Science, University of North Carolina, Chapel Hill
Toni Carbo Bearman, Executive Director, National Commission on Libraries and Information Science
Harold C. Cannon, Director, Division of Research Programs, National Endowment for the Humanities
Robert A. Caro, Authors Guild of America
Eileen Cooke, Director, American Library Association Washington, D.C., Office
Ann Eastman, Virginia Polytechnic Institute and State University
Anne Edwards, President, The Authors Guild
Hardy Franklin, Director, Martin Luther King Library, Washington, D.C.

Paul Goldstein, Professor, Stanford University Law School
William B. Goodman, Editorial Director, David R. Godine Publisher
Agnes Griffin, Director, Montgomery County Department of Public Libraries
Peter Heggie, Executive Secretary, The Authors Guild Inc.
Dennis Hyatt, Law Librarian and Associate Professor, University of Oregon
Richard Kleeman, Association of American Publishers
Deanna Marcum, Program Officer, Council on Library Resources, Inc.
Perry D. Morrison, Professor Emeritus, University of Oregon
William Z. Nasri, School of Library and Information Science, University of Pittsburgh
Ralph Oman, Chief Counsel, Senate Judiciary Subcommittee on Patents, Copyrights, and Trademarks
George Piternick, Professor Emeritus, School of Librarianship, University of British Columbia
Lelia B. Saunders, Director, Arlington County Department of Libraries
Thomas Stave, Assistant Professor and Head Documents Librarian, University of Oregon
John W. Sumsion, Registrar, Public Lending Right, Great Britain
Barbara Tuchman, Authors League of America
Robert Wedgeworth, Executive Director, American Library Association

Library of Congress:
The Librarian of Congress and Mrs. Boorstin
Carol A. Nemeyer, Associate Librarian for National Programs
John Y. Cole, Executive Director, Center for the Book
Linda Cox, Staff Assistant, Center for the Book
Lewis I. Flacks, Policy Planning Adviser, Copyright Office
Richard E. Glasgow, Assistant General Counsel, Copyright Office
David E. Leibowitz, Policy Planning Adviser, Copyright Office
Waldo H. Moore, Associate Register of Copyrights for Special Programs
Harriet L. Oler, Senior Attorney Adviser, Copyright Office
Dorothy Schrader, General Counsel, U.S. Copyright Office
Elizabeth Stroup, Director for General Reference

64: PLR COULD COST LIBRARIES MILLIONS

Edith McCormick

Sixteen "sample" public libraries in Great Britain began tallying loans according to author in January as the Public Lending Right, which took nearly 30 years to pass Parliament, finally went into effect.

The PLR plan is funded by a central government grant of £2 million. Beginning February 1984, authors will collect annual payments based on how many times their books were borrowed from British libraries. The scheme, based on loans from a controversial random sample of 16 of Britain's 6,000 libraries, is designed to yield between £5 and £5,000 per year to individual authors.

Visiting ALA in January, Keith Lawrey, secretary general of the Library Association, and Carl Earl, chair of the LA's London and Counties Branch, discussed with AL what the association's position has been on the PLR Act of 1979.

Lawrey said that though the association supported the fundamental principle that authors should be supported in some way by the state, "its major concern was that such financial support might come from government monies that would otherwise go to libraries."

PLR is administered by the same department, the Office of Arts and Libraries, that ultimately is responsible for the allocation of funds made to libraries. Said Lawrey, "The government will quickly forget that they said the money that was going to be available for PLR was going to be extra to what was already allocated [for libraries]. The net result is that the £2 million, or whatever it becomes, is effectively 2 million less spent overall as available resources to libraries."

Original sample was 72
Originally, a government-appointed body called the Technical Investigation Group recommended that a sample of 72 service points was the minimum needed for acceptable accuracy. Authors' groups feared that administering loans from so large a sampling would deplete the £2-million pot and campaigned to have the number reduced to 16. These were selected by the PLR Registrar, John W. Sumsion. Sumsion, who was appointed for five years, took his post Sept. 1, 1981.

Loans are recorded at the 16 sampling libraries by means of machine-readable codes, and this data is transcribed to magnetic tape cassettes for dispatch to the Registrar.

Earl fears the Registrar's office may get returns that don't reflect the borrowing habits of the country at large. He noted that Sumsion used only libraries with computer control systems already recording ISBNs that could easily input into his system. Also, Earl suggested, since one system seemed best suited to the operation, it appeared to have been a determining factor in the choice of samples, further diminishing the randomness.

"The way statistics have to be gathered and recorded becomes very expensive, and the administrative costs are going to take a high proportion of the total money allocated by Parliament," said Earl. "The majority of authors are going to get pence—literally, pence!" Authors can receive as much as £500 per title, but an upper limit of £5,000 has been decreed so popular authors won't drain the pool.

"The only people who are going to benefit are those authors, like Barbara Cartland, etc., who already are making more than an adequate living out of it."

Manipulation of returns
Will authors try to distort the returns to their advantage? Earl, who is deputy director of Kent County Library, said one author had come into a Kent sampling library to donate his books to the collection. "Like most libraries, we only accept donations if we can dispose of them as we think fit. So we transferred the donation to a library not being sampled."

Earl commented that it would be difficult to detect if a library worker were trying to boost the PLR "take" for a writer friend at the circulation level. He said that since no one had recorded pre-PLR returns at sampling libraries for a basis of comparison, it is now too late to set up a monitoring system.

"There are no safeguards built into this scheme. It's been done far too casually and has not been properly thought through," Earl said.

AL asked Earl if he felt PLR somehow tainted the principles of free and unencumbered library service.

"This is a personal view, and I have every sympathy with the aim of assisting young, up-and-coming authors who are trying to make a living by writing; but I don't think PLR is the way to assist them," Earl said. "One of the ways PLR could have operated was to charge the borrower for every loan: a few pence a book, say. Now we have a sort of dangerous precedent where people will say, 'Well, PLR is surely only another way of library charge.' The fact that the money comes as a pool from government is not really relevant."

Earl favors basing the payment to authors on the purchases made by libraries—such a plan is used in the Netherlands.

"The PLR plan introduced a concept that is dangerous to the idea that libraries should be completely free and open," said Earl, "and that pressures put on librarians will divert them from the freedom to select and choose stock in relation to the needs they perceive the users have."

Registrants so far
As of the second week in January, Registrar Sumsion told AL he had received applications from just over 3,000 authors. "I expect anywhere from 15,000 to 30,000 more, but I wish I knew." Since the system is set up so that an author who registers now stands to make no more than an author who registers the day before the close of the first pay period on June 30, Sumsion said writers had no incentive to rush their papers to his office.

In the Spring 1981 issue of Library Trends, Raymond Astbury of the Liverpool Polytechnic library school traced the origins and future of PLR in Britain. He reported that Writer's Action Group founder, Maureen Duffy, told him that authors will campaign for inclusion of reference books, nonbook materials, and nonpublic libraries within the PLR scheme. Keith Lawrey, however, believes their chances are "very slim."

"The government has now wiped it off the slate," he said. "The Registrar reports to Parliament on how the system operates. Any major changes are not very possible. PLR is with us and may be tampered with, but I doubt if it will change drastically."

A fact of legal life in 10 countries, public lending right will eventually have to be faced by American librarians, too. The low earnings of most writers in America and Canada make the PLR concept alluring—i.e., compensation commensurate with the number of readers who benefit. But a reading of the literature on PLR will show that the concept, put into practice, is a mixed bag.

65: THE NEW UNITED STATES "MANUFACTURING CLAUSE" OR A TORONTO PROMISE FULFILLED

Charles H. Lieb[+]

The various sections of the United States copyright law, together known as the "manufacturing clause", were first enacted in 1891, when at the same time, and as a trade-off, copyright protection was first granted to foreign authors under certain conditions. Their basic purpose quite simply was to require English language books offered for sale in the United States to be manufactured and bound in the United States. The method by which this was to be accomplished was also simple and direct - either the books would be produced in the United States or they would be denied copyright protection in the United States.

In 1955 the United States joined the Universal Copyright Convention and the manufacturing requirements were thereafter narrowed to include only English language works prepared by American authors or by foreign authors domiciled in the United States. In 1967 the United States became a party to the Florence Agreement (Agreement on the Importation of Educational, Scientific and Cultural Materials) under which it obligated itself to remove customs duties on books and related materials

---

+ with assistance from Robert W. Frase on the Agreement of Toronto which he reduced to writing, and which he signed for the United States Group.

imported from other countries which were parties to that Agreement. It more than complied with that obligation; - it removed customs duties not only on books and other materials entering from fellow-signatory countries, but from all other countries as well.

Thus, books and other materials covered by the Florence Agreement entering the United States from Canada have not been subject to United States import duties since 1967.

1. *The Agreement of Toronto* This was the situation when the so-called Agreement of Toronto was reached+ in February 1968. That Agreement called for reciprocal action on the part of the United States and Canada, - namely that the United States would exempt Canadian produced books from the United States manufacturing requirements, and in return Canada would enter the Florence Agreement, thus eliminating the Canadian 10% ad valorem duty which existed and still exists with certain exceptions on the import of United States books into Canada.

The Agreement of Toronto, between a group of ten organizations in the United States and a group of nine organizations in Canada, reads as follows:

AGREEMENT OF TORONTO

Representatives of the U.S. and Canadian business and labor organizations concerned with printing and publishing met in Toronto on February 16, 1968 to discuss three interrelated issues of mutual interest, namely, an exemption for Canada from the U.S manufacturing clause, Canadian acceptance of the Florence Agreement, and effective resistance to weakening of international copyright protection.

After a thorough discussion of all aspects of these interrelated issues, the following courses of action were unanimously agreed upon:

(1) The Canadian group will promptly inform the Canadian Government of the Toronto meeting and of the agreement to take parallel action on both sides

---

+ Agreement on February 16, 1968 was oral and was later reduced to writing and signed.

of the border to bring about exemption for Canada from
the U.S. manufacturing clause and the acceptance by
Canada of the Florence Agreement. The Canadian group
will urge the Canadian Government to accept the Florence
Agreement as soon as exemption for Canada has been
adopted by the U.S. Congress. It is noted that the
acceptance of the Florence Agreement can be accomplished
in Canada without the necessity of an Act of Parliament.

(2) The U. S. and the Canadian groups will cooperate
in urging their respective governments to consult and
work together to oppose the Stockholm Protocol or
similar actions weakening international copyright
protection which may be proposed under the Universal
Copyright Convention.

(3) The U.S. group will do its utmost to obtain incorporation of an exemption for Canada in the manufacturing
section of the bill to revise the U.S. copyright law
(S.597) now being considered by a U.S. Senate Subcommittee.
Specifically, the U.S. group will inform the Department
of State of the Toronto meeting and will urge the
Department (a) not to oppose an exemption for Canada
from the U.S. manufacturing clause, and (b) to work
closely with the Government of Canada in opposing
weakening of international copyright protection under
the Berne Convention or the Universal Copyright Convention. The U.S. group will also bring to the attention
of the appropriate subcommittee of the Senate and House
Judiciary Committees the recommendations of the Toronto
meeting with respect to the manufacturing clause amendment.

It is anticipated that cooperative efforts on, and resolution of, the foregoing issues in a mutually satisfactory
manner will lead promptly to definite future cooperation
between the United States and Canadian groups on the
removal of any remaining barriers to trade between the
two countries affecting the printing and publishing
industries.

[*Editors' Note:* Material has been omitted at this point.]

2. *Manufacturing Clause Phase-out* Congress in the recently
enacted omnibus copyright
revision bill, which became law on October 19,1976, Pub. L.
94-553, 94th Congress, made good on the American part of the
agreement. Commencing January 1, 1978, when the new Act takes
effect, Canadian produced books will be exempt from the manufacturing requirements. Indeed, Congress went further - it
decreed that on July 1, 1982 the manufacturing requirements
would be eliminated in their entirety, and that in the four and
one-half year interim the kinds of works required to comply
with the manufacturing clause would be reduced; the *in terrorem*
provisions which threaten the loss of copyright protection to
works which do not comply with the clause would be eliminated,
and the number of non-complying books that would be importable
into the United States would be raised from 1500 to 2000. For
good measure, Congress as of January 1, 1978 abolished that
confusing and confounding concept peculiar to American copyright law, ad interim copyright protection.

Publishers and authors will therefore have to live with the
existing manufacturing clause until January 1, 1978, and with
the watered-down clause until July 1, 1982. The manufacturing
clause after that date is scheduled for oblivion.+

The manufacturing clause as it exists today is ambiguous; the
case law dealing with is sparse and the relevant literature
contradictory. Because of its short remaining life, this
summary will not elaborate on the existing law and add to the
confusion. Instead, it will discuss the highlights of the new
manufacturing requirements found in Section 601 of the new Act,
and of the companion Section 602 of the same Act which for the

---

+ Note however that the Congressional Record for September 30,
1976 carries a letter from the Chairman (Senator McClellan of
Arkansas) and another member (Senator Scott of Pennsylvania) of
the Senate Subcommittee on Patents, Trademarks and Copyrights
to the Register of Copyrights requesting the Register to study
and report to the Congress on the economic implications of the
complete repeal of the manufacturing clause; the study to be
made in the early months of 1981 and the report to be filed on
or about July 1 of that year. The letter does not have the
force of law, but the Register of Copyrights has agreed to make
the study and submit the report.

first time will prohibit certain kinds of "buying-around"; each
to become effective January 1, 1978. The reader should be
cautioned however that these new sections require close reading,
and that what follows is merely a summary in most general terms.

As stated above, Canada is specifically exempted from the provisions of the section. Thus, manufacture in Canada will be
considered the same as manufacture in the United States. In
granting this exemption Congress in its Conference Report
stated its expectation that Canada would move promptly to adopt
the Florence Agreement and to take steps reciprocally with the
United States to remove the existing trade barriers; otherwise,
it said, it would expect that the exemption would be removed
(H.R. 94-1733, 94th Congr. 2d Sess).

3. *Covered Works* The new manufacturing clause will apply only
                      to a work consisting "preponderantly" of
nondramatic literary material in the English language and protected by copyright. It will not apply to works consisting
wholly or preponderantly of:

> dramatic, musical, pictorial or graphic works;
> foreign language, including bilingual and
> multilingual, works; or
> public domain material.

Where the work consists in part of material protected by the
manufacturing clause and in part of material not required to
be manufactured in the United States or Canada, the test will
be whether the work consists "preponderantly" of the protected
material. The word "preponderantly" is used not only in a
quantitative sense but also in terms of relative "importance".
Thus, for example, where the literary material in a work consists merely of a foreword or brief description or explanation
of pictorial material, the manufacturing requirement would not
apply to the work, in whole or in part. On the other hand, if
the English language nondramatic literary text exceeds the
pictorial material in importance, the manufacturing requirement
would apply, and this would be true notwithstanding that more
pages in the book might be devoted to the pictures than to the
text.

Obviously, a very considerable degree of personal judgment will
be required to determine the relative importance of the two
classes of material contained in the same work and pre-clearance
in such a case with the Copyright Office or the Customs Service
might be advisable.

4. *Covered Authors* The new manufacturing clause will apply only to works by an American citizen or by any other person domiciled in the United States. It will not however apply to the work of an American citizen if he has been domiciled outside the United States for a continuous period of one year immediately preceding the date of importation, nor will it apply if the author, through choice or necessity, arranges for first publication of his work by a foreign rather than a domestic publisher.

In the case of a work made for hire (a term of art defined with specificity in the Act) the clause will apply if the work in whole or in substantial part is prepared for a citizen or domiciliary of the United States or for a domestic corporation or enterprise, including a foreign subsidiary formed primarily for the purpose of avoiding the manufacturing requirement.

The new manufacturing clause will not apply, of course, to foreign works offered United States protection under the Universal Copyright Convention, or to any other foreign-authored work, or to a work co-authored by an American and a foreigner not domiciled in the United States if the foreign author is responsible for "any substantial part" of the work. Nor, of course, will the clause apply to a work made for hire if at least "a substantial part" of it is prepared for a foreigner not domiciled in the United States or for a foreign corporation.

Thus, if a substantial part of the work made for hire is prepared by an American at the instance of a foreign corporation it will be considered a foreign work. Conversely, if a substantial part of the work is prepared by a foreigner at the instance of an American corporation, it will be considered an American work.

The descriptive term "substantial part" may perhaps be quantified or otherwise explained in regulations to be prepared by the Copyright Office and the Customs Service. Unless and until that occurs, pre-clearance here too might be advisable.

5. *"Manufacturing"* Under the new Act if the work falls within the manufacturing requirement it will only be necessary that the protected portions of the work be "manufactured" in the United States or in Canada, and the publisher will be free to manufacture elsewhere the balance of the material in the work. In this connection the use of imported

"repro proofs" will finally receive official approval. The ma
ufacturing requirement of the new Act will be satisfied notwithstanding that the manuscript is set in type outside the
United States or Canada, provided that the plates from which
the copies are printed are made in the United States or Canada
and are not themselves imported, and provided of course that
the printing and binding is also done in the United States or
Canada. Similarly, the importation of computer tapes and, in
the writer's view, "repro films", from which plates can be prepared, will likewise be permitted.

6. *Enforcement* The purpose of the new clause, like that of th
present, is to induce the manufacture of
American-authored works in the United States during the phase-
out period, if more than a limited number of copies are to be
distributed in the United States - 2,000 under the new Act as
compared to 1,500 under the current Act.

Unlike the current act however, the new Act does not threaten
loss of copyright as a penalty for non-compliance. On the contrary, although it prohibits the importation into the United
States of non-complying copies and subjects them to seizure and
forfeiture if unlawfully imported, the new Act specifically
provides that violation of the manufacturing requirements will
not invalidate copyright in the work.

Instead, the new Act provides an infringer a defense in an infringement proceeding if he proves that copies of the work which
he has infringed were imported and distributed in the United
States in violation of the manufacturing requirements. The
defense however is limited to infringement of "nondramatic
literary material" (which is the kind of work sought to be protected by the manufacturing clause), and to infringement of any
other part of the work, the exclusive rights to which are owned
by the same person. In order to establish his defense, the infringer must prove (a) importation of the copyright-protected
copies in violation of the manufacturing requirements; (b) manufacture of the infringing copies in compliance with the manufacturing requirements, and (c) that the infringement began
before an authorized edition complying with the requirements
had been registered. Thus, by manufacturing a new edition in
the United States or Canada and by registering it in the Copyright Office the copyright owner will be able to reinstate his
full exclusive rights to the work.

7.   *"Buying-Around"*   Heretofore, a publisher exclusively licensed
                         to publish a work in the United States, or,
conversely, one who has granted foreign rights to others but has
retained exclusive United States rights, could not protect himself from the unauthorized importation of copies of that work by
a third party (a practice sometimes called "buying around"),
provided the imported copies were lawfully manufactured abroad.
Commencing January 1, 1978, following the example of British,
Canadian and Australian law, importation of that nature will
constitute an infringement of the exclusive right of American
distribution and will be actionable at law in the same manner
as any other infringement.

A word of caution is appropriate. From and after January 1, 1978,
one may safely rely on the territorial exclusivity which is an
essential feature of copyright and on the remedy afforded by
Section 602 to prevent unauthorized "buying around". However,
an agreement which goes beyond a grant of copyright rights (for
one or more countries) and states contractual restrictions or
prohibitions against sale or resale across national boundaries
or otherwise, may be challenged by the Department of Justice as
an agreement to divide markets in violation of the Sherman
Antitrust Act.

An important exception to the new prohibition against "buying
around" is that nonprofit libraries and educational organizations will be allowed to import up to five copies of a work for
their "library lending or archival purposes". Publishers of
scholarly books should note, however, that the five copy exemption will not apply if the importation is part of an activity
that constitutes "systematic reproduction of distribution" by
the library or other organization in violation of Sec. 108(g) (2)
discussed below. This exception to the exemption was added at
the same time that the "interlibrary proviso" was added to Sec.
108(g) (2), and after the Register of Copyrights testified that
the British Lending Library Division at Boston Spa in England
had become a major supplier of unauthorized photocopies of
journal articles to libraries throughout the world, including
the United States, and that if the practice continues it could
be considered a violation of Sec. 108(g) (2), were that section
applicable.

The result is far from clear. There is reason to believe, at
least in this writer's view, that when an American library receives copies from the British Lending Library which that library

made for the American library without authorization from the
copyright owner, the American library may subject itself to
liability as a vicarious infringer.

8. *"Piratical Copies"* The present Act prohibits the importation of "piratical" copies, i.e., those
illegally manufactured abroad, and the new Act retains that prohibition. It also excludes copies that, although lawfully made
abroad, would have been unlawful if United States copyright law
were applicable. A typical example would be a work by an
American author that was in the public domain in a foreign
country owing to the absence of copyright relations between
that country and the United States, but that is protected here.
At the risk of overemphasizing British Library lending practices
it should be noted that unauthorized copies made by the British
Library Lending Division might also be considered "piratical",
in which case their entry into the United States could be prohibited as such.

9. *Conclusion* The United States more than fulfilled its obligation under the Florence Agreement, – eliminating
import duties not only on books and other covered material coming in from other participants in the agreement, but from all
other countries including Canada as well.

Similarly, the United States has more than fulfilled the promise
made by the American group in the Agreement of Toronto, not only
by providing for the Canadian exemption commencing in 1978, but
by granting exemption for all in 1982.

388

66: CONGRESS VOTES TO KEEP MANUFACTURING CLAUSE BY OVERRIDING PRESIDENT REAGAN'S VETO

CONGRESS VOTES TO KEEP MANUFACTURING CLAUSE BY OVERRIDING PRESIDENT REAGAN'S VETO of the extension which requires that books and periodicals written in English by Americans and by foreigners who are living in the US must be printed and bound in the US or Canada if they are to have complete copyright protection. The bill on which Congress voted extends the manufacturing clause for four more years during which time the House Committee on the Judiciary, the administration, the Senate, and the industry itself expects to develop a policy to resolve permanently this question in a manner which will protect jobs and promote free trade. This, according to both the Senate and the House, is the ultimate objective of the bill. The clause in some variation has been part of the law since 1891.

Less than a week after the vote, the Authors League began making plans to challenge the constitutionality of the manufacturing clause and said that it would file suit in the very near future. According to a spokesman from the league, Congress in not supporting the presidential veto, "ignored the serious First and Fifth Amendment issues raised by the extension."

Irwin Karp, general counsel of the Authors League said, "Those familiar with publishing know that the great proportion of the jobs allegedly at risk involved material that's not even banned by the manufacturing clause, or is of minor copyright importance so that it could be freely exported whether or not the clause was extended." Opponents of the clause have repeatedly maintained that supporters were exaggerating the situation and distorting the intent of the law by lumping together with book manufacturing the manufacture of items such as matchbooks and cheese wrappers. "The real victims of the clause always have been American authors of books," Karp said. Karp believes that with the extension of the clause, "it is highly likely that if American publishers find it economically advantageous to have books manufactured in Japan or other countries they will simply use foreign rather than American authors, which permits them under the clause to import books without any restrictions."

Townsend Hoopes, president of the Association of American Publishers said, "We're very disappointed because we worked hard to defeat the proposed extension of the bill." Publishers and authors have not always agreed on publishing matters, but, according to Hoopes, they have been united in opposition to such issues as proposed postal rate increases and extension of the manufacturing clause.

The bill was returned with the following message from the president:

I am returning without my approval H.R. 6198, a bill that would extend for four years the "manufacturing clause" of the U.S. copyright law that expired on June 30, 1982.

The manufacturing clause requires that many printed materials be printed in the United States in order to enjoy copyright protection. The clause was written into law nearly a century ago, in an effort to strengthen our relatively new printing industry by limiting foreign competition. However, the "infant industry" justification for protecting our printing industry is no longer valid; our industry is now one of the most modern and efficient in the world.

During the recent Tokyo Round of Multilateral Trade Negotiations, our trading partners objected to the manufacturing clause as inconsistent with our international obligations. Extension of the clause, as provided in H.R. 6198, could result in increased international trade tensions that could endanger American jobs. I would further note that if the printing or publishing industry believes itself injured, or threatened by injury, due to the expiration of the manufacturing clause, it has the option of requesting relief under the Trade Act.

My administration has placed a very high priority on

strengthening free trade, and we are energetically seeking to remove artificial foreign barriers to American exports. We are confident that our free enterprise system will enable American products to face foreign competition in our own open market overseas, provided our access to those markets is not blocked by protectionist barriers that distort international competition.

Given the importance of our efforts to remove foreign trade barriers, it would be self-defeating to extend an artificial barrier of our own. For these reasons I cannot approve H.R. 6198.

Signed/ Ronald Reagan

Strom Thurmond (R-SC), who urged his Senate colleagues to vote to override the veto message of the president, spoke for many when he said that he did not believe that "our [US] foreign trade interests are adversely affected. Moreover," the Senator said, "expiration of the manufacturing clause, according to the Department of Labor, could lead to the loss of thousands of American jobs."

The creation of an artificial trade barrier, Thurmond said, is based on the assumption that the manufacturing clause prevents materials from the US from being printed in Britain or other European countries. Not a good reason, according to Thurmond, because very little material would be sent to Europe anyway. Thurmond sees the "real" competition to the US printing industry coming from the Near East and the Pacific Basin countries.

Continuing his argument, Thurmond told the Senate, ". . . a US Labor Department study dated June 15, 1981, concludes that expiration of the manufacturing clause would cause a decrease in demand for printing leading to a loss of 78,000 to 172,000 job opportunities in the printing and publishing industry. It also concludes that an estimated 170,000 to 367,000 job opportunities could be lost in related industries."

A statement by Senator Howard Metzenbaum (D-OH) reflected the recorded remarks of others: "I know of no issue that is more important to the people of this country at this time than the matter of employment of our people and the opportunities for people to have a job. Unfortunately, we have been losing too many of our jobs to foreign imports, and the fact that the manufacturing clause of the copyright law would expire or did expire on July 1, 1982, makes this issue that much more important."

Two senators spoke in favor of the president's action: Gordon Humphrey (R-NH) and Robert Dole (R-KS). Both gave more weight to the international trade issue. Senator Humphrey said: ". . . we are all upset at the nontariff trade barriers erected by Japan and other countries to our products. If we continue to extend barriers of the same kind, then we have no ground on which to argue against those erected by foreign nations. I see no particular reason why we should extend this protection to this particular industry. There is another side, another party involved here, those who own the copyrights. They are not free today to have their works printed wherever they wish and this is a freedom that, while it is denied to them, is available to other composers, musical composers, and others. (Now the provision applies only to copyrighted materials of a nondramatic nature, published in English by United States domiciled authors. It does not apply to works of art, musical compositions, dramatic works, sound recordings, or motion pictures.)

Mr. Thurmond answered this argument: ". . . the so-called manufacturing clause extends the full protection of our copyright laws to a book written by an American author living in this country only if the book is manufactured or printed in either Canada or in the United States. The law was enforced by banning the importation and distribution of any book written by an American author which is printed in a foreign country. This affords a strong inducement to our authors to use our printers here in the United States."

Senator Dole tole the senators, "I believe we ought to support the president's veto action in this case. The Labor Department study suggesting that there would be a large job loss as a result of the expiration of the manufacturing clause has been discredited rather effectively. The Congressional Research Service and the Council of Economic Advisors both have conducted studies and concluded that there would be little or no effect on employment as a result of expiration. There is every indication that this industry is healthy.

"In addition," Senator Dole said, "I would note that the clause, if extended, may well violate our GATT* obligations and is certainly inconsistent with them. There is a real risk that it will precipitate a GATT complaint and may cause retaliation by the Europeans, in particular, against US trade interests." Dole then asked that a copy of a letter to Representative Robert Kastenmeier (D-WI) from David Ladd, register of copyrights, be introduced into the record. The letter, which points up the disparity between the above two studies and that of the Department of Labor, is reprinted below.

December 17, 1981

Hon. Robert W. Kastenmeier,
House of Representatives
Washington, DC

Dear Rep. Kastenmeier: This supplements the Copyright Office's testimony concerning H.R. 3940. Most, but not all, of this supplementary information concerns the rather marked disparity between the results, in terms of economic effects, of the estimates of the Congressional Research Service and the Office of Foreign Economic Research of the Department of Labor. Although the latter report was not received into the record of your hearing, its conclusions drew attention there and, I note, in the Senate when S. 1880 was introduced. There are four points which must be considered by anyone evaluating the Labor Report.

1. The present manufacturing clause does not protect the number of job opportunities remotely as large as the Labor Report suggests, because the clause does not cover the range of printed material assumed by the Labor Report. Only nondramatic literary works consisting preponderantly of English-language material are covered. As construed by the courts, "preponderantly" means that the surface area of textual material must be measured against the surface area of illustrative and other nontextual material; only if the former outweighs the latter is the work within the clause's scope. (*Stonehill Communications, Inc.* v. *Martuge*, 512 F. Supp. 349 (S.D.N.Y. 1981)). Thus, estimates of lost job opportunities with respect to the printing of blankbooks, business forms, heavily illustrated catalogues, greeting cards and the like are not credible if based on the expiration of the clause, because such works, and the jobs of their manufacturers, are in no way affected by the clause. The Copyright Office report, which emphasized the book publishing industry, did not do so in an attempt to minimize the impact of expiration. Its emphasis was based on the historic fact that virtually all of

*General Agreement on Tariffs and Trade, which the US joined in 1948.

the debates, court cases, and Customs interventions have occurred with respect to books. Prior to the Labor Report, no one, including Mr. Nordberg, the economist hired by the Book Manufacturers' Institute, had ever suggested that such sectors of the printing industry as newspapers, commercial printing, "miscellaneous publishing," and "miscellaneous printing services" would in any way be affected by the expiration of the clause. I do not understand on what basis they were included in the Labor Report; and its conclusions should not be accepted unless their inclusion is explained.

Particularly troublesome is the inclusion of commercial printing. The Department of Labor adopts an Office of Management and Budget definition of commercial printing. As can be seen in the attachment, taken from the OMB's Standard Industrial Classification Manual, the output of the sector denominated commercial printing consists almost entirely of works not protected by the clause: bags, bread wrappers, calendars, cards, sheet music, post cards, bank notes, maps, and the like. Printers concerned about losing work in the manufacture of nonliterary works, such as these, have nothing to fear from the clause's expiration because they are not now protected. While no one seems to know how many jobs in the commercial printing sector are clause-related, that number is far smaller than indicated in the Labor Report.

2. The Labor Report fails to distinguish between printing and publishing, but at least 70% of jobs in the book industry are in publishing rather than printing, and thus not protected by the manufacturing clause. As was made clear at the hearing, these are, for all practical purposes, separate industries. Another division of the Department of Labor, the Bureau of Labor Statistics, distinguishes in its reports between book publishing and book printing, but does not do so with respect to other printing/publishing sectors. No one has suggested that publishers are going to lose jobs if the clause expires; thus one may reasonably — indeed, must — question the propriety of lumping printers and publishers together when predicting job losses. Interestingly enough, with respect to the book industry, 71.4% of those employed in August of 1981 were in publishing rather than printing.[1] To the extent that the Labor Report has combined these sectors, one should probably discount its estimates by a like percentage, since only printers will even arguably be affected. Based on the limited scope of the clause and the differences between printing and publishing, the Copyright Office believes that fair analysis of Table 2 of the Labor Report (p. 5) should keep the following factors in mind:

SECTOR, DESCRIPTION, AND COMMENT

26.01. — Newspapers, Although covered by the clause, they are too time-sensitive to go abroad even at the 2% high range prediction.

26.02. — Periodicals, They are far too time-sensitive to permit ocean transport from the Pacific Basin of anything like 15% of present output.

26.03. — Book Printing and Publishing, 70 percent of these jobs are publishing and thus not threatened. Of the remaining 30 percent, not all of the output is protected by the clause. (Illustrated works, works of foreign authors, etc.).

26.04. — Miscellaneous Publishing, Undefined in the Labor Report but, to the extent that this concerns publishing jobs, none should be lost through expiration.

26.05. — Commercial Printing, No one, including the supporters of the clause, has ever before suggested that commercial printing is at issue here. There is no evidence concerning the extent to which commercial printers' output is copyrighted. Only copyrighted literary works are covered by the clause; thus the data here must be discounted to whatever extent copyright is not claimed or the works are not literary.

[1] Employment and Earnings, October 1981, Bureau of Labor Statistics at 72.

26.06. – Manifold business forms, blankbooks, and binders. Few job opportunities are threatened here since the works tend to fall into two categories unaffected by the clause: uncopyrightable works and works in which no copyright is claimed.

26.07. – Greeting card Publishing. The publishing-printing dichotomy is at issue here, as is the quantitative distinction between literary and other works. Few if any jobs should be threatened, since most greeting cards contain vastly more illustrative than textual materials.

26.08. – Miscellaneous Printing Services, Also undefined in the Labor Report. It seems unlikely that its products are literary works whose manufacturers are protected by the clause, since such works appear in some of the previous categories.

Of all of the sectors listed in Table 2, then, only 26.03 (Book printing and publishing) has even the potential for being seriously affected by expiration, and even there the predictions should be reduced by at least 70 percent to account for the vast majority of that sector's employment being in publishing than printing.

3. The sources for the quantitative estimates in the Labor Report are open to question because its predictions concerning output decreases are explained not by resort to objective data but only upon subjective "informed judgments of analysts in industry, labor, and government." With respect to the book industry, it is clear that the 35-40% range of output loss is taken directly and unquestioningly from the report commissioned by the Book Manufacturers' Institute and prepared by E. Wayne Nordberg to buttress their arguments in support of extension of the clause. There is no reason why the United States government should adopt the numbers of an interested party without independent examination. With respect to other sectors, where the report predicts large job losses, no explanation at all is given for the predicted output losses. In addition, the Labor Report treats the manufacturing clause as having the effect of a 33% import duty on books because that is the subsidy paid by Australia to its book manufacturers. For the reasons articulated by CRS in its report and described in ours, the "Australian experience" is hardly relevant to the future of the US industries; and, even if it were, it is unclear how the clause, which prevents certain business from taking place, can be compared to a duty which increases transaction costs. Although the Labor Report cautions repeatedly against over-reliance on its data, "pro-clause" advocates appear to rely on its numeric conclusions and ignore such caveats. The importance of the caveats may be seen by examining two of them: At page 12, the Labor Report states:

"The lack of certain basic data, such as the percent of printed material in each sector that is actually copyrighted * * * prevented more accurate, point estimates."

Thus it is conceded that the percentage of copyrighted work is unknown. Since a critical issue in analyzing the effect of the expiration of the manufacturing clause is not merely whether a work is copyrighted, but also whether it is literary, the data become, of course, even more unreliable.

Then, at page 13, one reads: "The accuracy of the section one estimates rests on the assumptions * * * [which] are the informed judgments of analysts in industry, labor, and government. To the extent that these judgments are incorrect, the resulting estimates will be biased."

As stated above, these judgments do appear at best unexplained, if not clearly incorrect, thus meaning at least that an inference of bias would not be unjustified.

4. The Labor Department apparently assumes, incorrectly, that the clause's expiration will leave these jobs without alternative forms of protection. As I believe the hearing made clear, this is not at all the case. Expiration, combined with the protocol to the Florence Agreement, will place American printers on an equal footing with all other American workers.

Provable threatened harm will entitle them to relief in the same forum to which most industries now go: the International Trade Commission.

The position of the Copyright Office is that number of jobs and job opportunities potentially directly exposed by expiration, far from being in the hundreds of thousands, is in the range of 5,000 to 9,000 found by CRS. This is not to say that anywhere near this many jobs or opportunities would be lost however: growth in exports and domestic demand and the availability of conventional trade relief from the International Trade Commission should serve to prevent any significant losses whatsoever.

Since the hearing we have received information concerning possible retaliation against the United States if the clause is retained. According to persons involved in trade negotiations, the Common Market countries and Switzerland have at various times refrained from seeking trade relief against the United States on the belief that the clause would expire in 1982. As recently as last month the matter was raised at meetings in Washington in which the E.E.C. apparently manifested an intention to pursue relief under the General Agreement on Tariffs and Trade if the clause were to be retained. While the scope and effect of any retaliatory measures can not easily be predicted, it is fair to assume that they will be adverse to US interests. In addition, the British Embassy sent a letter to the State Department on December 9, 1981 in which it "note[s] with regret" the terms of H.R. 3940.

Thank you very much for the opportunity to amplify the record.

Sincerely yours,

David Ladd
Register of Copyrights

In the House of Representatives, Tom Railsback (R-IL) called attention to the fact that the bill represented a bipartisan effort, passing both houses with no objections, and then centered on the employment issue, saying "... I think it is very important that we recognize that it [the printing industry] is probably the most highly labor intensive of any manufacturing industry in the United States. As a result, wage differentials between the United States and low wage countries, such as Hong Kong and Singapore, are much more destructive to printing than to most other manufacturing industries." Railsback then supported this statement by recalling, "... during 3 days of hearings held by the Courts Subcommittee on this issue, it was well documented by several witnesses that the main threat to the American printing industry and to American jobs rests with the Japanese. The Japanese are prepared, we believe, to undertake the building of major facilities in the low wage Pacific basin countries, such as Singapore, Taiwan, and Malaysia. I think we all recognize the hard line that Japan has taken – enjoying access to American markets while maintaining a variety of subtle trade barriers to protect Japanese markets. What could be more ridiculous," Railsback asked, "than to let the manufacturing clause expire and simply hand over to Japan a big hunk of our nation's seventh largest industry, while receiving nothing in return from Japan?"

"Likewise," Railsback continued, "the Canadians have highly discriminatory mailing rates and significant tariffs ranging up to 'effective tariffs' of 40 percent on printing that US firms have attempted to ship into Canada. Because the manufacturing clause has been scheduled to expire, the Canadians have done virtually nothing to pull down these trade barriers. If the manufacturing clause is extended, we will have a basis on which to deal with the Canadian problems. The important point here is," Railsback stressed, "that the manufacturing clause has been scheduled to expire for 5½ years and yet how many countries have removed trade barriers as a result? I do not know of any."

Representative Bill Frenzel (R-MN) opposed the motion to override the veto by the president of H.R. 6198. "The statute discriminates against one single class of authors and denies them the copyright protection in a free and open market," said Frenzel. "In 1976," he continued, "the Judiciary Committee recognized that the manufacturing clause was the last vestige of an obsolete statute. They put the industry on notice that the clause was unjustified economically as well as "trade distortive" and set a termination date of July 2 of this year. The committee at that time wrote into its report:

After carefully weighing the arguments, the committee concludes that there is no justification on principle for a manufacturing requirement in the copyright statute, and although there may have been economic justification for it at one time, that justification no longer exists.

Frenzel then told the House that the manufacturing clause "clearly violates" our international obligations under the GATT, the Florence Convention, the Bern Convention, the Universal Copyright Convention, and other international agreements. Also, according to Frenzel, "it violates the principle of national treatment by not allowing importers the same treatment as domestic producers, and it violates the most-favored nation principle by providing Canada with an exemption to the requirement. Ironically," Frenzel said, "we [the US] exempted Canada, I am told, because we expected them to sign the Florence Convention, which they then did not do."

Frenzel thought it unlikely that the trading partners of the US "will accept this extension" without formal challenge. Specifically, Switzerland, Great Britain, and the EEC have "complained bitterly" and have served notice that they will take their complaint to the GATT and seek retaliation against our exports. "This means," said Frenzel, "that while we think we are protecting jobs in an industry which probably does not need it, we are likely to be sacrificing jobs in industries that are now exporting. In fact, one of them may be the export of books by the very same industry."

Frenzel reminded the House that it had always "pointed to the expiration date when we have discussed this with our trading partners and telling them we were going to conform our practice to the international agreements to which we have become a party. The president believes," Frenzel continued, "and quite rightly I think, that a further extension of the manufacturing clause will weaken his ability to secure additional markets abroad. Our goal of strengthening exports and our efforts to remove artificial foreign barriers to American exports will be made much more difficult if this bill becomes law."

Representative Edward J. Derwinski (R-IL) extended this argument: "The manufacturing clause was 'grandfathered' when we joined the GATT in 1948. We undertook then to bring such grandfathered legislation into conformity with the GATT as soon as practicable. Many of our fellow contracting parties in the GATT are of the view that grandfathered legislation loses its protection once it has been modified," Derwinski continued. "The manufacturing clause has already been modified, but our trading partners did not challenge us because we did lessen the coverage of the manufacturing clause. When our negotiators refused to negotiate the elimination of our nontariff barrier under the manufacturing clause (during the Tokyo Round of multilateral trade negotiations), our trading partners objected. Their objection was most understandable," Derwinski concluded.

US trading partners agreed not to press for negotiated elimination of the clause because it was scheduled to expire this year. Derwinski sees the outcome as the US pressing other countries to eliminate trade barriers, and defending "a piece of blatant protectionism." Derwinski raised doubts about the success of that defense because the grandfather clause protection may no longer apply. The result, he said, "could be the required payment of trade compensation by the United States to other countries, especially in areas where others seek increased import opportunities in our markets, or with the withdrawal of concessions benefiting US exports. The US agricultural sector is particularly vulnerable to retaliation," Derwinski warned, "as are other highly competitive export sectors."

The House and Senate votes on the question: "Will the House/Senate, on reconsideration, pass the bill, the objections of the President to the contrary notwithstanding?" were:

House: Year-324; Nays-86; Answered Present-2; Not Voting-21.
Senate: Yeas-84; Nays-9; Not Voting-7.

The bill became Public Law 97-215 July 13,1982.

Organized labor was reported to be "elated" by the vote. Rex Hardesty, a spokesman at the headquarters of the American Federation of Labor and Congress of Industrial Organizations, said "We think it saved a couple hundred thousand jobs, so we're glad to see the veto overridden. We lobbied hard for the extension and we hope the veto was overridden on the job issue."

67: THE AUTHOR & MORAL RIGHTS

Michael F. Schwartz

Attorney at Law

*Author agrees that producer shall have the unlimited right to vary,
change, alter, modify, add to and/or delete from the property and change
the sequence thereof and the characters and the description of characters. . . .
Author hereby waives the benefits of any provision of law known as
"droit moral" . . . and agrees not to institute . . . any . . . lawsuit . . . (for
defamation or mutilation of the property.*

This is a standard clause included in a typical contract between an
author and a producer, granting the use by the producer of a copyrighted
work of art. As is readily apparent, such a granting clause does not afford
the author much protection against subsequent distortions or
misrepresentations.

The American author is a captive audience of the exigencies of commercial distribution and the commercial marketplace. The author, whose
reputation has not preceded him or her to the bargaining table, must
contend with the vastly disproportionate bargaining power of the
entertainment industry. The relatively unknown author is desperately trying
to find an outlet for the exploitation of his or her work. The price that this
artist must pay in exchange for an often meager monetary reward is the
relinquishment of all creative control over his or her work. This is
somewhat analogous to selling your soul in order to pay the rent.

The rights of authorship can be divided into two fundamental categories: property rights and moral rights. The Federal Copyright Law
pertains to the property rights of ownership. On the other hand, a veritable
cornucopia of American jurisprudence, including the law of defamation,
privacy, unfair competition, breach of contract, common laws and most
recently, the Lanham Act, a Federal statute providing a remedy for false
designation of origin or false description or representation of work
products, envelops the issues raised by moral rights of authorship.

The Federal Copyright Law (and the 1978 revision) does not recognize
the existence of moral rights of authorship. It is designed to protect the
commercial value, or property rights of an author's creation and it grants
protection not to the creator as such, but to the owner of the copyright in
the work. Consequently, the protection afforded by this law is limited to
compensation for specific economic harm to the owner of the copyright.
Once the author sells or leases a copyright, a contract determines any and
all further rights in connection with that creation.

[*Editors' Note:* Material has been omitted at this point.]

THE EUROPEAN DOCTRINE

American jurisprudence does not recognize the European doctrine of moral rights or droit moral. Essentially, this doctrine focuses on two critical rights: the right of paternity and the right to integrity of the work. Under the concept of paternity, a creator has the absolute right to claim authorship of his work, to prevent his name from being used for a creation not his own and to prevent others from being named as the creator of his work. Under the concept of integrity, an author can prevent others from making changes that distort or mutilate his work.

Of course, inherent in all of this is a clash of philosophies: the owner's property rights versus the author's personal or moral rights.

In American jurisprudence, property rights have taken precedence and this has produced all sorts of unfortunate results.

One example can be found in litigation involving Vargas, a commercial artist and Esquire magazine. Vargas sought to have his name as creator of certain drawings entitled "Vargas Girls" appear with these drawings which he had sold to Esquire and which Esquire had reprinted under the title "Esquire Girls" without any creator credit. Under the moral rights doctrine Vargas would have an absolute right to claim authorship of his work. However, Vargas was forced to rely on contract law, claiming the magazine was under an "implied agreement" to give Vargas a credit for his drawings. The court rejected this contention, finding in effect, that absent specific language, there is no implied duty to give the artist or creator credit for his work.

Specific language or the lack thereof, in a contract, is often the achilles heel of the artist when locked in battle with the producer of a play or literary property over the rights granted or reserved pursuant to that contract. The standard contract in the industry will often find the artist granting all rights in his literary property to the producer except those rights specifically reserved by the artist and as specified in the contract.

The Dramatist Guild has broached this potential for abuse of the artist by turning the tables on the producer who is a signatory of the Guild's minimum basic production contract. This contract is designed so that the artist grants, sells or assigns to the producer certain specific rights, while reserving all rights not otherwise granted, sold or assigned.

Consequently, there is no blanket clause in a Guild contract in which the artist waives his moral rights in and to the play or literary property involved, but rather, a "reservation of rights" clause in which all rights not otherwise granted in the contract are reserved by the artist. The Dramatist Guild's minimum basic production contract is an effective method of protecting the moral rights of artists. Unfortunately, it is not an industry-wide institution.

A recent litigation involving the mutilation of a television script belonging to Monty Python, a British comedy group, by the American Broadcasting Co., has found the court in a surprising decision, holding for the first time, that distortion of a copyrighted work is actionable under the Lanham Act. Although recognition of such a Federal right increases protection for artists in America, it is still an inadequate substitute for droit moral.

395

VIII: INTERNATIONAL
ASPECTS

Papers 68 Through 71: Commentary

Jon A. Baumgarten and Charles H. Lieb, in the "International Copyright" portion (Paper 68) of their *Kirk-Othmer Encyclopedia* article on "Copyrights," have written such a clear, brief exposition on international aspects of copyright that a similar commentary on our part would be superfluous. Especially when we follow their information as we do, with a brief U.S. Copyright Office sheet (Paper 69) entitled "In Answer to Your Query: International Copyright."

One of us, Barbara Friedman Polansky, has commented in Paper 70 on "Recommendations for Settlement of Copyright Problems Arising from the Use of Computer Systems for Access to or the Creation of Works," a report issued by the United Nations Educational, Scientific, and Cultural Organization (UNESCO) and the World Intellectual Property Organization (WIPO). This document has been disseminated throughout the world for countries to consider as the basis for national legislation. "Of course," writes Polansky, "the proposed principles cannot serve as a complete model for any one country to endorse because the recommendations are compromises among existing [national] laws and rules of the international conventions." Nevertheless, Polansky urges, "We should become aware of this document and its recommendations, which might, some day, affect the U.S. Copyright Law and thus, inevitably, our rights as creators, copyright owners, and users of protected works."

Paper 71 by U.S. Register of Copyrights David Ladd, "To Cope With the World Upheaval in Copyright"—subtitled "Reflections on the Future Development of Copyright"—was commissioned by WIPO. Its main sections depict its scope: Introduction, Rationale of Authors' Rights and Copyright, The Challenges to Copyright Analyzed, WIPO/UNESCO Initiatives, and Recapitulation of Recommendations. This is a penetrating review of basics, problems (challenges), and vigorous measures for solutions at international as well as national levels.

BIBLIOGRAPHY

Caution on Berne Convention Urged by Officials, 1982, *Publ. Wkly.* **221**(19):17–18.

Copyright Office, 1983, *International Copyright Relations of the United States,* Circular R38a, Library of Congress, Washington, D.C.

Gabay, M., 1979, The United States Copyright System and the Berne Convention, *Copr. Soc. U.S.A. Bull.* **26**(3):202–220.

68: TRADEMARKS AND COPYRIGHTS

Jon A. Baumgarten

Paskus, Gordon & Hyman

Charles W. Lieb

Paskus, Gordon & Hyman

[*Editors' Note:* In the original, material precedes this excerpt.]

COPYRIGHTS

[*Editors' Note:* Material has been omitted at this point.]

International Copyright

The foregoing discussion has been directed toward copyright protection for works in the United States. Works originating in the United States are also subject to copyright protection in a great many foreign countries. The phrase international copyright is, however, something of a misnomer, for there is no single law or code of international copyright governing the protection in one country of works originating in others. There are a number of bilateral relations and multilateral conventions pursuant to which works originating in one country are entitled to protection in others. Two principal multilateral conventions are the Universal Copyright Convention, to which the United States is a party, and the Berne Convention, to which the United States does not belong. United States adherence to the Berne Convention is generally understood to be precluded, at the current time, because of the U.S. law's continued emphasis on the "formalities" discussed above in contravention of a fundamental Berne principle that copyright protection shall be free of any formalities (18). (However, works originating in the United States can gain protection in Berne countries by simultaneous publication in the United States and a country that is a member of the Berne Convention.)

Although treaties and conventions do impose certain minimal requirements on member states with respect to the type of protection to be accorded foreign works, in each case the actual nature of protection accorded by a foreign country is ultimately determined by its own law. Members of the Universal Copyright Convention cannot impose formalities as a condition to copyright protection of works originating in the United States that are unpublished or, if published, that contain the notice of copyright described above. (For this purpose, however, the symbol © must be used in the notice.)

The correlation among international copyright protection, political and cultural exchange between nations, and transcontinental communications technology has been widely noted (19). Yet on the international scene, no less than on the domestic, the tensions posed by new technology for copyright are increasingly being felt, and the problems of photocopying, computer usage, satellite and cable-television transmissions, and private audio and video recording are far from settled.

Another element of concern in the international copyright sphere has been the pressure brought by developing countries for severe limitations on the rights accorded to copyright owners. Although ostensibly based upon the need for simplified access to foreign works for purposes of local cultural development, among the more developed countries it is felt that these attitudes are frequently shortsighted. It is pointed out, for example, that if a particular country substantially decreases the amount of protection available to foreign works and thereby encourages use of such works without adequate compensation or the need to seek permission, the end result is likely to be the flooding of that country with foreign works to the detriment of that country's indigenous intellectual and publishing communities. There is a very clear historical example of such a development: the United States. Before 1891, the United States did not accord protection to foreign works and found its markets saturated with unauthorized, inexpensive reprints of works from the UK. The development of indigenous U.S. authorship and publishing quite clearly suffered in this situation. In the words of one contemporary observer (20):

"Why should the Americans write books, when a six-weeks passage brings them in our own tongue, our sense, science, and genius, in bales and hogsheads?"

[*Editors' Note:* Only the references cited in the preceding excerpt are reproduced here.]

BIBLIOGRAPHY

18. *N.Y.U.J. Int. Law Pol.* **9**, 455 (1977).
19. Eg, A. Ciampi in *Symposium on Practical Aspects of Copyright*, United International Bureau for the Protection of Intellectual Property, Geneva, 1968, p. 81
20. Remarks of Sydney Smith, quoted in R. Nye, *The Cultural Life of the New Nation, 1776–1830*, Harper & Row, New York, 1960, p. 250.

69: IN ANSWER TO YOUR QUERY: INTERNATIONAL COPYRIGHT

U.S. Copyright Office

There is no such thing as an "international copyright" that will automatically protect an author's writings throughout the world. Protection against unauthorized use in a particular country basically depends on the national laws of that country. However, most countries offer protection to foreign works under certain conditions which have been greatly simplified by international copyright treaties and conventions. There are two principal international copyright conventions, the Berne Union for the Protection of Literary and Artistic Property (Berne Convention) and the Universal Copyright Convention (UCC).

The UCC came into force in the United States on September 16, 1955. (See Circular R38a for a list of member countries.) Generally, the works of an author who is a national or domiciliary of a country that is a member of the UCC are eligible for protection under the UCC. Regardless of nationality or domicile, any author whose work was first published in a UCC country may claim protection under the UCC. If the published copies bear the notice of copyright in the form and position specified by the UCC, this notice will satisfy any other formal conditions a UCC member country would otherwise impose as a condition of copyright. A UCC notice should consist of the symbol © (C in a circle) accompanied by the year of first publication and the name of the copyright proprietor (example: © 1982 John Doe). This notice must be placed in such manner and location as to give reasonable notice of the claim to copyright.

An author who wishes copyright protection for his or her work in a particular country should first determine the extent of protection available to works of foreign authors in that country. If possible, this should be done before the work is published anywhere, because protection may depend on the facts existing at the time of first publication.

If the country in which protection is sought is a party to one of the international copyright conventions, the work generally may be protected by complying with the conditions of that convention. Even if the work cannot be brought under an international convention, protection under the specific provisions of the country's national laws may still be possible. There are, however, some countries that offer little or no copyright protection to any foreign works. For current information on the requirements and protection provided by other countries, it may be advisable to consult an expert familiar with foreign copyright laws. The U.S. Copyright Office is not permitted to recommend agents or attorneys or to give legal advice on foreign laws.

Reprinted from *In Answer to Your Query: International Copyright,* Library of Congress, Washington, D.C., 1982, 1p.

70: INTERNATIONAL RECOMMENDATIONS FOR HANDLING COPYRIGHT QUESTIONS ABOUT COMPUTER-GENERATED WORKS: WHAT ARE OUR CONCERNS?

Barbara Friedman Polansky

American Chemical Society
Washington, D.C. 20036

Throughout the world, authors and proprietors of copyrighted information are concerned with the electronic reuse of their material. We in the United States are still experiencing growing pains in coping with some of the provisions in the Copyright Act of 1976. Section 101 has been changed to include a definition of a computer program, and Section 117 has been amended to provide for limitations on exclusive rights for computer programs. Still, however, there are disagreements about copyright owners' rights, particularly in the field of data bases. With the ever-rapid advancement of computer technology and the increase of transborder data flow, we should keep abreast of international discussions and recommendations that may and can affect the U.S. Copyright Law and our rights as creaters, copyright owners, and/or users of protected materials.

We all know that information is valuable. It becomes more so when people want to use it and reuse it. Of course, there are certain limitations to use and reuse because of the exclusive rights that are afforded to copyright owners by law. On the other hand, statutory "fair use" permits certain uses that are considered not to infringe copyright. The factors that determine whether or not a use is permissible are so general that "fair use" is a much disputed section of the U.S. Copyright Law (Title 17, U.S. Code). To make matters more troublesome, laws enacted to protected proprietary rights cannot keep pace with the rapid advancement of technology. In 1980, the U.S. Copyright Act of 1976 was amended to include the definition of a computer program and to reword Section 117, regarding the limitations of exclusive rights for computer programs. But what about works that are generated by computers? Are these works proper subject matter for copyright? If so, who owns the copyright: the person who runs the computer program or the person who developed the software? These and other complex issues were discussed by an international committee of government experts on such matters. They wrote the document entitled "Recommendations for Settlement of Copyright Problems Arising from the Use of Computer Systems for Access to or the Creation of Works",[1] which I shall refer to as the recommendations document. The committee's meeting report, which accompanies the recommendations, will be referred to as the UNESCO/WIPO report.[2]

The recommendations document has already been disseminated throughout the world for countries to consider as national legislation. Of course, the proposed principles cannot serve as a complete model for any one country to endorse because the recommendations are compromises among existing natural laws and rules of the international copyright conventions. Nevertheless, we should be aware of this document and its recommendations, which might, some day, affect the U.S. Copyright Law and thus, inevitably, our rights as creators, copyright owners, and users of protected works.

The recommendations were first discussed in May 1979, when the Working Group on Copyright Problems Arising from the Use of Computers was convened by the United Nations Educational, Scientific and Cultural Organization (UNESCO) and the World Intellectual Property Organization (WIPO). These two groups are the specialized UN agencies that are responsible for administering the international copyright conventions.

There are two such conventions on copyright: the Berne Union, which is the oldest and which was formed in the 1890s by the western European powers, and the Universal Copyright Convention (UCC), which is administered by UNESCO. Nations that belong to the Berne Union do not have required copyright formalities and have the minimum standards of copyright protection. On the other hand, countries that belong to the UCC, including the United States, must abide by specified formalities, such as using a copyright notice, which consists of the word "Copyright" or the symbol ©, the name of the copyright owner, and the first year of publication. Because of the differences between the two copyright conventions, the UNESCO/WIPO recommendations were written as general principles.

UNESCO and WIPO have been and are working together to study computers and the use of computers with respect to copyrighted works. In December 1980, they convened the Committee of Government Experts on Copyright Problems Arising from the Use of Computers for Access to or the Creation of Works (hereafter referred to the Committe); this Committee was asked to study and act on the Working Group's report of June 1, 1979. The Committee's report of the 1980 meeting was distributed to various groups, including the American Chemical Society, for discussion and comment.[3]

In June 1982, the Second Committee of Government Experts met to discuss the draft recommendations and comments submitted by interested groups. This Committee adopted a final report which is dated August 13, 1982, and which was distributed to countries throughout the world. It includes participants' comments on the draft recommendations, international compromises, and points raised at the June 1982 meeting of government experts. The recommendations document is annexed to the UNESCO/WIPO report. Members of the Second Committee of Government Experts felt that the recommendations represented a "real and necessary step forward in the application of the international copyright conventions to the rapidly developing new technology and increasing transborder data flow".[2] They also felt that the document would prove to be a valuable guideline for national legislators.

The preamble to the adopted recommendations includes the following points: (a) high priority is being given to information policy on an international level; (b) due to the rapid development of information technology, users are able to have direct access to data bases through networks; (c) the practice of storing and retrieving copyrighted works in computer systems

† Presented before the Divisions of Chemical Information and Chemistry and the Law, and the Joint Board-Council Committee on Copyrights, Symposium on "Copyright and Ownership of Database Information", 185th National Meeting of the American Chemical Society, Seattle, Washington, March 22, 1983; American Chemistry Society: Washington, DC, 1983.

is likely to grow; (d) copyright plays an important role as a stimulus for creativity and the development of society.[1]

This is a good place to stop to review the basics of copyright, because point d is a principle of copyright which was based on the U.S. Constitution. Article I, Section 8, grants Congress the power "to promote the progress of science and useful arts by securing for limited times to authors and inventors the exclusive right to their respective writings and discoveries". So, "the primary purpose of copyright legislation is to foster the creation and dissemination of intellectual works for the public welfare; an important secondary purpose is to give creators the reward due them for their contribution to society".[4]

In order to better understand the complex issues presented in the recommendations document, it is helpful to know certain definitions given in the U.S. Copyright Law, which was enacted October 19, 1976, and which became effective January 1, 1978. Copyright protection, as described in Section 102, extends to "original works of authorship fixed in any tangible medium of expression, now known or later developed, for which they can be preceived, reproduced, or otherwise communicated, either directly or with the aid of a machine or device.... In no case does copyright protection ...extend to any idea, procedure, process, system, method of operation, concept, principle, or discovery...".[5] Other laws, such as patent laws, protect ideas, procedures, etc., independent of their forms of expression.

The important word to note in the definition of works protected by copyright is "fixed". Section 101 of the U.S. Copyright Law describes a work as being "fixed" in a "tangible medium of expression when its embodiment in a copy or phonorecord...is sufficiently permanent or stable to permit it to be preceived, reproduced, or otherwise communicated for a period of more than transitory duration...".[5] In other words, if a work is created on a word processor so that it is projected briefly on a screen or captured only momentarily in the memory of a computer, that work is not fixed and cannot be protected by copyright. On the other hand, computer data bases, which are electronic files of information "formed by the collection, assembly, and arrangement of preexisting materials or data, are clearly [protected], provided the resulting work as a whole consistutes original authorship".[6] Also, data bases are subject to copyright because a data base permits works to be "preceived, reproduced or otherwise communicated for a period more than transitory duration".[5]

This brings us back to some of the other points noted in the preamble of the UNESCO/WIPO recommendations document: (a) the use of new technologies should be more user friendly and provide for the appropriate protection of works; (b) because of the development toward international computerized information systems and the increase of transborder data flow, it is highly desirable to have international cooperation in reaching common and practical solutions for settling copyright problems; (c) in order to stimulate the creativity of authors but not hamper the dissemination of works in computer systems, legislation must take into account the legitimate interests of both copyright owners and users of protected works; (d) countries should be guided by the recommendations presented in the UNESCO/WIPO document when considering or enacting legal solutions and provisions governing problems which arise from the use of computers for accessing or creating works.[1]

The first major section of the final UNESCO/WIPO document is entitled "Subject Matter to Which the Recommendations Apply". The document regards such subject matter to be that which is considered to enjoy copyright protection because it constitutes intellectual creation or material which otherwise enjoys protection under copyright legislation. Bibliographic data per se, including the name of the author, title of the work, publisher, year of publication, and so forth, are not considered to be protected works. Subject to the given provisions of acceptable subject matter, protected works are listed as (a) full texts, or substantial parts thereof, and other complete representations of protected works, (b) abbreviated representations of works in the form of adaptations, derivative works, or independent works, (c) collections and compilations of information, including bibliographic data of several works, and (d) thesauri and similar works intended for the exploitation of computerized data bases.[1]

The Committee originally addressed the question of whether and what kinds of abstracts should be given copyright protection, but this topic proved highly controversial, and all mention of abstracts was subsequently eliminated in both the Committee's report and recommendations document.

The next section of the UNESCO/WIPO document is entitled "Rights Concerned". In the opening sentence, storage in and retrieval from computer systems are clearly noted as being acts of input and output. According to the recommendations, these acts involve at *least* the following rights of authors; (a) the right to make or authorize the making of translations, adaptations, or other derivative works; (b) the right to reproduce any work involved; (c) the right to make the work available to the public by direct communication; (d) the moral rights.[1] I will address moral rights later.

In the next section "Acts Concened" input of a copyrighted work into a computer system is defined as including reproduction of a work in machine-readable form and fixation of a work in the memory of a computer system. Any acts of input, such as reproduction, are subject to the author's exclusive rights and therefore require the copyright owner's permission. For the purpose of this section of the recommendations, a work is considered "reproduced" when it is "fixed in a form sufficiently stable to permit its communication to an individual".[1] The medium on which subject matter is fixed for storage purposes is not expressly mentioned in the recommendations document because the Committee felt that there was the possibility of new media being invented in the future. They agreed that more general and not limiting terminology be used in the final document.[1]

Output is also addressed under "Acts Concerned". Countries are requested to consider copyright protection for output of works from computer systems, whether such output is found to be a reproduction or a corresponding act (such as the production of a hard-copy printout, the fixation of texts, drawings, machine-readable forms, sounds, or audio–visual works in physical form, or the transmission of the contents of a data base into the memory of another computer system) or an act whereby a work is made available to the public (examples include visual images or other perceivable forms of a presentation of a work). The recommendations further state that countries should consider including in their national laws express recognition of the exclusive right of the author to make his work available to the public by means of computer systems. The author or copyright owner should have the sole right to control the destination of his work. Of course, this exclusive right may apply to the acts of input or output or of input only, which is the starting point of control.[1]

In the area of "Moral Rights", the general provisions in national and international law should apply. The United States does not have a section on "moral rights" in the U.S. Copyright Law. The closest provision that we have to ethical considerations is fair use, which is broadly described in Section 107 of the U.S. Copyright Act. The factors to be considered in determining whether use of a work is "fair use" include (1) the purpose and character of the use, including whether such use is of a commercial nature or is for nonprofit educational purposes, (2) the nature of the work, (3) the amount and substantiality of the portion used in relation to the work as a whole, and (4) the effect of the use upon the potential market for or value of the copyrighted work.[5]

"Limitations on Copyright" is the next section in the UNESCO/WIPO recommendations document. Countries are urged to give special consideration to the limitations permitted by the international conventions and provided for in national laws concerning the use of the copyrighted works in computerized systems. National laws may include, as exceptions to the exclusive rights, certain uses of protected works in computer systems, but such uses must be within the limits established by the international convention to which the country belongs.

It should be noted that Section 117 of the U.S. Copyright Law was amended to provide for limitations on exclusive rights concerning computer programs. The owner of a physical copy of a computer program may make or authorize the making of another copy or adaptation of that program provided that such action is necessary to use the program *or* that the copy made is for archival purposes only and that all such copies are destroyed when the owner of the computer program no longer has the right to possess it.

The next section of the UNESCO/WIPO document is "Administration and Exercise of Rights and Legislative Measures". The recommendations advise use of contractual agreements or other negotiated licenses to control input and output of copyrighted works. Moral rights are expressed again in this section of the document, which begins with the premise that "both authors and society at large are mutually interested in rapid and easy dissemination of works...". Countries are asked to consider taking measures to facilitate effective systems for both exercising and administering rights to works used in computer systems and to assess the practical possibilities of exercising moral rights.[1]

When freely negotiated licenses are not feasible, mandatory licenses may be introduced, provided they are in keeping with the provisions of the international copyright conventions. Although material in computer systems can be transmitted across international borders, the effect of a nonvoluntary license would only apply in the country in which the license had been prescribed. This conforms to the Berne Convention.

The last section of the UNESCO/WIPO report is titled "Use of Computer Systems for Creation of Protected Works". Computer software, which may enjoy protection under other national laws (e.g., patent, copyright, unfair competition, or trade secrets), is not included or dealt with in the recommendations document because some delegates felt that this subject was out of the Committee's realm. However, they also felt that computer software "could be discussed to a certain extent when considering creation of works with the use of computer systems". They understood that it would be difficult to "make a clear and complete distinction between a computer as a mere tool for the creation of works and the program used for that tool".[2] Because of this complex issue, the Committe decided to address the topic of computer software at another time; however, some delegates noted in the report that they were in favor of copyright protection for computer software.

The United States affords copyright protection to computer software. A computer program, as defined by the 1980 amendment to Section 101 of the U.S. Copyright Law, is "a set of statements or instructions to be used directly or indirectly in a computer in order to bring about a certain result".

Paragraph 14 of the UNESCO/WIPO recommendations document states the following: "Where computer systems are used for the creation of works, [countries] should basically consider them as a technical means used in the process of creation for achieving the results desired by human beings."[1] The Committee agreed that the recommendations on this subject should be flexible and that countries should consider the general principles given when applying them to concrete situations or practical problems.

One of the first drafts of the recommendations contained three paragraphs dealing with ownership of copyright in computer-generated works. Although these paragraphs were deleted in the final recommendations, they were included in the Committee's final report as possible applications of the general statements presented in the recommendations document:

(a) "If the program is capable of producing one work only, then the author who has given instructions or the composer and the programmer who not only provides technical assistance in utilization of the computer but whose contribution is a creative one should be considered the author or co-authors of the resulting work, as the case may be."

(b) "If the program is capable of producing different results and the author has himself made a choice among these results, he should be regarded as the author of the resulting work; if he has asked a programmer or another person to choose the elements for the composition of the final version, then this programmer or another person and the author himself should be normally regarded as co-authors to the extent that they make a creative contribution."

(c) "If the program is capable of producing different results but the final choice is made by a third party, the mere choice by itself should not be regarded as creative contribution."[2]

The following general principles, to which the Committee referred to in its report, appeared in paragraphs 15 and 16 of the final recommendations document:

15. "In order to be eligible for copyright protection, the work produced with the help of computer systems must satisfy the general requirements for such protection established by the international conventions and national law on copyright."

16. "In the case of works produced with the use of computer systems, the copyright owner in such works can basically only be the person or persons who produced the creative element without which the resulting work would not be entitled to copyright protection. Consequently, the programmer (the person who created the programs) could be recognized as co-author only if he or she contributed the work by such a creative effort."

At the suggestion of one delegate to the Committee, the final document covers works created by the use of computer systems in connection with commissioned works. The paragraph dealing with this subject mentions that the "matter of attribution of copyright ownership should be left to national legislation".[2]

What do these comments and recommendations mean to us? There is a possibility that they will be considered when our own copyright law is amended or completely revised, such as we experienced effective January 1, 1978. Our copyright law has already been amended to provide for the definition and limitations on exclusive rights concerning computer programs. It might not be too long until our law might include sections dealing with data bases, electronic publishing, downloading, or limitations on exclusive rights for the flow of transborder data. Who knows what inventions are around the corner that will affect us in our daily lives? The use of small computers for personal tasks, as well as for business purposes, is increasing. People are realizing more and more that information is valuable and will be readily available only for a fee.

What are some of our other concerns? Those that have already been voiced include the following.

(1) Is downloading permissible? Downloading is the electronic transfer of information from one data base to another, including that from an on-line data base service through one's own local microcomputer. At the Online '82 Conference &

Exposition, Carlos Cuadra, President of Cuadra Associates, Inc., said that "many publishers have come to accept the idea that there are legitimate reasons for the temporary retention of data obtained from an online search, and they have given [such] permission.... More and more users want to retain records permanently, to make them part of their own local electronic library." He urged publishers "to give immediate attention to...user needs and to develope pricing policies...that serve those needs, while protecting their own rights in the data".[7] Although I am not in a position to give any legal advice, I suggest you look at the contract you have with the copyright owner or data base producer. If you do not already have a contract and you are reusing information gleaned from an on-line system, perhaps you should request a copy. I suggest you ensure that what you want to do with data base information is permissible and spelled out in your agreement. Also, do not hesitate to seek legal advice. These steps might save you a lot of headaches (and possible lawsuits) in the long run. Keep in mind that the copyright owner has the exclusive right to determine the conditions under which data is made available to others.

(2) What happens to information after users receive it? This is an old and a present concern that we cannot really do anything about, except perhaps through negotiated contracts, licenses, and agreements. I still believe that most people are honest and would be willing to abide by the copyright law and by reasonable terms set by publishers.

(3) Does copyright infringement of works in a computer system occur at the point of input or output? The Subcommittee on Databases of the National Commission on New Technological Uses of Copyrighted Works, better known as CONTU, came to the same conclusion as the UNESCO/WIPO group: the act of storing a computerized data base in the memory of a computer is the exclusive right of the copyright owner.[8]

(4) Does "fair use" apply to computer-generated works? CONTU determined that fair use of machine-readable data bases follows "the same guidelines as are applicable to print materials. This means that the user could retrieve and use information derived from the data base, such as a citation or in fact, just as he would with any other copyrighted work. He may not, however, use a substantial portion of the data base without violating the owner's copyright."[8]

I am sure there are countless other concerns and questions that one may have with the copyrightability of computer-generated works or works accessed from computerized systems. It is well-known that users want and need information that is timely and cost effective. It is almost certain that "downloading will soon become a way of life",[9] and we will have to pay for the right to use and reuse that valuable resource known as information.

Until our copyright law and other laws catch up, or at least come close, to the rapidly advancing and ever-changing technology, I urge you to use good judgement concerning the use and reuse of copyrighted material. I leave you with a word of advice, which I have adapted from the late Joseph McDonald: Take not from others to the extent that you would be resentful if they took that from you.

REFERENCES AND NOTES

(1) UNESCO/WIPO/CEGO/II/7, Annex I, 1982: Recommendations for Settlement of Copyright Problems Arising from the Use of Computer Systems for Access to or the Creation of Works.

(2) UNESCO/WIPO/CEGO/II/7, Aug 13, 1982: Report of the Second Committee of Governmental Experts on Copyright Problems Arising from the Use of Computers for Access to or the Creation of Works, Paris, June 7–11, 1982.

(3) UNESCO/WIPO/CEGO/I/7, Feb 20, 1981: Report of the Committee of Governmental Experts on Copyright Problems Arising from the Use of Computers for Access to or the Creation of Works, Paris, Dec 15–19, 1980.

(4) Peters, M. "General Guide to the Copyright Act of 1976"; Copyright Office, Library of Congress: Washington, DC, 1977, p 1.1.

(5) Title 17, USC, Copyrights, Oct 19, 1976.

(6) Boorstyn, N., "Copyrights, Computers, and Confusion" *J. Patent Office Soc.* **1981**, *63* (5), 277.

(7) Cuadra Associates, Inc. *NFAIS Newslett.* **1982**, *24* (6), 9.

(8) Wolfe, M. "Copyright and Machine Readable Databases" *Online* (*Weston, Conn.*) **1982**, July, 54.

(9) Keenan, S. "The End User's Point of View" *ASIDIC Newslett.* **1982**, *No. 43*, p 6.

71: TO COPE WITH THE WORLD UPHEAVAL IN COPYRIGHT

David Ladd*

This article, commissioned by WIPO from a distinguished copyright scholar, Mr. David Ladd, the Register of Copyrights of the United States of America, begins a series of articles under the general title "Reflections on the Future Development of Copyright."

The series of articles will examine, from various points of view, fundamental concepts of copyright and thoughts about its future development in the light of the changing social, economic and technological environment. All the articles, as in the case of this one, will reflect the views of their authors, rather than any policy of the International Bureau of WIPO.

On the eve of the centenary of the Berne Convention in 1986, it seems necessary that the elements should be furnished for a basic appraisal of whether the copyright system in general and the Berne Convention in particular serve their purpose as fully as they could and should.

I. Introduction

A. The Stress on Authors' Rights and Copyright

This paper has been prepared to identify the major challenges confronting the present and future development of authors' rights and copyright,[1] and to recommend approaches towards more effectively engaging international organizations in meeting these challenges.

It does not purport to represent official views, either in WIPO or in the United States. The United States experience may, however, be instructive, because the early application of commercially significant technologies there compels groups interested in copyright — copyright users and copyright owners — to come to grips with these trends in their early stages. One may examine in these efforts both successes and failures, and thereby inform discussions and decision-making on similar problems elsewhere.

So successful have been these technologies in disseminating protected works that this very success has given rise to objections against *any* perceived obstacle to a work's enjoyment. Such objections are both economic and philosophical: they focus on payment for authors' rights and copyright; and, on philosophical and ideological grounds, those payments are increasingly called into question.[2] The focus in this paper is

---

* Register of Copyrights of the United States of America.

[1] The terms *authors' rights* and *copyright*, often used synonymously, are here frequently employed to emphasize that rights of authors and publishers are, while usually allied, nevertheless distinct.

[2] See, *e.g.*, M. Ficsor, "Disquieting Report from the Maginot Line of Authors," *Copyright*, 1982, p. 104; S. Stewart, "International Copyright in the 1980's" (18th J. Geiringer Memorial Lecture), 28 *Bulletin of the Copyright Society of the USA*, 1981, p. 351.

Reprinted from *Copyright* 19:289-300 (1983).

not upon any particular technology, although particular examples are used for illustration, but upon the cumulative and general impact of various technologies on copyright and ideas about the role of copyright.

B. The International Character of the Strains

The strains upon copyright are becoming increasingly international in character. And even in countries where they have not yet appeared, they are likely to do so soon, and in force. Photocopying, for example, is a copyright issue everywhere; and photocopying creates stubborn problems of reconciling the interests of authors and publishers with the growing non-commercial sectors of advanced societies. Such reconciliation often requires domestic accommodations to be made in copyright laws. But, more profoundly, the interaction of several technologies — broadcast and satellite transmissions, computer and computer-controlled optical disk storage and retrieval, and the technology for large-scale pirating and trafficking in pirated copies — presents problems of a different order. Purely domestic approaches cannot hope to contain them, because they are international problems often involving international commerce or transmissions, and thus requiring international solutions.

C. Need for International Solutions

In the hurly-burly of change, policy-makers must continuously and carefully not only watch and assess how various countries try to cope, but also search for *new* international solutions to increasingly international problems. This is easy to say, but hard to do. The international copyright positions taken by various States rarely proceed far in advance of domestic positions on the same questions. In a sense, the development of international law for new technologies requires us to search for solutions which permit variations at the state level, while moving steadily toward a substantial degree of international harmonization.

There is accordingly a renewed need for effective international cooperation through formal treaties and existing international organizations. In addition, we now need something in the nature of less formalized arrangements seeking to rationalize trade practices in the new technological and global environment. It is inevitable that change will cause the reexamination of not only conventional legal norms and familiar commercial practices, but also of the theoretical and doctrinal underpinnings of copyright as well. The future is uncertain — troublingly so, not only because events are fast-breaking and the problems are numerous, but because the once-shared vision and aspiration for a world community for authorship and authors' interests has faded. As we face an uncertain future, we must take care to ensure that the protection afforded by copyright is real as well as formal. However salutary the language of a treaty, the critical test is whether authors' rights and copyright are, in fact, protected and appropriate payments for the use of those rights are actually made.

D. The Essential Role of Non-Governmental Organizations

For decades, especially after the formation of the International Copyright Union, international cooperation extended the reach of authors' rights. As new forms of expression — the cinema, radio, television — appeared, domestic law-making served as a precursor of gradual elaboration of the Berne Convention. The *spirit* which gave birth to the Berne Union was so closely identified with the aspirations of artists and authors — and with their idealistic, and perhaps romantic, vision of a universal law guaranteeing equality and independence to all authors — that the modernization of Berne was made both more deeply urgent and easier. This is an historical point, but worth keeping before us: international copyright treaties and organizations were the legal expressions of a vision which originated with authors themselves. The direct precedents of the first international copyright convention — and later the newer Universal Copyright Convention — lay in the efforts of *non-governmental* organizations. The Congress of Authors and Artists (Brussels, 1858), its successors in Antwerp in 1861 and 1877, and the 1878 Congresses of Artists and of Authors in Paris, were meetings at which authors, artists, journalists, educators and political figures hammered out a consensus over what broad principles should protect authors' rights on a multinational basis.

Common international legislation on copyright and allied rights thus served the overall aims of creative persons: to advance the welfare of authors and their disseminators; to reduce national barriers to international cultural discourse and to let this discourse, ideally, lead to a better educated citizenry and greater international harmony. In any event, it is necessary that, in addressing the problems here presented, full recourse be had to those most directly affected — the authors and their organizations. No proxy, no government, no official, can represent their interests better than they can themselves.

E. Causes of the Diminished International Vision

The notions of a harmonious international copyright community just recited can be seen, in retrospect, to have been over-optimistic. Several factors may account for this.

First, the theory of authors' rights has inevitably become entwined with matters of international trade in copyrightable "objects" and has therefore been subject to powerful political pressures for protectionism. Fundamentally, this has permitted the re-introduction of reciprocity into practical copyright matters, to the detriment of an important principle for which international copyright stands: national treatment.

Second, to the extent that the dream of a universal copyright regime looked toward deeper integration of States into an international system of broader cooperation, two world wars in less than 30 years blighted those aspirations.

Third, the notion of international harmonization of copyright in 1886 did not encompass large sections of the world as we know it today; it was, in the main, a European vision reflecting the deepest feelings of Europe's leading cultural personages.

Fourth, in recent years international organizations have been timid in their extension, elaboration and perfection of protection for intellectual property. For decades, especially after the Berne Convention, international cooperation was extended to new forms of expression as they appeared. But in recent years the whole range of political and economic issues involved in today's international geopolitics have cast their shadow upon WIPO and Unesco. They have therefore become less and less able fully to adapt and perfect modes of protecting authors, and more and more preoccupied with political strivings of political groups. The results have been inevitable: either "consensus" positions so muted in compromise and vague in direction that decisive action in the service of authorship became virtually impossible; or a shift in focus away from protecting authors toward serving users.

None of this, however, detracts from the essential lessons to be drawn from the formative history of international copyright up to the development of the Universal Copyright Convention. First, recognition of authors' rights should be an essential part of the jurisprudence of all civilized countries; second, any effective international consensus on copyright must be based upon meeting the reasonable needs of *authors* and *copyright owners*, and therefore international initiatives in copyright must involve their support and commitment at all stages; third, while the principle of national treatment may thwart attempts to impose discriminatory rules upon foreign creations, this is not enough: international law on copyright should gradually raise the overall quality of authors' rights and adapt standards of protection to changing circumstances. Those changing circumstances are usually changes in technology and related alterations in markets for copyrighted works; but it must be conceded that, together with increased facilities for unauthorized uses, there has come a diminished appreciation of the central importance to our lives of authorship and copyright, and a growth in resistance to payment for use and enjoyment of protected works.

Perhaps ironically, the broadest international consensus in support of copyright and authors' rights flowered during the industrial age, when international cultural discourse and trade were not so extensive as they are today. The fact is that precisely at the time when telecommunications and related technologies are bringing the world closer together, many are uncertain about the proper role of copyright in this environment.

F. The Need for Reaffirmation of Goals and Ideals

What is needed now is a strong reaffirmation that it is in the common interest — the public interest — to support authorship everywhere; and that the recognition of the property rights of authors, within and among nations, is of inestimable importance to all persons. What is also needed is an effort to relate the elevated principles declared in international meetings and documents more directly to the *real* world of authorship and commerce. And, finally, the extension of authors' rights and copyright to new kinds of works must be examined against accepted philosophical and doctrinal principles so that the historical domain of authors' rights and copyright not be endangered, and that new species of creative works be effectively encouraged.

The means available to the international organizations to require or encourage compliance with internationally set norms in copyright are several:

1. affirmation or reaffirmation of principles to be effected within particular countries in accordance with local requirements;

2. declarations that specified conduct should be considered legal or illegal, to the end of establishing in a more positive way that such conduct is approved or disapproved, leaving to particular countries the modes of execution and enforcement;

3. establishment of model laws for national legislation;

4. alteration of existing treaties, or creation of new ones.

Intergovernmental organizations are composed, of course, of member States. The reference here to means available to them, and the several references later in this paper to what WIPO could do or should do, are meant as references to how governments could or should use the international organizations they have created.

II. The Rationale of Authors' Rights and Copyright

The rationale for authors' rights and copyright has been so exhaustively and philosophically explored time and time again that one may wonder why it is necessary to restate it here. There are several reasons: first, because in a period when the value of authors' rights and copyright are repeatedly challenged, time-honored and time-tested truths cannot be too frequently repeated.[3] Second, the term *copyright* is sometimes used to include in a shorthand way both authors' rights and copyright (the distinction between the two, and their separate roles, become relevant later in this paper). There is a third value, in addition to moral rights and economic rights, served by authors' rights and economic rights, which is not frequently articulated: the creation of a culture, an infrastructure, in which authors and artists may — to the extent the public supports their works — thrive. And fourth, it is important to assess these premises against the various ideological challenges to copyright now arising.

A. The Purpose of Copyright

Throughout history, human improvement has flowed from those gifted in "the exercise of the intellect." That surely was Tocqueville's meaning: "From the time when the exercise of the intellect became a source of strength and of wealth, we see that every addition to science, every fresh truth and every new idea became a germ of power placed within the reach of the people." [4]

Societies have usually, therefore, been concerned with encouraging those gifted "in the exercise of the intellect" — not merely the power of thought, but of creative imagination as well. Or, to use Tocqueville's words: "Poetry, eloquence and memory, the graces of the mind, the fire of imagination, depth of thought . . ." [5] The creative works of previous generations are among the richest treasures of our common heritage and are cherished as a grand collective human achievement.

These works have long been honored, and special care has been taken to nurture and protect the gifted who can open our eyes to a vision of life otherwise impossible. For scholars, priests, astrologers, shamans, poets, teachers, musicians and authors, means have been provided to foster them so that they might experience, reveal and teach.

The ways in which particular ages and societies have fostered authorship are many and varied: protected status or exemption from other work; royal, ecclesiastical or state patronage; academic posts and

tenure; government commissions, appointments, honors or subsidies. This support has extended both to creators and to organizations which bring creative works to wider and wider preservation, understanding, appreciation and enjoyment — schools, libraries, orchestras, learned academies, museums, broadcast enterprises, and even publishers and printers.

For the most part, until the 16th century, this support was largely a matter of the favor and largesse of the powerful. But at that time appeared a new and miraculous engine through which we might directly acknowledge, support, and pay tribute to the gifted to create and support traditions and cultures in which they may create, and thus enable their work in our behalf: copyright.

The central idea of copyright is to establish an instrument of property for which the public, in paying for its use, provides the resources to reward, and thus sustain and motivate, authors to create works with which people everywhere can inform, enlighten and enlarge themselves. At the same time, copyright, providing exclusivity, protects the publisher [6] for the values — production skills, business acumen, investment, and risk — he contributes in realizing the work and bringing it to the public for enjoyment and enrichment. These points are well understood and have been frequently stated. The argument for copyright is one of both justice and utility.

Moreover — and this is less frequently stated — collectively considered, authors' revenues from their audiences support subcultures, or communities of interest, technique, and tradition both within a given society and internationally. These subcultures foster an environment in which the author can be stimulated and inspired, and which, as a totality, at once carries a philosophical and esthetic tradition, collective knowledge of techniques and skills, and voluntary associations to honor and extend knowledge and experience. Individual artists and creators will appear in every society. But every society must strive to facilitate the growth of a culture which recognizes and sustains those who do appear, moves their works to realization, use, understanding and criticism, and thus cumulatively creates a legacy so that works of authorship can survive, together with the further works they inspire, for transmission to later generations. This consideration is of particular importance to developing nations — as it was historically in America — as they seek to strengthen and enlarge their own traditions, commerce and creative milieu.

---

[3] ". . . [the argument for copyright] is not as obvious as the popularist argument of cheap access to copyright works by the general public. Therefore the copyright argument needs to be put again and again in differing forms and in all countries. Once this is acknowledged the task of constantly arguing for the maintenance and development of copyright, which may at times appear repetitive or even tedious, becomes a necessary, even a noble pursuit, humanist in the best sense of the word." S. Stewart, "International Copyright in the 1980's — Part 2: Crisis in the 1980's," IFPI *News* No. 14, 1982, pp. 18-22, at 20.
[4] Comte Alexis de Tocqueville, 1 *Democracy in America* (New York), 1945, author's introduction at 5.
[5] *Ibid.*

[6] The term *publisher*, along with words derived therefrom, is used as a term of art in a broad sense in this paper to refer to any entrepreneur whose efforts lead to the public dissemination, performance, or display of works of authorship. In this extended definition, recording enterprises and motion picture producers, for example, are also "publishers."

As three American sociologists have reminded us, Gustave Flaubert once said that is was time to abandon the illusion that "books dropped like meteorites from the sky." That illusion still persists; the inspiration of authorship is confused with the drudgery of production. We must realize that:

> Ideas are the brain children of individuals; but books, in which ideas are given concrete shape so as to be conveyed to their intended audience, are the products of the collective work of members of publishing firms that specialize in the production and distribution of books. Thus, publishing houses are indispensable intermediary points in the diffusion of ideas. If the marketplace of ideas is to allow the blooming of many flowers, it is of the essence that there exist a publishing industry capable of fostering diverse intellectual and literary products that can compete for the attention of the public.[7]

Copyright, then, rewards and sustains not only authors, but their publishers as well.

B. *The Different Interests of Author and Disseminator*

The contributions of both the author and the publisher are necessary and, although their interests differ, they are allied. The author requires reward for his gift and effort; the publisher, compensation both for his technical skills and entrepreneurial contribution. Both those interests are frequently comprised in the term *copyright*. And indeed the publisher, by assignment or license, is often a surrogate for the author.

Even when rights are acknowledged and payment occurs, there are screens or baffles between royalties or payments collected and authors' hands: in nearly all cases authors do not themselves directly sell 'copies, nor do they authorize performance. Instead, they are represented by collecting societies or other intermediaries. With the spread of statutory and compulsory licenses, collecting societies grow ever more important. And in cases where distribution under such licenses is made by government organizations, the problem of equitable distribution may be even more acute.

We come now to the point whose brevity of statement here must not be allowed to belie its importance: copyright laws and organizations are more concerned with the definition and enforcement of rights against unauthorized use, and less about the relations between authors and publishers. It is essential, as a matter of justice, that the rewards of *copyright* penetrate through the bureaucratic layers of official or private societies to authors. Put bluntly, appropriate parts of the money which the public pays to use and enjoy protected works must truly reach the authors' hands. In this respect, both within nations and within the international organizations, increased

---

[7] Coser, *et al., Books, the Culture and Commerce of Publishing* (1982), p. 3.

attention must be given to how payments for the use of protected works are distributed as well as how they are collected. WIPO can, in a scholarly way, canvass and classify the various ways in which national regimes seek to safeguard authors' rights throughout the term of protection — as in the United States, where the law contains the termination right and limitations on the concept of "works made for hire" and, elsewhere, where *droit de suite* is in force. The very effort will focus attention upon the problem as well as suggest practical possibilities for national legislation.

The distinction between authors' rights and publishers' rights has become important in another respect. Copyright has been sought — often successfully — for new kinds of works less and less resembling the historical works of the imagination in which copyright finds its roots: computer programs, data bases and, in certain respects, industrial designs, including semiconductor chips. In these works, the character and quality of the creative faculty is so different from that of a novel, a film or a painting, so more nearly approaching inventorship as to raise the question of whether they should not be protected by some form of a neighboring right rather than copyright. The uncritical extension of copyright to such new kinds of works also arguably makes more vulnerable the protection of traditional works of authorship. For example, the term of 50 years *post mortem* has emerged out of a concern for the livelihood of an author and his family, but that purpose has less force for industrial-like works and, inadvertently and unwisely, may invite the calling into question of protracted terms of protection for *all* works.

International organizations should continue examining questions concerning computer-related and similar issues but they should do so without being so dazzled by technological progress that they lose sight of traditional authors and their works. In general, in considering the extension of copyright from its historic base in belles lettres to new technology-enabled or technology-containing works, questions should repeatedly be asked about the effects upon traditional copyright of extending copyright to new kinds of works and about the alternatives of new kinds of copyright-like protection outside copyright itself.

III. The Challenges to Copyright Analyzed

The sources of stress on copyright are various and rooted in change — in technology, in markets and other commercial practices, in shifts in public expenditure, and in international relations. Each stress is serious; together they are truly formidable. In sum, they have produced upheaval in the copyright world. It is useful to identify them and analyze them separately.

A. Technological and Market Changes

The first source of strain is technological change. Although technologies ultimately create new markets, their immediate effects are the disruption of customary and established channels for distributing copyrighted works. Even if these strains are transitional in nature, optimism for the long term should be guarded. Inequities built up during transitions can become vested. Shorter term accommodations may ultimately serve neither authors', publishers', nor users' interests. Many new technologies are widely diffused, creating difficulty in discovering or controlling essentially private uses which have public consequences. It is futile to try to impose, in traditional contract fashion, charges for such uses on a transactional basis. Authors' societies, copyright proprietors and a growing body of non-commercial users of copyrighted works now see the necessity of devising and legalizing indirect methods of monitoring such uses, charging for them and distributing the monies collected to the copyright owners whose works are used.

These general statements are readily grasped by a concrete illustration. For decades, copyrighted cinematic works were secure against unauthorized copying. This security arose, of course, from the nature of the necessary equipment and its expense. Motion pictures were released only for theatrical exhibition; the copyright owner did not part with ownership of the distributed prints; exhibition occured only in theaters; and no one dreamed of copying the films for personal use.

Together with television broadcasting, the videocassette recorder has changed all that: everyone can copy films in his own home, even if they were licensed only for broadcast; videocassette sales (authorized and piratical) constitute a new market; and videocassette rental shops spring up, constituting yet another market. The result: theatrical display, and its inherent controls available to the copyright owner, is being displaced. The application of copyright law to new technological uses is often doubtful and usually delayed; and in the period of doubt public and non-creative commercial interests exploit the ambiguities by occupying the new zone and resisting payment. If "windfall" profits are large enough, then these interests become powerful enough to extend the delay almost perpetually.

If one surveys, in addition to videotaping, the other new technologies, including photocopying, cable television, satellite transmissions and computers, certain common characteristics are discerned:

1. a trend toward the increased importance of display and performance rights for the dissemination of "traditional" works;

2. widespread consumer ownership of instruments for display, performance and copying [8];

3. the frequent occurrence, with the appearance of new technologies (e.g., cable and videorecording), of doubt or ambiguity about the very applicability of copyright control and, until the doubt is resolved, by legal interpretation or statutory change, the spread of unauthorized use which because of its large scope is difficult to bring within legal control; and

4. the practical unenforceability of traditional copyright rights by traditional means against uses which are increasingly private, not readily detectable, and yet enormous in scale.

The greatest danger thus presented is that copyright becomes irrelevant in actual practice. If one approaches new technology questions from a point of view which asks what the present law *is*, the chances are rather good that one's answer will reflect 19th-century assumptions about "good copyright policy," rather than late-20th-century reality. There is a substantial danger that exemptions reflecting earlier copyright laws, which focused upon the rights to publish and distribute copies of works to ultimate consumers, can be inadvertently and unwisely extended, thus creating an environment, unimaginable in earlier times, where their effects are far greater and less incidental to the broad commercial freedom copyright owners need to survive. Copyright principles are eternal — or should be to those who care at all about human progress and freedom — but the precise rules by which we achieve copyright's objectives must vary and may need substantial changes to meet substantially changed circumstances. In the ultimate analysis, the question is not whether a certain activity *is*, for example, a "fair use," but whether, in an emerging social and economic order, it *ought* to be within the control of authors so that they can maintain independent creativity.

To meet this need, two responses are possible: first, the clear formulation of national laws in broad prospective terms so as to encompass all significant uses of a protected work; and second, the fostering of usable licensing mechanisms where direct control by the author or the copyright owner is not possible, or greatly inefficient or inconvenient.

On the first point, the marvels of technology simply cannot be predicted beyond a near horizon and, therefore, statutes should never be drawn with exclusive rights tied firmly to any particular technol-

---

[8] To this list might be added technical capabilities to *adapt* protected work. Rather sophisticated features in home and institutional audio equipment permit the literal creation of personal musical anthologies, mixing broadcast performances with album cuts. The integration of word processing technologies with electronic publishing will eventually pose problems in sorting out adaptation rights in traditional literary works.

ogy. It is imperative to frame laws which declare in broad terms the various rights of which copyright is composed — reproduction, distribution, display and performance — so as to comprehend later unanticipated uses and to make this purpose an explicit objective of such laws. In this scheme, the protection founded by such a general declaration should be presumed to apply to each new technological use as it appears, with exceptions or exemptions to be permitted only when specifically provided.

If rights turn out to be unworkable, or too sweeping, or otherwise demonstrably against the public interest, they can be altered in response to the general will. It is far more difficult to do the reverse — to retrieve that which, with the passage of time, is seen to have been lost.

The usefulness and effectiveness of this technique has recently been demonstrated in the United States. There, home taping has been held — subject to review in our Supreme Court (and Congress) — to be an infringement of the generally stated exclusive right under copyright to control copying.[9]

WIPO should encourage, by whatever means at its disposal, the adoption of domestic laws which contain such general statements of the rights of copyright as to encompass the predictable future uses of protected works made possible by technology.

In the case of home taping, as in others, it is neither practical nor possible to control uses of protected works by assertion of these rights directly against the user. With respect to videorecording, therefore, indirect measurement of sales of tapes and machines used for recording, however imperfect, has been resorted to and is proposed in the United States. Where it is impossible to control and restrain use directly, it may be possible to make only an indirect measurement of actual uses and, under the mechanism of a blanket licensing scheme, to collect for them. The increased use of such non-voluntary licenses is likely inevitable. Since a compulsory license is a severe limit on the right of the author to control the exploitation of his works, it is essential that the international copyright community, under WIPO's leadership, develop clear principles about when such licenses are proper in order to protect authors, what their essential features should be, how they should be structured and managed once adopted, and under what conditions they should be abandoned.

Historically, there have been at least four reasons advanced for adoption of compulsory licenses:

(a) to overcome unacceptably high transaction costs, including the costs of finding the contracting partners for separate transactions, negotiating and settling the bargain, and completing arrangements for performance of private contracts;

(b) to provide a feasible means of legitimizing and collecting payment for the use of copyrighted works, when no present mechanism is found to exist (*e.g.*, the compulsory licenses, in place in Austria and West Germany and proposed in the United States, which require payments from manufacturers of videorecorders and/or tape as a part of recognizing the right of private videorecording);

(c) to correct a particular abuse of dominant bargaining position (as in the case of the original regime in the United States governing mechanical reproduction of music); and

(d) to subsidize, at least temporarily, a particular use to benefit the user industry, or the public which buys its service (*e.g.*, the original US cable license, which provided statutory rates constituting an income redistribution from copyright owners to cable operators by setting a royalty at a value substantially sub-market).

At the outset, one should note that the problems posed in (a) and (b) above can effectively be dealt with by voluntary systems. Significantly, some of the most important practical justifications for compulsory licensing go to the issue of comprehensive, *blanket* licensing, not to the need for *compulsion*.

One should keep those four justifications for mandatory licenses in mind when reviewing today's copyright/technologies-of-use issues. One sees, for example, in the case of photocopying and home taping, that the instruments for copying are widespread. Not only is ownership of videocassette recorders fast proliferating, but small photocopying machines suitable for home use have been on the market for some time. In any case, the copying is not visible to the copyright owner and the user has no notion how to acquire a license. The only way for the user to avoid violating the law, and for the copyright owner to be compensated, is by a mandatory license, with some indirect measurement or metering of use.

Compulsory licensing must, in some cases, be admitted. It is never the best, nor preferred, nor even welcome way of compensating authors, but sometimes, the only way. Every such licensing scheme should provide mechanisms for (1) setting the rates or fees, (2) collecting the royalties, and (3) dividing and distributing the collections. Fixing rates in a statute, or vesting the rate-setting power in a government tribunal, should be avoided whenever possible. The reason is straightforward: in such cases, the legislature itself, or the bureaucratic tribunal, will be too susceptible to popular and political forces who find it all too easy to take from the comparatively and numerically weaker creative minority and give to the numerically stronger.

---

[9] *Universal City Studios, Inc.* v. *Sony Corp. of America*, 659 F. 2d 963 (9th Cir. 1981).

The cable television compulsory license in the United States provides an interesting case study. Since 1978, the rates have been set in the copyright statute and adjusted by our Copyright Royalty Tribunal (CRT). Under the early — and low — adjustments, no one, not even the cable operators, contended that the rates resembled fair market values. A recent rate-making by the CRT, in which it raised the rates by a factor of roughly four in an attempt to approximate a fair market rate, has caused the cable industry to become as disenchanted with the CRT as were copyright owners when the rates were lower.

The broad disenchantment with the cable license, and its administration by the CRT, has shown itself in the debate on the home taping controversy. Some members of Congress, determined not to entrust to the CRT the administration of the compulsory license proposed for home taping, have sought an alternative: a period of voluntary good faith negotiations among the interested parties, followed, if that proves unsuccessful, by compulsory arbitration. This is a preferred mode: it retains some aspects of voluntary bargaining conduct and it reduces the opportunity for politically, and unfairly, reducing authors' compensation.

In the case of the compulsory licenses for cable and home taping, the use of a scheme more favorable to authors than a government-administered compulsory license was prejudiced for the simple reason that no organization existed to manage the collection and distribution of royalties.

This suggests an important initiative for WIPO: the preparation of models for collecting society schemes geared to new and foreseeable uses of protected works. In this work, WIPO could either take the lead, or encourage the work of present collection societies. But the purpose should be to develop a "science," to prepare models containing various alternatives, to the end that legislatures, confronted with a choice of kinds of administrative systems for compulsory licenses, could act with confidence that a licensing mechanism could be chosen and implemented on the basis of expertise and experience.

The fact that, at a given time, transaction costs are high and a compulsory license necessary must not prevent the reexamination of transaction costs and other market indicia after time has passed, industries have matured, and government intervention may have lost its utility. The need for reexamination may be seen in the cable-copyright experience in the United States. Partial copyright liability together with the compulsory license for cable was adopted in 1976, when it was probably necessary. Yet, as the technology and the industry developed, the supplying of copyrighted programming under contract (not under compulsory license) became possible. Several "pay television" services and cable networks now thrive. (Only over-the-air, or hertzian, transmissions

are subject to the compulsory license in the United States.) Because of these new services, over-the-air programming did not remain the only, and therefore indispensable, source of programs for cable; the pay television and cable networks acted as the focal point for acquiring, and paying for, copyrighted programs; and the possibility thus appeared of discontinuing the compulsory license and relying on contract, just as the broadcast services had always done.

In such cases it should be asserted and established, as a matter of principle, that when contract becomes a viable and workable alternative, compulsory licenses should be discontinued. In the United States, because the compulsory license has not been discontinued, cable, alone among all the program delivery services to the public — direct broadcast satellite, broadcast, videocassettes and the like — enjoys a privileged position that skews competition in favor of cable.

The copyright community should consider, and consider asserting, the following principles:

1. the exclusive right to authorize the dissemination of his works is a fundamental right of the author;

2. the right to fair compensation for the use of his work is an important component of his whole right, but not co-extensive with it;

3. voluntary contractual arrangements are the norm and should be compromised only in the face of the most compelling need;

4. if mandatory licenses are adopted, the author must be fairly compensated;

5. authors' compensation should not be less than would likely obtain under free contractual arrangements, were they possible; (i.e., authors should not be required to subsidize the uses of their works);

6. comprehensive licensing schemes and arrangements should be managed privately rather than by the government;

7. development of blanket licensing organizations, and of principles for their formulation and administration, should be a principal goal of international organizations concerned with copyright;

8. when conditions of technology, markets, or industrial organization permit, compulsory licenses should be discontinued.

B. Ideological Stresses

In many societies, "technology" refers to objects and processes which are tools one brings to meeting life's tasks. For calculating payrolls, the abacus and the high speed computer may be seen as essentially the same thing — though we may quibble about which is "better," and argue long about why. But "technology" is more than tools; it is itself an ideology, held by many to be the central theme of human history. The idea of "technology," underlying the value-laden goals of modernity, advancement — development — is more powerful and pervasive than any particular machine.

For this reason, we are inclined to view technologic growth as a generally positive thing, liberating us from pre-industrial and industrial age drudgeries and inhibitions. "Technology" is pressed, by its claque, into the service of freedom and inevitably becomes confused with freedom itself.

The encounter with technology reveals philosophical differences in and among societies, many of which have important consequences for authors' rights and copyright. The gravity of copyright-technology problems is exacerbated by the extent to which — just at the time copying technology is becoming greatly dispersed — ideological objection to payments to authors (or to anyone) are being voiced even more loudly.

The argument is that creative works — in these debates often regarded as a species of "information" — are so essential to education, informed public discussion and the enjoyment of life that they must be considered invested with a social obligation not applicable to other forms of property. Therefore, the curious argument runs, these works should not only *not* be specially rewarded because of their special value; instead, authors and copyright owners must be limited to the bare minimum necessary to evoke the work and sustain its dissemination. It must be owned that in many cases this rigorous demand flows not from necessity, but from a lack of appreciation of authors and their works and even a distrust for those who work with their spirit and mind.

The case is sometimes stated in terms of the need for "access." The authors' interests must yield, it is declared, to this need; and the means employed to compel the author to yield are various — exemptions, compulsory licenses with low rates, or refusals to extend copyright protection to new uses. Such arguments are frequently urged most enthusiastically, expansively and (in truth) expensively, by those who themselves reap large commercial profit from the unpaid-for uses.

In conjunction with the argument of the need for access has appeared the companion argument that protection should be accorded the author and the copyright owner, either in formulating legislation or enforcing rights, only upon a proof that economic "harm" or losses which would otherwise result. Thus, in the United States, both on the photocopying and home taping issues, advocates have argued that absent a showing of harm which is causally related to a particular activity, that activity should not be made subject to proprietary controls under copyright. Otherwise, it is asserted, the public's need for "access" — by copying or performance, for example — should prevail over the rights of the author and the copyright owner. Accommodating technologies of use to authors' rights has raised the fear that proprietary exclusivity can (and therefore *will*) be used to limit "access" to works, thereby thwarting the goal of achieving widest circulation of cultural and informational works.

In the United States, the battle for a comprehensive exemption to legitimize unauthorized home taping has involved enormous expenditure, and vast lobbying and propaganda efforts. It seems fair to ask whether the limitations on copyright which opponents of copyright liability are seeking will enhance public access to protected works. First, the problem is not proprietary restraints inhibiting access. The public already has paid for authorized access to cinematic works on television for *viewing*; thanks to the new technology of home videotaping, we are confronting access for *copying*, which is neither authorized nor paid for. When advocates plead access in order to curtail copyright, they frequently do not truly *mean* access. Access, they have — in sale or rental, or borrowing from libraries, or in authorized copies, or through transmissions. What is meant, however, is *convenience* in use, by acquiring actual ownership of unauthorized and unpaid-for copies.

These notions, in the context of accommodating copyright to new technology, appeared and were rejected recently in the United States — at least by the judiciary. In *Universal City Studios, Inc.* v. *Sony Corp. of America*, 659 F.2d 963 (9th Cir. 1981), the court rejected the idea that access, in the sense of convenience, can justify curtailment of copyright, or trigger fair or private use exemptions.

The case of *Encyclopaedia Britannica* v. *Crooks*, 542 F. Supp. 1156 (W.D.N.Y. 1982), raises another crucial aspect of contemporary copyright conflicts: copyrighted works are increasingly used on a wide, systematic and commercially significant way by large non-commercial user organizations. In *Encyclopaedia Britannica*, the user class was schools: a centralized media center videotaped broadcast transmissions for classroom use in many of the area's public schools. The scale of the operation, conflicting directly with copyright owners' sale, rental and broadcast markets, was held to be a copyright infringement.

The claims of non-profit user interests are difficult to resist because they often evoke universally approved social obligations such as education. In the United States the central value of publicly financed education cannot be overestimated. It has been the path to position and power for generations of impoverished immigrants and natives, and has represented the epitome of opportunity and social mobility. In a period of contracting economic growth, with sharply rising costs of education, all costs are scrutinized; and that includes the costs of teaching materials, including protected works, which include in turn not only books, but films and transmissions.

The *Encyclopaedia Britannica* case did not arise under the current US Copyright Act, but that law takes a view of how the demands of non-commercial users should be accommodated to copyright at least as strong as that of this case. In the revision of the law in the United States in 1976, the Congress rejected several general not-for-profit exemptions, providing instead, in the context of the sweeping, prospective exclusive rights of which copyright is composed, numerous specific and limited exemptions, many of which are in support of curricular educational use.

All this raises a general and difficult problem: granting that education is a paramount social obligation and acknowledging that its costs are high and rising rapidly, that alone does not solve the problem of attaining the social goals underlying protection of authors. Is it necessary to reach the goal of publicly supported education without giving reasonable compensation to authors for use of their works in educational missions? If not, are we defraying some educational costs by imposing upon authors an undue limitation on their rights and consequently their earnings?

This question is difficult in market-economy societies. It is even more severe in societies which distrust special rights for intellectuals, believe the work of the gifted to be heavily freighted with social obligation, and regard egalitarian imperatives as at least as important as individual reward.

Upon reflection, however, such arguments may not be admitted. Education is a general social obligation and should be generally supported. If works of authorship are required in education, then the fair response is to pay for their use with public funds. Otherwise such uses become, ironically, a special tax or penalty upon authors.

The problem will arise wherever governments — in schools, broadcast services, or elsewhere — require the use of protected works, and will be aggravated if the proportion of such government uses in relation to private uses rises.

WIPO should accordingly seek to establish the principles that

1. unauthorized general or mass use, whether all together or one-at-a-time by many, should not be allowed merely upon arguments of need for access, and

2. government uses should be paid for on a par with private payments for such use.

By the same token the idea of harm as a basis for protection must be rejected. The first and most important answer to that argument is that authors and publishers should be rewarded, and rewarded greatly, if the public expresses its favorable judgment on their works.

Nowhere is it stated that an individual author must be confined to the minimum incentive to put pen to paper or brush to canvas. Life is, in any event, rarely susceptible to such "fine tuning" — least of all, artistic and intellectual creation. Some few authors, moved by strong feeling or possessed of divine madness, might well create compulsively without regard to what reward might come, but that does not detract from the value of what they have created. Nor does it solve the problem of paying for the actual production and distribution of creative works. Others — no doubt the large majority — create not only to satisfy themselves, but to feed themselves and their families, and to acquire the creature and psychological comforts which everyone desires.

The point is that an author does not dedicate his life and talents to authorship, nor even decide whether he will create another, and yet another, work upon a precise prospective calculation of what each individual exertion will yield him. The overall level of economic and moral protection of creators is decisive to authors: does it *permit* (not guarantee) economic independence? Does it favor intellectual independence?

Beyond that, however, there are practical difficulties in defining and applying the concept of harm as a condition of copyright and reward. There is, in this context, no satisfactory consensus about the meaning of *harm;* and indeed those who urge this argument have failed to offer general definitions for it.

The unsatisfactory quality of this approach appears when one asks these questions in relation to the important copyright issues of the day:

1. What is the meaning of the term *harm?*

2. What kind or degree of harm will, by the use of the test, require permission or payment for use?

3. In the courts or in the legislature, who should bear the burden of proof — the creators and the copyright owners, or those who wish to use them, often to their own commercial advantage, without payment or permission?

No author, nor any copyright owner, can infallibly predict how a work will be accepted and rewarded by the public. No one can assess, *ex ante*, failure or success. All efforts, therefore, to forecast or divine what "harm" (or reward) will occur will fail and it is unjust to impose such a burden on the author or copyright owner at any point.

The "harm" motif is related to yet another argument to limit rewards to authorship and copyright — the argument of "double payment." In its crudest form, the argument is that once an author has realized income from the exercise òf *one* of his rights, he has forfeited his right to income from other copyright rights. Under this argument, revenues from publication extinguish the right to revenues from performance or from recording.

These ideological inroads must be resisted; and WIPO should put forward the following principles:

1. authors and copyright owners should not be confined to the bare minimum reward necessary to sustain their efforts, but should be entitled to rewards proportioned to the value of the use made of protected works;

2. accordingly, just compensation for use, not harm to the authors, however defined, should be the principle of copyright protection;

3. likewise, the author should be justly compensated for *all* uses of his works and not confined, by ideas of "exhaustion" or "double payment," to payment for only one, or a few, of such uses.

C. International Transactions and Payments

International organizations have been and are primarily concerned with the definition of rights. They are little concerned with the enforcement of rights or with international remissions of payments to authors and copyright owners. Because of important changes and developments, international organizations must come to grips with practical copyright enforcement problems and, in particular, the equity and effectiveness of international copyright royalty remittances.

That copyright problems are increasingly international in character has earlier been stated. Technological innovations sharply increase the possibilities of trans-border infringements and trans-border opportunities for income for authors and copyright owners. In both these areas, there is a need for expanded activities of WIPO.

In the case of trans-border uses of copyrighted works, problems have arisen with the reception of broadcast signals for retransmission by cable. For present purposes an even more startling illustration may be used. In some parts of the world, the satellite transmissions of cinematic works are being intercepted and, without authorization, rebroadcast, in at least one case on a government-owned broadcast service. In addition, in some cases, videocassettes of such cinematic works are being used for such broadcasts. And such practices are likely to spread.

In these cases, where international agreements do not clearly apply, or where their development would be too slow, WIPO should sponsor international fora where such problems may be exposed and discussed to the end that informed opinion may correct some abuses and foundations be laid for negotiated settlements or ultimately appropriate international agreements.

There is another tendency which WIPO should move to correct. There is a practice whereby monies collected by authors' societies and like institutions (whether on the basis of contract or compulsory licenses) are distributed not in proportion to the estimated volume of the use of the works of each author, but by giving preference to domestic authors. In other cases, such monies are dedicated to social or cultural purposes in the country of collection.

This trend should be denounced as an abuse of copyright. The monies for the use of protected works should flow to authors and copyright owners, whether domestic or foreign; and the social and cultural purposes to which monies are increasingly devoted should be served instead by public appropriated funds.

WIPO should therefore study the possibilities of persuading governments to see to it that the societies' international distributions are proper. This effort could consist of recommendations by the Berne Union Assembly and of international reporting sessions convened by WIPO in which governments could report on the experience of their nationals.

IV. WIPO/Unesco Initiatives

To try to deal with emerging foreseeable problems before they become insurmountable, international organizations should devote as much attention as possible to two important near-term issues: satellites and "electronic" libraries.

A. Satellites

An item of great concern to rights holders throughout the world is the rapidly changing and constantly expanding use of satellites in the distribution of copyrighted works.

In the United States alone, several important litigations have concerned the copyright ramifications of:

(a) individuals' private reception of non-broadcast satellite signals intended for reception only by cable systems;

(b) commercial cable systems' similar reception and retransmission without payment or authorization; and

(c) the scope of the compulsory license intended for cable systems and its applicability to certain satellite transactions.

Other problems will soon be thrust into full view, particularly those concerning direct broadcast satellite transmissions, in which individuals, rather than cable systems or similar entities, will be the intended recipients of signals relayed from satellites.

In retrospect it appears that the United States' "new" copyright law (now seven years old) was not written with recent satellite developments in mind. As entrepreneurs, courts and legislatures now try to resolve domestic conflicts, one should note that international disputes loom large. Even now, copyright owners in the United States are complaining about the uncompensated and unauthorized receipt and retransmission of satellite signals by foreign television networks.

As more satellites are launched and used throughout the world, similar issues will repeatedly arise. The time for serious examinations and work by and in international organizations is now. Among the important questions upon which an international consensus should be developed are:

1. How do the major multilateral copyright treaties deal with satellite issues?

2. Would the Brussels Satellites Convention, if it were widely adhered to, resolve pressing problems successfully?

3. Is some new treaty desirable and, if so, how can it be drafted both carefully and expeditiously?

This paper proposes no specific answers to these questions. It simply urges that they receive prompt consideration.

B. The Electronic Library

The tension generated between portions of the library and publishing communities by disputes concerning the photocopying of library materials may, in a short time, be exacerbated by new disputes: those concerning the placement into computer-accessible media of large portions of libraries' collections and, thereafter, the copying, transmitting and displaying of parts of those collections, on demand, at several (possibly remote) locations simultaneously.

Currently two pilot projects of this type are being carried out by large federal libraries in the United States. Although they are not identical, both are characterized by the use of electro-optical disks as the storage medium and the attendant possibilities of inexpensive disk reproduction and distribution. It might, for example, be physically and economically possible within a few years to provide dozens of large libraries with disks containing large parts of the collection of the Library of Congress. Such disks may contain musical and audiovisual works as well as "conventional" printed materials.

Obviously, two important goals collide when such systems are implemented: the preservation of cultural heritage (and the more mundane but also important recordation and organization of current information of all types), on the one hand, and the enforcement of authors' rights, on the other. As libraries throughout the world increase their use of electro-optical disks and related technologies, questions concerning how

copyright owners shall be compensated must be addressed early on if the answers are to be salutary for the author and publisher communities. Otherwise, if uncompensated unauthorized uses become the norm, what now look like serious problems may become intractable.

WIPO should attempt — together with international library organizations — to ensure that, in the development of the library of the near future, the creators of the works which libraries collect are not left out.

V. Recapitulation of Recommendations

Throughout this paper, many recommendations are made. They are repeated here:

— Authors and copyright owners should be *justly* compensated for all significant uses of their works.

— National laws should speak in broad prospective terms to reach that end.

— Payments for uses should reach authors and copyright owners — domestically and abroad — rather than being diverted to general purposes.

— WIPO should vigorously examine methods — such as termination and *droit de suite* — by which authors retain some control and derive some benefit for the continued use of their works.

— Unauthorized general uses — whether occurring on one occasion or as the sum of many single uses — should not be permitted upon arguments that copyright impedes "access" to copyrighted works.

— Governments should pay market rates for their uses of copyrighted works.

— New works should be protected and encouraged, but not at the expense of "traditional" works and historical copyright.

— Healthy international copyright requires the active participation of non-governmental experts and organizations.

— Treaties and model laws should be constantly examined, revised or replaced, if necessary.

— Compulsory licenses, adopted only if absolutely necessary, should be carefully drafted:

    — private collecting societies should be encouraged,

    — payments should be as close as possible to market-price payments, and

    — such licenses should be abandoned when no longer necessary.

— WIPO should help develop models and model laws concerning collecting societies and compulsory licenses.

IX: FUTURE
DEVELOPMENTS

Papers 72 Through 75

In this section we have assembled some important papers on the future of copyright—philosophical, targeted expositions on the future of copyright and the problems that will perplex it.

To lead off, we present Jon A. Baumgarten's remarks in "Will Copyright Survive the New Technologies? Should It?" (Paper 72). Among a list of seven impacts of technology on copyright owners he specifies:

> [Technology] has created innovative means of unauthorized use (e.g., database bleed-offs from broad or high-speed inquiries, or downloading) . . . . It has created an enormous public appetite for immediate "access" to copyrighted works, one having little patience with the niceties of property and contributing to resurrection of the old misguided shibboleths of copyright (e.g., as a "monopoly" or "obstacle to dissemination" as well as new ones (e.g., equating "public air waves" with "public domain" and creating a false dichotomy between the "private" interests of authors and publishers and a higher "public" good).

Nevertheless, Baumgarten concludes that copyright *should* survive:

> Although some specifics . . . may have to change . . . the basic principles of copyright, the dignity of creations of the intellect . . . and the encouragement of creative effort through economic reward (in the case of the learned societies, recoupment of publishing expenses, if not profit) will, I think, bear retention. The alternatives are not acceptable. . . .

A similar conclusion is derived by Dennis D. McDonald in Paper 73, "Copyright *Can* Survive the New Technologies." In looking at whether we should "abandon the concept of recovering some payment for usage," he says "not really . . . [because] it becomes more and more difficult to monitor it." Instead, he suggests greater application of price discrimination. For instance, having "owners of video-rental outlets . . . pay a higher rate for the purchases of videocassettes they intend to rent rather than sell." He believes that "people will become more aware of ownership rights only if the artists, writers, and producers speak more

419

directly to the public [on] the abuse of technology which essentially cuts off their earning potential." But he worries because he has not heard much of this from really famous people.

The next article, from *Information Hotline,* contains excerpts from the testimony presented at Congressional hearings on Copyright and Technological Change. Although we feel that Paper 74 makes fascinating reading, it seems likely that no reader will agree with all of the conclusions.

It is entirely appropriate that we conclude our compendium with an article by former U.S. Register of Copyrights David Ladd (Paper 75). He is as strong and clear an advocate of the importance of copyright as former Register Barbara Ringer was of author rights, per se, and is a very eloquent pleader for his cause.

In "The Future of Copyright," Ladd derives four "common characteristics," all worrisome, from his survey of the new technologies. However, he believes:

> [The copyright laws can] master, or even survive the new technologies . . . [if they are] framed in broad terms to relate the various rights of which copyright is composed—reproduction, distribution, display, and performance—so as to comprehend later anticipated uses and to make this purpose an explicit objective of such laws. . . . Such a strategy will work only if it is not undermined by expansive notions of fair use or by private use exemptions.

Ladd believes further that comprehensive arguments can be mounted against "the main attack on copyright . . . that copyright is in opposition to the free flow of information and the public's right to know and use. . . . What is needed is a searching reexamination of how strong copyright systems serve the important needs of all people." That, he says, is the purpose of copyright.

We join these experts in believing that copyright does indeed have a future, although it must occasionally change to keep pace with man's ingenuity. Perhaps some new ideas will come from the Office of Technology Assessment's 1984–1985 study on "Intellectual Property Rights in an Age of Electronics and Information," a study requested by Congress. As we concluded our Paper 1 in this volume:

> We see no other mechanism that could presently work better. We can only urge patience, good ethical practices, and cooperation instead of confrontation. If these can prevail, perhaps we can all withstand—to coin a phrase—the temptations of technology.

BIBLIOGRAPHY

Baumgarten, J. A., 1983, Commentary: Copyright at the Crossroads, *Billboard* **95**(46):10.

Weil, B. H., 1984, Legal Issues Affecting the Information Communities: Copyright, Trade Restrictions, National Security Classification, in *Information Transfer: Incentives for Innovation,* M. L. Neufeld, I. L. Sperr, R. J. Rowlett, Jr., and M. A. Miller, eds., National Federation of Abstracting and Information Services, Philadelphia, Pennsylvania, pp. 25–32.

72: WILL COPYRIGHT SURVIVE THE NEW TECHNOLOGIES? SHOULD IT?

Jon A. Baumgarten

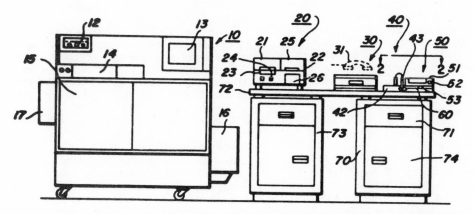

Diagram of patented Xerox copyright device

As early in 1945, a well known legal scholar described the relationship between copyright and technological innovation as follows:

> Copyright is the Cinderella of the law. Her rich older sisters, Franchises and Patents, long crowded her into the chimney corner. Suddenly the Fairy Godmother, Invention, endowed her with mechanical and electrical devices as magical as the pumpkin coach and mice footmen. Now she whirls through the mad mazes of a glamorous ball. [Chaffee, Reflections on the Law of Copyright, 45 Columbia L Rev. 504, 513 (1945).]

The "magical devices" noted by this scholar were motion pictures and radio. Since that time copyright has come face to face with over-the-air, cable, subscription and direct broadcast television; satellite, microwave, and laser interconnection, network, and delivery systems; photocopying and microform reproduction, further enhanced by electronic search capabilities; computer input, manipulation, retrieval, and transmission; vastly improved means of audio and video recording; object code, bubble and optical/digital storage; software and firmware; and so on.

Those of us fortunate to practice law on the cutting edge of copyright have to develop new vocabularies—where we once spoke of paragraphs, scenes, and lyrics, copying and paraphrasing, licenses and options, we now talk about bits, bytes and pixels, downloading, downlink intercepts, and reverse engineering, vertical blanking intervals, source code escrows, and beta testing. From the viewpoint of copyright proprietors, the result has not altogether been the "glamor" noted by the scholar.

To a great extent, and increasingly so, the new technologies tend toward erosion of both copyright owners' rights, and their abilities to control or secure compensation for the use of their works. Equally disturbing, these developments have contributed to popular, to political, and in some cases even to judicial denial of the fundamental legitimacy of copyright.

The "technological revolution" clearly holds great promise, but whether the copyright system will survive the headlong rush to fulfill that promise or be trampled in a technocratic stampede deserves the most careful consideration. This concern goes well beyond the particular interests of individual copyright owners, for our system is based on the Constitutional premise that the public interest is best served by assuring economic incentive to creative effort. This premise, I might add, has in the past proved itself manyfold in the richness of this country's scientific, intellectual, and artistic products and in the diversity of the channels of communication open for expression of the most conventional—or heretical—of views.

It has become increasingly fashionable, however inaccurate, for opponents of copyright in particular cases to point to the profiteering "greed" of copyright proprietors as the source of their claim to protection. This is an untenable stance, one that overlooks commercial realities and such factors as the impact of technology on prior markets, as well as the very Constitutional basis of copyright.

However, it is sufficient rebuttal, to recall that it was the American Chemical Society in its *amicus curiae* brief before the Supreme Court in *Williams & Wilkins v. U.S.* that pointed out that the continued vitality of the *not-for-profit* publishing sector, the learned societies, depended upon the prerogatives and principles of copyright—a conclusion echoed by

---

Baumgarten, who is a former general counsel of the U.S. Copyright Office, is a partner in the law firm of Paskus, Gordon & Hyman. He also serves as general counsel to the Association of American Publishers. This article is adapted with permission from remarks made in August to the division of chemical information of the American Chemical Society.

the American Institute of Physics, American Society for Testing and Materials, and the university presses.

Technology impact

Technology's impact on copyright owners undoubtedly takes several forms. It can be seen, for example, as having the beneficial effect of offering new or expanded market possibilities. But to stop there would be superficial, for it has other, troubling, effects (on prior or more traditional markets, as well as on the reality of those newly made possible).

- It has made reproduction of copyrighted works a simple and relatively inexpensive task, moving even commercial piracy to within easy reach and mobility (e.g., record, tape and computer software and chip piracy).
- It has decentralized unauthorized duplication, generating forms of infringement that assume significance principally when it is recognized that they might be viewed on a cumulative or aggregate basis (e.g., photocopying; concert bootlegging; off-air recording).
- It has changed the locus of infringement, moving it from public activity to private or semi-private contexts and raising practical problems of detection and enforcement, as well as concerns over intrusion (e.g., home audio and video recording; intra-corporate photocopying; program and data base appropriation).
- It has created innovative means of unauthorized use (e.g., data base bleed-offs from broad or high-speed inquiries, or downloading).
- It has distorted traditional roles played by "publishers" and "consumers" of copyrighted works; the consumer is now capable of serving as the publisher, creating copies as and when needed, on demand (e.g., photocopying; audio and video recording; software duplication). Although there are some who disagree, I suggest that a similar distortion can be discerned in the activities of library operations under the misnamed rubrics of inter-library "loan" of journals, and "document supply."
- It has called into question the applicability of conventional copyright principles to new contexts (e.g., the limits on protection of "fact works" as applied to data bases; and the provisions of proposed chip protection bills).
- It has created an enormous public appetite for immediate "access" to copyrighted works, one having little patience for the niceties of property and contributing to resurrection of the old misguided shibboleths of copyright (e.g., as a "monopoly" or "obstacle" to dissemination) as well as to new ones (e.g., equating "public air

waves" with "public domain," and creating a false dichotomy between the "private" interests of authors and publishers and a higher "public" good).

For copyright to survive, a number of steps must be taken, including education as to the values of the copyright system and the dignity of intangible property; copyright owners' own reexamination of existing permissions and marketing systems; litigation, where necessary; and innovative legislation. The latter may be particularly important, but practically quite difficult because of perceived political problems in causing alleged consumer "deprivations."

One of our problems, you see, is that the very speed of technology means that copyright owners are often playing catch-up, seeking relief after the public has become accustomed to appropriating the intellectual property of others "for free"—an attitude that is not easily countered. Yet, if copyright is to continue to serve the interests of both creators and society, our legislators must accept the admonition of Senator Charles McC. Mathias, Chairman of the Copyright Subcommittee of the Senate Judiciary Committee that:

... failing to protect [rights of copyright owners] is not excused by the fact that new technologies have made the protection of those rights more difficult. *The very ingenuity of our age that has produced these remarkable technologies should be able to devise the laws to accommodate them.* [Sen. Charles McC. Mathias, Cong. Rec., December 16, 1981 at S 15723 (emphasis added).]

I must concede, of course, that my conclusion to this point rests on an assumption—namely, that copyright *should* survive. This is an assumption that has, on occasion in the past and more often of late, been questioned. Technology, we are told by some, will make copyright obsolete. As you have probably guessed, I do not accept this assertion. Some specifics of copyright law may change—some may have to change—but the basic principles of copyright, the dignity of creations of the intellect as well as of physical labor and the encouragement of creative effort through economic reward (in the case of the learned societies, recoupment of publishing expenses, if not profit) will, I think, bear retention.

The alternatives, as I see them, are not acceptable: a diminishing of creative commitment and investment; a minimizing of alternative, even beneficially redundant, channels for expression; and the substitution of some institutional, central or official authority in the process of creation, selection, and publication.   ∎

73: COPYRIGHT *CAN* SURVIVE THE NEW TECHNOLOGIES

Dennis D. McDonald

An optimistic view about the chances of copyright survival in the brave new world of new technologies

Copyright is a type of law designed to protect certain rights of those who fix or record creative works in tangible form. It protects the form in which ideas are embodied, not the ideas themselves. Economists might talk in terms of copyright conferring a "monopoly" on the creator whereby the creator can use these ownership rights to his or her own advantage. The idea behind copyright laws is that the public good is advanced by the stimulus for creation which such ownership provides. The assumption is that the artist or writer who knows that financial benefits will flow from the act of creation will proceed to create, thus benefitting both himself/herself and society.

There is an obvious weakness in this argument since information is what economists call a "public good." In reality, it is very difficult to exclude any additional users from having access to information. Unlike other commodities information is not "used up" when it is used. Thus, copyright, right from the start, appears to be protecting a good whose use is difficult to control.

It is not always clear that copyright is a stimulus

McDonald is vice president of King Research, Inc. Rockville, Md. This article is adapted from remarks given at the Third Annual Alumni Day, College of Library and Information Services, University of Maryland, College Park.

for creation. In the case of scholarly communication, career advancement and a scientific culture which demands disclosure and dissemination of findings is the stimulus for creation—not copyright and the promise of royalties from photocopying. In addition, surveys of authors have shown that most authors do not make a full-time living from their craft but must instead rely on other sources of income for survival. Surely the prospect of copyright ownership cannot be a strong stimulus for creation in such cases.

Copyright and Technology

Perhaps the strongest threat to the concept of copyright is new technology--audiotape and videotape recorders, photocopying machines, satellite receiving antennas, pay-TV descramblers, and microcomputer disk drives. What these technologies have in common is that they all make it very easy to copy a recorded work without the knowledge of the work's owner.

It is the *ease* with which unauthorized copying can be performed which has caused some experts to suggest that the whole concept of copyright is dead. According to this view, which I refer to as the "strict constructionist" view, copyright was a concept which was born when moveable type was first developed. That was a time when copies of printed works were difficult and expensive to reproduce and obtain. Plus, it was easy to define what was meant by a work due to the relatively unitary and static nature of the works themselves and to the relatively small number of publishers in existence then.

Now recording and copying technology is widespread. Copies of works are regularly made legally or illegally, without the knowledge of the creator or owner. Perhaps, more importantly, modern technology makes it easier for anybody to become an author or publisher.

Expansion of authorship and publishing beyond the individuals and institutions who were traditionally in control of these functions means that in the future it may be more difficult to incorporate quality control and standards into the publishing process. Second, an expansion of interest in authorship or publishing may actually *increase* interest in intellectual property protection, since more people may become concerned about protecting their property rights.

Still, the pressure being put on copyright by new technology is caused by the ease with which works can be duplicated. Albums broadcast on the radio can easily be audiotaped. Movies broadcast on TV can be videotaped. Books and journals can be photocopied. Computer databases can be down-loaded and searched off-line. Computer software can be passed around and duplicated by all the members of a computer user group.

Much of this copying is perfectly legal, of course, since the law has incorporated "fair use" criteria for non-commercial uses. However, some strict constructionists have used this ease of duplicability to support their views of the obsolescence of copyright.

Sometimes it is even difficult to determine what is protected by copyright, a case in point being a database which is constantly updated from remote sites. Perhaps a case can then be made that a computerized work, since it is constantly changing, never truly becomes "fixed in a tangible form."

I don't think this is really a very strong argument against copyright. As far as I am concerned, the moment a work is fixed or recorded, even temporarily, it becomes susceptible to copyright or other forms of intellectual property protection. Questions about what is protected can be resolved. The economically important issue is how payments are made for use and copying, and whether or not the owner has any control over the circumstances in which the copying is done.

Payment

Ultimately, it seems likely that the distribution of all forms of intellectual property cannot be controlled directly by the creator, owner, or their direct li-

censees. Works become distributed, copied, accessioned into library collections. At some point the owner or distributor no longer can collect a fee for the copying or distribution of a work. How then does the owner recover a benefit from use or copying of a work which cannot be defined as fair use? And if an owner *cannot* recover a price for the use of his or her work, then aren't we saying that the concept of copyright is dead?

If it becomes more and more difficult to monitor usage, should we abandon the concept of recovering some payment in return for usage?

There are two general approaches to recovering payments. Either payment is tied to the number of times a work is used or copied, or it is tied to some other non-transaction mechanism. The Copyright Clearance Center is a good example of a system which ties its payments for institutional photocopying to the number of transactions. At the CCC, payments are based on either a census of all photocopying done by a member institution or on a sample taken during a specified time period, and the results are projected to an annual total in order to calculate royalty payments.

Non-transaction methods have been proposed for other media. For audiotapes and videotapes it has been suggested that taxes be placed on blank tapes or recording machines, the assumptions being that sales of these items parallel in some fashion unauthorized copying which currently takes place. The disadvantage of this last system, of course, is that everyone would have to pay the tax, regardless of whether he or she were involved in copying copyrighted material. And, a method--probably based on sampling--would have to be developed to divide up the proceeds thus generated.

Appropriateness of payment methods will differ significantly from industry to industry and institution to institution. For example, most photocopying machines in academic libraries are coin-operated. Use of such machines is normally not monitored by library staff. Any payment schemes concerning these machines would have to deal with the reality that a very large proportion of the items copied on these machines are not library materials at all.

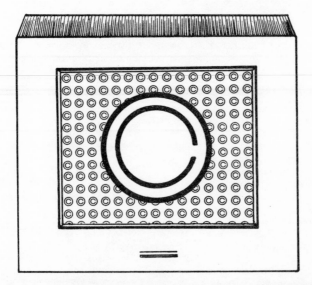

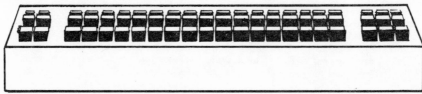

Software-swapping among owners of similar computers is very common. Not all of this software is necessarily covered by copyright. In fact, significant portions of micro-computer software written today is, based on my impression, designed to be in the public domain. So, figuring out any sort of transaction-based system for calculating how a software creator or manufacturer would be paid would probably be impossible to develop.

We may be moving into a period when transaction-by-transaction accounting and payment for the use of copyrighted materials is becoming increasingly obsolete for some works, because of the expense of collecting transaction data. One temporary exception to this is in the area of bibliographic database usage. As we shift from the use of printed indexes to online usage, data on user transactions can be collected that was previously unavailable. This is only a temporary advantage, however, due to the increasing availability of downloading as a searching aid. Downloading to a microcomputer for later searching again will potentially put a significant volume of search activity out of reach of the system operator, and hence out of reach for a transaction-by-transaction royalty accounting.

If it becomes more and more difficult to monitor usage, should we abandon the concept of recovering some payment in return for usage? Not really, since other mechanisms can be developed for compensating owners. One very commonly used method is price discrimination, where different classes of users are charged different rates according to their size or expected volume of usage. Librarians are already familiar with this practice since they often pay a higher rate for journal subscriptions than individual subscribers. Price discrimination should be used more explicitly as a method for licensing copyright-related activities such as copying and re-distribution. For example, perhaps owners of video rental outlets should simply pay a higher rate for purchases of videocassettes they intend to rent rather than sell. Or perhaps industrial libraries would pay a surcharge on journal subscriptions which would serve as a specific licensing fee for photocopying. In this way, the need to collect even samples of actual photocopying transactions could be avoided.

The chief drawback to such a scheme is that collecting royalty payments and distributing them to the copyright owners are two separate operations. Assuming the data could be collected, how important is it to distribute royalty payments to owners in perfect proportion to the copying of their works? Even now, there must be significant error in sample-based distribution schemes such as ASCAP's for broadcast music, the CCC's for serial publications, and the non sample-based distribution scheme for cable television compulsory licenses operated by the Copyright Royalty Tribunal. Errors can occur when the sample varies and a large number of items have a low transaction volume. The expense of collecting transaction data must then be traded off against the value of the works which are involved. It makes little sense to spend large sums of money to collect and distribute small amounts. Using license schemes for general classes of users would reduce overall operational costs, and selective sampling schemes could help "divide up the pie". So much the better if the distributor builds a copying licensing fee into the up-

---

It makes little sense to spend large sums of money to collect and distribute small amounts.

---

front subscription or purchase price, thereby negating the need for separate royalty collection and distribution mechanisms.

Other considerations

We would be sadly mistaken if we equated copyright with requirements for payment. Even though in the United States we do tend to emphasize the financial and economic aspects of copyright, it is interesting to note that in some other countries national copyright laws make legal distinctions between economic rights and what are usually called "moral rights." This refers to things such as the right not to be misquoted, the right not to have one's work plagiarized, and so on. Although copyright lawsuits both inside and outside the U.S. tend to focus on economic issues, I think that new information technology is going to make moral rights issues more important, simply because it is becoming simple to obtain access to and modify copyrighted works. We are seeing only the tip of the iceberg now.

For example, one of the things King Research is currently investigating for the National Institute of Education is the variety of ways information services are provided to the U.S. educational community. One thing we are finding is that many federally-supported educational information dissemination activities over the past 10 years have emphasized the "information

synthesis" function. Information service providers not only deliver a set of documents, they also scan through a variety of different sources, select, and evaluate what is appropriate, and then "repackage" what they select in a manner that frequently corresponds more to the needs of the user than to the integrity of the original source documents.

Modern information technology makes this repackaging and synthesis function easier to do. It makes it a lot easier to "take a little bit from here, a little bit from here, and a little bit from there. . ." before delivering a response to a requestor. It is very easy when repackaging information to lose information about sources, about authors, and the other things that are important to a scholar when documenting an original work. I hypothesize that in applied fields like engineering and education people are much more likely not to complain about the lack of traditional documentation when a practical, applied decision or problem is being attacked. It is in these fields where we may see an increase in "moral rights" disputes due to the ease with which information can be repackaged electronically. This may actually overshadow royalty payment problems if copyright owners move away from transaction-by-transaction accounting, especially when only "bits and pieces" of their works are involved.

I must admit that many of my feelings about copyright stem from a personal belief in the value of recorded thought. Many of our current problems concerning how to interpret copyright in the face of new technology would move closer to resolution if more members of the public were aware of the mental and physical energy which goes into creating a literary or artistic work. With the continuing increase in personal computer and videorecorder ownership, people will become more aware of ownership rights only if the artists, writers, and producers speak more directly to the public.

I am worried that this really won't happen. For example, the slippage in phonograph record sales during the recent recession was widely attributed in that industry to increasing off-the-air taping and unauthorized duplicaiton. (I tend to think it was due more to recession, an aging population, and a lack of innovation in music.) Yet when did you ever hear a Mick Jagger, a Luciano Pavarotti, or a Dolly Parton speak out publicly about the abuse of technology which essentially cuts into their earning potential? Never. Yet I think it is these same people, and famous authors such as James Michener, who could help ease our transition to new technology since they could make more people think between creativity and copyright. If we hear nothing from them, then I fear that the concept of copyright really *will* be threatened by new technology.   ■

74: COPYRIGHT LAW DEVELOPS "SEVEN YEAR ITCH" AS NEW TECHNOLOGY RENDERS RECENT REVISIONS OBSOLETE

How to keep the law current with rapid advancements in new technology was the question posed at the first of a series of Congressional oversight hearings on Copyright and Technological Change. Rep. Robert W. Kastenmeier (R-Wisc.) and members of his House subcommittee heard testimony that included such conclusions as:

- the ultimate purpose of copyright "is not to protect authors but rather to enrich the public domain"

- the flow of court decisions that force the future into historical arguments that become obsolete should be stopped. "The courts have the potential for crippling the future. They are increasingly exercising that potential."

- software will be much more important in our future economy than hardware (an estimate is given of 4:1)

- the growth in "value" of information raises the incentive to "steal" it — and the personal computer, the VCR, the audio cassette and at-home photocopying machines all provide easy access for illicit copying

- Congress may need to retain more staff members with sci/tech back-

grounds in order to advise more effectively on the results of the Congressional action on technology

- an entirely new science or discipline will be needed simply to keep track of developments in all of the others

- we talk today of "narrowcasting," *i.e.*, special interest programming for identifiable market segments rather than "broadcasting" which tried to appeal to the greatest mass of recipients.

Excerpts from the testimony heard by the House Subcommittee on Courts, Civil Liberties and the Administration of Justice are reprinted below.

> **Excerpts from the**
> **Statement of Robert W. Kastenmeier**
> *Chairman, House Subcommittee on*
> *Courts, Civil Liberties and*
> *Administration of Justice*

In about 500 B.C., the Greek philosopher Heraclitus observed that "nothing endures but change." The proof of that statement is its truth today. In our age, however, technology has accelerated the pace of change far beyond what Heraclitus might have dreamed. It is easy to forget that the movie industry is only about seventy years old; the television industry is reaching its fourth decade; and communications satellites are in comparison mere infants.

We, as a society, are entering a new age. The fundamental shift from an industrial to an informational society is no longer just a prediction but is becoming a reality. The majority of the American workforce is engaged not in the production of goods but in the creation, processing and distribution of information. Expanding information technology, from computers to satellites, from television to teletype, ensures that we will become even more of an information society in the future.

In this new society, it is predicted that information will be a key resource — the new capital. As the economic importance of information increases, the law of information — intellectual property law — assumes a critical function in shaping the new society. Similarly, the First Amendment, which ensures that both our society and our governmental system are free and relatively open, occupies a central role. We live in a society where creative ideas and thoughts are meant to compete with each other. Every resident of this country benefits from this relative openness.

Indisputably, the goals of government are to preserve fundamental civil liberties and human rights, to ensure equality among all citizens, and to protect private property. As relates to intellectual property law, a key question is how should these goals be best reconciled. In this important regard, this subcommittee not only has jurisdiction and expertise in the area of copyright but also is competent to handle diverse civil liberties issues.

Not long ago, this subcommittee — with the assistance of able academicians, lawyers and other distinguished experts — revamped the Copyright Law of 1909. The fruit of our labor was the Copyright Revision Act of 1976.

Yet just a few Congresses later, science has advanced beyond what was then barely on the horizon. Today, several bills before the subcommittee attempt to accommodate some of these technological developments. Pending before us are bills that would extend copyright protection to semiconductor chips, mask works, and computer software; that would set forth a legal framework for home taping; that would modify the first sale doctrine for audio and video rental; and that would delineate rights in the area of cable television. We plan to address some of these issues in separate legislative hearings.

. . .

As we consider these bills, however, we must also concern ourselves with larger issues. How should copyright law respond to technological change? Should copyright law accommodate changes initiating outside the law, or should copyright law attempt to delay change by preserving existing rights? How should the legal dividing lines be drawn between the sometimes competing demands of consumer and proprietor? It goes without saying that Congress has an important role to play in answering these questions. What we do not know in this regard is what role should be played by other governmental entities within the executive and legislative branches. Should new bureaucracies be created to solve problems or to reallocate resources? In a time of finite budgetary resources, we must ask how much taxpayer money should be spent in pursuit of legislative goals.

As the subcommittee with oversight responsibilities for the federal judicial branch of government, we know that the courts are being asphyxiated by delays and costs. With judicial review being a common feature of all copyright legislation, we need to know more about the role of courts in this area. Are courts doing a good job, or are specific issues that arise in the area of copyright and technology not amenable to judicial resolution? The *Universal* v. *Sony* litigation immediately comes to mind.

In short, the purpose of our hearings today and tomorrow is to refine these preliminary questions and to develop a body of knowledge and understanding that Congress can draw upon in the years to come. Technology has accelerated what already has been referred to as the "ever whirling wheel of change" so that it is not enough to react to past events. As members of Congress, fulfill our role in helping to shape it for the betterment of all Americans.

Excerpts from the
Remarks of Benjamin M. Compaine
Executive Director, Program on Information Resources Policy, Harvard University

It is my understanding that I was asked to testify today not as an authority on copyright but as a "futurist." Futurist, however, has something of a vague, blue-sky ring to it. I do not presume to predict the future. Instead, I will try to lay out some of the forces and trends put in motion by rapidly changing communications technology and then suggest some of the possible policy implications of these developments. My objective is to provide a context for your subsequent discussions of copyright. I have submitted a formal written statement which I request be included with the record of this hearing.

There was, not too long ago, a simpler era for the media industries, when a newspaper was a newspaper and television meant whatever the home receiver was able to pick up from one of three commercial networks. Cable operators merely brought a piece of wire into a home so the video image of what the networks were broadcasting might come in sharp — or come in at all — for many users.

By contrast, in the 1980s, participants in the media and allied arenas are faced by a rapid change in technology and by the blurring of the distinction that has characterized the individual media. For instance, the television set at home is being used for private showing of theatrical films or for displaying output from a distant computer; homes with cable service are able to view programming that is not available on the old-line networks, or, for that matter, anywhere off the air. The talk today is of "narrowcasting," *i.e.*, special interest programming for identifiable market segments rather than the broadcasting which tried to appeal to the greatest mass of recipients.

The changing environment that makes a precise definition of the media arena difficult simultaneously creates the potential for new opportunities for those involved in the media industry. It also should alert us to possible entry by new competitors, such as computer firms and telephone companies, which have not been traditionally viewed as being in the media business. This, then, may lead to new areas of conflict, not only in the market place, but among government regulators seeking to identify their territories and the new media forms and participants.

Since 1930, however, the center of the map has become filled with businesses that have elements of content as well as processing of content and/or transmission. Today, the information business is composed of increasingly convergent industries, and the media industry is converging with previously distinct industries.

An Alternative Scheme for Describing the Media

Given that terms that describe the media today — like "television,' "magazine," etc. — evoke connotations in most of us that may inhibit conceptualizing about the future media environment, the Program on Information Resources Policy has classification schemes that may be usefully substituted. The goal was to find a simple yet comprehensive framework which could classify the various roles and functions of traditional as well as newer technologies we have called the "media."

The framework we have settled upon, which combines pragmatic simplicity with reasonable inclusiveness . . . consists of three primary components: content, process and format. Organizations engaged in the mass media or communications business are usually engaged in creating, transmitting or processing information for display via one or more of several possible formats.

The content is the information that is provided by the supplier and received by the user. Information, as used in this paper, is broadly defined to encompass news, entertainment, music, commentary, advertising, numerical data, narration, etc. — essentially anything that is transmitted by the design of a sender or at the request of a receiver. (I recognize that information has other meanings growing out of a variety of disciplines, but seek here to use the broadest possible description.)

Process refers to both the handling and transmitting of the information. Among the processing functions are gathering, creating, and storing information. This would include a newspaper reporter researching and writing an article, storing it on a floppy disc for editing, hyphenation and justification by a computer for typesetting and make-up. Another example would be the activities leading to filming a movie, videotaping a tennis demonstration, or creating and providing an access to a computerized data base.

Examples of processing components are the transmission conduits, such as broadcasting, coaxial cable, mail and private parcel delivery, microwave, telephone and the storage/handling modes that include computers, printing presses and paper.

Format, as used in this schema, refers to the form in which the content is made available to the user or is handled by a processor. This may be as hard copy, such as printed words or pictures on paper. It may be an electronic visual representation, such as that created on a video display tube, and could be as words as well as pictures. It may be a mechanical visual representation such as that created by projecting movie film or micro-materials. It may be an aural representation, such as the sounds created by a vibrating speaker cone. And in many cases, several formats are combined, as in the case of most of the content displayed through a television set.

Traditionally, the "media" have been defined primarily by their format — newspaper, book, magazine, radio. More recently, process names have been used to denote the medium, such as "cable," "videocassette," "home computer," etc. Both cable and video cassette, for example, are merely alternative means to broadcasting for delivering content in a video/aural format. Similarly, newspaper publishers may find in the near future that some of what they now put onto paper as part of the traditionally printed product may be more efficiently delivered to the video terminals of only those subscribers requesting such information from the publisher's computer (like classified ads or stock prices). The "newspaper," therefore, may become a service using in part an ink-on-paper format and in part a video format. Increasingly, data base publishers have found that computer processing and video display of their content is an efficient and financially rewarding method of offering their services — although the content may be the same as that which existed in a print format.

Determining just what is content is far from clear, as seen in the computer software business. A floppy disk or other computer storage medium might have a program that enables users to create their own content. In that respect, a spreadsheet program like VisiCalc is much like a business form. But information, such as an article read via a computer termi-nal, has more in common with a traditional print magazine. Yet both are classified as "software" in the current jargon.

Future of New Processes and Formats

Electronic publishing is already a reality. It involves allowing users at home or in the office access to content stored in computers. To date, most of this content has been a repackaging of content originally prepared for print. Income received by publishers from electronically distributed content have been mostly considered extra revenue, much as videocassette revenue from motion pictures is still a relatively small portion of that income stream.

In the future, we may see an increasing volume of content created for and distributed primarily by electronic means. Among some speculative possibilities that various sources have suggested:

— Someday, the daily newspaper, already processed and stored in computers in the publisher's plant, could be "downloaded" to storage media of subscribers during the night via telephone or cable lines, instead of "rolling the press." The subscriber then views the newspaper on a portable flat, high resolution screen that could be carried to the porch, the bus or train.

— Publishers could mass produce their content in the form of "read only memory," or ROM. These computer chips could store the equivalent of a book or magazine. They would be sold in retail stores or sent via the mail.

— Books as well as archival information could be stored on optical video discs, for viewing also on a television screen.

— It is possible — though still not feasible — to have an on-demand on-line video library. That is, the types of video and audio programs and films that are today distributed by cable or cassette, disks or broadcast, could be digitized and stored in a computer, much the way text is stored today. Just as we can call up text information on demand, so may the user at home request to see a particular movie or other program. Then, that viewer and that viewer only, can watch the movie, while other viewers are choosing their own shows. Thus, while today we think of 35 or 54 cable channels being filled simultaneously, in the future, a household might need only two or three cable channels, because they will not have to choose from among the offerings provided by some programmer, but view whatever they want to see, whenever they want to see it, from a library of computer-stored video program. Moreover, once digitized, individuals could create their own programs, by assembling pieces or scenes that producers could provide. For example, they might first select one of several opening scenes, then decide on a comic scene instead of a tragic scene, and so on. This sort of "create your own programming" is already being offered on some optical video discs.

— Computers may be programmed to do more than just be passive storage and transmission devices. They could receive the downloaded newspaper I described a few minutes ago and be programmed to select out those types of articles that the individual subscriber likes to see: for example, the score of the local baseball team, any news about the airline industry, any want ads for used sailboats between 24 and 32 feet and costing less than $40,000. One day, we may have computers that can take a written work and create an abstract from it.

— Publishers of reference works, such as encyclopedias, are already providing online access to users with home computers. As telephone transmission speeds get faster, some customers could decide to have the entire work "downloaded" onto their own mass storage media. Then, after the one time charge for this transmission, they would not have to pay continuing royalties to either the owner of the reference material or the service bureau that provided the computer facility.

They could also make electronic copies to sell or just give to friends.

Implications for Copyright

The concept of copyright was not practical in a society when human memory was the primary repository of records and creativity and not enforceable in the pro-Gutenberg world. The modern notion of copyright is largely a function of the technology of the printing press. It made possible centralized control of the production process for written works.

In the mid-18th century, a confluence of factors, including the steam driven rotary press, made possible relatively cheap reproduction of print and lead to the democratization of the consumption of intellectual property. More modern media forms — film, phonograph records, radio and television broadcasting — shared with the printing press the mass production and distribution of many identical products, also relatively easily controlled by suppliers of the creative works. Thus, the print notion of copyright was readily transferable to these newer forms.

Today, we are looking at a substantial change in the nature of control. Starting with audio tapes and photocopying machines, we have seen a proliferation of inexpensive techniques for demicratizing the production of intellectual property. Video tape machines, floppy disks and other forms of computer-readable storage devices are making it easier for users of content to create, store, reproduce and transmit intellectual property. But instead of simply making a faithful duplicate of the original, computer programs can tinker with original content, creating an output that is fundamentally different from the content entered into the computer, yet which was not specifically anticipated by the creator of the algorithms in the computer program.

These fundamental changes give rise to questions may have to be addressed in the reconsideration of the nature of copyright. Among them are:

— Who is the "author" of "original" material created by a computer program, such as an abstract from a longer article: the computer programmer? the author of the original article or book? the owner of the computer? the computer?

— How does one measure which source has added what elements to a creative work if the digital editing and duplication process leaves no visible trail, unlike penciled marginal notes?

— How, if at all, can duplication and transmission of electronic works by users in the home or office be measured?

— How can one tell the difference between a legally authorized copy and a "bootleg" copy, particularly when dealing with textual material that has come from the computer of the publisher to the computer of the user?

— What mechanisms can ascertain that creators of intellectual property get compensated for their contributions without stunting the development of technological tools that are expanding the process and format options available for these creators?

The challenge for public policymakers is to construct laws and regulations that are flexible enough to respond to very uncertain technological developments and unpredictable market changes. We can be relatively accurate in predicting what the technology already in existence or in the laboratories makes possible. But wrong or premature regulation may stifle otherwise useful developments. Waiting too long to correct an inequity may result in the politically expedient necessity of having to grandfather many exceptions.

Excerpts from the
Testimony of Joseph F. Coates
J. F. Coates, Inc.

I am a futurist, that is, one who earns his living in the systematic study for public and private clients, of long-range trends in American and the global society and their implications for present day decisions. I believe that I can be most useful to the Committee in tracing out some of the major changes that should form a context for radically reconstructed legislation with regard to ownership and access to information, knowledge, and other intellectual property.

Before turning to the trends which are shaping the future, let me suggest several conclusions with regard to legislative needs. That should make clearer what the evidence I present is leading to.

First, it would be a serious mistake to improve the present body of copyright law incrementally. To force the future into a mold of the past and the present would do a disservice to the nation.

Second, actions should occur with some dispatch to stem the flow of court decisions which must force the future into historical arguments, categories, and decisions which are obsolete. The courts have the potential for crippling the future. They are increasingly exercising that potential.

Third, we must anticipate and develop images of the future which focus from the point of view of this committee's deliberation on the role of knowledge and information in shaping society. In that way, new legislation can create a future which will permit the flourishing of information as a commodity and management instrument in society, which, in turn, will stimulate socially, democratically, and economically desirable outcomes.

Finally, many of the dislocations which inevitably must occur in a period of rapid social, economic, and technological transition should be examined from the deeper perspective of desirable social futures, so as to mitigate the temptation to respond to the brief but pressing travail of the moment by sacrificing more socially desirable outcomes right around the corner.

Let me turn now to some major trends in American society, as clues to the implications for information, intellectual property, and questions of the rights of ownership and access.

The central and overarching trend is the continuing movement of the United States into the so-called post-industrial society. The characteristics of the post-industrial society are information industries and the crucial value of new knowledge in the creation of new business and industry out of the great knowledge machine, science, and technology. Complementing this rise of information and knowledge-related industries is a relative decline in the importance of manufacturing, processing, and handling of physical goods.

But there are few sharp breaks with the past. For example, the enormous productivity of agriculture is due in large part to the application of scientific and technological knowledge throughout food production, handling, and processing. Other successful new industries: telecommunications, electronics, microprocessing, genetics, chemistry, and materials, depend on new knowledge out of science and its application as technology.

The centrality of knowledge and information is also radically altering the pattern of the workforce. Depending upon the details of the count, 45–55% of the workforce is now in the information game. Only some 3% are in agriculture, and perhaps another 22% are engaged in the direct manufacture of products; the rest are in other forms of service.

The so-called post-industrial society, therefore, implies a fundamental shift in the concept of what is important in terms of ownership. In the pre-industrial era it was land. In the industrial era it was the instruments of production— physical goods and property. The flourishing of copyright and the patent system, its analog, resulted from issues framed around physical ownership. The copyright of books became important only when books could be easily printed and re- produced. In a very direct way, copyright is a child of the printing press. As the printing press and its analogs decline in importance, so must traditional copyright. Copyright applies to movies because, like books, movies can only be made or reproduced in a few places, permitting ready control and monitoring, but it does not apply to an individual per- formance on stage or in a concert hall.

With the shift of knowledge and information to center stage, economically, socially, and now politically, we must begin to rethink legislation, rules, customs, and regulations dealing with the concepts of property, ownership, and access.

The post-industrial or information-based society has led to the rise of "the intellectual commons." The mass flow of information to and fro in society creates a new intellectual commons in which ideas are generated, rapidly fall into common currency, and their origins or source are lost sight of. Increasingly, all Americans expect full, ready, free, and equal access to information. From a social point of view, that access is central to the preservation and strength of democratic institutions. As the Founding Fathers pointed out, democracy depends upon an informed electorate.

We must, therefore, stimulate and expand the intellectual commons as a safeguard and stimulant of democracy. Many trends move in this direction: the Freedom of Information Act, the National Environmental Policy Act, the openess of con- gressional hearings, are all part of the expanding intellectual commons. The technology of the Xerox machine and its imitators and descendants is a physical tool for stimulating the intellectual commons, as is the home video recorder. In part, the new issue becomes protecting legitimate rights to intellectual property in the face of the higher social legitimacy of that intellectual commons. This is an ascending issue because never before has power been so unequivocally based on knowledge.

A second trend of major importance is that technological devices are blurring many traditional distinctions that form the basis for our thinking about knowledge and information. Dis- tinctions between what is printed and not printed are rapidly blurring as Xerox or floppy discs and computers permit us to make a typewriter or keyboard into a miniature printing plant. As you are very familiar with here on Capitol Hill, a dictated letter can go through a word processor and become a thousand personal letters to a thousand constituents. Technology makes it possible to go directly from voice to electronics, from voice to voice, or from voice to electronics to print, or voice to electronics to print and voice. Soon it will be economically practical as it is now technologically feasible to go from voice to print. We have the capabilities of storage, not only in the traditional archival form, but electronically. Consequently, as technology blurs these distinctions, we must begin to think about what we want to do to positively manage these new technologies from a social point of view. Any legislative concept based merely on a printed or directly intelligible symbol is unsound.

It is worth noting that we are virtually bereft of any theory of the economics of information, and hence of any theory that would, from an economic point, guide fundamental legisla- tion on the cost and value of various mechanisms for preserv- ing the rights of ownership of and access to information.

Collateral to the rise of the information society is the rise to prominence of intellectual inventions. While we are

all well familiar with physical inventions, everything from spacecrafts to the styrofoam coffee cups, we tend not to think of the development of institutional, organizational, and conceptual means of solving problems as inventions. But they are inventions, and they are becoming important.

Let me cite two intellectual inventions. One was pay-as-you- go income tax, invented by Beardsley Ruml in World War II. Obviously, that is a major social invention having a profound value for society in terms of controlling inflation and being able to finance government expenditures. Ruml in no way benefitted from that, other than in satisfaction and prestige.

An interesting mixed case of an intellectual invention with a physical aspect is the highway cloverleaf. The cloverleaf is a major element in modern highway construction throughout the world, and yet to the best of my knowledge, the inventor of the cloverleaf never received any compensation and had no rights to that concept. It would seem perfectly reasonable that every cloverleaf built in the world as a device to speed trans- portation and save lives merits him a reward especially since we routinely reward people who invent such trivial or merely convenient things as styrofoam coffee cups and hula hoops. A major new need of the future will be to expand, elaborate, and perfect the concept of intellectual property and widen the variety of mechanisms for providing rewards.

Another derivitive consequence of the rapid pace of change in the information society is illustrated by the current concern over the illegal reproduction of video tapes and movies. Many things in our society, particularly but not exclusively in the area of entertainment and business (tip sheets and newsletters), have very high short-term economic value which rapidly decays. We may, therefore, need mechanisms which provide strong protection and severe sanctions for illegal use in the short run but become more relaxed and even are eliminated in the slightly longer run. Protecting information ephemera will be a growing problem.

Technology is also making possible infinite variations in written, printed, and graphic materials. In the same way that you on Capitol Hill can take a dictated letter and personalize it for every constituent, similar things can be done with books, voice and video tapes, graphics, maps, and so on. This creates problems and opportunities for protection.

An illustration of the problem of the new information soc- iety is the status of software. Traditionally, software was considered incidental to the development of hardware. As the price of hardware has fallen, and as the use of computers, both mainframe and micro permeates society, it is clear that the life-blood of that system is software, that is, programming. And there is no doubt in my mind that ownership rights should be attached to software, which incidentally is the basis for tax and revenue. But the role of software in various systems dif- fers, and what the rules for protection should be is quite blurred. The need to clarify those points is enormous. The possibilities of minor variations on copyrighted software type are great. One must look out for the potential predatory practices in which minor variations effectively neutralize or infringe the rights of the developer.

Many of these questions would be best solved by mech- anisms that take them out of the formalized court procedures and encourage other kinds of mechanisms such as mediation and arbitration. But again those laws should have built-in safeguards against proceduralization, which is increasingly the bane of our world. So long as the vast legions of lawyers have a stake in complexity, they will work diligently to complexify these matters to feather their own nest, while the longer term interests of society and individuals are thwarted. Forcing the new information technology into old copyright is a bonanza for lawyers and a blow to progress.

Trends in technology are creating new kinds of information

and new kinds of potential copyright, ownership, and access issues. Take, for example, the case of space flights which remotely collect geographic information. These overflights now raise the issues as to who should have the right to deal with that information. It is truly a new perspective on the world; whether any precedent fits is an interesting question. Should someone have the right to information about your property if that right gives them a marginal advantage in knowing something about your property, such as the likelihood of a mineral or oil deposit, which, in turn, may let them effectively cheat you on a purchase of land or mineral rights? This issue is not only a domestic but increasingly an international affair.

Technology is also creating problems about the residence or the location of information. Vast amounts of Canadian business data are now stored in the United States, for example. The residence of data creates conflicts of ownership rights and access in terms of conflicting laws in different countries.

Theft, undesirable practices, and new uses of information are all creating turbulence. I would like to cite a few, to suggest the severity of the consequences of attempting to solve them in terms of already established categories. As we well know, people who own home videos often wish to copy a commercially available tape for their own showing. On the other hand, others are copying these things for re-selling, which is piracy or counterfeiting. The industry is concerned about this, but rather than looking for innovative long-term solutions, they are off on a traditional response based on precedent to constrain the right to reproduce this material. One industry suggests building a tax into the cost of video equipment to repay for the losses from theft, thus raising the price of the equipment. This is clearly an anti-social move because the effect would be to discourage the general use of the new equipment, whereas common sense, business sense, and social interest say, keep the price at a level that will expand use of the new equipment.

Similarly, the print industry, particularly scientific publishers, have been concerned about preventing reproduced copies of their material from circulating. And again we created a foolishly, elaborate system for protecting our rights, rather than finding innovative ways of effectively dealing with the issue. There is very little evidence to suggest that their solution has done anything but create an institutional annoyance and has not stopped the copying of scientific journal information. Again, short-term interests have blinded publishers to long-term alternatives and have led to a stultifying rather than an expansive solution. Bad law lends to its own neglect and to the ultimate disrespect for all law.

Technology is also affecting our language. "Hardware," "software," "micro," "modem," "byte," "bit," "mouse," and "light pen" are becoming common expressions. But the technology has more severe effects on the very style in which we structure information. The technology will inevitably modify our grammar as well as our vocabulary. We are also beginning to think in new linguistic styles as graphics, charts, figures, and tables become more commonplace. And finally, the printed word as seen through the computers and word processors is much more flexible and interactive. I do not know what the consequences of this are for copyright, but the changing nature of language certainly should be considered in your deliberation.

Science is creating some truly new questions in terms of the legal categorization of things increasingly important to the economy such as genetically produced products. By virtue of being living organisms they are the embodiment of a message. It could also be considered a composition of matter. In one case it would be a candidate for copyright; in the other, for patent protection. The one crucial question is what will best serve society over the next several decades.

As a final note of technological change, let me point out that the rapidly evolving technology of encryption may have a radical effect on issues of copyright and protection, since encryption may offer for the first time the practical equivalent of trade secrets accompanying the broad and wide dissemination of knowledge and information in the marketplace. Broadly disseminated information could be understandable only to those who have the key. Whether that is good or bad, and whether that should be encouraged or discouraged, is so new as to be a totally open question.

Finally, in the area of trends, let me note the integration of the global economy is leading even to the export of white collar work. Daily flights from New York City to the island of Jamaica carry white collar work back and forth. The well known Chinese copies by Taiwan and Hong Kong or printed matter have already expanded to Chinese copies of information technology and devices. Integration of the global economy has encouraged worldwide theft of films and video. And the integration of the global economy makes it quite plausible that by the end of the century the software capital of the world could very well become India with its vast repository of under-utilized scientists and engineers trained to the doctoral level. A blobal perspective must be integrated into the future deliberations about copyright and the role of ownership and access on our post-industrial globe.

Let me suggest an image of the future which would inform your deliberations. In my judgement, by the turn of the century, the average American household will have in use and at its disposal telematics equipment, that is, telecommunications and computer equipment and collateral support equipment, equal in value to the average family car. As this technology permeates society, legislation on copyright, that is, legislation framing the rights to ownership and access and use, should take into account the need to promote and stimulate this intrinsically democratizing, fundamentally revolutionary, and central economic and social wave sweeping over American society.

**Excerpts from the
Statement of David Lange**
Professor of Law, Duke University

As you know, copyright is an amalgam of property law principles bent to the service of a rather simple bargain. A limited term of protection against copying is granted to an author's original expression in exchange for the dedication of that expression to the public domain at the end of the term. The public ordinarily benefits at least twice from this bargain: once, when the original expression is first created, and then again when the expression is added to the public domain from which anyone may borrow freely to fashion new works. Although a copyright belongs to an author during its term, the ultimate purpose of this bargain is not to protect authors but rather to enrich the public domain. The cardinal principle in copyright law, then, is that any decision to extend the law or to recognize new interests ought to be based on a realistic expectation that one day the public domain will bear new fruit.

If the law were as simple as this bargain, there would be few occasions for betrayal of the public domain. Unfortunately, however, though the bargain is simple in concept, it is the essence of complexity in practice. Property law is inherently difficult. Worse, there are terms of art at work in this field of law which are as defiant of conventional understanding as the idea of a vest with sleeves. Speak of writing and the ordinary person thinks of words on a page; but in copyright terminology, a "writing" takes on constitutional dimensions. It may include music, painting and sculpture, as well as photography, motion pictures, sound recordings and more. Similarly, the idea of an "original" expression must be understood as having a distinctive copyright significance. Creativity, in the conventional sense, plays only a minor role in copyright law. What "originality" requires is not invention (which is more nearly the separate province of patent law) but rather an absence of copying. And so it goes from one peculiar term to the next. In copyright law we have a complex system of rules made even more complex by an *ad hoc* terminology. The potential for confusion is immense. And when there is discord the loudest voices tend to be raised in the service of particular copyright interests rather than on behalf of the public domain.

An additional, intensely human phenomenon also accounts for the occasional betrayal of the public domain. The bargain between an author and the public, so simple and gratifying when first struck, can appear virtually Faustian as the end of a copyright term approaches. Few proprietors of successful works can brave the passage of those works into the public domain with a simple show of cheerful equanimity. To the contrary, copyright lawyers are often asked to play the role of Daniel Webster as they seek some imaginative way to cheat the Devil and avoid the public domain. The consequence of these undertakings is a hellish collection of intellectual property theories just beyond the edges of copyright — theories in unfair competition, trade secrets, rights of publicity, trademarks and the like — which the inventive lawyer relies on in an effort to keep the author's property in his work alive forever.

Beyond these commonplace occasions for betrayal of the public domain, there is the still more pervasive fact that the subject matter of this species of property is completely intangible. A book in its physical form is something we can see and touch; but the copyright in that book is an abstraction beyond the evidence of our senses. We "see" a copyright only imperfectly, inexactly, as a kind of reflection in our mind's eye. To be sure, when we speak of a personal property interest in the physical copy of a book, we have to understand that legal conception of property as an abstraction — but at least we understand what the subject matter of the property interest is. Our senses tell us what the book feels like, what it looks like, how much it weighs and so on. In copyright, however, the unavoidable conceptual complexities inherent in all property law are magnified many times by the fact that no one can ever be sure that anyone else understands the subject matter of the law in the same way. I show you copies of two novels — one, *Moby Dick* by Herman Melville; the other, *Jaws* by Peter Benchley. Anyone who can see can tell one copy from the other. But no one can be sure whether *Jaws* itself is a "copy" of *Moby Dick* in the sense in which that term is used in copyright. We can agree on the consequences of copying — at least enough to be able to make some sense of the law — but as to the fact of copying itself we must always entertain some doubt. Our senses cannot help us and our minds may differ.

Of course, these troublesome attributes of copyright have not kept it from evolving into a subject of great practical utility. Our conceptual grasp of the law sometimes exceeds our practical grasp of definitions — sometimes, like Mr. Justice Stewart in the obscenity cases, we must content ourselves with "knowing" a copyrightable interest only when we "see" it. If we are not unduly distressed by the role intuition must then play in the law, we can get by. But there is still an unusual and nagging potential for misunderstanding in the law of copyright, a vulnerability which is particularly apt to result in betrayal of the public domain when this law is subjected to the stresses and pressures that accompany efforts to secure recognition for new technology.

The betrayals I have in mind are likely to take one of two forms. On the one hand it is possible that an interest will receive insufficient recognition in law because it is insufficient-

ly recognized in fact. Choreography once was excluded from the full protection of copyright on just this ground. An art form inadequately understood by most of us in its own terms, it was protected under the 1909 Act only when presented in a form of expression we could appreciate. Sound recordings are another example of expression which the law of copyright may once have rejected because of an unwillingness to come to terms with a peculiarity in the medium of expression itself. Indeed, it might be said that sound recordings offer the best example of what can happen when the law of copyright fails to meet the challenge of a new technology so that a legitimate form of expression fails in turn to achieve adequate recognition and protection. Arguably, had it not been for the passage of the Sound Recording Amendment of 1971, the vulnerability of the recording industry ot "piracy" might have brought that industry to ruin. I do not mean to endorse this argument; I merely acknowledge its plausibility in order to make a point beyond it — namely, that insufficient copyright protection can mean reduced incentives to the production of expression and thus ultimately reduced contributions to the public domain.

A more serious form of betrayal, however, takes place when an interest is protected which ought not be — or when an interest is given excessive or misconceived protection. In either case something may then be withheld from the public domain which properly belongs there. And in either case, technology may be implicated in the error. I think, for example, that if the technology of the chromolithograph had not distracted Mr. Justice Holmes (in *Bleistein* v. *Donaldson Lithographing Co.*, 188 U.S. 239 (1903)) he might have written a more thoughtful opinion on the eligibility of advertising for copyright protection. More recently, in a case involving the sole motion picture record of the assassination of President Kennedy (*Time, Inc.* v. *Bernard Geis & Associates*, 293 F. Supp. 130 (S.D.N.Y. 1968)), the court might have come to a more secure conclusion had it understood that public access to the event itself could not possibly be foreclosed by the law of copyright — in other words, had the court understood that the copyright owner's claims in that case were profoundly misconceived.

In these examples and many others, the law of copyright has failed to respond adequately to the challenges posed from time to time by new technology. In the deepest sense, perhaps, the explanation for these failures may be found in the intangibility of the subject matter of copyright and the vulnerability of the law to misunderstanding. This dilemma is inherent in the subject and cannot altogether be avoided. And yet, because a mistake in copyright law is potentially quite serious, with adverse consequences for the public domain running well beyond the initial mistake itself, it is important that we attempt to meet each new copyright proposal with the most painstaking efforts at careful, independent analysis. In one sense, to be sure, that analysis inevitably must be *ad hoc*. Precisely for that reason, however, it ought to be undertaken against a rigorous background of procedure agreed upon in advance and applied uniformly from case to case.

In effect, what I propose is a kind of civil procedure for new copyright legislation — a system imposing the legislative equivalent of burdens of proof and adverse presumptions to be met by anyone who proposes to extend the scope of existing copyright protection or who proposes protection for a new interest. For the latter kind of proponent, there might well be additional threshold tests intended to identify those new forms of expression which are sufficiently like existing copyright interests to deserve further consideration. No proposal ought to be rejected out of hand merely because it involves expression in a new form. If the expression is otherwise conceptually akin to the established subject matter of copyright, if it meets at least the established minimum requirements of originality, and if the new medium can be seen

434

as reasonably analogous to the established "writings" which are the province of statutory copyright, then it would seem that the proponent ought to have at least an attentive audience as he argues the new interest's entitlement to recognition. I would suggest, however, that even when these threshold requirements have been met, the new interest ought to face a still challenge amounting to a heavy burden of proof and a clear presumption against recognition. Each new copyright interest, by definition, represents a potential encroachment into the territory of the public domain. No new interest ought ever to be recognized unless and until the consequences of that encroachment have been explored in the fullest practical sense. It is reasonable to require the proponent of a new interest to bear the burden of showing why any intrusion into the public domain ought to be allowed — and equally reasonable to presume that the public domain will be protected until that burden has been discharged.

How, then, can the proponent of a new interest meet this additional burden and overcome the presumption against recognition? First, I would suggest, he must demonstrate the susceptibility of the new expression to a reasonably clear and satisfactory statutory definition — and, equally important, to a clear, common conceptual understanding — so that the dimensions of the resulting copyright are intelligible. An interest that cannot be defined and cannot be understood probably should not be made the subject of copyright protection. Computer programs in FORTRAN or BASIC, for example, probably meet this test; but programs in microchip reduction may not.

Second, a proponent must succeed not merely in defining the interest in an affirmative sense; he should be able to define it as well in terms of what it is not. No new interest should be recognized unless the public domain adjacent to that interest is fully redefined and reaffirmed. If, for example, it proves necessary to legislate in the so-called field of "home recording" it will be equally important to affirm the nature of those private rights which are not to be affected. Copyright is an essentially provincial field of law; it ought not be permitted to encroach too far or too easily into private lives.

Third, a proponent ought to be expected to sponsor a careful competitive analysis of all the costs and benefits of the proposed legislation. If, for example, the motion picture industry is to suggest that the "first sale" doctrine ought to be revised in the case of video cassettes, then it must also explain how and why the tape rental industry should bear the adverse consequences, if any, of that change. What may be at stake in a case like this are economic interests developed in reliance on a well-established concept amounting to a vested interest in the public domain. If so, it will not ordinarily be sufficient merely to say that the proposed legislation will extend the benefits of copyright to existing proprietors or make them more secure. To the contrary, unless a superior claim can be shown on some other ground, the interest derived from the public domain should prevail. Even dire warnings about the likelihood of industry-wide retrenchment should not lead automatically to changes in the copyright law. Copyright can be an efficient form of institutional bargain, but it is not intended to save buggy-whip manufacturers from ruin.

Fourth, a proponent should be able to show how the new legislation ultimately will enhance the public domain. Unless this is likely to be a practical consequence, new or extended protection will be unwarranted.

Finally, a proponent must be able to defend the new interest in terms of all of the principal provisions of the copyright law — or else suggest how *ad hoc* provisions can be fashioned which will meet the more particular requirements of the new interest without simultaneously converting the entire field into Balkan provinces. If, for example, microchip

programs are to claim the protection of copyright, should all provisions of the present law apply? Should the term of protection be the same as it is for conventional books written by conventional authors? Should these programs be impressed with some form of compulsory license? Should the provisions for remedies be revised? If the answers to these and similar questions require substantial rewriting of the existing Act, then it is likely that the law of copyright ought not to extend to this form of interest. After all, when a garment requires sleeves it makes little sense to call it a vest.

In outlining these questions, and in suggesting the propriety of others like them, I do not suppose that Congress or this subcommittee ought to be bound by any rigid approach to the delicate task of decision-making. I intend merely to describe the general nature of a procedure that ought to attend the passage of new copyright legislation. Ordinarily, a proponent ought to bear the burden of establishing the need for the legislation against the weight of an adverse presumption. The ultimate issues will not necessarily be easier to resolve, but the interposition of that presumption will make it less likely that the public domain will be ignored or too easily thrust aside as new interests and new technologies command increasing attention.

Excerpts from the
Testimony of Fred W. Weingarten
Program Manager, Communication and Information Technologies Program, Office of Technology Assessment

A number of OTA studies have touched on the topic of copyright protection, and they have, on occasion, raised intellectual property issues that OTA regards as important and worthy of consideration by Congress. For example, in the report *Computer-Based National Information Systems*, OTA projected future developments in computer technology and developed a general overview of the relevant policy issues that would confront Congress over the next decade. Briefly discussing computer software protection, OTA concluded:

". . . the issue of computer software protection appears sufficiently important and unsettled to warrant continued congressional attention."

In the report *Informational Technology and Its Impact on American Education*, we looked to see whether the lack of adequate protection for computer software and data bases might be a barrier to the development of computer-based curriculum. OTA compared and evaluated the use of five basic types of protection: trade secrets, trademarks, patents, the law of unfair competition, and copyrights. Each of these mechanisms appears to protect information to some degree — some more than others — but each also has significant limitations. Three specific questions regarding educational software were raised:

- How should software be protected, while recognizing the competing interests of groups who use software or benefit from its use?

- How can piracy and the various types of misappropriation of software be better dealt with?

- How can the incentives be increased for software innovation, especially educational software, given the limitations and costliness of the existing remedies for its protection?

Technological Trends

It has become common in the press and popular literature to speak about the new "Information Society" or "Information Age." Whether or not such statements suffer from journalistic exaggeration, we are clearly in the middle of a fundamental transformation of the way information is created, stored, transmitted, and used, not just in our own society, but worldwide. These changes are based on rapid technological advances in both computers and communications which have been brought about by progress in such fundamental areas as microelectronics, photonics, and satellites. These advances are providing us with a vast smorgasmoard of new products and services.

But change in technology, *per se*, is only part of the story. Along with technological innovation, we are experiencing changes in the way that technology is used and offered in the marketplace. These changes in industry structure may generate as many public policy issues — particularly with respect to the area of intellectual property — as does the technology itself. Both trends must be taken into account.

I will concentrate on five areas of change that seem most relevant to the purposes of this subcommittee:

1. The variety of choice.
2. The increasing storage and use of information in electronic form.
3. The enhanced social and economic value of information.
4. The changing marketplace.
5. The internationalization of information technology and services.

After briefly describing these changes, I will outline some possible issues and policy questions to which these trends may give rise.

Variety of Choice

One way in which intellectual property has always been protected has been to keep it secret or to make it exclusive. Before the advent of public libraries, for example, often only scholars or other select groups of individuals had access to collections of books, documents, and manuscripts. Similarly, today in some cases, we limit access of information to those who own it or who can pay for it as in the case of proprietary information and commercial data bases. The increased availability and diversity of new information technologies to the public will enhance the public access to information. Thus it may undermine the protection of some form of intellectual property.

Not so long ago, if we were average home or business consumers of information technology we had only a few choices open to us. For communication services, we had, what is referred to in the telephone community as POTS (for Plain Old Telephone Service). For video, we had a relatively few channels of broadcast television. For audio, AM and FM radio, plus records and magnetic tape were our choices. Computers were large, expensive beasts and there were relatively few in number (at least as compared with current figures).

Now look at what is or will soon be happening.

Under the stimulus of technology and deregulation, vendors are bringing to market a wide variety of specialized communication services. There are local networks for use within an office to tie together word processors, desk-top computers, and mainframe computers. Specialized carriers are beginning to provide new media that compete with the telephone company's "local loop" of copper wire. Cellular radio offers low cost and widely available mobile telephone service. Two-way interactive cable, originally conceived of as a system to distribute television programming, is being adapted to provide data communication for business transactions. AT&T and its competitors are all developing new enhanced long distance services, based on satellites, fiber optics, or even an old fashioned microwave radio. By the next century, communications engineers see us as approaching what they refer to as an Integrated Services Digital Network (ISDN), in which one can transmit information of any type (voice, video, facsimile, computer data) at high speed between any two points on earth — all over an interconnected network.

A similar diversity also characterizes the computer market. Supercomputers, large mainframes, mini's, and desktop or personal computers are all commercially available. At the smallest end of the scale, it becomes hard for a consumer to even recognize that he or she is purchasing a computer — microprocessors are now standard components of a myriad of products. The capability of these machines continue to grow rapidly with performance/cost ratios nearly doubling every two years.

For television watchers, traditional broadcasting is now being challenged by two-way cable, low power broadcast, direct broadcast satellites, multipoint distribution, video disks (both optical and capacitance), video cassettes and, in the future, high definition television. Audio technology is experiencing new competition. AM stereo is becoming available and an audio laser disk has recently been introduced to the market.

We should not leave out of this list the advent of new technologies for the creation of video and audio programming. Computer graphics is coming of age as far as it is becoming increasingly cost-effective for commercial producers to invest in very large scale computer capacity to generate graphical imagery. (Supercomputer manufacturers cite the entertainment industry as a new market for their machines.) Much advertising that we see on television depends on computer graphics, as do the high tech special effects of movies such as "Tron." Some graphics experts say that we are within a decade of being able to create fully realistic images, even of people, by computer graphs. In the same way, sound generation is advancing for applications that range from the creative — providing a new medium for performance, to the more mundane — as a cost effective replacement for a human voice.

All of these new technologies supplement, extend, or improve in some sense existing information services provided to the home or office. Some other proposed services and products seem to be new in concept, as well. For example, Teletext and Videotext services will not only provide to the home or office terminal access to information in a new form but also a host of new types of services. Promoters are already experimenting with electronic news, in-house shopping and banking, and electronic mail. Remote medical consultation, education, and other social services could also be provided.

Electronic Digital Information

Because many of the new information and communications technologies will require that information can be handled in an electronic and digital form less and less information will be maintained in traditional paper form.* Office automation will accelerate this trend. With the proliferation of word processors and personal desk-top computers new information will originate in an electronic form, with paper being used for copies. Automated tellers, supermarket checkout systems, and other computer-based transaction systems also collect and create information in digital electronic form. Moreover, all forms of information — telephone conversations, audio and video recordings, photographs, and television signals — can and, in the future, will be stored, communicated and accessed in electronic digital form.

Because electronic information is vulnerable in new ways — for example, such as systems failure and misappropriation — this increased use of information in electronic form has implications for the protection of intellectual property. And intellectual property laws, designed to protect information stored on paper, may become increasingly less effective in an electronic age.

The Information Market

In part spurred by technological innovation, we are experi-

---

*The term "Digital" is a technical term that refers to information that is stored or transmitted in the form of binary bits.

encing the rapid growth of a market for information. On the demand side, for example, business is starting to view information and knowledge as a critical factor of production. Innovation, the creation of new products and services, both generates and is based on the use of information. Some futurists even maintain that, by the end of this century, most workers will be employed in an information, or knowledge, industry and that information will be the principal export commodity from any highly industrialized nation. A major problem that affects many public policy questions including that of intellectual property rights is how to measure the value of information as a market commodity.

The challenge for intellectual property legislation will be in protecting the content of information systems. Computers need programs and data. Broadcasters need programming. Videotex providers need information services. We use the term "software" to refer to this content. In somewhat simplified terms, software is the information processed and delivered by information technology.

By many measures, it seems reasonable to expect that software will be much more important in our future economy than hardware. For many, if not most, information technologies, the market resembles that for razors and blades; few machines and many programs. Video game suppliers have been operating on this theory since they first came to market. Large computer installations, have long passed the crossover point where investments in software outweigh those in hardware. Some estimates place the ratio at four dollars of investment in software for every dollar invested in hardware. As a result, the commercial market for computer software is growing rapidly. One market research group predicts, for example, that computer software sales in the US will triple from $4.5 to $13.5 billion by 1986. While owners of small computers are not yet to the point of such major proportional investments in software, they are expected to approach it over the next few years. Moreover, providing information services and producing information software entails a growing proportion of employment. In 1982, the Bureau of Labor Statistics estimates that over 751 thousand people were working as programmers and system analysts — far more than those employed to manufacture computers.

Changing Industrial Structure

Intellectual property issues will also be affected by changes in the structure of the information industry, many of which will be due to actions taken by the federal government. The most significant of these changes will be in the direction of increased competition. Although the impact of these changes are bound to be significant, their exact nature is still unclear.

The best known change is the deregulation and break-up of AT&T. Deregulation will, in effect, allow the entry of eight very large firms into the information product and services industry (those firms being AT&T and the seven regional operating companies). The expectation and hope of those promoting deregulation is that with the research and manufacturing capability of the telephone companies released in the competitive marketplace, the rate of innovation and marketing of new products and services will be accelerated.

Also, the recent tendency of the FCC to allow for greater freedom in the use of the broadcast spectrum will have a major impact on the structure of several markets. For example, private broadcast communication systems will bypass, and increasingly compete with, local telephone facilities.

The structure of the domestic industry will also be affected by increased international competition. Whereas in the past, the United States has held an unchallengeable lead in innovation in information technology, competition has picked up considerably. In the hardware market, we are already long past the point where foreign nations follow our lead. In computers, Japanese firms are now competitive at all levels. In

consumer electronics, the Japanese have led the way in VCR and, now, audio optical disk technology. The French and British, among others, have been in the forefront in developing Teletext and Videotext. There is no reason to believe that competition will not become equally severe in the software areas, raising the economic stakes for US firms and increasing the pace of innovation.

Internationalization of Information Technology

Information systems are becoming increasingly international. In the first place, the technology is, in some sense, inherently international in that it ignores national boundaries. Broadcast satellites and high-power radio and television transmitters regularly spill across national boundaries. And the value of telecommunications systems is enhanced when they are interconnected. Hence, there has always been an incentive to connect systems across national boundaries, an incentive reflected in the current move toward the ISDN.

The international market for programming will continue to grow. Broadcasters, seeking to fill an insatiable supply of entertainment and information channels with video programming are turning to foreign sources and are, in turn, selling US programs abroad. The BBC has long been a cultural mainstay of American Public Broadcasting, and the British have a fascination for <u>Dallas</u>, but that market will broaden substantially.

Faced with these trends, international diplomacy and commerce is increasingly finding that international information flow and trade pose important and very difficult problems among nations. Among these problems are questions pertaining to the protection of intellectual property.

Questions and Implications

The advance of technology, the changing industry structure, and the enhanced value of information raise a number of questions about the protection of intellectual property. Given the conflict of basic interests involved — the future of the US economy, fairness, and the needs to preserve the basic rights of citizens, these issues need to be explored by Congress when considering legislation affecting intellectual property.

Balance of Societal Interests

In an information age, the social and political value of information and knowledge will be enhanced. And individuals, if they are to effectively participate in and equitably share the benefits of an information society, will need to have greater access to knowledge and information. The door to social and economic opportunity will be more widely open to the literate — to those who have access to and know how to use information resources. Yet, as OTA pointed out in its education report, the trend toward an information marketplace, where more and more information is bought and sold, could overrun those public interests and create a new underclass based on lack of access to education and to information.

American concerns have traditionally sought to provide free public access to information. Public libraries were predicated on that belief. For example, many of the public libraries built by Andrew Carnegie at the turn of the century have above their doors the phrase "Free to All." Similarly, public schools, dating back to the 1860s, were created in the belief that only an educated, literate society can govern itself.

In ancient China the public's right to information was provided for in a somewhat different fashion. I have been told, for example, that in China at that time it was not considered a crime to steal a book. The story may be apocraphal, but the point it illustrates is valid.

While social and political concerns may call for providing increased access to information, economic concerns may call for greater information protection and exclusivity. Earlier, for example, we observed that information technology and, in particular, information products and services, are becoming major components of the US economy. The implication of that observation is that policies that encourage the innovation and the development of that industry are vital to the health of the US economy. Certainly, the information industry argues that strengthened protection of its inventions is vital to stimulating the development of new product and services.

Intellectual property law addresses the conflict between the need to protect rights to information in order to increase the incentive for innovation and the need to insure the freest possible flow of information. In an information society, the stakes are higher on both sides of that equation and mechanisms for protection of intellectual property become both more important and more difficult.

Feasibility of Protection
Given the changing nature of information, the trends in information and communications technologies, and the changing nature of the information market, a number of fundamental questions are raised about our ability to effectively control the use of information in traditional ways. There are a number of problems with the traditional mechanisms:

- Information in electronic form does not seem to fit comfortably into the centuries old models that underlie intellectual property protection.

- The growth in "value" of information raises the incentive to "steal" it.

- Technology, widely and inexpensively available, carries with it the capability of misappropriating it. The personal computer, the VCR, the audio cassette, soon even the in-home Xerox machine, all provide easy access for illicit copying.

Given these problems, we may need to develop new techniques to protect intellectual property that are more appropriate to electronic technologies.

Potential Market Distortions
One of the most noticeable characteristics of information technology is the trend toward an extraordinary diversity of products and services. Some of these will compete directly with each other, some will offer significant differences. All, however, will be in competition for limited consumer and business dollars, and not all will survive the test of the marketplace. In this intensely competitive marketplace, with large sums at stake, firms will be looking for any advantage. In some cases, they will see the ability to protect their information products as providing an important competitive edge.

Changes in the copyright law may favor one product or service, or one technology or type of company over another. A public policy question arises as to the extent that Congress should consciously try to influence that outcome or should concentrate on trying to provide a "neutral playing field" for the competitors. In our education study, for example, some publishers told us that, in the absence of adequate copyright protections, they would continue to concentrate on the mass market for video games rather than on more expensive, longer payoff educational software.

Related Laws and Alternatives
Copyright is only one area of law now struggling to remain relevant in the face of changes in information technology and the need to protect property interests. OTA's education study listed five areas of law. To the list of five presented earlier, I would add a sixth, computer crime legislation — that is, legislation that specifically makes it a federal crime to use computers as tools in the conduct of criminal activities.

In addition to legal controls, there are also technological ones. Piracy can be reduced, for example, by encrypting cable and broadcast television signals and by developing more sophisticated copy protection for computer programs. Of course, mitigating against the development of security technology is the growing sophistication of those who wish to break the protection and steal information.

Thus, an important question is the role copyright protection plays with respect to these other forms of control. It may be that certain intellectual property problems brought before this subcommittee would be better handled through changes in patent law, criminal law, or simply left to the technologists for solution.

Conclusion
For the foreseeable future, Congress will be the focus of numerous efforts to modify and update copyright law. Several bills have already been introduced this year and are now under consideration by the subcommittee. The flow will not likely ease up. These pressured arise, at least in part, both from the rapid advances in information technology and from the growing importance of information and innovation in our society.

In responding to these legislative proposals, Congress will need to adopt a broad perspective that includes at least three dimensions — 1) technological breadth, 2) pace of change, and 3) mechanism of protection.

Technological Breadth — The future holds in store for us a wide variety of new information services and new mechanisms for delivering them. While these technologies are diverse, they are similar insofar as their primary utility rests in the "software," or information base that makes them do work, entertain us, or inform us. Hence, copyright law affects them all, and consideration of modifications to that law need to account for the full range of technologies.

Pace of Change — Rapid change is another characteristic of today's information technology. This change is due both to technological innovation and competition in the marketplace. A very promising product or service may not survive in the marketplace, either because consumers do not want it or because another, even more attractive substitute comes along to take its place. One of the natural hazards of legislating in this environment is that the time frame for legislation is slower than that for innovation. By the time the law is changed, the problem may be different. It will be important to take a long-term view of technological development in assessing legislative options.

Mechanisms for Protection — The notion of protecting information rights is imbedded in a number of laws, ranging from copyright and patents to bills on computer crime and personal privacy. In addition, advances in security technology may allow information producers to protect their products better by controlling their distribution and use. Finally, in the international arena, US protections interact with those of foreign governments. As we experience increasing transnational flows of information, the relationship between US law and those of foreign governments needs to be taken into account. Otherwise, dissonance between those laws may inadvertently disrupt a desired flow of information.

> **Excerpts from the**
> **Statement of John F. Banzhaf III**
> *Professor of Law, National Law Center*
> *George Washington University*

Twenty years ago the computer industry was in its infancy, but already a large and rapidly growing baby. There were over 20,000 large computers in operation at the time valued at over five billion dollars, and an estimated one billion dollars had already been spent on computer programs to operate them. Yet, strangely enough, there was virtually no legal protection available for these programs, and thus little incentive to develop general purpose programs or to share existing programs, except as a computer sales tool.

Why was this? The Copyright Office had a policy against recognizing copyright protection for programs, apparently based upon a lack of understanding of what they were and the various forms in which they existed. Technical people familiar with programs probably had no knowledge of the copyright law, and of its possible application to protect these newly emerging and very valuable forms of intellectual property. Even the lawyers who presumably represented entities in the computer industry did not know enough about the two fields — computer programming and copyright law — to put the two together and make a persuasive case for copyright protection.

So, by default, the task fell to me as a second-year law student at Columbia Law School. As part of a project to see if computer programs could be copyrighted, I wrote two programs — one on paper and one on magnetic tape — and brought them down to the Copyright Office seeking registration. After some discussion, including my explanation of what they were and how they worked, the Copyright Office reversed its previous policy and on May 4, 1964 agreed for the first time to reigster and recognize copyrights on computer programs.

This was my first major exposure to the wide and probably growing gap between people knowledgeable about law, and those knowledgeable about science and technology: a gap which in another context was referred to by C.P. Snow as "The Two Cultures."

My next experience with this critical communications gap occurred shortly thereafter. My copyright law research had led me, of course, to realize that Congress was then considering a major revision of the statutory copyright law; the first major revision since almost the turn of the century. Yet in searching through all of the study committee records I found only three references to the possible impact of data processing on the copyright law, or of the possible need to amend the copyright law to deal with this major new development. And, Mr. Chairman, all of these references began by saying, "Well, I don't feel competent, because I don't understand these machines well enough," or "I don't understand this business either."

So, on June 17, 1965, virtually upon my graduation from law school, I appeared before another House Judiciary Subcommittee to testify "as the sole and very unofficial representative of the data processing community." I pointed out the need to amend the proposed copyright revision to accommodate data processing, and suggested an amendment. No one from the industry or elsewhere supported this proposal, nor did anyone from any other group oppose it.

As difficult as it may be to believe, this already major industry — probably the fastest growing new industry at that time with clear implications for the future — was totally ignored in considering copyright law revisions. I can only suggest that the reason, once again, was the inability of people in one field to know about and keep up with important developments in another — a problem which is already growing more and more serious as scientific knowledge and even scientific disciplines multiply, and as the rate of technological development continues to accelerate.

What then can Congress do to deal with this problem, and to prevent such serious oversights from happening again? One answer might be to seek to recruit and retain more staff members with scientific and technical backgrounds. Such people might be better able than those without such backgrounds to determine which technologies would be affected by Congressional action, or would be most in need of it. They might also be better able to communicate with people in these fields, and to seek out their input when specialized information might be useful.

As a simple example of the latter problem, I can cite from my own experience the reapportionment area, where lawyers and legislators adopted a number of weighted voting schemes to deal with the "one man, one vote" Supreme Court mandate. None of the lawyers on either side of these issues apparently realized that there might be mathematical problems involved with these plans, nor that there existed a branch of mathematics — called "game theory" — designed to deal with it. And naturally the people who knew about the mathematics paid little attention to the problems of reapportionment. It was only the fact that I came across the problem doing research for another law review article, and was aware of the existence of this mathematical discipline, which resulted in their analysis and eventual ban.

Another far-reaching proposal for dealing with this problem of emerging technologies is to consider setting up a special committee in each House of Congress composed solely of legislators with scientific or technical backgrounds — much as the Judiciary Committees are composed of legislators with legal backgrounds. As to which of these disciplines — law or science — is more important in dealing with these problems, I can only say that most scientists I know can read and understand a judicial opinion or a statute a lot better than most lawyers can read and understand a research report, an equation, or a statistical analysis.

In the longer run we will probably even have to even do more. Looking probably no later than the year 2000, I would suggest that we will need an entirely new science or discipline simply to keep track of developments in all of the others. Such a scientific discipline — NEXIALISM: the science of joining in an orderly fashion the knowledge of one field of learning with that of other fields — has already been proposed by author A.E. van Vogt. Unless some progress in this direction is made soon, none of us will be able to keep up with anything, and we may literally find ourselves drowning in our own data.

Returning to the field of copyright law, I would suggest that I see no logical, legal, or policy reason why computer chips should not be entitled to copyright protection. Indeed, I will go even further and join my colleague Professor Irving Kayton and predict that genetically engineered works — *i.e.*, spliced and recombinant DNA microorganisms created by molecular biologists and genetic engineers — can also be protected under the new copyright law, just as computer programs were found to fit within the old law. Indeed, even further reaching applications, including long-chain polymer organic compounds, and organic data-processing devices, could enjoy copyright protection under the existing statute.

But this does not mean, of course, that Congress should not carefully examine and reevaluate the copyright statute in response to changing technological development. Although the protection may be upheld under the existing statute, this certainly doesn't mean that there will be the requisite certainty for financial planning, or the most appropriate scope of protection.

I recall that when I sought copyright protection for computer programs, the principal barrier was a turn-of-the-century case involving player piano rolls with holes in them. Although I have as much respect for precedent as the next lawyer, I could not see why copyright protection for computer programs recorded on magnetic tape should depend on whether a clever lawyer could adequately distinguish punched paper tape from magnetic recording tape.

In concluding, Mr. Chairman, I would like to say a word in

favor of copyright protection. Although I was at one time a patent attorney, and although as an investor I have several technical patents, I nevertheless always had a soft spot in my heart for copyright protection. Patents are probably more prestigious, and provide a broader scope of protection than copyrights, in the sense that no one may practice the subject matter of the patent even if they independently discover it. But patents are expensive and difficult to get, seem to be regularly struck down by the courts, and provide a very broad monopoly.

In contrast, copyrights are very easy and quick to obtain, tend to be sustained, and although providing a limited protection only against copying, they also provide a wide range of very effective enforcement mechanisms. In short, the tradeoff seems to be a good one — the creator prevents others from copying his original work at very little expense, and is thereby encouraged not only to create but to share his creation. In turn, the public gains the use of the work at a cost which is kept reasonable by the threat that an exorbitant fee will encourage others to duplicate the work — *e.g.*, a computer program, a chip, etc. — without copying from the copyright holder, and then make it available to the public for less.

75: THE FUTURE OF COPYRIGHT

David Ladd

Securing it, in a time of rapid technological and political change, should be seen as a humanist endeavor

This audience needs no primer from me to understand that the principal source of strain on copyright is the succession of marvelous new machines for using and enjoying protected works, appearing at a wrenching pace. You know, firsthand, the problems of reprography, of the control of inputting protected works into electronic information systems, of the rapidly oncoming electronic libraries and of piracy, which in many parts of the world is rampant.

Nowadays a vast new array of technological innovations continues to test our understanding of authorship and copyright and our will to vindicate their values. Authors' and publishers' rights become difficult to enforce as we move away from the print culture and confront a surge of space-age apparatus that enables the broad-based dissemination and simultaneous reception by huge audiences of almost unimaginable quantities of creative works.

In the copyright world there is a prevailing mood of dread that brilliant technologies will overwhelm authorship and copyright. There is danger. But the greater danger is that of despairing and accepting that result as inevitable. Or of doing nothing to avert it.

As one surveys the various new technologies, including photocopying, cable television, satellite transmissions, computers and videotaping, certain common characteristics emerge:

1. A trend toward the increased importance of display and performance for the dissemination of "traditional" works.

2. Widespread consumer ownership of instruments for display and performance, and for copying for such display, performance and use.

Ladd is the U.S. Register of Copyrights, and this article was adapted from a speech he made recently to the International Publishers Association meeting in Mexico City.

3. The appearance, along with new technologies, of doubt or ambiguity about the very applicability of copyright control, and, until the doubt is resolved, the unchecked spread of unauthorized uses which are then difficult to bring within legal control (for example, cable and videorecording).

4. The practical unenforceability of traditional copyright rights by traditional means against uses which are increasingly private, not readily detectable and yet enormous in scale.

Copyright in the past—at least in those countries with highly developed jurisprudence in intellectual property—adapted, and adapted rather well, to technological change.

The Library of Congress Test

Technological innovation is not new. But its pace is now unprecedentedly fast, and accelerating.

I won't attempt to discuss the multitude of problems in accommodating copyright to these new technologies. But there is an important project underway in the Library of Congress in the United States which I would like to focus upon, because it embodies so much of the hopeful opportunities and anxious dangers which we sense are rapidly enveloping us.

The Copyright Office in 1983 issued a comprehensive report evaluating that portion of our copyright law which specifically deals with library and archival reproduction and distribution of works. Of course, the central concern of that report was the central problem in 1975: library photocopying. And, while photocopying is still a vigorously, and often bitterly, debated issue, a major portion of our report was given over to the newer technologies, including computerization of library services, electronic publishing, new machine-readable formats for publications, and the like.

We tried to keep in mind the Librarian of Congress's constant reminder that new technologies are not necessarily, not even generally (in his term),

"displacive." Print publishing will not disappear, not even atrophy. Electronic libraries will not eclipse reprography: at some point a user will usually print out a hard copy which, earlier, he or she would have photocopied. But as we prepared the report, we realized as well that analogizing the highly automated, telecommunications-linked libraries of the future (serving a population where home computing and personal reprography will be normal) to the age of the coin-operated photocopier was fruitless.

Roughly contemporaneous with our photocopying report, the Library of Congress embarked upon an experiment to study and apply optical disk technology to the preservation and organization of collections and to reference services to such collections. This is, as I see it, a paradigm of contemporary legal and political problems in copyright and a testing ground for determining whether we can effectively prepare for the future on some basis other than sacrifice of authors' rights.

The system will encompass various kinds of works, including print materials, photographs, and cinematic works, stored on optical disk, catalogued, randomly accessible and incredibly compacted. There will be the potential for display and print-out at remote stations as well as on site. The disks themselves can be cheaply replicated.

The implications are obvious and staggering. Large parts of the Library's holdings, technologically speaking, can be immediately available by telecommunication links throughout our country and throughout the world, and indeed the database—that is, much of the Library's vast holdings—will be able to be transferred in duplicate optical disks to London, La Paz, Jakarta or Irkutsk.

Is not the imminence of such a system, whether at the Library of Congress or elsewhere, cause for both optimism and dread? Optimism, because it promises untold efficiencies in providing library services—by which we mean mostly works of authorship—in

Reprinted from *Publ. W'kly* **225**(22):24-26 (1984).

The Future of Copyright   25

remote corners of the globe, with obvious benefits to impoverished and developing countries. Dread, because if copyright is not provided for—creatively, thoughtfully and effectively—copyright can be grievously hurt. And I suggest that two things will be necessary to contain this revolution: domestic laws which anticipate this new electronic miracle and an international order with minimal common standards of protection or an international treaty providing them.

Because of technological innovation and its tempo, it is illusory to believe that we can deal with these new technologies piecemeal and one-by-one. Rather, copyright laws must, if they are to cope, be crafted with declarations of rights broad enough to encompass new technologies of use as they appear, with any limitations specifically enumerated and defined. That indeed was the approach of the comprehensive recodification of our law in the Copyright Act of 1976.

In the revision process which culminated in that Act, my predecessor, Abraham Kaminstein, counseled against "confining the scope of an author's right on the basis of present technology so that, as the years go by, [the] copyright loses much of its value because of unforeseen technical advances."

Our 1976 Act sought to do so. The act itself provides a framework of broad exclusive rights limited only by express limitations and the fair use doctrine. If copyright laws are to master, or even survive, the onslaught of new technologies, they must be framed in broad terms to relate the various rights of which copyright is composed—reproduction, distribution, display and performance—so as to comprehend later unanticipated uses and to make this purpose an explicit objective of such laws. Needless to say, such a strategy will work only if it is not undermined by expansive notions of fair use or by private use exemptions.

But what I have said goes to how copyright can adapt and survive. What of the will to have it do so?

Ready, cheap and often free access is a demand increasingly appearing in copyright policy debates and lawsuits. And support for this demand frequently arises both from commercial interests who deem those interests to be affected by payment for use of protected works and also by public or publicly supported constituencies understandably concerned with maximum utilization of works of authorship. This debate has emerged in international meetings I have attended, but it appears in blunt form in the United States in the two

opinions—the majority and the dissent—in the recent Betamax case and in our current legislative debates.

Stephen Stewart, Q.C., of the United Kingdom, in his 1980 Geiringer Lecture at New York University, identified a major contemporary challenge to copyright and explained it so aptly that I quote from his lecture at length:

"The next challenge is one which goes to the very root of copyright. It is a doctrine which is not new, but which assumed much greater importance in the 1960s and 1970s and will, I fear, gather strength in the 1980s as the economic recession develops. It is known as 'consumer politics.' Applied to copyright, the doctrine means that the consumer should have the widest possible access to all copyright material at the lowest possible cost and, in many cases, free. Almost everybody in our modern society is a consumer of copyrights in several respects: as a reader of books, newspapers, or other printed copyright material, as a listener to music, as a viewer of television or as a parent of a child at school who should have his school books cheap or free,

to name only the most common uses.

"Thus, put in electoral terms, on most copyright issues the overwhelming majority of voters are on one side and a comparatively very small number of voters, who are copyright owners, are on the other side of the argument. Furthermore, only a tiny fraction of this small number of copyright owners becomes millionaires, but it is those few who are constantly in the public eye. No politician, even if he is the opposite of a populist, could totally ignore this when taking a position on a copyright issue. The counter-argument, as you all know, is that without copyright, the liberty of the subject, including the liberty of speech and the freedom of expression in literature and the arts, would be in danger and ultimately some of the values of Western civilization would be at risk. But this counter-argument is not as obvious as the populist argument of cheap access to copyright works by the general public. Therefore, the copyright argument needs to be put again and again in differing forms and in all countries. Once this is acknowledged,

the task of constantly arguing for the maintenance and development of copyright, which may at times appear repetitive, or even tedious, becomes a necessary, even a noble, pursuit, humanist in the best sense of the word."

How, then, to embark upon this "noble" and "humanist" pursuit?

First, we must never abandon the idea of the author's right. For countries standing in the European tradition, and for those countries which are members of the Berne Convention, its defense will be easier: in those countries, the philosophical basis of copyright is rooted in the idea that an author's work is the extension of his personality; the foundation idea of the author's right as a natural right dominates the jurisprudence; and the Berne Convention, reflecting its European origins, has higher minimal standards from which all debate on copyright issues departs.

Technological change has made copyright issues ever more international in nature. For the past century, authors, governments and international organizations have struggled with international copyright issues. Many of these, however, were refinements of local issues, such as, "How shall the state of A treat the works of a national of the state of B?" Now, however, issues involving international traffic in copyrighted materials inhere directly in technological progress. And in transborder information flow, and specifically in internationally operating electronic libraries, those problems will be particularly acute.

But whether in national regimes or international commerce, the case for copyright must be continually made.

Although the principal argument for copyright has always been one of justice, there is another argument no less vital: copyright is an instrument of freedom, and a basic one at that. Copyright is intended to support a system, a macrocosm, in which authors and publishers compete for the attention of the public—independent of the political will of the majority, the powerful and, above all, the government—no matter how startling, disturbing or controversial their experience, views or visions.

Copyright sustains both authors and publishers. More relevantly, copyright supports a system, a milieu, a cultural marketplace which is important in and of itself. If the system's variety is injured, then so too is freedom.

But those grounds—justice and vitality in fostering diversity and freedom—are not where the current debate on copyright has moved. The main attack on copyright is that copyright is in opposition to the free flow of information and

> **Although the principal argument for copyright has always been one of justice, there is another argument no less vital: copyright is an instrument of freedom, and a basic one at that**

the public's right to know and use. And here the challenge is greatest, and those who prize copyright and all its benefits must elaborate the arguments and collect the evidence to persuade that:

1. With and because of copyright, works of authorship are available in an abundance and variety never known before and at declining costs.

2. Copyright policy should aim at plenty for consumers, in which plenty there is an opportunity for the excellent to emerge.

3. Curtailment of copyright not only deprives authors of payment, but appropriates the values whch the entrepreneur adds in making the author's work available.

4. Limitations on copyright do not necessarily lower costs to the public; they frequently transfer value from copyright owners into the pockets of other commercial interests.

5. Vast benefits in employment and revenues flow from the exploitation of copyrighted works, aside from royalties to authors and profits to publishers.

6. Where profits are momentarily large, they are balanced both by losses from failures and by entry of new authors and entrepreneurs in search of those profits.

7. Public uses of protected works—by which I mean primarily government uses—should not be borne as a subsidy from authors and publishers, but paid for as a social cost.

8. To constrain revenues to copyright will have a debilitating effect, not always immediately visible, but appearing sometimes only over the long run.

Implementing Copyright

Whatever one may think of the comparative merits of economic planning and free markets, or of government as an instrument of wealth redistribution, government should abstain as much as possible from intervention in the copyright world and willingly forbear from setting or affecting the value or price of works of authorship. Better to trust the consumers' choices in what they will pay to read, see and hear. Thus, authors and authors' publishers will succeed or fail as the public decides, diversity and freedom will be served, and authors' works will continue to flow to the public in quantity and ever declining costs.

What is needed is a searching reexamination of how strong copyright systems serve the most important needs of all people. That is its purpose. That is its historic and present achievement. The results should be a revitalized appreciation of copyright and furthering what Mr. Stewart has called the "noble" and "humanist" endeavor of leading the public to that understanding and appreciation, too.

Copyright Update

Unlike in the other parts of this book, this Copyright Update commentary is not followed by selected texts, since this is a revised second printing of the book and not a second edition. We believe that the chief contribution of this update is the Recent References list that follows our brief commentary.

Both this commentary and the reference list are categorized to follow the same outline as the main parts of the book. In both, we cover the important copyright developments that have occurred since the first printing of this book; the reference list also contains citations that further illuminate other aspects of the original text. All additions have been included in the revised Index.

I. Overview and Basics

U.S. adherence to the Berne Convention, which had in recent years received much attention, is now a fact. In October 1988, Congress finally passed the enabling legislation, and the Senate ratified the Berne treaty, effective in early 1989. Preserving/obtaining effective international-copyright protection, averting possible Berne-nation retaliation, allowing U.S. participation in Berne management, strengthening U.S. trade negotiations, and better protecting new technologies were among the reasons for making the few necessary changes in the U.S. Copyright Statute, chief among which is the Berne-required removal of formalities, particularly for foreign works. Mandatory registration as a precondition to lawsuits is now required only for domestic works, as a compromise, and use of the copyright notice is no longer mandatory (albeit recommended). Citations in Part VII of the Recent References report the moral-rights debate, and other parts report other Berne aspects.

Regarding computer software, the Copyright Office has decided that separate registration and deposit of computer-screen displays is not required. It has proposed demand deposit for machine-readable copies for use in a new Library of Congress reading room. Considerable attention has been focused on revised, more reasonable deposit requirements for databases and computer programs.

II. Creators and Owners

The Copyright Office and other interested parties are looking at giving better copyright protection to architectural, photographic, and choreographic works. The U.S. Customs Service has proposed new regulations for notifying copyright owners of unauthorized imports of works produced abroad for foreign markets. Claiming illegal photocopying, certain publishers, initially under the aegis of the Association of American publishers (AAP), have filed a class-action suit against Texaco; the new Association for Copyright Enforcement (ACE) (see Part IV of this commentary) is now participating with AAP. Other related developments are touched on under Parts III and IV.

III. Users

The British Library Document Supply Center (BLDSC) has reported high costs in using the optical disks from the ADONIS experiment. In regard to unauthorized U.S. imports of photocopies from the BLDSC, it has been pointed out elsewhere that what may be "unauthorized but legal" in one country (such as the U.K.) can become "unauthorized and illegal" when imported into another, because of differing national copyright laws.

In the main, however, libraries now seem to be more concerned with proper use of copyrighted materials, including use of videotapes and computer software; recent publications show fewer broad interpretations. One of us (Weil) has recently reviewed the technological ways in which pertinent articles are being *identified* (computer searching of bibliographic databases), *delivered* (still chiefly as photocopies), or *stored* locally in computers for later use (downloading, local-area networks.). These uses are having a negative effect on journal subscriptions, spurring publisher attention to copyright licensing.

IV. Intermediaries/Information Services

"The collective administration of [copy]rights" is receiving much more attention, here and abroad. "RROs" (reproduction rights organizations), such as the Copyright Clearance Center in the U.S., are already collecting and distributing millions of dollars annually from users of copyrighted materials, despite noncompliance by many or most. The Association for Copyright Enforcement (ACE), representing some U.S. publishers and authors, has been organized and funded to "halt illegal copying, recover damages, and bring such copying under license," with emphasis on the new technologies as well as photocopying.

V. Basic Issues

Fair use, databases, abstracts (including primary-publisher and abstracts-service relations), and works-for-hire definitions continue to receive much debate and attention.

In regard to bibliographic-database reuse of "author abstracts," most of the primary journals still willingly permit this, although every now and then a publisher requests licensing. The National Federation of Abstracting and Information Services has recently issued a booklet describing the mutual benefits of the several points of cooperation among "Primary and Secondary Information Services."

The copyrightability of compilations continues to receive attention. Some courts have ruled that one does not necessarily need to apply the same criteria for compiling telephone directories as for compiling other factual compilations in deciding whether a use is fair. Also, in deciding whether to register a work, the Copyright Office no longer extends telephone-directory criteria to other factual compilations.

VI. Technological Issues

Technological aspects and impacts are touched on in most of the parts of this book; the recent literature is replete with further consideration of these issues and with the issues elucidated in the papers in Part VI of this volume. New issues include copyright ownership and rights to create computer colorizations of black-and-white motion pictures. Copyright protection for computer software, and its enforcement, continue to attract much attention.

At least for the present, the Library of Congress and publishers are said to have struck a policy balance in connection with the inclusion of copyrighted material in the LC optical-disk project. However, the Patent and Trademark Office has not yet indicated whether it will change its plans to include in its new, computerized patent-examiner database copies of the copyrighted literature cited in its patent-application work without seeking copyright permissions.

A very elaborate (but much-criticized) study on "Intellectual Property Rights [Copyright] in an Age of Electronics and Information" was made and reported on by Congress' Office of Technology Assessment in April 1986. Among its various proposals, OTA recommended that Congress establish a mechanism to evaluate the intellectual property system. No actions have been taken on its recommendations.

VII. Legislative and Judicial Issues

Chief among the new issues in this area is the claim by several states that they are immune to suits for money damages in copyright-infringement cases. Appeals of court decisions upholding such immunity appear to place this issue on the path to possible Supreme Court consideration. In an unrelated case, the Supreme Court has already ruled that Congress must include specific language if it intends that general laws are to override the Constitutional (Eleventh Amendment) doctrine of [State] sovereign immunity. While Congress did not intend to grant such immunity in passing the Copyright Statute, it does not seem to have said so in so many words; some studies indicate that it may be necessary to seek appropriate Congressional revision of the Copyright Statute. At present, copyright owners can only seek injuctions against future violations, not damages for past ones (except possibly against individual State employees).

First-sale-doctrine and rentals issues continue to receive attention. Congress is considering legislation to regulate computer-program (software) rentals. Legislation governing videocassette (motion-picture) rentals is said to be unlikely.

After one five-year extension, the Manufacturing Clause (discussed in Paper 65 in this book) has been allowed to disappear, but it is said that proponents are still lobbying for its reenactment.

As mentioned earlier, protection of author (creator) "moral rights," discussed in Paper 67 in this book, became a live issue in the debate on U.S.

adherence to the Berne Convention. Although moral rights are not specifically mentioned in the U.S. Copyright Statute, it is generally felt that it includes sufficient language on them to satisfy Berne requirements. Nevertheless, Congressional consideration of moral-rights issues (including works for hire) is anticipated in 1989.

Deeming it no longer needed nor desirable, the Association of American Publishers and the Register of Copyrights have withdrawn their previously reported support (Papers 59 and 60 in this book) for an "umbrella-statute amendment" that would have permitted some rigidly limited photocopying from works not registered by their publishers with the Copyright Clearance Center or not otherwise licensed for copying.

VIII. International Aspects

Agencies of the U.S. Government are paying a vast amount of attention to strengthening international copyright protection for U.S. proprietors. The U.S., Europe, and Japan are attempting to strengthen GATT, the General Agreement on Tariffs and Trade, to provide global protection for intellectual property rights against piracy, etc. Adhering countries would be obligated to write national laws that would conform with a GATT intellectual property code. In GATT's enforcement mechanism, retaliation could be applied to any GATT area of trade, not just intellectual property.

As mentioned earlier, the recent U.S. adherence to the Berne Convention strengthens the U.S. position. One early concern was whether a revised GATT would contain an international copyright code differing from the Berne Convention.

The Commission of the European Communities has embarked on an extensive study of copyright laws requiring immediate action because of technology. Also, the World Intellectual Property Organization (WIPO), which administers the Berne Convention, has scheduled a sequence of meetings designed to develop a model copyright law "for the harmonization of national legislations." The emphasis of these meetings is on new technologies.

IX. Future Developments

As is evident from many of the recent references reported under specific parts, but not here, the copyright literature continues to be replete with forecasts that the new technologies will make copyright protection for intellectual properties much more difficult and less effective. We have already mentioned the study by Congress' Office of Technology Assessment, listed under Part VI in the Recent References, and the European Commission and WIPO studies. The situation is so complex that it is not surprising that no one has come forth with a clear and acceptable general solution.

RECENT REFERENCES

I. OVERVIEW AND BASICS

Baumgarten, J. and Meyer, C.A., 1987, The United States and Berne Convention—1987, *RIGHTS* 1(3):1,2.

Berne Convention Implementation Act of 1988 [S. 1301 and H.R. 4262], 1988, *Congressional Record—Senate,* Oct. 5, 1988, pp. S14544-S. 14547;—*House,* Oct. 12, 1988, pp. H10091-H10098. Also, Berne Convention for the Protection of Literary and Artistic Works [Senate Ratification], *Congressional Record—Senate,* Oct. 20, 1988, pp. S16939-S16941.

Copyright Office, Library of Congress, 1988, Registration Decision, Registration and Deposit of Computer Screen Displays, *Fed. Register* 53(112):21817-20.

Copyright Office, Library of Congress, 1988, Registration of Claims to Copyright: Mandatory Deposit of Machine-Readable Copies: Proposed Rulemaking, *Fed. Register* 53(153):29923-25.

Final Report of the Ad Hoc Working Group on U.S. Adherence to the Berne Convention, 1986, *Columbia—VLA Law and the Arts J.* 10(4):513-735.

Stuller, J., 1988 (June), Your Guide to Copyright, *Writer's Digest,* pp.28-32.

II. CREATORS AND OWNERS

AAP Files Comments on [U.S. Customs Service] Proposed [Imports] Notification Regulations, 1987, *AAP Monthly Report* 4(6):2.

Are Photographs Coming Into Their Own?, 1988, *RIGHTS* 2(2):7, 8, 14, 15.

Bach, S.L., 1986, Music Recording, Publishing, and Compulsory License: Toward a Consistent Copyright Law, *Hofstra Law Rev.* 14(2):370-403.

Besen, S.M. and Kirby, S.N., 1987, *Private Copying Appropriability and Optimum Copying Royalties,* Rand Corp., Santa Monica, CA.

Brennan, T.C., 1987, The Copyright Royalty Tribunal—An American Perspective, *Copyr. Soc. U.S.A. J.* 34(2);148-165.

Copyright Office, Library of Congress, 1988, Notice of Inquiry; Works of Architecture, *Fed. Register* 53(110):21536-38.

Labaton, S., 1988(July 25), New Group [ACE] to Sue to Aid Copyrights, *New York Times,* p.D2.

Lieb, C.H., 1987, The "Texaco Case": A Class Action Approach to Unauthorized Photocopying, *RIGHTS* 1(3):7,8.

Low, C., 1986 (Nov. 16), A Battle Royal Over Art Royalties, *Insight,* pp. 63, 67.

Oman, R., The Compulsory License Redux: Will It Survive in a Changing Marketplace?, *Cardozo Arts & Entertain. Law J.* 5(1):37-50.

Singer, B.A., In Search of Adequate Protection for Choreographic Works: Legislative and Judicial Alternatives, *Univ. Miami Law R.* 38(2):287-321.

III. USERS

Bradbury, D., 1987, *ADONIS: The View of the Users [BLDSC],* 110-SER-3/SCIE-6-E, 53rd IFLA Council and General Conference, Brighton, U.K., pp.23-10, 23-11.

Line, M.B., 1988, Whose Rights?, *RIGHTS* 2(2):5, 14.

Moskowitz, D.B., 1987 (Sept. 14), Copying Others' Software Can Mean Trouble for Corporations, *The Washington Post,* Washington Business Section, p.22.

Nasri, W.Z.,1987, *Legal Issues for Libraries and Information Managers,* The Haworth Press, New York.

Reed, M.H., 1987, *The Copyright Primer for Libraries,* American Libraries Association, Chicago, or National Education Association, Washington, DC.

Copyright Update

Reed, M.H. and Stanek, D., 1986 (Feb.), *Library and Classroom Use of Copyrighted Videotapes and Computer Software,* Separate (insert) from *Amer. Libr.*

Weil, B.H., 1987, The Many Routes to Published Information, *Schol. Publ.* 18(4):263-270.

IV. INTERMEDIARIES/INFORMATION SERVICES

Bringing Photocopying Under Control [RROs], 1987, *RIGHTS* 1(1):12, 13.

CCC Distributes $1 Million, 1988, *RIGHTS* 2(2);10.

Collective Administration of Rights: Wave of the Future?, 1987-88, *RIGHTS* 1(4):10-12.

Hoffman, A.C., 1988, Electro-Copying and Collective Administration of Rights, *RIGHTS* 2(1):2, 11, 12.

Miller, P.A. and Levine, A.J., 1985, *The Information Executive's Guide to Intellectual Property Rights,* Information Industry Association, Washington, D.C.

Publishers Call for Copyright Enforcement [GATT, Berne, RROs, EC, BLDSC], 1988, *RIGHTS* 2(2):1,2, 11-13.

Stern, B.T., 1987, *ADONIS: The Experience to Date,* 13-SER-2/SCIE-2-E, 53rd IFLA Council and General Conference, Brighton, U.K., pp.23/8-23/10.

V. BASIC ISSUES

Abrams, F., 1987, First Amendment and Copyright [Fair Use], *Copyr. Soc. U.S.A. J.* 35(1):1-12.

Asser, P.N., 1986, Relations Between Primary and Secondary Publishers, *NFAIS Newsletter* 28(1):6,7.

Bremner, J. and Miller, P., 1987, *Guide to Database Distribution: Legal Aspects and Model Contracts,* National Federation of Abstracting and Information Services, Philadelphia, PA.

Drew, S., 1985 (June), Online Databases: Some Questions of [Library] Ownership, *Wilson Lib. Bull.,* pp. 661-663.

Cochran Introduces Latest Work-for-Hire Bill, 1987, *AAP Monthly Report* 4(6):2.

Hardy, I.T., 1988 Copyright Law's Concept of Employment—What Congress Really Intended [Work for Hire], *Copyr. Soc. U.S.A. J.* 35(3):210-258.

Hunter, K., 1987, New Technologies, Publishing, and Copyright: An Introduction to Database Publishing, *RIGHTS* 1(2):1, 12-15.

Lloyd, F.W. and Mayeda, D.M., 1986, Copyright Fair Use, The First Amendment, and New Communications Technology: The Impact of Betamax, *Fed. Communication Law J.* 38(1):59-103.

Patry, W.F., 1985, *The Fair Use Privilege In Copyright Law,* Bureau of National Affairs, Washington, DC.

Primary and Secondary Information Services: Basic Information [Roles] from NFAIS, 1988, National Federation of Abstracting and Information Services, Philadelphia, PA.

VI. TECHNOLOGICAL ISSUES

Bader, E.K., 1986, A Film of Different Color—Copyright and the Colorization of Black and White Films, *Cardozo Arts and Entertain. Law J.* 5(2):497-543.

Business and the Law: Copyrights and Software, 1987 (May 11), *New York Times,* p.D2.

Clapes, A.L., et al., 1988, Silicon Epics and Binary Bards: Determining the Proper Scope of Copyright Protection for Computer Programs, *UCLA Law Rev.* 34:1493-1594.

Cooper, F.L. III and Sapronov, W., 1986, Software Protection and Pricing in a LAN Environment, *Jurimetrics J.* 26(2):162-180.

Copyright Office, Library of Congress, 1988, Copyright Registration for Colorized Versions of Black and White Motion Pictures, Final Rule, *Fed. Register* 53(153):29887-90.

450

Copying the Look and Feel of Computer Software: Fair Competition or Copyright Violation?, *Comput. Law & Intellect. Prop. CLIPNOTES* 2(2):1, 4-8.

Demas, S., 1985, Microcomputer Software Collections [Loan Policies for], *Special Libr.* 76(1):17-23.

Duggan, J.T. and N.V. Pennella, 1988, The Case for Copyrights in "Colorized" Versions of Public Domain Feature Films, *Copyr. Soc. U.S.A. J.* 34(4):333-379.

Fantel, H., 1985, The Big-Dish Satellite Antenna Is Becoming a Best Seller, *New York Times* 134 (46, 372):H-26.

Fetterman, D.J., 1986, The Scope of Copyright Protection for Computer Programs: Exploring the Idea/Expression Dichotomy, *Washington and Lee Rev.* 43(4):1373-1411.

Garman, N., 1986, Downloading—Still a Live Issue, *Online* 10(4):15-25.

Gerrard, L., 1988, The Question of Ownership of Academic Software, *Schol. Publ.* 19(2):116-119.

LC Optical Disk Policy Strikes User/Publisher Balance, 1986(Nov.), *Amer. Libr.*, p. 746.

Library of Congress, Network Advisory Committee, 1987, *Intellectual Property Rights in an Electronic Age* [Proceedings], Network Planning Paper No. 16, Cataloging Distribution Service, Washington, DC.

Office of Technology Assessment, U.S. Congress, 1986, *Intellectual Property Rights in an Age of Electronics and Information,* OTA-CIT-302, U.S. Government Printing Office, Washington, DC.

Samuelson, P., 1988(September), Is Copyright Steering the Right Course [re software engineering]?, *IEEE Software,* pp. 78-86.

Sherman, C.H., et al., 1988, *Computer Software Protection Law*, Bureau of National Affairs, Washington, DC.

Soat, J., 1985, Thou Shalt Not Copy, *Automated Office* 46(12):13.

Williams, M.E., 1985, Electronic Databases, *Science* 228(4698):445-456.

VII. LEGISLATIVE AND JUDICIAL ISSUES

Brown, R.S., 1988, Adherence to the Berne Copyright Convention: The Moral Rights Issue, *Copyr. Soc. U.S.A. J.* 35(3):196-209.

Copyright Office, Library of Congress, 1988, *Report of the Register of Copyrights—Library Reproduction of Copyrighted Works (17 USC 108),* Washington, D.C. NTIS Report PB 212014 (Paper Copy A99).

Karp, I., 1986, Reflections on the Copyright Revision Act: Sovereign Immunity, *Copyr. Soc. U.S.A. J.* 34(1):53-71.

Milestone in Struggle to Get States to Obey Copyright Law, 1988, *Inf. Times* 7(3):4.

PLI Copyright Conference Covers Judicial, Legislative Developments [state immunity, compilations, Berne, works for hire, licensing and fair use], 1988, *BNA's Patent, Trademark, Copyr. J.* 36(884):147-149.

Register of Copyrights, 1988, *Copyright Liability of the States and the Eleventh Amendment,* Report, Washington, DC.

Stern, R.H., 1986, *Semiconductor Chip Protection,* Law & Business, Clifton, NJ.

Symposium: The Semiconductor Chip Protection Act of 1984 and Its Lessons, 1985, *Minn. Law Rev.* 70(2):263-579.

VIII. INTERNATIONAL ASPECTS

Anti-Piracy Fight Advances, 1988, *RIGHTS 2(2):9, 10.*

Altbach, P.G., *International Copyright in Comparative Perspective: Problems and Quandries,* Proceedings, 9th Annual Meeting of the Society for Scholarly Publishing, Washington, DC.

Baumgarten, J., 1987, *Principles of International Copyright Protection,* Proceedings, 9th Annual Meeting of the Society for Scholarly Publishing, Washington, DC.

451

Commission of the European Communities, 1988, *Green Paper on Copyright and the Challenge of Technology: Copyright Laws Requiring Immediate Action,* Communication from the Commission.

Copyright Office, Library of Congress, 1985, *Announcement: U.S. Senate Ratifies Brussels Satellite Convention,* Washington, DC.

Copyright Protection in Asia, 1988, *Publ. Weekly* 223 (13):1, 2.

Smith, M.B., 1987, U.S. Policy and Actions on Intellectual Property Protection, *RIGHTS* 1(1):6-10.

Smith, M.B., 1988(June), Protecting Copyright Through the GATT, *Anti-Piracy News & Copyr. Rev.* 13;1,2.

INDEX

About the Editors

BEN H. WEIL has had a long career in information management and systems and as an author and editor. He was born in St. Joseph, Mo., and received the B.S. and M.S. degrees in chemical engineering from the Universities of Missouri and Wisconsin. He has managed information centers at Gulf Research & Development Company, the Georgia Tech Engineering Experiment Station, Ethyl Corporation Research Laboratories, and Exxon Research and Engineering Company. Since retiring from Exxon Research in 1982, he has been president of Ben H. Weil, Inc., doing information consulting, including copyright compliance.

Mr. Weil is the author or editor of six books and over 400 papers and articles, many of the latter on copyright. He became a member of the American Chemical Society's new Joint Board-Council Committee on Copyrights in 1968, serving as chairman from 1970-1977 and as a consultant from 1980 through 1984. From 1971-1975 he was chairman of the Proprietary Use/Rights Committee of the American Society for Information Science. He has served on the Proprietary Rights Committee of the Information Industry Association since 1971, and has served several terms on the Copyright Committee of the National Federation of Abstracting and Information Services, twice as its chairman.

In 1977, on loan from Exxon Research to the Association of American Publishers, he designed and put into operation the Copyright Clearance Center, Inc., on whose board he then served for eleven years.

Mr. Weil has been a member, fellow, and officer of many scientific and information societies, from whom he has received numerous awards. He continues to be active in most of these organizations.

BARBARA FRIEDMAN POLANSKY has been copyright administrator for the American Chemical Society's Books and Journals Division since late 1979; she is also staff liaison to the ACS' Joint Board-Council Committee on Copyrights. Originally from Rome, N.Y., she grew up in York, Pa., and now lives in Chevy Chase, Md. In 1975 she received the B.S. degree from the Pennsylvania State University where she majored in operations management. Prior to her present position she was production editor for one of the science journals of the American Geophysical Union.

Mrs. Polansky is very active in professional organizations. In 1982, she cofounded the Copyright Round Table (Washington, D.C.). She is a member of The Copyright Society of the U.S.A., the Rights and Permissions Advisory Committee of the Association of American Publishers, and the Copyright Committee of STM (International Group of Scientific, Technical and Medical Publishers).

From 1983 to 1984 she served as the copyright news columnist for the newsletter of the Society for Scholarly Publishing. She was 1983-1984 Chairman of the Potomac Valley Chapter of the American Society for Information Science (ASIS), and in the fall of 1984 she became content editor for that chapter's newslettter. In late 1985, she served in a six-month contracted position as Executive Director of the American Copyright Council.

In addition to these activities, Mrs. Polansky has presented and published many papers on copyright, some of which are included in this book.